Praise for *Director in a Nutshell*

"A massive road atlas into the territory known as Director and Shockwave. Offers vital details for developers of every interest level, including coverage of many topics rarely even mentioned in other books. I want copies for everyone on the Director QA team."

—Buzz Kettles, Senior Quality Designer, Macromedia Director Team

"A great piece of work of which Bruce can be very proud. I would describe it as 'a Direct-L Killer.' If it doesn't kill off all the questions on the Direct-L listserv, it will at least cut down the volume."

—Peter Small, Author of *Lingo Sorcery* and *Magical A-Life Avatars*

"This is the first book that provides the under-the-hood details that benefit Director developers of all levels. More thorough and accurate than any other reference available."

—Marc Canter, Inventor of Director, Canter Technology

"In Multimedia Gulch, the hotels don't have bibles on the bedside tables— they have copies of Director in a Nutshell.*"*

—Roy Pardi, Director of Multimedia, JuniorNet, Inc.

*"*Director in a Nutshell *covers all the new features of Director 7 and will surely become the default reference for Director users of all levels. I keep only two Director books on my desk: Macromedia's* Lingo Dictionary *and* Lingo in a Nutshell. Director in a Nutshell *will join them as soon as I get my copy."*

—Roger Jones, Throbbing Interactive

Praise for the Companion Volume,
Lingo in a Nutshell

DIRECTOR
IN A NUTSHELL

A Desktop Quick Reference

DIRECTOR
IN A NUTSHELL

A Desktop Quick Reference

Bruce A. Epstein

O'REILLY®

Beijing · Cambridge · Köln · Paris · Sebastopol · Taipei · Tokyo

Director in a Nutshell

by Bruce A. Epstein

Published by O'Reilly & Associates, Inc., 101 Morris Street, Sebastopol, CA 95472.

Editor: Tim O'Reilly

Production Editor: Nancy Wolfe Kotary

Printing History:

> March 1999:   First Edition.

This book is printed on acid-free paper with 85% recycled content, 15% post-consumer waste. O'Reilly & Associates is committed to using paper with the highest recycled content available consistent with high quality.

ISBN: 1-56592-382-0

Table of Contents

Preface

You are holding in your hands one half of *Bruce's Brain in a Book*. The other half of my brain is in the companion book, *Lingo in a Nutshell*. These books are the distillation of years of real-life experience with countless Director projects plus many hours spent researching and testing new features of Director 6, 6.5, and 7. While they can be used separately, they are ideally used as a single two-volume reference that costs less than most single Director books.

Director in a Nutshell focuses on the "concrete" aspects of Director—the Cast, the Score, Projectors, MIAWs, media (graphics, sound, digital video, and text), Director's windows, GUI components (buttons, cursors, menus), and Shockwave. *Lingo in a Nutshell* focuses on the abstract concepts in Lingo, such as variables, scripts, Behaviors, objects, mouse and keyboard events, timers, math, lists, strings, and file I/O.

If you already know a lot about Director or have been disappointed by the existing documentation, these are the books you've been waiting for. They address many of the errors and omissions in Macromedia's documentation and many third-party books. There is no fluff or filler here, so you'll miss a lot if you skim.

What Are These Books and Who Are They For?

Director in a Nutshell and *Lingo in a Nutshell* are Desktop Quick References for Director and Lingo developers who are familiar with Director's basic operation and need to create, debug, and optimize cross-platform Director and Shockwave projects. These books are concise, detailed, respectful of the reader's intelligence, and organized by topic to allow quick access to thorough coverage of all relevant information.

Because Lingo and Director are inextricably linked, I have kept all information on a single topic within a single chapter, rather than breaking it along the traditional Director versus Lingo lines (with the exception of Chapter 10, *Using Xtras*, in this book and Chapter 13, *Lingo Xtras and XObjects,* in *Lingo in a Nutshell*). Don't assume that all the Lingo is consigned to *Lingo in a Nutshell*; *Director in a Nutshell* includes a lot of Lingo and you should be familiar with the Lingo basics covered in *Lingo in a Nutshell*.

This book (*Director in a Nutshell*) should not be confused with the third-party books that merely rehash the manuals; nor should it be considered an introductory book. It is exceptionally valuable for non-Lingo users but also covers Lingo related to those aspects of Director mentioned earlier. *Lingo in a Nutshell* covers both the basics of Lingo and its most advanced features. Each book covers both Windows and the Macintosh.

To describe these books as "beginner," "intermediate," or "advanced" would be misleading. Strictly as a comparison to other books on the market, you should consider their *coverage* extremely advanced, but the text itself is accessible to Director users of all levels. *Lingo in a Nutshell* allows Director users to take full advantage of Lingo's power, and *Director in a Nutshell* helps users of all levels deal confidently with the spectrum of Director's media types and features.

What These Books Are Not

These books are not a rehash of the Director manuals or Help system, but rather a complement to them, and as such are unlike any other books on the market.

These books are not a celebration of Director as multimedia Nirvana. They are for people who know that Director has many quirks and some bugs and want to know how to work around them quickly and effectively.

These books are not courses in graphic design, project management, Photoshop, HTML, or JavaScript. They will however help you integrate your existing skills and external content into Director's framework.

These books are not a Director tutorial, because I assume that you are familiar with the basics of Director's Cast, Score, Stage, and menus. They are not for people who need hand-holding. They are for people who can apply general concepts to their specific problem and want to do so rapidly.

These books are not perfect—errors are inevitable—so use them as a guide, not gospel. (These are the most thoroughly researched books ever written on Director and correct many errors and omissions in other sources.) While these books cannot anticipate all circumstances, they do provide the tools for you to confidently solve your specific problems even in the face of erroneous or incomplete information.

About This Book

Director in a Nutshell covers everything about content development and delivery in Director. It covers media and user interface elements and the Lingo to control them. It is divided into three major sections:

Part I, *Director's Core Components*
> Chapter 1, *How Director Works*, explains Director's event-driven model and how it affects playback and screen imaging, and covers the hidden details of how the Score, Cast, and Lingo interact.

Chapter 2, *Being More Productive*, provides many tips and shortcuts to save you days over the course of a project, including details on hardware and software for development and testing and a primer on Windows and the Mac OS.

Chapter 3, *The Score and Animation*, covers animation techniques and optimization, the Score window and sprite manipulation, markers, and the Tempo channel. If you've had trouble adjusting to Director 6's new Score, this chapter is a gold mine. It also covers the Lingo for Score navigation, Score recording, and analyzing corrupted Score notation.

Chapter 4, *CastLibs, Cast Members, and Sprites*, covers all aspects of cast library management, importing assets into Director, linking to external media, and Cast window shortcuts. It also covers the Lingo for manipulating castLibs, cast members, and sprites, including comprehensive tables of supported media formats and all cast member and sprite properties for each asset type. It also includes several utilities to analyze and debug your Cast.

Chapter 5, *Coordinates, Alignment, and Registration Points*, covers Director's multiple coordinate systems (Stage-relative, monitor-relative, member-relative, and MIAW-relative) that determine sprite and window positioning. It also covers cast member registration points and Director's alignment tools. It tabulates the coordinate systems and units used by various Lingo keywords.

Chapter 6, *The Stage and Movies-in-a-Window*, covers the commands and operations that control the Stage and manipulate Movies-in-a-Window. It covers panning and scaling window views, communicating between windows, and setting window types and window properties.

Part II, *Delivery and Optimization*

Chapter 7, *Cross-Platform and OS Dependencies*, covers all cross-platform issues, including the differences in Lingo and Director amongst the Macintosh and various flavors of Windows.

Chapter 8, *Projectors and the Runtime Environment,* covers the options for creating runtime versions of your Director project for each platform. It also covers the Lingo to analyze various system properties at runtime, including determining the playback platform and the CD-ROM's drive letter. It also details differences between the authoring environment and Projectors.

Chapter 9, *Memory and Performance,* covers optimizing your project's performance and minimizing its memory usage. It details the memory and disk space required for each media type and lays out a memory budget for Director projects. It covers the Lingo that analyzes and controls memory allocation and cast member preloading, idle loading, purging, and unloading. It covers techniques to detect and fix memory leaks and to optimize all aspects of your project's performance.

Chapter 10, *Using Xtras,* covers installing and using Xtras in your Director projects. It describes in detail the Xtras that come with Director and tells you which ones you need to ship with your Projector and where to put them. See also Chapter·13 in *Lingo in a Nutshell.*

Chapter 11, *Shockwave and the Internet,* covers Shockwave delivery and creating linked CD-ROMs that access Internet-based content. It details which

Shockwave plug-ins are required for each browser on each platform, and covers the differences between Shockwave and standalone Projectors.

Part III, *Multimedia Elements*

Chapter 12, *Text and Fields*, covers the commands and operations for field and text cast members, including choosing the right type of text cast member and D7's new font cast members. See also Chapter 7, *Strings*, and Chapter 10, *Keyboard Events*, in *Lingo in a Nutshell*.

Chapter 13, *Graphics, Color, and Palettes*, covers the different types of graphical cast members and the Paint window. It includes a crucial explanation of palette management in Director, plus tips on solving palette problems. It also covers D7's new color model, vector shapes, and animated GIFs.

Chapter 14, *Graphical User Interface Components*, covers buttons, checkboxes, alert dialog boxes, cursors, and menus, and their control via Lingo. It also includes details on the Custom Cursor and Popup Menu Xtras.

Chapter 15, *Sound and Cue Points*, covers sound playback and manipulation, including *puppetSounds*, external sounds, Shockwave Audio (SWA), and cue points. It also covers sound mixing under Windows.

Chapter 16, *Digital Video*, covers video playback and manipulation via the Score and Lingo, including QuickTime and Video for Windows, plus details on QuickTime 3 and the QT3 Xtra.

Refer to *http://www.zeusprod.com/nutshell/appendices* for additional appendices on Flash, ActiveX, PowerPoint, Java, shipping checklists, and more.

Conventions Used in This Book

The following typographic, grammatical, and stylistic conventions are used throughout *Director in a Nutshell*.

 The turkey icon designates a warning relating to the nearby text.

 The owl icon designates a note, which is an important aside to the nearby text.

Typographical Conventions

- Lingo keywords (*functions*, *commands*, and *property names*) are shown in *italic*, except in tables, where they are only italicized when necessary to distinguish them from the surrounding text. Italic in tables usually indicates replaceable values.

- *Arguments*, *user-specified*, and *replaceable* items are shown in *italic constant width* and should be replaced by real values when used in your code.

- New terms are shown in *italic* and are often introduced by merely using them in context. Refer to *http://www.zeusprod.com/nutshell/glossary.html* for details.

- Options in dialog boxes, such as the *Tab to Next Field* checkbox, are shown in *italic*.

- Menu commands are shown as MenuName ➤ MenuItem.

- Constants such as TRUE, FALSE, and RETURN are shown in Courier.

- #symbols are preceded by the pound (#) character and shown in Courier.

- Optional items are specified with curly braces ({}) instead of traditional square braces ([]), which Lingo uses for lists. For example:

  ```
  go {to} {frame} whichFrame
  ```

  means that the following are equivalent:

  ```
  go whichFrame
  go to whichFrame
  go to frame whichFrame
  go frame whichFrame
  ```

- Allowed values for a property are separated by a vertical bar (|). The following indicates that *the checkBoxType* property can be set to 0, 1, or 2:

  ```
  set the checkBoxType = 0 | 1 | 2
  ```

Grammatical and Stylistic Conventions

- Most Lingo properties start with the word "the," which can lead to sentences such as, "The *the member of sprite property* can be changed at runtime." I often omit the keyword *the* preceding properties to make sentences or tables more readable, but you should include the "the" in your Lingo code.

- Lingo event handlers all begin with the word "on," such as *on mouseUp*. I often omit the word "on" when discussing events, messages and handlers, or in tables where the meaning is implied.

- Be aware that some Director keywords are used in multiple contexts such as the *on mouseUp* event handler and the *the mouseUp* system property. The intended usage is discernible from context and is stated explicitly only in ambiguous circumstances.

- I use terminology fairly loosely, as is typical among Lingo developers. For example a "*mouseUp* script" is technically "an *on mouseUp* handler within a script." The meaning should be clear from the context.

- I capitalize the names of Director entities, such as the Score, the Stage, the Cast, and the Message window. I don't capitalize general terms that refer to classes of items, such as sprite scripts.

- Most handler names used in the examples are arbitrary, although handlers such as *on mouseUp* that trap built-in events must be named as shown. I use variable names like *myThing* or *whichSprite* to indicate items for which you

should substitute your own values. When in doubt, see Chapter 18, *The Lingo.
Keyword and Command Summary*, in *Lingo in a Nutshell* or Director's online
Help.

- I use few segues and assume you will re-read the material until it makes
  sense. As with a Dali painting, you must revisit the text periodically to discover details that you missed the first time.

Examples

- Example code is shown monospaced and set off in its own paragraph. If a
  code fragment is shown, especially using the put command, it is implicit that
  you should type the example in the Message window to see the result. Any
  text following "--" is the output from Director (shown in constant width),
  or a comment from me (shown in *italic constant width*):

```
set x = 5     -- Set the variable x to 5
put x         -- Display the value of x
-- 5
```

- Long lines of Lingo code are continued on the next line using the Lingo continuation character (¬) (created using Opt-Return or Opt-L on the Macintosh or Alt-Enter under Windows):

```
set the member of sprite (the currentSpriteNum) = ¬
    member "Hilighted Button"
```

- If you have trouble with an example, check for lines that may have been erroneously split without the Lingo continuation character (¬). Remember to use
  parentheses when calling any function that returns a value. Otherwise you'll
  either see no result or receive an error.

```
rollover          -- wrong
rollover()        -- wrong
put rollover      -- wrong
put rollover()    -- correct
```

- I sometimes use the single-line form of the *if...then* statement in an example
  for brevity. You should use multi-line *if...then* statements in your code. See
  Chapter 1, *How Lingo Works*, in *Lingo in a Nutshell* for details on the *if* statement.

```
-- This will usually work
if (x > 5) then put "It's True!"
-- But this is more reliable
if (x > 5) then
    put "It's True!"
end if
```

- If a handler is shown in an example, it is implied that the handler has been
  entered into the appropriate type of script. Unless otherwise specified, mouse
  event handlers such as *mouseUp* belong in sprite scripts, frame events handlers such as *exitFrame* belong in frame scripts, and custom utilities belong in
  movie scripts. I often show a handler followed by an example of its use. Type
  the handler into a movie script, and then test it from the Message window. If I

don't show a test in the Message window, either the handler does not output a visible result or it is assumed that you will test it yourself if you are interested:

```
-- This goes in a script, in this case a movie script
on customHandler
   put "Hello Sailor!"
end customHandler

-- This is a test in the Message window
customHandler
-- "Hello Sailor!"
```

- The output shown may vary inconsequentially from the results you see based on your system setup. Most notably, the number of decimal places shown for floating-point values depends on your setting for *the floatPrecision* property.

- If the output of a handler is extremely long, the results will not be shown in their entirety or may not be shown at all.

- The examples are demonstrative and not necessarily robust, and in them I assume that you provide valid inputs when applicable. It is good practice to include type checking and error checking in your actual Lingo code, as described in Chapter 3, *Lingo Coding and Debugging Tips*, and Chapter 1 in *Lingo in a Nutshell*. I often omit such checking to keep examples shorter and focused on the main issue.

- Some examples, particularly the tests performed from the Message window, are code *fragments*, and won't work without help from the studio audience. You should ensure that any variables required by the examples (particularly lists) have been initialized with meaningful values, although such initialization is not shown. For example:

```
put count (myList)
```

assumes that you have *previously* set a valid value for *myList*, such as:

```
set myList = [1, 7, 5, 9]
```

- Some examples allude to text or field cast members, such as:

```
set the text of field "Memory" = string(the freeBlock)
```

It is implied that you should create a text or field cast member of the specified name in order for the example to work.

- Screenshots may not match your platform exactly.

- I present a simplified view of the universe whenever my assumptions are overwhelmingly likely to be valid. You can intentionally confuse Director by setting bizarre values for a property or performing malicious or unsupported operations, but you do so at your own risk. I cover situations where errors might occur accidentally, but you should assume that all statements presented as fact are prefaced by, "Assuming you are not trying to screw with Director just for fun . . . ." When necessary, I state my assumptions clearly.

- The myriad ways to perform a given task are shown when that task is the main topic of discussion, but not if it is peripheral to the subject at hand.

When incidental, I may show the clearest or most expedient method rather than the most elegant method.

- Following an example, I occasionally suggest ways to modify the code as a Reader Exercise. Solutions to Reader Exercises are posted at:

  http://www.zeusprod.com/nutshell/exercises/

- Examples are usually self-contained, but they may rely on custom handlers shown nearby. If an example builds on previous examples or material cross-referenced in another chapter, it is assumed that the relevant handlers have been entered in an appropriate script (usually a movie script).

New Features in Director 7

Director 7 is a great leap forward. There are no major changes to the Score or sprite messaging as in the D6 upgrade from D5, but there are many new features added on top of those in D6 and D6.5. For a complete list of new features, bugs, differences from D6, tips on updating movies from D6, and outstanding issues in both Director 7 and Shockwave 7, see the D7 FAQs starting at:

http://www.zeusprod.com/nutshell/d7faq.html

See Macromedia's summary of new features at:

http://www.macromedia.com/software/director/productinfo/newfeatures/

For documentation not available in the printed manuals or online Help, see:

http://www.macromedia.com/software/director/how/d7/

Select the *Fun* tab in the *About Director* window (under the Apple menu on the Macintosh or the Help menu under Windows) for demos of many new features including alpha channels, RGB colors, text and fonts, quads, rotation and skew, Flash 3, vector shapes, and animated GIFs.

If you need one or more of D7's new features, then upgrade. Regardless, take some time to learn D7 before creating a commercial product or upgrading a project from D6. The initial consensus is that D7 is extremely stable for a major revision. By the time you read this the D7.0.1 maintenance release should be available at *http://www.macromedia.com/support/director/upndown/updates.html*.

The Director 7 Shockwave Internet Studio includes these items which are not in the standalone Director upgrade:

- Behavior Library Palette (only limited Behaviors are included with standalone D7).

- Multiuser Server (Director for Windows includes the Windows server only, and Director for Macintosh includes the Macintosh server only, and you'll need the version that matches your web server. Linux and Unix versions are anticipated.)

- Macromedia Fireworks.

- Sound editor: Sound Forge XP (Windows) or Bias Peak LE (Macintosh).

Director 7 Features by Category

The major new features of Director 7 fall into several categories.

System architecture:

- D7 is based on a new playback engine first introduced as part of Shockwave 6.0.1, but completely different than the D6 engine. As such, it has many new features (especially dynamic sprite distortion), but also has new quirks.

- The Shockwave playback engine is now a system-level component (like QuickTime) that can be used by multiple browsers and so-called Slim Projectors. Slim Projectors can be under 200 KB and can even download missing components or Xtras from the Internet. Director 7 and Shockwave 7 continue the trend towards modularization by using many Xtras, which you can omit if the feature is not needed.

- The underlying engine is the same in all versions of Shockwave 7 for all browsers, Director 7 on both Macintosh and Windows, plus the new Shock-Machine (a local Shockwave player). Expect to see fewer differences across playback platforms than in prior versions. Any playback environment can adopt Shockwave's security hobbles by declaring itself as a "safe" environment by setting *the safePlayer* to TRUE.

Score, animation, authoring, and playback improvements:

- The Stage is a standard window that can be closed or moved during authoring, or placed in front of all MIAWs (D7.0.1 fixes a bug in this regard).

- New sprite properties and media types create eye-popping animation with minimal cast members (ideal for Shockwave delivery).

- Colorize, skew, rotate, and mirror bitmaps, Flash, animated GIFs, text, and vector shapes on Stage or using the Sprite Toolbar and Sprite Inspector.

- Quad distortion performs 3D-like effects at runtime on text, bitmaps, and animated GIFs. Reverse the corners to see the "back" of a sprite or twist it into a bowtie.

- Up to 1000 sprite channels and 999 frames per second playback.

- Dynamic z-ordering of sprite channels via Lingo (the *locZ of sprite* property).

- Alpha channels (partial transparency) and runtime dithering.

- Multiple monitors supported under both Windows and Macintosh.

- The Paint window supports 16-bit and 32-bit painting.

- Dynamic selection of sound mixer, including QT3 Mixer, under Windows.

- Improved ink effects, sprite colorization, and blend. True RGB color model allowing colorizing of sprites in all color depths.

- Capture the Stage into a cast member using *the picture of the stage*, or crop it with the new *crop()* command.

- Improved grid snapping that uses the nearest corner or side instead of the registration point to snap a sprite to the grid.

Media improvements and additions:

- D7 includes all the import and export media features added in D6.5 including QuickTime 3, Flash 2, ActiveX, Java Export, PowerPoint import, and custom animated cursors, plus new support for Flash 3, MPEG 3, and improved QuickTime 3 support.

- New animated GIF members, plus JPEG and GIF import, and support for internal compressed JPEG, GIF, and animated GIF assets.

- Text cast members allow anti-aliased text to be edited, rotated, skewed, and colorized at runtime. Some support for hypertext links, HTML import, and RTF styles, including superscripts and subscripts. Text, field, and script cast members are no longer limited to 32 KB.

- Compressed font cast members that can be used by both text and fields to provide platform-independent fonts without requiring font installation.

- Programmable vector shapes for dynamic Bézier curves, charts and graphs, splines, and polylines.

- PhotoCaster Lite (which allows import of separate Photoshop layers) and a demo version of the Beatnik sound Xtra are included.

Lingo improvements include:

- Dozens of new Lingo commands (see *http://www.zeusprod.com/nutshell/ d7lingo.html*).

- Scripts no longer limited to 32 KB.

- Improved *traceLoad* features and new *getStreamStatus()* function.

- Debug MIAWs in the D7 debugger.

- Lingo script colorization (I don't like it, personally).

- Library Palette provides many built-in Behaviors (included in Director 7 Shockwave Internet Studio only).

- Improved timers and Y2K-compliant date functions.

D7 supports streamlined JavaScript-like dot notation (a.k.a. dot syntax). Dot syntax is a shorthand way to specify member and sprite properties. It is available in most situations, and doesn't require the keyword set. For example:

```
sprite(5).loc = point (50, 100)
member(2, 3).directToStage = TRUE
```

can be used instead of:

```
set the loc of sprite 5 = point (50, 100)
set the directToStage of member 2 of castLib 3 = TRUE
```

D7's new bracket syntax is useful with lists. For example:

```
x = exampleList[1]
someList[7][4] = "newValue"
```

can be used instead of:

```
x = getAt (exampleList, 1)
setAt (getAt(someList, 7), 4, "newValue")
```

For many more examples and details, see Chapters 4 and 12, and *http://www. zeusprod.com/nutshell/dotsyntax.html.*

Shockwave 7 and Internet-related improvements:

- Shockwave 7 (SW7) uses a single system player and *Xtras* folder even if using multiple browsers. Automatic incremental upgrades of Shockwave 7 components (smaller downloads). A progress bar now appears to indicate movie downloading status.

- Automatic downloading of digitally signed Xtras and improved security against potentially damaging Xtras in Shockwave

- More convenience: Preview in Browser and a built-in Web 216 (browser-safe) palette. Improved AfterShock (although animated GIF export was dropped). Better streaming management, including *getStreamStatus()*. Support for web standards (HTTPS, XML, simple text HTML tags including tables, post FORM data with *postNetText*, and Java export).

- Multiuser Server (included with the Director Studio only) can create multiplayer games, chat rooms, and shared on-line databases. The Multiuser Xtra also allows peer-to-peer connections.

- ShockMachine is an enhanced player offering the ability to save and play Shockwave movies locally, with full screen playback, volume controls, and custom caching, without requiring a browser.

What's Missing in Director 7

Director 7 has a boatload of new features, but the following were dropped since D6, or not added, though widely hoped for, in D7:

- Macromedia's *Learning Lingo* manual has been incorporated into the *Using Director* manual. Many of the new features are documented on-line only (see URL cited earlier). D7's help system is no longer context-sensitive, but this may be fixed in D7.0.1.

- There is no native ability to render common HTML tags beyond limited support for HTML in text members. You still need an Xtra to "put a browser inside Director."

- No improvements have been made to Director's ability to handle DVD and MPEG video formats since version 6.0. The support for DVD is limited, but can be augmented with the DirectMedia Xtra from Tabuleiro da Baiana (*http:// www.tbaiana.com*).

- There is still not support for random access to SWA files. Macromedia justifies this by saying that most SWA files are streamed from the internet and therefore random access is impractical. Use QT3 movie audio tracks, which can be accessed randomly, instead.

- There is no easy way to permanently attach multiple Behaviors with custom properties to a sprite via Score Recording, although the new *scriptList of sprite* property provides read-only access to attached Behaviors and their current properties.

- D6 rich text is obsolete and has been replaced by D7 text members.

- QuickTime 2 is not supported. QuickTime 3 is required, although Video for Windows AVI files are still supported under Windows.

- SoundEdit 16 has been replaced by Bias Peak LE in the Macintosh Studio package. Extreme 3D and xRes have been supplanted by Fireworks.

- D7 does not support 68K Macs (requires a PPC or G3, and Mac OS 7.5.3 or higher) or Windows 3.1 (requires Windows 95/98/NT and a Pentium).

- RSX/DirectSound sound mixing is not supported in D7 as it was in D6, but D7.0.1 includes a DirectSound mixer that doesn't require RSX.

- No improvements or additions have been made to D7's project management capabilities. There is still no source code or version control system and no improved tools for collaboration among multiple developers.

- The widely rumored spell-checker and encryption Xtras have yet to surface.

Director Resources

The best thing about Director is the extended community of developers that you can torment for assistance. This book notwithstanding, Director is 90% undocumented. Visit Macromedia's web site frequently, and plug into the broader Director community via mailing lists and newsgroups.

Online Resources

The following resources are mandatory for serious Director developers. Links to additional URLs cited throughout this book can also be found at *http://www. zeusprod.com/nutshell/links.html.*

Director in a Nutshell and Lingo in a Nutshell

O'Reilly and Associates:

> *http://www.oreilly.com/catalog/directnut/*
> *http://www.oreilly.com/catalog/lingonut/*

Example code, bonus chapters, links to all URLs in the books:

> *http://www.zeusprod.com/nutshell*

Web Review—all things browser- and web-related:

> *http://www.webreview.com/*

Macromedia

Macromedia home page and mirror sites:

> *http://www.macromedia.com*
> *http://www-euro.macromedia.com*
> *http://www-asia.macromedia.com*

Director 7 new features, upgrade policy, and online docs:

> *http://www.macromedia.com/support/director/how/d7/*
> *http://www.macromedia.com/software/director/productinfo/newfeatures/*
> *http://www.macromedia.com/software/director/upgrade/*

Director 7.0.1, D6.5 Service Pack for Windows and other updaters:

> *http://www.macromedia.com/support/director/upndown/updates.html*

Director Developers Center (searchable database of tech notes and tips):

> *http://www.macromedia.com/support/director/*
> *http://www.macromedia.com/support/sdirector/ts/nav/*
> *http://www.macromedia.com/support/director/how/subjects/*

Shockwave Developer Center:

> *http://www.macromedia.com/shockwave/*
> *http://www.macromedia.com/support/director/how/shock/*

Dynamic HTML and Shockwave:

> *http://www.dhtmlzone.com/swdhtml/index.html*

Director-related newsgroups:

> *http://www.macromedia.com/support/director/interact/newsgroups/*
> *news://forums.macromedia.com/macromedia.plug-ins*
> *news://forums.macromedia.com/macromedia.director.basics*
> *news://forums.macromedia.com/macromedia.director.lingo*

Priority Access (fee-based) technical support:

> *http://www.macromedia.com/support/techsupport.html*
> *http://www.macromedia.com/support/director/suprog/*

Beta program:

> *http://www.macromedia.com/support/program/beta.html*

Director feature suggestions:

> *mailto:wish-director@macromedia.com*

Phone support:

> MacroFacts (fax information): 800-449-3329 or 415-863-4409
> Technical support: 415-252-9080
> Main Operator: 415-252-2000

User groups:

> *http://www.macromedia.com/support/programs/usergroups/worldwide.html*

Developer Locator (find a Director or Lingo developer in your area):

> *http://www.macromedia.com/support/developer_locator/*

Macromedia User Conference (UCON) May 25–27, 1999, in San Francisco, CA:

> *http://ucon.macromedia.com*

Web Sites and Xtras

Zeus Productions (my company) technical notes and Xtras:

http://www.zeusprod.com

UpdateStage (monthly technical articles and the Director Quirk List and Xtras):

http://www.updatestage.com
ftp://ftp.shore.net/members/update/

Director Online Users Group (DOUG)—articles, interviews, reviews:

http://www.director-online.com

Maricopa Director Web (the mother ship of Director information):

http://www.mcli.dist.maricopa.edu/director/tips.html
ftp://ftp.maricopa.edu/pub/mcli/director

Lingo Behavior Database (example Behaviors):

http://www.behaviors.com/lbd/

Links to additional third-party web sites:

http://www.mcli.dist.maricopa.edu/director/net.html
http://www.macromedia.com/support/director/ts/documents/
tn3104-dirwebsites.html

Third-party Xtras:

http://www.macromedia.com/software/xtras/director

FMA Online (links to many Xtra developers):

http://www.fmaonline.com

Xtras developer programs:

http://www.macromedia.com/support/program/xtrasdev.html
http://www.macromedia.com/support/xtras.html

Apple QuickTime and developer sites:

http://developer.apple.com
http://quicktime.apple.com

Mailing Lists

If you have the bandwidth, these mailing lists are often useful resources for Director, Shockwave, Xtras, and Lingo questions (see the Macromedia newsgroups listed earlier). These mailing lists generate a *lot* of email. Subscribe using DIGEST mode to avoid hundreds of separate emails each day.

DIRECT-L (Director and Lingo):

Send the following in the body (not subject) of an email to *listserv@uafsysb. uark.edu*:

```
SUBSCRIBE DIRECT-L yourFirstName yourLastName
SET DIRECT-L DIGEST
```

Archives: *http://www.mcli.dist.maricopa.edu/director/digest/index.html*
MailList: *http://www.mcli.dist.maricopa.edu/director/direct-l/index.html*

Lingo-L (Lingo):

> *http://www.penworks.com/LUJ/lingo-l.cgi*

ShockeR (Shockwave):

> Send the following in the body of an email to *list-manager@shocker.com*:
>
> ```
> SUBSCRIBE shockwave-DIGEST yourEmail@yourDomain
> ```
>
> Archive: *http://ww2.narrative.com/shocker.nsf*
> MailList: *http://www.shocker.com/shocker/digests/index.html*

Xtras-L (Xtras for Director):

> Send the following in the body of an email to *listserv@trevimedia.com*:
>
> ```
> SUB XTRAS-L yourFirstName yourLastName
> ```

Flash Resources

Flash newsgroup:

> *news://forums.macromedia.com/macromedia.flash*

Flasher mailing list:

> Send the following in the *body* of an email to *list-manager@shocker.com*:
>
> ```
> SUBSCRIBE Flasher yourEmail@yourDomain
> ```

Flash Pad:

> *http://www.flasher.net/flashpad.html*

Flash discussion group:

> *http://www.devdesign.com/flash*

We'd Like to Hear from You

We have tested and verified all of the information in this book to the best of our ability, but you may find that features have changed (or that we have made mistakes). Please let O'Reilly know about any errors you find by writing:

O'Reilly & Associates, Inc.
101 Morris Street
Sebastopol, CA 95472
800-998-9938 (in U.S. or Canada)
707-829-0515 (international/local)
707-829-0104 (fax)

You can also send us messages electronically. To be put on the mailing list or request a catalog, send email to:

> *nuts@oreilly.com*

To ask technical questions or comment on the book, send email to:

> *bookquestions@oreilly.com*

Dedications

Director in a Nutshell is dedicated to Zoë, who likes the ostrich on the cover; to Ariel, who has been waiting most of her life for me to finish this book; to Zachary, who has been waiting his *entire* life for me to finish this book; and to Mildred Krauss, the most literate, intelligent, and sincere person I've had the good fortune to be related to.

In memoriam

I wish to acknowledge the passing of my great-uncle Mark Daniel. It is with great personal sadness that I mourn his departure from the world into which, as the family obstetrician, he brought me and my siblings. May those who knew and loved him take comfort in the lives that he touched while he was here.

Acknowledgments

I am indebted to many people, some of which I've undoubtedly omitted from the following list. Please buy this book and recommend it to friends so that I can thank the people I've forgotten in the next revision.

My deep appreciation goes out to the entire staff at O'Reilly, whose patience, professionalism, and unwavering dedication to quality are directly responsible for the existence and depth of this book. Special thanks goes to my editors Katie Gardner and Troy Mott, who I put through heck if not hell, for their tolerance and perseverance; to the series editor Tim O'Reilly for recognizing the genuine article; to Edie Freedman, whose choice of an ostrich that looks like me for the cover made my wife amorous; and to Seth Maislin, for his index par excellence. My thanks also to Sheryl Avruch, Frank Willison, Robert Romano, Mike Sierra, and the O'Reilly production staff, including Clairemarie Fisher O'Leary, Nicole Gipson Arigo, Ellie Cutler, and Jane Ellin, who turn a manuscript into a book; to the sales and marketing staff, who bring home the bacon; and to all the O'Reilly authors in whose company I am proud to be.

I must especially thank Nancy Kotary, my production editor, for her tireless and heroic efforts on this book. Nancy is truly the epitome of what an editor should be—an invisible hand that improves a manuscript without detracting from the author's voice or content. I credit Nancy with turning me from a writer into a true author.

This project would not have happened without the efforts of my agent, David Rogelberg of Studio B Productions (*http://www.studiob.com*). He was instrumental in the development and genesis of both *Director in a Nutshell* and *Lingo in a Nutshell*, for which I am forever grateful. My thanks also to Sherry Rogelberg and to the participants of Studio B's Computer Book Publishing list (particularly John Levine).

The quality of the manuscript reflects my excellent technical reviewers, all of whom made time for this semi-thankless job despite their busy schedules: Lisa Kushins, who verified items to an extent that astounded me and provided feedback that improved every chapter she touched; Hudson Ansley, whose keen eye and unique perspective also improved the book immeasurably; and Mark Castle (*http://www.the-castle.com*), who helped shape the style and content from the earliest stages. My thanks also goes out to all my beta readers, who provided useful feedback, particularly Roger Jones, John Williams, Ted Jones, and Alex Zavatone, and to the reviewers who were kind enough to peruse the manuscript and offer the choice quotes you'll find on the back cover.

I can not begin to thank all the Macromedians who develop, document, and support Director, many of whom provide technical support on their own time on various mailing lists. My special thanks goes to Buzz Kettles, for all his feedback regarding Shockwave audio and sound mixing. My thanks again to Lalit Balchandani, David Calaprice, Jim Corbett, Landon Cox, Ken Day, Peter DeCrescenzo, David Dennick, John Dowdell, Mike Edmunds, John Embow, Eliot Greenfield, Jim Inscore, David Jennings, James Khazar, Leona Lapez, S Page, Andrew Rose, Joe Schmitz, Bill Schulze, Michael Seery, Werner Sharp, Karen Silvey, Gordon Smith, Joe Sparks, John Thompson, Karen Tucker, John Ware, Eric Wittman, Doug Wyrick, and Greg Yachuk, all of whom fight the good fight on a daily basis. A special thanks to Stephen Hsu of Puma Associates, for the use of his equipment. My thanks goes out to the wider Director community many of whom I thanked in *Lingo in a Nutshell*, and to Jeff Buell, Kurt Cagle, Marc Canter, Chino, Jamie Ciocco, Jim Collins, Rob Dillon, Greg Griffith, Colin Holgate, Marvyn Hortman, Richard Hurley, Jeremy Scott Knudsen, Brian Kromrey, Renfield Kuroda, George Langley, James Newton, John Nyquist, Daniel Plaenitz, Andrew Rose, Gary Rosenzweig, Terry Schussler, Brian Sharon, John Taylor, Michael Weinberg, Mark Whybird, and Charles Wiltgen, whom I did not.

I still owe a debt of gratitude to Professor David Thorburn, who taught me more about writing than anyone before or since. Please send any complaints to him.

I want to acknowledge both my immediate and extended family, especially my parents (you know who you are), whose love and encouragement molded me into a reasonable facsimile of an adult; and to my wife Michele, whose love and encouragement made these books possible.

I'd like to thank you for taking the time to read this book. It is not a static lecture, but an ongoing conversation between you the reader and me the author. Feedback from many customers, clients, and friends has already shaped its content and, with any luck, will shape many future revisions. Let us see if we can learn some things about Director and something about ourselves in the process.

—Bruce A. Epstein
Franklin Park, N.J., March 1998

"Wisdom consists of knowing when to avoid perfection."
—Confucius

PART I

Director's Core Components

CHAPTER 1

How Director Works

This chapter explains what Director does behind the scenes and how the Cast, the Score, the Stage, and Lingo interact. You will learn how, why, and when Director does (and doesn't) send messages and process user events. (Refer also to Chapter 2, *Events, Messages, and Scripts*, in the companion volume, *Lingo in a Nutshell*.) This chapter will help you make intelligent design decisions and debug hitherto vexing problems. It assumes that you are familiar with the mechanics of using Director's Score and Cast windows. If not, refer to Macromedia's *Using Director* manual and to the *Show Me* demonstration movies that come with Director. See also Chapter 3, *The Score and Animation,* and Chapter 4, *CastLibs, Cast Members, and Sprites.* If you are unfamiliar with Lingo, you should read Chapter 1, *How Lingo Thinks*, and subsequent chapters in *Lingo in a Nutshell* to understand the Lingo used throughout this book.

Director's Frame-Based Model

This section describes how Director's Score and Cast interact when playing your Director movie file. This forms the basis of most Director development, so slog through the introductory paragraph, and you'll soon be in "Aha!" territory.

The Score, Frames, and the Playback Head

Director has its roots in traditional animation. Each frame of the Score represents a slice of time, and the elements in the sprite channels are overlaid (sprites in higher channels usually appear in the foreground) to create the final image on the Stage. An individual frame of the movie is *static*—animations are created by moving sprites over successive frames (i.e., over time). The Stage displays the current frame as indicated by the position of the *playback head* (the red rectangle and vertical line) in the Score window, but Lingo changes are not processed until the playback head advances or an *updateStage* command is issued. Furthermore, Lingo can override the Score notation for individual sprite channels (this is called puppeting), and *the updateLock* property can prevent Director from redrawing the Stage.

Unless directed otherwise, Director automatically proceeds left to right through each frame of the Score, displaying sprites and obeying the Effects channels that control sounds, transitions, palettes, and tempos. As the playback head moves, Director repeatedly checks for user events and redraws the Stage as necessary.

Sounds are triggered and graphics redrawn only when there is a *change* from the previous frame. Director redraws only the portion(s) of the Stage that change.

Director automatically generates *events* or *messages*, such as *prepareFrame, enterFrame, exitFrame*, and *idle*, as the movie plays (but generates only *idle* events if the movie is paused with the *pause* command).

Director incurs additional overhead in certain special frames of the Score. Avoid looping in the first or last frame of the Score. In the first frame, Director initializes many movie attributes. Extend the sprites in the first frame into adjacent frames and use a later frame for interactivity instead. In the last frame of the movie, Director also incurs additional overhead and does not always behave consistently. Instead of looping in the last frame, create dummy frames at the end of your Score, so that your final meaningful frame is not the last frame in the Score.

For example, put this frame script in the script channel of a dummy frame beyond your last "real" frame:

```
on exitFrame
   nothing -- dummy script
end
```

Director performs faster with the playback head moving forward than looping in a frame or moving backward. You may see a hitch in an animation as Director's playback head loops backwards. Consider *tweening* (extending) the animation over additional frames in the Score for smoother playback.

Although the size of the Score notation is usually dwarfed by media, the entire Score is always loaded when a movie starts (or downloads via Shockwave) and remains in memory during playback. If your Projector takes a long time to start up, either minimize your Score or use a dummy loader movie (see "Stub Projectors" in Chapter 8, *Projectors and the Runtime Environment*).

Director stores and recognizes only the *changes* of sprite attributes from one frame of the Score to the next, similar to video "differenced" frames. This reduces the size of the Score notation, but can prevent Director from recognizing changes between frames. The end of a sprite is not considered a change. Properties for that channel are not updated until another sprite with different properties begins in that channel. If you check the *rollover()* of a nonexistent sprite, Director will use the bounding box of the last sprite to occupy that sprite channel.

Similar to the concept of video keyframes, the Score includes periodic keyframes (full records of sprite properties). The Score's hidden keyframes should not be confused with *sprite* keyframes created explicitly by the developer. Score keyframes require more storage than *difference* frames, but they allow Director to recreate any frame without deriving it from the beginning of the Score.

Don't confuse the *length* of the Score in frames with the size of the Score *notation* as stored to disk or held in RAM. The length of sprite spans within the Score has negligible effect; extending a background sprite over 500 frames adds only about 1 KB. The size of the Score notation depends mainly on the number of sprite channels used and the frequency of changes from frame to frame, not the number of frames. Reduce the size of your Score by joining individual cells and removing unneeded keyframes within sprite spans.

Each additional sprite channel adds about 90 bytes to the Score notation. Additional storage is required when a new sprite occurs or attributes of the sprite change. In D6, it doesn't matter if you skip sprite channels; using channel 120 does not cause Director to store information for all the unused channels that precede it. In D7, unused channels *do* affect performance; limit the number of channels under `Modify` ➤ `Movie` ➤ `Properties` and see *the lastChannel* property.

Effects Channels

The following is a brief overview of the Score Effects channels. Refer to "Lingo Overriding the Score" later in this chapter for more details.

Tempo Channel

Director plays every frame of an animation regardless of how long it takes. It attempts to keep pace with the Tempo channel's frame rate setting (such as 30 fps), but is not guaranteed to do so. Your animation and soundtrack may get seriously out of synch.

 Director is frame-based, not time-based. The Tempo channel sets a maximum frame rate (preventing Director from running too quickly on higher-end machines), *not* a minimum or guaranteed frame rate.

You can synchronize media using the Tempo channel to wait for a sound or digital video to end or to reach a cue point, or by using time-based media (QuickTime or AVI files). You can also use the Tempo channel to wait for a fixed amount of time, or for the user to click the mouse or press a key.

The Tempo frame rate affects how often Director checks for user events, such as mouse clicks. A Tempo less than five frames per second results in a sluggish response to mouse and keyboard events.

In Director 6 and 7, the Tempo channel's *Wait* options no longer lock out other interactivity as they did in Director 5 and earlier versions.

Palette Channel

The Palette channel controls Director's color display when using an 8-bit color depth (256 colors) or lower. It has no effect in 16-bit or higher color depths (thousands or millions). See Chapter 13, *Graphics, Color, and Palettes.*

Only one palette can be active at any time. At color depths higher than 8-bit (256 colors) Director largely ignores palettes, and won't perform palette fades and color cycling.

Transition Channel

The Transition channel adds visual effects such as wipes and dissolves to your movie. Transition execution time is inexact and performance varies across platforms.

Transitions occur after the *prepareFrame* handler but before the *enterFrame* handler. See Table 16-1 in *Lingo in a Nutshell* for a list of transition types and see "Transition Channel" in Chapter 3 for many important details.

Sound Channels

The Sound channels allow you to place sounds directly in the Score. Although the Score shows only two Sound channels, Lingo can access up to eight sound channels. Score sounds are triggered only when a change in the Sound channel occurs from one frame to the next. Because animations are frame-based but sounds are time-based, synchronization is not guaranteed. The number of frames over which a sound is tweened does not necessarily affect its duration. The sound may be cut off if not tweened out over enough frames (at a given tempo). The sound will end when it is complete, even if tweened out over additional frames (unless its *loop* option or *loop of member* property is set).

Take care to avoid conflicts with Score sounds when using sound channels 1 and 2 via Lingo (refer to Chapter 15, *Sound and Cue Points*).

Sprites

This section provides a very brief overview of sprites. You should be familiar with Chapter 4, *Sprites*, in Macromedia's *Using Director* manual.

Sprite References

The Score does not contain any assets such as graphics, video, or sound; it contains *references* to the assets physically stored in the cast libraries (which may in turn point to external files on disk). A Score reference is called a *sprite*, and a sprite always points to a cast member by its *cast member number*, which is like a coat-check tag. To get your coat back, you give the clerk your tag, and he matches the number on the tag to the coat hanger. When the playback head enters a frame, Director reads the sprite references and loads the corresponding cast members by number. This is very efficient, because a single cast member can be used as a sprite in multiple frames or in multiple sprite channels in the same frame, yet be stored only once on disk.

 If you move a cast member in the Cast window, Director automatically updates the Score's sprite reference(s) to point to the new cast member number. If you cut and paste cast members, the sprites references *don't* update.

Your Lingo is never updated automatically, even when moving cast members. Refer to cast members by name rather than by number to avoid breaking your Lingo code if a cast member moves. Use global variables to refer to sprite channels to make your Lingo easier to update when a sprite moves to a different channel or use *the currentSpriteNum* to refer to a sprite.

Sprite Properties

Each sprite can have attributes such as its location, ink effect, and size. All sprites share some core properties, but each type of sprite (bitmap, digital video, field) has properties that are meaningful only for that specific asset type. Most sprite properties can be set via both the user interface and Lingo.

A sprite is just a collection of *properties* (attributes). A sprite refers to a cast member, but it is not the cast member itself. Changing a sprite's properties affects only a single sprite. Changing a cast member's properties affects all sprites that reference it.

To change the graphic displayed by a sprite at runtime, change its *member of sprite* property, which can be changed independently of other sprite properties. Use Edit ➤ Exchange Cast Members to change a sprite's cast member permanently during authoring.

Sprite Spans

In Director 5, a *sprite* was a single cell (i.e., a sprite reference in a single frame). In Director 6 and later, a sprite can span a *range* of frames. A sprite span often uses the same cast member throughout its life, but each cell in a sprite span can use a different cast member, just as a sprite's location can change in each cell along its span.

You can work with a sprite span as a unified object, which is often easier than working with individual cells over a series of frames. The *beginSprite* message is sent when the playback head first enters a sprite span and the *endSprite* message is sent when the playback head leaves the sprite span. A frame script can span multiple frames and receives these messages too. In D7, the new *startFrame* and *endFrame of sprite* properties indicate the extents of a sprite's span.

Puppet Sprites

The Score is most useful for creating predetermined animations. Lingo can override the Score settings to create variations that are impossible or prohibitive with the Score alone. Overriding a sprite's Score properties via Lingo is called *puppeting*. Director 6 and later automatically puppet and unpuppet sprite properties in most cases. To move a sprite, you can dynamically change its *loc of sprite* property at runtime. Changing *the member of sprite* property changes the cast member (such as a bitmap) displayed on the Stage, just as switching coat-check tags would result in your receiving a different coat from the cloak room.

Scripts and the Script Channel

Script cast members attached to the Script channel (i.e., *frame scripts*) are executed as the playback head moves through the Score. These typically contain Lingo handlers that move the playback head to another frame or cause it to loop in the current frame. The *prepareFrame, enterFrame, idle,* and *exitFrame* messages are sent to the frame script whenever the playback head moves or loops in a single frame. A frame script can span multiple frames and receives the *beginSprite* message when the playback head first enters its span, and the *endSprite* message when the playback head leaves it, just as a sprite script would.

The Script channel is often used to execute Lingo in response to the playback head moving, but it also receives mouse and keyboard events not trapped by sprites.

Each sprite in the Score can have one of more Lingo scripts, called *sprite scripts,* attached to it. Attaching Behaviors (i.e., scripts) to sprites allows them to react to user events, such as mouse clicks.

Lingo scripts can also be piggybacked onto a cast member directly rather than attached to a sprite. These are called *cast scripts* and are not contained in separate cast members but are added to existing cast members such as bitmaps. When a cast member is placed in the Score, the resulting sprite automatically has access to that cast member's cast script. Refer to Chapter 2 in *Lingo in a Nutshell* for more information.

Cast Members

Most assets are stored in the Cast, including text, bitmaps, and shapes. The Cast also contains items that are used in the Score, but never appear on the Stage, such as transitions, palettes, and scripts. All cast members have properties, some of which are specific to a particular data type; a bitmap's properties include its width, height, and bit depth, and a sound's properties include its sampling rate and number of channels. Many properties, such as a sprite's location, can be set on a per-sprite basis, but some cannot. For example, the state of radio buttons, the width of text fields, and the *directToStage* property of digital videos can be changed only on a per-member basis.

When you change a cast member, all sprites referencing that cast member are affected. This can include sprite references in multiple movies if the assets are stored in an external cast library. You can change entire cast libraries wholesale to, say, facilitate internationalization. See Chapter 4.

Some assets, notably sounds, Flash movies, and video, can reside external to the cast (i.e., they are externally *linked*). Linked assets always point to external files by name. Any changes to the contents of the external file are incorporated automatically. If an external file is missing, Director will either ignore the asset or ask the user to locate it.

Storage and Loading

At any given time, only the cast members required in the current frame must reside in RAM. The majority of assets can remain on disk (or even on the Web). Director does a good job of automatically loading cast members as they are needed and unloading them as required to free up RAM for still other cast members as the animation progresses. It is best to create your presentation and see how it runs on the target platform, before tweaking the preloading and unloading of assets as described in Chapter 9, *Memory and Performance*.

When you save a movie file, Director appends the edits made since the last save. Whenever you edit or delete a cast member, the old data stays in the movie file until you use File ➤ Save and Compact or File ➤ Save As.

Director stores cast members from internal casts in the order in which they are used in the Score, not the order in which they appear in the Cast window. Cast members in external casts *are* stored in the order in which they appear in the Cast window.

Drawing to the Stage

The Stage is the user's viewport into your Director presentation. Placing a cast member directly on the Stage creates a sprite in the Score, but not all sprites in the Score are necessarily visible (they may be off-Stage, etc.).

Before Director displays a frame, it assembles all the assets in an offscreen buffer. Some assets, such as digital video and Flash movies, can bypass the offscreen rendering and are drawn *direct-to-Stage*. This is faster, but may prevent Director from knowing when it must refresh portions of the screen.

Lingo changes to sprite properties are not reflected on the Stage until an *updateStage* is issued or the playback head moves (including looping in a single frame using *go the frame*).

Director renders the upcoming frame in its offscreen buffer before displaying the final result on the Stage, in the following steps:

1. Director loads cast members as needed for the upcoming frame, unloading other assets as required.

2. Director sends the *beginSprite* event to any sprites whose spans begin in the upcoming frame (it is also sent to the frame script if the frame script span begins anew). You can perform initialization or override Score properties in an *on beginSprite* handler in a score script.

3. Director sends the *prepareFrame* event to all sprites and the script channel in the upcoming frame. The *on prepareFrame* handler is called every time the playback head moves, so use *on beginSprite* instead for one-time initialization.

4. Director notes those areas of the screen than have changed from the previous frame. Sprites that haven't changed aren't redrawn unless they were previously covered by another sprite that has since moved.

5. Director doesn't draw those sprites whose sprite channel is muted in the Score or whose *visible of sprite* property is set to FALSE.

6. Director renders sprites that do not draw themselves direct-to-Stage. Sprites in higher channels may obscure those in lower channels. (Sprite channel 1 is in the background, and higher channels are in the foreground.) Each sprite is rendered according to its ink effect, blend value, foreColor, etc.

7. Director renders sprites whose *trails of sprite* property is TRUE and are not direct-to-Stage, again in back-to-front order. In D7, sprites with trails may mistakenly erase nearby pixels.

8. Director draws only the *changing* areas of the new frame from the offscreen buffer to the Stage, exclusive of areas covered by direct-to-Stage sprites. Transition and palette effects are executed as the new frame is drawn.

9. Director triggers any sounds in the current frame's Sound channels. There may be a lag before the sound is audible, especially when using multiple Sound channels under Windows. See Chapter 15 for details.

10. Direct-to-Stage sprites such as digital video or Flash sprites draw themselves to the Stage. They are drawn in the foreground above all other sprites using the *copy* ink effect. Because they bypass Director's offscreen buffer, they perform faster, and direct-to-Stage sprites can also be rendered "between" frames during idle periods; if using a direct-to-Stage Flash or QuickTime sprite whose frame rate is faster than the Director tempo, they will be rendered multiple times per Director frame for smoother playback. Two overlapping direct-to-Stage sprites will repeatedly redraw over each other and should be avoided.

11. Director sends *enterFrame*, *stepFrame*, *idle*, and *exitFrame* events as described in Chapter 2 of *Lingo in a Nutshell*. StepFrame events allow items in *the actorList* to update themselves for the next frame, and *idle* events allow a sprite to perform background tasks.

Messages are sent to sprite Xtras during the drawing process (see *http://www.macromedia.com/support/xtras/xdks/xdk_d6a4/docs/html/mmdg/mmdgc2.htm*).

Director will not redraw any sprites behind a direct-to-Stage video if there is no change in the sprite from the previous frame of the Score. Move the sprite or use a transition to force Director to refresh its sprite area after the video completes.

Sprites that appeared in previous frames but not in the current frame are automatically erased unless one of the following is true:

- The trails property was applied to the sprite.
- The sprite has been manually puppeted via Lingo.
- They are digital video or Flash sprites played direct-to-Stage, in which case artifacts may be left.

A sprite may not appear on the Stage if:

- Its sprite channel is muted in the Score.
- Its *visible of sprite* property is set to FALSE.
- The Score notation or its *loc of sprite* property places it off-Stage.
- It is obscured by another sprite, including sprites in higher channels, sprites with a higher *locZ*, and direct-to-Stage sprites.

- It was manually puppeted in another frame, in a state where that sprite was not visible, such as being located off-Stage.

- Its *width of sprite* or *height of sprite* is zero or its *skew of sprite* is 90 or 270.

- Its properties were puppeted to make it visible, but the Stage has yet to be refreshed.

- It is an unstroked (i.e., *the lineSize of member* is zero), unfilled shape sprite.

- It is a digital video sprite with no video track or the video track disabled.

- It is a Flash or vector shape member or sprite with its *imageEnabled* property set to FALSE.

- It is a Shockwave Audio (SWA) sprite.

- Its *blend of sprite* property is set to zero.

- Its ink effect makes it impossible to see on the given background.

- Its foreground color makes it impossible to see because it is the same color as the background.

- The *member of sprite* points to a missing or invalid cast member.

- A sprite was puppeted with nothing in that sprite channel. You must manually set the *loc, width, height, member,* and *foreColor of sprite* properties.

A sprite may not appear, or may appear as a red "X" if the cast member is unavailable, because:

- An external asset, such as a digital video file, is missing.

- The asset has not yet been downloaded from the Internet.

- Memory is low (in which case some sprites can't be loaded).

- A missing sprite Xtra, such as the Flash Xtra, is required for that asset type.

- The sprite requires QuickTime or a similar extension, and the correct version is not installed.

Lingo Versus the Score

The toughest thing about Director is the quirky interaction between the Cast, the Score, and Lingo. Experience will teach you whether the Score or Lingo is best suited to a particular task, although a hybrid approach is often optimal.

At one extreme, all sprite properties, sounds, palettes, and transitions are controlled solely by the Score. This requires that the presentation plays exactly as laid out in the Score, which is adequate for most slide shows or self-running demos. The Tempo channel can be used to wait for sounds, cue points, a fixed time, or mouse clicks.

At the other extreme is the so-called *one-frame movie*, which has been erroneously promoted as the Holy Grail of Director development. The Score has many strengths, and it is foolish to try to duplicate all its features solely through Lingo. Capitalize on *both* the Score's and Lingo's strengths. Use the Score for static items or predefined animations and Lingo for dynamic sprites and to add interactivity.

Use the Score to position fixed sprites, and use Lingo to jump between different frames in response to user choices. Lingo is also required when an animation needs to change randomly, such as for an arcade game, or change under user control, such as for a drawing game.

Lingo and the Playback Head

Director was originally only an animation tool. Lingo was added later, and the marriage is not perfect. The order in which Director sends messages, runs Lingo handlers, updates the Stage, plays sounds and video, and performs transitions can be extremely confusing. When does Director execute Lingo, and when does it obey the Score? At any moment, "where" is Director, in Lingo or in the Score?

Director gives the illusion of doing two things at once by quickly alternating between its two masters—the Score and Lingo. The position of the playback head determines which frame's information is read from the Score, but the current Lingo handler executes *independently* of the playback head.

The playback head can be moved to a different frame from Lingo while a script is being executed. Director continues to execute the remainder of the current Lingo handler, even following a *go to* command. Example 1-1 illustrates this point.

Example 1-1: The Playback Head Versus Lingo Execution

```
on exitFrame
  go to frame 10
  alert "The alert command was executed"
end exitFrame
```

Note that the alert message is posted even though the *go to* command moves the playback head. This same phenomenon can cause handlers to be executed in an unexpected sequence. Suppose the following *mouseDown* handler (which jumps to frame 20) is attached to a button in frame 10; a *mouseUp* handler is also attached:

```
on mouseDown
  beep
  go to frame 20
end mouseDown

on mouseUp
  alert "MouseUp was detected in frame 10"
end mouseDown
```

In frame 20, a separate sprite (in the same position on the Stage as the first button) also has a *mouseUp* handler attached:

```
on mouseUp
  alert "MouseUp was detected in frame 20"
end mouseDown
```

What happens?

1. The user depresses the mouse on the button in frame 10.

2. The *mouseDown* script's *go to frame 20* command sends the playback head to frame 20.

3. The *mouseUp* event is detected in the destination frame, not the original frame. The *mouseUp* handler in frame 10 is never executed.

Because the playback head moved between the issuance of the *mouseDown* and *mouseUp* events, the *mouseUp* event was unexpectedly detected in the destination frame (frame 20). Avoid jumping to a different frame during a *mouseDown* handler to prevent this. If necessary, wait within the *mouseDown* handler until *the mouseUp* property is TRUE, indicating that the mouse has been released.

Lingo Execution and Stage Updating

Director was designed around the assumption that Lingo handlers are brief and that control is quickly relinquished to Director's Score. While a lengthy Lingo handler is executing, the Stage does not update and Director does not process events. Furthermore, Lingo commands that affect the Score channels do not go into effect immediately, but are held up (*buffered*) until the playback head moves or an *updateStage* command is issued. This allows you to make several changes without the user seeing the interim steps. For example, you might use a *puppetTransition* when moving a sprite onto the Stage, as follows:

```
on showIt
  set the loc of sprite 5 = point (150, 200)
  -- Transition type 1 is a wipe right
  puppetTransition 1
  updateStage
end showIt
```

The following commands do not take effect until the Stage is redrawn:

Sprite property changes (*loc of sprite, member of sprite,* etc.)
puppetSprite
puppetPalette
puppetSound
puppetTransition
puppetTempo

Use *updateStage* to trigger Lingo's puppet commands and display sprite changes on the Stage. Use the *updateLock* property to prevent Director from redrawing the Stage when going to another frame or during Score Recording.

Director's designers assumed that you would exit the current Lingo handler after issuing certain commands. The playback head does not move instantaneously when a Lingo command affecting it is issued. If you issue a *go* command, the destination frame's *enterFrame* handler will be executed, followed by the remaining statements after the *go* command, followed by the destination frame's *exitFrame* handler. Some commands may be "postponed" until the remainder of the handler is completed, most notably *delay* and *open.*

Attach the Frame script in Example 1-2 to the Script channel and play the movie. Open the Message window to see the results.

Example 1-2: Unexpected Sequence of Execution

```
on exitFrame
  put "Before the delay, the time is" && the long time
  delay 300
  put "After the delay, the time is" && the long time
end exitFrame
```

Notice that the *delay* occurs after both *put* statements have been executed, not between them, as one might expect. Place commands in separate *exitFrame* handlers in successive frames of the Score to ensure the desired order of execution.

Lingo Interferes with Director's Event Handling

Generally, Director processes events only when the playback head is moving and Lingo is not being executed. Director does not process mouse and keyboard events while a Lingo handler is executing, such as during a *repeat* loop. Director does not issue *prepareFrame*, *enterFrame*, and *exitFrame* handlers if the movie has been paused using the *pause* command. Keep your Lingo handlers, especially *on idle*, brief to allow Director to process user events.

Within a *repeat* loop, you can use *updateStage* to refresh the Stage, and you can manually check for mouse and keyboard activity using *the mouseDown* and *the keyDown* properties. While a *repeat* loop is executing, Director will buffer all the mouse clicks and not send them onto the appropriate sprites until the current Lingo handler completes. Instead of looping within a *repeat* loop or using *pause*, use *go to the frame* to loop in a frame while still allowing Director to issue frame events and process user events.

The *clickOn* and *key* properties do not update within a Lingo handler. The initial value when the handler is called is the only value reported until the handler completes. The *stillDown* property does not update within a repeat loop. To obtain the current state of the mouse and keyboard, check *the mouseDown* instead of *the stillDown* and *the keyPressed* instead of *the key*.

Lingo Overriding the Score

A number of Lingo commands override the notations in the Score, but their interaction is quirky.

Auto-puppets versus manual puppets

Prior to Director 6, a sprite channel was either completely under Lingo's control (*puppeted*) or completely under the Score's control (*unpuppeted*) at any given time. There were no compromises, although control could be switched between the two methods by manually puppeting or unpuppeting the sprite channel with the *puppetSprite* command or *the puppet of sprite* property.

When manually puppeting a sprite, the puppeted sprite takes its initial properties from the single frame in the Score in which you issue the *puppetSprite* command. (Therefore, if you puppet a sprite in a frame where that channel is empty, the initial sprite properties are undefined.) Once puppeted, the entire sprite channel is completely under Lingo control, and that sprite will not update in any way without explicit instruction from Lingo. The channel remains under Lingo control until you explicitly *unpuppet* the sprite using *puppetSprite spriteNum, FALSE*. See also "The truth about puppeting" in the D6 *ReadMe* file.

Director 6 introduced *auto-puppeting*. To change a sprite's location by setting *the loc of sprite*, you need not explicitly puppet the sprite channel. Director will automatically puppet the individual property you've changed, but *all other properties of that sprite will continue to obey the Score notation*. Best of all, any auto-puppeted properties automatically cancel themselves when that sprite span ends. You still have the option of explicitly using the *puppetSprite* command to control a sprite channel manually.

The *puppetSprite* command puts the entire Score sprite channel under Lingo control. Auto-puppeting places only selected properties of the current sprite span under Lingo control.

The following properties of a sprite are auto-puppeted whenever the property is set: *backColor, blend, editable, foreColor, height, ink, loc, locH, locV, member, moveable, rect,* and *width*. Auto-puppeting of individual properties has no effect on *the puppet of sprite* property.

Puppeting perils

When a sprite channel is unpuppeted, the sprite does not immediately revert to reflect the Score settings—manually puppeted sprites or auto-puppeted properties retain their puppeted values until the Score affects a change to that property value or a *go to frame* or *playFrame* command is executed.

Remember that the Score stores only *changes* from one frame to the next. For example, if two adjacent sprite's spans in a single channel share the same *locH* value, no change is recorded in the Score where the first sprite ends and the second begins. If the *locH* of the first sprite has been set via Lingo, the auto-puppeted value will "stick" for the second sprite. To combat the problem, you can explicitly record a sprite's Score-based properties in its *beginSprite* handler before making Lingo changes, and explicitly restore its properties in its *endSprite* handler.

Some developers have reported poor results when relying on Director to automatically unpuppet auto-puppeted attributes. If necessary, puppet and unpuppet sprites manually.

Cast, Score, and Lingo Cooperation

Many Director developers envision the Score and Lingo as being pitted against each other, but you should structure your Cast and Score to cooperate actively with your Lingo code.

Organize your Cast and Score such that it makes your Lingo easier to write and maintain. Use markers to identify frames regardless of the frame number. Use cast member names to identify members regardless of their cast member numbers. For example, using the same name for a button and for the marker that it jumps to allows you to reuse the same Lingo script for many buttons:

```
on mouseUp me
   go (the name of the member of sprite (the spriteNum of me))
end
```

The Cast

Every asset, script, and transition appears in the Cast, but may not necessarily be used in the Score. Movie Scripts, Parent Scripts, fonts, and custom cursors are used by Director, but never appear in the Score. Puppeted bitmaps and sounds may never appear in the Score, but are still required by Lingo at runtime. Place assets that are to be used as puppets into dummy frames in the Score, so that they are stored near similar assets when the file is saved. This also prevents them from being flagged as "unused" in the *Find Cast Member* dialog box.

To access a series of cast members, place them sequentially in the Cast, such that your Lingo code can simply increment the *memberNum of sprite* property to find the next one. Example 1-3 changes sprite 5's graphic when the button is clicked. It might be used for a slide show.

Example 1-3: Cooperation Between the Cast and Lingo

```
on mouseUp
   set the memberNum of sprite 5 = the memberNum of sprite 5 + 1
end
```

Note that the script in Example 1-3 always uses the next cast member in the Cast. You need to ensure that your slide show's elements are stored sequentially in the Cast for this to work. You might add Lingo to detect that you've reached the end of the slide show and start back at the first slide. The revised script assumes that your last cast member in the slide show is named "Last Slide" and that the first one is name "First Slide" with an arbitrary number of cast members between them:

```
on mouseUp
   if the member of sprite 5 = member "Last Slide" then
     set the member of sprite 5 = member "First Slide"
   else
     set the memberNum of sprite 5 = the memberNum  ¬
       of sprite 5 + 1
   end if
end
```

Note that we named our cast members so that Lingo can refer to them by name, not by member number (which may change). Name cast members consistently to simplify your Lingo. The script in Example 1-4 will work for any cast member whose highlighted button state is named the same as the default button state with the word "hi" appended. For example, if the original state of a button is named "my button" and the highlighted state is named "my button hi", the script will highlight the button on rollovers.

Example 1-4: Naming Cast Members to Make Lingo Easier

```
property spriteNum, origName
on beginSprite me
  set origName = the name of the member of sprite spriteNum
end beginSprite

on mouseEnter me
  set the member of sprite spriteNum = origName  && "hi"
end mouseEnter

on mouseLeave me
  set the member of sprite spriteNum = origName
end mouseLeave
```

 A cast member's name and its position *relative* to other cast members are your primary tools for simplifying Lingo that manipulates cast members. Do not rely on the *absolute* position of cast members in your Lingo code.

Place assets and scripts that are used in multiple movies (or even multiple projects) in external cast libraries, rather than maintaining separate copies in each movie's internal cast.

The Score

Your Score should be beautiful and suggest a natural structure or pattern. Similar sections such as user menu screens should each occupy the same number of frames in the Score. They should be separated by the same number of blank frames. They should each have markers (with sensible names) in the same relative positions (such as to mark the beginning of the scene).

Consistent use of markers simplifies the Lingo needed to jump to different frames in the Score. Instead of having ten different Lingo scripts each jumping to a different frame, you can just write one reusable script using *go next*.

Consistent use of sprite channels simplifies the Lingo to manipulate sprites. Suppose you have ten buttons, and as the user clicks each one you want to change the color of a secondary sprite. If you place each button sprite in the channel preceding the sprite it is supposed to affect, you can use a script such as:

```
on mouseDown
  set the foreColor of sprite(the clickOn + 1) = random(255)
end
```

If attached to a sprite in channel 10, this will change the color of sprite 11; if attached to a sprite in channel 12, this will change the color of sprite 13, etc.

Your Score should have symmetry. Consistent use of markers and sprite channels are your primary tools for simplifying Score-related Lingo.

Always use the same sprite channel for a button or graphic that is used throughout the Score. For example, your background should always be in channel 1, and your Help button might always use channel 15. Use the same sprite channel for different sprites of a similar nature that are used in different scenes. For example, in each scene using digital video, always place your digital video cast member in the same sprite channel. This enables use of a single global variable throughout your movie to access that particular sprite or channel.

How Director Runs Your Movie

By understanding the specific sequence of events that Director performs when it runs your movie, you can better plan and debug your project. Refer to "How Director Executes Your Projector" in Chapter 8 for important details on the Projector environment, where the start-up procedure varies markedly on the two platforms.

Director Startup

When the Director application starts, the following takes place:

1. When the Director authoring environment is launched, it allocates a certain amount of memory for itself.

2. Director loads Xtras from the *Xtras* folder located in the same folder where Director is installed. Xtras such as QuickTime 3 may require extra memory or system extensions, or may fail to initialize.

3. On Windows only, Director reads the *DIRECTOR.INI* file located in the same folder as Director (see Appendix D in *Lingo in a Nutshell*).

4. On Windows only, the Projector temporarily installs the *DIRDIB.DRV* video driver in the *C:\WINDOWS\SYSTEM* folder. Some anti-viral software may object. I've encountered conflicts when running D4 Projectors simultaneously with programs that use DirectX video drivers.

5. On Windows only, Director 6 and earlier may temporarily install *MACROMIX. DLL* in the *C:\WINDOWS\SYSTEM* folder to mix multichannel audio. (If you're using QT3, you can install the QT3Mix sound mixer instead. See Chapter 15.) Again, some anti-viral software may object. Refer to Macromedia TechNote #03130.

6. Director reads the *LINGO.INI* file, if any, located in the same folder as Director, and runs any *on startUp* handler it finds there (see Appendix D in *Lingo in a Nutshell*).

7. Director loads QuickTime and/or Video for Windows if needed and not already loaded.

Movie Startup

When you open and run a Director movie file, the following occurs:

1. Director reads the movie's *initial load segment*, which contains the movie properties, Score, and cast member header information. Cast member media is loaded independently.

2. The movie's internal font map is loaded. The *FONTMAP.TXT* file from the same folder where Director is installed is used for any new movies.

3. The movie's entire Score is loaded into memory. The Score is usually small, so this is a problem only for large movies with a lot of Score changes. Combine individual cells into sprite spans if possible.

4. Director attempts to locate external castLibs and posts a *Where is...?* dialog box if it can't find them.

5. The header information describing each cast member is read.

6. Director issues a warning if Sprite or Transition Xtras are needed for certain cast members but not loaded. It may also issue errors for missing MIX Xtras that are required for linked sounds or bitmaps. This cannot be trapped with *the alertHook.*

7. The cast members in the movie's castLib(s) are loaded according to each castLib's *preLoadMode of castLib* property. All script, font, and shape cast members are loaded.

8. Director allocates a new graphics drawing context for the Stage, erasing any trails or old sprites.

9. The monitor depth may be switched on the Macintosh if *the switchColorDepth* is TRUE (see the *Reset Monitor to Movie's Color Depth* option under File ➤ Preferences ➤ General and under File ➤ Create Projector ➤ Options). In D7, this causes a flash even if the monitor depth is already correct.

10. The Stage's size and position may change based on the *centerStage* and *fixStageSize* properties (see the *StageSize* options under File ➤ Preferences ➤ General and under File ➤ Create Projector ➤ Options).

11. Refer to Chapter 6, *The Stage and Movies-in-a-Window*, for details on which system properties are reset when a movie is played.

12. Director runs the *prepareMovie* and *prepareFrame* handlers before displaying the first frame of the new movie.

13. Director loads the cast members required for the first frame of the movie.

14. Director streams external assets from disk, or loads new cast members as needed or explicitly instructed.

15. Network assets are cached in an invisible temporary folder.

The Grand Scheme of Things

If Director were an animal, its skeleton would be built of *properties*. Properties are attributes of an item and can usually be read and changed. Understanding the property hierarchy will help you comprehend Director's structure. The very incomplete list in Table 1-1 should get you started.

Table 1-1: Director's Property Hierarchy

Category	Examples	See
System	colorDepth, deskTopRectList, quickTimePresent	Chapters 8 and 9
Projector	fixStageSize, platform	Chapters 8 and 9
Movie	stageTop, stageLeft, paletteMapping	Chapters 6, 8, and 9
Window	drawRect, title	Chapter 6
Score	selection, frameTempo	Chapter 3
Sprites	locH, locV, member	Chapter 4
Cast library	preloadMode	Chapter 4
Cast members	width, height, depth	Chapter 4
Asset type properties	digitalVideoType	Chapter 4
Xtras	Custom properties	Chapter 10
Behaviors and parent scripts	ancestor, spriteNum	Chapter 12 in *Lingo in a Nutshell*
Lists	Custom properties	Chapter 6 in *Lingo in a Nutshell*

For a more complete list of properties, see Table 4-10 and the following web sites:

http://www.macromedia.com/software/xtras/docs/html/drref/drtypes.htm
http://www.macromedia.com/software/xtras/docs/html/drref/drtypndx.htm

Macromedia TechNote #06203 lists Director properties by object:

http://www.macromedia.com/support/director/how/subjects/propertylist.html

For a complete list of all Lingo commands and keywords, see Chapter 18, *Lingo Command and Keyword Summary*, in *Lingo in a Nutshell*.

Tradeoffs in Director

You wouldn't expect a luxury car to get the best gas mileage, nor an economy car to include a fancy stereo, and you should be aware of the compromises inherent in any project design. The key to Director development is to understand and balance various tradeoffs. Something that shortens the download time of a Shockwave movie may degrade the animation's performance. Other design choices may improve performance at the expense of greater RAM or disk usage.

Throughout the remainder of the book, we'll discuss the strengths and weaknesses of various techniques. The optimal approach depends on your specific project requirements.

CHAPTER 2

Being More Productive

By its very nature, multimedia is multidisciplinary; you need to know at least a little about a lot of different things. This chapter provides an overview that will help you identify and fill in many of your weak spots and thus save you time. It also covers Director's shortcuts that didn't belong in any other chapter.

Plan Ahead

If you attempt to create or manage a large multimedia project on your own without *significant* prior experience, you risk extreme stress and possible financial ruin. Hire experienced and competent professionals to help design, manage, and implement your project. Inexperienced people will cost you more in the long run even at significantly lower hourly rates. You have been warned.

For many additional tips on hiring appropriate staff or contractors, project management, and the multimedia production process, see *Multimedia Demystified: A Guide to the World of Multimedia from Apple Computer, Inc.* (Random House).

Plan your project before starting production:

- Specify the scope and exact nature of the project. Manage your clients' expectations firmly. You can't hit a moving target.

- Create a storyboard on paper or using Director's File ➤ Print ➤ Stage command. (See the *Print* dialog box's *Scale 50%* and *Storyboard Format* options.)

- Create a production schedule and timeline for milestones (leave time for beta-testing). When you've completed your estimate, quintuple it. Seriously.

- Get the client's approval in writing at every phase of the process.

- Specify the supported target platforms. Use the guidelines in Chapter 7, *Cross-Platform and OS Dependencies*, to decide which features you will be able to support on the desired platforms.

- See "Determining the Appropriate Minimum Hardware Playback Platform" (an article I wrote), at *http://www.macromedia.com/support/director/how/expert/ playback/playback.html*.

- Research Director's capabilities and limitations before committing to Director as an authoring tool and before planning your project around a feature that will require an Xtra.

- Outline a memory budget. Be mindful of performance during the development phase. Don't rely on last-minute optimization.

- Outline a disk space and bandwidth budget for CD-ROM or Shockwave delivery.

- Draw up a contract outlining all parties' rights and responsibilities. See the book *Software Development: A Legal Guide* by Nolo Press (*http://www.nolo. com*). At a minimum, draw up a letter of agreement outlining the key features and deliverables.

- For Shockwave development, refer to the list of known limitations in Chapter 11. Consult *http://www.macromedia.com/support/director/how/d7/* for details on creating and customizing Java applets using the Director for Java player.

- Research content preparation and test sample content before preparing the remainder.

- Decide on your color depth and any custom palette(s). Using an 8-bit palette gives the best performance and widest compatibility, but requires palette management if using more than one custom palette. See Chapter 13.

- Create a prototype including sample assets of each type and adjust the screen layout, buttons, and interactivity based on client or user feedback.

- Be organized. Don't start off on sloppy footing; it will just get worse. Keep track of all assets meticulously and ensure that the latest assets are incorporated into each revision.

- Obtain licenses for Xtras, QuickTime distribution, and copyrighted content as necessary. Comply with Macromedia's *Made with Macromedia* logo requirements, as described on the Director 7 CD.

- Create and maintain a bug database.

- See the optimization checklists in the appropriate chapters, and see *http://www.zeusprod.com/nutshell/appendices/checklists.html* for details on the files you'll need for your CD-ROM, bug report forms, and guidelines for creating installers.

- Refer to Chapter 3, *Lingo Coding and Debugging Tips*, in *Lingo in a Nutshell* for ways to plan and use Lingo.

If you have not previously implemented all the required features in earlier projects, expect to run into significant difficulties. Uncharted waters are littered with shipwrecks. Above all: test early, test often (TETO), and test on all target platforms (TOATP).

Avoiding Lost Time

You can waste a lot of time if you have problems with your hardware and software. Here are some tips for saving time:

- Obtain the appropriate hardware and software as outlined later in this chapter.

- Use a separate machine for development versus testing.

- Adopt a cautious approach to new software and hardware. It is called the "bleeding edge" for good reason.

- Beta testing is a good way to get a jumpstart on the future, but it takes a lot of time and is often not worth the hassle. Inexperienced developers should rely on released software instead.

- Avoid beta versions of system software. Macromedia will not support beta versions of Windows 98. Upgrade to the release version if appropriate.

- Whenever a new version of Director, Shockwave, QuickTime, Netscape Navigator, Microsoft Internet Explorer, or other major software is released, there are bound to be incompatibilities. Avoid switching to a new version close to your ship date (i.e., use D6 if you don't need D7's features).

- Take advantage of the Director-related resources cited in the Preface. A few well-phrased questions can save you weeks of frustration.

- There is nothing so costly as having to redesign your project or redo your content upon encountering a show-stopping limitation that you could or should have anticipated. Plan ahead based on the guidelines in this book and test your prototypes at each phase.

Obtain the following as warranted to avoid lost work or lost time:

- Current virus protection software.

- Surge protectors for all equipment, including phone lines.

- Uninterruptible power supply (UPS), especially in regions prone to storms or power fluctuations.

- A fast and convenient data backup system. Create permanent archives on CD-Rs or digital tapes. Use rewritable media only for temporary backups. Perform a complete "image" system backup of your entire machine once a week. Back up your new data every day or even twice a day.

- A fast and reliable Internet connection, including a secondary ISP to avoid downtime, and possibly a mirror site for your web server.

- Suitable contingency plans for hardware problems, such as extra equipment or a service contract. Lease or obtain loaner equipment when hardware needs repair.

Always do the following:

- Save original content, such as uncompressed video, full-resolution scans, and 32-bit artwork, before dithering to an 8-bit palette.

- Save a working copy of your Lingo code to a different movie file before making major changes.

- Save your source Director movies, and be sure to obtain the source from sub-contractors. Lingo cannot be recovered from protected or compressed Director files.

Hardware and Software You'll Need

Director is a demanding application, and you'll have other applications running concurrently. Many developers don't have thousands of dollars to lay out for hardware and software, but don't be penny-wise and pound-foolish; the aggravation and indirect costs it can spare you makes hardware a wise investment. The following sections provide a comprehensive list, not a mandatory one; buy the components that are most likely to affect your productivity.

Identify and remedy bottlenecks in your development. Don't buy something until you need it (prices always fall), but invest in hardware and software promptly when the need arises. If you are constantly quitting and restarting applications, buy more RAM. If your disk space is low, buy a hard disk. If you do a lot of graphic and Score work, get a bigger monitor or dual monitors.

Buy, borrow, or lease the computers you need and set up some way to transfer files between them. Many $100,000 projects have been delayed for want of a $1,000 test PC and a $50 Ethernet card to transfer files to it.

Multiple Monitors

You can attach multiple monitors to a Macintosh or Windows 98 PC by installing a secondary video card. Some special Windows 95/NT cards support multiple monitor outputs. For a large list of video cards supported by Windows 98 for multiple monitors, see:

   http://www.microsoft.com/hwtest/hcl/

Office and Work Environment

Multimedia development is remarkably stressful. Carpal tunnel syndrome, back pain, eyestrain, and tension headaches are extremely common and should not be ignored. Your own physical well-being depends heavily on your physical environment's ergonomics. Get a supportive chair (armrests reduce elbow strain), a comfortable keyboard, an efficient mouse with proper mousepad (or trackball, graphics tablet, etc.), and a pleasing monitor (with a swivel stand). Ensure that you have adequate lighting, desk space, shelving, file cabinets, phone lines, staff, office space, capital, and so on to be maximally productive.

Don't neglect your body and mind. Get sleep. Avoid punishing your body with caffeine and other common stimulants. If you drink, stick with fine, hand-crafted

---

beers. You will be more productive if you get regular exercise (force yourself to take a five-minute walk every day), eat real food (not junk food), and avoid work at least one day a week. All religious implications aside, as my Rabbi says, "It need not be a particular day each week, but set aside time for yourself and your family. We all need daily sleep and weekly rejuvenation. Wherever and whenever it may be, make your own Sabbath." You'll find many technical problems easier to solve if you return to them after a day's rest.

Above all, attempt to keep life, clients, deadlines, career, money, health, and family in perspective. This book should go a long way to helping you spend less time pulling your hair out over Director, but it can't help with every aspect of your project. Few of us are doing work that will matter 50 years from now. Relax and enjoy life—it is too short. If you are honest with your clients or employer, you will find that they are human too. If you encounter an unreasonable client or boss, remember that you can always decline a project or quit a job.

Development Environment

If you spend a lot of time developing in Director, your development system should have adequate horsepower. Take the time to properly configure your system. Eliminate unnecessary and potentially destabilizing extensions or beta software. Back up frequently.

Either platform—hardware recommendations:

- 64 MB of RAM (minimum); playback requires 12 MB RAM available, preferably 32 MB installed
- 1 GB of hard disk space for applications
- 2 to 4 GB of hard disk space for data files for a large project
- 4X CD-ROM or higher
- 56 Kbps Internet access—preferably higher (cable modem, T1)
- Removable storage—Zip, Jaz, SyQuest, tape backup, etc.
- CD-R burner (mandatory if creating CD-ROMs)
- $832 \times 624 \times 256$–color monitor (preferably large monitor or dual monitors, supporting thousands or millions of colors)

Either platform—software recommendations:

- Director for Macintosh and Windows
- Flash for Macintosh and Windows if using vector graphics
- QuickTime 2.1.2 (Windows), QuickTime 2.5 (Macintosh), QuickTime 3.0 (Macintosh and Windows) required for D7
- Photoshop (Adobe), Freehand or Fireworks (Macromedia), or similar graphics editing tool (for simple art you can use the Paint window)
- deBabelizer (*http://www.equilibrium.com*) or similar graphics batch processing tool
- Peak LE or Sound Edit 16 (Macintosh), Sound Forge or Cool Edit (Windows)

- Video editing and compression software, such as MoviePlayer (Apple), Premiere (Adobe) and Media Cleaner (formerly Movie Cleaner Pro from Terran Interactive)

- Web browser to read HTML documentation

- Adobe Acrobat Reader to read PDF documentation

- HTML editor (BBEdit, HomePage, DreamWeaver)

- Resource editor (ResEdit for Macintosh)—see Chapter 8, *Projectors and the Runtime Environment*, for details on Windows resource editors

- Utilities to decode, unstuff, and unzip downloaded files (see *http://www.zeus-prod.com/site/zip.html*)

Macintosh-specific hardware and software:

- PowerPC or G3 processor

- System 7.6.1 or later for development (Mac OS 8 also recommended for testing)

- Projectors require 7.5.3 or later; Shockwave 7 requires 7.6.1 or later

- QuickTime extension

- AppleScript extension

Director 6.x can run on a 680x0 Macintosh, but D7 and many newer features in D6.5 require a PowerPC or G3.

Windows-specific hardware and software:

- Pentium, Pentium II, or Pentium III processor

- Windows 95/98 or Windows NT 4.0

- QuickTime for Windows

- Sound card

- Speakers

Shockwave development (see Chapter 11):

- Microsoft Internet Explorer (MIE) and Netscape Navigator for Macintosh and Windows (versions 3.x, 4.x, and 5.x)

- AOL browser for Macintosh and Windows (free trial versions available)

- Shockwave plug-ins for Netscape

- Shockwave ActiveX Control for MIE

- A web server to which you can upload your Shockwave movies

- FTP software to upload your Shockwave movies

Testing Environment

As a bare minimum for testing, you will need at least one computer that runs each OS that you intend to support. Refer to Chapter 8 for details on determining an appropriate playback platform.

Test performance on your minimum target playback machine; your development machine is not an appropriate benchmark. Test from a CD-ROM, not just a hard drive. The Windows platform tends to be more restrictive than the Macintosh. Do not wait until the last minute to port your project to Windows. Plan ahead to avoid surprises. Test from a Projector, not just the authoring environment, especially when delivering for laptops, which tend to be quirky.

Find a compatibility test lab where you can test your product or hire a third-party beta-testing company to perform compatibility tests for you. Consider a beta program if you have a reliable customer base.

Macintosh development and delivery

For Macintosh delivery, you will need separate 68K and PowerPC-based Macintoshes, running various versions of System 7.x and Mac OS 8.x. You can boot from Zip cartridges to test different OS versions on the same machine. Perform compatibility tests on the CPUs you intend to support, such as 68040, 601, 603, 604, and G3 processors, including iMacs. While Macintosh hardware is very consistent, variations do exist. For example, 68040 Macs don't work well with Projectors set to *Use Temporary System Memory* and are not supprted by D7. Users' hardware configurations and software extensions will vary widely, especially with the various laptop and clone models now available. For example, iMacs support different screen resolutions than other desktop models.

Windows development and delivery

For Windows delivery, you will need a machine that can run Windows 3.1, Windows 95/98, and Windows NT. (A Macintosh running SoftWindows, VirtualPC, or similar emulator is not a reliable substitute.) Director 5 included a Windows 3.1 development environment, but with Director 6, you must develop under Windows 95/98 or NT 4.0, even if you are delivering for Windows 3.1 or NT 3.5.1. You can test 16-bit projectors under Windows 95, but you should also test them under Windows 3.1. Director 7 doesn't support Windows 3.1 at all.

Use a *boot manager* such as System Commander from V Communications (*http://www.v-com.com*) or Boot Manager, included with Partition Magic from PowerQuest (*http://www.powerquest.com*), or multiple bootable external drives to test multiple versions of Windows on a single PC. You should test each flavor of Windows on all supported CPUs (486, Pentium, Pentium with MMX, and Pentium II). You will also need to do extensive compatibility testing on a wide variety of sound and video cards. Refer to the Software Publisher's Association site for specifications for MPC3-compliant Windows computers (*http://www.spa.org/mpc/mpc3. htm* and *http://www.spa.org/mpc/stand.htm*). Don't forget to test Windows 3.11 and various flavors of Windows NT (NT 3.5.1, NT 4.0, and NT Server).

If you must release a product concurrently with a new OS or CPU, join the appropriate hardware or software beta program to obtain early access for testing.

Simplifying Testing

Invest in the hardware and software necessary to facilitate file transfers and testing across various machines. Purchase Director for both Macintosh and Windows if delivering for both platforms. Install the Director development environment on all the computers you intend to test to ease debugging. It is much harder to debug and impossible to make corrections if only a Projector is installed. (If using Director 5, you should install Director for Windows under Windows 3.1 as well.)

 Being a lazy human, you will not test unless it is convenient to do so. Set up an easy way to transfer files between computers. By using a stub Projector, as described in Chapter 8, you can quickly test without rebuilding your Projector. Test early, test often.

Ensure that your test machines have adequate disk space, CD-ROM drives, sound cards, speakers, and RAM as well. A crippled test machine is useless.

File transfers

Set up a network connecting all the machines on which you intend to test. With the right type of network you need not necessarily copy the files to other machines. You can perform crude testing by running the project over the network off the main server (this also simulates the lower performance of a CD-ROM).

You may need Ethernet cards ($50 to $75) for your PCs, Ethernet transceivers ($20 to $50) for your Macintoshes, a small Ethernet hub ($50) and networking software. You can hook up a peer-to-peer network without a hub, but then you'll need cross-over cables instead of the standard Ethernet cables, and the hubs are cheap and the standard cables come with the Macintosh Ethernet transceivers. PC MACLAN for Windows ($100 to $175) by Miramar Systems (*http://www.miramarsys.com*) is an inexpensive way to set up a small Ethernet-based network. Netopia/Farallon (*http://www.netopia.com* or *http://www.farallon.com*) sells networking solutions (PhoneNet and EtherWave). Asanté (*http://www.asante.com*) and Dayna (*http://www.dayna.com*) also sell inexpensive Ethernet hardware. DAVE (*http://www.thursby.com*) allows a Mac to mount a PC's shared volumes over Ethernet peer-to-peer with the PC running standard MS TCP/IP. See *http://www.macwindows.com* for ways to connect Macintoshes and PCs and share peripherals among them.

Removable media

In lieu of a network, you can use removable media for both Macintosh and PCs, such as Iomega Zip drives (*http://www.iomega.com*). I don't recommend this route, because it is constrained by the size of the cartridge (100 MB in the case of basic Zip cartridges, although larger media abound) and often requires you to copy the same file between cartridges and hard drives. If you go the removable route, buy a drive for each machine so that you can transfer a data cartridge without moving the entire drive. You can also use a CD-ROM burner to transfer data, but burning CDs can be time-consuming and is not sensible for small, iterative changes. In short, set up a network instead. It's well worth the extra effort.

If you are delivering your software via CD-ROM you should *definitely* buy a CD-R burner and a stack of blank CD-Rs.

Configuring Your System

The following are some configuration tips to make your system perform better and to make Director easier to access:

- You can check your Director version, serial number, organization name, and username during authoring using the *About Director* box, or *the productVersion, serialNumber, organizationName,* and *userName* properties.

- To reregister your copy of Director, delete the invisible *BRAND.BRD* file and re-enter your company information and serial number.

- To avoid the "Please Register" reminder, either register via one of the electronic methods or print the registration form to a file.

- See "OS Shortcuts and Tips" later in this chapter for a primer on the Mac OS and Windows.

- In D7, disable *Auto Coloring* under File ➤ Preferences ➤ Script and reduce the number of Score channels under Modify ➤ Movie ➤ Properties (the default is 150 and the maximum is 1,000).

Configuring Your Macintosh Computer

These tips should help make Director easier to launch and use on the Macintosh:

- Use aliases as shortcuts to frequently used items.

- Create an alias on your desktop using the Finder's File ➤ Make Alias command (Cmd-M).

- Add an alias to your Apple Menu by placing it under *Mac HD:System Folder:Apple Menu* or use the "Add Alias to Apple Menu" utility under *Apple Extras:AppleScript:Automated Tasks.*

- Create a hierarchical menu under your Apple Menu by placing items within subfolders within the *Apple Menu* folder. Desktop aliases are readily accessed from file selection dialog boxes and are great for drag-and-drop operations.

Create aliases to the following:

- All installed versions of Director (D5.0.1, D6.0.2, D6.5, D7, D7.0.1, etc.)

- Director's *Help* file, so that you can access the help system without starting Director

- Frequently used tools including browsers, HTML editors, resource editors, graphics programs, sound programs, and utilities

- Macintosh *Preferences* folder and Director *Xtras* folder

- Current project folder and content folders (graphics, sounds, etc.) for easy access via File ➤ Import, Insert ➤ Media Element, or File ➤ Open dialog boxes

To automatically open a document or start an application such as Director when your computer boots, place an alias to it in the *Startup Items* folder within the System folder.

Performance improvement suggestions:

- Install at least 64 MB of real RAM and shut off Virtual Memory in the *Memory* Control Panel.

- Allocate at least 20 MB to Director using the Finder's File ➤ Get Info command.

- When running Director, close all other unneeded programs, including Macintosh Control Panels.

- Turn off the *Calculate folder size* option in the *Views* Control Panel.

- Turn off unnecessary file sharing under the Finder's File ➤ Sharing menu. Macintosh file sharing takes a long time to start up. Turn it off using the Sharing Setup Control Panel.

- Minimize the extensions in use via the *Extensions Manager* Control Panel. Your computer will reboot faster and be more stable.

Configuring Your Windows Computer

Windows uses shortcuts, which are similar to Macintosh aliases. Create shortcuts using the right mouse button. Add a shortcut to the top level of the Windows Start Menu by dropping it onto the Start Menu icon or adding it to the *C:\Windows\ Start Menu* folder. Add the items described earlier in this chapter for the Macintosh Apple Menu to your Windows Start Menu.

To automatically open a document or start an application such as Director when Windows boots, place a shortcut to it in the *C:\Windows\Start Menu\Programs\ Startup* folder.

Director 6.5 for Windows does not properly save your user preferences. The Director 6.5 Service Pack solves the problem.

Performance improvement suggestions:

- Install at least 64 MB of real RAM, but let Windows manage your memory (as specified in the *System* Control Panel). Windows becomes unusable if there is insufficient swap disk space.

- Avoid double-clicking documents (Director files, HTML files, etc.) to open them. Each time you do this, Windows opens another copy of the application. Instead, use the File ➤ Open command from within the application.

- Minimize the number of files in your *Xtras* folder as described earlier.

If your Windows system disk is very full and there is not enough free space, as required to install many applications, use Partition Magic by PowerQuest (*http://www.powerquest.com*) to reallocate some of the partitioned space to drive C without destroying data. It also moves applications to other drives to free up disk space.

I use System Commander by V Communications (*http://www.v-com.com*) to boot multiple flavors of Windows on a single CPU. It includes an excellent manual, but can quickly become complicated if you haven't planned well. V Communications also sells utilities (Gate and On Stage) that automate software testing.

For many additional details on configuring Windows 95/98 and NT, see *Windows Annoyances* and *Windows 98 Annoyances* (David A. Karp; O'Reilly & Associates).

Working with Multiple Director Files

Director can open only one movie file at a time, but there are several tricks you can use to work with multiple castLibs and multiple movies at once. Each serialized copy of Director is licensed only for a single computer. Contact Macromedia for larger licenses.

Running multiple copies of Director
Separate copies of Director can each open a different movie file. Under Windows, a second copy of Director will open if you double-click Director's icon or a DIR or CST file in the File Explorer. On the Macintosh, duplicate the Director application to create a second copy that you can run independently (Director complains only if two copies with the same serial number are running on two different computers). Running multiple copies may cause palette flickering if your monitor is not set to thousands or millions of colors.

Check *the productVersion* or *the applicationPath* in the Message window to confirm the version of Director in use, and its location (important when installing new Xtras to make sure you put them in the right place).

Transferring assets between multiple movies
On the Macintosh, you can cut and paste cast members between two movies open in separate copies of Director. Under Windows, you must either close the movie from which you are copying assets (or set it to read-only), or copy only one cast member at a time.

External castLibs
You can open a nearly unlimited number of linked or unlinked external castLibs simultaneously. Use an external castLib linked to two movies to share or copy assets between them, or use an unlinked external castLib as a conduit.

MIAWs
Although you cannot easily view their Score or internal castLib, you can open multiple MIAWs in addition to the main movie on the Stage. D7 allows you to debug Lingo in unprotected MIAWs.

Maintaining Multiple Versions of Director

I strongly recommend keeping multiple versions of Director available on your system. I keep D5.0.1, D6.0.2, D6.5, D7, and D7.0.1 installed. You may need them to debug or revise an old project or for compatibility testing. For example, Director 5 supported authoring under Windows 3.1, and Director 5 may be useful to debug Director 5–compatible Lingo or XObjects.

Exercise extreme caution when switching to a major new revision of Director. Unforeseen problems will crop up. Many quirks have been reported in D7. Maintenance releases such as D7.0.1 are usually much safer, although never foolproof.

Naturally, new releases often fix old bugs. Check whether the latest free upgrade to which you are entitled fixes bugs you've encountered. That said, there is a big distinction between testing a new (or previous) version and blindly shipping with it. I recommend against changing versions close to a ship date unless it fixes a known bug that affects you *and* if sufficient time is allowed for complete compatibility testing. If you are not having problems and have performed thorough tests, you are probably better off shipping with the "known quantity."

Many developers complain about the high price of Director upgrades. In my experience they are usually well worth it if you need their new features. At least learn about the upgrade before deciding whether it is for you. You can get free upgrades if you participate actively in Macromedia's beta program (see the Preface).

You may need to reinstall or upgrade third-party Xtras after upgrading. Use aliases or shortcuts to share Xtras among multiple versions of Director.

Starting the desired version with multiple copies of Director installed

On the Macintosh, each movie or castLib file is associated with a specific major version of Director via the document's Creator Code. The Creator Code for Director 7.x is MD00, but differs from the Creator Code used by D6.x (MD97), D5.x (MD95), D4.x (MD93), and D3.x (MMDR). For example, if multiple versions of D6.x are installed, the version most recently installed on the System disk is ordinarily used.

If both Director 5 and 6 are installed under Windows, Director 5 may open even when you double-click a Director 6 file (and cause an error message because it cannot read the file). If Director 7 is installed after Director 6, even D6 files will open in D7 when double-clicked. Starting Director manually (perhaps via an alias or shortcut) guarantees that the desired copy of Director is started.

Under Windows, the .DIR file extension (and other extensions, such as .CST) are "tied" to only one application. To change the default application for these extensions to a different version of Director:

1. Click the right mouse button on the Start Menu and choose **Explore** to open the File Explorer.

2. Choose **View ► Options** in the File Explorer to open the *Options* dialog box.

3. Deselect the *Hide MS-DOS file extensions for file types that are registered* checkbox (this shows all file extensions, including .DIR, while exploring).

4. Select the *File Types* tab in the *Options* dialog box.

5. Scroll down the alphabetical list of registered file types until you find the entry for *Macromedia Director Movies*. Highlight it and click the *Edit* button. The *Edit File Type* dialog box appears.

6. Change the *Description of Type* to *Macromedia Director X Movie* if desired.

7. Highlight the item labeled *open* in the Actions list, then click the *Edit* button.

8. Click the *Browse* button and browse to the desired version of Director.

9. Click *OK* to dismiss the editing action dialog box, then click *Close*, then *Close* again to accept the changes.

To choose the version of Director for Windows with which to open a DIR file, place shortcuts to various versions of Director in *C:\Windows\SendTo*. Then right-click on a DIR file and choose Send To from the pop-up menu.

Mastering Director

Director is an exceedingly complex program and most developers use only a small portion of its features. Invest the time to familiarize yourself with its capabilities and reread the documentation and revisit this book periodically. If you encounter a time-consuming task, there's probably an easier way to perform the operation. Take advantage of the resources listed in the Preface, and ask other developers if you are stuck.

Even if you aren't a programmer, you can create utilities in Lingo that save time during authoring or analyze the Cast and Score. For example, you might write a utility to check for cast members with an incorrect color depth. See Example 3-9 in Chapter 3, *The Score and Animation*, and Examples 4-4 through 4-8 in Chapter 4.

Help and Manuals

The Director 6 and 7 Help systems include a lot of information that is not in the manuals, plus many useful *Show Me* demonstration movies. In D6, choose *Show Me* from the Help menu or from the Help Contents window for demonstrations of many of Director's new features. In D7, the ShowMe movies are under *Contents: Getting Started: Director ShowMe Movies* in the online Help.

The Macromedia manuals have substantially improved their coverage of real-world issues. They also do an excellent job of explaining the Score, Paint tools, Palette Window, etc. I assume you are familiar with the Macromedia manuals; I don't repeat the tutorial information here. If you don't have the manuals, pick up a basic third-party book such as *Inside Director 6 with Lingo* (New Riders) or *Director 7 Demystified* (PeachPit/Macromedia Press).

The *Learning Lingo* manual from earlier versions of Director has been folded into the *Using Director* manual in D7. Many of D7's new features are documented online. See *Web Links* under the D7 Help menu, or *Contents: Getting Started: Director Developer's Center* in the online Help.

The Help menu under Windows appears immediately to the right of the Window menu. On the Macintosh, it appears as a "?" icon at the far right of the menubar. Table 2-1 outlines the Help functions.

Table 2-1: Director Help Functions

Function	Macintosh	Windows
Help ➤ Director Help	Help key	F1
Help ➤ Help Pointer	Cmd-?	Ctrl-? or Shift-F1
Lingo Help (new in D7)	Ctrl-click on Lingo keyword	Right-click on Lingo keyword
About box	Apple Menu ➤ About Director	Help ➤ About Director

The context-sensitive Help Pointer doesn't work in D7.0, because Macromedia changed the Help system late in the beta phase. It may be fixed in D7.0.1.

Director 6.5 uses HTML documentation for its new Xtras. Specify your preferred browser under File ➤ Preferences ➤ Network and check the *Launch When Needed* option. See *http://browserwatch.internet.com/browser.html* for browsers with smaller footprints than MIE and Netscape.

For help on a Lingo keyword in D6, highlight the word, then click on the Help Pointer icon at the right edge of the Toolbar, or use one of the keyboard shortcuts. In D7, use Ctrl-click (Mac) or right-click (Windows) and choose Lingo Help. Use the Lingo pop-up menus in the Script and Message windows to check a keyword's syntax.

Being More Productive Within Director

Director has an overwhelming number of features, and no one remembers them all. This section gives an overview of the biggest time-savers.

Productivity tips:

- Minimize the number of files in the *Xtras* folder by removing unused Xtras and non-Xtras files such as HTML documentation sometimes installed there.

- Custom palettes make Director's interface harder to read. During authoring, set the monitor to a higher depth to avoid color changes when working with one or more custom palettes. Set it to 256 colors for testing if applicable.

- Use onion-skinning to align the registration points of cast members or create animations with a series of cast members.

- Use the *Align* windoid to align sprites on the Stage.

- Use the Score to manipulate sprites as described in Tables 3-14 and 3-15. Use View ➤ Sprite Labels, View ➤ Zoom, and View ➤ Display to configure the Score display.

- Edit sprite paths directly on the Stage. See Table 3-13.

- Use File ➤ Preferences ➤ Cast ➤ Label ➤ *Number:Name* to display the name and number of each cast member in the Score script popup, the Cast window, and the Sprite Toolbar (or Sprite Inspector). Also set Cast preferences to display smaller thumbnails and display no more than the necessary number of cast member slots in the Cast window.

- Make effective use of external castLibs. See Chapter 4.

- Use external editors for bitmaps, sounds, and other common asset types under File ➤ Preferences ➤ Editors.

- Familiarize yourself with the Animation Wizard, Widget Wizard, Button Library, and Palette Library under the Xtras menu in D6 (obsolete in D7).

- See the premade Behaviors under Windows ➤ Library Palette in D7.

- Use the Sprite Inspector or Sprite Toolbar to manipulate sprite properties.

Mouse, keyboard, and command shortcuts:

- Learn the keyboard shortcuts for common and repetitious tasks listed in tables throughout this book and *Lingo in a Nutshell.*

- Use Ctrl-click (Macintosh) or the right mouse button (Windows) to open context-sensitive pop-up help menus, especially in the Score and on the Stage (see Tables 2-4, 3-11, and 3-12). Consider obtaining a multi-button programmable mouse on the Macintosh to make access easier.

- Under Windows, use the Alt key to access the pull-down menus for commands without keyboard shortcuts.

- Use Shift-Enter to hide all non-Stage windows when playing a movie (Cmd-1 or Ctrl-1 hides non-Stage Windows in D6, but not in D7).

- Use the shortcut Toolbar under Window ➤ Toolbar.

- Use the Paint window shortcuts described in Chapter 13.

- Use the numeric keypad to start and stop the movie (plus other functions). See Table 2-9.

- Use the function key shortcuts. See Table 2-11.

- Use Edit ➤ Repeat, Cmd-Y (Macintosh), or Ctrl-Y (Windows), to repeat the previous operation.

In D7, the Stage can be closed like any other window. In D6, to get the Stage out of your way:

- Set the Stage's size to 16×16 and position it in the corner of the screen using Modify ➤ Movie ➤ Properties.

- Position the Stage on a secondary monitor if you have one.

- Create a movable, resizable Macintosh Stage as described under "Changing the Stage on the Macintosh" in Chapter 6.

- Set *the visible of the stage* = 0.

Importing tips:

- Use Cmd-R (Mac) or Ctrl-R (Windows). Think "Rimport" to remember that the shortcut uses the R key.

- Example 4-5 finds linked files that reside in different folders and Example 4-7 imports small linked files.

- See "Importing tips, annoyances, and caveats" in Chapter 4.

Lingo tips:

- Write Lingo utilities and tool Xtras to monitor memory or other system properties, perform repetitive tasks, analyze the Cast and Score, and perform Score Recording.

- Use the Lingo Debugger, Message, and Watcher windows as described in Chapter 3 in *Lingo in a Nutshell*.

- Develop a library of common utility scripts and keep them in an external castLib that you can link to each movie.

- Use the Behavior Inspector to attach and manage multiple Behaviors per sprite and use Behaviors and parent scripts to create re-usable code.

- Use Macromedia and/or third-party Xtras when necessary.

- Styled and colorized text can be very slow to edit in the Script window. Disable script colorization in D7 under File ➤ Preferences ➤ Script.

Director's auto-indent feature can become very slow for large scripts, especially under Windows and when using formatted text. To insert a multiline structure, such as a *repeat* loop, without affecting the existing indentation:

1. Press Return four or five times to open blank lines at the desired point.

2. On the first open line, type *repeat with x = 1 to 69*, but don't press Return.

3. At the bottom of the open space, type *end repeat*.

4. Now press Return. Because you've ended the *repeat* loop already, there is no need for extensive, slow reindentation.

5. Add the desired statements within the body of the *repeat* loop.

A similar technique can be used with *on...end, if...then...end if,* and other multiline structures.

Shortcuts in Director

Instead of trying to memorize specific keyboard combinations for each window, note the modifier keys in Tables 2-2 and 2-3 used throughout Director. In Table 2-2, which covers menu accelerator (shortcut) keys, A represents the appropriate alphanumeric character. Note that the Command (Cmd) key on the Macintosh is often labeled with a "cloverleaf" or "propeller" symbol.

The Ctrl and Alt keys under Windows always do the same thing as the Cmd and Option keys (respectively) on the Macintosh. For example, *the commandDown* property reflects the state of the Cmd key on the Macintosh and the Ctrl key under Windows, and *the optionDown* property reflects the state of the Option key on the Macintosh and the Alt key under Windows. Note that although *the controlDown* reflects the state of the Ctrl key on both platforms, the Macintosh Ctrl key is used to simulate Windows right mouse clicks and has little relation to the Windows Ctrl key.

Table 2-2: Menu Accelerator Key Overview

Operation	Mac	Win
Menu accelerator key	Cmd-*A*	Ctrl-*A*[1]
Extended or opposing action[2]	Cmd-Shift-*A*	Ctrl-Shift-*A*
Alternative meaning unrelated to standard GUI usage[3]	Opt-*A* Cmd-Option-*A*	Alt-*A* Ctrl-Alt-*A*
Context-sensitive menu (authoring) or right mouse click (playback)	Ctrl-click[4]	Right mouse button
Pull-down menu selection	No keyboard shortcut	Alt-*A*

[1] The Ctrl key is used for most Director shortcuts under Windows; notable exceptions are Alt-F4 (Exit) and F1 (Help).
[2] For example, Cmd-] inserts a frame; and Cmd-Shift-] inserts multiple frames. Cmd-R imports files and Cmd-Shift-R exports files.
[3] For example, Cmd-P is used for Print and Cmd-Opt-P for Play.
[4] Prior to Director 5, the Ctrl key was used for other shortcuts on the Macintosh. As of Director 5, it always brings up a context-sensitive menu during authoring.

Table 2-3 covers keys that create, modify, or extend selections.

Table 2-3: Standard Selection Modifiers

Selection	Mac	Win	Notes
Extend	Shift	Shift	Extends the Cast, Score, text, or palette selection.
Toggles current or discontiguous selection	Cmd or Shift	Ctrl or Shift	Adds or removes the clicked item from the current selection or selects discontiguous items.
Copy (drag modifier)	Option	Alt	Duplicates the object being dragged in Cast, Paint, Text, Field, Markers, Script, or Score window. Use to open additional windows (see Table 2-7).
Constrain	Shift	Shift	Constrains movement horizontally or vertically, or constrains aspect ratio (circle, square, etc.).

Double-clicking selects a word or blank line in the Text, Field, and Script windows. Triple-clicking selects all text.

Menu Shortcuts

Most menu commands are grouped by topic in other chapters, but this section discusses menus that cut across multiple topics.

Director provides numerous context-sensitive menus that are accessed with the right mouse button under Windows or by Ctrl-clicking on the Macintosh. In the second column of Table 2-4, each shortcut is prefixed with the name of the menu on which each command typically appears.

Table 2-4: Context-Sensitive Menus

Click in This Window	For Quick Access to These Menu Options
Toolbar Control Panel Tool Palette Sprite Inspector Text Inspector Memory Inspector Align Tweak Onion Skin	Window ➤ Toolbar, Control Panel, Tool Palette, Sprite Inspector, Text Inspector, or Memory Inspector Modify ➤ Align or Tweak View ➤ Onion Skin File ➤ Preferences ➤ General ➤ Show Tool Tips

Behavior Inspector	**Top Pane:**
	    Parameters...
	    Script...
	    New Behavior...
	    Clear Behavior
	Events Pane:
	    New Event...
	    Clear Event
	Actions Pane:
	    New Action...
	    Clear Actions

Text or Field window	Edit ➤ Cut Text, Copy Text, or Paste Text Font (typeface), Font Size, or Font Style Modify ➤ Font..., Paragraph..., or Cast Member Properties...
Message window	Edit ➤ Cut Text, Copy Text, Paste Text, Find Handler... Control ➤ Watch Expression Wrap
Script window and Debugger window (bottom pane only)	Edit ➤ Cut Text, Copy Text, or Paste Text Font... Comment Uncomment Control ➤ Toggle Breakpoint, Ignore Breakpoints, or Watch Expression Edit ➤ Find Handler..., Go to Handler, Lingo Help Control ➤ Recompile All Scripts Modify ➤ Cast Member Properties..., Wrap
Video window (D6) QuickTime window (D7) AVI window (D7)	Edit ➤ Cut Video, Copy Video, or Paste Video Fit to Window Modify ➤ Cast Member Properties...

Table 2-4: Context-Sensitive Menus (continued)

Click in This Window	For Quick Access to These Menu Options
Paint window[1]	Edit ➤ Paste Bitmap View ➤ Zoom In or Zoom Out Modify ➤ Cast Member Properties...
Score window and Sprite Toolbar	Varies depending on area of Score in which you click. See Table 3-11.
Stage	Varies depending on whether you click on sprite or on Stage. See Table 3-12.
Cast window	Edit ➤ Cut,[2] Copy,[2] Paste, Edit Cast Member,[2] or Launch External Editor[2] Find in Score (Edit ➤ Find ➤ Selection) File ➤ Import[3] Insert ➤ OLE Object[3] (Windows only) Modify ➤ Cast Member Properties[2] Edit ➤ Cast Member Script[2] Modify ➤ Cast Properties
Library Palette	Show Names
Markers, Watcher, Vector Shape, and Color Palettes windows	No pop-up menu (can use keyboard shortcuts for standard cut, copy, paste, and select all).

[1] After making a selection in the Paint window, Ctrl-clicking, or right-clicking within the selection, the pop-up menu includes the Flip, Rotate, Distort, Filter, Color, and Repeat Effects.
[2] Available only when clicking on an occupied cast member slot.
[3] Available only when clicking on an unoccupied cast member slot.

File menu

Table 2-5 lists the File menu commands. See also Table 4-3 for details on the formats supported by the various File ➤ Save commands.

Table 2-5: File Menu Commands and Accelerators

File Menu Option	Macintosh	Windows
New Movie[1,2]	Cmd-N	Ctrl-N
New Cast[2]	Cmd-Opt-N	Ctrl-Alt-N
Open[2,3]	Cmd-O	Ctrl-O
Close[1]	Cmd-W	Ctrl-F4
Save[2]	Cmd-S	Ctrl-S
Save As	None	Alt-F,A
Save and Compact	None	Alt-F,V

Table 2-5: File Menu Commands and Accelerators (continued)

File Menu Option	Macintosh	Windows
Save All[2]	None	Alt-F,L
Revert	None	Alt-F,R
Import[2,4]	Cmd-R	Ctrl-R
Export	Cmd-Shift-R	Ctrl-Shift-R
Create Projector...	None	Alt-F,T
Save as Shockwave Movie[2]	None	Alt-F,W
Save as Java[5]	None	None
Page Setup	Cmd-Shift-P	Ctrl-Shift-P
Print[2,6]	Cmd-P	Ctrl-P
Preferences...	Cmd-U (General)	Ctrl-U
General		Alt-F,F,N
Network		Alt-F,F,S
Score[7]		Alt-F,F,R
Sprite		Alt-F,F,C
Cast		Alt-F,F,P
Paint		Alt-F,F,E
Editors		
Script		
Preview	None	F12
Send Mail[8]	N/A	Alt-F,M
Quit (Mac) or Exit (Windows)	Cmd-Q	Alt-F4

[1] File ➤ Close closes only the current window. To close the current Director movie, use File ➤ New Movie or the Toolbar icon.
[2] Function appears on the Toolbar in D7.
[3] The File menu also shows recently opened movie files and cast files.
[4] See Table 4-4 for supported import file types and Table 4-5 for additional media types inserted via the Insert menu.
[5] File ➤ Save As Java requires the Java Export Xtra included with D6.5 and D7.
[6] Director can print the Stage, Score, Scripts, Cast Text, Cast Art, Cast Thumbnails, and Marker Comments. More options, including storyboarding, are available when printing the Stage. Director does not print puppeted sprites but does print muted sprite channels.
[7] Important Score-related preferences are accessible via the context-sensitive Score pop-up menu. See Table 3-11.
[8] Windows only. Enabled only when you have a MAPI server installed and active and a movie file is open. For example, if using Eudora, select the MAPI icon under Tools ➤ Options and set the *Use Eudora MAPI server* option to *Always*.

Edit menu

Table 2-6 lists the Edit menu commands, including important commands for finding items. Some menu items may be inactive or may vary slightly depending on the currently active window and selection.

Table 2-6: Edit Menu Commands and Accelerators

Edit Menu Option	Macintosh	Windows
Undo[1]	Cmd-Z	Ctrl-Z
Repeat	Cmd-Y	Ctrl-Y
Cut[1]	Cmd-X	Ctrl-X
Copy[1]	Cmd-C	Ctrl-C
Paste[1]	Cmd-V	Ctrl-V

Paste Special
   Insert
   As PICT (Mac only)
   Using OLE (Windows only)
   Relative
	None	None

Clear	Delete	Delete or Backspace
Duplicate	Cmd-D	Ctrl-D
Select All	Cmd-A	Ctrl-A
Invert Selection (see Color Palettes window)	None	Alt-E,V
Find Text	Cmd-F	Ctrl-F
Find Handler[2]	Cmd-Shift-;	Ctrl-Shift-;
Find Cast Member[1]	Cmd-;	Ctrl-;
Find Selection[3]	Cmd-H	Ctrl-H
Find Again	Cmd-G Cmd-Opt-F	Ctrl-G Ctrl-Alt-F
Replace Again	Cmd-Opt-E	Ctrl-Alt-E
Edit Sprite Frames	Cmd-Opt-]	Ctrl-Alt-]
Edit Entire Sprites	Cmd-Opt-[	Ctrl-Alt-[
Exchange Cast Members[1]	Cmd-E	Ctrl-E
Edit Cast Member	None	Alt-E,M
Launch External Editor	Cmd-, (comma)	Ctrl-, (comma)

[1] Function appears on Toolbar.
[2] Highlight a handler name and use the *Go To Handler* button in the Message or Script window to find a handler in a movie script that matches the highlighted name. In the Script window, use Option-click (Macintosh) or Alt-click (Windows) as a shortcut.
[3] Can be used to find cast member used in the Score, or highlighted text in Field, Text, or Script windows.

Other menus

The View menu incorporates many different functions that don't necessarily form a coherent group. See Tables 3-14 and 3-15 for details on the commands that affect sprite paths and the Score display. See Table 3-17 for commands that move the playback head among various markers. The View menu changes for the active window.

The Insert menu incorporates commands affecting the Score frames and sprite keyframes (see Tables 3-1, 3-6, 3-15, and 3-18) and commands to insert new cast members (see Tables 4-5 and 4-7).

The Modify menu incorporates commands to modify castLib, cast member, sprite, frame, and movie properties (see Tables 3-1, 3-3, 3-4, 3-6, 3-15, 4-2, and 4-8), align sprites (see Table 5-6), and affect text and fields (see Table 12-5).

The Control menu incorporates commands to control the playback head (see Table 3-17) and for Lingo debugging and compilation (see Table 3-4 in Chapter 3 in *Lingo in a Nutshell*).

The Xtras menu includes numerous completely unrelated items (depending on which Xtras are installed) such as Tool Xtras, bitmap filters, Behavior libraries, PowerPoint Import, and Shockwave audio settings. It also includes the *Update Movies* option. See Table 4-3 and "The Xtras Menu" in Chapter 10.

The Window menu is covered in detail in Table 2-7. The Help menu is covered in Table 2-1.

Director's Windows

Director has over 20 separate windows in several broad classes: so-called *primary* windows (Score with optional Sprite Toolbar, Cast, and Stage), *media* windows (Paint, Text, Field, Color Palettes, QuickTime, Vector Shape, and Script), *secondary* windows (Markers, Message, Debugger, Watcher), and *inspectors* and *windoids* (Control Panel, Toolbar, Tool Palette, Library Palette, Behavior Inspector, Sprite Inspector, Text Inspector, Memory Inspector, Align, Tweak, and Onion Skin). You'll need a very large monitor or multiple monitors for serious production work.

Cmd-1 (Mac) or Ctrl-1 (Windows) opens and closes the Stage window in D7. In D6, these shortcuts hide all non-Stage windows. In D7, use Shift-Enter to play the movie and hide the non-Stage windows.

Option-click or Shift-click (Macintosh) or Alt-click (Windows) the close box of a Director window to close all non-inspector windows. The same shortcut used with an inspector closes all inspector windows. (Option-Cmd-W doesn't close all windows as it will in the Macintosh Finder.)

Table 2-7 lists all window types (most are accessed via the Window menu). Cmd-Shift-H (Mac) or Ctrl-Shift-H (Windows) toggles the Paint tools in the Paint window, the Sprite Toolbar in the Score, and the button toolbar in the Text, Field, Message, and Script windows.

Table 2-7: Window Menu Shortcuts

Operation	Macintosh	Windows
File ➤ Close[1]	Cmd-W	Ctrl-F4
Window ➤ New Window[2]	Opt-click "+" button	Alt-click "+" button or Alt-W,N
Window ➤ Toolbar	Cmd-Shift-Opt-B	Ctrl-Shift-Alt-B
Window ➤ Tool Palette	Cmd-7	Ctrl-7
Window ➤ Library Palette[3]	None	None
Window ➤ Inspector ➤ Behavior[3]	Keypad * or Cmd-Opt-;	Keypad * or Ctrl-Alt-;
Window ➤ Inspector ➤ Sprite[3]	Keypad / or Cmd-Opt-S	Keypad / or Ctrl-Alt-S
Window ➤ Inspector ➤ Text	Cmd-T	Ctrl-T
Window ➤ Inspector ➤ Memory	None	None
Window ➤ Stage[3]	Cmd-1	Ctrl-1
Window ➤ Control Panel[3]	Cmd-2	Ctrl-2
Window ➤ Markers	Cmd-Shift-M	Ctrl-Shift-M
Window ➤ Score[2,3]	Cmd-4	Ctrl-4
Window ➤ Cast[2,3]	Cmd-3	Ctrl-3
Window ➤ Paint[3,4]	Cmd-5	Ctrl-5
Window ➤ Vector Shape[3,4]	Cmd-Shift-V	Ctrl-Shift-V
Window ➤ Text[2,3,4]	Cmd-6	Ctrl-6
Window ➤ Field[2,4]	Cmd-8	Ctrl-8
Window ➤ Color Palettes[4]	Cmd-Opt-7	Ctrl-Alt-7
Window ➤ Video[2,4] (D6 #digitalVideo)	Cmd-9	Ctrl-9
Window ➤ QuickTime[2,4] (D7 #quickTimeMedia)	Cmd-9	Ctrl-9
Window ➤ AVI Video[4] (D7 #digitalVideo)	N/A	Alt-W,V
Window ➤ Script[2,3,4,5]	Cmd-0, Cmd-Shift-U	Ctrl-0, Ctrl-Shift-U
Window ➤ Message[3]	Cmd-M	Ctrl-M
Window ➤ Debugger	Cmd-` (accent)	Ctrl-` (accent)
Window ➤ Watcher	Cmd-Shift-` (accent)	Ctrl-Shift-` (accent)
View ➤ Onion Skin	None	Alt-V,O

Table 2-7: Window Menu Shortcuts (continued)

Operation	Macintosh	Windows
Modify ➤ Align	Cmd-K	Ctrl-K
Modify ➤ Tweak	Cmd-Shift-K	Ctrl-Shift-K

1 File ➤ Close closes the active window.
2 See "Multiple Window Views" later in this chapter.
3 Function appears on the D7 Toolbar.
4 Double-clicking the thumbnail of a cast member of the given type opens up the corresponding media editor window.
5 Cmd-Shift-U (Macintosh) or Ctrl-Shift-U (Windows) opens the first movie script.

Multiple window views

If the corresponding window type is the active window, the keyboard shortcuts in Table 2-7 will close the window. If it is not already the active window, it will be opened and/or brought to the front.

Use Window ➤ New Window while the appropriate window type is already active to create multiple Score, Cast, Text, Field, QuickTime, Vector Shape, or Script windows.

The Option key (Macintosh) or Alt key (Windows), in combination with any gesture that brings up a window, creates a new instance of that window type (for window types that support multiple instances). For example, Option-double-clicking or Alt-double-clicking on a script cast member in the Cast window opens the script in a new Script window. Similarly, Option–clicking or Alt-clicking the "+" button in the Text, Field, QuickTime, Vector Shape, or Script windows creates a new window of the appropriate type.

If multiple windows of a given type are open, they appear in hierarchical menus under the Window menu. Internal and linked external castLibs, plus multiple open Cast windows, are listed under the Window ➤ Cast menu. Holding down the Option or Alt key while selecting an existing castLib from the *Choose Cast* pop-up list in the Cast window creates a new Cast window.

Prior to D6, only one Score window existed. In D6 and D7, you can open multiple views, but there is still only one Score per movie.

Multiple Cast, Text, Field, and Script windows can show different views of a single entity. For example, two Script windows can be used to view different portions of a single long script. Unfortunately, all views synchronize to show the insertion point if the script is edited. Likewise, multiple views of a single castLib all synchronize if you double-click a cast member's thumbnail.

You cannot open multiple views of the other window types shown in Table 2-7 such as the Paint window or Color Palettes window (although the Sprite Inspector and Sprite Toolbar show the same information). There is no way to split a single Script, Score, or other window into multiple "panes." You must create a separate window instead.

Media Windows

Figure 2-1 shows the standard buttons that appear at the top of the media (Script, Paint, Text, Field, QuickTime, and Vector Shape) windows. See also Figure 4-1.

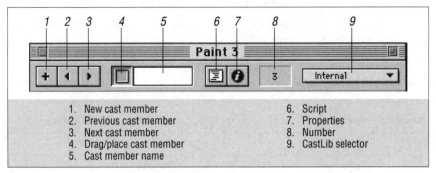

1. New cast member
2. Previous cast member
3. Next cast member
4. Drag/place cast member
5. Cast member name
6. Script
7. Properties
8. Number
9. CastLib selector

Figure 2-1: Standard media editor buttons

Table 2-8 shows the interface shortcuts to open media editors and edit member properties.

Table 2-8: Cast Member and Sprite Editing Shortcuts

Action	Command
Open the cast member in the appropriate media editor (Script, Paint, Text, Field, Quick-Time, Vector Shape, and Color Palettes)	Choose appropriate option from Window menu or use keyboard shortcuts in Table 2-7. Choose Edit ➤ Edit Cast Member. **Double-click on:** • Thumbnail in the Cast window, Sprite Inspector, or Sprite Toolbar • Sprite or sprite span in the Score (may need to triple-click in some cases) • Sprite on the Stage
Open additional editing windows[1]	Option-click (Mac) or Alt-click (Windows) the right or left arrow buttons or plus (+) in the media editor window (see Figure 2-1). Choose Window ➤ New Window
Modify cast member's properties (opens Cast Member Properties dialog box)[2]	Click the "i" button in the media editor window (see Figure 2-1). Click the "i" button on Stage overlay (see View ➤ Sprite Overlay ➤ Show Info). Cmd-double-click (Mac) or Ctrl-double-click (Windows) a sprite on the Stage. Ctrl-click (Mac) or right-click (Windows) a sprite on the Stage or in the Cast and select Cast Member Properties. **Highlight cast member in Cast window, then use:** • The "i" button in the Cast window • Cmd-I (Mac) or Ctrl-I (Windows) • Modify ➤ Cast Member ➤ Properties

[1] Multiple media editor windows of a given type appear hierarchically under the Window menu.
[2] If you select multiple cast members, the Properties dialog box shows the cast members' type (or "Multiple"), the number of items selected, their total size, and their *Palette* and *Unload* settings. If the palette is the same for all selected items, it can be changed en masse, and the *Unload* setting can always be changed for all selected items.

To edit properties of member types implemented via Xtras (QuickTime 3, Flash, Vector Shape, Text, Font), double-click the cast member or click Options in the member property dialog box.

Numeric Keypad and Function Key Shortcuts

Table 2-9 lists the one-button shortcuts that use the numeric keypad. The Num Lock key must be off if using a PC keyboard that has dual function keys on the numeric keypad.

Table 2-9: Numeric Keypad Shortcuts

Keypad Key	Operation	Macintosh	Windows
=	Show/hide cursor	None	None
/	Sprite Inspector	Cmd-Opt-S	Ctrl-Alt-S
*	Behavior Inspector	Cmd-Opt-;	Ctrl-Alt-;
–	Toggle Stage between black and *the stageColor*	None	None
+	Hide sprite selection handles, path, and info overlay on Stage	None	None
Enter	Toggle Stop/Play	Cmd-Opt-P	Ctrl-Alt-P
Shift-Enter	Hide non-Stage windows and Play movie	Shift-Cmd-Opt-P	Shift-Ctrl-Alt-P
. (period)	Stop	Cmd-Opt-.	Ctrl-Alt-.
0	Rewind[1]	Cmd-Opt-R Cmd-Shift-← Shift-Tab	Ctrl-Alt-R Ctrl-Shift-← Shift-Tab
1	Step backward[1]	Cmd-Opt-←	Ctrl-Alt-←
Shift-1	Previous keyframe in selected sprite[1]	None	None
2	No shortcut assigned	N/A	N/A
3	Step forward[1]	Cmd-Opt-→	Ctrl-Alt-→
Shift-3	Next keyframe in selected sprite[2]	None	None
4	Previous marker[1,2]	Cmd-←	Ctrl-←
5	Show current frame in Score (use *Center Current Frame* button)	None	None
6	Next Marker[1,2]	Cmd-→	Ctrl-→
7	Mute sounds (toggle)	Cmd-Opt-M	Ctrl-Alt-M

Table 2-9: Numeric Keypad Shortcuts (continued)

Keypad Key	Operation	Macintosh	Windows
8	Loop Playback (toggle)	Cmd-Opt-L	Ctrl-Alt-L
9	No shortcut assigned	N/A	N/A
Num Lock	Should be off in most cases	N/A	N/A

1 Moves playback head.
2 If there is no next or previous marker the playback head moves 10 frames in the specified direction.

Table 2-10 lists additional keys that are between the numeric keypad and the main keyboard. Do not confuse them with the similarly named keys that sometimes appear on the keypad itself (especially on PC keyboards).

Table 2-10: Supplemental Keys

Key	Usage
Page Up	Scroll up one screen in Cast, Score, Message, Script, Text, or Field window.
Page Down	Scroll down one screen in Cast, Score, Message, Script, Text, or Field window.
Home	Top of Score or Cast window; beginning of line in Script, Text, Field, or Message window.
End	Last channel in Score or last used cast member slot in Cast; end of line in Script, Text, Field, or Message window.
Left arrow[1]	Move cursor left one character or sprite left one pixel.
Right arrow[1]	Move cursor right one character or sprite right one pixel.
Up arrow[2]	Move cursor up one line or sprite up one pixel.
Down arrow[2]	Move cursor down one line or sprite down one pixel.

1 In the Cast window, Cmd-→ and Cmd-← (Macintosh) or Ctrl-→ and Ctrl-← (Windows) advance to the next/previous used cast member slot. In the Score window they move the playback head to the next/previous marker.
2 In the Cast window, Cmd-↑ and Cmd-↓ (Macintosh) or Ctrl-↑ and Ctrl-↓ (Windows) cycle through the movie's castLibs.

Table 2-11 shows function key shortcuts (which are primarily designed for Windows) and the equivalent Macintosh shortcuts. All are new as of Director 6 except F1, Alt-F4, and Ctrl-F4. Note that the F1 and F2 keys perform different actions on Macintosh and Windows, the F3 and F4 keys are Macintosh-only, and the F5, F8, F9, and F10 keys are Windows-only in D6, but cross-platform in D7.

Table 2-11: Function Key Shortcuts

Function Key	Operation	Win	Mac	Windows Alternative	Macintosh Alternative
F1	Help ➤ Director Help	✓	*Undo*	Alt-H,D	Help Key
Shift-F1	Help ➤ Help Pointer	✓		Ctrl-?	Cmd-?
F2	Edit cast member name in Cast window and media editors	✓	*Cut*	Ctrl-Shift-N	Cmd-Shift-N
F3	Edit ➤ Copy		✓	Ctrl-C	Cmd-C
F4	Edit ➤ Paste		✓	Ctrl-V	Cmd-V
Ctrl-F4	File ➤ Close Window	✓	*Paste*	Alt-F,C	Cmd-W
Alt-F4	Quit	✓		Alt-F,X	Cmd-Q
F5	Control ➤ Run Script	✓	✓	Alt-C,U	Cmd-Shift-Opt-↑
F6	Edit ➤ Find ➤ Cast Member	✓	✓	Ctrl-;	Cmd-;
Shift-F6	Edit ➤ Find ➤ Handler	✓	✓	Ctrl-Shift-;	Cmd-Shift-;
F7	Modify ➤ Cast Member ➤ Script	✓	✓	Ctrl-'	Cmd-'
Shift-F7	Modify ➤ Sprite ➤ Script	✓	✓	Ctrl-Shift-'	Cmd-Shift-'
F8	Control ➤ Step Into Script	✓	✓	Alt-C,T	Cmd-Shift-Opt-→
F9	Control ➤ Toggle Breakpoint	✓	✓	Alt-C,G	Cmd-Shift-Opt-K
Shift-F9	Control ➤ Watch Expression	✓	✓	Alt-C,W	Cmd-Shift-Opt-W
Alt-F9	Control ➤ Ignore Breakpoints	✓		Alt-C,O	Cmd-Shift-Opt-I
F10	Control ➤ Step Script	✓	✓	Alt-C,I	Cmd-Shift-Opt-↓
F11	Insert ➤ Remove Frame	✓	✓	Ctrl-[	Cmd-[
F12 (D6)	Insert Frame	✓	✓	Ctrl-]	Cmd-]
Shift-F12 (D6)	Insert ➤ Frames...	✓	✓	Shift-Ctrl-]	Shift-Cmd-]
F12 (D7)	File ➤ Preview in Browser	✓	✓	Alt-F,B	None

OS Shortcuts and Tips

This section gives some quick tips to make you more productive outside of Director, especially if you are inexperienced on one or more platforms. Luckily, Director hides most of the platform-dependent issues from you (see Chapter 7). See Chapter 14, *External Files*, in *Lingo in a Nutshell* or *http://www.zeusprod. com/technote/filepath.html* for details on the differences between file names on the major platforms. See also Chapter 9 for details on memory configuration.

There is a mind-boggling array of freeware and shareware utilities to assist you in various OS-related functions on both Windows and the Macintosh. I recommend installing only those few utilities that improve your productivity measurably, as excessive extensions can destabilize your system. Director-Online has an article on Director developers' favorite utilities at *http://www.director-online.com/features/ zavs_brain/zavshead10.html.*

What Every Windows Developer Should Know

There is no way for me to cover even a fraction of what you need to know about Windows to debug Windows configuration issues competently. Search Macromedia's Tech Notes for appropriate troubleshooting hints. There are hundreds of Windows tricks covered in *Windows Annoyances* by David A. Karp. Buy a copy even if you know Windows well.

Here is a one-minute primer on things to know about Windows:

Start Menu, Control Panel, Find File, and Run options
> You can add shortcuts to your programs to the Windows Start Menu (see "Configuring Your Windows Computer" earlier). Use Start ➤ Settings to access Windows Control Panels (especially the *Display* and *System* Control Panels). Use Start ➤ Find to search for files (* is a wildcard character; for example, search for *.DIR to find all Director movie files). Use Start ➤ Run to run applications and test command-line arguments.

Taskbar
> The Taskbar contains the Start Menu, plus icons for each "visible" running application (other invisible processes can be viewed by hitting Ctrl-Alt-Del once). Use Start ➤ Settings ➤ Taskbar to configure the Taskbar. Use Alt-Tab to cycle among running applications (see Table 2-12).

Right mouse click
> Use the right mouse button on the desktop and throughout Windows to access context-sensitive menus. Right-click on the Start Menu to open the File Explorer. Inside the File Explorer, use the right mouse button to copy or move a file (the default action when dragging an EXE file is to create a shortcut).

Windows System folder
> Most Windows system files of interest are under the "Windows" and "Windows System" folders, which are usually named *C:\Windows* and *C:\ Windows\System* under Windows 95/98, and *C:\WINNT* and *C:\WINNT\ System* under Windows NT. Browse around these directories using the File Explorer and you'll find many wondrous things, including the *C:\Windows\ Start Menu\Programs* folder. Use the FileIO Xtra's *getOSdirectory()* method to locate the Windows folder.

Windows file types and drives
> Windows file types are identified by a three-letter extension such as .DIR for Director movie files or .BMP for bitmap files. Each file type is associated with one and only one executable program (EXE file) via the *WIN.INI* and/or Windows Registry file. Windows drives are assigned drive letters. See Example 8-6.

INI files

Windows uses INI (initialization) files to configure the OS and set options for applications. Director's *DIRECTOR.INI* file is covered in Appendix D, *The DIRECTOR.INI and LINGO.INI Files*, in *Lingo in a Nutshell*. The *LINGO.INI* file does not follow the true Windows INI file format (as described at *http://www. zeusprod.com/technote/ini.html*). The most important Windows INI files are the *SYSTEM.INI* and *WIN.INI* files in the *C:\Windows* directory.

Windows Registry file

The Windows Registry file includes information about Windows and the installed applications. Although used heavily under Windows 95, 98, and NT, it also exists under Windows 3.1. It supersedes much of the functionality of the *WIN.INI* file. Examine the Registry by typing `RegEdit` under `Start ➤ Run.`[*]

Other important Windows files

Besides the *WIN.INI*, *SYSTEM.INI*, and Registry files, the *AUTOEXEC.BAT* and *CONFIG.SYS* files control what Windows does at startup and also load device drivers. Examine these files by typing `SysEdit` under `Start ➤ Run.`

AutoRun

Windows can be configured to play a CD-ROM automatically when it is inserted. See "AutoRun under Windows" in Chapter 8.[†]

DLLs, DirectX, RSX, and other drivers

Many applications install so-called *drivers* in your Windows System folder, which control the video card, sound card, and other devices. These are usually in the form of DLL files, and in some instances may conflict with Director. It is important to compatibility-test against a wide variety of consumer PCs with a variety of commercial software and common drivers installed. See especially "Sound Mixing Under Windows" in Chapter 15.

Safe Mode

Windows 95 can be started in so-called *Safe Mode*, a diagnostic mode used to troubleshoot your Windows installation. Start in Safe Mode by holding down the `F8` key while Windows boots.

MS-DOS Prompt

If the `Start ➤ Run` menu option is insufficient, you can access a command-line interface using `Start ➤ Programs ➤ MS-DOS Prompt`. (See Appendix B, "MS-DOS Crash Course" in *Windows Annoyances*.)

If *any* of the above items were unknown to you, you should really learn more about Windows. There are many good books besides *Windows Annoyances*, including *Windows 95 in a Nutshell* (Tim O'Reilly and Troy Mott, O'Reilly and Associates).

---

[*] See Chapter 3, *The Registry*, of *Windows Annoyances*, and also see *Inside the Windows 95 Registry* (written by Ron Petrusha and also published by O'Reilly and Associates).

[†] See also "Turning Off the CD-ROM AutoRun" in Chapter 4, *Advanced Customization Techniques*, of *Windows Annoyances*.

Macromedia included a wonderful booklet, *Multimedia Essentials for Windows*, with Director 4 for Windows. Though outdated, it explains many Windows basics, and is available from *http://www.zeusprod.com/nutshell/downloads/*.

Table 2-12 lists some of the most common shortcuts under Windows.

Table 2-12: Windows OS Shortcuts

Shortcut	Usage
F1	Help.
Ctrl-F4	Closes a window.
Alt-F4	Closes an application.
F5	Refreshes a directory listing.
F8	Hold down the F8 key while Windows boots to start in *Safe Mode*, *Safe Mode with Networking*, or other special mode for troubleshooting.
Ctrl-Esc	Opens the Start Menu.
Alt	Opens pull-down menus. Use letters, arrow keys, and Enter key to make selections.
Alt-Tab	Cycles amongst open applications.
Alt-Esc	Sends active application to back.
Ctrl-Alt-Del	Press it once to display a list of running tasks from which you can terminate a hung application. Press it twice to reboot.

What Every Macintosh Developer Should Know

If you are a Windows developer, you may be lost when you need to port to the Macintosh. Again, there is no way for me to cover even a fraction of what you need to know about the Macintosh to debug Macintosh configuration issues competently. Search Macromedia's Tech Notes for appropriate troubleshooting hints. Here is a one-minute primer on things to know about the Macintosh:

Macintosh menubar
> The Apple Menu at the left of the menubar can be configured by adding or removing items from the *Apple Menu Items* folder within the *System* folder. From the Finder, the Help menu at the right of the menubar accesses the Macintosh Guide and a very useful summary of shortcuts. Click on the icon at the far right of the menubar to open the `Application` menu and choose from among currently running application.

System folder
> The Macintosh *System* folder contains both the *System* and *Finder* files (i.e., the Mac OS itself), and need not necessarily be called "System Folder." Use the FileIO Xtra's *getOSdirectory()* method to locate it. It includes the *Apple Menu Items, Control Panels, Extensions, Preferences* and *Startup Items* folders. See the *About the Mac OS* folder under the *Apple Extras* folder in the root of the System disk for details on each of these folders and their contents.

Extensions folder

The *Extensions* folder contains drivers loaded when the Macintosh boots. The extensions to load can be customized with the *Extension Manager* Control Panel or disabled entirely by holding down the Shift key when rebooting.

Resource forks

Macintosh program files contain *resource forks* that hold cursors, dialog boxes, strings, and other resources used by the program. These can be edited with *ResEdit* (free from Apple) or another resource editor.

Macintosh file types and drives

A Macintosh file's format is identified by a hidden four-character case-sensitive File Type, such as MV97 for a Director 6 movie file. Each document is associated with one and only one application (program) via a hidden four-character case-sensitive Creator Code. Unlike under Windows, different files with the same File Type can be associated with different applications. Macintosh drives are identified by a name of up to 27 characters. See Chapter 14 in *Lingo in a Nutshell*, *http://www.zeusprod.com/technote/filepath.html*, and *http://www.zeusprod.com/technote/filetype.html*.

Desktop folder

Desktop folder is an invisible folder that contains items on the desktop. Items on the desktop are specified as *Drive:desktop folder:desktopItem*.

Desktop database

The *Desktop database* is a hidden database of all installed applications and the file types that they understand. It can be rebuilt by holding down the Command and Option keys while rebooting.

AppleScript

AppleScript is a general scripting language used to control the Mac OS and communicate between AppleScript-aware applications. Many Macintosh applications will respond to AppleScript commands, and many utilities for the Mac OS are written in AppleScript. You can test AppleScripts using the *AppleScript Editor* under the *Apple Extras:AppleScript* folder in the root of the System disk. Director responds to basic Apple Events. Use the zScript Xtra (*http://www.zeusprod.com/products/zscript.html*) for additional control over sending and receiving Apple Events.

Gestalt

The Macintosh doesn't use individual toolbox calls to obtain system information as does Windows; it uses a single *gestalt* toolbox call with various *gestalt selectors*.

Each case-sensitive, four-character, gestalt selector obtains a single piece of information about the installed software and hardware. With the proper gestalt selector you can determine almost anything about the Macintosh (see Chapter 8). The OSutil Xtra includes a *gestalt* method. For example, using OSutil, this call returns the Mac OS version:

```
set OSversion = OSgestalt("sysv")
```

A list of gestalt selectors can be obtained from:

http://www.bio.vu.nl/home/rgaros/gestalt/

Macintosh productivity tips

Mouse button

Consider buying a two-button mouse with right-button emulation software to access context-sensitive menus on the Mac. (By default, this requires the Ctrl key plus a mouse click).

Managing Macintosh windows

The *WindowShade* Control Panel allows you to hide a window temporarily by double- or triple-clicking in its titlebar. See Table 2-12 for important shortcuts.

Find File

The Finder's File ➤ Find command (Cmd-F) can find files by attributes other than the filename and can also search on multiple attributes via the *More Choices* button. To check a file's File Type, change the search criteria to *file type* and drop the file onto the middle of the dialog box. To search for all Director 7.x movie files, specify a file type of "MV07". *Find File* can limit searches to the desktop, the current Finder selection, or local drives. Choose *Find File Shortcuts* from the Help menu while *Find File* is the active application for much more information.

Files and folders

To refresh a Macintosh directory listing, close the folder and re-open it.

To open the parent folders containing a folder, Cmd-click on the folder's name in its window's titlebar. A pop-up folder hierarchy appears.

Use the Finder's *View* menu to view files by different attributes (see the *Views* Control Panel); click a column's heading to sort by its value.

Type the first few letters of a filename to jump to it in a folder or dialog box.

Utilities

Default Folder is shareware that provides convenient access to multiple recently used folders:

http://www.stclairsoft.com/DefaultFolder/index.html

QuickKeys (from CE Software, *http://www.cesoft.com/products.html*) is a macro utility that allows you to automate frequently repeated tasks with a single keystroke. You can also use AppleScript to automate tasks.

Table 2-13 lists key combinations that can be held down while rebooting to affect the Macintosh in some way.

Table 2-13: Mac OS Key Combinations While Rebooting

Hold Down While Rebooting	Usage	Wait Until
Cmd-Option	Rebuild the desktop	Confirmation dialog box appears.
Cmd-Option-P-R	Zap Parameter RAM (PRAM)	The Macintosh makes its startup sound three times, then release the keys.
Shift	Disable all extensions	"Extensions off" message appears.
Space	Displays Extension Manager	Extensions Manager appears.

Table 2-14 lists some of the most common shortcuts on the Macintosh.

Table 2-14: Mac OS Shortcuts

Key Combo	Usage
Cmd-Option-Esc	Force quit (abort) a frozen program.
Cmd-Arrow	Expand (right arrow) or collapse (left arrow) selected folder (or click triangle when viewing by name, etc.).
Cmd-Option-Arrow	Expand (right arrow) or collapse (left arrow) all subfolders within selected folder (or Option-click triangle when viewing by name, etc.).
Cmd-Shift-?	Macintosh Guide providing Macintosh help.
Cmd-drag	Cmd-drag a window's titlebar to move it without making it active.
Cmd-Option-W	Close all open windows (or Option-click a window's close box).
Option-*selection*	Hold down the Option key while selecting an application to hide all windows of previous application.
Option-drag	Copy a file instead of moving it.

Screen Grabs

Table 2-15 shows how to take a screen grab at the OS level. To take a screen grab via Lingo in D7, use *the picture of the stage* or *the picture of window* properties. In D6, or to capture areas outside Director's Stage, use an Xtra such as the freeware ScrnXtra (*http://www.littleplanet.com/kent/kent.html*) or the PrintOMatic Xtra (*http://www.printomatic.com*). For full-motion screen recording, see utilities such as CameraMan, Lotus ScreenCam, and Microsoft Camcorder. (See also the VCap and VSnap video and frame capture utilities at *http://www.penworks.com/xtras/*.)

Table 2-15: Operating System Screen Grab Shortcuts

Screenshot	Mac[1]	Win[2]
Screen grab	Cmd-Shift-3	Print Screen
Capture rectangular area	Cmd-Shift-4	Requires third-party utility[3]
Capture a specific window	Cmd-Shift-Caps Lock-4	Alt-Print Screen

[1] Macintosh screen grabs are created as PICT files named "Picture *n*" in the root level of the System disk and are accompanied by a camera shutter sound. Hold down the Ctrl key to capture to the clipboard instead of a file. Capturing a window or rectangular subsection of the screen requires Mac OS 7.6 or later.
[2] Windows Print Screen functions always copy a bitmap of the specified area to the clipboard from which it can be pasted into other applications. Within Director for Windows Alt-Print Screen also captures the full screen. Capturing a window works only from the File Explorer.
[3] See *http://www.zeusprod.com/site/scrncapt.html* for some third-party screen-capture utilities.

CHAPTER 3

The Score and Animation

This chapter covers the mechanics of using the Score. In this chapter, I assume that you are familiar with the basic operation of the Cast and Score to create animations as described in Macromedia's *Using Director* manual.

Animation Techniques

Most people use Director primarily for cell animation, but there are many ways to create animations and pseudo-animation effects. Examine Director's example movies and any movie for which you have the source to see how various animation techniques are accomplished. The best approach depends on the effect you seek and the performance, memory, disk space, and bandwidth limitations of each technique.

Most animations are not as interesting to the end user as the animator would like to think. Performance is often more important than perfection. There is always a delay when cast members are loaded. You can preload the animation, or accept the multiple small delays as it plays. In all cases, reduce, reduce, reduce!

Table 3-1 compares the strengths and weaknesses of various animation techniques. Throughout the table, the term *storage* indicates RAM and disk usage and implies greater downloading time. Low bandwidth techniques, such as shapes with custom tile patterns, are ideal for Shockwave. Score animation techniques do not guarantee the tempo or synchronization. Use digital video and cue points for accurate timing. See also "Animation Optimization" later in this chapter.

Table 3-1: Animation Technique Comparison

Animation Technique	Strengths	Weaknesses
Control ➤ Real-Time Recording	Simulates natural, fluid movements.	Inexact, but can be tweaked afterwards.
Control ➤ Step Recording	Exact keyframe positioning.	Tedious for longer animations.

Table 3-1: Animation Technique Comparison (continued)

Animation Technique	Strengths	Weaknesses
Scaling bitmap cast members in real time	Low storage/bandwidth.	Poor runtime performance, and poor quality scaling.
Scaling and rotating members in the Paint window	Sprite drawing is fast, provided cast members are loaded.	Multiple cast members require high storage and bandwidth.
Rotating cast members in real time	Low storage/bandwidth.	Requires Xtra in D6.5 and earlier.[1] Processor-intensive.
Alpha channel compositing	Anti-aliases a single cast member over various backgrounds. Low storage/bandwidth.	Requires Alphamania Xtra (*http://www.medialab.com*) in D6.5 and earlier. Native in D7. Works best in 32-bit color. Processor-intensive.
Modify ➤ Sprite ➤ Tweening (formerly *In-Between Special*)	Extensive control over lead-in, lead-out, and curvature.	Difficult to create exact paths, such as circles (use Lingo or Score Recording).
Path manipulation on-Stage	Excellent visual control of path over time.	Can be tedious and inexact.
Edit ➤ Paste Special ➤ Relative	Seamlessly extends an animation sequence.	Can be tedious for repetitive animations. Use film loops instead.
Insert ➤ Film Loop	Treats a multi-sprite animation as a single entity.	Limited control via Lingo.
Modify ➤ Frame ➤ Palette ➤ Color Cycling	Fast performance with low storage/bandwidth. Illusion of flowing water or changing lights.	Requires graphic skills and a custom palette. Works only in 8-bit (256 colors).
Modify ➤ Frame ➤ Palette ➤ Fade to Black/White	Smooth visual transition, especially when switching to new palette.	Works only in 8-bit (256 colors). Can't fade pure white or pure black pixels on Windows.
Modify ➤ Frame ➤ Palette ➤ Palette Transition	Gives cool psychedelic transition.	Looks bad if the effect is unintentional. Switch palettes while screen is black instead. Works only in 8-bit (256 colors).
Colorizing sprites (Tools Palette color chips or *foreColor* and *backColor*)	Fast with minimal storage/bandwidth (1-bit cast members). Ideal for Shockwave.	Prior to D7, colors depend on palette and may be inconsistent at color depths other than 8-bit.
Shape sprites (Window ➤ Tool Palette)	Minuscule storage/bandwidth. Can use custom tile patterns.	Draws more slowly than bitmaps. Shapes limited to lines, rects, and ovals.
Digital Video (QuickTime or Video for Windows)	Excellent scalability and synchronization. Quality and compression depend on source and codec.	High bandwidth. Requires QT or VFW software. Limited sprite layering and ink effect support. Works poorly with transitions.

Table 3-1: Animation Technique Comparison (continued)

Animation Technique	Strengths	Weaknesses
Insert ➤ Media Element ➤ QuickTime 3 (or File ➤ Import in D7)	Supports a wide range of animation and transition effects and even sprite animation.	Requires QT3 Xtra. Not supported under Windows 3.1 or 68K Macs.
Insert ➤ Media Type ➤ Shockwave Flash Movie (or File ➤ Import in D7)	Flash animation files are compact and scalable.	Requires Flash Asset Xtra. Not supported under Windows 3.1 or 68K Macs.
Modify ➤ Frame ➤ Transition	Easy to create visual effects if you have the proper transition.	Performance and appearance may vary on different machines and platforms.
ZoomBox	Creates zooming effect from one sprite to another.	Limited usefulness.
Blend and other ink effects (Modify ➤ Sprite ➤ Properties)	Good for subtle fade-ins and fade-outs. Requires only one cast member.	Processor-intensive. Will not work with digital video. Works best at higher color depths. See Example 13-5.
Xtras ➤ Wizards ➤ Animation Wizard	Great for panning and zooming text for titles and bulleted lists.	Limited number of operations; uses only rich text cast members. Obsolete in D7.
Score Recording	Gives complete control over sprite animation and effects channels.	Requires Lingo programming. Can't record Behaviors easily.
Insert ➤ Control ➤ Custom Button	Easily creates animated buttons with up to eight different states.	Limited to button rollovers and highlights. Buggy. Obsolete in D7.
Lingo-based animation	Gives complete control over sprite animation. Dynamic or exact animations possible.	Can be complex to implement and debug. Difficult to tweak animation as is easily done in Score.
Xtras ➤ Import PowerPoint File	Leverages content developed in PowerPoint.	Reads only PowerPoint 4.0 files. Not all features supported.
Quad, skew, rotate, and Vector Shapes in D7	Requires few cast members.	Processor-intensive. Requires D7.

[1] The QuickTime 3 and Flash Asset Xtras can rotate the image within the bounding box of their respective sprites. The third-party Effector Set (*http://www.medialab.com*) or Cast Effects Xtra (*http://www.penworks.com/xtras/castfx*) can also rotate cast members in real time. These Xtras are all processor-intensive may not be supported on all platforms. D7 includes native support for real-time rotation of bitmap, Flash, text, animated GIf, and vector shape cast members.

Animating with Director's Score

Table 3-2 explains the new sprite properties used to flip, rotate, and distort sprites in Director 7. Rotation and skew are in measured in degrees. Use the rotation/skew tool (see Figure 14-1) to rotate or skew a sprite as shown in the *Rotating a sprite* and *Skewing a sprite* Show Me movies in the D7 online Help. Use the Tab key to switch between the rotation/skew and selection tools. Use the rotation tool in the center of the sprite to perform rotation; use the same tool on an edge of the sprite's bounding box to skew the sprite.

Table 3-2: Director 7 Sprite Transformation Properties

Property	Notes
flipH of sprite	Boolean property that flips a sprite across its own (possibly rotated and skewed) "vertical" axis. See the *Flip Horizontal* button in the Sprite Inspector.
flipV of sprite	Boolean property that flips a sprite across its own (possibly rotated and skewed) "horizontal" axis. See the *Flip Horizontal* button in the Sprite Inspector.
locZ of sprite	Adjusts a sprite's z-ordering (the paint layer in which it is drawn). Sprites with a higher *locZ* are drawn in the foreground (the default is the sprite number). Mouse events obey the sprite channel order, not the z-order.
mapMemberToStage (sprite *n*, *pointInMember*)	Returns point on Stage corresponding to point within member, accounting for transformations. Returns *<Void>* if point is outside member bounds.
mapStageToMember (sprite *n*, *pointOnStage*)	Returns point within member, accounting for transformations, corresponding to point on Stage. Returns *<Void>* if point is outside member bounds.
obeyScoreRotation of member	If TRUE, Flash members use D7's Score rotation. If FALSE (default for movies upgraded from D6.5), uses the *rotation of member* Flash property.
quad of sprite	Specifies arbitrary four corners of bitmap, text, or animated GIF sprite, such as [point(*x1, y1*), point(*x2, y2*), point(*x3, y3*), point(*x4, y4*)]. Coordinates can be floats. Exchanging the first or last two points creates a bowtie effect. Must be set via Lingo.
rotation of member	Rotates QuickTime display (in degrees) within sprite's bounding box.
rotation of sprite	Rotates sprite bounding box, in degrees. Can be set in Sprite Inspector.
scale of member scale of sprite	Scales viewable member area within sprite bounding box. For QuickTime sprites, the *scale* is a list (the default is [100.0, 100.0]) and *the crop of member* must be TRUE. For Flash and vector shapes, the *scale* is a percentage (the default is 100.0). See *scaleMode* in Table 13-4.
skew of sprite	Setting the skew can tilt or flip a sprite. Default is 0.0. A *skew* of 180 reverses a sprite. A *skew* of 90 or 270 hides a sprite (displays it on edge). Can be set in Sprite Inspector.

The *flipH, flipV, rotation,* and *skew of sprite* properties affect the bounding box of bitmap, text, Flash, vector shape, and animated GIF sprites, but not other sprite types. QuickTime 3 sprites can be rotated within their bounding boxes using *the rotation of member.* The *quad of sprite* is settable for bitmaps, animated GIFs, and text sprites, but it read-only for other sprite types. When the *quad of sprite* has been set, the *rotation, skew, flipH,* and *flipV of sprite* properties are ignored. The *quad* and *locZ of sprite* properties must be set at runtime via Lingo; they are not stored in the Score permanently, nor can they be set via the Sprite Inspector.

The Modify ➤ Transform menu options (also available using Ctrl-click (Mac) or right click (Windows) on a sprite in the Score or on the Stage) initiate or undo various transformations. The mirror transformations reflect a sprite across the Stage's axes, whereas the *flipH* and *flipV* properties reflect the sprite across the sprite's possibly rotated and skewed axes. If the regPoint is in the center of the object, *flipH* and *Flip Horizontal in Place* have the same net effect, as does *Mirror Horizontal* in place if the sprite is not rotated or skewed. Create an asymmetric cast member with an off-center regPoint and then rotate it to see the difference between the various transformations. For many more details on sprite transformations, see *http://www.zeusprod.com/nutshell/transforms.html*.

The following transformations are available under Modify ➤ Transform:

Rotate Left
> Decreases *rotation* by 90 degrees (rotates around regPoint).

Rotate Right
> Increases *rotation* by 90 degrees (rotates around regPoint).

Mirror Horizontal
> Flips across Stage's vertical axis passing through regPoint by setting the *rotation* to 180 − *rotation* and the *skew* to 180 − *skew*. *FlipH* is not affected.

Mirror Vertical
> Flips across Stage's horizontal axis passing through regPoint by negating the *rotation* and setting the *skew* to 180 − *skew*. *FlipV* is not affected.

Flip Horizontal in Place
> Flips across sprite's vertical axis passing through regPoint. Toggles *flipH* and adjusts *locH of sprite* as necessary so that *rect of sprite* is unchanged.

Flip Vertical in Place
> Flips across sprite's horizontal axis passing through regPoint. Toggles *flipV* and adjusts *locV of sprite* as necessary so that *rect of sprite* is unchanged.

Reset Width and Height
> Resets *width* and *height of sprite* to cast member dimensions, and sets *stretch of sprite* to FALSE, but other properties don't change.

Reset Rotation and Skew
> Resets *rotation* and *skew* to 0, but other properties don't change.

Reset All
> Resets *height, width,* and sets *stretch, rotation, skew, flipH,* and *flipV* to 0. But original *loc of sprite* can't be reset automatically.

Creating animations with cast members

Table 3-3 shows some of the special options for creating and modifying animations using one or more cast members.

Film Loops

Film loops are convenient to deal with an animation or multiple sprites as a single entity. See Macromedia's *Using Director* manual for a basic explanation of film loops. Film loops effectively increase the number of sprite channels available,

Table 3-3: Animation Operations in the Cast and Score

Action	Command
Center a sprite on Stage	Drag the square *Drag Cast Member* icon from the Cast window or one of the media editor windows directly to the Score, or use Cmd-Shift-L (Mac) or Ctrl-Shift-L (Windows).
Create a single sprite span from selected cast members	Highlight cast members, then choose Modify ➤ Cast to Time or hold down Option (Mac) or Alt (Windows) when dragging from Cast to Score, or use Cmd-Shift-Opt-L (Mac) or Ctrl-Shift-Alt-L (Windows).
Lay out selected cast members in separate sprite channels	Highlight cast members, then drag to Score. Each becomes a sprite of the default duration. See File ➤ Preferences ➤ Sprite.
Reverse a horizontal sequence of frames	Highlight sprites in the Score, then choose Modify ➤ Reverse Sequence or Cmd-drag (Mac) or Ctrl-drag (Windows) the first keyframe past the end of the sprite.
Rearrange sprites from a vertical column (frame) to a horizontal channel	Highlight multiple channels in *one* Score frame, then choose Modify ➤ Space to Time. (Use with single-frame sprites, or when editing individual sprite frames.)
Create a film loop	Highlight sprite(s) in the Score, then choose Insert ➤ Film Loop (film loop is created in Cast, not Score) or copy sprites to clipboard, then paste into a single cast member.
"Unwrap" a previously created film loop	Copy a film loop castmember to clipboard. Then highlight a single cell in the Score and paste film loop from clipboard.

although film loops using an excessive number of sprites can slow animation. You can apply ink effects and Behaviors to sprites before incorporating them into a film loop, which can even include sounds in the Sound channels. The film loop itself can also be moved over time, have Behaviors and inks applied, and so on.

Use film loops to animate a stationary sequence of bitmaps such as a clock face, a single bitmap changing location, or any sprite properties changing over time.

The *regPoint of member* property for a film loop is its center and cannot be set manually, but you can change the *regPoint of member* of a constituent cast member within the film loop to change its relative position.

Because a film loop refers to other cast members, those cast members must not be deleted. Likewise, the Custom Cursor Xtra (new in D6.5) uses a series of cast members to create an animation much like a film loop. The Score of a Director movie imported as an unlinked member is converted to a film loop. The Custom Button Editor Xtra (new in D6 but obsolete in D7) is not like a film loop, in that bitmaps used within a custom button can be deleted if not needed elsewhere.

Film loops animate in lock step with the main Score (one frame in the film loop for each frame in the Score). A film loop always begins at its first frame; there is no Lingo control over the frame position *within* a film loop (you can use a global variable in a *prepareFrame* handler to track the film loop's current frame number).

In D4, looping in a single frame did not allow a film loop to animate. In D5 and later, a film loop will animate when looping in a single Score frame using *go the frame* but not when waiting via *pause* or via the Tempo channel. The latter can be used to start and stop a film loop mid-stride, but will also pause other animations.

To simulate the starting and stopping of a film loop independent of other animations, swap its sprite's *member of sprite* property for a stationary bitmap. Set a film loop's *loop of member* property or the *Loop* checkbox in its Properties dialog box to cause it to loop continuously. If the *loop* property is FALSE, the film loop will remain on its last frame after playing once through.

When changing member properties at runtime, Director may not redraw the film loop as expected. When setting *the loop of member* property at runtime, also reset *the media of member* property to force Director to recognize the change:

```
set the loop of member "loop" = FALSE
set the media of member "loop" = the media of member "loop"
```

Furthermore, when setting *the regPoint of member* or *picture of member* of any constituent cast members, you might need the following to update the film loop:

```
set the crop of member "loop" = the crop of member "loop"
```

A film loop's *the media of member* property is akin to *the score* property of a MIAW (or of the main movie itself). You can copy *the media of member* of film loops to *the score* property of MIAWs and vice versa. You can construct film loops at runtime by first performing Score recording in a MIAW.

See James Newton's tips on film loops at *http://www.director-online.com/howTo/ UD_articles/UD27.html.*

Animation Optimization

There are many fine graphic artists who create beautiful graphics but don't understand how to optimize them for real-time playback. As the Director expert, it is your job to work with graphic artists to help them create content appropriate for Director. These techniques can reduce storage space requirements dramatically, which translates into faster load times and less memory usage.

Common errors committed by graphic artists with a print background:

Repeating full-screen graphics when only minor elements change
Large static portions of graphics should be created as separate cast members and used as separate sprites. For example, animate a dog's wagging tail or barking head as a series of cast members, but use a separate cast member for its immobile body. If the graphics are rendered by a 3D program you should trim each frame by hand in the Paint window. This preserves the original registration points and can lead to a huge reduction in file size.

Embedding elements in the background
The background should be separate from any elements that change, move, or require interactivity. If an element is embedded in the background, it cannot be animated or scripted separately. Director doesn't import individual paint layers of a Photoshop document separately, but the third-party Photocaster Xtra (*http://www.medialab.com*) will do so. D7 includes Photocaster Lite.

Imperfect alignment and subtle size changes

Even a one-pixel shift is readily apparent in Director. All elements that are invariant from frame to frame should be separate cast members anyway, but if an element is repeated, it should be *exactly* the same size and in the same place in each frame. All buttons should have consistent sizes and alignment. Highlighted, depressed, or rollover versions of buttons should be the exact size of the original. Your Lingo code will be much easier to implement if graphics that have similar purposes are all a consistent size. Imagine a multiple choice exam in which the user clicks within ovals to fill out an answer sheet. There may be too many ovals to use a separate sprite for each one. Consistent size and spacing of the ovals makes it much easier to determine which one the user clicked and allows a single cast member to be used to fill in each oval.

Too high a frame rate, or too many intermediate steps in an animation

Reduce animation rates to 12–15 fps (frames per second) to reduce the number of cast members required. Using 15 members within a film loop instead of 50 reduces the animation by 70%. If needed, blur the cast members in a graphics editor to simulate motion.

Too high a color depth

Using 8-bit (indexed) color reduces overhead by 50% versus 16-bit color and by 75% versus 32-bit color. In all cases, save the original high-color artwork in case you need to redither it.

Only one palette can be active at any given time when using 8-bit color

All elements used on a single screen or within a single scene should have the same palette. Using one palette throughout the entire presentation simplifies matters greatly. Any palette switch will be obvious, unless you use a transitional screen containing only colors common to both palettes (or just black). Create one or more custom palettes in deBabelizer or a similar tool to maintain image quality.

Reserved colors must be in the same positions in each palette

Any elements that are used on multiple screens with different palettes must use only reserved colors that are stored in the same place in each custom palette. If designing for Windows or cross-platform, the Windows reserved colors should be used at the beginning and end of the custom palette. Refer to Chapter 13 for important details.

Anti-aliasing against the wrong background

Anti-aliasing a graphic against a white background in Photoshop causes gray pixels at the edges and results in a halo effect when displayed against a dark background. Anti-alias against the background color on which the object will be displayed in Director, don't anti-alias, or use sprites that are dynamically anti-aliased (Alphamania, text, Flash, or D7 bitmaps with an alpha channel).

Animating large objects or too many objects

Large graphics animate slowly because Director must redraw too much of the screen. Animate fewer, smaller graphics in larger increments to make your animations faster.

Using slow ink effects

Stick to the faster ink effects such as *copy*, *matte*, and *background transparent* and avoid slower ink effects such as *blend*. Digital Video and Flash Assets perform much better when played direct-to-Stage and non-copy ink effects should be avoided.

Using too large a Stage

For consumer products, you should use a 640×480 Stage. An 832×624 Stage requires 70% more RAM and should be used only when you can control the playback platform, such as for a kiosk or dedicated sales force.

Drawing graphics in the wrong size

Resized (stretched) bitmap sprites are very slow. Create all graphics in the size in which you expect to use them on-Stage. Use Modify ➤ Transform Bitmap (or scale them in Photoshop or deBabelizer before importing). Trim any graphics larger than the Stage.

Using Edit ➤ Exchange Cast Members to swap cast members of different sizes may result in stretched sprites. Use the *Restore* button in the *Sprite Info* dialog box or Modify ➤ Transform ➤ Reset Width and Height to reset them to their natural size. If using a single cast member at multiple sizes, scaling it may be preferable to creating multiple cast members. You must balance load time, RAM usage, and performance in your situation. Flash, vector shape, shape, and field cast members scale without performance degradation, but scaling field cast members changes their bounding box, not the size of the text.

Failure to test cross-platform

The appearance and performance of an animation may depend on the platform, especially when using transitions. Graphics in the same palette tend to appear darker under Windows than on the Macintosh.

Excessive bandwidth

The larger an animation, the more disk storage it requires and the longer it takes to load. Animation speeds may suffer if other media—such as audio—is being used simultaneously. Reduce the animation or eliminate the peripheral activity that is slowing down the animations.

The Score

Director 6's Score is radically different from earlier versions and includes a Sprite Toolbar and customizable views. (The D7 Score is identical to D6's Score, although the Sprite Toolbar includes new fields shown in Figure 3-2.) In D6 and later, sprites span a range of frames over time rather than occupying a single cell. Sprites can be manipulated as a single object without manually highlighting individual cells. You can manually insert keyframes at any point in a sprite. Tweening between keyframes is automatic; sprite paths can be manipulated directly on Stage.

A sprite span covering a range of frames is somewhat insulated from other sprite spans in the same channel. A sprite can be thought of as part of a *scene* lasting for some portion of the channel. The cast member, location, and other properties of a sprite can vary during a sprite span, but the attached Behaviors (i.e., sprite scripts) always apply to the entire sprite span.

Changing a single sprite property via Lingo affects only the current sprite span, except for *the puppet of sprite* (or *puppetSprite* command) and *the visibility of sprite* which affect the entire *channel*. Refer to "Auto-puppets versus manual puppets" in Chapter 1 for details. Sprites receive several new messages in D6 and D7 (*begin-Sprite, endSprite, mouseEnter, mouseLeave*, and *prepareFrame*), making them much easier to manage than in earlier versions.

The most notable improvements to the Score since D5 are the ability to manipulate sprites as unified objects and the availability of multiple Score windows, zooming options, and a highly visible (red) playback head indicator. The most notable drawback is that the sprite shuffling buttons were replaced with keyboard shortcuts (see Table 3-15) and the window layout is somewhat inefficient. A single window with split views would be preferable to multiple Score windows, and there is no way to "remember" more than one Score window setting.

Figure 3-1 shows the elements of the Director 6 and 7 Score for comparison to the Director 5 Score. Note that in Figure 3-1, items in bold apply to D5, D6, and D7. Items 27 through 31 (in italic) apply to D5 only, and the unbolded items between 1 through 26 apply to D6 and D7 only.

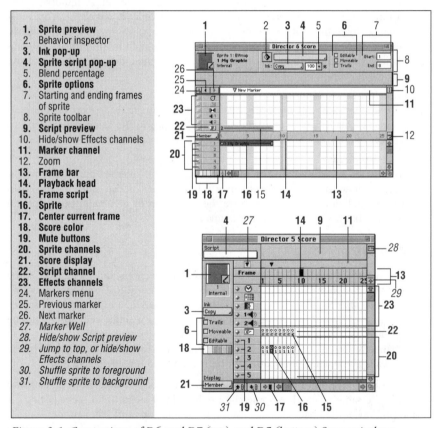

1. **Sprite preview**
2. Behavior inspector
3. **Ink pop-up**
4. **Sprite script pop-up**
5. Blend percentage
6. **Sprite options**
7. Starting and ending frames of sprite
8. Sprite toolbar
9. **Script preview**
10. Hide/show Effects channels
11. **Marker channel**
12. Zoom
13. **Frame bar**
14. **Playback head**
15. **Frame script**
16. **Sprite**
17. **Center current frame**
18. **Score color**
19. **Mute buttons**
20. **Sprite channels**
21. **Score display**
22. **Script channel**
23. **Effects channels**
24. Markers menu
25. Previous marker
26. Next marker
27. *Marker Well*
28. *Hide/show Script preview*
29. *Jump to top, or hide/show Effects channels*
30. *Shuffle sprite to foreground*
31. *Shuffle sprite to background*

Figure 3-1: Comparison of D6 and D7 (top) and D5 (bottom) Score windows

D6 and D7 use new gestures to select and move sprites, set the current frame or select multiple frames, select channels, add markers, and perform other actions. Table 3-4 compares the Score in D5 to that in D6 and D7. See Figures 3-2 and 5-4 for details on D7's updated Sprite Toolbar and Sprite Inspector.

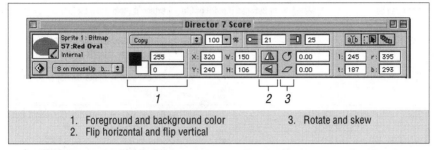

1. Foreground and background color
2. Flip horizontal and flip vertical
3. Rotate and skew

Figure 3-2: Director 7 Score's Sprite Toolbar

The So-Called Director 5 Style Score Preference

The File ➤ Preferences ➤ Score ➤ *Director 5 Style Score display* option in D6 and D7 doesn't truly provide a Director 5–style Score. It displays sprites as individual cells, but doesn't change the features of the Score window or the gestures required to manipulate sprites and the playback head. Shut off the *Tween Size and Position* preference under File ➤ Preferences ➤ Sprite to prevent D6 and D7 from automatically recalculating tweened sprite frames when a sprite keyframe changes.

Do not cling to the Director 5–style Score. The updated Score is closely tied to sprite paths, auto-tweening, auto-puppeting, and new sprite messages, and is much more powerful once you get used to it.

Table 3-4: Director 5, 6, and 7 Score Comparison

Feature	Director 5	Director 6 and Director 7
Score window(s)	Single window with limited config-urability.	Multiple configurable views, zooming, and Sprite Toolbar and Sprite Inspector.
Playback head indicator[1]	Filled rectangle in Frame number area.	Red line running vertically through Score window.
Number of Sprite channels	48	120 in D6, up to 1000 in D7
Sprite spans	Sprite is a single cell. Each cell is independent, with manual retweening.	Sprites span multiple frames and have optional keyframes.
Sprite properties	Manual puppeting overrides entire sprite channel, until unpuppeted.	Auto-puppeting overrides individual sprite properties for life of current sprite only (manual puppeting of entire channel still available).
Tween sprite attributes besides position and size	Modify ➤ In-Between Special.	Modify ➤ Sprite ➤ Tweening. Retweening is automatic. D7 tweens colors.

Table 3-4: Director 5, 6, and 7 Score Comparison (continued)

Feature	Director 5	Director 6 and Director 7
Tween/extend a sprite over more frames	Highlight span of frames and use Modify ➤ In-Between (Cmd-B or Ctrl-B).	Click and drag last frame of sprite to extend it (hold down the Opt or Alt key to extend single-frame sprites) or position playback head and choose Modify ➤ Extend Sprite (Cmd-B or Ctrl-B).
Sprite paths	None.	Choose View ➤ Sprite Overlay ➤ Show Paths.
Sprite keyframes	None.	Choose View ➤ Keyframes (Cmd-Shift-Opt-K or Ctrl-Shift-Alt-K).
Thumbnail, Ink, Trails, Moveable, Editable, and Script pop-up options	Built into Score window.	Included in optional Sprite Toolbar or floating Sprite Inspector.
Show/hide script preview area	Show/hide script preview button.	Edit ➤ Preferences ➤ Score ➤ Script Preview.[2]
Show/hide Effects channels	Show/hide Effects channel button.	Button has new appearance and position, but similar function (see Figure 3-1).
Shuffle sprite channels forward or back	Shuffle forward and shuffle back buttons at bottom of Score.	Drag sprites manually or use keyboard shortcuts in Table 3-15.
Tempo channel	Maximum tempo 120 fps. Waits for end of sound or digital video.	Maximum tempo 500 fps in D6, 999 fps in D7. Waits for cue points in sounds, digital video, and SWA.
Add markers	Drag marker from Marker Well. Default name is empty.	Click in Marker channel or use Insert ➤ Marker. Default name is "New Marker."
Frame scripts	Single script can be attached to each frame of Script channel.	Single Behavior can span a range of frames in Script channel and receives new messages.
Frame events sent	*enterFrame, stepFrame, exitFrame, idle.*	Added *prepareFrame, beginSprite,* and *endSprite* messages.
Sprite scripts	Single script can be attached to each cell.	Multiple Behaviors can be attached to a sprite as a whole. New Behavior Inspector.
Sprite events sent	*mouseUp, mouseDown, rightMouseUp, rightMouseDown, stepFrame.*	Added *beginSprite, endSprite, mouseEnter, mouseLeave, mouseWithin, mouseUpOutside, new, prepareFrame, enterFrame,* and *exitFrame* messages.
Muted channels	Muted sprite channels still receive events.	Muted sprite channels don't receive events. Invisible sprites do.

Table 3-4: Director 5, 6, and 7 Score Comparison (continued)

Feature	Director 5	Director 6 and Director 7
Jump to top of Score	Show/hide Effects channel button jumps to top.	Home key.
Select a sprite over a range of frames	Double-click one of the cells in the range.	Single-click unified sprite span or double-click if editing individual frames.
Duplicate selected cells	Opt-Cmd-drag (Mac) or Ctrl-Alt-drag (Windows).	Opt-drag (Mac) or Alt-drag (Windows).
Select entire channel[3]	Double-click channel number at left of Score.	Single-click or double-click channel number at left of Score.
Select entire frame	Single-click in frame number bar and drag over one frame.	Double-click in frame number bar.
Pasting entire frames	Insertion point set between two frames by single-clicking in frame number area.	Insertion point can be set only by selecting a frame or cell. Pasting frames results in at least one frame or cell being overwritten.
Pasting sprites	Will overwrite existing sprites without warning.	If no room is available, you can optionally overwrite existing sprites, truncate sprites being pasted, or insert frames.
Frame number readout while scrolling	Frame number readout shown as horizontal thumb slider is dragged.	No readout. Score scrolls as thumb slider is dragged.[4]
Step frame recording[5]	Option-click (Mac) or Alt-click (Windows) on sprite channel's number or drag a cast member to Score.	Use Control ➤ Step Recording.
Real-Time recording[6]	Hold down Ctrl-Spacebar while dragging sprite.	Can also use Control ➤ Real-Time Recording.
Display menu	At bottom left of Score window. Inaccessible if Score window shows less than eight channels.	Adjacent to frame number bar, and accessible via View ➤ Display.
Motion display mode	*Motion* display pop-up mode shows movement and cast member type.	Replaced by *Location* display and sprite paths. Still available with *D5 Style Score display* mode.
Script display mode	*Script* display shows sprites with cast-member scripts as "+".	Renamed *Behavior* display mode. Only *D5 Style Score display* shows cast member scripts as "+".
Extended display mode	Shows cast member type and motion.	Cast member type and motion display available in *D5 Style Score display* mode only.

Table 3-4: Director 5, 6, and 7 Score Comparison (continued)

Feature	Director 5	Director 6 and Director 7
Cell coloration	Empty and nonempty cells may be colored (defaults to white).	Only occupied cells can be colored in D6 mode (defaults to light purple).
Drag-and-drop	Preference setting can be toggled at any time using the spacebar when dragging.	Always on in D6 mode. Preference setting in *D5 Style Score display* mode.
Cell selection	Can select any range of cells.	Use Opt key (Mac) or Alt key (Win) to select both occupied and unoccupied cells in D6 mode.
Preferences	File ➤ Preferences ➤ Score.	Can also use shortcut menu[2] to set preferences.

[1] Director 5 includes a *Playback Head Follows Selection* option under File ➤ Preferences ➤ Score. In D6 and D7, if you select a sprite on Stage, the playback head always jumps to the corresponding frame.
[2] Using Ctrl-click (Mac) or right-click (Windows) in the Score window gives quick access to several commonly used Sprite and Score preference settings. See Table 3-11.
[3] In D6 and D7, single-clicking a channel number selects the individual sprites within the channel (empty frames are not highlighted). If a sprite channel is not being used, all the empty frames in the channel are highlighted. This is an easy way to check whether a channel is used anywhere in the Score. Double-clicking selects both occupied and unoccupied frames.
[4] Use Opt-drag (Mac) or Ctrl-drag (Windows) to prevent the Score from updating until you release the slider. For 68K Macs running D6, the default behavior is the same as D5 (use Opt-drag or Ctrl-drag to reverse the behavior).
[5] Step Frame recording is indicated by a red dot to the left of the affected Score sprite channels. Turn it off under D5 by clicking the red button while holding down Opt (Macintosh) or Alt (Windows). Turn it off under D6 or D7 using Control ➤ Step Recording.
[6] Real-Time recording is indicated by a red circle in D5 or a red arrow in D6 and D7 to the left of the affected Score sprite channels. Turn it off under D5 by releasing the Ctrl key and spacebar. Turn it off under D6 and D7 using Control ➤ Real-Time Recording.

I use the *Director 5 Style Score display* occasionally to:

- Work with movies updated from earlier versions of Director.
- See more sprite channels when zoomed out (in D6-style display, the vertical size of sprite channels is independent of the zoom factor).
- Display sprite motion (indicated by arrows in the Score) rather than location.
- Turn off drag-and-drop.
- See cast member scripts (indicated by a plus sign) while in Script/Behavior display mode.

Changing How the Score Window Looks

The commands in Table 3-5 change the Score's appearance, but do not change its content or move the playback head. Most aspects of the Score retain the Director 6 style regardless of the *Director 5 Style Display* preference setting, which affects only the sprite cell area.

Table 3-5: Score Window Appearance

Action	Menu Command	Mac	Win
Display sprites as individual cells as in Director 5	Edit ➤ Preferences ➤ Score ➤ Compatibility ➤ Director 5 Style Score Display	Ctrl-click for menu[1]	Right-click for menu[1]
Edit a chosen sprite span as individual cells	Edit ➤ Edit Sprite Frames	Cmd-Opt-]	Ctrl-Alt-]
Show sprite position and path over time	View ➤ Sprite Overlay ➤ Show Info or Show Path	Cmd-Shift-Opt-O, or Cmd-Shift-Opt-H	Ctrl-Shift-Alt-O, or Ctrl-Shift-Alt-H
Display Score in monochrome without regard to current palette	File ➤ Preferences ➤ General ➤ User Interface ➤ Classic Look (Monochrome)	Ctrl-click for menu	Right-click for menu
Include Script Preview area in Score	File ➤ Preferences ➤ Score ➤ Options ➤ Script Preview	Ctrl-click for menu	Right-click for menu
Show sprites by Cast Member, Behavior, Location, Ink, Blend, Extended	View ➤ Display or *Display* pop-up in Score window	None	Alt-V,D
Configure *Extended* display mode	File ➤ Preferences ➤ Score ➤ Extended Display	Ctrl-click for menu	Right-click for menu
Show/hide Effects channels	Use show/hide Effects channels button, or see Table 3-11	None	None
Zoom in or out from 12% to 1600%	View ➤ Zoom ➤ Wider, View ➤ Zoom ➤ Narrower, or *Zoom Menu* button in Score Window	Cmd- - (minus) Cmd- + (plus)	Ctrl- - (minus) Ctrl- + (plus)

[1] Ctrl-click (Macintosh) or right-click (Windows) accesses a context-sensitive shortcut menu in the Score window and on Stage. See Tables 3-11 and 3-12.

Effects Channels

Table 3-6 shows techniques for adding elements to the Effects channels (Tempo, Palette, Transition, Sound1, Sound2, or Script channel). Double-clicking an empty cell of an Effects channel brings up the proper window to add the corresponding element type. Double-clicking an occupied cell allows you to edit the existing settings for that channel.

Changing a Script or Transition in the Effects channels modifies the corresponding cast member and therefore affects all uses of that cast member throughout the Score.

Table 3-6: Director 7 Sprite Transformation Properties

Property	Notes
flipH of sprite	Boolean property that flips a sprite across its own (possibly rotated and skewed) "vertical" axis. See the *Flip Horizontal* button in the Sprite Inspector.
flipV of sprite	Boolean property that flips a sprite across its own (possibly rotated and skewed) "horizontal" axis. See the *Flip Horizontal* button in the Sprite Inspector.
locZ of sprite	Adjusts a sprite's z-ordering (the paint layer in which it is drawn). Sprites with a higher *locZ* are drawn in the foreground (the default is the sprite number). Mouse events obey the sprite channel order, not the z-order.
mapMemberToStage (sprite *n*, *pointInMember*)	Returns point on Stage corresponding to point within member, accounting for transformations. Returns *<Void>* if point is outside member bounds.
mapStageToMember (sprite *n*, *pointOnStage*)	Returns point within member, accounting for transformations, corresponding to point on Stage. Returns *<Void>* if point is outside member bounds.
obeyScoreRotation of member	If TRUE, Flash members use D7's Score rotation. If FALSE (default for movies upgraded from D6.5), uses the *rotation of member* Flash property.
quad of sprite	Specifies arbitrary four corners of bitmap, text, or animated GIF sprite, such as [point(*x1, y1*), point(*x2, y2*), point(*x3, y3*), point(*x4, y4*)]. Coordinates can be floats. Exchanging the first or last two points creates a bowtie effect. Must be set via Lingo.
rotation of member	Rotates QuickTime display (in degrees) within sprite's bounding box.
rotation of sprite	Rotates sprite bounding box, in degrees. Can be set in Sprite Inspector.
scale of member scale of sprite	Scales viewable member area within sprite bounding box. For QuickTime sprites, the *scale* is a list (the default is [100.0, 100.0]) and the *crop of member* must be TRUE. For Flash and vector shapes, the *scale* is a percentage (the default is 100.0). See *scaleMode* in Table 13-4.
skew of sprite	Setting the skew can tilt or flip a sprite. Default is 0.0. A *skew* of 180 reverses a sprite. A *skew* of 90 or 270 hides a sprite (displays it on edge). Can be set in Sprite Inspector.

Palette effects include fades and color cycling and work only in 256-color (8-bit) mode. To apply a palette effect over time, select a range of frames in the Palette channel, then use Modify ➤ Frame ➤ Palette. Use the menu option in D5 (or with the D5 Style Score mode in D6) to edit a Palette channel entry in a single frame without editing adjacent entries. Custom palettes must be created separately before they can be used in the Palette channel.

The Modify ➤ Frame ➤ Sound dialog box is also convenient for testing sounds in the Cast. Ctrl-click (Mac) or right-click (Windows) directly on the Stage to insert effects quickly.

Tempo Channel

Double-click in the Score's Tempo channel or choose Modify ➤ Frame ➤ Tempo to access the Tempo channel properties dialog box. (The Tempo channel is ignored in Shockwave movies; use the Lingo alternatives to the Tempo channel shown following, and in Table 3-7, and Example 15-4.)

In D6 and D7, the Tempo channel's *Wait* settings no longer monopolize Director's attention, as in previous versions. *Idle* messages and mouse events are now processed even while waiting via the Tempo channel.

The Tempo channel controls the movie's tempo (i.e., frame rate) and more:

Tempo

The *Tempo* option sets a maximum desired frame rate from 1 to 500 frames per second (fps) in D6, or up to 999 fps in D7. It does not guarantee that your animation plays at the specified rate. Use a tempo that the lowest supported computer will achieve, such as 10 fps, depending on your product and target platform. Test and optimize your product to make it work at the desired speed.

An *idle* event is sent during each frame, so any *idle* handler is called very frequently if the movie's Tempo is fast. Consider lowering the frame rate if using an *on idle* hander. The *puppetTempo* overrides the Tempo setting only as long as the playback head moves *forward*. The puppetTempo setting is canceled by the *go* command moving the payback head backward or looping in a frame. Set the *puppetTempo* after any *go* command. See also *the frame-Tempo* property in the online Help.

Wait

The *Wait* option pauses the playback head for a fixed time from 1 to 60 seconds. Use a custom handler or the *delay* command to wait for fractional seconds or longer than one minute.

Wait for Mouse Click or Key Press

When waiting for a user action via this Tempo channel setting, a blinking cursor is shown. To wait for a mouse-click, but not a keypress, use:

```
on exitFrame
  if not the mouseDown then
    go the frame
  end if
end
```

To wait for a keypress only, use:

```
on exitFrame
  go the frame
end

on keyDown
  go the frame + 1
end
```

Wait for Cue Point

This option waits for a cue point within (or end of) a sound, digital video, or SWA (Shockwave Audio) sprite. If the *Cue Point* option is set to *Next*, Director will wait until the end of the media if it has no cue points or loop points. You must update the *Channel* option manually if you move a sound or sprite to a different channel. Refer to Chapters 15 and 16 for additional details on media playback and synchronization with cue points.

Table 3-7 summarizes the Tempo channel options and related Lingo.

Table 3-7: Tempo Channel Options

Option	Usage	See Lingo Commands
Tempo	Set a desired tempo from 1 to 999 frames per second (500 fps in D6)	puppetTempo, the frameTempo
Wait Interval	Wait for a fixed interval in seconds	delay, the timer
Wait for Mouse Click or Key Press	Wait indefinitely for user action	on mouseDown, the keyDown, on keyDown
Wait for Cue Point	Wait for a cue point in a sound, digital video, or SWA cast member	on cuePassed, isPastCuePoint
Wait for End	Wait for end of a sound or digital video without cue points	duration of member, movieTime of sprite, movieRate of sprite, soundBusy

To play an animation at an absolute rate, or to maintain perfect lip sync, you must use QuickTime or Video for Windows. You can export your Director movie in QuickTime format (on the Macintosh and under Windows in D7) or AVI format (under Windows) and then reimport it back into Director as a cast member. Cue points are less exact but allow you to synchronize audio with Score animations.

Transition Channel

The Transition channel adds visual effects such as wipes and dissolves. Transition execution time is inexact and performance varies across platforms. You can select the chunk size and *minimum* execution time of a transition but cannot limit the *maximum* execution time. Palette transitions, fades, and color-cycling are performed in the Palette channel, not the Transition channel, and do not work at monitor depths above 8-bit (256 colors). You can use a dissolve transition when going to a black or white screen to simulate a fade to black or fade to white palette transition at higher depths.

Transitions occur when entering the frame in which they are placed (after the *prepareFrame* event but before the *enterFrame* event). Director compares the contents of the previous frame with the contents of the upcoming frame to determine the changing area over which the transition will occur (unless the entire Stage area is chosen for the transition).

A transition will execute even when no visible change occurs between two frames. Never loop in a frame with a transition, as it is very slow, even though nothing appears to be happening.

Transitions occur over the entire Stage or the minimum area encompassing the sprites that have changed, including any digital video sprites. Especially under Windows, stop any digital videos before performing transitions.

Transition performance varies with the complexity of the transition, the size of the transition area, and the platform. Dissolves are noticeably chunkier under Windows than the Macintosh. The *dissolve bits fast, dissolve pixels,* and *dissolve bits* transitions work under 32-bit color despite claims in Macromedia documentation to the contrary.

QuickTime 3 supports many new transitions, which must be added in an external tool, such as MakeEffectMovie (*http://www.apple.com/quicktime/developers/tools. html#effects*), but will play back in Director via the QT3 Asset Xtra.

Several third-party Transition Xtras that add new visual effects are available:

- XtraZone—dissolve and fade transitions: *http://www.xtrazone.com.*

- DM Transitions—Dedalomedia Interactive: *http://www.dmtools.com.*

- Sharkbyte Killer Transitions: *http://www.sharkbyte.com.*

- Xaos Tools Trans-X (Mac-only). The Director 5 CD for Macintosh includes the Xaos Tools Trans-X LE transition dissolve on the Macintosh, but there is no Windows version.

- Zeus Productions (my company) shareware TranZtions: *http://www.zeusprod. com/products/tranz.html.*

Table 3-8 lists the Lingo pertaining to transitions.

Table 3-8: Transition-Related Lingo

Command	Usage
the changeArea of member	If TRUE, transition occurs over only the minimum bounding rectangle of screen changes. If FALSE, transition occurs over entire Stage.
the chunkSize of member	Number of pixels per step (from 1 to 128) in the transition. Larger chunk size is faster. Smaller chunk size is smoother.
the duration of member	Minimum (not maximum) duration in milliseconds. Use a larger *chunkSize* to minimize duration.
the frameTransition	Number of cast member used in Transition channel.

Table 3-8: Transition-Related Lingo (continued)

Command	Usage

puppetTransition[1]	Transition cast members can be specified by member name, member number, or integer code (1 to 52):
	
	`puppetTransition member "whichMember"`
	`puppetTransition member memberNum`
	`puppetTransition transitionCode {,time} ¬`
	`    {,chunkSize } {, changeArea}`
	
	time is in 1/4 second increments (0 to 120)
	
	chunkSize is in pixels (1–128)
	
	changeArea is TRUE | FALSE
	
	`puppetTransition 0 -- cancel a transition`

the transitionType of member[1]	An integer code from 1 to 52 representing the type of transition (wipe, reveal, etc.). Transition Xtras may return 0.
the type of member	The *type of member* returns #transition for Transition cast members although Transition Xtras may return different symbolic codes.

[1] See Table 16-1 in *Lingo in a Nutshell* or see ***puppetTransition*** in the online Help for a list of integer transition codes (1 to 52).

Some transition types ignore some transition properties, and the defaults may vary. For example, *the changeArea* property is always TRUE for wipe transitions.

PuppetTransitions are a one-time occurrence and do not override the Transition channel permanently. Transitions will complete suddenly (perform a jump cut) when the user clicks the mouse or presses a key during authoring, but only key presses will interrupt a transition in a Projector. A *puppetTransition* command is overridden by subsequent *puppetTransition* commands (including *puppetTransition 0*) before the next screen update. *PuppetTransition 0* does not override transitions in the Transition channel as will other *puppetTransition* commands.

Markers

A marker is a convenient way to refer to a particular frame in the Score. Use Markers to refer to a frame by name even if its frame number changes. The words "marker" and "label" are often used interchangeably. Technically, a marker has an optional label name. To create a marker, simply click in the marker channel (it is easy to create markers accidentally when you are trying to edit existing ones).

Markers can be viewed and edited en masse in the Markers window (see Figure 3-3).

A marker's name is always shown on the first line of the righthand pane of the Markers window and is also shown in the Score. You can add a hidden comment to a marker in the Markers window by entering RETURN at the end of its name in the righthand pane and then typing more text. Long marker names may wrap onto subsequent lines, but only the text after the RETURN is treated as a comment. A single marker's name and comment are limited to 255 characters combined.

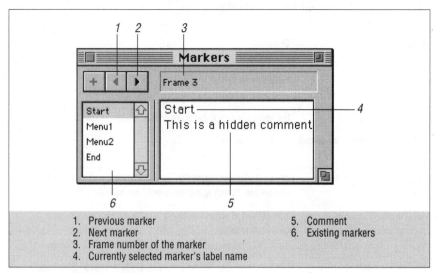

1. Previous marker
2. Next marker
3. Frame number of the marker
4. Currently selected marker's label name
5. Comment
6. Existing markers

Figure 3-3: Markers window

Comments can not be read via Lingo (they don't appear in *the labelList*), although they can be created via Lingo. More than 32K of label names and comments may cause all the labels to be lost. Editing a marker's name in the Score's marker channel deletes any hidden comments attached to that marker.

Table 3-9 summarizes the commands that manipulate Markers, including the ability to print them. (Refer to Table 3-19 for Lingo commands that navigate amongst existing markers and to Table 3-17 for commands that move the playback head between existing markers.) Operations using *the frameLabel* always apply to the marker in the current frame.

Table 3-9: Marker Manipulation

Action	Command
Open Markers window	Cmd-Shift-M (Mac), Ctrl-Shift-M (Windows), or Window ➤ Markers.
Add a marker	Insert ➤ Marker, click in Marker channel or use: `set the frameLabel = "newLabel"` In D5, drag a new marker from the Marker Well.
Move a marker	Drag it in the Marker channel.
Delete a marker	Drag it off the Marker channel or use: `set the frameLabel = 0`
Copy a marker	There is no way to copy a marker directly. If you copy entire frames, any markers are copied, too.

Table 3-9: Marker Manipulation (continued)

Action	Command
Rename a marker	Select a marker in the Marker channel or in the Markers window and type in new name or use: `set the frameLabel = "renameLabel"`
Get list of markers	Use *Marker* pop-up in the Score, Marker window, or *the labelList*.
Get or set the marker in the current frame	Use *the frameLabel*.
Jump to an absolute or relative marker	Use *go* or *play* with the *marker( )* or *label( )* function as shown under the next section, "Checking marker names," and in Table 3-19.
Add a comment to a marker	Type RETURN at end of marker name in the Markers window and add comments or use: `set the frameLabel = "name" & RETURN & "comment"`
Print marker comments	File ➤ Print ➤ Print Marker Comments or File ➤ Print ➤ Print Stage ➤ Options (Choose Scale = 50%, Storyboard Format, Marker comments).
Terminate new sprites before reaching the next marker	File ➤ Preferences ➤ Sprite ➤ Span Duration ➤ Terminate at Markers.

When importing PowerPoint presentations, Director creates a marker label for each slide. See *http://www.zeusprod.com/nutshell/examples/* for a utility to insert markers at fixed intervals in the Score.

Checking marker names

To obtain the frame number associated with a label, use either of these:

```
put label ("labelName")
put marker ("labelName")
```

The parentheses are mandatory in the previous example. *Label( )* and *marker( )* return the first label with the specified name, although there may be additional markers with the same name.

You can use *the frameLabel* to get or set the current frame's label.

Converting the labelList to a true Lingo list

The movie property *the labelList* returns a text string of the existing labels separated by RETURN characters (one label to each line). Empty labels appear as blank lines. The handler in Example 3-1 converts *the labelList* to a true Lingo list so that we can conveniently manipulate it with Lingo's list functions.

Example 3-1: Converting the labelList to Lingo List Format

```
on convertLabelsToList
  set myLabelList = []
  -- Convert the labelList from a text string
  -- to a true Lingo list
```

Example 3-1: Converting the labelList to Lingo List Format (continued)

```
   repeat with x = 1 to the number of lines in the labelList
      add (myLabelList, line x of the labelList)
   end repeat
   return myLabelList
end convertLabelsToList


put convertLabelsToList()
-- ["KeyTest", "New Marker", "SWAtest ", "", "New Marker"]
```

Later, we'll use this Lingo list to detect potential errors with our marker names.

Reader Exercise: Modify the example to create a list that contains frame labels and their frame numbers. You could then create utilities to sort label names alphabetically or search for labels containing a given string, or to search and replace a string within marker label names.

Preventing common label name errors

One typically uses a label's name to jump to a frame with a marker, such as:

```
   go label ("labelName")
```

One common error is to use the incorrect label name, resulting in a "Frame not defined" script error. The problem might be a typo in either your *label()* call or the marker label itself. Leading and trailing spaces are allowed in label names, but they are usually unintentional.

Another common error is to have two frames with the same label name, as with the name "New Marker" in Example 3-1. The *label()* function will always return the first matching label, never the latter one(s).

The *examineList()* utility Example 3-2 checks any Lingo list of strings for duplicate entries and warns if any entries contain spaces. Director treats label names in a case-insensitive manner, but the *getPos()* command is case-sensitive. We convert all strings to uppercase when adding them to our test list to ensure that we detect conflicting label names regardless of their case.

Example 3-2: Examining a List of Strings for Potential Errors

```
on examineList verifyList
  set testList = []
  repeat with x = 1 to count (verifyList)
    -- Convert strings to uppercase for comparison
    set thisItem = makeUpperCase(getAt(verifyList, x))
    -- Check if item has any unwanted spaces
    if thisItem contains SPACE then
      put "Space(s) in item" && x & ":" && thisItem
    end if

    -- Check if item is unique
    if getPos (testList, thisItem) then
      put "Duplicate item" && x & ":" && thisItem
    else
      -- If it's unique, add it to the list
```

```
      add (testList, thisItem)
    end if
  end repeat
end examineList

on makeUpperCase upString
  repeat with x = 1 to length(upString)
    set thisChar = charToNum (char x of upString)
    -- Convert ASCII "a" through "z" to uppercase
    if thisChar >= 97 and thisChar <= 122 then
      put numToChar (thisChar - 32) into char x of upString
    end if
  end repeat
  return upString
end makeUpperCase
```

Let's analyze the list of labels constructed using *convertLabelsToList()*:

```
  put examineList (convertLabelsToList())
  -- "Space(s) in item 2: NEW MARKER"
  -- "Space(s) in item 3: SWATEST "
  -- "Space(s) in item 5: NEW MARKER"
  -- "Duplicate item 5: NEW MARKER"
```

Run this utility to ferret out potentially troublesome marker names.

Reader Exercise: Modify it to complain about labels named "New Marker" that were added unintentionally or to ignore spaces in the midst of a label name. You might use this utility with the *checkScore* utility in Example 3-9. (I use Example 3-2 again in Chapter 4 to detect potential errors in cast member names.)

Being More Productive in the Score

The following tips will make you more productive in the Score.

The Playback Head is a Key Player

Director 6 and 7 use a very different paradigm than D5 to select and tween sprites. In Director 5, one generally highlights the range of sprite cells of interest, and, for example, uses the in-between command to extend a sprite to the end of a highlighted area. In Director 6 and 7, tweening is automatic and one generally selects either sprites or empty Score cells, but not both.

In Director 6 and 7, the playback head's position determines the frame at which to split or extend sprites, insert keyframes, and so on. Its position is independent of the Score selection.

The following commands rely on the playback head position.

Under the Insert menu:

- Keyframe
- Remove Keyframe
- Frames

- Remove Keyframe

- Marker

Under the **Modify** menu:

- Split Sprite

- Extend Sprite

You can't click and drag to extend or shorten multiple sprites. To adjust the length of multiple sprites, use this:

1. Select one or more sprites in the Score. Use **Cmd**-click (Mac) or **Ctrl**-click (Windows) to select discontiguous sprites.

2. Click *once* in the frame number bar to move the playback head without canceling the selection.

3. Choose **Modify ➤ Extend Sprite**, **Cmd-B** (Mac), or **Ctrl-B** (Windows).

If the playback head is within a sprite's span, this technique shortens the sprite by moving its tail to the left. If the playback head is outside the sprite, the sprite's head or tail is extended to reach it.

Use the Sprite Inspector to enter a starting or ending frame manually for one or more selected sprites. Use this technique to move the head of multiple selected sprites to the right.

Using multiple Score views

You can open multiple Score windows using **Window ➤ New Window** when the Score is already the active window. Each Score window's zoom factor, Sprite Toolbar, *Display* mode, Script Preview area, and *Director 5 Style display* mode can be configured independently. You can't open or close multiple Score windows in unison—you must recreate them each time they are closed.

Use multiple Score windows to:

- View discontinuous frames from multiple areas of the Score.

- View discontinuous sprite channels in a given frame.

- View the Score at different magnifications. Use one window as an overview, and another for your working view.

- View the Score in both the D6/D7 and D5 styles simultaneously.

Table 3-10 lists some of the biggest time-savers when working in the Score.

Table 3-10: Saving Time in the Score

Action	Menu Command	Mac	Windows
Open Score window	Window ➤ Score	Cmd-4	Ctrl-4
Open additional views of the Score window	Choose Window ➤ New while Score window is in foreground	None	None

Table 3-10: Saving Time in the Score (continued)

Action	Menu Command	Mac	Windows
Find where a cast member is used in the Score	Edit ➤ Find ➤ Find Selection	Cmd-H	Ctrl-H
Find next occurrence of cast member in Score	Edit ➤ Find Again	Cmd-G Cmd-Opt-F	Ctrl-G Ctrl-Alt-F

To find where a cast member is used in the Score, first highlight a cast member in the Cast window, which must be in the foreground to start the search, then press Cmd-H or Ctrl-H. If more than one cast member is selected, Director searches the Score for the first selected cast member only. For subsequent searches, press Cmd-G or Ctrl-G. The Score window can remain in the foreground.

Context-sensitive popup menus

Table 3-11 lists context-sensitive menus available in the Score window. Use Ctrl-click (Mac) or right-click (Windows) to bring up a different shortcut menu based on where in the Score you click (the Effects channels, the sprite channels, or elsewhere).

Table 3-11: Score Shortcut Pop-up Menus

Click in Sprite Channel Cells	Click in Effects Channel Cells	Click Elsewhere in Score Window
Edit ➤ Edit Sprite Frames	Edit ➤ Edit Sprite Frames	View ➤ Display
Edit ➤ Edit Entire Sprite	Edit ➤ Edit Entire Sprite	View ➤ Sprite Toolbar
Edit ➤ Cut Sprites	Edit ➤ Cut Sprites	Prefs ➤ Script Preview
Edit ➤ Copy Sprites	Edit ➤ Copy Sprites	Effects Channels (show/hide)
Edit ➤ Paste	Edit ➤ Paste	View ➤ Show Keyframes
Edit ➤ Select All[1]	Insert ➤ Insert Frame	View ➤ Sprite Labels
Insert ➤ Insert Keyframe	Insert ➤ Remove Frame	Prefs ➤ Score Preferences
Insert ➤ Remove Keyframe	Modify ➤ Frame ➤ Tempo	Prefs ➤ Sprite Preferences
Modify ➤ Sprite ➤ Tweening	Modify ➤ Frame ➤ Palette	Prefs ➤ Director 5 Style Display
Modify ➤ Arrange[1]	Modify ➤ Frame ➤ Transition	
Modify ➤ Transform[1]	Modify ➤ Frame ➤ Sound	
Modify ➤ Sprite ➤ Properties	Modify ➤ Frame ➤ Frame Script	
Window ➤ Inspectors ➤ Behavior		
Modify ➤ Sprite ➤ Script		
Modify ➤ Font[1]		
Modify ➤ Cast Member ➤ Properties		
Modify ➤ Cast Member ➤ Script		
Edit ➤ Edit Cast Member		
Open Cast[1]		

[1] New in D7.

Table 3-12 lists context-sensitive menus available on the Stage with Ctrl-click (Mac) or right-click (Windows).

Table 3-12: Stage Shortcut Pop-up Menus

Ctrl-Click or Right-Click a Sprite on Stage	Ctrl-Click or Right-Click the Stage Itself
Edit ➤ Edit Sprite Frames	Edit ➤ Paste
Edit ➤ Edit Entire Sprite	Edit ➤ Select All
Edit ➤ Cut Sprites	Modify ➤ Frame ➤ Tempo
Edit ➤ Copy Sprites	Modify ➤ Frame ➤ Palette
Edit ➤ Paste	Modify ➤ Frame ➤ Transition
Edit ➤ Select All	Modify ➤ Frame ➤ Frame Script
Insert ➤ Insert Keyframe	View ➤ Sprite Overlay ➤ Show Info[1]
Insert ➤ Remove Keyframe	View ➤ Sprite Overlay ➤ Show Paths
Modify ➤ Sprite ➤ Tweening	Live Dragging[1]
Modify ➤ Arrange	Modify ➤ Movie ➤ Properties
Modify ➤ Transform	Window ➤ Inspectors ➤ Behavior
Modify ➤ Sprite ➤ Properties	
Window ➤ Inspectors ➤ Behavior	
Modify ➤ Sprite ➤ Script	
Modify ➤ Font	
Modify ➤ Cast Member ➤ Properties	
Modify ➤ Cast Member ➤ Script	
Open Cast	

[1] Live Dragging updates coordinates shown by View ➤ Sprite Overlay ➤ Show Info.

Editing sprite paths and keyframes on the Stage and in the Score

Director 6 treats a sprite span as a unified object and allows you to view and edit a sprite's path over time. You define keyframes in the animation and Director automatically tweens the intermediate frames.

You can edit a sprite's path directly on the Stage using View ➤ Sprite Overlay ➤ Show Paths. Add keyframes to set a sprite's location in a given frame explicitly. You can only indirectly affect the position of tweened frames.

A sprite's on-Stage path appears as a series of lines connecting large dots (*keyframes*) and small dots (*tween frames*), as shown in Figure 3-4. Keyframes are the anchor points of the animation, and the tween frames' positions depend on the settings under Modify ➤ Sprite ➤ Tweening.

To view keyframes in the Score window, turn on View ➤ Keyframes when the Score is active. Remember that the playback head's position is used to insert keyframes and extend sprites in the Score. For tweening purposes, Director treats a sprite span as a single unit whether its being viewed as a solid bar (D6/D7 made) or as a collection of individual cells (D5 mode).

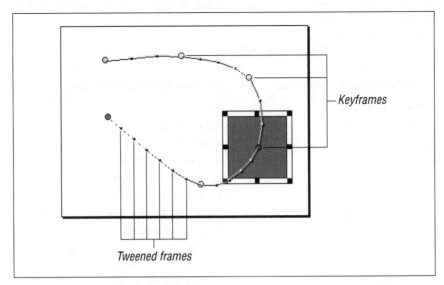

Figure 3-4: Sprite path on the Stage

Table 3-13 shows the shortcuts when editing a sprite's path on the Stage.

Table 3-13: Editing Sprite Paths on the Stage

Action	Mac	Windows
Show path on Stage (View ➤ Sprite Overlay ➤ Show Paths)	Cmd-Shift-Opt-H, or Ctrl-click on the Stage.	Ctrl-Shift-Alt-H, or right-click on the Stage.
Show sprite at a keyframe (moves playback head)	Double-click a keyframe (large dot).	Double-click a keyframe (large dot).
Move a keyframe	Click and drag any keyframe.	Click and drag any keyframe.
Create a keyframe anywhere along a sprite's path	Option-drag a tween frame (small dot).	Alt-drag a tween frame (small dot).
Select only current keyframe of sprite	Option-click the sprite.	Alt-click the sprite.
Delete a keyframe (delete key deletes entire sprite)	Double-click keyframe, then Ctrl-click and choose *Remove Keyframe*.	Double-click keyframe, then right-click and choose *Remove Keyframe*.
Alter tweening attributes (Modify ➤ Sprite ➤ Tweening)	Cmd-Shift-B	Ctrl-Shift-B

Table 3-14 lists other actions that can be performed directly on the Stage.

Table 3-14: Other On-Stage Shortcuts

Action	Mac	Windows
Open cast member media editor	Double-click	Double-click
Edit cast member properties	Cmd-double-click	Ctrl-double-click
Select or unselect multiple sprites individually	Shift-click	Shift-click
Change ink effect of all selected sprite(s)	Cmd-click	Ctrl-click
Show sprite information on the Stage (View ➤ Sprite Overlay ➤ Show Info)	Cmd-Shift-Opt-O	Ctrl-Shift-Alt-O
Change opacity of sprite information panel	Drag small horizontal line (at right side of panel) up and down	Drag small horizontal line (at right side of panel) up and down
Hide sprite selection handles, path, and Info overlay on the Stage	Keypad +	Keypad +
Hide cursor	Keypad =	Keypad =
Real-Time recording	Cmd-Spacebar-drag the sprite	Ctrl-Spacebar-drag the sprite
Move sprite by 1 pixel	Arrow keys	Arrow keys
Move sprite by 10 pixels	Shift-arrow keys	Shift-arrow keys
Stage shortcut menu	Ctrl-click on the Stage	Right-click on the Stage

Manipulating sprite spans and keyframes in the Score

Table 3-15 shows the commands that manipulate sprite spans.

Table 3-15: Sprite Channel Manipulation

Action	Menu Command	Mac	Win
Shuffle sprites up and down	Modify ➤ Arrange ➤ Bring To Front Modify ➤ Arrange ➤ Move Forward Modify ➤ Arrange ➤ Move Back Modify ➤ Arrange ➤ Send To Back	Cmd-Shift-↑ Cmd-↑ Cmd-↓ Cmd-Shift-↓	Ctrl-Shift--↑ Ctrl-↑ Ctrl-↓ Ctrl-Shift-↓
Move a sprite using drag and drop	File ➤ Preferences ➤ Score ➤ Compatibility ➤ Director 5 Style Score Display ➤ Allow Drag and Drop	Spacebar causes opposite behavior	Spacebar causes opposite behavior
Duplicate a sprite span	Edit ➤ Copy and Edit ➤ Paste	Opt-drag sprite[1]	Alt-drag sprite[1]

Table 3-15: Sprite Channel Manipulation (continued)

Action	Menu Command	Mac	Win
Select single cell of sprite	None	Opt-click	Alt-click
Edit sprite span(s) as individual cells	Edit ➤ Edit Sprite Frames	Cmd-Opt-]	Ctrl-Alt-]
Edit entire sprite as a single unit	Edit ➤ Edit Entire Sprite	Double-click Cmd-Opt-[	Double-click Ctrl-Alt-[
Create new keyframe (and optionally extend existing sprite)	Select single cell, then use Insert ➤ Keyframe or move the on-Stage sprite	Opt-drag existing keyframe.[1] Opt-click then press Cmd-Opt-K or move on-Stage sprite, or Opt-drag.	Alt-drag existing keyframe.[1] Alt-click then press Ctrl-Alt-K or move on-Stage sprite or Alt-drag
Select multiple keyframes	None	Cmd-click	Ctrl-click
Remove selected keyframe(s) in sprite(s)	Select sprite(s) or individual keyframe(s), then use Insert ➤ Remove Keyframe	None	Alt-I,E
Select the entire sprite span or just the current frame	File ➤ Preferences ➤ Sprite ➤ Stage Selection	Ctrl-click for Sprite preferences	Right-click for Sprite preferences
Set sprite preferences	File ➤ Preferences ➤ Sprite ➤ Span Defaults	Ctrl-click for Sprite preferences	Right-click for Sprite preferences
Set default sprite span width	File ➤ Preferences ➤ Sprite ➤ Span Duration	Ctrl-click for Sprite preferences	Right-click for Sprite preferences
Split selected sprite(s) at playback head location	Modify ➤ Split Sprite	Cmd-Shift-J	Ctrl-Shift-J
Join selected sprites	Modify ➤ Join Sprite	Cmd-J	Ctrl-J
Extend selected sprite(s) to playback head location	Modify ➤ Extend Sprite	Cmd-B	Ctrl-B
Change cast member used in selected sprite(s)	Edit ➤ Exchange Cast Member	Cmd-E	Ctrl-E
Select discontiguous sprites	Shift-click on the Stage	Cmd-click in the Score or on the Stage	Ctrl-click in the Score or on the Stage
Clear sprites (not copied to clipboard)	Edit ➤ Clear Sprites	Delete	Backspace

Table 3-15: Sprite Channel Manipulation (continued)

Action	Menu Command	Mac	Win
Copy sprites to clipboard[2]	Edit ➤ Copy Sprites	Cmd-C	Ctrl-C
Cut sprites to clipboard[2]	Edit ➤ Cut Sprites	Cmd-X	Ctrl-X
Paste sprites from clipboard[2]	Edit ➤ Paste Sprites	Cmd-V	Ctrl-V
Select all channels	Edit ➤ Select All	Cmd-A	Ctrl-A
Paste relative to other sprites, or paste as PICT	Edit ➤ Paste Special	None	Alt-E, A

[1] Opt-dragging (Mac) or Alt-dragging (Windows) adds a keyframe and extends the sprite if you click on a keyframe (including the first or last frame of a sprite span) and can be used to extend single-frame sprites. These option keys duplicate the sprite if you click and drag a non-keyframe.
[2] Save the movie before copying frames or sprites between movies.

Moving around in the Score

Table 3-16 summarizes commands that change the portion of the Score visible in the Score window without moving the playback head.

Table 3-16: Commands that Change the Score View

To Jump View	Command	Shortcut
Frame containing playback head	Click *Center Current Frame* button	None
Up one page	Click above thumb slider in vertical scrollbar	Page Up key[1]
Down one page	Click below thumb slider in vertical scrollbar	Page Down key[1]
Scroll left and right	Scrollbars	Click to left or right of thumb slider in scroll bar to jump more
Top of Score	*Top* button (D5 only)	Home key[1]
Bottom of Score	None	End key[1]
First frame	Drag thumb slider in horizontal scrollbar	Keyboard commands move playback head (see Table 3-17)
Last frame	Drag thumb slider in horizontal scrollbar	Keyboard commands move playback head (see Table 3-17)

[1] You cannot use the Page Up, Page Down, Home, and End keys on the numeric keypad to affect the Score view. Use the separate keys of the same name that exist between the keypad and the main alphanumeric keys on most extended keyboards.

Moving the playback head

Table 3-17 summarizes commands that move the Score's playback head. I recommend using the keypad shortcuts.

Table 3-17: Moving the Playback Head

Playback Head	Menu Command	Mac	Windows	Keypad
Step one frame forward[1]	Control ➤ Step Forward	Cmd-Opt-→	Ctrl-Alt-→	3
Step one frame back[1]	Control ➤ Step Backward	Cmd-Opt-←	Ctrl-Alt-←	1
Next keyframe of sprite	None	None	None	Shift-3
Previous keyframe of sprite	None	None	None	Shift-1
Rewind to first frame[1,2,3]	Control ➤ Rewind	Cmd-Shift-← Cmd-Opt-R Return or Shift-Tab	Ctrl-Shift-← Ctrl-Alt-R Enter or Shift-Tab	0
Jump to last frame	None	Tab Cmd-Shift-→	Tab Ctrl-Shift-→	None
Play movie[1,2]	Control ➤ Play	Cmd-Opt-P	Ctrl-Alt-P	Enter
Hide non-Stage windows and play movie[4]	Works with keyboard but not menu option (Control ➤ Play)	Shift-Cmd-Opt-P	Shift-Ctrl-Alt-P	Shift-Enter
Stop movie[1,2,4]	Control ➤ Stop	Cmd-.(period)[5] Cmd-Opt-.(period)	Ctrl-. (period)[5]	. (period)
Go to next marker[6]	View ➤ Marker ➤ Previous	Cmd-→	Ctrl-→	6
Go to previous marker[6]	View ➤ Marker ➤ Next	Cmd-←	Ctrl-←	4
Go to any marker[6]	View ➤ Marker menu,[7] Marker pop-up menu, or Markers window	None	None	None
Go to any frame	Click in any frame	go frame X	go frame X	None
Set playback head to Loop[1]	Control ➤ Loop	Cmd-Opt-L	Ctrl-Alt-L	8

1 There is also a Control Panel button for this action. See Window ➤ Control Panel.
2 There is also a Toolbar button for this action. See Window ➤ Toolbar.
3 Use the Return key (Mac) or Enter key (Windows) on the main keyboard, not the numeric keypad, to jump to the beginning of the Score.
4 Director's menubar becomes invisible, but is accessible by clicking at the top of the monitor.
5 Cmd-. (Macintosh) or Ctrl-. (Windows) will ordinarily quit the Projector. If the *Play Every Movie* option is checked when the Projector is built, Director will go to the next movie instead.
6 See also the *go loop, go next, go previous, go marker( )*, and *label( )* commands. Moves ten frames at a time if there are no markers.
7 The View ➤ Marker menu always includes the *Previous* and *Next* marker options. It also includes the names of up to three markers to the left of the playback head and up to three markers to the right of the playback head.

Control Panel

The Control Panel starts, stops, advances, and rewinds the movie. See the *Actual Tempo Display* button under the *Control Panel* window in the online Help. It displays the actual playback rate in FPS (frames per second), SPF (seconds per frame), elapsed time in seconds, or elapsed total (includes speed of Effects channels). Having the Control Panel open, especially in elapsed total mode, can reduce playback speed.

Copying, inserting, and deleting Score frames

Table 3-18 summarizes how to copy, add, and delete entire frames from the Score.

In Director 6 and 7, double-click in the frame number bar and then drag (or Shift-click) to select multiple frames. Single-clicking moves the playback head but not the Score selection.

Table 3-18: Copying, Inserting, and Deleting Frames

Action	Menu Command	Mac	Windows
Insert (duplicate) multiple frames[1]	Insert ➤ Frames	Cmd-Shift-]	Ctrl-Shift-] Shift-F12
Insert (duplicate) single frame[1]	None	Cmd-]	Ctrl-] F12
Remove single frame	Insert ➤ Remove Frame	Cmd-[	Ctrl-[F11
Remove multiple frames	Select multiple frames and use Edit ➤ Cut or Edit ➤ Clear	Cmd-X or Delete	Ctrl-X or Backspace
Copy frames from a different movie	Edit ➤ Copy, switch movies, Edit ➤ Paste	Cmd-X, switch movies, Cmd-V	Ctrl-X, switch movies, Ctrl-V

[1] The *Insert Frame* option duplicates the current frame. There is no direct command to insert blank frames unless the frame you are duplicating happens to be blank. When pasting sprite spans that are too big to fit into the currently open area of the Score, Director will prompt you to insert blank frames. See the *insertBlankFrames( )* utility in Example 3-6.

When copying a single cast member, the actual data is copied to the clipboard, because it is of a type that the OS can recognize. But when copying sprites, entire frames, or multiple cast members, the actual data is not placed on the clipboard. Instead, a *scrap tag* that identifies the original assets' location is placed on the clipboard. An example of this is:

```
Macromedia Director animation from:
MacHD:Nutshell:Test
Channels 8 to 8
Frames 30 to 42
```

or:

```
Macromedia Director cast from:
MacHD:Nutshell:Test
3 cast members 9 to 11
```

If copying between movies, the data referenced by the scrap tag will be read from the source file on disk. If you've made changes, save the source movie before switching movies so that the scrap tag points to the intended assets.

When copying frames from one movie to another, follow these steps:

1. Save the current movie.

2. Select and copy the desired frames to the clipboard.

3. Close the current movie.

4. Open the destination movie.

5. Set the insertion point by double-clicking in the frame number bar.

6. Pasting frames from the clipboard overwrites at least one frame in the Score. Choose Insert ➤ Frame to create a dummy frame that we can sacrifice in step 7.

7. Paste from the clipboard on top of the sacrificial frame. The data is pasted at the point of the Score selection, not necessarily at the playback head's position.

Steps 1, 3, and 4 are not necessary when working within a single movie. Step 6 is not necessary in Director 5, which allows you to set an insertion point *between* frames by single-clicking the frame number bar. If a single occupied cell is the insertion point, it will be overwritten by the pasted sprites without any warning.

When copying sprites or frames between movies, Director also transfers any necessary cast members to the new movie.

Score Lingo

This section lists details on navigation in the Score.

Lingo Navigation

Commands that move the playback head can be used either in a frame script (usually in an *on exitFrame* handler) or in a sprite script (usually in an *on mouseDown* or *on mouseUp* handler).

Use *play* to temporarily jump to another frame or movie, and *play done* to return to the original departure point.

You can use multiple *play* commands in succession, but there must be a *play done* corresponding to each one. If you don't need to return to where you've left off, use *go* instead of *play* to jump to a frame or movie.

In the following examples, the curly braces ({}) represent optional words or phrases:

```
go {to} {frame} whichFrame {of movie whichMovie}
go {to frame whichFrame of} movie whichMovie
```

```
play {frame} whichFrame {of movie whichMovie}
play {frame whichFrame of} movie whichMovie
play done
```

Don't confuse the keyword *frame*, which is optionally used in the *go* and *play* commands, with the system property *the frame*, which represents the current frame number.

In Table 3-19, `whichFrame` is either an integer frame number, a property such as *the frame*, or a call to the *marker()* or *label()* functions, which return frame numbers, such as:

```
go to the frame -- This loops in the current frame.
go frame 50
go marker("labelName")
go label ("labelName")
```

Table 3-19: Lingo for Navigation

Action	Command
Wait for a specific time or event	Use Tempo channel, delay *nTicks*, or see "Playback Head Control" later in this chapter
Get the current frame number	`put the frame`
Loop in the current frame	`go the frame`
Loop back to the most recent marker	`go loop`
Loop back to the previous marker	`go previous`
Jump to next marker	`go next`
Jump to a marker by name	`go marker("labelName")` `go label ("labelName")`
Jump to a relative marker	`go marker(x)` –n: nth marker to left of current frame –1: previous marker to left of current frame 0: marker in current frame or previous marker to left 1: next marker to right of current frame n: nth marker to right of current frame
Jump to a marker or frame number	`go whichFrame`
Jump temporarily to a marker or frame number	`play whichFrame`
Return from a temporary jump to a frame or movie	`play done`
Jump to a Director file in same folder[1]	`go movie "movieName"`

Table 3-19: Lingo for Navigation (continued)

Action	Command
Jump to a specific frame in different Director file (in same folder)[1]	`go frame whichFrame of movie "movieName"`

Jump to a Director file in a subfolder below current movie's folder[1]	`if the platform contains "Mac" then`
	`  go movie the pathName & "folder:movieName"`
	`else`
	`  go movie the pathName & "folder\movieName"`
	`end if`

Jump temporarily to a Director file[1]	`play movie "movieName"`
Jump temporarily to a specific frame in different Director file[1]	`play frame whichFrame of movie "movieName"`

Jump temporarily to a different Director file in a subfolder[1]	`if the platform contains "Mac" then`
	`  play movie the pathName & "folder:movieName"`
	`else`
	`  play movie the pathName & "folder\movieName"`
	`end if`

Prevent the Stage from updating when changing frames[2]	`set the updateLock = TRUE`
Go to a Shockwave movie from a local projector	`gotoNetMovie("url")`
Play a Shockwave movie in a browser	`gotoNetPage("url", "targetFrameOrWindow")`
Control a Shockwave movie from the browser	JavaScript and VBscript can control the position of a Shockwave movie's playback head. See Chapter 11, *Shockwave and the Internet,* for details.

[1] When specifying a Director movie file, do not include the .DIR file extension. Director will find it automatically. It will also find .DCR and .DXR extensions, so you don't need to update your code when you prepare (protect or burn) your movies for Projector playback. Shockwave, however, requires the .DCR extension to find a movie.

[2] *The updateLock* is not entirely reliable in preventing the screen from updating, especially when modifying elements in the destination frame. See "Score Recording" later in this chapter.

Commands following a *go* command are executed, because the first *go* command moves the playback head but does not exit the handler. In the following example, the second *go* command is always executed:

```
on keyDown
  if the key = "y" then
    go frame "Yes"
  end if
  go frame "No"
end
```

The previous example should be rewritten as:

```
on keyDown
  if the key = "y" then
    go frame "Yes"
```

```
   else
      go frame "No"
   end if
end
```

Commands following a *play* command are executed, but not until a *play done* command returns control to the original script. Commands following *play done* are never reached. If the *play* command is called from a sprite script, *play done* returns the playback head to the original frame. If the *play* command is called from a frame script, *play done* returns the playback head to the *following* frame.

Don't use a *go* command to return from a *play* command. Unless a matching *play done* command is issued for each *play* command, memory will be consumed. Don't use more than one *play* command in a single script; use two successive frame scripts if necessary.

The *play movie* command is not fully supported from inside a *tell* command. When *play movie* is issued from inside a *tell* command, it will be treated like a *go movie* command.

To implement a history list, it is best to use *go* commands. Example 3-3 implements a fairly simplistic history feature, but gives you an idea of the procedure. *GoToNew* adds an item to the history. *GoBackward* and *goForward* trace your steps. They should be placed in a movie script and called from a Behavior.

Example 3-3: Implementing a History List

```
global gHistory, gHistPointer

on goToNew frameNum
   if not listP(gHistory) then
      set gHistory = []
      set gHistPointer = 0
   end if
   -- Enter this into the history
   set gHistPointer = gHistPointer + 1
   addAt gHistory, gHistPointer, frameNum
   -- Delete any future beyond this point
   repeat while count(gHistory) > gHistPointer
      deleteAt (gHistory, gHistPointer + 1)
   end repeat
   go frameNum
end goToNew

on goBackward
   if not listP(gHistory)or gHistPointer < 2 then
      -- Can't go back. There is no history.
      beep
   else
      set gHistPointer = gHistPointer - 1
      go getAt (gHistory, gHistPointer )
   end if
end goBackward

on goForward
   -- Beep if there is no future
```

Example 3-3: Implementing a History List (continued)

```
  if not listP(gHistory) or gHistPointer = 0 then
    beep
  else if gHistPointer >= count(gHistory) then
    beep
  else
    set gHistPointer = gHistPointer + 1
    go getAt (gHistory, gHistPointer)
  end if
end goForward
```

It is trivial to modify Example 3-3 to go to different movies instead of frames within the same movie. Simply use *go movie* in place of *go* and pass in a movie name (or full movie path) instead of a frame number to *goToNew*.

The Director 7 Library Palette includes Behaviors that implement a history list of sorts.

Playback Head Control

The Tempo channel is rather coarse. It can wait only in increments of 1 second (up to a maximum of 60 seconds) and does not work in Shockwave. The *delay* command causes the playback head to loop in the frame until a specified number of ticks elapses (a tick is 1/60 of a second). During a *delay*, mouse and keyboard events are ignored, except for certain key events that abort the Projector.

Delay doesn't work when the playback head is not moving. Any statements in an *on exitFrame* handler preceding *delay* execute repeatedly in Director 5, but execute only once in Director 6 and 7. Commands after *delay* are executed before the wait occurs, as demonstrated by Example 3-4.

Example 3-4: Incorrect Use of Delay

```
on exitFrame
  put "Hello"
  delay 2 * 60
  put "Hello again"
end
```

The following don't work when the Director movie is paused:

- *prepareFrame* events
- *enterFrame* events
- *exitFrame* events
- *stepFrame* events
- Animation of film loops
- Looping sounds

Note that *idle* events are sent even while the movie is paused. Avoid the *pause* and *continue* commands to stop and start the playback head. Use the following frame script instead of *pause* to wait in a frame:

```
on exitFrame
  go the frame
end exitFrame
```

Use the following frame script instead of *continue* to advance the playback head:

```
on exitFrame
  go the frame + 1
end exitFrame
```

Waiting for Events

Remember that Director automatically dispatches events to appropriate scripts. Wait in a frame using the earlier *exitFrame* script containing *go the frame*. Attach event handlers (*mouseUp*, *keyDown*, etc.) to sprites to react to user events.

 Do not confuse *waiting* for an event to occur with *processing* the event once it occurs. If a user event is not the desired one, exit your event handler. Allow Director to continue waiting for events by looping in the frame. Your event handler will get called at the next event.

Suppose you are waiting for the user to enter the RETURN key in an editable field. Attach the script in Example 3-5 to the field sprite.

Example 3-5: Processing an Event

```
on keyDown
  if the key = RETURN or the key = ENTER then
    go frame "Check User Entry"
  else
    -- Send other keystrokes onto editable field.
    pass
  end if
end if
```

Note that if the user hits anything other than the RETURN or ENTER key, we simply send it onto the field sprite. You should not attempt to wait for the user to hit the correct key *within* a *keyDown* handler. Instead, we branch to another frame only when the desired key is detected. In all other cases, we allow the handler to complete without going to another frame. Control returns to the *go the frame* command in our *exitFrame* handler, which will continue to wait for more keyboard and mouse events.

Controlling the Score Channels via Lingo

Lingo can control the Effects channels (Tempos, Transitions, Palettes, and Sounds), but the persistence of the change varies with each command. Some commands are permanent until canceled manually, others are one-time shots, and still others are cancelled only when the playback head moves backward in the Score. None of these commands take effect until the playback head moves or *updateStage* is called. Table 3-20 shows Lingo commands that override the Score notation to control the Effects channels and sprite channels.

Table 3-20: Puppeting the Effects and Sprite Channels

Lingo Command	In Effect Until
set the *property* of sprite *whichSprite* = *value*	Affects single sprite property until current sprite span ends (implicit auto-puppeting).
puppetSprite *whichSprite*, TRUE | FALSE	Overrides entire sprite channel until manually canceled with *puppetSprite FALSE* command (explicit puppeting).[1]
puppetPalette *whichPalette* {, *speed*} {, *nFrames*}	In effect until Director encounters another Palette setting in the Palette channel[2] or the playback head loops backward in the Score (or in the same frame). In that case, the most recent Palette setting to the left of the current frame takes effect. See Chapter 13.
puppetSound	Overrides specified sound channel until manually canceled with the *puppetSound 0* command (*sound playFile* can override puppet sounds). See Chapter 15 for details on syntax.
puppetTempo[3]	Sets frame rate until Director encounters another Tempo setting, or until the playback head loops backward in the Score (or in the same frame), due to a *go* command, in which case it uses the most recent Tempo setting.
puppetTransition	*PuppetTransition* is a one-time occurrence. Transitions in the Transition channel continue to be obeyed. See Table 3-8.

[1] Setting *the puppet of sprite* property has the identical effect as using the *puppetSprite* command.
[2] The *puppetPalette* command can only initiate a palette switch. It can not initiate palette fades or color cycling as can the Palette channel.
[3] The *puppetTempo* command can only change the frame rate. It can not simulate the "wait" settings in the Tempo channel.

Score Recording

You can modify and create sprites in the Score via Lingo using Score Recording. Although this is theoretically possible from a Projector, you would ordinarily perform Score recording only during authoring. Use an *on prepareFrame* handler at runtime to analyze or modify a frame before it is drawn. A Score recording session begins with *beginRecording* and must be terminated with *endRecording*, especially before a subsequent *beginRecording* command.

The *beginRecording* command cannot be used in an *on enterFrame* handler. Use an *on exitFrame* handler instead. A sprite in a newly recorded frame adopts the previous properties for that channel unless overridden explicitly by setting new properties for that sprite.

Table 3-21 lists commands most commonly used during Score Recording. You would usually set sprite properties such as the *member*, *locH*, *locV*, and *rotate of sprite* properties as well.

Table 3-21: Score Recording

Command	Result
beginRecording	Starts Score recording session.
clearFrame	Clears Effects and sprite channels in the current frame.
deleteFrame	Deletes the current frame from Score.
duplicateFrame	Duplicates the current frame.
endRecording	Ends a Score recording session.
the frameLabel[1]	Gets or sets marker label string of current frame.
the framePalette[1]	Sets palette in current frame, or gets latest palette setting (not necessarily set in current frame). Can't be used to create palette fades or color cycling.
the frameScript[1]	Gets or sets script number attached to Script channel of current frame.
the frameSound1[1]	Gets or sets sound in Sound channel 1 of current frame.
the frameSound2[1]	Gets or sets sound in Sound channel 2 of current frame.
the frameTempo[1]	Sets frame rate, or gets latest Tempo setting (not necessarily set in current frame). Does not read or set other Tempo wait options.
the frameTransition[1]	Gets or sets Transition number of current frame.
go frame	Move playback head to a frame for recording.
insertFrame	Same as *duplicateFrame*. Does not insert blank frames. See Example 3-6.
the media of member	Represents the Score-like contents of a film loop. Can be tested and set to the Score of a MIAW.
the scoreColor of sprite	Sets the color of a sprite cell (integer 0 to 5); not particularly reliable.
the scoreSelection	Returns a Lingo list of lists indicating the currently selected cells in the Score.
the score	Represents the entire Score of the main movie of a MIAW. Can be assigned to film loop's *media of member* property.
the scriptNum of sprite	Attaches a single script to a sprite. Attached Behaviors assume default parameters. The *scriptList of sprite* cannot be set.
the tweened of sprite	If TRUE, creates tweened frames. If FALSE, creates keyframes.
the type of sprite	Sets the type of a sprite to an appropriate cast member type, such as 16.
updateFrame	Commits changes to current frame of Score.
the updateLock	If TRUE, prevents the screen from updating when the playback head moves or *updateFrame* is used.[2]

Table 3-21: Score Recording (continued)

Command	Result
the updateMovieEnabled	If TRUE, changes to unprotected, uncompressed movies will automatically be saved when exiting the movie.

1 The frame properties can be tested at any time, but most can be set only during a Score recording session. *The frameLabel* can be set at any time (see the *Markers* section).
2 The *updateLock* is not always reliable. Director may redraw fields despite *the updateLock* being TRUE.

Markers are copied along with entire frames. When you delete a frame with a marker, the marker is deleted, too. If you duplicate a frame with a marker, the marker is not duplicated—it is just pushed one frame to the right. Example 3-6 inserts one or more blank frames in the Score.

Example 3-6: Inserting Blank Frame

```
on insertBlankFrames numFrames
  if voidP(numFrames) or not integerP(numFrames) then
    set numFrames = 1
  end if

  beginRecording
    repeat with n = 1 to numFrames
      -- Create the new frame
      duplicateFrame
      updateFrame
      -- Back up the playback head
      go the frame -1
      -- Clear the stuff in the frame
      clearFrame
      updateFrame
    end repeat
  endRecording
end insertBlankFrames
```

For an extensive example of Score Recording in D6, see Xtras ➤ Wizards ➤ Animation Wizard. You can open the Animation Wizard Director movie to examine its source code.

Field cast members display on Stage during Score Recording even if *the update-Lock* is TRUE. Use D7 text cast members instead. There is no documented way to attach multiple Behaviors and set their parameters during a Score Recording session, but they can be attached dynamically at runtime.

The scoreSelection and frame properties

Besides setting the current frame's properties during a Score recording session, you can read them using *the frameSound1, the frameSound2, the frameTransition,* and *the frameScript*. You could, for example, write a utility to find all the frames where a given transition is used. Note that *the frameTempo* and *the frame-Palette* return the latest setting in effect, even if it was set in an earlier frame. If no palette has been set in the palette channel, *the framePalette* reports the default palette from `Modify` ➤ `Movie` ➤ `Properties`. Note also that *the frameTempo* and *the framePalette* can not simulate all the options of their respective channels.

Currently selected frames and sprites are indicated by *the scoreSelection* property, which returns a list of lists of the form:

```
[[startChan1, endChan1, startFrame1, endFrame1] ¬
    {, [startChan2, endChan2, startFrame2, endFrame2]} ]
```

Each sublist indicates the starting and ending channel and frame numbers of a portion of the selection. Unlike D5, in D6 and D7, a separate sublist is used for each channel of the Score's selection (*startChan* and *endChan* within each sublist are always the same). Selecting frames 1 to 50 of channels 3 and 4 would result in:

```
put the scoreSelection
-- [[3, 3, 1, 50], [4, 4, 1, 50]]
```

If two non-adjacent sprites in a single channel are selected, the list will contain separate sublists for each. Use the `Option` (Mac) or `Alt` key (Windows) to select both occupied and unoccupied cells in a rectangular block in the Score. Use the `Command` key (Mac) or `Ctrl` key (Windows) to select discontiguous sprites.

The sprite channels within *the scoreSelection* range from 1 to 120 in D6 (or up to 1000 in D7). The Effects channels are represented in *the scoreSelection* using the negative numbers shown in Table 3-22. Note that the codes for Sound channels 1 and 2 are –2 and –1, respectively, despite other documentation to the contrary.

Table 3-22: The scoreSelection Codes

Code	Indicates
1 to 48 in D5 1 to 120 in D6 1 to 1000 in D7	Sprite channels
0	Frame Script channel
–1	Sound channel 2 (not 1)
–2	Sound channel 1 (not 2)
–3	Transition channel
–4	Palette channel
–5	Tempo channel

The scoreSelection can also be set, but it will be split into sublists for each channel in the specified area when retrieved from Lingo:

```
set the scoreSelection = [[1,2,1,50]]
put the scoreSelection
-- [[1, 1, 1, 50], [2, 2, 1, 50]]
```

Score Recording requires an existing transition cast member when setting *the frameTransition*. Example 3-7 creates one dynamically.

Example 3-7: Creating a Transition Cast Member via Lingo

```
on createTransition transType, duration, chunkSize, changeArea
    -- TransType is an integer code from 1 to 52
    -- Duration is in milliseconds, chunkSize is from 1 to 128
    -- and changeArea is TRUE or FALSE
    set newTrans = new (#transition)
    set the transitionType of newTrans = transType
    set the duration       of newTrans = duration
    set the chunkSize      of newTrans = chunkSize
    set the changeArea     of newTrans = changeArea
    return newTrans
end createTransition
```

In Example 3-8, note that *the framePalette* uses negative numbers to refer to built-in palettes and positive numbers to refer to custom palette cast members. The *frameTempo* expects an integer, and *the frameLabel* expects a string (or 0 to delete a marker). The *frameSound1*, *frameSound2*, *framePalette*, *frameTransition*, and *frameScript* accept cast member numbers. There is nothing to prevent you from setting them to the improper type of cast member, which you should avoid.

Example 3-8: Score Recording the Effects Channel

```
on recordFrame
  beginRecording
    set the frameLabel = "My Label"
    set the frameTempo = 15
    set the framePalette = -1
    set the frameTransition = createTransition (5, 1000, 20, TRUE)
    set the frameSound1 = member "mySound"
    set the frameSound2 = member "another sound"
    set the frameScript = member "myScript"
    updateFrame
  endRecording
end recordFrame
```

Preventing Problems

When I receive a project to debug, the Score notation has often been maimed to some degree. Score notation errors are usually caused by ill-advised cutting and pasting of cast members in the Cast window. Another potential cause is phantom Score references created by abortive attempts to add a Score script, as explained in Example 2-2 in Chapter 2 of *Lingo in a Nutshell*.

The result is that the Score may contain references to incorrect types of cast members. For example, a reference in the Script channel may point to a cast member that isn't a script, or a reference in a sprite channel may point to a cast member that is a script instead of a bitmap. Similarly, the Effects channels may contain references to the wrong type of cast member. Example 3-9 analyzes the Score and diagnoses these problems. Place such utilities in an external cast and link it to your movies or incorporate it into a separate MIAW (copy the MIAW to the *Xtras* folder to add it to the **Xtras** menu). Rewrite Example 3-9 to use *tell the Stage* from your MIAW to analyze the main movie's Cast and Score rather than the MIAW's.

Walking the Score

To examine the Score (channel by channel and frame by frame) is often called *walking the Score*. Example 3-9 flags these potential problems:

- The Frame Script referring to a non-script cast member

- The script number attached to a sprite referring to a non-script cast member (works for first Behavior only)

- Ink effects other than Copy, Matte, and Background Transparent

- Stretched sprites (shapes, buttons, and fields excepted)

- Sprites that refer to cast members of invalid types, especially *#empty* cast members

If it finds any of these problems, this example displays the sprite and frame number so that you can inspect it in the Score. You can specify a range of frames to check:

```
checkScore 1, 50
```

If you don't specify a range of frames, it checks the entire Score.

Example 3-9 is not intended to be comprehensive or particularly robust. It can easily miss potential problems or cause spurious warnings, but it is a great start. Use it as a basis to create other utilities that analyze, search, or modify the Score. You could analyze the highlighted portion of the Score as indicated by *the scoreSelection*.

Example 3-9: Walking the Score to Check for Problems

```
on checkScore startFrame, endFrame
  if voidP(startFrame) then set startFrame = 1
  if voidP(endFrame)   then set endFrame  = the lastFrame

  -- Check the maximum number of channels for this version
  case (integer (char 1 of the productVersion)) of
    6: set numChannels = 120
    7: set numChannels = the lastChannel
    otherwise: set numChannels = 48
  end case
  -- Prevent screen from updating while checking Score
  set the updateLock = TRUE
  put "Checking frames:"  && startFrame && "to" && endFrame
  repeat with f = startFrame to endFrame
    go frame f
    -- Print a status message periodically
    if (f mod ((endFrame - startFrame + 1)/10)) = 0 then
      put "Checking frame" && f
    end if
    -- Verify the frame script's type
    if the frameScript then
      if the type of member ¬
        (the frameScript) <> #script then
        put "Bad FrameScript Reference, Frame:" && f
      end if
    end if
    repeat with s = 1 to numChannels
      if the memberNum of sprite  s <> 0 then
```

Example 3-9: Walking the Score to Check for Problems (continued)

```
      -- Verify the sprite scripts' types
      -- This only works for first attached Behavior
      if the scriptNum of sprite s then
        if the type of member ¬
              (the scriptNum of sprite s) <> #script then
          put "Bad Script Reference, Frame:" ¬
              && f && "Sprite"  && s
        end if
      end if
      -- Check for slow inks
      case (the ink of sprite s) of
        0, 8, 36:  -- Copy, Matte or BG Transparent are OK
        otherwise:
          put "Suspicious Ink, Frame:" && f && ¬
              "Sprite" && s && the ink of sprite s
      end case
      -- Check for suspicious stretched sprites
      if the stretch of sprite s then
        case (the type of member ¬
            (the memberNum of sprite s)) of
          #shape, #button, #field: nothing
          otherwise
            put "Suspicious Stretch, Frame:" && f ¬
                && "Sprite" && s
        end case
      end if
      -- Check for suspicious member types
      set thisType = the type of member ¬
            (the member of sprite s)
      case (thisType) of
        #empty, #script, #palette, #transition, #sound: ¬
          put "Suspicious sprite type, Frame:" && f && ¬
              "Sprite" && s && thisType
          put "member" && the member of sprite s
      end case
    end if
  end repeat
end repeat
set the updateLock = FALSE
put "Done checking"
end checkScore
```

Reader Exercise: Incorporate Example 13-2, which checks for potential problems with Marker names, into the *checkScore()* utility in Example 3-9. Add your own improvements to check for slow or suspicious Score usage (e.g., digital video sprites perform best when their dimensions and *loc of sprite* properties are multiples of 8). Update Example 3-9 to check the contents of the undocumented *scriptList of sprite* property in D7 instead of the older *scriptNum of sprite* property. See also the undocumented methods within the UI Helper Xtra to read Behaviors and their parameters from the Score in D6. See also Examples 4-4 through 4-8 for utilities that check cast members as well as the "Sure?" utility at *http://www.reference.se/sure/*.

CHAPTER 4

CastLibs, Cast Members, and Sprites

This chapter covers importing assets, using the Cast window, and the Lingo that manipulates castLibs, cast members, and sprites. If you are unfamiliar with sprites and cast members, refer to the tutorials in Macromedia's *Using Director* manual.

Cast Libraries

Director assets are stored as cast members within *castLibs* (cast libraries, or simply *casts*). The Cast window is shown in Figure 4-1.

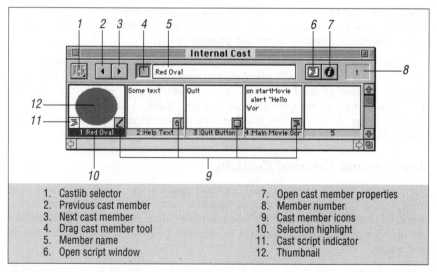

1. Castlib selector
2. Previous cast member
3. Next cast member
4. Drag cast member tool
5. Member name
6. Open script window
7. Open cast member properties
8. Member number
9. Cast member icons
10. Selection highlight
11. Cast script indicator
12. Thumbnail

Figure 4-1: Cast window

Prior to Director 5, cast members were referred to using the *cast* keyword (which, though obsolete, is still supported for backward compatibility). In conversation, the word *cast* refers to a castLib, not an individual member, but Lingo uses the keyword *castLib* to refer to cast libraries and the keyword *member* to refer to members (i.e., cast members) within a cast library.

Director supports both internal and external castLibs. A movie always contains at least one internal castLib, which may have zero cast members. You can optionally create additional internal castLibs, which are private to a single Director movie (although a MIAW can access the main movie's cast using *tell the Stage*). External castLibs are often linked (attached) to one or more movies, but they can also be used as standalone libraries during authoring (so-called "floating" castLibs).

An *internal* (*unlinked* or *embedded*) cast member is one in which the data is incorporated directly into the Cast and stored in Director's internal format for the given data type. For example, text cast members are always embedded. If an asset has been imported as an unlinked cast member, you do not need to distribute the original asset file with your Projector, but it should be kept in case you need to modify it and reimport it.

A *linked* cast member is one that points to an external file containing the data of interest. Some cast members, such as digital videos, are always linked.

 The external asset files associated with linked cast members must be distributed with your Projector.

Some cast members—notably sounds and bitmaps—can be either linked or unlinked. Don't confuse a linked (external) castLib with linked cast members (which can reside in either internal or external castLibs).

You can sometimes access external assets without creating a cast member. The *sound playFile* command will play an arbitrary external WAVE or AIFF file. Some Xtras also access external files without necessarily creating a new cast member. The FileIO Xtra can read an external text file. External assets can be accessed dynamically by changing a cast member's *fileName of member* property to point to a new file.

Multiple and External CastLibs

You can link (attach) one or more external castLibs into your movie and open multiple Cast windows to view them simultaneously. External castLibs are convenient for holding assets that are used in more than one movie. You can use multiple internal or external castLibs to organize assets such as graphics, sounds, and scripts.

Any asset used in more than one movie should be stored in an external castLib. This eases maintenance, reduces storage requirements, and ensures consistency across movies. Keeping common scripts in an external castLib eases testing, editing, and debugging.

If you drag a cast member between two castLibs (either internal or external) that are linked to the same movie, it is moved (not copied) from the original castLib to the destination castLib.

All external castLibs need not be linked to the current movie. Use `File ▶ New ▶ Cast` to create a new external castLib and `File ▶ Open` to open an existing unlinked external castLib. Unlinked castLibs do not appear in the Cast window castLib selector and are not accessible via Lingo, but dragging a cast member from an unlinked external castLib to another castLib will copy it to the destination castLib.

If you place a cast member from an unlinked external castLib onto the Stage or into the Score, Director prompts you to link the castLib to the current movie or to copy the cast member to one of the castLibs already attached. If the unlinked castLib's names contain the word "Library" (such as the D6 Behavior Library), Director automatically copies cast members to the first internal castLib without prompting.

You can repeatedly drag Behaviors from any unlinked external castLib (such as the Behavior Library) directly to the Score; only one copy of the Behavior will be copied to your internal cast. (Director uses a unique internal ID number to prevent duplicate copies of a single Behavior.) Any modification to the Behavior's script or its cast member name will cause Director to import a fresh copy the next time the Behavior is applied.

The D6 Widget Wizard uses Score Recording and often inserts multiple copies of the same bitmaps and Behaviors into your internal cast. Apply Behaviors by hand as per the Widget Wizard's help instructions to avoid rampant duplication when using the same widget multiple times.

In D7, the Library Palette Window replaces `Xtras ▶ Behavior Library`. Add your own Libraries to the Library Palette by placing castLibs containing Behaviors in the *Xtras/Libs* folder or one of its subfolders. See the many useful existing Behaviors in the Library Palette that comes with the Director Multimedia Studio (but not the standalone version).

Great uses for external castLibs

There are numerous reasons to use external castLibs, even when an asset is not used in multiple movies:

Collaboration
> By placing the different assets in different castLibs, multiple developers can work on the same project semi-independently. An artist can update graphics and deliver them in a new external cast library, or a sound designer can provide replacement sounds.

Smaller backups and downloads
> By separating assets in external castLibs, you can back up only the data that has changed. The time and disk space savings can be significant. If collaborating remotely, you need not upload 10 MB of graphics and sounds to change the Lingo.

Use caution when moving cast members within an external castLib. Although Director will try to update the movie's Score to reconcile changes in the castLib, it is safest to tell collaborators not to move any cast members in an external castLib.

Internationalization of multilanguage versions

Store text, field, and bitmap cast members that need to be translated to different languages into an external castLib. Place the translated assets into the same cast member positions as the originals. Don't forget culture-specific images, such as mailboxes, police, taxicabs, and flags, and beware of items that might offend local users. For example, in some countries, a "thumbs-up" sign is an obscenity equivalent to the middle finger in the U.S. (Note that the Macintosh "counting fingers" animated hand cursor never shows the thumb up by itself. It starts and ends with the innocuous pinkie.)

Source code security

If you are a consultant, you can keep your Lingo scripts in a protected external castLib. You can withhold the source code permanently or until you've been paid without otherwise hindering delivery and testing.

Pseudo-editing multiple movies

Placing scripts, graphics, or sounds in an external castLib makes it easy to edit related items used in different movies without switching between movies. Although Director can't open two movies at once, you can open external castLibs from different movies and edit them simultaneously.

Script, asset, and Behavior libraries

You can create external castLibs of utility scripts (such as those in this book), common sounds (mouse-clicks and your company jingle), and graphics (your company logo). If you place your castLib in your *Xtras* folder, it will appear under the `Xtras` menu. Give the castLib a name containing the word "Library" (with or without a .CST extension) and Director 6 will copy assets from it without prompting. In D7, use the *Xtras/Libs* folder.

Disadvantages of external castLibs

External castLibs have their limitations:

Assets are not necessarily stored in the optimal order

When you use `File` ➤ `Save and Compact` on a Director movie, the cast members in any internal castLibs are stored in the order in which they are used in the Score. When compacted, cast members in external castLibs are stored in the order in which they appear in the Cast window.

Because external castLibs are usually accessed by multiple movies' Scores, there is no single optimal storage order. Rearrange them manually to improve load times or use `Modify` ➤ `Sort` ➤ *Usage in Score*.

Limited number of castLibs

In theory, you can attach an unlimited number of internal and external cast libraries to a Director movie. The 16-bit version of Director 5 for Windows 3.1

and 16-bit Projectors were limited to 12 external castLibs. This limit was removed in Director 6, but the maximum number of file handles under Windows 3.1 is set by the *CONFIG.SYS* file, not by Director. Avoid an excessive number of castLibs (more than six or so). Even in D7, an inordinate number of castLibs slows a movie's startup.

Potential conflicts in Lingo

System event handlers (such as *startMovie, idle, exitFrame, mouseDown, mouseUp,* and *keyDown*) within movie scripts in an external castLib might be called unintentionally for any movie to which that castLib is linked. Likewise, duplicate handler names in movie scripts of multiple castLibs will conflict.

Potential conflicts in cast member names and references

Having two cast members with the same name would prevent you from referring to the second one by name. When using multiple castLibs, cast member references should include the castLib, such as:

```
member whichMember of castLib whichCast
```

or in D7 notation:

```
member(whichMember, whichCast)
```

Collaboration must be undertaken with caution

If you change the Score while someone else is changing an external castLib you must reconcile the file versions at some point. See "Adjusting Score references to external cast libraries" later in this chapter.

Memory leaks and bugs

Some bugs occur only when using an asset in an external castLib. For example, there have been problems with sounds in external castLibs not being released from memory and occasional problems with Xtra cast members in external castLibs. If you encounter what seems like an obscure problem, try moving the asset to an internal castLib. (Also upgrade to the latest version of Director. Director 6.0.1 fixed a problem with moving film loops between castLibs in D6.0, and D7.0.1 fixes problems with fonts in external casts.)

Unlinking and relinking external castLibs

If you use **Modify ➤ Movie ➤ Casts ➤** *Remove* to unlink a castLib, Director will ask you whether to remove all Score references to it. This indicates that the movie uses some of the members stored in the castLib and you should cancel the operation. If your goal is to replace an external castLib, you can set *the fileName of castLib* property or use **Modify ➤ Cast ➤ Properties** to modify the link. Alternatively, you can close the movie and then move or delete the external castLib. When you reopen the movie, Director will prompt you to locate the missing castLib, allowing you to specify a different castLib.

 If the Score uses cast members from an external castLib that is replaced, the members in the replacement castLib must use the same *memberNum* positions as in the original castLib.

To export an internal castLib to an external castLib file, use *save castLib* and specify an external file as the destination.

There is no documented Lingo to create and attach a new castLib at runtime. You can create and attach a dummy castLib during authoring and reassign its *fileName of castLib* property as needed. The following unsupported Lingo works in most cases:

```
importFileInto findEmpty(1), "myFile.cst"
```

Search the Direct-L archives for the phrase "importFileInto castLib" for details and caveats.

The freeware CastControl Xtra will attach and detach castLibs at runtime (*http://www.magna.com.au/~farryp/director/xtras/*).

```
-- The first parameter sets the name of castLib property.
-- The second sets the fileName of castLib property.
AttachCastLib internalName, filePath
```

CastControl can detach a castLib by number or by name, but don't attempt to detach internal castLibs (attempting to detach the first internal castLib crashes):

```
detachCastLib 3
detachCastLib the name of castLib 3
```

The CastEffects Xtra (*http://www.penworks.com/xtras/castfx*) can also create and link a new castLib dynamically at runtime (and it can scale, rotate, and extract images at runtime). Also see the Effector Set Xtra (*http://www.medialab.com*), which can transform (scale, rotate, etc.) cast members at runtime, although D7 adds native support for these features.

Shared Cast versus external cast libraries

In Director 3 and 4, only a single external castLib known as the *Shared Cast* was allowed. The Shared Cast was actually a standard Director file whose cast members were accessible from the main movie. The main movie would automatically look for a Shared Cast file in the same folder (there was no explicit link between the main movie and the Shared Cast). To use separate Shared Casts, you needed to place movies in different folders. Members in the Shared Cast appeared at the end of the main movie's Cast window and were distinguished by italicized names and numbers. To prevent conflicts, the cast members in the Shared Cast had to use cast member slots after those used by the main movie(s).

Director 5 and later support multiple external castLibs that are explicitly linked into a movie and can reside anywhere. (In Director 6 and 7, external castLibs can even reside on the Internet.)

When updating a movie from D4 to D6, the Shared Cast is renamed *SHARED.CST* and linked as an external castLib to all movies updated in the same batch. In D4, the Shared Cast's cast members always used the same cast member slots. To simulate this when updating to D6, *the number of member* of the first cast member slot of castLib 2 (presumably the new *SHARED.CST* file) is *kludged* (rigged) to coincide with the first used cast member number in the old D4 *SHARED.DIR* (Shared Cast) file. If the old D4 Shared Cast "started" at cast member 100, when updated to D6, *the number of member 1 of castLib 2* reports 100, not 131073, as it would for movies created from scratch in D6. Furthermore, this holds true for whichever castLib is castLib 2 in the updated movie, even if it is not *SHARED.CST!* This can wreak havoc if *SHARED.CST* is not the second castLib.

In D5 and later, the castLib number of any external castLib will depend on the number of internal castLibs and the order in which external castLibs are attached. The number of the first external castLib is always one greater than the number of internal castLibs. Table 4-1 outlines the use of the Shared Cast or external castLibs in Director.

Table 4-1: Shared Cast Versus External CastLibs

Version	External CastLib Name	Notes
Director 3.1.3	Shared Cast (Mac), *SHRDCST.DIR* (Windows)	File format was not cross-platform. Shared Cast resided in same folder with main movie. D6 will not update from D3.1.3.
Director 4	*SHARED.DIR* (unprotected) or *SHARED.DXR* (protected)	Cross-platform file format, but Shared Cast still resided in same folder with main movie. D7 will not update from D4.
Director 5	*<AnyName>.CST* (unprotected), *<AnyName>.CXT* (protected), or *<AnyName>.CCT* (Shockwave)	Multiple external castLibs allowed. CastLibs can use any name and can reside in any folder.
Director 6 and 7	Same as Director 5.	Shockwave casts can be used locally or reside at any URL.

Adjusting Score references to external cast libraries

Moving, adding, or deleting cast members in an external castLib affects all Director movies that link to that castLib, including ones that are not open when the changes occur. Director tracks these changes via a cast member's unique internal ID. It prompts you to update the Score references the next time you open a movie using that external castLib (as shown in Figure 4-2) even if the altered cast members in the external castLib are not used in the current movie.

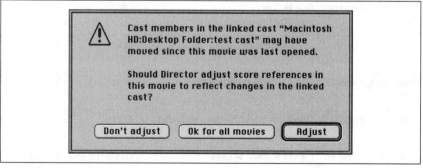

Figure 4-2: Adjusting references to linked castLibs

The three possible responses to the dialog box are not particularly intuitive:

Adjust

> Adjusts all Score references to accommodate any moved cast members. This is the default option and usually the correct choice. If a cast member has been deleted, Director does not remove the Score reference but will point to a nonexistent cast member unless the cast member slot is reused.

Don't adjust

> Leaves the Score alone. This is a dangerous option, because it is likely that the sprite references in the Score will point to wrong or nonexistent cast members. If you choose this accidentally, quit Director without saving the current movie, and then reopen the movie. If you really don't want to adjust the Score references, you must save the movie after hitting this option to prevent being warned again. You'll need to make some other change to enable the File ➤ Save option, or use File ➤ Save As or File ➤ Save and Compact instead.

Ok for all movies

> This is the vaguest prompt of all time. In Director 4, this option was named *Don't Warn Me Again*. It does *not* adjust the Score and prevents Director from warning you if other movies using the same external castLib need to be updated. Use this only if you added cast members to an external castLib but did not move or delete any cast members. If you choose this by mistake, quit Director without saving the current movie.

Cast Library Mechanics

Table 4-2 shows the commands that manage internal and external cast libraries.

Table 4-2: Working with CastLibs

Operation	Menu Command	Mac	Win
Open/Close Cast window	Window ➤ Cast	Cmd-3	Ctrl-3
Open more Cast windows	Window ➤ Cast ➤ *CastLibName* Window ➤ New Window	Opt-click castLib pop-up	Alt-click castLib pop-up
Open unlinked external Cast	File ➤ Open or use Toolbar button.	Cmd-O	Ctrl-O
Open Behavior Library (D6)	Xtras ➤ Behavior Library	None	None
Open Java Behaviors (D6.5)	Xtras ➤ Behavior Library for Java	None	None
Open Library Palette (D7)	Window ➤ Library Palette or use Toolbar button	None	None
Create, link, remove, or modify castLibs in use	Modify ➤ Movie ➤ Casts	Cmd-Shift-C	Ctrl-Shift-C

Table 4-2: Working with CastLibs (continued)

Operation	Menu Command	Mac	Win
Create a new castLib	File ➤ New ➤ Cast Modify ➤ Movie ➤ Casts ➤ New Choose *New Cast* from Cast window castLib pop-up or use Toolbar button.	Cmd-Opt-N	Ctrl-Alt-N
Switch castLib displayed in a Cast window	Use *Choose Cast* pop-up in Cast window.	Cmd-↑ Cmd-↓	Ctrl-↑ Ctrl-↓
Link to existing castLib on local drive on Internet	File ➤ Import ➤ Director Cast Modify ➤ Movie ➤ Casts ➤ Link Choose Internet button in file selection/import dialog box.	Cmd-R Cmd-Shift-C	Ctrl-R Ctrl-Shift-C
Change castLib fileName, name, or preLoadMode	Modify ➤ Cast Properties Modify ➤ Movie ➤ Casts ➤ Properties	Ctrl-click in Cast window	Right-click in Cast window
Change preferences for cast member thumbnails	File ➤ Preferences ➤ Cast or Context pop-up in Cast window	None	Alt-F, F, C
Sort cast members	Select cast members, then choose Modify ➤ Sort.	None	None

Compacted, protected, and compressed castLibs

There are three "formats" for both Director movies and castLibs:

Standard format (including "Compacted" movies)
> The standard Director formats are the well-known movie (DIR) and castLib (CST) files used primarily during authoring. They can also be used with a Projector (if left external rather than embedded in the Projector) and even played locally via a Shockwave-enabled browser. *Compacted* movies and castLib files are different only in that compacting removes any deleted cast members and optimizes cast member order and Score notation. Compacting a file does not protect or compress the assets beyond Director's native cast member compression.

Protected format
> Protected movie and castLib files (DXR and CXT) are marginally smaller than their DIR and CST counterparts because they don't include cast member thumbnails or human readable scripts (i.e., the *scriptText of member*). Protected files cannot be opened in Director and are intended to remain external to a Projector. Protected files are compacted (as is done to standard files using File ➤ Save and Compact), but assets are not compressed.

Compressed (Shockwave or "Shocked") format
> Compressing a file compresses the assets for Shockwave or local playback and protects the assets (as with protected movies). You should manually compact the file before compressing it. Compressed movie and castLib files

(DCR and CCT) are measurably smaller than their standard or protected counterparts, but compressed files must be decompressed as they are loaded into RAM. This trade-off yields better streaming performance over the Internet, where download time is at a premium. Director 6 and 7 include the ability to use DCR and CCT files wherever DXR or CXT files are allowed (even with a local Projector) but the space saved may not justify the slower load time when using local files on a CD-ROM.

In D6 and D7, internal sounds are compressed as SWA if *Compression* is enabled under Xtras ➤ Shockwave for Audio Settings. In D7, JPEG and GIF images imported with the *Include Original Data for Editing* option will be retain their JPEG and GIF compression when shocked.

Note that you should generally use Director movie and castLib files of the same genre; protected movies (DXR files) should use protected castLibs (CXT files), and compressed movies (DCR files) should used compressed castLibs (CCT files).

Table 4-3 lists commands that save movies and castLibs in various formats. Saving the main movie saves both its internal castLibs and the Score. Some commands also save the external castLibs linked to the main movie. None of the commands saves MIAWs, which must be opened as the main movie to be edited.

Table 4-3: Saving and Converting CastLibs and Movies

Command	File Type	Compact	Compress	Protect	Replace Original	Batch
File ➤ Save[1,2]	DIR or CST				✓	
File ➤ Save As[3]	DIR or CST	✓			Optional	
File ➤ Save and Compact[2]	DIR or CST	✓			✓	
File ➤ Save As Shockwave movie	DCR or CST		✓	✓		
File ➤ Save as Java[4]	DJR	✓		✓		
File ➤ Save All[1,5]	DIR or CST				✓	
Xtras ➤ Update Movies ➤ Update[6]	DIR or CST	✓				✓
Xtras ➤ Update Movies ➤ Protect	DXR or CXT	✓		✓		✓
Xtras ➤ Update Movies ➤ Convert to Shockwave movie(s)	DCR or CCT		✓	✓		✓

[1] Performs "incremental" save. Option is active only if changes have been made, and only those movies or castLibs that have changed are saved.
[2] This command saves the "active entity" and its components. If the active window is associated with the main movie or any of its externally linked casts, all of these components are saved if necessary. To save an unlinked external castLib, make sure it is the active window.
[3] If the main movie is active, File ➤ Save As saves only the movie, *not* its external castLibs. If a linked or unlinked external castLib is active, it saves only the active castLib and not the main movie.
[4] Creates a Java (DJR) file and optional Java source and class files. Requires Java Export Xtra included with D6.5 and D7.
[5] Saves any open movies or castLibs that have been modified.
[6] Batch updates movies and castLibs from D4 or D5 to D6, or from D5 or D6 to D7.

CastLib preferences

The File ➤ Preferences ➤ Cast option, except for the Label option, can be set separately for each Cast window. They are not castLib properties and cannot be accessed via Lingo.

Maximum Visible

> Controls the number of thumbnails (from 512 to 32,000) visible in the Cast window. Set it slightly larger than *the number of members of castLib* to afford finer control with the vertical scrollbar in the Cast window and to improve performance marginally. If you set it too low, you won't see all available cast members, but can still access them via the media editor windows.

Row Width

> Controls how many thumbnails are displayed across the Cast window. The fixed options (8, 10, and 20) prevent the cast members from wrapping as the Cast window size changes. When using a fixed number of thumbnails per row, if the Cast window is too narrow, cast members will seem to be missing. Use *Fit to Window* to wrap the display to the window's width.

Thumbnail Size

> Use a smaller thumbnail size to see more cast members.

Label

> Controls whether the cast member number, name, or both are shown in the Cast window, Sprite Toolbar, Sprite Inspector, and in the Score when the *Display* mode is *Member*.

Media Type Icons

> Set this to *All Types* to display the small icons shown in Figure 4-3 to identify each asset type within its cast member thumbnail in the Cast window, Sprite Toolbar, and Sprite Inspector.

Show Cast Member Script Icons

> Select this option to distinguish cast members with cast member scripts attached. A small icon (separate from the media type icon) appears at the left of the thumbnails in the Cast window, Sprite Toolbar, and Sprite Inspector. To visually distinguish sprites with attached cast member scripts, use the Director 5 Style Score with the *Behavior* display mode (cast scripts are indicated by "+" signs if no sprite script is attached).

Importing, Inserting, and Creating Assets

You will often create your assets in some external program and then import them into Director. You can also create bitmaps, text, and buttons in Director. Shockwave audio can be exported from SoundEdit or Peak LE on the Mac, or created using the Xtras ➤ Convert WAV to SWA option under Windows.

Director requires the MIX (Media Information Exchange) Xtras to import various sound and bitmap formats. Without the MIX Xtras (in the *MIX* subfolder of the *Xtras* folder), the corresponding file types will not appear in the File Import dialog box or work via drag-and-drop.

Importing Media into the Cast

Director for Macintosh will import files with either a recognized file extension or the corresponding Macintosh File Type shown in parentheses in Table 4-4. Macintosh File Types are always four characters, case-sensitive, and space-sensitive (the spaces in "BMP " and "RTF " are required). Director for Windows files imports files based only on their three- or four-letter extension. Name all your files with no more than eight characters followed by a three-letter extension. It will make life easier, when copying files across networks with some Windows systems.

Refer to the TechNote, "File Types, Creator Codes and Extensions" at *http://www.zeusprod.com/technote/filetype.html* and Chapter 14 in *Lingo in a Nutshell* for more details on Macintosh File Types and cross-platform file names.

A database of Macintosh Creator Codes and File Types is available from:

http://www.angelfire.com/il/szekely/index.html

QuickTime Pro reads and writes numerous file formats:

http://quicktime.apple.com

DeBabelizer by Equilibrium Technologies reads and writes numerous file formats:

http://www.equilibrium.com/ProductInfo/DB3/DB3ReadersWriters.html
http://www.equilibrium.com/ProductInfo/DBPro/ProReadersWriters.html

IrfanView32 is a freeware graphics file viewer for Windows 95/98/NT:

http://members.home.com/rsimmons/irfanview/

The Shockwave 6.0 plug-in supported any linked bitmap and sound types for which MIX Xtras were installed. The Shockwave 6.0.1 plug-in recognizes GIF, JPEG, and audio files without any Xtras, but ignores any installed MIX Xtras.

Table 4-4 shows the file formats that can be imported using File ➤ Import or via drag-and-drop. Drag-and-drop import uses the default import settings. For example, you can't use drag-and-drop to create a linked sound, because the default is to create an unlinked sound. Refer to Macromedia's *Using Director* manual for additional details on importing, and see "Import options: To link or not to link" later in this chapter. See also Table 4-5 for additional media types not imported via the File ➤ Import menu option and requiring Sprite asset Xtras as described in Chapter 10. The Director 6 and 7 CDs contain sample graphics and audio files under *Macromedia/Support*, with which you can practice importing each media type.

Table 4-4: Supported Import File Formats

Asset Type	Notes	Mac	Win
All Files	Shows all asset types	Shows only recognized file types	Imports unknown types as OLE
Bitmap Image[1,2]	All supported graphical types (including PICTs; JPEG import requires QuickTime)	.BMP ('BMP '), .GIF ('GIFf'), .JPG, .JPEG ('JPEG'), .LRG, .PCT, .PIC, .PICT ('PICT'), .PNT ('PNTG'), .PSD ('8BPS'), .TGA ('TPIC'), .TIF ('TIFF')	.BMP, .DIB, .EPS , .FCC, .FCI, .GIF, .JPG, .LRG, .PCD, .PCT, .PCX, .PIC, .PICT, .PNG, .PNT, .PSD, .TIF, .TGA, .WMF
PICT	PICTs only	.PCT, .PIC, .PICT ('PICT')	.PCT, .PIC, .PICT
Palette[1,2]	Create palette in deBabelizer or Photoshop	.PAL ('8BCT'), imported with bitmap[2]	.PAL, imported with bitmap.[2] Photoshop CLUT
Scrapbook	Mac only	'scbk'	N/A
PICS	Mac only	.PICS ('PICS')	N/A
FLC and FLI	Win only (AutoCAD)	N/A	.FLC, .FLI
Sound[3]	Supports uncompressed and IMA-compressed sounds	.AIF, .AIFF ('AIFF'), .AIFC ('AIFC'), .WAV, .WAVE ('WAVE'), System 7 SND ('sfil'), .au ('ULAW'), .SWA ('SWaT'), .MP3 ('MPG3')	.AIF, .AIFF, .AIFC, .WAV, .WAVE, .au, .SWA, .MP3
Director movie[4]	Director 5, 6, or 7 movie files	.DIR ('MV07', 'MV97', 'MV95'), .DCR ('FGDM'), .DXR ('M!07', 'M!97', 'M!95')	.DIR, .DCR, .DXR
Director Cast[5]	Director 5, 6, or 7 cast files	.CST ('MC07', 'MC97', 'MC95')	.CST
Digital Video	Mac: QuickTime Win: Video Clip	.MOV ('MooV'), .MPG, .MPEG ('MPEG'), .AVI ('VFW ')	.MOV, .AVI, .MPG, .MPEG
Rich Text (D6)[1,6] Text (D7)[1]	MS Word creates RTF files	.RTF ('RTF '), .TXT ('TEXT'), .HTM, .HTML	.RTF, .TXT, .HTM, .HTML
Animated GIF	New in D7	.GIF ('GIFf')	.GIF
Shockwave Flash	New in D7; use Insert menu in D6.5	.SWF ('SWFL')	.SWF

[1] This asset type can also be created in Director on either platform.
[2] When importing bitmaps containing custom palettes, Director optionally imports the palette as well.
[3] Director 6 doesn't import SWA via File ➤ Import; D7 does, but they are converted to standard internal sounds. The Sun AU Import Xtra included with D6.5 and D7 is required to import .au sound files. Some compressed WAVE files are not supported.
[4] Importing a Director Movie file directly into the Cast (unlinked) imports all its assets as separate cast members. Its Score becomes a film loop, and its scripts, bitmaps, sounds, and so on are each transferred as separate cast members.
[5] Importing a Director Cast file does not create a cast member. It simply links an existing castLib into the current movie. See Modify ➤ Movie ➤ Casts. ImportFileInto can link to cast files at runtime.
[6] A new rich text cast member is created whenever a page break or column break is encountered. HTML files are imported as rich text cast members, but none of the HTML tags are obeyed in D6. D7 imports HTML files as text members and supports basic tags.

File import notes

All bitmaps are imported at 72 dpi (dots per inch). A 300 dpi bitmap will appear about four times larger upon import. Director flattens a Photoshop document's multiple paint layers rather than importing then as separate elements. Either export the layers as separate images from Photoshop, or use the Photocaster Xtra (*http://www.medialab.com*) to import the Photoshop layers as separate cast members automatically (Photocaster Lite is included with D7).

The following file types use the file extensions shown in parentheses: xRes (.LRG), Photoshop 3.0 (.PSD), MacPaint (.PNT), and TARGA (.TGA). The Windows-only Postscript (.EPS), Photo CD (.PCD), Windows Meta-File (.WMF), and .PCX formats are imported with the ImageMark MIX Xtra. It imports only the TIFF preview available in some EPS files and not true EPS data. The ImageMark Xtra is not included with D7, so the EPS, PCD, WMF, and PCX formats are no longer supported. The ImageMark MIX Xtra is not licensed for redistribution (i.e., it is for authoring only).

In Director 5, all PICT files were imported at 32-bit, but Director 6 removes this limitation. Under Windows, 16-bit PICT files will import at the current color depth or as 24-bit PICTs. Set your monitor to 16-bit color (thousands) to import PICTs at 16-bit. QuickTime is required to view JPEG-compressed PICT files. In Director 6 and 7, under Windows, PICT files should use a .PCT extension, whereas in Director 5, the .JPG extension was required for JPEG-compressed PICTs.

The Photoshop CLUT palette file import was briefly released with D6.0.2 and reintroduced in D7. Custom palettes are typically imported along with the bitmap file in which they are embedded. In D7, GIFs imported via File ➤ Import can be imported as either bitmap or animated GIF members.

Additional media types

Table 4-5 shows additional supported media types that are not imported via the File ➤ Import menu option and don't support drag-and-drop. Data types used by sprite Xtras must be inserted using the Insert menu or Xtras menu in D6.5, although some are imported via File ➤ Import in D7. To import Freehand files, you must convert them to Flash format. Note that the .MOV extension is used for both QTVR and linear QuickTime movies, although the two are quite different.

Table 4-5: Additional Supported Formats

Asset Type	To Add Element	Mac	Win
ActiveX[1,2]	Insert ➤ Control ➤ ActiveX	N/A	.OCX
Shockwave Audio[3,4,5]	Insert ➤ Media Element ➤ Shockwave Audio	.SWA ('SwaT')	.SWA
Other Sound formats	Copy Sound Edit 16 and scrapbook sounds to clipboard and paste into the Cast window	N/A	N/A
Custom Cursor[1]	Insert ➤ Media Element ➤ Cursor	None	None
OLE[6]	Insert ➤ Media Element ➤ OLE Object	N/A	Various

Table 4-5: Additional Supported Formats (continued)

Asset Type	To Add Element	Mac	Win
QTVR 1.0	Don't import. See Chapter 16.	.MOV ('MooV')	.MOV
QTVR 2.0[1]	Insert ➤ Media Element ➤ QuickTime 3	.MOV ('MooV')	.MOV
QD3D	See Chapter 16.	'3DMF'	.QD3D
QuickTime 3[1,5,7]	Insert ➤ Media Element ➤ QuickTime 3	.MOV ('MooV'), .AVI ('VfW ')	.MOV, .AVI
Push button, check box, radio button	Use Tool Palette or Insert ➤ Control	Cmd-7	Ctrl-7
Fields	Cut and paste text into fields, use FileIO, or Insert ➤ Control ➤ Field	Cmd-8	Ctrl-8
Flash[1,5,8]	Insert ➤ Media Element ➤ Shockwave Flash movie (D6.5). Insert ➤ Media Element ➤ Flash Movie (D7).	.SWF ('SWFL')	.SWF
PowerPoint[1,9]	Xtras ➤ Import PowerPoint File	.PPT	.PPT

[1] Requires an Xtra included with D6.5 and D7.
[2] The ActiveX Xtra is for Windows only.
[3] Requires an Xtra included with D6.0.x, D6.5, and D7.
[4] SWA can be created using Sound Edit 16 on the Macintosh or Xtras ➤ Convert WAVE to SWA under Windows.
[5] Also imported via File ➤ Import in D7.
[6] OLE is for Windows only. Any file extensions not recognized by Director For Windows are imported as OLE cast members. See Edit ➤ Paste Special ➤ Using OLE. OLE objects created under Windows appear as bitmaps on the Macintosh.
[7] Quicktime 3 supports dozens of media formats, although some of these are usually imported directly. For example, GIF and JPEG files should be imported as bitmaps instead of Quicktime 3 cast members. In D7, import QT3 cast members via File ➤ Import. See Chapter 16.
[8] D6.5 supports Flash 2. D7 supports Flash 2 and Flash 3.
[9] Only PowerPoint 4.0 files are supported. Save PowerPoint 97 files in PowerPoint 4.0 format before importing.

Linked and Unlinked Media Types

Table 4-6 shows each asset type as returned by *the type of member* property, and whether it is linked (asset file remains external) or unlinked (data is embedded into the Cast and stored in Director's native format). Linked assets must be distributed with your Projector.

Some asset types, such as *#digitalVideo*, have additional subtypes reported by a second Lingo property.

Table 4-6: Media Types and Subtypes

Media Type	Notes	Linked?
#ActiveX[1]	Requires ActiveX control included with D6.5 and D7 (Windows only).	Yes
#alpha[1]	Requires Alphamania Xtra (*http://www.medialab.com*).	No

CastLibs & Sprites

Table 4-6: Media Types and Subtypes (continued)

Media Type	Notes	Linked?
#animGIF[1]	New In D7. See Insert ➤ Media Element ➤ Animated GIF, and File ➤ Import.	Optional
#bitmap	Only unlinked images can be edited in Paint window.	Optional
#btned[1]	Requires Custom Button Editor Xtra. Source bitmaps used for custom button can be deleted. Obsolete in D7.	No
#button	See *buttonType of member* (#checkBox, #pushButton, #radioButton).	No
#cursor[1]	Requires Custom Cursor Xtra included with D6.5 and D7.	No
#digitalVideo	QT2.x or AVI files in D6. In D7, used only for AVI files under Windows. See *digitalVideoType of member* (#quickTime or #videoForWindows).	Yes[2]
#empty	Unoccupied cast member.	N/A
#field	See *boxType of member* (#adjust, #fixed, #limit, #scroll).	No
#filmloop	Cast members used by film loops must be retained.	No
#flash[1]	Requires Flash Asset Xtra included with D6.5 and D7.	Optional
#font[1]	New in D7. See Insert ➤ Media Element ➤ Font.	No
#movie	Only linked Director movies become #movie cast members. If imported as unlinked, the components are imported as different types.	Yes
#ole	Windows-only; treated as #bitmap on Macintosh.	Yes
#palette	See *palette of member* and *paletteRef of member* in Table 13-8.	No
#picture	Use *Import PICT file as PICT* option. Can't be edited in Paint window.	No
#PopMenu[1]	Requires PopUp Xtra (*http://www.updatestage.com/xtras*).	N/A
#QD3D_Xtra[1,3]	Requires QD3D Xtra (included on D6 CD and free from Macromedia).	Optional
#QuickTimeMedia[1,2,3]	Requires QuickTime 3 Asset Xtra included with D6.5 and D7.	Yes
#richtext	To find rich text members, search for members of type *Text* under Edit ➤ Find ➤ Cast Member in D6.5. Obsolete in D7. See #text.	No
#script	See *scriptType of member* (#score, #movie, #parent).	No
#shape	See *shapeType of member* (#line, #oval, #rect, #roundRect).	No
#sound	AIFF and WAVE sound files can be playing using *sound playFile* without a cast member reference. See also #SWA.	Optional
#SWA[1]	Requires SWA Xtras.	Yes
#text[1]	New in D7. Replaces #richText and supersedes #field cast members. (#text type also referred to #field cast members in D4.)	No

Table 4-6: Media Types and Subtypes (continued)

Media Type	Notes	Linked?
#transition	See *transitionType of member* in Table 16-1 in *Lingo in a Nutshell*.	No
#vectorShape[1]	New in D7. See Window ➤ VectorShape.	No
#xtra[1]	Xtras generally report a custom type name. If the required Xtra is missing, sprite may appear as a red X on the Stage.	Xtra-dependent

[1] To find this cast member type (and all Xtra cast members) search for members of type Xtra under Edit ➤ Find ➤ Cast Member in D6. In D7, Vector Shape, QuickTime 3, Flash, Animated GIF, Cursor, Font, and SWA cast members can be searched for individually.
[2] Digital Video cast members are always linked. Don't import QTVR movies as #digitalVideo cast members. Use the QTVR Xtra or the QT3 Xtra instead. QuickTime 2 videos can be imported as #digitalVideo or inserted as #QuickTimeMedia in D6.5. QuickTime 3 videos should be inserted as #QuickTimeMedia.
[3] QD3D cast members can be inserted as #QD3D_Xtra cast members if the QD3D Xtra is installed. They can also be inserted as #QuickTimeMedia if the QT3 Xtra is present.

The *new* command creates cast members on the fly. See Example 3-7. Figure 4-3 shows the icons for most of the media types in Table 4-6. Note that the larger rectangular icons indicate linked assets. Note the new icon for Behavior scripts in D6 and D7.

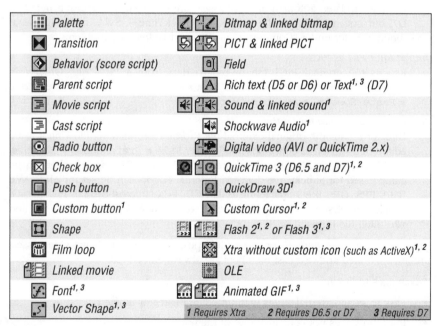

Figure 4-3: Media type icons

Import options: To link or not to link

Refer to the *Import Command* entry in the online Help for details on the basic use of the Import dialog box. The *Internet* button lets Director import files (which can end up either linked or unlinked) from a URL. When you import a bitmap with a custom palette or with a different color depth than the current movie, Director will prompt you with additional import options. See Chapter 13 for details.

There are four possible import modes:

Standard Import

Imports media directly into the Cast. Regardless of the external file's format, bitmaps and sounds that are imported in this mode are converted to Director's internal data formats. Once imported, you can't distinguish between a TIFF, PICT, BMP, and so on. If importing a Director movie file, this causes the imported movie's assets to be copied as individual cast members into the main movie's Cast.

Link to External File

Assets remain in external file(s) and are pointed to by the *fileName of member, URL of member,* or *streamName of member* property (see Example 4-5 and the *linked of member* property). This is relevant for AIFF, WAVE, bitmap, PICT, animated GIF, Flash, and Director movie cast member types. Linked filenames are updated automatically for the current platform (Director changes the drive letter and path separators as long as the file's position relative to the Director movie is maintained). Stick with DOS-style "eight dot three" filenames for maximum compatibility. The *fileName of member* updates automatically for assets imported via the Insert menu in D7, but not in D6.5. See the "Can't find QuickTime 3, SWA, or Flash files at runtime" entry under "Common Importing and Linked File Problems."

Import PICT File as PICT

Retains the original PICT (shape-based) data from a PICT file. Otherwise, Director converts the imported PICT into a bitmap cast member. See Edit ➤ Paste Special ➤ As PICT (Mac only).

Include Original Data for Editing

Director retains the original external file's format information, allowing it to be edited in an external editor specified under File ➤ Preferences ➤ Editors. In D7, use this option to allow internal GIF and JPEG cast members to be compressed for Shockwave delivery. External editors can be set for AIFF, AVI, BMP, EPS, GIF, JPEG, MacPaint, PAL, PCD, PCX, Photoshop 3.0, PICT, PNG, QuickTime, System 7 *snd* resource, Sun AU, TARGA, TIFF, WAVE, WMF, and xRes LRG file formats.

The import mode is ignored for some file types. For example, digital video assets are always linked and text cast members are always embedded.

Advantages to linking:

- Easy to swap external assets without editing Director movie or cast.
- Importing does not consume a lot of memory.
- Size of castLib is minimized.
- Audio streams from disk at runtime, using less memory.

Disadvantages to linking:

- External unprotected assets must be included with the Projector.
- Linked graphics load more slowly because they are not stored in Director's native file format.
- Linked audio streaming from disk may interfere with loading of other assets.
- Linked sounds don't obey *the loop of member* setting.
- Linked sounds are immediately purged from memory.
- Requires MIX import Xtra(s) at runtime.
- Palettes not always handled properly (see Chapter 13).

Advantages to importing directly into the Cast:

- Movie's assets are contained within Cast or Projector, offering some security, and not requiring external files to be included with the Projector.
- Uses fewer external file handles, although this is rarely an issue.
- Internal audio remains in memory and can be looped.
- Assets are stored in order in which they are used in Score.
- Assets are stored in Director's native format for faster loading.
- Does not require MIX import Xtra(s) at runtime.

Disadvantages to importing directly into the Cast:

- Cast can grow very large.
- Memory can run low when importing.
- Memory can run low when playing large sounds.
- Large sounds must be loaded in their entirety before playing.

Import short or frequently used sounds into the Cast. Leave longer sound files on disk and link to them instead. Before playing an internal sound, Director loads the entire sound into memory. Using linked cast members or *sound playFile* streams the data from disk as it is needed. While it uses less memory, streaming from disk may interfere with the loading of other assets.

Importing tips, annoyances, and caveats

Here are some tips on importing efficiently:

- Drag and drop to import files from the desktop.
- Files are imported in the order in which they are provided by the operating system, not the order in which they are added in the *Import* dialog box, nor necessarily in alphabetical order. Select the newly imported cast members and choose Modify ➤ Sort to rearrange them by their name or another attribute.
- Use the Macintosh shareware *Default Folder* extension to make it easier to import media from a variety of subfolders without manually navigating among them.

- When you select items to import in the *Import* dialog box, Director always jumps to the beginning of the available file list. For easier importing, move all the files to be imported into a separate folder, then use the *Add All* button.

- If importing most but not all files in a folder, first use *Add All*, then remove the ones that you don't want to import.

- Imported assets may be scattered around the Cast. Select an empty area in the Cast with enough room to import all assets together before importing.

- If you run out of memory while importing, you should allocate more RAM or import in multiple steps and save between imports. Separate the files into temporary folders and import one folder at a time.

Watch out for these issues:

- Director 6 and 7 use the name of the imported file to name the new cast member but strip off the file extension (unlike D5). If you import two files with the same filename but different extensions, they will be given identical cast member names. See "Checking for duplicate cast member names" later in this chapter. You could write you own utility to add an appropriate extension to each cast member, such as a .BMP extension to bitmap cast members.

- On the Macintosh, you can preview sounds and graphics in the File ➤ Import dialog box, but only before adding them to the import list.

- Some cast member types are always linked or embedded regardless of the mode chosen for importing the files. See Table 4-6.

Common importing and linked file problems

Some common problems with importing and linked files are:

Where is . . . ? (File Can't Be Found)
If you link to an external asset file, Director will look for that file when the cast member is needed. You must distribute any external asset files with your Projector. Director automatically converts the linked file path to a path that is relative to the Director movie. It also adjusts the file path from Macintosh to Windows (or vice versa). You should obey Windows 3.1's more restrictive file-naming conventions on any other OS if you intend to distribute under Windows 3.1. Refer to the TechNote, "Path and File Specifications" at *http://www.zeusprod.com/technote/filepath.html.*

If Director can't find a file, it will bring up the dreaded *Where is . . . ?* dialog box. Simply point to the new location for the asset, and Director will update *the fileName of member* property accordingly when you save the file. If you don't have the asset available and don't want to change the link, hit *Cancel* and Director will prompt you again next time you use the file. Test linked files from within your Projector. If a link is incorrect, you will be prompted every time the Projector runs, because Director doesn't save changes automatically from a Projector.

The simplest way to avoid the problem is to keep external files in the same folder with the Director movie or Projector. In any case, always keep files in the same relative positions during development and runtime. Refer to the *checkLinks()* utility in Example 4-5.

If Director can't find a movie file needed for a *go to movie* or *play movie* command, you will also be prompted to find the movie. However, Director will not update your Lingo code, even during authoring, and you will get the same error message until you update your Lingo code manually.

Can't find QuickTime 3, SWA, or Flash files at runtime
When inserting assets via the `Insert` menu (QuickTime 3, SWA, Flash, and others), Director 6.x does not automatically create a relative path. Thus, when the assets are moved or burned onto a CD, Director won't be able to find them. Replace the absolute path in the cast member properties dialog box with a relative path using the @ operator to represent the folder in which the Director file resides (it does *not* represent the castLib's folder, which may differ). For example, if a QT3 movie *myVideo.mov* is in a subfolder named *Video*, edit the file name to read *@/video/myVideo.mov* (without quotes) or set its *fileName of member* property to `"@/video/myVideo.mov"` (with the quotes). D7 handles this automatically; there is no need to use the @ operator.

Running out of memory
Assets imported into Director are stored temporarily in memory. If you import many large items, Director will use up all of its available memory. Import fewer items, then save your Director file to free up memory for additional importing. Avoid using *importFileInto* at runtime, as it consumes memory. Import bitmaps at a lower color depth or link to external assets instead of importing them into the Cast, and avoid importing large rich text files. Also allocate more memory to Director.

Bitmaps registration points
Director ignores the registration points set in other programs, such as Photoshop. Use Photocaster (*http://www.medialab.com*) to maintain registration when importing Photoshop documents, or use `Edit ➤ Launch External Editor`, which retains regPoint information (see `File ➤ Preferences ➤ Editors`). The regPoint may display incorrectly when changing *the fileName of member* property. You may need to set the *regPoint of member* and then force Director to recognize it by setting *the picture of member* property to itself:

```
set the regPoint of member whichMember = point (x, y)
set the picture of member whichMember = ¬
    the picture of member whichMember
```

Imported bitmap is wrong size in Paint window
The bitmap was saved at the wrong resolution, such as 96 dpi or 300 dpi. All bitmaps should be saved at 72 dpi before being imported into Director.

Custom palette not imported
Save the bitmap in indexed color mode with an adaptive palette in Photoshop, deBabelizer, or similar graphics program. Director will detect and optionally import the palette along with the bitmap. Custom palettes embedded in QuickTime movies are not recognized. Attach such palettes to a dummy bitmap and import that instead.

Director 6.5 for Macintosh includes a new PICT Import Export Xtra that prevents Director 6.5 from recognizing the custom palette in a PICT file during import. It should be removed from the *Xtras:MIX* subfolder (don't forget to restart Director). Reinstall it only when using the *Save as Java* function.

Creating Media Within Director

Table 4-7 shows the shortcut commands used to create assets within a Director movie.

Table 4-7: Creating and Inserting Media Within Director

Action	Command	Mac	Win
Import Cast Members	File ➤ Import, drag and drop into Cast window, context-sensitive pop-up in Cast window, or Toolbar button	Cmd-R	Ctrl-R
Export frame(s)	File ➤ Export	Cmd-Shift-R	Ctrl-Shift-R
Add bitmap[1]	Insert ➤ Media Element ➤ Bitmap, or Window ➤ Paint	Cmd-5, then hit + button	Ctrl-5, then hit + button
Add rich text[1] (D6) Add text (D7)	Insert ➤ Media Element ➤ Text, or Window ➤ Text	Cmd-6, then hit + button	Ctrl-6, then hit + button
Add palette	Insert ➤ Media Element ➤ Palette	Cmd-Opt-7	Ctrl-Alt-7
Add vector shape	Insert ➤ Media Element ➤ Vector Shape, or Window ➤ Vector Shape	Cmd-Shift-V	Ctrl-Shift-V
Record sound[1,2]	Insert ➤ Media Element ➤ Sound	None	N/A
Add push button, radio button, or checkbox	Insert ➤ Control..., or use Window ➤ Tool Palette	Cmd-7	Ctrl-7
Add field[1]	Insert ➤ Control ➤ Field, or use Window ➤ Tool Palette	Cmd-8	Ctrl-8
Add custom button[3]	Insert ➤ Control ➤ Custom Button	None	None
Add film loop	Insert ➤ Film Loop or copy sprite(s) and paste into cast member slot	None	None

[1] These asset types can be copied from other applications and pasted into Director via the clipboard. Some information, such as rich text formatting, may be lost in the transfer.
[2] Only the Macintosh version of Director supports recording sounds. Under Windows, you'll need an Xtra, such as Focus 3 SoundFX Xtra (*http://www.focus3.com*) or Sound Xtra (*http://www.updatestage.com/xtras*).
[3] Requires Custom Button Editor Xtra. (Obsolete in D7.)

Exporting

Director exports the Stage area only. Reduce the Stage size to the desired output size before exporting. (Prior to D7, the Stage width is limited to multiples of 16 pixels.) If the export fails, make sure that the visible area of the Stage is not blank. Director exports the data in the Score only—any puppeted sprites are ignored. Director does not export individual cast members, but you can copy sounds, text, and bitmaps to the clipboard and then paste them into an appropriate program or place sprites on the Stage to export them. Many Xtras, such as the ScrnXtra (*http://www.littleplanet.com/kent/kent.html*) will capture the screen and export it to a file.

Director 6 for Macintosh exports in PICT, PICS, Scrapbook, and QuickTime 2 formats. Director 6 for Windows can export a DIB file sequence (BMP), or in Video for Windows (AVI) format. The D7 QT3 Export Xtra supports QT3 export on both Macintosh and Windows.

When exporting in QuickTime or Video for Windows format, transitions are not included and each sound may be exported as a separate audio track. Use Adobe Premiere or similar tool to add visual transitions and SoundEdit 16 or similar tool to remix the audio tracks.

Working with Cast Members

If you replace a cast member, all sprites that reference it will use the new asset. This can be great if you want to replace a button on every screen, but troublesome if you meant to replace only some occurrences.

Cast Member Loading

There are three possible settings for castLib loading under Modify ➤ Cast Properties. These control the overall loading of a castLib's assets:

When Needed
This is the default mode; loads cast members on demand prior to drawing the frame in which they are needed.

Before Frame One
This mode loads as many cast members as possible in the order in which they are needed in the Score. This increases the initial load delay, but to the extent that memory is available, animations will perform more quickly.

After Frame One
This mode behaves the same as *Before Frame One*, except that it displays the first frame as quickly as possible before proceeding to load more data.

Refer to *the purgePriority of member* property and Chapter 9, *Memory and Performance*, for details on loading and unloading individual cast members.

Dynamic Linking to Cast Members at Runtime

If at all possible, import all assets ahead of time during authoring. Avoid importing assets at runtime, as it consumes excessive amount of memory. Use *importFileInto* during authoring only. To link dynamically to an external sound, digital video, or bitmap member, set *the fileName of member* property.

If you attempt to set *the fileName of member* property to an invalid file, the property won't update. Check *the fileName of member* after setting it to determine if the relinking succeeded. Even if there is insufficient RAM to read the external file, *the fileName of member* will update. Check that the *picture of member* property is nonzero to confirm that the import succeeded.

Setting *the fileName of member* works best when replacing a cast member with an external file of the same type. Create a dummy cast member ahead of time for each data type that you intend to import. If necessary, create a dummy cast member on the fly, using the *new()* function. For example, assuming that the PICT file is in the same folder as the Director movie:

```
set dummy = new (#picture)
set the fileName of dummy = the moviePath & "someFile.PCT"
```

You may need to force Director to update the link using:

```
set the fileName of dummy = the fileName of dummy
```

Note that all sprite properties are not updated when setting *the fileName of member* property. This is especially a problem when using, for example, Quick-Time movies with differing frame rates. Likewise, palettes for external files are not well-behaved if the palette changes at runtime. Problems with the registration point are common.

Linking to text files is not supported. To read text files on the fly, you can use the FileIO Xtra and assign the result to a text or field member.

Sorting and Searching for Cast Members

To sort cast members, select the ones to be sorted or choose Edit ➤ Select All and then Modify ➤ Sort. You can sort cast members by the order in which they are used in the Score, their media type, name, or size. Use the *Empty at End* sort option to eliminate any unused cast member slots.

Use Edit ➤ Find ➤ Selection to search for a given cast member in the Score. Use Edit ➤ Find ➤ Cast Member to locate cast members with a particular name, media type, or palette. You can search all castLibs or limit the search to a single castLib, and list the matching cast members in name or number order. In D6, search for cast members with a Type of *Xtra* to find SWA cast members (searching for *Sound* cast members won't suffice) or to find other Xtra asset types added in D6.5 (QT3, Flash, Custon Cursors, and ActiveX). In D7, you can individually select the new types (Vector Shape, QuickTime 3, Flash, Animated GIF, Cursor, Font, Shockwave Audio) that were lumped together under "Xtras" in D6 and still appear if you search for Xtras in D7. You can use *Select All* to highlight all the found cast members in the Cast window.

Deleting unneeded cast members

Use the *Usage (Not Used in Score)* option under Edit ➤ Find ➤ Cast Member to find unused cast members. Movie script cast members are never shown as unused, even though they don't appear in the Score. If a film loop is used in the Score, its constituent members are considered to be used in the Score also. These cast members must be kept handy, as they are not embedded in the film loop. Similarly, cast members included in Custom Cursor members must remain in the cast. Conversely, graphics embedded into Custom Button cast members in D6 may be discarded if not used elsewhere.

Cast members that are not used in the Score may still be used. Parent scripts, fonts, and Custom Cursors are shown as unused in the Score, even though you may well need them. Do not delete them.

So-called unused cast members that are in fact used as *puppetSprites* should be placed in dummy frames of the Score near other related sprites. This prevents them from being flagged as unused and optimizes their storage order on disk for faster loading. Delete truly unneeded cast members and use File ➤ Save and Compact to reduce the Director movie's size permanently. Never clear cast members from external castLibs, unless you are sure that other Director movies don't use them either.

Cast Window Shortcuts

The Cast window (Figure 4-1) contains many options that are common to the media editors (Figure 2-1), such as the arrow buttons, the script icon, and the properties icon. It also contains a castLib pop-up menu and a cast member number display.

You can select multiple cast members to check their cumulative size or modify their purge priorities all at once. If you select only bitmap cast members, you can also set their default palette.

To list all the colors used in one or more cast members, select the cast member(s) in the Cast, and then use the Palette window's *Select Used Colors* option.

Table 4-8 lists Cast window shortcuts. Refer to the tables in Chapter 3 for details on creating and manipulating sprites.

Table 4-8: Cast Window Shortcuts

Action	Command	Mac	Win
Cut, copy, paste, or edit cast members	Edit menu, or ontext-sensitive menu	Ctrl-click	Right-click
Modify cast member properties[1]	Modify ➤ Cast Member ➤ Properties (see also Table 2-8)	Cmd-I	Ctrl-I
Modify cast member script	Modify ➤ Cast Member ➤ Script, or use *Script* button.	Cmd-' (apostrophe). Opt-*Script* button opens new script.	Ctrl-' (apostrophe). Alt-*Script* button opens new script.
Edit in appropriate internal media editor	Edit ➤ Edit Cast Member, or select thumbnail and press Return. Double-click thumbnail in Cast, Sprite Inspector, or Sprite Toolbar	None	Alt-E,M

Table 4-8: Cast Window Shortcuts (continued)

Action	Command	Mac	Win
Edit in external editor	Edit ➤ Launch External Editor (see File ➤ Preferences ➤ Editors)	Cmd-, (comma)	Ctrl-, (comma)
Edit cast member name[2]	Click in cast member's name area	Cmd-Shift-N	Ctrl-Shift-N
Switch displayed castLib	Use castLib pop-up menu	Cmd-↑ Cmd-↓	Ctrl-↑ Ctrl-↓
Open additional Cast windows	Window ➤ Cast ➤ *castLib*	Opt-click castLib pop-up	Alt-click castLib pop-up
Jump to specific cast member	Type its number quickly in cast member number field	None	None
Jump to next or previous occupied slot	Click on desired cast member, or use arrow buttons in media editor.	Cmd-→ Cmd-←	Ctrl-→ Ctrl-←
Jump to first cast member	Scroll to top of vertical scrollbar	Home key[3]	Home key[3]
Jump to last used cast member	Use vertical scrollbar	End key[3]	End key[3]
Page up or down one screen in Cast	Click above or below vertical scroll slider	Page Up or Page Down key[3]	Page Up or Page Down key[3]
Select a range of cast members	Select first cast member, then Shift-click last cast member	Shift-click	Shift-click
Select all cast members	Edit ➤ Select All	Cmd-A	Ctrl-A
Create new cast member	Click + button in media editor window	Cmd-Shift-A	Ctrl-Shift-A
Select discontiguous cast members	Edit ➤ Find ➤ Cast Members	Cmd-click	Ctrl-click
Delete single cast member (copies to clipboard)	Edit ➤ Cut Cast Members	Cmd-X	Ctrl-X
Copy cast member(s) to clipboard	Edit ➤ Copy Cast Members	Cmd-C	Ctrl-C
Clear multiple cast members (does not copy to clipboard)	Edit ➤ Clear Cast Members	Delete key	Delete or Backspace key
Duplicate cast member(s)	Edit ➤ Duplicate	Cmd-D, or Opt-drag	Ctrl-D, or Alt-drag
Find or select cast member by name, type, palette, or usage in Score	Edit ➤ Find ➤ Cast Member	Cmd-;	Ctrl-;

Table 4-8: Cast Window Shortcuts (continued)

Action	Command	Mac	Win
Find where used in Score	Select cast member, then Edit ➤ Find ➤ Selection	Cmd-H	Ctrl-H
Exchange cast member used in a sprite[4]	Select sprite, then select cast member, then Edit ➤ Exchange Cast Members, or use Toolbar	Cmd-E	Ctrl-E
Sort cast members by usage in Score, name, size, type	Select at least two cast members then choose Modify ➤ Sort	None	None
Place cast member at center of Stage	Drag *Drag Cast Member* tool in Cast window or media editor to Score	Cmd-Shift-L	Ctrl-Shift-L
Move cast members within Cast window	Select and drag or select, release mouse, and use *Drag Cast Member* tool	None	None
Lay out selected cast members over time	Modify ➤ Cast to Time	Cmd-Shift-Opt-L	Ctrl-Shift-Alt-L

[1] The online Help for "Keyboard Shortcuts" under "Cast window and cast editor shortcuts" is outdated in D6. Ctrl-clicking a thumbnail doesn't edit cast member properties in D5, D6, or D7 as it did in D3 and D4. On the Macintosh, it opens a context-sensitive menu, and under Windows it toggles the selection of discontiguous cast members.
[2] This shortcut was added in D6.0.1.
[3] Use the Home, End, Page Up, and Page Down keys that exist between the numeric keypad and the main keyboard, not the ones on the numeric keypad itself.
[4] Option-double-clicking or Alt-double-clicking does not exchange cast members as claimed in the online Help.

Moving and Copying Cast Members

Director prevents accidental deletion of cast members by disabling Edit ➤ Cut Cast Members (Cmd-X or Ctrl-X) when more than one cast member is selected. Use Edit ➤ Clear Cast Members instead.

Deleting cast members that are used in the Score is fraught with peril. Use File ➤ Find ➤ Cast Members ➤ *Usage* to ensure that the cast members are not used in the Score. Also make sure that they are not used via Lingo.

When you delete a cast member using Edit ➤ Cut Cast Members, Director copies the cast member to the clipboard, which can be slow and may overflow memory for large cast members. If you don't need to paste the cast member, use Edit ➤ Clear Cast Member or the Delete key to delete the cast member instantly. Director prompts you to confirm the deletion only when deleting multiple selected cast members.

Moving cast members in the Cast window

The square *Drag Cast Member* icon (see Figure 4-1) always represents the currently selected cast members. To move the cast members, you need not drag the selection around the Cast window or wait for it to scroll. Instead, use the following:

1. Highlight one or more cast members and release the mouse.
2. Scroll using the keyboard or Cast window scrollbars.
3. Drag the square icon to the destination. It acts as a proxy for the original selection.

You can also drag the square icon from the Cast window or any of the media editor windows (such as the Paint window) to the Stage or Score.

Whenever you move a cast member, Director updates the Score, but won't update any Lingo code. Refer to cast members by name from within Lingo to avoid problems if they move. Cutting and pasting cast members does not maintain the correct Score references, and should be used with caution or not at all.

Copying cast members between movies

When you copy multiple cast members, a *scrap tag* that identifies the original assets' location is placed on the clipboard instead of the actual cast member data.

When copying cast members between two movies, save the source file first, or the scrap tag may point to the wrong stuff.

You can also copy cast members between movies by using an unlinked external castLib as a conduit:

1. Use File ➤ New ➤ Cast to create an unlinked external castLib.
2. Drag the cast members from the first movie's castLib to the conduit castLib.
3. Close the current movie and open the destination movie.
4. Drag the cast members from the conduit castLib to the second movie's castLib.

When copying sprites or frames, Director also transfers any necessary cast members to the new movie, including linked cast members, which remain linked.

You can replace an entire cast library, and the Score will use the new cast members. This is ideal for simplifying project management (or internationalization), but works only if all the cast members in the replacement cast have the same location as those in the original cast. Otherwise, it wreaks havoc.

Common cast member-related errors

These are some of the most common errors when working with cast members:

Editing a cast member used in multiple places
Editing a script, bitmap, field, or text cast member that is used in multiple frames or sprites of the Score causes a universal change whether intended or not. Changing the width, height, or text of a field or text cast member or the *hilite of member* property of a button cast member changes them everywhere throughout the Score. Use separate cast members if necessary.

Incorrect Score references

If you move member(s) in the Cast, the Score will update automatically to point to the cast members' new locations, but there are several actions that can lead to incorrect Score references.

Changing a cast member's position via cutting and pasting will not update the Score. You can (carefully) paste a replacement cast member into the old one's position in the Cast window, but if you copy and paste cast members incorrectly, a Score reference might point to the wrong type of asset. For example, the sound channel may point to a bitmap cast member. Errant script references can be created if you cancel a new script, as described in Example 2-2 in *Lingo in a Nutshell*. This can be very confusing and difficult to debug. See Example 3-9 to detect this type of corruption.

If you delete a cast member that is referenced in the Score, Director won't be able to find it. Director will repeatedly try to load the nonexistent cast member, and this may crash Director. Use Edit ➤ Find ➤ Cast Member ➤ *Usage* to make sure a cast member is not used before deleting it.

Corrupted files or cast members errors

Though not common, it is not exceedingly rare for a file or individual cast member to become corrupted. If a file appears corrupt, use File ➤ Save As or File ➤ Save and Compact to recover it. In severe cases, copy and paste the Score and/or cast members to a new movie. If an individual cast member is corrupted (as indicated by an "Error Unpacking Cast Member" error), replace it with a backup or placeholder. Use Edit ➤ Find ➤ Selection to find where it is used in the Score and to remind you of the nature of the lost cast member. Use Edit ➤ Clear Cast Members instead of Edit ➤ Cut Cast Members to delete corrupted cast members.

Do not use older versions of Norton Utilities on a Mac OS8 HFS+ file partition, as it can corrupt your files.

Memory errors

An "Out of Memory" or "Not Enough Memory To Load This Cast Member" error may indicate that the Score is trying to load a non-existent cast member. If low on memory, use Edit ➤ Clear Cast Members instead of Edit ➤ Cut Cast Members. The latter attempts to copy the item to the clipboard, which is slower and requires more memory. Save the file frequently to free memory consumed by pending changes.

CastLib and Cast Member Lingo

Most Lingo member-related commands accept a cast member reference of the form:

```
member whichMember {of castLib whichCast}
```

where *whichMember* and *whichCast* can be names or numbers, such as:

```
member "Headline"
member "Headline" of castLib 7
member "Background" of castLib "newArt"
member 1 of castLib 3
```

or, in D7 notation:

```
member("Headline")
member("Headline",7)
member("Background", "newArt")
member(1,3)
```

 D7 will not tolerate member references of the form *member (x) of castLib y*. Convert them to *member (x,y)*. See the D7 *ReadMe* file for details.

If the optional castLib is not specified, Director may assume the first (internal) castLib, *the activeCastLib*, or the current castLib of a sprite's associated member depending on the command used, so specify an explicit castLib when in doubt. It is generally a good idea to refer to castLibs by name rather than number in case the order of castLibs changes.

The *erase member* command deletes cast members without a confirmation. The *move member* function does not update the Score notation to reflect the cast member slot changes, which will probably lead to incorrect Score notation.

Access Speed and Name Caching

You can refer to cast members by number, but because cast member numbers may change, you should access members by name. Director always finds the first cast member with the specified name, so you should take care to avoid duplicate cast member names (see Example 4-4).

Prior to Director 5, accessing cast members by name was slow, because Director looked up the cast member each time. As of Version 5, Director caches the names of cast members the first time they are used. Subsequent accesses by cast member name are comparable in speed to access by cast member number. Even so, cast members that appear earlier in the cast are found more quickly the first time when searching by name.

The number of member property is convenient for finding a member by name; it returns −1 if the member is not found:

```
put the number of member "existing member"
-- 5
put the number of member "nonexistent"
-- -1
```

Director does not cache script name references. The following can be very slow:

```
repeat with x = 1 to 100
  set myObj = new (script "Parent Script")
end repeat
```

The following can be significantly faster when creating many script instances:

```
set n = the number of member "Parent Script"
repeat with x = 1 to 100
```

```
        set myObj = new (script n)
    end repeat
```

If you add or delete cast members during authoring, the name cache may become inaccurate. For example, deleting a cast member may not be reflected immediately in *the number of member* property, which should return –1, but instead returns the old member number:

```
put the number of member "deleted member"
-- 7
```

Closing and reopening the file should reset the name cache.

Table 4-9 covers Lingo commands that operate on a castLib or create, move, or delete members within a castLib. See Table 4-10 for a complete list of cast member and sprite properties.

Table 4-9: CastLib and Cast Member Lingo

Lingo	Usage
the activeCastLib	Returns the number of the currently selected castLib. Buggy in D7.0, but fixed in D7.0.1.
castLib *whichCast*	Refers to a castLib within an expression, e.g.: `put the name of castLib whichCast`
the castLibNum of member *whichMember*	Returns the number of the castLib containing a particular cast member. (Read only.)
duplicate (member *fromMember* {of castLib *fromCast*} {, member *toMember* of castLib *toCast*})	Duplicates the specified cast member. Returns new cast member position.
erase (member *whichMember* {of castLib *whichCast*})	Deletes the specified cast member (dangerous!). Always returns 0.
the fileName of castLib *whichCast*	Returns the complete path to a castLib file.[1] Can be set for external castLibs.
findEmpty(member *whichMember* {of castLib *whichCast*})	Finds the next available cast member slot in a castLib. If you don't specify a castLib, it assumes castLib 1, not *the activeCastLib*.
importFileInto member *whichMember* {of castLib *whichCast*}, *fileNameOrURL*	Imports an asset into a castLib. Not recommended at runtime, because it consumes memory.
member *whichMember* {of castLib *whichCast*}	Refers to a member within an expression, e.g., `put the name of member 1 of castLib 1`
member (*whichMember*, *whichCast*)	Refers to a member in D7 notation.
move (member *fromMember* {of castLib *fromCast*} {, member *toMember* of castLib *toCast*})	Moves the specified cast member, but does not update Score notation! Existing cast member in destination will be replaced. Returns new cast member position.

Table 4-9: CastLib and Cast Member Lingo (continued)

Lingo	Usage
the movieFileFreeSize	Returns the number of bytes saved by performing a File ➤ Save and Compact to purge deleted members.
the name of castLib *whichCast*	Specifies the name of the castLib. Can also be set.
new(#*memberType*)	Creates a new cast member on the fly. Returns the member reference of the newly created cast member.
the number of castLib *whichCast*	Returns the number of a castLib specified by name.
the number of castLibs	Returns the totals number of castLibs (both internal and external) attached to the movie.
the number of members of castLib *which-Cast*	Returns the number of the highest cast member slot used in a castLib even if those cast members have been deleted.
the preLoadMode of castLib *whichCast*	Determines when cast members will be loaded. See Modify ➤ Cast ➤ Properties.
save castLib *whichCast, destinationFile*	Stores a castLib to disk. Use it to export an internal castLib. Works with external protected castLibs.
saveMovie *destinationFile*	See Chapter 6, *The Stage and Movies-in-a-Window.*
the selection of castLib *whichCast*	Specifies the cast member(s) highlighted in the specified castLib. Can be tested and set.

1 The *fileName of castLib* of the first internal castLib is the same as the movie's complete path. The *fileName of castLib* of any secondary internal castLibs is EMPTY. The *fileName of castLib* of an external cast is its complete file path. This property can be set for external castLibs, but any changes are ignored if the specified file does not exist. Setting this property for internal castLibs has no effect.

The utility in Example 4-1 displays all the castLibs and indicates whether they are internal or external.

Example 4-1: Listing Internal and External castLibs

```
on showCastLibTypes
  repeat with i = 1 to the number of castLibs
    case (the fileName of castLib i) of
      EMPTY, the moviePath & the movieName:
        set castLibType = "Internal"
      otherwise
        set castLibType = "External"
    end case
    put "CastLib" && i && the name of castLib i && castLibType
  end repeat
end showCastLibTypes
```

Creating New Cast Members on the Fly

The *new(#memberType)* function (see Example 3-7) returns a cast member reference only if it succeeds. It returns error code –2147219501 if the desired type is not available, perhaps because of a missing Xtra. For example, *new(#flash)* will fail if the Flash Asset Xtra is not available. Beware—if you get *#memberType* as a return value, you most likely have an *on new* handler in a movie script that is intercepting the *new()* function call. Any *on new* handlers should reside in score scripts or parent scripts only.

When you create a new cast member on the fly, you may need to set its properties, such as its *picture of member, media of member,* or *text of member.* Note that *new(#script)* creates a movie script. Set *the scriptType of member* to *#score* or *#parent* as needed. Note that *new(#shape)* creates a #rect. Set *the shapeType of member* to *#roundRect, #oval,* or *#line* as needed.

Cast Member and Sprite Properties

Cast member and sprite properties are at the heart of Lingo and Director. A single cast member has a single set of member properties, but each instance in which it is used as a sprite can have a unique set of sprite properties. Sprite properties always pertain to the sprites in the current frame. Sprites that have been manually puppeted while in another frame override the current frame's Score notation.

There is no easy way to read or set the properties of sprites in frames other than the current frame. In D6 and D7, it is best to have a sprite change its own properties when that sprite is finally reached. If necessary, store the new sprite properties in global or property variables that can be accessed in the *on beginSprite* handler, which is called before a sprite is drawn.

To check sprite properties in another frame, use something of the form:

```
set oldFrame = the frame
set the updateLock = TRUE
go frame someFrame
if the property of sprite someSprite = someValue then
  statement(s)
end if
go frame oldFrame
```

Understanding cast member and sprite properties

Most cast member and sprite properties can be set via Lingo, and many read-only properties can be set indirectly or via Director's interface. For example, you can change a cast member's width and height using Modify➤Transform Bitmap, or change the *left, top, right,* and *bottom of sprite* properties by setting *the rect of sprite* property. D7, unlike D6, allows you to set the *left, right, top,* and *bottom of sprite* directly as well. Some properties are available via Lingo only, such as *the media of member* and *the currentTime of sprite* properties.

It is often possible to guess whether a property pertains to cast members, sprites, or both. Cast member properties tend to be attributes that don't change or are intrinsic to the cast member itself, such as *the sampleRate of member.* Sprite properties often pertain to a cast member's use on the Stage at a given time, such as *the loc of sprite*. (A cast member does not have a location on the Stage, so a *loc of member* property would make no sense.) Some properties, such as *the width*, are both cast member and sprite properties. A cast member has an intrinsic width, but it can also be resized on-Stage when it is used as a sprite.

All cast members share some properties, but each cast member type may also have unique properties. Likewise, all sprites share some properties, but each sprite type may also have unique properties. Table 4-10 lists the cast member and sprite properties for each asset type. Be sure to test *the type of member* before testing asset-specific properties, such as:

```
if the type of member whichMember = #shape then
  -- We're sure it is a shape, so we can check the shapeType
  if the shapeType of member whichMember = #oval then
    put "We found an oval"
  end if
end if
```

To check if a cast member is empty, use:

```
if the type of member whichMember = #empty then...
```

To check if a sprite is empty, use:

```
if the memberNum of sprite whichSprite = 0 then...
```

or:

```
if the type of sprite whichSprite = 0 then...
```

Lingo Syntax for Cast Member and Sprite Properties

Although not shown explicitly, all cast member and sprite properties shown in Table 4-10 are specified as:

```
the property of member whichMember
the property of member whichMember of castLib whichCast
the property of sprite whichSprite
```

In D7, you can use the equivalent dot notation:

```
member(whichMember).property
member(whichMember, whichCast).property
sprite(whichSprite).property
```

Don't confuse member properties with *the member of sprite* and *memberNum of sprite* properties, which determine a sprite's cast member (such as a bitmap) and can be changed at runtime to change a sprite's appearance.

To refer to a sprite's member, use *the member of sprite* or *memberNum of sprite* property:

```
set the member of sprite (the currentSpriteNum) = ¬
    member whichMember
set the memberNum of sprite (the currentSpriteNum) = ¬
    someMemberNumber
```

In D7, you can use:

```
sprite(the currentSpriteNum).member = member whichMember
sprite(the currentSpriteNum).memberNum = someMemberNumber
```

The *number of member*, *member of sprite*, and *memberNum of sprite* properties all differ. *The member of sprite* uniquely identifies a cast member by both its castLibNum and position (*memberNum*) within that castLib. The *memberNum of sprite* is the integer slot number of a cast member, but does not uniquely identify a cast member, because it doesn't include the castLibNum. The *number of member* property converts a member reference into a unique integer regardless of its castLib.

 Adding an integer (*n*) to the *number of member* or *memberNum of sprite* property will indicate a cast member *n* slots away from the original member. Adding an integer to *the member of sprite* doesn't work and results in a zero value.

Note that two sprites may have the same *memberNum*, but actually be two different cast members in two different castLibs. (If using only one castLib, this isn't an issue.)

```
put the member of sprite 11
-- (member 5 of castLib 2)
put the member of sprite 12
-- (member 5 of castLib 1)
put the memberNum of sprite 11
-- 5
put the memberNum of sprite 12
-- 5
```

For backward compatibility the obsolete *castNum of sprite* property returns a unique number identifying the cast member. For members in the first castLib, it is identical to *memberNum of sprite* property. For members in subsequent castLibs, it is equal to:

```
(the castLibNum of sprite) * 65536 + the memberNum of sprite
```

For example:

```
put the member of sprite 11
-- (member 5 of castLib 2)
put the castNum of sprite 11
-- 131077
```

Use *the number of the member of sprite* instead of the obsolete *the castNum of sprite* to obtain this unique number:

```
put the number of the member of sprite 11
-- 131077
```

The *number of member* property reports a different value in movies updated from D4 that used a Shared Cast than it ordinarily does for movies created from scratch in D6. See "Shared Cast versus external cast libraries" earlier in this chapter.

The obsolete *cast of member* and *cast of sprite* properties are not meaningful and should not be used.

A nonexistent member returns the number –1:

```
put the number of member "Nonexistent"
-- -1
```

In D7 notation, *member ("nonexistent").number* generates an error for non existent members.

If a sprite channel is empty, its *member* and *memberNum* properties are as such:

```
put the memberNum of sprite 50
-- 0
put the member of sprite 50
-- (member 0 of castLib 0)
```

You'll often see this *incorrect* attempt to change a sprite's cast member:

```
set the member of sprite 5 = the member of sprite 5 + 1
```

Adding an integer to *the member of sprite* fails because *the member of sprite* is a complex structure. Adding an integer to it performs an implicit type conversion that results in a value of zero!

```
put the member of sprite 5
-- (member 2 of castLib 1)
put the member of sprite 5 + 1
-- 0
```

However, adding an integer to *the memberNum of sprite* works because *the memberNum of sprite* is an integer:

```
put the memberNum of sprite 5
-- 2
put the memberNum of sprite 5 + 1
-- 3
```

Use the following to switch a sprite to display the next cast member in the same castLib:

```
set the memberNum of sprite 5 = the memberNum of sprite 5 + 1
```

The previous example calculates *the memberNum of sprite 5*, and then increments it by one. It does not calculate *the memberNum of sprite 6*.

Use parentheses to refer to a different sprite number, in this case, sprite 6:

```
set the memberNum of sprite 5 = the memberNum of sprite (5 + 1)
```

Set *the member of sprite* instead of *the memberNum of sprite* to switch to a new cast member in a different castLib:

```
set the member of sprite 5 = member 7 of castLib 3
```

The *memberNum of member* property always reflects the offset of the cast member slot from the beginning of its castLib. It doesn't change unless you move the cast member in the Cast window. The *memberNum of sprite* doesn't change unless you set it via Lingo (or edit the Score or move the cast member while the movie is halted).

The *castNum of sprite, number of member, member of sprite,* and *castLibNum of sprite* properties can vary with the number or order of castLibs attached to a given movie. A single external castLib may have a different castLib number in two movies to which it is attached.

To refer to a sprite itself within a script attached to the sprite use *the currentSpriteNum,* such as:

```
on mouseDown
  set the loc of sprite (the currentSpriteNum) = the clickLoc
end mouseDown
```

You can also use *the spriteNum of me* property (note the required *me* parameter):

```
on mouseDown me
  set the loc of sprite (the spriteNum of me) = the clickLoc
end mouseDown
```

This can also be rewritten as follows (note that *spriteNum* is declared as a property variable):

```
property spriteNum
on mouseDown me
  set the loc of sprite spriteNum = the clickLoc
end mouseDown
```

Some properties, such as *the scale of sprite* and *the duration of member,* use different units when applied to different asset types. Others differ markedly for internal and external assets (*the fileName of member* is EMPTY for internal members, but contains the external filename of linked assets; conversely, *the media of member* is meaningful for internal members only). Some properties are stored permanently in the Score; others such as the *rect of sprite* and *the quad of sprite* are secondary properties derived from the Scored properties at runtime.

Setting member and sprite properties

Setting a member property makes a permanent change to the target cast member. Member properties are usually set via *Cast Member Properties* dialog boxes instead of Lingo. The latter is most useful when writing authoring-time utilities. Setting member properties at runtime is allowed, but not necessarily reliable. For example, you cannot reliably change the *directToStage of member* digital video property at runtime. Instead of changing the property at runtime, create two versions of the same cast member with different values for the *directToStage* property and swap a sprite's *member of sprite* as necessary to switch between them.

Auto-puppeted properties and manually puppeted sprites that have been unpuppeted get reset automatically only when a change occurs in the Score. See "Auto-puppets versus manual puppets" in Chapter 1, *How Director Works,* for details.

If possible, set sprite properties instead of member properties at runtime. For example, set a field's *editable of sprite* property rather than its *editable of member* property. Member properties usually update immediately. Sprite properties don't update until the Stage is redrawn using *updateStage* or by the playback head advancing.

Because edits to fields affect the cast member, they appear immediately. (This is a problem in Score Recording even when *the updateLock* is TRUE.) When setting member properties at runtime, you can force Director to recognize them by setting the *picture* or *media of member* property to itself, as shown in Example 4-2.

Example 4-2: Setting Member Properties at Runtime

```
set the regPoint of member "myBitmap" = point (50, 38)
set the picture  of member "myBitmap" = ¬
  the picture of member "myBitmap"
set the loop of member "myFilmLoop" = TRUE
set the media of member "myFilmLoop" = ¬
  the media of member "myFilmLoop"
```

By contrast, sprite properties are intended to be both read and set at runtime. Setting a sprite property at runtime via Lingo causes that setting to temporarily override the Score notation. Change a sprite's properties permanently by editing it in the Score or on the Stage when the movie is halted. Lingo changes to sprite properties are stored permanently only if they are made during a Score Recording session.

Table 4-10 is a complete list of member and sprite properties, listed alphabetically by asset type (see the remaining chapters for frame, window, movie, and system properties). The table does not repeat the common properties shared by all cast members (excluding *#empty* ones). Not all member and sprite properties are settable, and all properties are not meaningful for all member types. For example, the *editable* property applies only to text and field assets. Properties such as *rect*, *width*, *height*, and *loc*, apply only to members that have a pictorial representation (bitmaps, shapes, text, video, Flash, etc., but not SWA, transitions, palettes, fonts, or scripts). Obsolete properties (the *cast* and *castType of member* and the *cast*, *castNum* and *immediate of sprite*) are omitted.

Table 4-10: Cast Member and Sprite Properties

Media Type	Cast Member Properties	Sprite Properties
All types (prior to D7)	castLibNum, fileName,[1] height, loaded, media, mediaReady, member, memberNum, modified, name, number, picture, purgePriority, rect, regPoint, scriptText, size, type, width	backColor, blend, bottom,castLibNum, constraint, cursor, foreColor, height, ink, left, loc, locH, locV, member, memberNum, moveableSprite, puppet, scoreColor, scriptInstanceList, scriptNum, rect, right, stretch, top, trails, type, tweened, visible, visibility, width
New properties in D7	thumbnail	bgColor, blendLevel, color, endFrame, flipH, flipV, locZ, quad, rotation, scriptList, skew, startFrame, volume

Table 4-10: Cast Member and Sprite Properties (continued)

Media Type	Cast Member Properties	Sprite Properties
#ActiveX[2]	Each imported ActiveX control has its own custom member properties.	Each imported ActiveX control has its own custom sprite properties.
#animGIF[3]	directToStage, linked, fixedRate, playbackMode	See common properties.
#bitmap[4]	alphaThreshold,[3,] depth, dither,[3] palette, paletteRef, picture, useAlpha[3]	See common properties.
#btned[2] (obsolete in D7)	behavesLikeToggle, enabled, initialToggleState, labelString	behavesLikeToggle, enabled, isToggle
#button	alignment, backColor, buttonType, font, fontSize, fontStyle, foreColor, hilite, lineHeight, text	See common properties.
#cursor[2]	automask, cast memberList, cursorSize, hotSpot, interval, type	N/A (see *the cursor of sprite* for other sprite types)
#digitalVideo (used for QT2 in D6, and AVI only in D7)	center, controller, crop, cuePointNames, cuePointTimes, digitalVideoType, directToStage, duration,[5] frameRate, loop, pausedAtStart, preLoad, sound,[6] startTime, stopTime, track, tracks, timeScale, video	currentTime,[7] mostRecentCuePoint,[7] movieRate, movieTime, startTime, stopTime, volume[7]
#empty	memberNum, number, name, type (other common properties not supported)	See common properties (most evaluate to zero for empty sprites).
#field[8]	alignment, autoTab, backColor, border, boxDropShadow, boxType, dropShadow, editable, font, fontSize, fontStyle, foreColor, lineCount, lineHeight, margin, pageHeight, picture,[9] rect, scrollTop, text, wordWrap	editable, rect
#filmloop	center, crop, loop, media, sound, regPoint (read-only)	See common properties.
#flash[2,10]	actionsEnabled, bufferSize, buttonsEnabled, clickMode, eventPassMode, fileName, fixedRate, frameCount, frameRate, linked, loop, pathName, pausedAtStart, percentStreamed, playBackMode, posterFrame, preload, quality, rotation, sound, state, streamMode, streamSize, type, URL Also valid for #vectorShape: broadcastProps, centerRegPoint, defaultRect, defaultRectMode, directToStage, flashRect, imageEnabled, originH, originMode, originPoint, originV, regPoint, scale, scaleMode, static, viewH, viewPoint, viewScale, viewV	bytesStreamed, buttonsEnabled, bytesStreamed, clickMode, directToStage, eventPassMode, fixedRate, frame, loop, mouseOverButton, originH, originMode, pausedAtStart, playBackMode, playing, quality, sound Also valid for #vectorShape: imageEnabled, originPoint, originV, rotation, scale, scaleMode, static, viewH, viewPoint, viewScale, viewV

CastLibs & Sprites

Table 4-10: Cast Member and Sprite Properties (continued)

Media Type	Cast Member Properties	Sprite Properties
#font[3]	bitmapSizes, characterSet, font, fontStyle, name, originalFont, height, width	N/A (never used as a sprite)
#movie	center, crop, loop, scriptsEnabled, sound	See common properties.
#ole	See common properties.	See common properties.
#palette	See common properties (palette and paletteRef not supported).	N/A (never used as a sprite)
#picture	picture (palette and paletteRef not supported)	See common properties.
#QD3D_xtra[2]	See Table 16-19.	See Table 16-19.
#QuickTime-Media[2,11]	center, controller, crop, cuePointNames, cuePointTimes, directToStage, duration, fileName, frameRate, invertMask, isVRmovie, loop, mask, pausedAtStart, preload, regPoint, rotation, scale, sound, timeScale, translation, type, video	currentTime,[7] duration, isVRmovie, loopBounds, mostrecentCuePoint,[7] mouseLevel, movieRate, movieTime, mRate, mTime, rotation, scale, startTime, stopTime, timeScale, translation, volume,[7] volumeLevel, VRfieldOfView, VRhotSpotEnterCallback, VRhotSpotExitCallback, VRmotionQuality, VRmovedCallback, VRnode, VRnodeEnterCallback, VRnodeExitCallback, VRnodeType, VRpan, VRstaticQuality, VRtilt, VRtriggerCallback, VRwarpMode
#richtext (obsolete in D7)	pageHeight, picture, scrollTop, text (authoring only) (other properties available for #field members are *not* supported)	See common properties.
#script	scriptText, scriptType	Scripts themselves are never sprites, but can be attached to sprites (see *the scriptNum, scriptList,* and *scriptInstanceList of sprite* properties for other sprite types).
#shape	filled, lineDirection,[3] lineSize, pattern, shapeType	blend, blendLevel, lineSize
#sound	channelCount, cuePointNames, cuePointTimes, loop, sampleRate, sampleSize	currentTime of sound,[7] mostRecentCuePoint of sound,[7] volume of sound[7]

Table 4-10: Cast Member and Sprite Properties (continued)

Media Type	Cast Member Properties	Sprite Properties
#SWA[2]	bitsPerSample, bitRate, copyrightInfo, cuePoint-Names, cuePointTimes, duration,[5] numChannels, percentPlayed, percentStreamed, preLoadBuffer, preLoadTime, sampleRate, soundChannel, state, streamName, url, volume	currentTime,[7] mostRecentCuePoint,[7] volume[7]
#text[3]	alignment, alpha, antiAlias, antiAliasThreshold, autoTab, backColor, bgColor, border, bottom-Spacing, boxType, charSpacing, color, drop-Shadow, editable, firstIndent, fixedLineSpace, font, fontSize, fontStyle, foreColor, lineCount, line-Height, HTML, hyperlinks, leftIndent, lineSpace, kerning, kerningThreshold, margin, pageHeight, paragraph, picture, preRender, rightIndent, RTF, saveBitmap, scrollTop, selection, selectedText, tabCount, tabs, text, topSpacing, use Hypertext-Styles, wordwrap	editable, rect
#transition	changeArea, chunkSize, duration,[5] transitionType	N/A (never used as a sprite)
#vectorShape[3]	antiAlias, backgroundColor, closed, endColor, fill-Color, fillCycles, fillDirection, fillMode, fillOffset, fillScale, gradientType, strokeColor, strokeWidth, vertexList See also #flash entry.	See also #flash entry.
#xtra	Xtra-dependent. See common properties.	Xtra-dependent. See common properties.

[1] See the *streamName of member* and *url of member* properties for SWA cast members.
[2] Requires an Xtra.
[3] New in D7.
[4] The *hilite of member* property does not apply to bitmaps and does not coincide with the *Hilight When Clicked* option in the Bitmap Cast Member Properties dialog box (there is no Lingo equivalent).
[5] The *duration of member* has different time units for digital video, SWA, and transition cast members.
[6] The *sound of member* is a Boolean property of digital video cast members. For any other type member, it simply returns (*sound memberNum*).
[7] Use the *currentTime of sound, mostRecentCuePoint of sound*, and *volume of sound* properties when referring to #sound cast members in the sound channels. Use the *currentTime of sprite, mostRecentCuePoint of sprite*, and *volume of sprite* properties when referring to #digitalVideo, #QuickTimeMedia, and #SWA cast members in the sprite channels.
[8] The *textAlign, textFont, textHeight, textSize*, and *textStyle of member* properties for field cast members are obsolete and have been replaced by the *alignment, font, lineHeight, fontSize*, and *fontStyle* properties.
[9] The Shockwave 6.0.1 plug-in does not support the *picture of member* property for fields.
[10] The author-time Flash Xtra's *showProps(member)* and *showProps(sprite)* methods list the Xtras' supported member and sprite properties.
[11] Use the *movieRate, movieTime*, and *volume of sprite* properties in D7, and the *mRate, mTime*, and *volumeLevel* of sprite properties in D6.5. The VR-related sprite properties apply only if the *isVRmovie of member* property is TRUE. In D7, the sprite properties beginning with "VR" are deprecated and replaced by properties of the same name with out the "VR" prefix, such as *fieldOfView, hotSpotEnterCallback*, and so on.

Cast member and sprite property idiosyncrasies

Two or more sprite properties may not always return consistent information, and some properties return the wrong information. There are a number of idiosyncrasies pertaining to specific properties:

CastType versus type and memberType

The obsolete *castType of member* property returns *#text* for field cast members, whereas the *type of member* property returns *#field* for the same cast members. In D7, the *#text* type was recycled. A *type of member* of *#text* now identifies a new asset type that replaces *#richText* in D7. The misdocumented *memberType of member* doesn't exist and shouldn't be used. The *type of sprite* property returns 0 for empty sprites, and 16 for all other sprites; use this to find the type of asset associated with a sprite:

```
put the type of the member of sprite whichSprite
```

Width and height of graphic sprites

When swapping cast members for a sprite, the *height* and *width of sprite* may not update properly. Use *the height of the rect of sprite x* and *the width of the rect of sprite x* instead.

Width and height of field and text sprites

Although the properties of each sprite instance are usually unique, the *width of sprite* and *height of sprite* properties can not be set independently for different sprites created from the same field or text cast member. All field or text sprites created from a single cast member use the same width and height.

Hilite of sprite for buttons

The *hilite of member* of a button can be set only on a cast member basis. There is no *hilite of sprite* property. You must create separate cast members to create independent buttons.

Video sprite properties

The *center, controller, crop,* or *directToStage* properties cannot be set for digital video *sprites*. These can only be set on a cast member basis. Duplicate the cast member to apply different member properties.

Rich text properties lacking Lingo access

Director 6 does not provide Lingo access to the rich text cast member properties that are accessible for fields, such as *alignment, font, fontSize,* and *fontStyle*. These attributes can be set for multiple selected rich text cast members using the Text Inspector, Modify ➤ Font, or Modify ➤ Paragraph. Additional attributes must be set individually using the cast member properties dialog box. See Chapter 12, *Text and Fields*. In D7, use new *#text* members for which runtime properties are settable.

Changing cast member and sprite properties

Table 4-11 lists the convenient places to alter different sprite and cast member properties. Changing sprite properties in the *prepareMovie* and *startMovie* handlers is not reliable.

Table 4-11: When and Where to Change Member and Sprite Properties

To Change Sprite Properties When:	Use These Types of Handlers:
Playback head enters a sprite span	*on beginSprite*
Playback head leaves a sprite span	*on endSprite*
Cursors rolls over sprite	*on mouseEnter, on mouseWithin,* and *on mouseLeave*
User clicks on sprite	*on mouseUp, on mouseDown, on rightMouseUp,* or *on rightMouseDown*
Before frame is drawn	*on prepareFrame* (or *on stepFrame* if sprite is included in *the actorList*)
After frame is drawn	*on exitFrame* (avoid *on enterFrame*)
No other events are being processed	*on idle*

 When you puppet a sprite manually, its initial values are taken from the frame in which you issue the *puppetSprite* command. Avoid puppeting an empty sprite channel. Use an offscreen placeholder sprite, if necessary, and then set the *loc of sprite* to bring it on-Stage.

If you puppet an empty sprite channel, you must manually set the *width, height,* and *member of sprite* properties, and must often set the *loc* and *foreColor of sprite* properties, too.

In D7, the new *locZ of sprite* property (which defaults to the channel number but can be increased or decreased) changes the order in which sprites are layered. In prior versions, you cannot change a sprite's z-ordering directly. You could simulate it by swapping sprite properties with a sprite in a different channel. For example, to create a sprite that appears in front of all other sprites, you can set the properties of a placeholder sprite in the highest numbered channel.

Changing a Sprite's Properties Based on User Actions

It is common to modify a sprite's properties to make it respond to user actions. For example, you might change the cast member of a sprite when the user rolls over it or clicks the mouse. You should avoid hardcoding cast member names and sprite channel numbers, and instead create generalized handlers as described in Chapters 1 and 9 in *Lingo in a Nutshell.* You can use the Lingo properties *the currentSpriteNum, the clickOn, the spriteNum of me, the rollover, the member of sprite,* and *the memberNum of sprite* to create flexible handlers that will work when attached to any sprite in any channel.

Example 4-3 assumes that a highlighted and depressed version of the sprite's cast member are stored in the next two cast member positions. It highlights the button when the mouse rolls on the sprite and shows a depressed state when the mouse button is pressed. It handles the case where the users rolls on and off the sprite while holding the mouse down, and resets the sprite when the mouse rolls off or is released. Place this in a sprite script and attach it to a sprite.

Example 4-3: Multistate Button Behavior

```
property pOrigMember

on beginSprite
  set pOrigMember = the member of sprite (the currentSpriteNum)
end

on mouseEnter
  if the stillDown then
    set addCast = 2
  else
    set addCast = 1
  end if
  set the memberNum of sprite (the currentSpriteNum) = ¬
    the memberNum of pOrigMember + addCast
end

on mouseLeave
  set the member of sprite (the currentSpriteNum) = pOrigMember
end

on mouseDown
  set the memberNum of sprite (the currentSpriteNum) = ¬
    the memberNum of pOrigMember + 2
end

on mouseUp
  set the member of sprite (the currentSpriteNum) = pOrigMember
  go next
end
```

Cast Utilities

The following sections contain utilities that manage cast members.

Checking for duplicate cast member names

In Example 3-9, you saw how to cycle through every sprite channel of every frame of the Score. In this example, we cycle through each cast member of each castLib. This can be used as the basis for other utilities that perform some check on all the cast members.

Example 4-4 creates a Lingo list of all the cast member names. Using the *examineList()* utility from Example 3-2, we can check the cast member names for duplicates or potentially extraneous spaces:

```
examineList (buildCastmemberNamesList())
```

Example 4-4: Checking for Troublesome Cast Member Names

```
on buildCastmemberNamesList
  set nameList = []
  -- Create a list containing castmember names
  repeat with i = 1 to the number of castLibs
    repeat with j = 1 to the number of members of castLib i
      -- Find cast members with names
      set thisMember = member j of castLib i
      if the type of thisMember <> #empty then
        if the name of thisMember <> EMPTY then
          add (nameList, the name of thisMember)
        end if
      end if
    end repeat
  end repeat
  return nameList
end buildCastmemberNamesList
```

Finding linked cast members

The utility in Example 4-5 finds all cast members that have links to external files and reports if the specified path is not in the same folder as the current Director movie. Add clauses to the *case* statement as needed to handle the different properties for linked file paths.

Example 4-5: Checking for Linked Cast Members

```
on checkLinks
  -- Create a list containing castmember names
  repeat with i = 1 to the number of castLibs
    repeat with j = 1 to the number of members of castLib i
      set thisMember = member j of castLib i
      case (the type of thisMember) of
        #SWA: set linkPath = the streamName of thisMember
        #flash: set linkPath = the pathName of thisMember
        otherwise: set linkPath = the fileName of thisMember
      end case
      if linkPath <> EMPTY then
        if (linkPath starts the moviePath) then
          put "Linked" && thisMember & ":" && linkPath && "OK"
        else
          put "Linked" && thisMember & ":" && linkPath && ¬
              "not in same folder as DIR movie"
        end if
      end if
    end repeat
  end repeat
end checkLinks
```

Reader Exercise: Modify Example 4-5 to check whether the specified files exist and to verify that the file paths obey the Windows 3.1 file naming requirements. You might use an appropriate Xtra to copy the files to the local directory, and reset the *fileName, streamName,* or *pathName of member* property. You might even sort the files into different subdirectories based on their media type. You can also modify the example to find and check linked castLibs using *the fileName of castLib* property.

External file sizes

The *size of member* property does not return meaningful data for most externally linked files. To obtain the actual size of an external file on disk, use Example 4-6, which returns the size in KB. It requires the FileIO Xtra and returns –43 as an error code if the file cannot be found and other negative numbers for other errors. (See Chapter 14 and Appendix E, *Error Messages and Codes*, in *Lingo in a Nutshell*.)

Example 4-6: Determining External File Sizes

```
on getSize extMember
  -- Returns the file size of an external asset, in KB
  -- This assumes that the FileIO Xtra is installed
  set fileObj = new (Xtra "FileIO")
  if objectP(fileObj) then
    -- Get the file's length
    openFile (fileObj, the fileName of member extMember, 1)
    set errCode = status (fileObj)
    -- A negative code indicates an error
    if errCode < 0 then
      return errCode
    else
      set fileSize = getLength (fileObj) / 1024.0
      set fileObj = 0
      return fileSize
    end if
  else
    -- Make up an error code if new() fails.
    return -1
  end if
end getSize
```

Importing linked cast members

The utility in Example 4-7 imports linked bitmap and sound cast members that are less than 1024 KB (1 MB) into the cast. It uses the *getSize()* utility from Example 4-6 to calculate the size of the external file. Note that it preserves the cast member name, which is ordinarily destroyed by *importFileInto*. It should be used during authoring, not at runtime, and requires the FileIO Xtra as well as the MIX Xtras to import any linked data types. I've used a *case* statement so that you can easily modify it to import other data types. See also Example 4-5.

Example 4-7: Importing Small Externally Linked Files

```
on importLinks
  -- This iterates through all members in all castLibs
  repeat with i = 1 to the number of castLibs
    repeat with j = 1 to the number of members of castLib i
```

Example 4-7: Importing Small Externally Linked Files (continued)

```
        set thisMember = member j of castLib i
        set linkPath = the fileName of thisMember
        if linkPath <> EMPTY then
          set size = getSize(thisMember)
          -- This only imports small #bitmaps and #sounds
          -- and does not import other data types
          case (the type of thisMember) of
            #bitmap, #sound:
              -- If no error and it is less than 1024 KB
              if size > 0 and size <= 1024
                put "Importing" && thisMember && linkPath
                -- importFileInto destroys name, so save it
                set oldName = the name of thisMember
                importFileInto (thisMember, linkPath)
                set the name of thisMember = oldName
              else if size = -43 then
                -- The file may have been too big to import. Print
                -- an error message if the file was not found.
                put "Couldn't find" && thisMember && linkPath
              end if
          end case
        end if
      end repeat
    end repeat
  put "Done Importing links"
end importLinks
```

Counting cast members

The *number of members of castLib* property reports the last used member, not the number of occupied cast member positions. Example 4-8 counts the actual number of used cast members. I've used a *case* statement so that you can easily modify it to count cast members of specific data types (you'll need additional variables besides *n*).

Example 4-8: Counting Cast Members in a castLib

```
on countMembers
  -- Count the number of occupied castmember slots
  repeat with i = 1 to the number of castLibs
    set n = 0
    repeat with j = 1 to the number of members of castLib i
      case (the type of member j of castLib i)
        #empty: nothing
        otherwise: set n = n + 1
      end case
    end repeat
    put "CastLib" && i && "has" && n && "cast members" && ¬
    "(last member:" && the number of members of castLib i & ")"
  end repeat
end countMembers
```

CHAPTER 5

Coordinates, Alignment, and Registration Points

Director can determine the position of the cursor, sprites, mouse clicks, the Stage, and more, but the coordinates are not all relative to the same origin. Whatever the reference frame (the Stage, monitor, or bounding box of a cast member), the origin (0,0) is always at the upper left. All coordinates are measured in pixels.

Horizontal coordinates increase left to right. Vertical coordinate *increase* as you move *down* (points that are lower on the screen have a larger vertical coordinate, although this is erroneously inverted on Windows NT in D7.0). Negative coordinates are above and/or to the left of the origin.

See Tables 3-2 and 13-4, and *http://www.zeusprod.com/nutshell/d7.html* for a full discussion of D7's new vector shapes, and the *rotation, scale, skew, flipH, flipV,* and *quad* properties.

Registration Points and Alignment

The *left, top, right, bottom, width, height,* and *rect of sprite* properties describe a sprite's bounding rectangle on Stage, but the *loc, locH,* and *locV of sprite* properties represent the location of a single representative point—the registration point of the sprite's associated cast member. D7's new *locZ of sprite* property determines the drawing order of sprites.

Registration Points

For bitmaps created in Director, the *regPoint of member* is set to the center of whatever you've drawn at the time you first close the Paint window, flip to a different cast member, or click the regPoint tool (see Figure 13-6). Once fixed, the regPoint does not move when you edit the bitmap or when you duplicate the entire cast member. Change a bitmap's regPoint in the Paint window using the regPoint tool. Double-clicking the regPoint tool centers the regPoint automatically. A bitmap's regPoint can reside outside the bounding box of the bitmap itself. The regPoint is fixed for most asset types; the regPoint for a digital video is always its center, and the regPoint for a field, shape, or D6 rich text cast member is always its upper-left corner. The regPoint for D7 text members defaults to the upper left, but can be set via Lingo. Figure 5-1 shows a cast member and its regPoint.

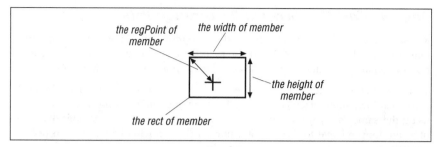

Figure 5-1: Member coordinates

The *regPoint of member* property reflects the position of the member's regPoint relative to the upper-left corner of the bounding box of the bitmap in the Paint window. The *locH, locV,* and *loc of sprite* properties reflect the position of the regPoint of the sprite's cast member and are relative to the upper left of the Stage, as are the other coordinates shown in Figure 5-2.

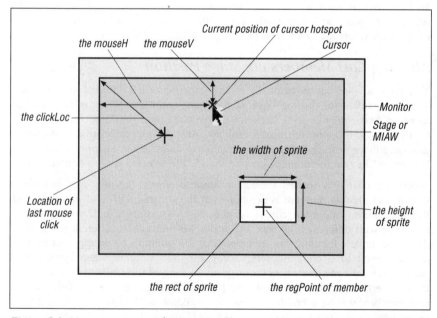

Figure 5-2: Mouse, cursor, and sprite coordinates

The *regPoint* of a bitmap cast member used with the *cursor* or *cursor of sprite* command is used as the cursor's hotspot.

Director's *constraint of sprite* property limits a sprite's location based on the bounding box of another sprite. It constrains the *loc* of a sprite (i.e., the location of its regPoint), but the constrained sprite's bounding box may extend well beyond the constraining sprite's area. Examples 5-5, 5-6, and 5-7 check whether a sprite's *rect* is within a particular area.

Aligning Cast Members via Registration Points

Registration settings in Photoshop or other programs are ignored when importing bitmaps into Director. Use Photocaster (*http://www.medialab.com*) to maintain registration among different paint layers when importing a Photoshop document.

You can align cast members on Stage by aligning their regPoints manually in the Paint window, then placing their regPoints at the same location on Stage (i.e., using the same *loc of sprite*). You can move an individual cast member that's part of a film loop relative to the rest of a film loop by moving its registration point in the Paint window or setting its *regPoint of member*.

Director displays bitmaps with their regPoints centered in the Paint windows so that you can use Onion Skinning to align the regPoints of multiple cast members. In practice, using Onion Skinning to align registration points manually is exceedingly difficult. Refer to the excellent *Onion Skinning* ShowMe movie in the D6 online Help for details. Remember that moving the regPoint in one direction generally offsets the graphic in the *opposite* direction.

Many idiosyncrasies regarding the use of the Paint window and its effect on the registration point are discussed under "Registration point and selections" in Chapter 13, *Graphics, Color, and Palettes*.

Aligning Cast Members via Stage Position

You can also align sprites manually on the Stage by setting different *locH* and *locV* values, regardless of the regPoints of their cast members. When tweaking alignment on Stage relative to a background template, use the Mute buttons in the Score to toggle a sprite channel's visibility. Any movement relative to the background will be readily apparent. Remember to unmute the channel when done. Use the "+" key on the numeric keypad to hide the selected sprite's handles.

When you change a sprite's *member of sprite* property, the new cast member is drawn such that its regPoint is positioned at the original *locH* and *locV*, not such that the sprite's upper-left corner on the Stage is maintained. If you swap cast members with different regPoints, the sprite will move to a different position on the Stage. Ensure that any cast members that are going to be swapped at runtime are registered to a common reference point. Swapping between bitmaps and digital video cast members is not a problem, as long as the regPoint for the bitmap is at its center (the default). Swapping between bitmaps and shape, field, or text cast members will be a problem unless the regPoint for the bitmap is moved to its upper-left corner (not the default) or the *locH* and *locV* are adjusted to compensate for the offset, as shown in Example 5-1. The regPoint for D7 text members can be adjusted to match the bitmap's regPoint instead.

Director Coordinates—Points and Rects

Before going any further, you should understand two special data types, *points* and *rects* (rectangles), which are both types of lists. Many functions and properties return points and rects or require them as parameters. In D7, points and rects can contain floating-point coordinates. In prior versions, coordinates are always converted to integers.

Point and rect lists

A point is a list of two coordinates in *x, y* order, such as:

```
put the clickLoc
-- point(107, 69)
```

A rect is a list of four coordinates in *left, top, right, bottom* order, such as:

```
put the rect of the stage
-- rect(96, 72, 736, 552)
```

A rect can also be specified as two points, but is immediately translated into the *left, top, right, bottom* form:

```
put rect(point(0, 0), point(640, 480))
-- rect(0, 0, 640, 480)
```

You can access the elements in a rect or point like any other list, such as:

```
set xCoord = getAt (the clickLoc, 1)
set yCoord = getAt (the clickLoc, 2)
set leftEdge = getAt (the rect of window 1, 1)
set topEdge  = getAt (the rect of window 1, 2)
```

or, in D7 notation:

```
xCoord = the clickLoc[1]
yCoord = the clickLoc[2]
rightEdge = window(1).rect[3]
bottomEdge = window(1).rect[4]
```

You can also access the elements using the undocumented point properties (*locH, locV*) and rect properties (*left, top, right,* and *bottom*), such as:

```
set xCoord = the locH of the clickLoc
set yCoord = the locV of the clickLoc
set leftEdge = the left of the rect of window 1
set topEdge  = the top  of the rect of window 1
```

or, in D7, notation:

```
xCoord = the clickLoc.locH
ycoord = the clickLoc.locV
leftEdge = window(1).rect.left
rightEdge = window(1).rect.right
```

You can determine the size of a rect using the undocumented rect properties *width* and *height*:

```
put the width of the rect of the stage
-- 640
put the height of the rect of the stage
-- 480
```

You can determine whether a list is a point or rect using the *ilk()* function:

```
put ilk (the clickLoc, #point)
-- 1
put ilk (the clickLoc)
-- #point
put ilk (rect(point(0, 0), point(640, 480)), #rect)
-- 1
put ilk (the rect of the stage)
-- #rect
```

Note that the while some commands can accept any four-coordinate list in lieu of a rect, these alternatives are not identified as rects by the *ilk()* function:

```
put ilk ([0, 0, 640, 480], #rect)
-- 0
put ilk (list(0, 0, 640, 480), #rect)
-- 0
```

The older QTVR 1.0 Xtra specifies rectangles as a string of four coordinates in quotes, such as `"50, 75, 120, 250"`, not as a true Lingo rect structure.

Prior to D7, you cannot directly set a sprite's *left, right, top,* or *bottom of sprite* coordinates. In D7, setting one of these properties will stretch the sprite's width or height accordingly. Example 5-1 positions a sprite's upper left at the specified point regardless of the position of the cast member's regPoint or whether the sprite is stretched.

Example 5-1: Positioning the Upper Left of a Sprite

```
on setSpriteUpperLeft s, leftCoord, topCoord
  -- s is the sprite number. leftCoord and topCoord are
  -- the coordinates of the desired location.
  -- Determine the offset of the upper-left corner from regPoint
  set offset = the loc of sprite s - ¬
     point(the left of sprite s, the top of sprite s)
  set the loc of sprite s = point(leftCoord, topCoord) + offset
end setSpriteUpperLeft
```

The offset from the upper left of the sprite to the regPoint of the sprite is calculated using the *left, top,* and *loc of sprite* properties. The offset is equivalent to *the regPoint of member* only if the sprite is not stretched.

Geometric examples

Example 5-2 calculates the area of the specified rectangle or two points that define a rectangle. It accepts the coordinates as either a rect, a list of four coordinates, four separate integers, two points, or two lists of two coordinates.

Example 5-2: Calculating a Rectangle's Area

```
on rectArea param1, param2
  set error = FALSE
  if the paramCount = 1 then
    -- User specified a rect, or a list or four points
    set rect1 = param(1)
    if listP(rect1) then
      if ilk (rect1, #rect) or count (rect1) = 4 then
        set point1 = point(getAt(rect1, 1), getAt(rect1, 2))
        set point2 = point(getAt(rect1, 3), getAt(rect1, 4))
      else
        set error = TRUE
      end if
    end if
  else if the paramCount = 2 then
    -- User specified two points
    set point1 = param(1)
    set point2 = param(2)
    if not ((ilk(point1, #point) or count(point1) = 2) and ¬
            (ilk(point2, #point) or count(point2) = 2)) then
      set error = TRUE
    end if
  else if the paramCount = 4 then
    -- User specified four coordinates
    set point1 = point(param(1), param(2))
    set point2 = point(param(3), param(4))
  else
    -- Wrong number of parameters
    set error = TRUE
  end if
  if error then
    alert "Specify one rect or two points"
    return -1
  else
    set width  = abs(getAt(point1, 1) - getAt(point2, 1))
    set height = abs(getAt(point1, 2) - getAt(point2, 2))
    return width * height
  end if
end rectArea

put rectArea (rect (0, 100, 50, 110))
-- 500
put rectArea ([0, 100, 50, 110])
-- 500
put rectArea (point(0,100), point (50, 110))
-- 500
```

Example 5-3 determines the distance between two points.

Example 5-3: Distance Between Two Points

```
on distance pt1, pt2
  if ilk(pt1, #point) and ilk(pt2, #point) then
    set h = the locH of pt1 - the locH of pt2
    set v = the locV of pt1 - the locV of pt2
    set dist = sqrt (h*h + v*v)
    return dist
  else
    return -1
  end if
end distance

put distance (point(0,0), point(3,4))
-- 5.0000
```

Stage-Relative Versus Monitor-Relative Coordinates

Some Lingo coordinates are given relative to the upper-left corner of the Stage (Stage-relative) and others are given relative to the upper-left corner of the main monitor (monitor-relative). In a multi-monitor setup, the main monitor is the one containing the menubar, but not necessarily the Stage. Stage-relative coordinates allow the Projector to play back on any size monitor, independent of the Stage's position (and, to some extent, its size). Monitor-relative coordinates are required to locate objects outside the confines of the Stage. The origin (0,0) is the upper-left corner of either the Stage or the monitor, depending on which Lingo property you're using. If the Stage itself is in the upper-left corner of the monitor, the two origins will coincide. You should test on a monitor larger than your Stage to ensure proper operation.

The coordinates of the cursor, sprites, and mouse clicks are given relative to the Stage's upper-left corner. The coordinates of the Stage itself, MIAWs, and secondary monitors are given relative to the main monitor's upper-left corner (or relative to the window when the Projector is played *In a Window* under Windows).

Converting between coordinate systems

To allow the user to move a sprite but limit its range to the Stage area, you must reconcile the Stage-relative and monitor-relative coordinates. A sprite is off-Stage left if its horizontal coordinate is negative. It is above the Stage if its vertical coordinate is negative.

 To determine if a sprite is beyond the right or bottom edge of the Stage, you must compare the sprite's position to the *width* and *height* of the Stage, not *the stageRight* and *the stageBottom*.

Figure 5-3 shows Stage-relative and monitor-relative coordinates.

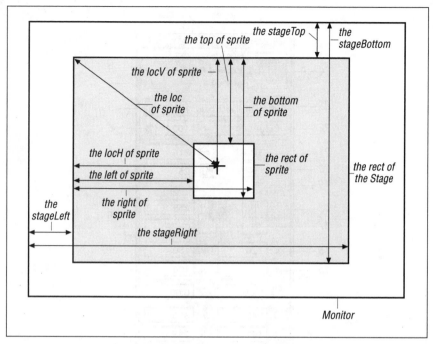

Labels in figure:
- the top of sprite
- the stageTop
- the stageBottom
- the locV of sprite
- the loc of sprite
- the bottom of sprite
- the locH of sprite
- the rect of sprite
- the left of sprite
- the rect of the Stage
- the stageLeft
- the right of sprite
- the stageRight
- Monitor

Figure 5-3: Stage and sprite coordinates

Figure 5-4 shows the Sprite Inspector. The same information is shown in the Score's Sprite Toolbar.

Example 5-4 is useful for checking whether Stage-relative coordinates such as those used by *the loc of sprite* are on the Stage. It first calculates the Stage's width and height. The *stageBox()* function returns the rect of the Stage relative to itself, rather than relative to the monitor.

Example 5-4: Translating Between Coordinate Systems

```
on stageWidth
  return the width of the rect of the stage
end stageWidth

on stageHeight
  return the height of the rect of the stage
end stageHeight

on stageBox
  return rect(0, 0, stageWidth(), stageHeight())
end stageBox
```

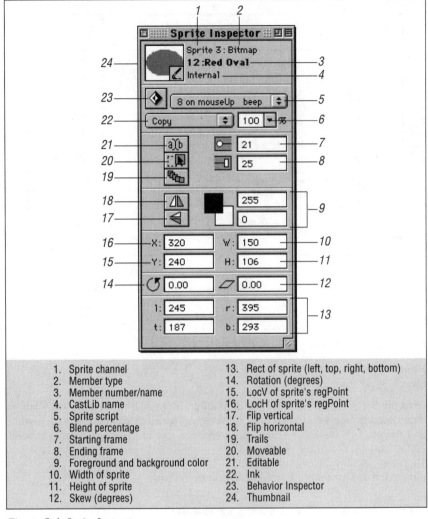

Figure 5-4: Sprite Inspector

1. Sprite channel
2. Member type
3. Member number/name
4. CastLib name
5. Sprite script
6. Blend percentage
7. Starting frame
8. Ending frame
9. Foreground and background color
10. Width of sprite
11. Height of sprite
12. Skew (degrees)
13. Rect of sprite (left, top, right, bottom)
14. Rotation (degrees)
15. LocV of sprite's regPoint
16. LocH of sprite's regPoint
17. Flip vertical
18. Flip horizontal
19. Trails
20. Moveable
21. Editable
22. Ink
23. Behavior Inspector
24. Thumbnail

Example 5-5 uses the handlers from Example 5-4 to check whether a sprite's regPoint (as indicated by *the loc of sprite*) is on the Stage. Note the use of the *inside()* function.

Example 5-5: Constraining a Sprite's regPoint to the Stage

```
on regPointOnStage spriteNum
  if the memberNum of sprite spriteNum = 0 then
    return FALSE
  end if
  if inside(the loc of sprite spriteNum, stageBox()) then
    return TRUE
```

Example 5-5: Constraining a Sprite's regPoint to the Stage (continued)

```
else
  return FALSE
end if
end regPointOnStage
```

Check whether the regPoint of sprite 4 is on Stage:

```
put regPointOnStage (4)
-- 0
```

Recall that the regPoint is only one representative point. You need to check the bounding box of the sprite separately. Example 5-6 checks whether any portion of a sprite's bounding box is on the Stage.

Example 5-6: Checking Whether a Sprite Is Partially On the Stage

```
on onStage spriteNum
  if the memberNum of sprite spriteNum = 0 then
    return FALSE
  end if
  set rect1 = the rect of sprite spriteNum
  if intersect (rect1, stageBox()) = rect(0,0,0,0) then
    return FALSE
  else
    return TRUE
  end if
end onStage
```

Check whether sprite 5 is anywhere on Stage:

```
put onStage (5)
-- 1
```

Example 5-6 can be used to check whether the entire sprite is off the Stage, using *not onStage(n)*. Example 5-7 checks whether any portion of a sprite is off the Stage.

Example 5-7: Checking Whether a Sprite Is Partially Off the Stage

```
on offStage spriteNum
  if the memberNum of sprite spriteNum = 0 then
    return TRUE
  end if
  set rect1 = the rect of sprite spriteNum
  if union (rect1, stageBox()) = stageBox() then
    return FALSE
  else
    return TRUE
  end if
end offStage
```

Member Coordinates

Table 5-1 lists cast member coordinate properties, which are measured relative to the upper-left corner of the cast member's bounding box in the Paint window. Only *the regPoint of member* can be set via Lingo. The remaining properties can be set indirectly by selecting the cast member and choosing Modify ➤ Transform Bitmap.

Table 5-1: Member Coordinate Properties

Lingo Command	Usage or Data Type	Relative To
the height of member	Vertical height of cast member	Cast member's top and bottom edges
the rect of member	rect(*l, t, r, b*) of cast member	Upper left of cast member bounding box; the left and top coordinates are always (0,0)
the regPoint of member	point(*h, v*) of registration point of cast member	Upper left of member's bounding box; regPoint is always (0,0) for shape and field members, and centered for digital video
the width of member	Horizontal width of cast member	Cast member's left and right edges

Sprite Coordinates

Table 5-2 lists sprite coordinate properties, which are generally measured relative to the upper-left corner of the Stage. See also Tables 3-2 and 5-4.

Table 5-2: Sprite Coordinate Properties

Lingo Command	Usage or Data Type	Relative To
the bottom of sprite[1]	Vertical coordinate of bottom edge of sprite	Top of Stage
the constraint of sprite[2]	Constrains *loc of sprite*	Constraining sprite's bounding box
the height of sprite	Vertical height of sprite on Stage	Self
the left of sprite[1]	Horizontal coordinate of left edge of sprite	Left of Stage
the lineSize of sprite	Pixel thickness of shape sprite's border	Border of sprite
the loc of sprite	Location of regPoint of sprite's cast member, defined as point(*h, v*)	Upper left of Stage
the locH of sprite	Horizontal coordinate of regPoint of sprite's cast member on the Stage	Left of Stage
the locV of sprite	Vertical coordinate of regPoint of sprite's cast member on Stage	Top of Stage

Table 5-2: Sprite Coordinate Properties (continued)

Lingo Command	Usage or Data Type	Relative To
the locZ of sprite	Controls Z-ordering, seems buggy in D7	Other sprites
the quad of sprite	Specifies four corner points of sprite [*upperLeftPt, upperRightPt, lowerRightPt, lowerLeftPt*]	Upper left of Stage
the rect of sprite	rect(*l, t, r, b*) of sprite's bounding box	Upper left of Stage
the right of sprite[1]	Horizontal coordinate of right edge of sprite	Left of Stage
sprite *sprite1* intersects {sprite} *sprite2*	Boolean indicating whether bounding boxes of *sprite1* and *sprite2* intersect	Sprite's bounding box; *matte* ink uses sprites' outlines
sprite *sprite1* within {sprite} *sprite2*	Boolean whether *sprite1* is within *sprite2*	Each other
spriteBox *whichSprite, l, t, r, b*	Obsolete, use *rect of sprite* instead	Upper left of Stage
the stretch of sprite	Boolean indicating whether sprite is stretched	Cast member's original size
the top of sprite[1]	Vertical coordinate of top edge of sprite	Top of Stage
the width of sprite	Horizontal width of sprite on Stage	Self

[1] Prior to D7, the *left, top, right,* and *bottom of sprite* cannot be set directly. Set the *rect, width, height, loc, locH,* or *locV of sprite* to set them indirectly.
[2] The *constrainH( )* and *constrainV( )* functions are not sprite properties. They do not constrain a sprite's movement automatically as can *the constraint of sprite*. Use them instead to constrain the *locH* or *locV* property of a sprite manually. See Table 5-4.

Mouse and Cursor Coordinates

Table 5-3 lists cursor and mouse coordinates, which are measured relative to the upper-left corner of the Stage.

Table 5-3: Mouse and Cursor Coordinates

Lingo Command	Usage or Data Type	Relative To
the mouseH	Horizontal coordinate of cursor's hotspot[1]	Left of Stage
the mouseV	Vertical coordinate of cursor's hotspot[1]	Top of Stage
the mouseLoc	point (*h, v*) of cursor's hotspot[1]	Upper left of Stage
the clickLoc	point (*h, v*) of last mouse-click	Upper left of Stage

[1] A custom cursor's hotspot is defined by the regPoint of the bitmap member used as the cursor.

Example 5-8 adds some useful functions that are absent from Director 6, although D7 supports the new property *the mouseLoc*.

Example 5-8: Useful Coordinate Utilities

```
on clickH
  return the locH of the clickLoc
end

on clickV
  return the locV of the clickLoc
end

on mouseLoc
  return point (the mouseH, the mouseV)
end
```

The *mouseH* and *mouseV* are negative if the cursor is above or to the left of the Stage. They are greater than *stageWidth()* or *stageHeight()* if the cursor is below or to the right of the Stage.

Example 5-9 allows the user to drag a sprite. It gives much faster response than the *Moveable* option in the Sprite Inspector (at the potential expense of other animation). In Director 5, you must manually puppet the sprite to move it via Lingo, but auto-puppeting in Director 6 and 7 does this for you. Example 5-9 accounts for the potential offset between the mouse click location and the regPoint of the sprite's cast member to prevent the sprite from jumping when it is first clicked. The D7 Library Palette includes additional Behaviors.

Example 5-9: Dragging a Sprite

```
on mouseDown me
  set mySprite = the spriteNum of me
  -- Determine the offset of the mouse click from the regPoint
  set offset = the loc of sprite mySprite - the clickLoc
  repeat while the stillDown
    -- Move the sprite wherever the mouse goes
    set the loc of sprite mySprite = ¬
        point (the mouseH, the mouseV) + offset
    updateStage
  end repeat
end mouseDown
```

Rect and Point Manipulation

The rects or points used with the commands in Table 5-4 are usually either Stage-relative or monitor-relative. See also Table 5-2.

Table 5-4: Rect and Point Lingo Commands

Lingo Command	Usage or Data Type	Relative To
the bottom of rect	Vertical coordinate of bottom edge (fourth element) of rect	Any rect
constrainH(*constrainingSprite, integer*)	Clips an integer, usually a horizontal coordinate	Constraining sprite's left and right coordinates relative to Stage
constrainV(*constrainingSprite, integer*)	Clips an integer, usually a vertical coordinate.	Constraining sprite's top and bottom coordinates relative to Stage
the height of rect	Vertical height of rect	Any rect
inflate (*rect, widthChange, heightChange*)[1]	Returns rect (*left – widthChange, top – heightChange, right + widthChange, bottom + heightChange*)	Original rect
inside (*point, rect*)	Boolean indicating whether *point* is located within *rect*	Each other
intersect (*rect1, rect2*)	Returns *rect* representing intersection of *rect1* and *rect2*	Each other
the left of rect	Horizontal coordinate of left edge (first element) of rect	Any rect
the locH of point	Horizontal coordinate (first element) of any point	Any point
the locV of point	Vertical coordinate (second element) of any point	Any point
map(*targetRect, sourceRect, destRect*)	Returns a new *rect* that has the same relationship to *targetRect* as *destRect* has to *sourceRect*	Relationship of *sourceRect* to *destRect*
map(*targetPoint, sourceRect, destRect*)	Returns a new *point* that has the same relationship to *targetPoint* as *destRect* has to *sourceRect*	Relationship of *sourceRect* to *destRect*
mapMemberToStage( )	Returns the point onStage corresponding to point in sprite	Accounts for sprite transformation. See Table 3-2.
mapStageToMember( )	Returns the point in member corresponding to point on Stage	Accounts for sprite transformation. See Table 3-2.
offset (*rect, horizChange, vertChange*)	Displace a rect(*l, t, r, b*) by *horizChange* and *vertChange* (can be negative)	Original rect
point (*horiz, vert*)	Defines a point(*h, v*)	N/A
#point	Returned by ilk (point(*h,v*))	See ilk in online Help or *Lingo in a Nutshell*

Table 5-4: Rect and Point Lingo Commands (continued)

Lingo Command	Usage or Data Type	Relative To
rect()	Defines a rect (*left, top, right, bottom*) or rect (point(*left, top*) point(*right, bottom*))	N/A
#rect	Returned by ilk(rect(*l,t,r,b*))	See ilk
the right of rect	Horizontal coordinate of right edge (third element) of rect	Any rect
union (*rect1, rect2*)	Returns rect representing union of *rect1* and *rect2*	Each other
the top of rect	Vertical coordinate of top edge (second element) of rect	Any rect
the width of rect	Horizontal width of rect	Any rect
zoomBox(*startSprite, endSprite* {, *delayTicks*})	Creates zooming effect from one sprite to another	Rects of sprites

1 *Inflate* is a function, not a command. It might be used as:
```
set the rect of sprite whichSprite = inflate (the rect of sprite whichSprite, 10, 20)
```

The Stage, MIAWs, and Monitor Coordinates

Table 5-5 lists coordinates and properties that are relative to the monitor rather than the Stage. Note that the coordinates of the Stage itself are given as monitor-relative. When a Projector is run in a window (prior to D7.0.1, available under Windows only), the coordinates are relative to the window, and not necessarily the monitor. Refer to Chapter 6, *The Stage and Movies-in-a-Window*, for more information.

Table 5-5: Stage-, Monitor-, and Window-Relative Coordinates

Lingo Command	Type or Units	Relative To
the centerStage	Boolean indicating whether Stage is centered	Center of monitor
the deskTopRectList	List of rect(s) of monitor(s), such as [*rect*(0, 0, 832, 624)]	Upper left of main monitor
the drawRect of window the drawRect of the stage	rect (*l, t, r, b*) of visible portion of MIAW or Stage	Upper left of MIAW's window, or upper left of Stage
the fixStageSize	Boolean indicating whether Stage size changes when switching movies	Stage size of initial movie
the rect of window the rect of the stage	rect (*l, t, r, b*) of MIAW's window or of Stage; buggy in D7.0, fixed in D7.0.1	Upper left of main monitor or Projector window

Lingo Command	Type or Units	Relative To
the stage	Represents the Stage itself in expressions	N/A
the stageBottom	Vertical coordinate of bottom edge of Stage	Top of main monitor
the stageLeft	Horizontal coordinate of left edge of Stage	Left of main monitor
the stageRight	Horizontal coordinate of right edge of Stage	Left of main monitor
the stageTop	Vertical coordinate of top edge of Stage	Top of main monitor
the sourceRect of window the sourceRect of the stage	MIAW's original Stage rect (*l, t, r, b*) defined under Modify ➤ Movie ➤ Properties.	Upper left of main monitor or Projector window
window *n*	Represents window *n* in expressions	N/A

Alignment in the User Interface

Director includes numerous tools for sizing and aligning sprites and the Stage itself, as listed in Table 5-6. See Tables 12-8, 12-10, and 12-11 for text-related coordinates.

Table 5-6: Adjusting Coordinates in the Interface

Usage	Menu Command	Mac	Win
Rearrange sprite channel order	**Modify ➤ Arrange...**		
	Bring To Front	Cmd-Shift-↑	Ctrl-Shift-↑
	Move Forward	Cmd-↑	Ctrl-↑
	Move Back	Cmd-↓	Ctrl-↓
	Send To Back	Cmd-Shift-↓	Ctrl-Shift-↓
Align sprites' top, bottom, left, right, center, or regPoint[1]	Modify ➤ Align, or D6 Toolbar	Cmd-K	Ctrl-K
Tweak sprite's horizontal and vertical position	Modify ➤ Tweak	Cmd-Shift-K	Ctrl-Shift-K
Move sprite one pixel	Click and drag on Stage	Arrow keys	Arrow keys
Move sprite ten pixels	Click and drag on Stage	Shift-arrow keys	Shift-arrow keys

Table 5-6: Adjusting Coordinates in the Interface (continued)

Usage	Menu Command	Mac	Win
Constrain sprite movement to either X or Y direction on Stage	Shift-drag on Stage	None	None
Align items using a grid (uses nearest corner in D7)	**View ➤ Grid...** Show Snap To Settings...	Cmd-Shift-Opt-G Cmd-Opt-G	Ctrl-Shift-Alt-G Ctrl-Alt-G
Center sprite's regPoint (not necessarily its *rect of sprite*) on Stage	Drag it from Cast window or media editor directly to Score	Cmd-Shift-L	Ctrl-Shift-L
Move registration point of bitmap in Paint window	Select regPoint tool and click in Paint window	G (selects tool) Opt-arrow keys	G (selects tool) Alt-arrow keys
Center regPoint in Paint window	Double-click regPoint tool	None	None
Align *regPoints* of multiple bitmaps in Paint window	View ➤ Onion Skin	None	Alt-V,O
Modify original cast member dimensions[2]	Modify ➤ Transform Bitmap Double-click bit-depth display in lower left of Paint window	None	Alt-M,T
Show sprite path and information on Stage	**View ➤ Sprite Overlay...** Show Info[3] Show Path Settings	Cmd-Shift-Opt-O Cmd-Shift-Opt-H	Ctrl-Shift-Alt-O Ctrl-Shift-Alt-H
Show sprite x (*locH*), y (*locV*), width, height, and left, right, top, and bottom	View ➤ Sprite Toolbar[4]	Cmd-Shift-H	Ctrl-Shift-H
Show sprite x (*locH*), y (*locV*), width, height, and left, right, top, and bottom	Windows ➤ Inspectors ➤ Sprite[4]	Cmd-Shift-S Keypad /	Ctrl-Shift-S Keypad /
Choose pixels, centimeters, or inches as default units[5]	File ➤ Preferences ➤ General ➤ Text Units	None	None
Text and Paint window rulers	View ➤ Rulers	Cmd-Shift-Opt-R	Ctrl-Shift-Alt-R
Show sprite location and change in location in Score	File ➤ Preferences ➤ Score ➤ Extended Display	None	None
View sprite's location in the Score	View ➤ Display ➤ Location, or Display pop-up in Score	None	Alt-V,D

Table 5-6: Adjusting Coordinates in the Interface (continued)

Usage	Menu Command	Mac	Win
Choose whether to tween sprite's size and position	File ➤ Preferences ➤ Sprite ➤ Span defaults	None	None
Determine custom line width for Paint window tools	File ➤ Preferences ➤ Paint ➤ Other line width Double-click custom line width button in Paint window	None	Alt-F,F,P
Set Stage size and position[6]	Modify ➤ Movie ➤ Properties	Cmd-Shift-D	Ctrl-Shift-D

[1] Click in one of the nine cells in the Align windoid to quickly set the horizontal and vertical alignment options. Click outside the cells' edges to set the alignment along one axis while resetting the other axis to *No Change*. Alignment by regPoints must be chosen manually from the alignment pop-up menus.

[2] A bitmap will not always resize the exact dimensions specified in the *Transform Bitmap* dialog box. Transformations that adjust the size by less than one percent may have no effect. Resize bitmaps in another program, such as deBabelizer or Photoshop.

[3] Select the *Live Dragging* option in the context-sensitive pop-up menu on the Stage (see Table 3-12) to update Sprite Info as a sprite is dragged.

[4] The Sprite Inspector (see Figure 5-2) is a floating windoid version of the Score Window's optional Sprite Toolbar. Switch between the Sprite Inspector's three possible display orientations by clicking the zoom box in its upper-right corner.

[5] The Text Units setting affects the ruler in the Text cast member window, which is marked in either centimeters or inches. If the preference is set to "pixels," the ruler is shown in inches, not pixels (at least in the U.S.).

[6] Prior to D7, the width and left offset of the Stage will be rounded down to the nearest multiple of 16. The Stage's height and width must each be at least one pixel. The Stage's offset can only be negative if using a second monitor to the left or top of the main monitor. Otherwise, setting a negative Stage position centers the Stage on screen. D7.0.1 fixes some bugs in Stage positioning with multiple monitors.

Registration

CHAPTER 6

The Stage and Movies-in-a-Window

This chapter covers the configuration and manipulation of the Stage and Movies-in-a-Window (MIAWs), including communication between them. Throughout this chapter, the movie running on the Stage is referred to as the "main movie," and "movie" refers to either the main movie or a MIAW.

Director 7 introduces some differences in the way the Stage and MIAWs are implemented. Most notably, the Stage is now a moveable and closeable window during authoring, and MIAWs no longer share the Stage's offscreen buffer. The initial release of D7.0 introduced some bugs in MIAW handling. In particular, MIAWs will disappear behind the Stage and modal MIAWs do not behave properly. These bugs should be fixed in D7.0.1. See *http://www.zeusprod.com/nutshell/miaws.html* and the D7.0.1 ReadMe for the latest information.

The Stage

The Stage is the viewport within which animation occurs. Any sprite placed off-Stage will not be visible, even if the monitor is larger than the Stage.

Refer to Chapter 1, *How Director Works*, for a description of on-Stage imaging and the offscreen buffer. Refer also to the discussion of direct-to-Stage video in Chapter 16, *Digital Video*.

The Stage as a Window

On the Macintosh, prior to D7.0.1, the Projector's Stage was always an immovable rectangular window with a one-pixel border, a two-pixel drop shadow, and no titlebar, zoom box, close box, or resize box.

In all versions of Director for Windows, and D7.0.1 or later on the Macintosh, the options under File ► Create Projector include *Full Screen,* which creates a fixed Stage without a titlebar, or *In a Window,* which places the Projector in a moveable window. The latter includes an optional titlebar (including a zoom box,

166

close box, and resize box under Windows) as determined by the *Show Title Bar* option.

Although it is not included in *the windowList*, the Stage shares most window-related properties with MIAWs and receives some window-related events. During authoring in D6, the Stage is typically behind all other Director windows and automatically disappears when another application comes to the foreground. In D7, it is treated like any other window in the stacking order.

To play the movie and hide all windows except the Stage, hold down the Shift key while pressing the Enter key on the numeric keypad. Director's menubar becomes invisible on the Macintosh (and under Windows if Director's window is maximized), but is accessible by clicking at the top of the monitor.

Positioning the Stage

The Stage's size and location are set for each movie under Modify ➤ Movie ➤ Properties (see Figure 6-1). These settings may be overridden when a new movie is loaded, based on the File ➤ Create Projector ➤ Options or File ➤ Preferences ➤ General settings. Note that prior to D7, the Stage's width and the position of its left edge must be multiples of 16. The Stage must be at least one pixel square. The size of a Shockwave movie is determined by the EMBED or OBJECT tag used to embed it in an HTML page. The Stage's size determines the dimensions of exported QuickTime, AVI, PICT, BMP, and PICS files (see File ➤ Export).

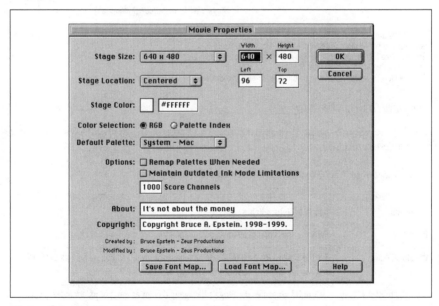

Figure 6-1: Director 7 Movie Properties dialog box

Table 6-1 explains the options that control the Stage's size and location. The Stage size cannot be changed via Lingo. Check the *deskTopRectList* to ensure that the monitor dimensions are large enough to accommodate your Stage, especially if using a Stage larger than 640×480 pixels.

Table 6-1: Stage Size and Location Settings

Action	Command
Set a movie's window size and position.[1]	Stage Size and Stage Location settings under Modify ➤ Movie ➤ Properties, or Cmd-Shift-D (Macintosh) or Ctrl-Shift-D (Windows)
Use the new movie's settings for the Stage's size and location, not the previous movie's settings.	Use *Movie Settings* option[2,3] or *set the fixStageSize = FALSE*
Ignore the new movie's settings and use the Stage's size and location of previous or first movie.	Set *Match Current Movie* or *Match First Movie*[2,3] option, or *set the fixStageSize = TRUE*
Force the Stage to be centered on a large monitor.	Set *Center* option[2,3], or *set the centerStage = TRUE*
Cover the desktop surrounding the Stage.[4]	*Full Screen* option[3]
Play Projector in a window.	Uncheck *Full Screen* or modify the Stage's WIND resource[5] (Macintosh), or check *In a Window*[3] (Windows)
Change Projector window's appearance.	Set the *Show Title Bar* option[3] (Windows), or modify the Stage's WIND resource[5] (Macintosh)

[1] The Stage's size and location may be overridden by the *General Preferences* and *Projector Options*.
[2] Set during authoring mode under File ➤ Preferences ➤ General.
[3] Set when creating a Projector under File ➤ Create Projector ➤ Options.
[4] See "Hiding the Desktop" in Chapter 8.
[5] See "The Stage's windowType-Related Attributes" later in this chapter.

Properties of the Stage

Besides the window-related properties that the Stage shares with MIAWs, Table 6-2 lists Stage-related Lingo.

Table 6-2: Stage Size, Position, and Window Commands

Command	Usage or Return Value
the stage	Refers to the Stage itself when defining window-like properties or using *tell*.
the stageColor[1]	Set the Stage's (or a MIAW's) background color from 0 to 255. (Also sets desktop color in full-screen Projector.) See Modify ➤ Movie ➤ Properties.
the bgColor of the stage	New in D7. Specifies the Stage's background color as rgb() or paletteIndex() color.

Table 6-2: Stage Size, Position, and Window Commands (continued)

Command	Usage or Return Value
the picture of the stage	New in D7. Captures current Stage's image.
the stageLeft, the stage-Top, the stageRight, the stageBottom	Coordinates of the Stage's edges relative to monitor's upper-left corner.
the fixStageSize and the centerStage	Determine whether the Stage will change size and be centered when the next movie is started. Affects next movie, not current movie. Has no effect on MIAWs. See File ➤ Preferences ➤ General and File ➤ Create Projector ➤ Options.

[1] Each MIAW has its own *the stageColor* property, despite the name's implication. To get the Stage's background color from a MIAW, use:

```
tell the stage to put the stageColor
```

Try to use the same Stage size, position, and color throughout the different movies in a project. Test on a large monitor to ensure proper alignment. Setting *the stageColor* equal to itself is a good way to refresh the entire Stage, such as:

```
set the stageColor = the stageColor
```

Movies-in-a-Window

A *Movie-in-a-Window* is a standard, protected, or compressed Director movie file that is displayed in a subwindow instead of on the Stage. MIAWs appear either behind or in front of the Stage in separate windows. They are not layered like sprites; use film loops or movie cast members to layer multiple elements within a single window.

Create a MIAW as you would any Director movie, bearing in mind the limitations described later in this chapter. Even though Director can open multiple MIAWs, only one movie can be edited at a time. In D7, Lingo from unprotected MIAWs can be debugged in the Debugger window. To debug MIAWs, which are not accessible in the Debugger window prior to D7, use the techniques in Chapter 3, *Lingo Coding and Debugging Tips*, in *Lingo in a Nutshell*.

MIAWs can be embedded in a Projector, as long as the *Play Every Movie* option is unchecked, but I *strongly* recommend keeping them external to your Projector. Use Xtras ➤ Update Movies to protect the MIAW instead. MIAWs can be DIR, DXR, or DCR files.

The *open window* command creates a new MIAW (or opens an existing one), whereas *go movie* changes the movie being played in the target window (either the Stage or an existing MIAW). The *open* command (without the *window* keyword) opens external executable programs, and should never be used with Director movies.

The Stage and MIAWs

MIAW Suggested Uses

MIAWs sometimes cause more problems than they solve, because of their limitations and potential conflicts with the main movie (especially in D7.0, so upgrade to D7.0.1). There are, however, many legitimate reasons to use MIAWs:

As floating tool palettes or windoids
MIAWs are ideal for auxiliary windows, such as a Help system. Use *moveTo-Front* to keep a floating palette windoid in the foreground or use an appropriate *windowType*, such as 49.

As custom dialog boxes
MIAWs are ideal for fancy dialog boxes that give the user more options than the standard alert dialog box.

For tool Xtras
MIAWs are ideal for authoring-time tools that modify or analyze the main movie. For example, the D6 Widget Wizard is a MIAW written in Lingo. Such tool Xtras can be protected DXR files to preserve code privacy. Set *the exit-Lock* to TRUE within your MIAW to prevent it from being halted along with the main movie during authoring.

The more esoteric purposes for MIAWs include:

As a surrogate Stage
The Stage window generally cannot be modified or repositioned as easily as a MIAW. You can hide the Stage using *set the visible of the stage = FALSE* and use a MIAW as a pseudo-Stage instead.

To overcome the sprite channel limit
A MIAW can extend the number of sprite channels beyond the 48 available in Director 5 (as can film loops). It is ill-advised to go beyond Director 6's 120 sprite channels for performance reasons, and D7 allows up to 1,000 sprite channels.

As a way to manipulate film loops
Because each MIAW has its own Score, they can be used to create and edit film loops dynamically. The trick is to use MIAW's *the score* property in conjunction with *the media of member* of a film loop.

As a "holding area" for reusable assets
In Director 4, before multiple external cast libraries were available, MIAWs could act as repositories for scripts and media. Use external cast libraries instead in D5, D6, and D7.

MIAWs Versus the Stage

While MIAWs have almost all the capabilities of the main movie, there are some notable limitations:

- MIAWs have their own Score, but their Palette settings are ignored. (The Tempo, Transition, and Sound channels work inside MIAWs.)

- MIAWs can't be used with Shockwave. Embed multiple Shockwave movies in an HTML page instead.

- MIAWs share global variables with the Stage and other MIAWs. If creating a Tool Xtra, use unique global variable names, such as *gCoolToolMyVar*, to minimize the chance of conflicts or (preferably) use property variables.

- MIAWs use memory and processing power until *forget window* is used.

- MIAWs do not have direct access to the scripts or Score of the main movie or its internal or external cast libraries (unless they share an external cast). Use *tell the stage* to access the main movie's Cast and Score from a MIAW.

- MIAWs share the sound channels with the main movie, so you cannot have both the main movie and a MIAW use sound channel 1 at the same time.

- The *pass* command will forward events from a MIAW to the Stage, but otherwise events may be intercepted by MIAWs.

What Movies Do and Don't Share

When using MIAWs or simply switching between movies using *go movie* or *play movie*, it is vital to understand which components are shared between movies and which are private to a single movie. The following lists are not necessarily definitive, but they'll steer you clear of the most common errors.

What movies share

MIAWs share the following with each other and with the main movie:

- Available memory and CPU time

- Palette (controlled by the Stage only)

- System sound channels (Score sound channels can be used in MIAWs)

- Offscreen imaging buffer (prior to D7)

In Director 4, each MIAW would open a copy of the Shared Cast, if any (this didn't work with protected Shared Casts). In D5, D6, and D7, the Shared Cast is superceded by external castLibs that can be linked to one or more movies, including MIAWs. You may need to set external castLib files to read-only if they are shared between the main movie and a MIAW or multiple MIAWs at the same time.

These properties and variables are shared across all MIAWs and the main movie. Changes to any of these values affect all movies:

- All global variables

- *the alertHook*

- *the applicationPath*

- *clearGlobals* (clears globals in the main movie and all MIAWs; in Director 6 and 7, it also clears *the actorList* in the movie from which it was called)

- *the framePalette* (value is always that of the main movie)

- *the frontWindow* (read-only; always represents window in foreground regardless of which movie it is checked from)

- *puppetPalette* (affects all movies when called from main movie; disabled in MIAWs)

- *the stageLeft, stageTop, stageRight, stageBottom, rect of the stage* always represent the location and dimensions of the main movie (the Stage size may change when using *go movie* or *play movie* to change the main movie).
- *the windowList* (never includes the Stage)
- Xtras that are open and accessible
- XLibs that have been opened manually with *openXlib* (no longer recommended)

What movies don't share

When using *go movie* or *play movie* to start a new movie, the following properties are all independent of the previous movie:

- *the visible of sprite* for all sprite channels is set to TRUE
- *the puppet of sprite** for all sprite channels is set to FALSE
- Sprite properties stored in the Score are reset to their Scored values*
- Sprite properties not stored in the Score (*the cursor of sprite*, etc.) are reset
- *the frameTempo*
- *the frameSound1*
- *the frameSound2*
- *the frameTransition*
- *the keyDownScript** is set to EMPTY
- *the keyUpScript** is set to EMPTY
- *the mouseDownScript** is set to EMPTY
- *the mouseUpScript** is set to EMPTY
- *the movieName*
- *the moviePath*
- *the name of castLib*
- *the number of castLibs*
- *the pathName*
- *puppetTempo*
- *puppetTransition*

Except for *the visible of sprite* property, all sprite properties are restored when using *play done* to return to a movie following a *play movie* command. If using *go movie*, the state of the movies are not stored and retrieved (so it uses less memory than *play movie*).

---

* During authoring, many of these properties are reset whenever the movie is halted or played. Therefore, they cannot be set and tested reliably from the Message window unless the movie is playing without interruption. For best results, set these properties from a Lingo script.

When a new movie starts, Director closes the old graphics context (drawing context) for the Stage and opens up a new one, purging trails and any sprites from the Stage. Refer to "Movie Startup" in Chapter 1 for more details on what happens when Director starts and loads a movie, including potentially changing the monitor color depth and Stage position.

The following are not reset when going to a new movie:

- custom menus
- *the actorList**
- *cursor*
- *the timer*
- *the timeoutKeyDown*
- *the timeoutLapsed†*
- *the timeoutMouse*
- *the timeoutPlay*
- *the timeoutScript*

Some properties, such as *the timeoutScript* and *the actorList*, are not reset when using *go movie* or *play movie*, yet each MIAW still maintains an independent copy of the properties.

Each MIAW's tempo and playback head are independent of the main movie. Set *the exitLock* to TRUE within your MIAW to prevent it from being halted when the main movie is stopped. If a MIAW is halted inadvertently, try restarting it by using *forget window* and then reopening it.

Each MIAW remembers its own playback head position (i.e., *the frame*), which doesn't change when the window is opened and closed. To reset the MIAW to frame 1 when it is reopened, you must either use *forget window* to first dispose of it or specify *go frame 1* in an *on openWindow* handler.

A MIAW continues to run even when it is not the active window (even if invisible or closed) unless its *Pause When Window Inactive* option is checked under Modify▶Movie▶Playback.

Each MIAW has its own independent copy of the properties listed earlier (*actorList, cursor, timer, timeoutKeyDown*, etc.) plus the following:

- The Score and sprites, excluding the Effects channels
- *the activeWindow* (always returns the window from which it is checked)

---

* Each MIAW has its own *actorList*. *The actorList* remains intact when branching to a different movie using *go movie* or *play movie*. This will cause problems if *the actorList* refers to specific entities that don't exist in the new movie, such as scripts from the previous movie. In Director 6 and 7, *clearGlobals* also clears *the actorList* of the movie from which it is called, but not *the actorList* of other movies.

† Whereas every MIAW and the main movie have independent timer properties, *the timeout-Lapsed* property can be reset by events in any other movie window. *The timeoutLapsed* is reset to zero when using *go movie* or *play movie* only in those movies in which *the timeoutPlay* is TRUE.

- *the exitLock*
- *the frame*
- *the stageColor*
- *startTimer*

Declaring and Using MIAWs

Assuming that you've created an appropriate Director movie, you can open it as a MIAW using the *open window* command:

```
open window "movieName"
```

Referring to a new window by an arbitrary name adds it to *the windowList* and allows you to set its attributes before using *open window* as shown in Example 6-1. Use *windowPresent()* to check if a window exists without adding it to *the windowList*.

Example 6-1: Setting a MIAW's Attributes Before Opening It

```
set testWindow = window "miaw1"
set the fileName of testWindow = "HelpWin"
set the rect of testWindow = rect (0, 100, 200, 400)
open testWindow
```

The following will not work unless window 1 already exists:

```
set the fileName of window 1 = "HelpWin"
```

If you are creating a MIAW to be used as a Tool Xtra, place it in Director's *Xtras* folder and restart Director. Select the MIAW Tool from the **Xtras** menu, instead of using the *open window* command.

Open MIAWs from the Stage, not from other MIAWs. Otherwise, a MIAW becomes the child of the MIAW from which it was spawned and won't be managed or purged properly. If necessary, have a MIAW instruct the Stage to open the second MIAW, as shown in Example 6-2.

Example 6-2: Opening a Second MIAW from a MIAW

```
tell the stage
  set the fileName of window "SubWindow" = "windoid"
  open window "SubWindow"
end tell
```

Starting MIAWs and the Great White Flash

The *rect* of a MIAW may appear white before the MIAW's contents appear, because a MIAW is an OS-level window, which is allocated and drawn in separate steps. As John Dowdell writes, "It's this contrast with Director's smooth [off-screen-buffered] internal drawing that makes normal system behavior seem so unusual."

To reduce the delay:

1. Use the *preLoadMovie* command.

2. Open the window off-Stage, then bring it on-Stage using *the rect of window.*

3. Open the window while it's invisible, then set *the visible of window* to TRUE.

MIAWs are also redrawn whenever the *windowType, rect,* or *drawRect of window* properties change. If the entire screen flashes (versus just the area of the new window), it might indicate that *the colorDepth* is changing. Make sure that the MIAW does not have any cast members with the wrong bit depth (see Example 13-1).

The windowList

The windowList is a linear list showing each MIAW's *name of window* property (not its *title* or *fileName*), even if it is not currently visible. If there are no MIAWs, *the windowList* is an empty list ([ ]) because the Stage is never included. To determine the number of existing MIAWs, use *count (the windowList)*, as shown in Example 6-3.

Example 6-3: The windowList

```
put the windowList
-- []
open window "miaw"
open window "foo"
set the rect of window "nonexistent" = the rect of the stage
put the windowList
-- [(window "miaw"), (window "foo"), (window "nonexistent")]
put count (the windowList)
-- 3
```

Referring to Windows by Name or Number

To refer the Stage or a MIAW, use a *windowID* of one of these forms:

the stage
> You can use *the stage* as a **windowID** for many MIAW-related commands. *The stage* always represents the main movie.

window *windowNumber*
> Where *windowNumber* is the MIAW's position in *the windowList* between 1 and *count(the windowList)*.

window "*windowName*"
> Where *windowName* is the window's *the name of window* property, not its *title* or *fileName*. If two MIAWs have the same name, the first one is used.

A window's number can vary, and a hard-coded **windowID** can be cumbersome to use repeatedly, so it is convenient to assign a **windowID** to a variable, such as:

```
global gSomeWindow
set gSomeWindow = window "mySubWindow"
```

Omit the keyword *window* when using *the stage* or using a function or property that returns a complete `windowID`, such as *the activeWindow*, or when it is already part of a variable.

The *windowPresent()* function accepts only the window's *name*, without the *window* keyword, and doesn't accept a window number.

Correct examples of window-related commands:

```
set testWindow = window "myWindow"
set the windowType of testWindow = 1
set the visible of the stage = TRUE
close the activeWindow
if windowPresent ("myWindow") then...
open window "myWindow"
```

Incorrect examples of window-related commands (compare to previous):

```
set testWindow = window "myWindow"
-- The variable "testWindow" already includes "window"
set the windowType of window testWindow = 1
-- Don't use "window" with "the stage"
set the visible of window (the stage) = FALSE
-- Don't use "window" with "the activeWindow"
close window the activeWindow
-- Don't use "window" with windowPresent()
if windowPresent (window "myWindow") then...
-- If you omit "window", "open" tries to launch an application!
open "myWindow"
```

Window Properties

Various properties of MIAWs or the Stage can be tested or set via Lingo using:

the *property* of window *whichWindow*

where *whichWindow* is a window name in quotes or a window number, or:

the *property* of the stage

or in D7 notation:

```
window(whichWindow).property
(the stage).property
```

D7's new *the stage.picture* property can be assigned to *(new(#bitmap)).picture* to create a screen grab.

A complete discussion of these window properties follows. Only the *drawRect* and *visible* properties can be set usefully for the Stage:

drawRect of window
fileName of window
modal of window
name of window
rect of window
sourceRect of window
title of window

titleVisible of window
visible of window
windowType of window

The Wind-X Xtra (*http://www.ncimedia.com/pages/director/swindex.shtml*) is a convenience utility to learn and manage MIAW creation. It has a nice GUI, and shows Macintosh, Windows 3.1, and Windows 95/98/NT versions of each *window-Type* without switching platforms.

Source Movie, Name, and Title

In the simplest case, you'll specify a movie to open by name, such as:

```
open window "myMovie"
```

which opens the file *myMovie*, *myMovie.DIR*, *myMovie.DXR*, or *myMovie.DCR*. (Director looks for them automatically in that order.)

MIAW's name, fileName, and title

In the previous case, the *name*, *fileName*, and *title of window* properties all equal *"myMovie"*. If *"myMovie"* can't be found, a file browser dialog box appears. Even if the user picks a different file, *the fileName of window* is still "myMovie".

Use this to determine the external file path for a MIAW:

```
tell window n
    put the moviePath && the movieName
end tell
```

The name of window is used to refer to a window in *the windowList*. *The fileName of window* is used to change the source movie used as the MIAW and can even be a URL. Use *downloadNetThing* before setting a MIAW's *fileName of window* property to a URL. If the specified movie cannot be found, changes to *the fileName of window* property are ignored. *The title of window* affects the name in the MIAW's titlebar, if any.

A single Director file can be used as *the fileName of window* for multiple MIAWs. A MIAW can even use the same Director file as the Stage. Use the Macintosh Finder's *Get Info* command or the Windows File Explorer's *Properties* command to set the Director movie file (and any castLibs) to read-only to prevent conflicts when using it concurrently in more than one window.

The Stage's name, fileName, and title

Refer to the Stage using *the stage*, not *the name of the stage*, which returns 0 (zero). Use *the movieName* and *the moviePath* to read the current movie's path, and *go movie* or *play movie* to play a different movie on the Stage. The title in the Stage's titlebar under Windows, if any, is the name of the Projector, not the name of the current movie file. Prior to D7, setting *the title of the stage* has no effect under Windows. The title of the Macintosh Stage (which defaults to "Stage") can be set in D7.0.1, or in prior versions if you've replaced the default Stage window with a custom WIND resource that includes a title bar. See "Changing the Stage on the Macintosh" later in this chapter.

The Buddy API Xtra (*http://www.mods.com.au/budapi*) can set a window's title under Windows. The MHT-Icon Xtra (*http://www.meetinghousetech.com/tools/tls_index.html*) will set a Windows's Projector's icon and the Stage window's title.

WindowType Attributes

The *windowType, modal*, and *titleVisible of window* properties affect a window's appearance and the user's interaction with it. There is no explicit Lingo control over whether a window has a resize box, zoom box, or close box; these are intrinsic to a window's *windowType*. The presence (or absence) of a titlebar determines whether a window is moveable by the user (any MIAW can be moved via Lingo by setting its *rect of window* property). The *modal* and *titleVisible* properties are ignored unless *the windowType* is –1 or 0.

modal

The Boolean *modal of window* property determines whether mouse clicks are allowed outside a MIAW of *windowType* 0 or –1. Other *windowTypes* are modal by definition, but this is not reflected in, nor affected by, the *modal* property. Modal windows may not work properly in D7.0 but should be fixed in D7.0.1.

titleVisible

The Boolean *the titleVisible of window* property determines whether a MIAW of *windowType* 0 or –1 displays a titlebar. The titlebar measures 20 pixels high and is not included in *the rect of window* dimensions. The *title of window* property can be set for any *windowType* with a titlebar.

windowType

The windowType of window is an integer code as shown in Figures 6-2, 6-3, and 6-4, and Table 6-3 that determines the appearance of the MIAW's framing window. The default *windowType* is –1. Some *windowType* codes are platform-specific. MIAWs are always drawn in the native OS's style, and their appearance may vary across Mac System 7 and OS 8 and Windows 3.1, 95, 98, and NT.

On the Macintosh, you can add custom window types by copying new WDEF (window definition) resources to the resource fork of Director or a Projector using ResEdit. Each new WDEF is assigned a *resourceID* and creates a family of 16 window types accessed by setting the *windowType* to (*resourceID*× 16) through (*resourceID*× 16) + 15. For example, the first window variation for a WDEF with a *resourceID* of 32 would be 512. See Figure 6-5.

For more information on borderless WDEF resources, see:

> *http://www.trevimedia.com/donationware.html*
> *ftp://ftp.trevimedia.com/pub/utilities/NoBorderWDEF1.0a.sit*

For the Round Window WDEF (see its *About...* box for instructions), see:

> *ftp://ftp.maricopa.edu/pub/mcli/director/sit/round-window.sit.hqx*

Other WDEFs may be found in public Macintosh programming or Hypercard archives. Adding a custom WDEF is unsupported, and ResEdit can permanently disfigure an application. Make a backup and proceed with caution.

You can use sprites, a linked movie cast member, or the Border Xtra from Media Connect (*http://www.mcmm.com*) to simulate a borderless or irregular MIAW. The Border Xtra for Windows that works with Director 6 will not work in D7, but an update is anticipated.

Figure 6-2 shows the primary *windowType* codes for Macintosh MIAWs. All windows in the figure are 125 pixels wide by 50 pixels high and are spaced evenly. The spacing appears uneven because *the rect of window* property is independent of the titlebar, border, and shadow of the window. *WindowTypes* 6, 7, 9, 10, 11, 13, 14, and 15 are valid, but not useful. Compare with Figure 6-4.

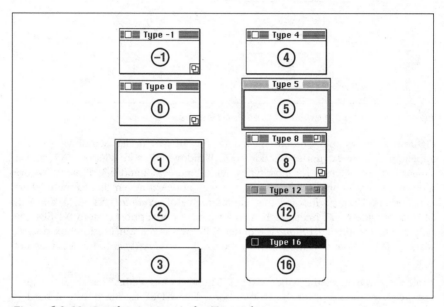

Figure 6-2: Macintosh primary windowType styles

Figure 6-3 shows some additional *windowType* codes for Macintosh MIAWs. The even numbered types 48–62 are a family of windoids convenient for tool palettes. The odd-numbered types 49–63 (not shown) are the same, except that their title-bars dim when they lose focus. Type 517 is not included with Director, but is part of the family of oval windows included in the Round Window WDEF cited earlier in this section (assuming that the Round Window is WDEF resource 32). Other variants 512–527 produce round windows with a titlebar, shadow, and other features.

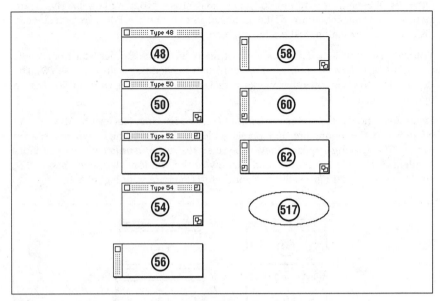

Figure 6-3: Macintosh extended windowType styles

Figure 6-4 shows the *windowType* codes for MIAWs under Windows 95. The appearance is similar under Windows 3.1, Windows 98, and Windows NT, and is similar to the Macintosh for most types. As in Figures 6-2 and 6-3, all windows are the same size and are evenly spaced, but may appear uneven due to the titlebars and borders. Under Windows, the minimum size of *windowTypes* –1, 0, and 8 is 112 pixels wide by 27 pixels high. Windows does not support custom WDEFs; the only useful extended *windowType* under Windows is 49, but its closebox doesn't work in D7.0. Note that the minimize button in *windowTypes* 8 and 12 does not work.

Table 6-3 summarizes the window types. The border of a MIAW is always at least one pixel wide (except for the custom borderless WDEF for Macintosh or border-less window Border Xtra for Windows). A window is moveable if it has a titlebar, and must be moved via Lingo if it does not. Windows without a close box must be closed manually via Lingo. The close box calls the *on closeWindow* handler, but does not perform a *forget window* command automatically. See "Opening, Closing, Forgetting, and Stacking MIAWs," later in this chapter.

The Buddy API Xtra (*http://www.mods.com.au/budapi*) can modify the buttons appearing in a window's titlebar under Windows.

WindowTypes listed as modal in Table 6-3 may not always remain in front in D7.0.

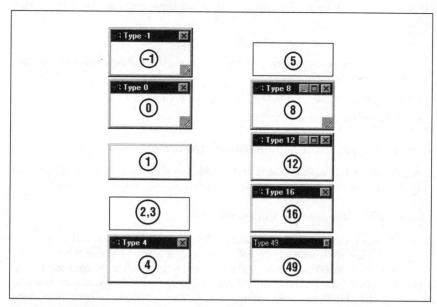

Figure 6-4: Windows 95 windowType styles

Table 6-3: Macintosh and Windows windowType Attributes

WindowType	Titlebar	Resize	Zoom	Border	Close Box	Modal
–1: Default	✓[1]	✓[1]			✓	No[2]
0: Document	✓[1]	✓[1]			✓	No[2]
1: Alert[3]				Thick		✓
2: Plain						
3: Plain with shadow				Shadow		
4: Document	✓				✓	
5: Movable	✓[4]			Thick[4]		✓
8: Document	✓	✓	✓		✓	
12: Document	✓		✓		✓	
16: Rounded Rect	✓			Rounded	✓	
48: Windoid[4]	✓	No[5]	No[5]		✓	
49: Windoid		No			✓	

[1] Defaults to yes, but depends on *the titleVisible of window* property.
[2] Defaults to no, but depends on *the modal of window* property.
[3] WindowType 1 creates an alert window that can live outside the Stage under Windows.
[4] Macintosh only.
[5] See Figure 6-3 for variations with resize and zoom boxes.

There is no such thing as a transparent Stage window, but you can simulate one using these steps:

1. Set *the visible of the stage* to FALSE.

2. Save a screen grab to a new cast member using the ScrnXtra (*http://www.little-planet.com/kent/kent.html*).

3. Use the screen grab as a background sprite in channel 1.

4. Set *the visible of the stage* to TRUE.

The Stage's windowType-Related Attributes

Changing *the windowType, modal,* and *titleVisible of the stage* have no effect, and the values returned by these properties are generally meaningless.

Changing the Stage on the Macintosh

A Macintosh Projector's Stage can have a titlebar in D7.0.1, which makes it moveable, but it does not have a zoom box, close box, or resize box. Use the *Show Title Bar* option (new in D7.0.1) under File ➤ Create Projector ➤ Options to add a title bar to a D7.0.1 Projector. In D6, the Mac Stage's window could be changed by editing the WIND resource named "Stage". Open WIND resource 1000 using ResEdit and select one of the window types as shown in Figure 6-5.

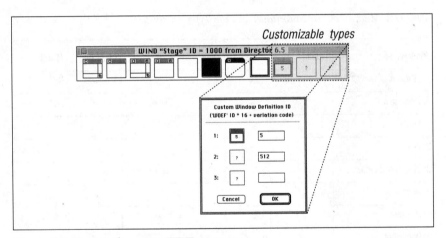

Figure 6-5: Macintosh custom WIND resources

To use a custom WDEF for the WIND resource, double-click one of the customizable window types shown in Figure 6-5. In the dialog box that appears, enter the WDEF *resourceID*× 16 (that is, if the WDEF *resourceID* is 32, enter 512).

You can edit the WIND resource in a single Projector, in the *Director 6.0 Resources* file (in which case it applies to future Projector builds), or in Director itself (which affects only authoring).

The Stage's default title is "Stage". Change it using:

```
set the title of the stage = "Custom Window Name"
```

or eliminate the title using:

```
set the title of the stage = EMPTY
```

Changing the Stage under Windows

Under Windows, the Stage can be set be set to *Full Screen*, in which case it is similar to the default Macintosh Stage (no titlebar, zoom box, close box, or resize box, nor is it moveable) and includes a desktop cover. Or the Stage can be set to *In a Window* mode, in which case it looks like a standard Windows application, and is moveable with an optional titlebar, zoom box, close box, and resize box. Select your preference under File ➤ Create Projector ➤ Options when creating your Projector.

Under Windows, *the title of the stage* defaults to the name of the Projector. *The titleVisible of the stage* defaults to TRUE, but it is only visible when played *In a Window* with the *Show Title Bar* option selected. The titlebar may prevent the bottom of the Stage from fitting on the screen if the Stage size is the same as the monitor dimensions.

During authoring, *Maximize* the Director 6 application window to eke out a few extra pixels at the top of the monitor if your Stage is as big as the monitor. This will hide the menu when the Stage is the only active window, giving you even more visible area. You'll still be able to *Minimize* the Director 6 application, but will need to quit and relaunch D6 to unmaximize its main window. In D7, use View ➤ Full Screen (Ctrl-Alt-1) to see the entire Stage if it is as big as the monitor.

Window Rects, Cropping, Panning, and Zooming

The *rect, sourceRect,* and *drawRect of window* properties determine a window's size and location, and the graphics displayed within it. They can be used to crop, pan, and zoom a MIAW.

None of the *windowType* styles includes scrollbars, even if the window is bigger than the monitor. You can simulate a titlebar, resize box, zoom box, close box, and even a scrollable window using standard sprites and custom Lingo.

Moving and cropping a MIAW's size and location

The rect of window determines the size and location of the visible portion of the MIAW or the Stage. The coordinates are monitor-relative (or relative to the Projector window if a Windows Projector is played *In a Window*), not Stage-relative, and exclude the titlebar, borders, and drop shadow, if any. On the Macintosh, a MIAW, unlike a sprite, can be positioned outside *the rect of the stage*.

Under Windows, if playing the Projector *Full Screen*, a MIAW can be positioned anywhere; in D6, if playing a Projector *In a Window*, MIAWs (except for *windowType* 1) must reside within the Projector window's bounds. In that case, to play a large MIAW from a smaller Stage, you must use *windowType* 1. You can instead use a large Stage window, but set *the visible of the stage* to FALSE to hide it. Then open a small MIAW to use as a surrogate Stage, and open a separate larger MIAW as originally desired. By opening the MIAWs from the Stage, they become children of the Stage window and can be placed anywhere within the Stage's bounding area (even though it is invisible).

The allowable position of MIAWs of various types relative to the Stage may be different in D7.0 and D7.0.1. See *http://www.zeusprod.com/nutshell/miaws.html* for current information.

The default *rect* of a MIAW is determined by its *Stage Location* and *Stage Size* as set under Modify ➤ Movie ➤ Properties when it was last edited.

The *left, top, right, bottom, width,* and *height of the rect of window* can be tested, but setting them has no effect. Instead, set *the rect of window* to change a MIAW's dimensions or position. The *stageLeft, stageTop, stageRight,* and *stageBottom* properties are shorthand for *the left of the rect of the stage,* etc. Setting *the rect of the stage* has no effect prior to D7.0.1. In D7.0, *the rect of the stage* does not update when the Stage window is moved during authoring, nor can it be set effectively. In D7.0.1, set it using:

```
set the rect of the stage = rect (ltrb)
```

The sourceRect of window gives the monitor-relative rectangle of a MIAW's original stage. The *sourceRect* can be changed only during authoring via Modify ➤ Movie ➤ Properties (which doesn't update the *sourceRect* until you close and reopen the movie). Use *the sourceRect* to restore a window to its default size and position, such as:

```
set the rect of window n = the sourceRect of window n
```

If *the rect of window* is smaller than *the sourceRect of window,* the MIAW content will be cropped. The window will show the upper left of the original movie, unless *the drawRect* has been altered.

When *the rect of window* is used under a Projector played *In a Window,* it is relative to the Stage window, not the monitor, as in other configurations. The *rect of the Stage* itself is always monitor-relative.

Window visibility—hiding a MIAW or the Stage

Changing *the visible of window* property hides or shows a MIAW, or you can use the *close* command, which also works for the Stage, such as:

```
set the visible of window whichWindow = FALSE
close window whichWindow
set the visible of the stage = FALSE
close the stage
```

You can determine whether a window is open by checking its *visible* property.

The *moveToBack* and *moveToFront* commands may cause MIAWs to obscure part or all of the Stage. In D7.0, MIAWs will disappear behind Full Screen Projectors, but this is fixed in D7.0.1. For MIAWs only, you can also set *the rect of window* somewhere offscreen. Use *forget window* to dismiss a window permanently.

If the *right* coordinate of *the rect of window* is less than the *left*, or the *bottom* is less than the *top*, the window may not appear or it may appear at the size of the default *sourceRect*.

Panning and zooming a MIAW or the Stage

The drawRect determines what section of the original MIAW appears within a window's frame and can be used to scale or pan the content in the window. The *drawRect* coordinates are relative to the *MIAW's own original Stage*, and default to its original dimensions. The left and top coordinate always default to zero, and the width and height default to match the MIAW's original Stage.

If the *drawRect*'s dimensions differ from *the rect of window*'s proportions, the contents of the MIAW are scaled. Text in fields and text members does not scale, and scaling bitmaps may degrade performance severely. To scale text, change its *fontSize of member* property or use bitmapped text instead.

To scale a MIAW's contents, perform the following steps. First, the default *drawRect* can be stored in a variable, as:

```
set origDrawRect = rect (0, 0, ¬
    the width  of the sourceRect of window n, ¬
    the height of the sourceRect of window n)
```

Then, to zoom out, decrease the size of the *drawRect*:

```
-- A scaleFactor of 2 zooms out by a factor of 2
set the drawRect of window n = origDrawRect / scaleFactor
```

Or, to zoom in, increase the size of the *drawRect*:

```
-- A scaleFactor of, say, 3 zooms in by a factor of 3
set the drawRect of window n = origDrawRect * scaleFactor
```

To reset the original zoom factor, use:

```
set the drawRect of window n = origDrawRect
```

Also see the *inflate(rect)* function in the online Help and the D7 *ShowMe* demo "Using the Lingo map() function."

Example 6-4 pans the content in a MIAW without scaling it.

Example 6-4: Panning MIAWs' Content

```
on panMIAW wName, endH, endV, numSteps, relative
  -- Get the starting position, for both panning
  -- and for relative positioning
  set startH = the left of the drawRect of window wName
  set startV = the top  of the drawRect of window wName
  -- Maintain the previous dimensions of the drawRect
  set widthH  = the width  of the drawRect of window wName
  set heightV = the height of the drawRect of window wName

  if relative then
    -- Position relative to current position, not (0,0)
    set endH = endH + startH
    set endV = endV + startV
  end if
```

Example 6-4: Panning MIAWs' Content (continued)

```
if numSteps > 0 then
   -- Pan smoothly from old to new position
   set incrH = float (endH - startH) / numSteps
   set incrV = float (endV - startV) / numSteps
   repeat with x = 1 to numSteps
      set nextH = startH +  x * incrH
      set nextV = startV +  x * incrV
      set the drawRect of window wName =  ¬
         rect (nextH, nextV, nextH + widthH, nextV + heightV)
   end repeat
else
   -- Jump to new position, be it relative or absolute
   set the drawRect of window wName =  ¬
      rect (endH, endV, endH + widthH, endV + heightV)
end if
end panMIAW
```

The following command smoothly pans the content in window "miaw1" from its current position until its upper-left corner is at the absolute position (100, 200). The pan occurs in ten steps.

```
panMIAW "miaw1", 100, 200, 10, FALSE
```

The following command immediately moves the content of window "miaw1" 100 pixels left and 200 pixels up from its current position.

```
panMIAW "miaw1", -100, -200, 0, TRUE
```

The border of the MIAW does not change in Example 6-4, as it is dependent only on *the rect of the window.*

Reader Exercise: Modify the example to change *the drawRect of the stage*, which will scale or pan the Stage's content, or to change a MIAW's *the rect of window*, which will move the MIAW's window frame across the screen without changing its content.

Window Focus and Active Windows

A window might lose or gain focus due to several commands (*moveToFront*, *moveToBack*, *open window*, *close window*, *forget window*, or *visible of window*) or a user action. Lingo's terminology regarding window focus is confusing. *The activeWindow* evaluates differently within each MIAW. *The frontWindow* is the same regardless of the MIAW from which it is evaluated. It changes only when the window in the foreground changes. Both properties are read-only. Refer to the *on activateWindow* and *on deactivateWindow* handlers under "MIAW messages."

activeWindow

> The *activeWindow* does not indicate the foremost window with focus, but rather the "current" window, either *(the stage)* or window *"windowName"*, in which a script is executing. It is convenient when a window must operate on itself (see Example 6-8). Example 6-5 detects whether the current movie is being run on the Stage or in a MIAW.

frontWindow

> The *frontWindow* indicates the foremost window with focus. During authoring, it returns (*the stage*) or (*window "windowName"*) unless another authoring window (such as the Cast or Score) is open, in which case it returns VOID. In a Projector, *the frontWindow* returns (*the stage*) only if no MIAWs are open, or if the Stage is forced to the front using *moveToFront* (or all MIAWs are moved back with *moveToBack*).

windowPresent("windowName")

> The *windowPresent()* function indicates only whether a window is on *the windowList*—the window may be closed (i.e., invisible). Example 6-6 counts the number of *open* (visible) windows.

Example 6-5: Differentiating a MIAW

```
on isMIAW
  if the activeWindow = (the stage) then
    return FALSE
  else
    -- the activeWindow is (window "windowName")
    return TRUE
  end if
end isMIAW
```

Example 6-6: Counting Visible Windows

```
on countVisibleMIAWs
  set winCount = 0
  repeat with x in the windowList
    if the visible of x then
      set winCount = winCount + 1
    end if
  end repeat
  return winCount
end countVisibleMIAWs
```

Reader Exercise: Modify Example 6-6 to check whether a visible window's *rect of window* property is onscreen as well.

Opening, Closing, Forgetting, and Stacking MIAWs

There are five commands (plus the *visible* property) that open and close MIAWs, change the stacking order, and remove MIAWs from memory. These commands affect the visual display of windows, and also call the event handlers as shown in Table 6-4.

Table 6-4: Commands to Open, Close, Forget, and Stack MIAWs

Command	Result	Calls Event Handler
moveToFront *windowID*[1]	Brings a window to the foreground	*on activateWindow*[2]
moveToBack *windowID*[1]	Sends a window to the back (last in stacking order)	*on deactivateWindow*[2,3]

The Stage and MIAWs

Command	Result	Calls Event Handler
open *windowID*,[1] or set the visible of *windowID*[1] = TRUE	Shows a window	*on openWindow*[4]
close *windowID*[1], or set the visible of *windowID*[1] = FALSE	Hides a window	*on closeWindow*[5]
forget window *whichWindow*[6]	Removes a MIAW from memory	*on closeWindow*

[1] *windowID* can be either *the stage* or *window whichWindow*.
[2] The *activateWindow* and *deactivateWindow* messages are not sent to the Stage.
[3] The *deactivateWindow* message is not reliably sent to MIAWs from within Windows Projectors, despite being sent during authoring.
[4] The *openWindow* message is sent only if the window was not previously open.
[5] The *closeWindow* message is sent only if the window was not previously closed.
[6] Don't use *forget the stage*, as it can cause a crash.

Closing a window does not remove it from memory or from *the windowList*; it just hides it from view. Use *forget window* to eliminate a window entirely. The following event handler forgets a window, so that Director can remove it from memory, whenever it is closed (such as via the closebox) or hidden:

```
on closeWindow
   forget window the activeWindow
end
```

When you *forget* a window, the numbers of subsequent windows in *the windowList* decrease by 1. Example 6-7 disposes of all MIAWs by repeatedly forgetting the first window remaining. Do not simply use *set the windowList = [ ]*.

Example 6-7: Disposing of All MIAWs

```
on killMIAWs
  repeat while count (the windowList)
    forget window 1
  end repeat
end killMIAWs
```

MIAW Messages

MIAWs and the Stage receive messages (sent because of Director, Lingo, or the user's actions) as shown in Tables 6-5 and 6-6. See Chapter 2, *Events, Messages, and Scripts,* in *Lingo in a Nutshell* for a detailed description of the order of events that are sent when a MIAW is opened and closed and when a movie is played using *go movie* or *play movie*. MIAWs also receive the standard messages (*prepareFrame, enterFrame, exitFrame, idle,* etc.).

Except for *on startUp*, the event handlers in Tables 6-5 and 6-6 must be placed in movie scripts.

Table 6-5: Movie-Related Event Handlers

Event Handler	Event Sent When
on startUp	Sent to *LINGO.INI* only when Projector is first started. (Not used for Shockwave.)
on prepareMovie[1]	Sent to a new movie that is starting *before* the first frame is drawn. Issued in Shockwave if Browser issues *Play( )* command. *PrepareMovie* is new as of D6. Some commands such as *quit* will not work in a *prepareMovie* handler and are better left for the *startMovie* handler.
on startMovie[1]	Sent to a new movie that is starting, *after* the first frame is drawn. Issued in Shockwave if Browser issues *Play( )* command.
on stopMovie[2]	Sent when a movie ends, including when using *quit* (but not *halt*), or when using *go movie* or *play movie* to start a new movie. Issued in Shockwave if Browser issues *Stop( )* command or user browses to new page.

[1] *prepareMovie* and *startMovie* events are sent to both the main movie and MIAWs.
[2] The main movie's *on stopMovie* handler is not called when using the *halt* command or when the user kills the Projector using a keyboard shortcut. MIAWs don't receive *stopMovie* events. See *on closeWindow* and *on deactivateWindow*.

The Lingo command *close window* is two words and should not be confused with the *on closeWindow* handler. Similarly, *open window* is a command, but *on openWindow* is a handler that gets called each time a window opens. Likewise, *the activeWindow* is a property that indicates the currently active window, but *on activateWindow* is a handler that gets called when a window is activated.

Table 6-6: Window-Related Event Handlers

Event Handler	Event Sent When
on activateWindow[1]	MIAW attains focus.
on closeWindow	*Close window* is issued, *forget window* is issued for an open window, *visible of window* is toggled to FALSE, or user clicks window close box.
on deactivateWindow[1,2]	MIAW loses focus.
on moveWindow[1]	User drags MIAW, but not when *rect of window* is repositioned via Lingo.
on openWindow	*Open window* is issued, or *visible of window* is toggled to TRUE.
on resizeWindow[1]	MIAW is resized by user with resize handles, but not when *rect of window* is changed via Lingo.
on zoomWindow[1]	User clicks zoom box (no way to tell if it is minimized or maximized).

[1] The Stage does not receive these messages.
[2] In D6 for Windows, the *deactivateWindow* message is never sent to MIAWs, even if the user clicks on the Stage or another application.

Window focus

When the focus shifts from one window to another, the *on deactivateWindow* handler is called for the MIAW losing focus before the *on activateWindow* handler is called for the window gaining focus. *The activeWindow* property, as always, equals the current window and can be used to perform any cleanup before losing focus. The MIAW receiving focus can then take appropriate action in its *on activateWindow* handler, as shown in Example 6-8. Modal windows should never lose focus until they are dismissed, but this is buggy in D7.0 (and fixed in D7.0.1).

Example 6-8: Gaining and Losing Focus

```
-- Place this handler in a movie script of the MIAW losing focus
on deactivateWindow
  set the title of the activeWindow to "Out of Service"
end
-- Place this handler in a movie script of the MIAW gaining focus
on activateWindow
  set the title of the activeWindow to "Ready for Action"
end
```

A MIAW gains focus and its *on activeWindow* handler is called if it did not already have focus and one of the following occurs:

- *open window* is used
- Its *rect of window* property is set
- Its *visible of window* property is set to TRUE
- All other windows are somehow deactivated
- It is brought to the foreground by a user click or the *moveToFront* command

A MIAW's *deactivateWindow* handler is called if one of the following occurs:

- *forget window* is used when the window is already closed or invisible
- *close window* is used when the window is open and visible
- Its *visible of window* property is set to FALSE
- Another window becomes active
- It is sent to the background by the *moveToBack* command

Communication Between MIAWs and the Stage

To pass information between MIAWs and the Stage, use global variables or global lists. Use the *tell* command to control the Stage from a MIAW or vice versa.

You can use the form *tell windowID to command,* such as:

```
tell the stage to go frame 50
```

Or you can use the a *tell...end tell* structure, such as:

```
tell window 1
  someHandlerName()
end tell
```

The previous example presumes that an *on someHandlerName* handler exists in a movie script of the MIAW. Messages can also be directed towards a specific sprite or script.

You can also use local variables within a *tell* statement, such as:

```
repeat with x = 1 to 50
  tell window 1 to put the name of member x
  tell window 2 to put the name of member x
end repeat
```

The following makes the main movie wait in a frame while any MIAWs exist:

```
on exitFrame
  if count (the windowList) then
    go the frame
  end if
end
```

MIAW Anomalies

MIAWs can cause unintended side effects. Use them sparingly and with caution.

MIAW bugs in D7.0

At press time, many of the outstanding issues with MIAWs in D7.0 are expected to be remedied in D7.0.1. These include focus problems with modal MIAWs, *windowType 49* not working properly, and MIAWs disappearing behind full-screen Projectors.

MIAWs not supported in Shockwave

MIAWs cannot be used in Shockwave, although an HTML page can contain multiple Shockwave movies that can communicate via JavaScript or using *setPref* and *getPref*.

MIAWs and keyboard events

A MIAW that has focus will intercept *keyDown* events even if it does not have any editable text fields. The main movie will receive *keyUp* events without any special accommodations. See Chapter 10, *Keyboard Events*, of *Lingo in a Nutshell* for solutions to the problem. Also see *the modal of window* property.

MIAWs and mouse events

Sprites on the main Stage can receive rollover events even when they are obscured by a MIAW placed over the Stage. See Chapter 9, *Mouse Events*, in *Lingo in a Nutshell* for solutions.

A MIAW will continue to receive and process events over its *rect of window* until it is forgotten (using *forget window*). Closing or hiding the window is not sufficient. If you intend to keep a hidden window around, set its *rect of window* off-Stage so that it does not trap any events unintentionally.

Sound conflicts

Recall that the Stage and MIAWs share the available sound channels. A MIAW may interfere with a sound in the main movie. Either wait for the sound to finish before opening the MIAW or play the sound from the MIAW.

Not releasing memory

MIAWs are not removed from memory until they are forgotten using the *forget window* command (*close window* merely hides the window). Even then, MIAWs that access objects will not be removed from memory until the objects they reference are cleared. Clear any references to objects from within your MIAW in your cleanup routine (either *closeWindow* or *deactivateWindow*).

Palettes

The Palette channel and the *puppetPalette* command are ignored within a MIAW. Use the same palette for MIAWs and the main movie or use a higher color depth (16-bit or 32-bit) in which palettes are irrelevant. The MIAW can tell the Stage to perform a *puppetPalette* command, as shown in Example 6-9.

Example 6-9: Initiating a Palette Change from a MIAW

```
on changePaletteFromMIAW paletteNum
  tell the stage
    puppetPalette paletteNum
  end tell
end changePaletteFromMIAW
```

Tempo and Transitions channels and performance

Each MIAW can have its own Tempo channel delays and frame rate setting separate from the main movie. Each MIAW can perform transitions independently of the main movie.

Beware of using many MIAWs, MIAWs with a high frame rate, and transitions in MIAWs. MIAWs can hog the CPU and severely degrade the main movie's performance. Even if a MIAW is closed or invisible, it still steals processor time. Use *forget window* to dispose of unneeded MIAWs. A MIAW will continue to loop even if the original movie from which it was created was not set to loop.

Conflicts with MUI

The MUI Dialog Xtra may conflict with open MIAWs. Close any MIAWs before using a MUI Alert or custom MUI dialog box or any feature of Director that uses MUI, such as the Behavior parameters dialog box. See *http://www.macromedia.com/support/director/ts/documents/unexpected_error.htm*.

Myron Mandell reports some success with using the MUI Xtra from MIAWs, but also reports that a modal MUI Alert dialog box cannot be dismissed when called from a modal MIAW on the Macintosh. He suggests the workaround shown in Example 6-10.

Example 6-10: Using MUI with a MIAW

```
if the platform contains "Macintosh" then
  set the modal of the activeWindow to FALSE
  displayMUIalert()  -- This is a custom handler
  set the modal of the activeWindow to TRUE
else
  displayMUIalert()  -- This is a custom handler
end if
```

PART II

Delivery and Optimization

CHAPTER 7

Cross-Platform and OS Dependencies

Director is remarkably similar across the Macintosh, Windows 3.1, 95, 98, and NT platforms. This chapter highlights the differences across platforms and across the various flavors of Windows. See also Macromedia's *Using Director* manual and Macromedia TechNote #03120 covering cross-platform issues.

Keep in mind that hardware varies widely. You must perform compatibility testing as described in Chapter 2, *Being More Productive*. See the same chapter for primers on the Mac OS and Windows, plus useful shortcuts.

Never diverge your Director movie file or Lingo code for different platforms. You will have to test and debug everything twice, which defeats the purpose of using Director. Use *the platform* to branch to platform-specific code instead.

This chapter lists the *intended* differences between platforms. There may also be platform-specific bugs. Consult the following sources to help determine whether a bug is platform-specific or machine-specific:

- Macromedia Tech Notes: *http://www.macromedia.com/support/director/ts/nav*

- UpdateStage's Mile High Quirk List: *http://www.updatestage.com/buglist.html*

- DOUG Bugbase: *http://www.director-online.com*

Chapter 18, *Lingo Keyword and Command Summary*, in *Lingo in a Nutshell* flags commands that vary between Macintosh and Windows.

Planning Your Cross-Platform Strategy

With planning, you can create a cross-platform product for only marginal additional effort. Without planning and testing, conversion may prove painful.

Test early. Test often. Test on all target platforms (including multiple browsers under multiple OSes for Shockwave or Internet-enabled Projectors). You have been warned.

You can't effectively test and debug cross-platform unless you have Director installed on both Macintosh and Windows computers and some easy way to transfer files between them. See "File transfers" in Chapter 2.

Cross-Platform Compatibility

The following items are the same across all major platforms or will work on all platforms if you obey the least common denominator (most stringent requirements), usually imposed by Windows 3.1:

- Director movie files (unprotected, protected, and compressed).

- Director castLib files (unprotected, protected, and compressed).

- Internal (embedded) cast members, including sounds and bitmaps.

- The vast majority of Lingo commands (exceptions follow).

- Many Xtras, such as the FileIO Xtra, have nearly identical syntax on all platforms, although variations may exist for individual methods.

- Some external document formats (such as PDF and HTML). Many external applications, such as Adobe Acrobat, are available cross-platform.

- External AIFF, SWA, and WAVE sound files.

- QuickTime 2 digital video files prepared to play on non-Apple platforms. Most QT3 files are cross-platform, except some codes, such as MPEG video.

- The same custom palette can often be used across platforms, although appearance may vary. See Chapter 13.

- Folders and filenames that obey the Windows 3.1 "eight-dot-three" short filename convention will also work under Windows 95/98/NT. ("Eight-dot-three" names also work on the Macintosh, although Macintosh file paths use a different format. See Chapter 14, *External Files*, in *Lingo in a Nutshell*.) In many cases, long filenames will confuse network software and CD-ROM burning software (depending on the setting, it will often truncate them to eight-dot-three format and add an "!" at the beginning of the name or a "~1" at the end). In rare cases, a Windows 95/98 user may disable long filename support, which will disrupt a shortcut pointing to a Projector with a long filename, for instance. Windows NT sometimes requires short filenames.

- Director converts the external file paths for linked cast members imported via File ➤ Import and linked castLibs automatically, assuming that the assets are in the same relative position to the Director movie. In D7, but not D6, it also adjusts paths for assets inserted via Insert ➤ Media Element automatically.

The following areas are always different across platforms:

- The Director authoring tool must be purchased separately for Macintosh and Windows. The Studio edition includes different Sound editors for Mac and Windows.

- Projectors need to be built separately for each platform, and the build options are slightly different across platforms.

- The D7 Multimedia Studio edition includes the Multiuser Server for only one platform (Mac or Windows). Unix and Linux versions are not available as of March 1999, but are expected.

- Many third-party Xtras must be purchased separately for Macintosh and Windows, and some are not available on all platforms.

- Some Macromedia Xtras, such as the ActiveX Control Xtra, are platform-specific or may not support Window 3.1 and 68K Macs.

- Many external applications are available on only one platform or operate significantly differently on different platforms.

- Some external document types (such as DIB files) are not cross-platform.

- OLE and ActiveX cast members and controls are Windows-only.

- AppleScript is Macintosh-only.

- Video for Windows (AVI) files are Windows-only, although they can be imported as QuickTime 3 members in D6.5 or D7 on a PowerMac.

- In D5 and earlier, WAVE audio files are supported under Windows only.

- Installers must be created separately for each platform.

- Anything that controls external devices is platform- and device-dependent (*mci* commands are Windows-only).

- *ReadMe* files often contain platform-specific instructions. Macintosh *ReadMe* files should be in SimpleText format. Windows *ReadMe* files should be plain text (TXT) files to be read by Notepad or MS Write. HTML format can be used on both platforms.

- Windows drive letters are machine-specific.

- File paths, such as that of the *Preferences* folder used by *getPref* and *setPref* and the System Preferences folder, are platform-specific.

- Any file paths to external sound files played via *sound playFile* are platform-specific, although proper paths can be created for each platform.

- The ability to run a CD automatically (AutoRun) when it is first inserted is different under Windows 95/98 and the Macintosh and is not supported under Window 3.1. See Chapter 8.

- Platform-specific configuration files, such as the Windows Registry file.

- Keyboard shortcuts to quit a Projector.

- Restart and shutdown commands (see Chapter 8).

Configuration-specific issues

The following items will vary with the user's configuration and may affect your production to varying degrees. For example, the size of the monitor limits the number of entries in a custom menu under Windows and also limits the number of configurable parameters in a Behavior during authoring (see *http://www.update-stage.com/previous/970801.html#item3*).

- Size, number, and color depth of monitors
- Video card and driver
- Sound card (should be SoundBlaster-compatible under Windows)
- Installed RAM, available RAM, and virtual memory configuration
- Installed drivers and extensions, including RSX, DirectX, etc.
- CD-ROM speed
- CD-ROM drive letter under Windows (varies depending on installed drives)
- Windows OS version or build including Service Packs, or Mac OS version
- Processor (486, Pentium, Pentium II, 68K, PowerPC, G3)
- Free hard drive space
- Network configuration
- Installed fonts
- QuickTime or Video for Windows availability and version
- Browser and plug-ins available
- Internet connection type and speed (modem, ISDN, T1, etc.)
- External applications' availability and version (such as Adobe Acrobat)

 Laptops, especially IBM Thinkpads, are notorious for nonstandard sound and video cards and drivers. Perform compatibility tests on popular laptops.

Refer to "Determining the Playback Platform" in Chapter 8 to detect the runtime environment including the platform type.

Porting Checklist

Here is a short checklist of things you can do to ensure that your product works cross-platform and under all flavors of Windows:

- Use Windows 3.1–compatible (eight-dot-three) short filenames.
- Use flattened and deforked QuickTime digital video files.
- Use cross-platform formats for any external sounds (AIFF, SWA, or WAVE).
- Use cross-platform formats for any external bitmaps (PICT, JPEG, GIF).
- Use a tempo that is achievable on all target platforms.

- Create Stub Projectors for each platform to access common Director assets.

- Do not bundle Xtras into your Projector.

- Avoid platform-specific Lingo.

- Avoid techniques that have platform-specific quirks, such as MIAWs.

- Avoid playing multichannel sound under Windows, if possible.

- Plan for platform-specific keyboard shortcuts.

- Avoid dissolve transitions, which are chunky under Windows.

- Avoid pure white or pure black pixels when using palette fades.

- Manage text and fonts as described in Chapter 12.

- Use 8-bit (256 color) graphics with a custom palette.

- Create a hybrid CD using Toast or similar ROM-burning software.

- Test early. Test often. Test on all target platforms.

Plan ahead

The largest portion of most multimedia projects is content preparation, which also tends to be the most platform-dependent aspect. Refer to the guidelines in the following section to avoid painful revisions.

Cross-Platform Differences

This section outlines the platform-specific issues in Director, including those related to the operating system, media elements, Xtras, external files, and Lingo.

Authoring Versus Playback

Authoring is remarkably similar on both platforms. The main difference during authoring is the keyboard shortcuts on the two platforms. Most keyboard shortcuts on the Macintosh use the Command and Option keys, whereas Windows uses the Control and Alt keys. Both platforms support the numeric keypad and the function keys for shortcuts. During authoring under Windows, context-sensitive menus are accessed with the right mouse button. The Macintosh uses Ctrl-click instead.

The external software required to accomplish a given task may not be available on both platforms. For example, Apple's QuickTime VR Authoring Studio requires a Power Macintosh, but can create QTVR files to be used on any platform.

Make-or-Break Decisions

Table 7-1 lists the things that would prevent you from being able to support a given platform, as might platform-dependent third-party Xtras. Some 32-bit Xtras that access internal Windows data structures, such as the TaskXtra from Little Planet (*http://www.littleplanet.com/kent/kent.html*), may support Windows 95/98, but not Windows NT. If your project includes external applications or demos that run only on limited platforms, you can choose not to support other platforms; or provide a warning that not all features are available.

Director 7 and Shockwave 7 do not support 68K Macs or Windows 3.1. Stick with D6 if supporting older platforms.

Table 7-1: Cross-Platform Limitations

If You Support This	You Cannot Use
Windows 3.1	Director 7, QuickTime 3, MUI Dialog, Custom Cursor, Flash, QD3D, DirMMX, and Alphamania Xtras. Graphics that require color depths greater than 8-bit. Non-direct-to-Stage QuickTime. Excessive numbers of external files.
Windows 95/98/NT	16-bit DLLs (XObjects) that cannot be relocated in memory. Non-direct-to-Stage QuickTime is supported for QuickTime 3, but not QuickTime 2.
Macintosh 68K	Director 7, QuickTime 3, Custom Cursor, Flash, and QD3D Xtras. Video for Windows (AVI). ActiveX or OLE cast members.
Power Mac	ActiveX or OLE cast members. Video for Windows (AVI) requires QuickTime 3.

Platform and Processor

Naturally, *the platform* and *the machineType* properties vary across platforms. *The platform* command returns "Macintosh,68K", "Macintosh,PowerPC", "Windows,16", or "Windows,32" (in the Director for Java Player, it returns "Java *version, browser, OS*").

The machineType returns 256 for all Windows PCs and an integer code for each Macintosh. The *runMode* returns "Author" (in Director), "Projector" (in Projectors), "Plugin" (in Shockwave), or "Java Applet" (in the Java Player). Refer to Chapter 8 for more details, including those on deciphering the Windows OS version and the installed CPU using Xtras.

Platform specifics

Only Windows supports the *DIRECTOR.INI* file (see Appendix D, *The DIRECTOR.INI and LINGO.INI Files*, in *Lingo in a Nutshell*). Director for Windows has supported the *LINGO.INI* file since D4, but it wasn't supported on the Macintosh until D5.

D7 has unofficial/undocumented support for Projector configuration parameters stored in a *Projector.INI* file. See *http://www.zeusprod.com/nutshell/otto.html* for details.

Director does not directly support platforms other than Macintosh and Windows. Past versions have partially supported OS/2, and there was even a 3DO-compatible player. Unix support is limited to the new Java Export Xtra that ships with D6.5 and D7 and creates a Java applet (although there was an old SGI-compatible player for Director 4). The Flash Player, but not Director, has been ported to Linux.

Windows 3.1 limitations

Windows 3.1 (and any 16-bit Windows Projector) is the most restrictive platform. D7 does not support Windows 3.1 at all and D6 supported Windows 3.1 Projectors, but not authoring. The number of simultaneous open files was limited to 20 in D5. Although the limit was raised to 100 open files in D6, the number of available file handles is limited to the value specified in the Windows *CONFIG.SYS* file.

Whereas Projectors can run under Windows 3.1 in higher color depths, graphics in Director's offscreen buffer are drawn only at an 8-bit depth. QuickTime video (which bypasses Director for Windows' compositing buffer) will use thousands of colors, but bitmaps of any depth will be displayed as 8-bit, with a corresponding reduction in color fidelity. Use 8-bit graphics with a custom palette instead.

16-bit Windows Projectors, even when played under Windows 95/98/NT, always use 8-bit color (256 colors).

The timer resolution under Windows 3.1 is fairly coarse. It measures only within about 4 ticks (and there are actually 62.5 ticks per second instead of the nominal 60). Consider using a dummy digital video sprite with a silent audio track for more accurate timing.

Under Windows 3.1, very large projects may exceed the limits of the Lingo Symbol Table. See *Lingo Table Archaeology*, available at *http://www.zeusprod.com/nutshell/chapters/symtable.html*.

The length of text strings may be limited under Windows 3.1. For example, the older *FileIO.DLL* (XObject) for Windows was limited to transferring 64 KB of data from or to an external text file in a single operation. Larger amounts of data had to be read in 64 KB chunks.

There are unconfirmed reports that the *on prepareMovie* handler is not called in Windows 3.1 Projectors in D6.

32-bit Windows 95/98/NT OSes and Windows NT quirks

Although Windows 95, 98, and NT are all 32-bit operating systems, they are far from identical. Even "Windows 95" can vary dramatically depending on which of the numerous patches released by Microsoft have been installed. (Many of these are installed by Internet Explorer, but uninstalling IE does not remove all of the files.)

Director 7 for Windows builds only 32-bit Projectors, but D6 and earlier versions could also create 16-bit Projectors. Windows 95/98 can run either type, but 32-bit Projectors are strongly preferred. Although you can theoretically use a 16-bit (Windows 3.1) Projector under Windows NT, a 32-bit (Windows 95/NT) Projector is highly recommended. Even so, the majority of Windows playback anomalies are reported under Windows NT, particularly those involving sound and video.

 If supporting NT, test on NT. You have been warned. See *http://www.zeusprod.com/nutshell/nt.html* for NT-specific quirks. Don't bundle Xtras into a Projector if supporting NT.

Although it theoretically shouldn't matter, reports are that Projectors built on an NT machine run better under NT than Projectors built under Windows 95/98. It has also been reported that Projectors that access multiple movies within the Projector crash with an "Exception: access violation" error under NT. (This despite the fact that the Lingo code works fine on other platforms.) Use a stub Projector with a single small movie in it, leaving other Director movies external. (I recommend this approach anyway.)

If you use a Lingo command, FileIO method, or Xtra that attempts to read from a nonexistent drive, it will cause a "Drive not ready. Abort?, Retry?" error under Windows NT, but not under Windows 95. See Example 8-6.

There have not been clear reports of trouble specific to Windows 98, but neither has Director been used by the developer community under Windows 98 for long. Some unconfirmed quirks in QT3 playback have been alleged. If delivering for Windows, test on all flavors, including Windows 98.

Director 7 (and to a lesser extent D6) supports multiple monitors under Windows 98. Test on multi-monitor systems, as they are more likely to be used by a consumer with the advent of Windows 98.

Hardware to beware

Here is a list of some of the types of hardware that can cause problems. For example, one user reported that PCs with dual processors crash when viewing their Shocked web site. Some hardware problems may be beyond your control, but any of these components should raise a red flag:

- Networked drives, especially CD-ROMs
- CD-ROM drives that may not read all one-off "pre-master" CDs, especially very fast CDs
- Laptop computers (most have nonstandard sound and video cards and drivers, especially Thinkpads)
- Dual- or multi-processor machines
- Multiple monitors and/or video cards
- Various printer incompatibilities or older printer drives
- Testing from a Jaz drive
- Testing from a system configured with multiple OSes and Boot Manager
- Custom hardware, such as video cameras, MIDI synthesizers, or VideoDiscs

Projectors and Runtime Issues

Macintosh and Windows platforms require separate Projectors that can only be built with the version of Director for their respective platforms. Prior to D7, you may wish to build more than one Projector for Windows, and even for the Macintosh, depending on the platforms you intend to support. D7 supports only PowerPC Projectors for Macintosh, and 32-bit Projectors for Win 95/98/NT.

Prior to D7.0.1, the *In a Window* Projector creation option pertains only under Windows. The *Reset Monitor to Match Movie's Color Depth* and *Use System Temporary Memory* Projector creation options pertain only to the Macintosh.

Windows Projectors are allocated memory as needed, whereas Macintosh Projectors receive a fixed memory allocation. Refer to Chapter 9, *Memory and Performance*.

Note that Projector names should obey the same filenaming conventions as other files for a particular platform. Windows Projectors should have an *.EXE* file extension but cannot be named *COMM.EXE*, which is reserved for the Windows OS. The default Windows 3.1 Projector name under D6, *PROJECTOR.EXE*, should be renamed to less than 8 letters to work under Windows 3.1.

If a Macintosh Projector is double-clicked more than once, only one copy of the Projector will be launched. It is possible to launch multiple copies of a single Windows Projector by double-clicking it several times. See Chapter 8.

Under Windows, Director may require write access to the Windows system directories in order to install temporary drivers, but such privileges are often denied under Windows NT.

Bundled Xtras are copied to the system disk at runtime and may cause an error opening *C:\WINNT* or *C:\TEMP* on NT machines, especially those with a hard disk partition larger than 4 GB. Don't bundle Xtras into your Projector—use an Xtras folder instead. See Chapter 10, *Using Xtras*.

The *saveMovie* command works on the Macintosh even for movies embedded within a Projector. On Windows, it only works with movies external to the Projector.

See Chapter 8 for many more Projector and runtime issues including the different methods for autostart/autoplay on the two platforms.

Memory and performance

Performance and available memory vary greatly across different machines running the same OS and across different platforms. Test your project early and often on machines with varying amounts of RAM and processing power.

If you test only on your development machine, you'll probably find that your project runs slowly on your target machine, and requires more than the minimum specified memory.

Macintosh applications (including Projectors) generally receive a fixed amount of memory (as set in the Finder's File ➤ Get Info window). Macintosh Projectors built with the *Use System Temporary Memory* option will also access additional RAM available to the system beyond their fixed pool of memory. (I don't recommend this option, because it causes trouble on 68040 Macs.) The File ➤ Preferences ➤ General ➤ *Use System Temporary Memory* option allows Director to access additional system memory during authoring.

Windows applications, including Projectors, share a common pool of memory. More RAM is made available to an application as needed. You can use Director 6 for Windows' File ➤ Preferences ➤ General ➤ *Limit Memory Size* option to simulate playback on a machine with less installed RAM. This option is not available in D7.

The inherent difference in the memory allocation scheme for Windows and Macintosh means that the values returned by certain memory commands are less meaningful under Windows, where memory changes dynamically. (The Memory Inspector also shows different information on the two platforms.)

The platform differences affect the following memory-related commands:

> *the memorySize*
> *the freeBlock*
> *the freeBytes*

The Windows-only *DIRECTOR.INI* file includes some options affecting disk swap space used for Projectors and during Authoring. Refer to Chapter 9 and to Appendix D in *Lingo in a Nutshell* for details on the following options:

```
[Memory]
ExtraMemory = kilobytes
SwapFileMeg = megabytes
```

The following commands affect how often Director for Macintosh allows the processor to service other requests (see Chapter 9). These commands have no effect under Windows or in Shockwave:

> *the cpuHogTicks*
> *the netThrottleTicks*

The Stage and MIAWs

The appearance of the Stage window varies under Macintosh and Windows, as described in Chapter 6, *The Stage and Movies-in-a-Window*, and Chapter 8. Not all *windowTypes* can be positioned outside the Stage boundaries under Windows, particularly prior to D7. The *deactivateWindow* message is not reliably sent to MIAWs from Windows Projectors. Custom window definitions (WDEFs) are supported on the Macintosh only.

MIAWs are not supported in Shockwave on either platform.

Palettes

Windows palette requirements are more restrictive than Macintosh palettes. Most of these issues can be avoided by using thousands or millions of colors, but that is not supported under Windows 3.1, and it degrades performance relative to 8-bit mode. See Chapter 13, *Graphics, Color, and Palettes.*

8-bit (256-color) palettes and reserved colors

Cross-platform products do not need different palettes on the different platforms. (Do not be misled by palette names such as "System – Mac" and "System – Win.")

Under Windows, the first ten and last ten palette positions are used by the OS to draw the user interface. If the colors in those positions do not match the colors in the default Windows palette, dialog boxes and other Windows components will

---

appear in the wrong colors. Because many graphics programs put the darkest colors at the end of a palette, Windows dialog boxes (which use those palette positions) may be unreadable and appear almost solid black when using a custom 8-bit palette.

Under Windows, it is best to use the reserved colors in the first and last ten positions of any custom palettes. Therefore, the built-in "System – Win" palette is a better cross-platform choice than the "System Mac" palette, which doesn't reserve the Windows colors. (The "System – Win" palette is the corrected version of the "System – Win (Dir 4)" palette that was not the true Windows default palette.) Versions of the built-in palettes with the first and last 10 colors reserved are included in D6 under Xtras ➤ Libraries ➤ Palettes. When creating custom palettes, the first and last ten positions can be reserved using deBabelizer (*http:// www.equilibrium.com*), Photoshop, or even Director's Color Palettes window.

4-bit (16-color) palettes

In the exceedingly rare case when the monitor is set to display only 16 colors, the VGA palette is the only 4-bit Windows palette allowed, whereas Macintosh 4-bit palettes can contain any 16 colors.

Gamma

Windows monitors tend to display the same RGB (or HSB) values somewhat darker than Macintosh monitors, because Windows monitors tend to have a lower gamma. Test your graphics on all target platforms before committing to a particular palette or consider using different palettes on the two platforms (not recommended).

Palette fades

On either platform, the first color (index 0) in any palette must be pure white, and the last color (index 255) must be pure black. Avoid having pure white or pure black in other palette positions (use off-white and off-black instead), because any pixels using those colors will be remapped to the first and last index. Windows cannot fade the first and last palette positions, so black pixels remain black and white pixels remain white during a palette fade. Palette fades work only in 8-bit mode (256 colors). At other depths, a jump-cut is performed and sprites may disappear from the Stage.

Platform-specific palette problems

Windows dialog boxes of any sort, such as alert boxes or file browser dialogs, can corrupt custom Windows palettes. Use the following in the *DIRECTOR.INI* file to prevent palette conflicts:

```
[Palette]
Animation = 0
```

This severely slows down palette fades in Director. Refer to Chapter 13 for complete details and for alternative solutions if you are using palette fades.

Playing QuickTime movies with different custom palettes on the Macintosh can lead to an incorrect palette. QuickTime 2 for Macintosh ordinarily uses the first custom palette and ignores subsequent palette changes. Refer to Chapter 13 for details on resetting the Macintosh QuickTime palette with the FixPalette XObject (*http://ftp.macromedia.com/downloads/*). It is not needed with QuickTime 3.

Monitors

Don't forget to test computers at various monitor color depths and sizes. You should generally center your Projector on larger screens and make sure it fits on smaller screens. Table 7-2 shows the typically supported monitor resolutions. Note that 640×480 is common to both platforms, although you could use an 800×600 Stage on an 832×624 Macintosh, for example.

Table 7-2: Monitor Resolutions

Platform	Monitor Resolutions
Macintosh	640 × 480
	800 × 600 (iMac only)
	832 × 624
	1024 × 768
	1152 × 870
Windows	640 × 480
	800 × 600
	1024 × 768
	1280 × 1024

Refer to *the centerStage* and *the deskTopRectList* properties, as covered in Chapter 8.

Dual monitors

Windows 98 and Windows NT support dual monitors, as does the Macintosh. Even Windows 95 can use dual monitors with a special video card. Test your product on a dual-monitor setup to ensure compatibility. Custom menubars, if any, appear on the primary monitor. Full-screen Projectors don't cover secondary monitors.

Monitor color depth

Macintoshes tend to perform better than Windows machines at higher color depths, but 8-bit (256-color) monitors are still the lowest common denominator. Palette fades work only in 8-bit mode (256 colors). The offscreen compositing buffer is always 8-bit under Windows 3.1, regardless of *the colorDepth* and *the fullColorPermit* settings. When using a Windows 3.1 (16-bit) Projector, graphics will be mapped through the current 8-bit palette even at higher color depths.

The *colorDepth* property can be tested under Windows, but it can be set reliably only on the Macintosh. On most Windows 95 PCs, setting *the colorDepth* does nothing. Some Macintoshes may be able to display millions of colors without being able to display thousands of colors (16-bit). Macintoshes set to millions of colors return 32 as *the colorDepth*. Windows machines set to millions of color return 24 as *the colorDepth*. Refer to Chapter 13 for details on setting and testing *the colorDepth*.

If a flash occurs when switching between movies on the Macintosh, but not under Windows, usually the monitor color depth is being reset to match the highest depth bitmap, and it is not a palette-related issue. Disable the *Reset Monitor to Match Movie's Color Depth* option when building your Macintosh Projector. See Example 13-3, which finds cast members with an aberrant *depth of member* setting.

The following color-related Lingo commands are platform-dependent:

> *the backColor of member* (uses different palette mappings)
> *the backColor of sprite*
> *the colorDepth* (can only be set reliably on the Macintosh)
> *the colorQD* (should always be true for all supported systems)
> *the foreColor of member* (uses different palette mappings)
> *the foreColor of sprite*
> *the fullColorPermit* (ignored under Windows 3.1)
> *the switchColorDepth* (ignored under Windows)

Transitions

Transition performance varies widely across machines, and transition times are not guaranteed. Pixel dissolves are noticeably chunkier and slower under Windows. Performing a transition while a digital video is playing is egregiously slow under Windows, but less so on the Macintosh.

Macromedia's *Lingo Dictionary* entry for the *puppetTransition* command claims that the *Dissolve Bits, Dissolve Bits Fast, Dissolve Pixels*, and *Dissolve Pixels Fast* transitions don't work at 32-bit color depths, but they work fine on both Power Macs and under Windows 95. Third-party transition Xtras may not be supported on all platforms, or may perform so poorly on some platforms as to be unusable.

Media

If prepared properly and limited to appropriate file formats, the same media can be used on all platforms. All internal (embedded) cast member types are completely cross-platform. Refer to Table 4-4 for supported file formats.

Graphics file formats

Some graphics formats importable on Windows are not supported on the Macintosh. Once imported into the Cast, the format of the original file is irrelevant, and can be brought over to the Macintosh.

Digital video

The most common cross-platform digital video solution is to ship QuickTime movies prepared for cross-platform playback and the QuickTime for Windows installer. Most Macintosh consumer products assume that the user already has the QuickTime Extension installed. QuickTime 2.x's features varied somewhat between Macintosh and Windows. QuickTime 3 is highly similar across platforms, but Director supports QT3 cast members only on PowerMacs and Windows 95/98/NT. QT3 supports MPEG video on the Macintosh, but not Windows. Refer to Chapter 16, *Digital Video*, for complete details on cross-platform digital video caveats and differences.

Refer particularly to the following Lingo properties:

> *the controller of member*
> *the digitalVideoType of member* (*#videoForWindows* or *#quickTime*)
> *the directToStage of member*
> *mci* (supported under Windows only)
> *the quickTimePresent*
> *quickTimeVersion()* (requires QT3 Xtra included with D6.5 and D7)
> *the timeScale of member*
> *the videoForWindowsPresent*

Sound

There are significant differences between audio playback on the two platforms (covered in detail in Chapter 15, *Sound and Cue Points*). Ignore them at your own peril! Depending on the method used and the Windows configuration, there may be unacceptable latency when playing multiple sounds, or some sounds may not play at all under Windows.

To maximize cross-platform compatibility, use either internal sound cast members or external SWA, AIFF, or WAVE files. (AIFF files were the only cross-platform format in Director 5.) See Table 15-1 for supported sound formats.

All audio should have one of the PC-compatible sampling rates (11.025, 22.050, or 44.1 kHz) and not the variations that are Macintosh-specific (11.127, 22.254 kHz, or other variations).

Director 6.5 and D7 support cue points in WAVE files, in addition to the AIFF, SWA, and digital video cue points supported in D6.0.x.

Sound volumes, especially those set by *the soundLevel* command, may vary across platforms. Sound fades also behave differently under Windows than on the Macintosh.

Director for Macintosh can record sounds (authoring-only) using Insert ➤ Media Element ➤ Sound. Only Windows supports *mci* commands for playing audio from external devices.

The methods of creating SWA-compressed sounds vary cross-platform.

Windows laptops in particular tend to have nonstandard sound cards. Obtain the latest drivers and test early on the targeted laptops.

Refer to Chapter 15 in this book and to Appendix D in *Lingo in a Nutshell* for details on these and other numerous Windows settings that affect audio mixing, buffers, and volume, including *MixMaxChannels* and the *SoundLevel* settings.

Other data types

OLE cast members are supported under Windows only (using Edit ➤ Paste Special ➤ Using OLE). On the Macintosh, they are treated as bitmaps.

PICTs are supported on both platforms, but can be maintained as PICTs only on the Macintosh (using Edit ➤ Paste Special ➤ As PICT).

QuickTime 3, Flash, Custom Cursor, QuickDraw 3D, and the new Animated GIF, Vector Shape, Font, and Text cast members are supported only on Power Macs and Windows 95/98/NT (not Windows 3.1 or 68K Macs).

The Alphamania Xtra (see *http://www.medialab.com*) is not supported under Windows 3.1, and requires 32-bit cast members on other platforms (although playback can be at 8-bit or 16-bit color depths).

User Interface

The appearance of various menus, dialog boxes, colors, and fonts is platform-dependent. A Windows Projector will look like a standard Windows application, and a Macintosh Projector will look like a standard Macintosh application. The MUI Dialog Xtra is supported on the Macintosh and Windows 95/98/NT only (not Windows 3.1).

Mouse

Windows mice have two or three buttons, whereas Macintosh mice usually only have one button. The right mouse button can be detected separately under Windows and simulated with a Ctrl-click on the Macintosh. Mouse response tends to be more sluggish under Windows, and the double-click interval may vary.

Refer to these properties and handlers in Chapter 9, *Mouse Events*, in *Lingo in a Nutshell*:

> the emulateMultiButtonMouse
> the rightMouseUp
> the rightMouseDown
> on rightMouseDown
> on rightMouseUp

Keyboard and modifier keys

The keys used to quit a Projector vary on the Macintosh and Windows. Windows uses Ctrl-Q, Ctrl-., Escape, Alt-Tab, and Alt-F4 to either quit the Projector or temporarily switch programs. Ctrl-Q does not quit Projectors in D7.0 for Windows—use Escape or Alt-F4. The Macintosh uses Cmd-Q, Cmd-., and Escape to quit the Projector. (*The exitLock* property locks out the keyboard combinations that are used to quit Projectors on each specific platform.) Refer to Chapter 10 in *Lingo in a Nutshell* to trap these key combinations.

The Alt key is used to access menus under Windows, and the Control key is used for keyboard menu shortcuts. On the Macintosh, the Command key is used for keyboard menu shortcuts.

These keyboard properties behave slightly differently on the two platforms:

* The *commandDown* property indicates whether the Command key on the Macintosh or the Control key under Windows is being pressed (*the controlDown* indicates the state of the Control key on both platforms).

* The *optionDown* property indicates whether the Option key on the Macintosh or the Alt key under Windows is being pressed.

The keyCode property returns the same values on both the Macintosh and Windows, even for function keys, arrow keys, and the numeric keypad. However, Macintosh and Windows treat upper- and lowercase characters differently. See "String Comparisons" later in this chapter. Some keys and their key codes may be specific to a given platform if they don't appear on both keyboards.

Fonts

The same fonts generally aren't available on both platforms. D7 allows you to embed custom fonts in new *#font* cast members for use by *#field* and *#text* cast members. In earlier versions, you can use *#richtext* or *#bitmap* cast members, which maintain their appearance without requiring fonts, but require a lot of RAM for large amounts of text. Use field cast members and the *FONTMAP.TXT* file to map fonts across different platforms in D6 and earlier. Refer to the "Fonts and Formatting" section in Chapter 12, *Text and Fields*.

The *fontStyle of member* field property supports the same settings on both platforms, but the "condense," "extend," "outline," and "shadow" attributes are only apparent on the Macintosh.

Menus

Menus operate somewhat differently on different platforms, as detailed in Table 14-6. Only the Macintosh supports styled text (bold, italic, etc.) for menu items and the display of a checkmark next to menu items. Refer to "Menus" in Chapter 14, *Graphical User Interface Components*, for additional details.

Macintosh menus can exceed the screen dimensions and scroll automatically, but are limited to about 255 items. Scrolling menus are not supported under Windows; although long Windows menus include a *More...* option, selecting *More...* leads to an empty dialog box. So under Windows, your custom menu must fit on one screen. Use the PopUp Xtra described in Chapter 14 to create hierarchical menus instead.

Cursors

You can either use one-bit cast members or a cursor resource ID to define a cursor and its mask, but not all cursor resources are supported on both platforms. Use one-bit cast members as cursors to guarantee cross-platform usage (copy the bitmaps of cursor resources into the Paint window to create bitmap cast members from them). The Custom Cursor Xtra included with D6.5 and D7 is supported on Power Macs and Windows 95/98/NT only (not Windows 3.1 or 68K Macs). Refer to *the cursor of sprite* property and *cursor* command under "Cursors" in Chapter 14.

Xtras

Xtras, XObjects, XFCNs, XCMDs, and DLLs are all platform-specific. Xtras and XObjects can be created for each platform, but a given Xtra or XObject file works on one platform only. XFCNs and XCMDs are Macintosh-only. DLLs are Windows-only. Make sure that the necessary Xtras are available for the platforms you intend to support. Look for Xtras that work the same on all platforms.

Both platforms allow Xtras to be bundled into Projectors (not recommended), but XObjects, XFCNs, and XCMDs can also be added manually to a Macintosh Projector's resource fork. The *XTRAINFO.TXT* file is used to translate Xtra names between platforms.

For a given task, you may need an Xtra on one platform but not the other. For example, the Macintosh does not allow the user to eject a CD manually, and thus an Xtra is required for this. Under Windows, a CD can be ejected manually by the user or automatically using *mci* commands.

Refer to Chapter 10 in this book and to Chapter 13, *Lingo Xtras and XObjects*, in *Lingo in a Nutshell* for additional details.

External Files

External files and applications can vary dramatically across platforms. The biggest difference is the way that drives, paths, and filenames are specified on the two platforms. For maximum compatibility, limit folder names to eight characters and filenames to eight characters with a three-letter extension. Do not use spaces or long filenames. When burning CD-ROMs, you should also obey the more stringent ISO 9660 file-naming standard that allows only alphanumeric characters and underscores (no hyphens or other characters).

Table 7-3 lists some basic cross-platform differences for external files.

Table 7-3: External File Differences

Item	Macintosh	Windows
CD and drive identifiers	CD drives identified by fixed name	Drive identified by varying letter depending on installed devices, such as D, E, or F
File path spec	*MacHD:myFolder:myFile.doc*	*D:\myFolder\myFile.doc*

Table 7-3: External File Differences (continued)

Item	Macintosh	Windows
File path separator	All items separated by colons (:)	Drive letter separated by colon and backslash (:\); folders separated by backslash (\)
File type determined by	Optional three-letter extension, or internal File Type (four-character case-sensitive code)	Mandatory three- or four-letter file extension
File structure	Files can contain both resource and data forks	Files contain data forks only
Text file lines separated by	Carriage return (CR)	Carriage return and line feed (CR/LF)

Keep in mind that some FileIO Xtra commands vary cross-platform and any command involving long filenames may not work as expected under Windows. For example, FileIO under Windows sometimes ignores spaces in long filenames. Also, Director's behavior when you omit a file extension may differ under Windows and on the Macintosh. For example, using *go movie "someName"* without specifying the .DIR extension will fail if there is a Windows subfolder named *someName* in the same directory.

See Chapter 14 in *Lingo In a Nutshell* for details on external files, the FileIO Xtra, and the following Lingo.

These external file commands are supported on the Macintosh only:

> *closeDA* (obsolete)
> *closeResFile* (obsolete)
> *getFinderInfo* (FileIO Xtra)
> *openDA* (obsolete)
> *openResFile* (obsolete)
> *setFinderInfo* (FileIO Xtra)
> *showResFile* (obsolete)

These commands use different path specifications on Macintosh and Windows:

> *the applicationPath*
> *closeXlib* (obsolete)
> *createFile* (FileIO Xtra)
> *the fileName of castLib*
> *the fileName of member*
> *the fileName of window*
> *getNthFileNameInFolder* (sees hidden files on Mac but not Windows)
> *getOSdirectory* (FileIO Xtra; Mac System Folder or Windows folder)
> *getPref* (uses different folders on Mac and Windows)
> *go movie*
> *the moviePath*
> *open*

open...with
openFile (FileIO Xtra)
openXlib (obsolete)
the pathName (obsolete system property)
the pathName of member
play movie
the searchPath (obsolete)
the searchPaths
setFilterMask (FileIO Xtra; Mac file types or Windows file extensions)
setPref (uses different folders on Mac and Windows)
showXlib
sound playFile
the streamName of member
the URL of member

Note that Director automatically adjusts the file paths for linked cast members imported via File ➤ Import, but not via the Insert menu in D6. D7 addresses the problem.

Math

The speed of math operations may be somewhat faster on Windows machines, although you wouldn't notice unless you were doing a large number of calculations. For some overflow or undefined conditions, the Windows and Macintosh platforms may return different values, especially in regard to NAN (error code indicating "Not a Number") or INF (error code indicating "Infinite"), as follows:

On the Macintosh:

```
put log(-1)
-- NAN
```

Under Windows:

```
put log(-1)
-- 0.0000000000e+0
```

The maxinteger and maximum float values

The maxInteger and the highest allowed float value are the same on both platforms, but the Macintosh and Windows handle overflow conditions differently. Both Macintosh and Windows:

```
put the maxInteger
-- 2147483647
```

On the Macintosh:

```
put the maxInteger + 1
-- -2147483648
put 1e309
-- INF
```

Under Windows:

```
put the maxInteger + 1
-- -0
put 1e309
-- -INF
```

Some implicit type conversions may differ across the two platforms. When comparing operands of disparate types (such as lists and integers), always perform explicit type conversion (using *integer()*, *float()*, etc.) to ensure that they operate as intended.

Prior to D7, the *random()* function returns a different series of values on the two platforms, even with the same initial *the randomSeed*. In D7, both platforms return the same series of random numbers. See Chapter 8, *Math (and Gambling)*, in *Lingo in a Nutshell.*

String Comparisons

Director sometimes relies on the underlying OS-dependent system calls to implement a particular feature. If Macintosh and Windows perform an operation differently, you may be in for a surprise. One notable case is string comparisons.

Director for Macintosh string comparison ranks the characters as follows:

"A" < "a" < "B" < "b", etc.

But Director for Windows string comparison ranks them as:

"a" < "A" < "b" < "B", etc.

Therefore, the same comparison may return different results on Macintosh and Windows.

On the Macintosh:

```
put "a" < "A"
-- 0
```

Under Windows:

```
put "a" < "A"
-- 1
```

String comparisons involving inequalities (>, <=, >, and >=) are case-sensitive. Comparisons using equals (=), not equals (<>), or the *offset()*, *contains*, and *starts* string commands are case-*insensitive*. The solution is to rely only on the equals (=) and not-equals (<>) operators, or first convert all characters in both strings to the same case (see Example 3-2).

Both the Macintosh and Windows rank characters with *diacritical marks* (accents, umlauts, etc.) along with the standard alphanumerics—but again, they vary slightly between platforms.

On the Macintosh:

"A" < "Ã" < "a" < "ã"

Under Windows:

> "a" < "A" < "ã" < "Ã"

Refer to Appendix C, *Case-Sensitivity, Space-Sensitivity, and Sort Order*, in *Lingo in a Nutshell* for details and utilities to address the problems.

Dates and Times

The timer resolution varies on the different platforms. It is accurate within approximately four ticks under Windows 3.1, but is accurate within one tick under Windows 95/98/NT and on the Macintosh. In D6 for Windows, there are 62.5 ticks per second. In D7, there are 60 ticks per second on both platforms. D7 also adds *the milliseconds* property for more accurate timing.

The format of dates and times can vary wildly depending on the user's country and system configuration. D7's new *systemDate()* and *date()* functions return and manipulate Y2K-compliant dates independently of the user's configuration.

The *timeScale of member* property has different defaults for QuickTime on the Macintosh, QuickTime for Windows, and Video for Windows. See Chapter 16.

Error Codes

Some error codes are shared on both platforms. For example, the FileIO Xtra uses Macintosh-style error codes on both platforms. Other error codes are platform-specific. See Appendix E in *Lingo in a Nutshell* for details.

Internationalization

Markets in the United Kingdom, Japan, Korea, Germany, France, Scandinavia, India, Israel, and other countries can all provide significant additional revenues. When localizing software, keep in mind that both the standard hardware and software configuration may differ significantly from the U.S. in addition to the obvious cultural and language differences. For example, in Japan. the first hard drive on a PC typically is labeled A:, not C: as in the U.S. Testing on the hardware and on localized versions of software (Mac OS and Windows) typical to that country is crucial. Director is available in English, Japanese, German, and French.

Set *the romanLingo* property to TRUE when working with multibyte languages, and refer to Chapter 4 for more internationalization hints.

When preparing for internationalization:

- Store text strings in a separate external castLib to make them easily replaceable.

- Fonts may vary widely across international platforms, including accents and other diacritical marks. See Chapter 12 in this book and Appendix A, *ASCII Codes and Key Codes*, and Appendix C in *Lingo in a Nutshell*.

- Leave more room for text strings, prompts, and button labels in foreign languages that are sometimes more verbose than English.

- Avoid bitmaps with culture-specific or potentially culturally offensive icons, symbols, and colors.

- Leave voice narration audio external to the Director movie, or in an external castLib for easy substitution.

- Date and time formats can vary dramatically in different countries. In the U.S, the month typically precedes the day in the *short date* format, but this is reversed in most countries. Use D7's new *systemDate()* and *date()* functions, or use an Xtra (such as DateMaster from *http://www.penworks.com*) in prior versions of Director to return a language-independent date.

CHAPTER 8

Projectors and the Runtime Environment

Runtime Projectors

Projectors are platform-specific applications that allow you to distribute your Director project to users who don't own Director. (Macintosh Projectors have the APPL file type, and Windows Projectors have an .EXE extension.) A browser with the Shockwave plug-in substitutes for a Projector, so don't create a Projector for Shockwave applications. The D7 ShockMachine will also allow playback without a Projector.

You need Director for Macintosh to create a Macintosh Projector, and Director for Windows to create a Windows Projector. Although D6 does not run under Windows 3.1, you can create a Windows 3.1 Projector using Windows 95, 98, or NT.

Director 7 and Shockwave 7 support only PowerMacs and Windows 95/98/NT. Developers supporting Windows 3.1 or 68K Macs must use D6.5 or SW6 or earlier. D7.0 Windows Projectors won't run on systems that don't have the *MSVCRT.DLL* present, such as virgin Win95 OSR2 installations. See *http://www.updatestage.com/bwlist.html* and place a copy of the DLL in the folder with your Projector.

Although Director is very similar across platforms, testing on your target platform(s) is vital. If you don't own Director for the eventual delivery platform, you are fighting with one hand tied behind your back. Spend the money for the appropriate versions of Director and a computer to run them on.

If necessary, hire an experienced consultant to port and debug your product and create your Projector for another platform. Be sure to comply with the Macromedia licensing agreement, as described in the *Made with Macromedia* folder on the Director CD (you must include Macromedia's logo in order to distribute Projectors royalty-free).

How Director Executes Your Projector

Once built, a Projector is like any other executable program. Before I explain how to build a Projector, I'll summarize what occurs when your Projector is run. Ordinarily, the user will start your Projector by double-clicking its icon in the Macintosh Finder or the Windows File Explorer. On the Macintosh, only one copy of an application can be launched. Under Windows, the user can inadvertently launch multiple copies if they repeatedly double-click a Projector's icon. The Launcher utility included with D5 and D6 should prevent this, or the BuddyAPI Xtra can be used to quit a Projector if it detects that a duplicate copy is running.

Use AtticMedia's (*http://www.atticmedia.com*) Load Once utility to prevent multiple double-clicks on an icon from starting multiple copies of a Windows application (the free version posts an advertisement).

Projector startup

These are the steps taken by the Projector at startup:

1. The OS launches the Projector when it is double-clicked, as it would any other application.

2. The Projector loads Xtras from the *Xtras* folder located in the same folder as the Projector (not from Director's *Xtras* folder).

3. Xtras bundled with the Projector are unbundled into a temporary folder (I recommend against bundling Xtras).

4. On Windows only, the Projector reads the *<ProjectorName>.INI* file (renamed from the *DIRECTOR.INI* file), if any, located in the same folder as the Projector.

5. On Windows only, the Projector temporarily installs video and sound drivers as described under "Director Startup" in Chapter 1, *How Director Works*.

6. Director reads the *LINGO.INI* file, if any, located in the same folder as the Projector, and runs any *on startUp* handler it finds there. See "Using LINGO.INI to create a flexible Stub Projector," later in this chapter.

7. All global variables are reset to VOID and system properties are reset to their default values. Refer to Chapter 6, *The Stage and Movies-in-a-Window*, for details on which system properties are reset when a movie is played.

8. Refer to "Movie Startup" under "How Director Runs Your Movie" in Chapter 1 for details on how Director loads and runs a Director movie.

9. If the movie uses cast members that require Sprite Xtras, QuickTime, or Video for Windows, but these elements are not installed, a warning may be issued and those cast members will not appear on Stage.

Projectors always start at the first frame of the first movie embedded within the Projector. See *http://www.zeusprod.com/technote/restore.html* for a technique that uses an external file to jump immediately to a different frame or movie from within a Projector. This can be used to restore the Projector to the user's last position.

If your Projector displays a "Made with Macromedia" splash screen whenever it starts or ends, it was created with a "Not For Resale" or "Educational" version of Director. Register your copy of Director using a commercial serial number to avoid the splash screen. (Delete the invisible *BRAND.BRD* file in the Director application's folder and restart Director to enter a new serial number.) Even then, you must include the "Made with Macromedia" logo somewhere in your production (usually the credits) to avoid a licensing fee.

To speed the startup of your Projectors:

- Use a Stub Projector containing only a small loader movie with a minimal Cast and Score.

- Specify a realistic minimum CD-ROM speed, RAM requirement, and processor speed for your presentation.

- Instruct the user to quit other applications, and shut off network services.

- You can't create a progress box before your Lingo code has actually begun, but you can set a custom wait cursor (cursor type 4) or display a greeting to reduce the perceived delay. Use introductory sounds, which can delay the loading of other assets, with caution.

- Don't bundle Xtras into your Projector. Leave them in an *Xtras* folder, and include only the minimum necessary Xtras.

- You may consider copying your Projector to the user's hard drive, but this is unnecessary in the vast majority of cases if you've optimized your presentation properly.

- Do not perform preloads at the start of your Projector or set castLibs to be preloaded (using *the preLoadMode of castLib* or `Modify ➤ Cast Properties`). Consider idle loading if necessary.

- Use the Load Once utility from AtticMedia or a splash screen such as Fast Splash (*http://www.ames.net/bsmith*) or Splash Screen 99 (*http://www.fantazm.com*) to prevent the impatient user from accidentally launching multiple Windows Projectors.

Stub Projectors

Rebuilding your Projector for multiple platforms and OS versions every time the project changes becomes tedious. A *Stub Projector* is built from a single dummy Director movie that merely transfers control to an external Director movie file that performs the real work.

Stub Projectors are ideal because:

- They rarely need to be rebuilt even if your first Director movie changes.

- Your Projector will always access the latest version of the Director movies.

- Stub Projectors are small. They can be copied to the hard drive with the data remaining on the CD, and they will start up quickly. There was a D5 bug under Windows 95 that required free space on the user's hard drive equal to the size of the Projector! A Stub Projector's small size minimized the issue.

- Although Projectors are unique to a given platform, the DIR, DXR, DCR, CST, CXT, and CCT files are all *binary-compatible* (the same file can be used on Macintosh and Windows). Using identical external files on all platforms, you can fit a 500 MB cross-platform project on a single hybrid CD; multiple Projectors for Macintosh and Windows add only a few megabytes each.

The only drawback to a Stub Projector is that your project does not include everything in a single file. If you insist on bundling everything into a Projector (which I don't recommend) you should still use a Stub Projector during development. When you bundle the DIR files into the Projector, you can specify the order of the movies to optimize load times. When using a Stub Projector, you should manually arrange the files on the CD in the order in which they'll be used (competent CD-ROM burning software, including Toast (*http://www.adaptec.com*), allows you to place files in any order).

Creating STUB.DIR

To create the stub movie to use as the basis for your Projector, follow these steps:

1. Use File ➤ New ➤ Movie to create a new Director movie.

2. Double-click in the Script channel of the first frame to create a frame script. (Stub Projectors may not work if you create a movie script but no frame script.)

3. Add the following *on exitFrame* handler (you'll need to type in only the middle line, as Director automatically provides the rest):

```
on exitFrame
  go movie "INTRO"
end
```

4. Replace *INTRO* with the name of the first Director movie in your project, but omit the file extension. Director will look for *INTRO*, *INTRO.DIR*, *INTRO.DXR*, or *INTRO.DCR* automatically in that order.

 Omit the .DIR extension so that you won't need to rebuild your Projector when you protect or compress your external files. Shockwave requires the .DCR extension, but doesn't use Projectors anyway.

---

5. Use Modify ➤ Movie ➤ Properties to set the Stage's size (usually 640×480) and background color (usually black). (In Director 4, use File ➤ Movie Info to set the Stage's size and the color chip in the Control Panel window to set its color.)

6. To avoid a "palette flash" of the desktop when the Macintosh Projector starts, use the Macintosh System palette. Under Windows, you can use a palette with the Windows interface colors reserved in the first and last ten entries (see the sample palettes available in D6 under Xtras ➤ Libraries ➤ Palette Library). Subsequent movies can use the same palette on both platforms, because the desktop will be covered. Perform palette switches when the Stage is black.

7. Use **File ➤ Save** to save the file as *STUB.DIR* and use it to build your Projector (see "Creating Your Projector," later in this chapter). See also "Creating and Using Stub Projectors" at *http://www.zeusprod.com/technote/ stub.html* for details and additional stub Projector techniques for both D6 and D7.

Using LINGO.INI to create a flexible Stub Projector

Projectors always look for a *LINGO.INI* file and run its *on startUp* handler. You can use global variables to create a Stub Projector whose behavior can be modified by changing the external *LINGO.INI* file. Create the following *LINGO.INI* file in a text editor such as SimpleText or Notepad:

This goes in your external *LINGO.INI* file:

```
on startUp
  global gMovieName
  -- Set gmovieName to your first movie's name
  set gMovieName = "INTRO"
  -- This prevents math errors under D5 and D6 for Windows.
  if string(0.0)= "a" then nothing
end
```

Modify the *STUB.DIR* created earlier to use the following frame script instead:

```
on exitFrame
  global gMovieName
  go movie gMovieName
end
```

After creating a Projector from the revised *STUB.DIR*, you won't have to rebuild it if your first movie's name changes. Simply modify the *LINGO.INI* file to point to a new movie file. I call this a *FlexStub Projector*. You read it here first. (See Appendix D in *Lingo in a Nutshell* for details.)

 You must distribute this *LINGO.INI* file with your Projector. Always distribute a *LINGO.INI* containing at least one command with your Windows Projector; some Windows machines running multimedia shells will complain if no *LINGO.INI* file is present.

The *on startUp* handler in the *LINGO.INI* can set any global variable (even ones not used by *STUB.DIR*). This can be used to configure your Projector for debugging without modifying the Projector itself.

Creating Your Projector

You will create at least one Projector (except for Shockwave applications), and often multiple Projectors for different platforms, as follows:

1. Choose **File ➤ Create Projector**.
2. Select one or more Director movie files to be incorporated into the Projector. You can also add Casts and Xtras manually to the Projector. (If you've followed my advice, you'll add only *STUB.DIR*.)

3. Set the Projector options using the *Options* button (see Figures 8-1 and 8-2).

4. Click the *Create* button to create the Projector.

Refer to Macromedia's *Using Director* manual or to the online Help for the basic mechanics of adding Director files to your Projector.

Macintosh Projector types

Figure 8-1 shows the Macintosh *Create Projector* and *Options* dialog boxes in Director 6. See Figure 8-3 for new options in D7.

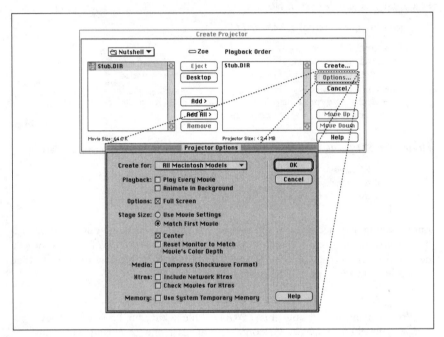

Figure 8-1: Macintosh D6 Projector creation options

The following Projector types are available in D6 under the *Create for* option. D7 for Macintosh supports only PowerMac/G3 Projectors.

Standard Macintosh
> The smallest Macintosh Projector type, this will run on all Macintoshes but is intended for 68K (680x0-based) models. It runs in emulation mode on Power Macs (including the new Macintosh G3 family), providing less than optimal performance.

Power Macintosh Native
> This Projector will not run on older (68K) Macintoshes. It is most appropriate if your application requires a PowerMac or G3, or for a dedicated kiosk.

All Macintosh Models
> This option creates a *Fat Binary* Projector, composed of Standard (68K) Macintosh and Power Macintosh Native halves. The Mac OS automatically determines which half to launch based on the installed CPU. This option creates the most

compatible but largest Projector. Although it requires more disk space, it allegedly uses the same amount of RAM as would separate Standard Macintosh and
Power Macintosh Only Projectors. Create two separate Projectors to allocate
different amounts of memory for 68K Macs and Power Macs.

Windows Projector types

Figure 8-2 shows the *Projector Options* dialog box for Director 6 under Windows.

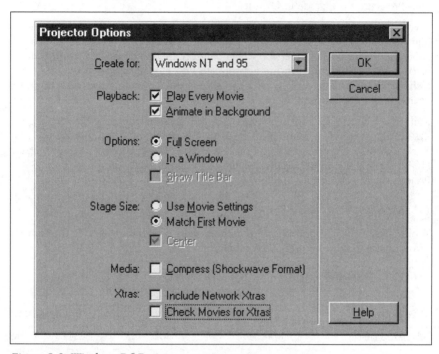

Figure 8-2: Windows D6 Projector creation options

D6 for Windows supports two different Projector types under the *Create for*
option: *Windows NT and 95* and *Windows 3.1*. D7 for Windows supports only
Win 95/98/NT development and playback (not Windows 3.1). Although you can't
develop under Windows 3.1 or NT 3.5.1, D6 can create Windows 3.1–compatible
Projectors (Director 5 supported Windows 3.1 authoring as well). *Windows 3.1*
(16-bit) Projectors will play on Windows 3.1 and 95/98 platforms. *Windows 95 and
NT* (32-bit) Projectors will play only on Windows 95/98 and NT. Some NT systems
can run 16-bit applications, but I strongly recommend using a 32-bit Projector if
supporting Windows NT.

The upgrade disk from Director 5 to Director 6.0 did not build Windows 95/98/NT
Projectors correctly due to a manufacturing flaw. (The Projector would crash with
the error, "Windows can't execute this archive because it is in an invalid format.")
Unrelated to this, Director 6.0 16-bit projectors running under Windows 3.1 with
SHARE.EXE installed could cause "Invalid Projector File" errors. The 32-bit

Projector problem was solved by a patch, and the Windows 3.1 problem could be solved by setting the 16-bit Projector to read-only.

The upgrades to D6.0.2 or D6.5, obtainable at *http://www.macromedia.com/support/director/upndown*, solve these projector-related bugs. Anecdotal evidence suggests that Projectors built with Windows NT work better under NT than those built with Windows 95/98. (Macromedia claims that there is no difference.)

D7.0 Projectors require *MSVCRT.DLL*. Place a copy of this DLL in the folder with your Projector, or upgrade to D7.0.1.

If you build both 16-bit and 32-bit Windows Projectors, you can use the Launcher utility (on the D6 for Windows CD under *X:\GOODIES\LAUNCHER*) to launch either the 16-bit or 32-bit version depending on the Windows platform. Launcher uses an INI file to branch to the appropriate Projector, thereby imitating a Macintosh Fat Projector. Alternatively, you can either direct users to a particular Projector or install only the proper Projector.

Xtras must match the Projector type, not the platform: 16-bit Projectors require .X16 Xtras (even when running on a 32-bit OS) and 32-bit Projectors require .X32 Xtras. Likewise, if you are using QuickTime 2 for Windows, the installed version (16-bit or 32-bit) must match the Projector type. QT3 supports only 32-bit Projectors.

Projector size comparison

Table 8-1 shows the approximate minimum sizes of Projectors in D4 through D7 incorporating only a tiny *STUB.DIR* movie.

Table 8-1: Macintosh and Windows Projector Sizes

Projector Type	D7	D7 with Xtras	D7 Slim[1]	D6.x	D5.0.1	D4.0.4
Windows 3.1 (16-bit)	N/A	N/A	N/A	1,207 KB	911 KB	677 KB
Windows 95/NT (32-bit)	1,400 KB	2,160 KB	107 KB	1,477 KB	1,378 KB	N/A
Standard Macintosh (68K)	N/A	N/A	N/A	1,016 KB	713 KB	288 KB
Power Macintosh Native	2,170 KB	3,046 KB	207 KB	1,458 KB	1,062 KB	654 KB
All Macintosh Models	N/A	N/A	N/A	2,350 KB	1,652 KB	1,068 KB

[1] Size of Slim Projector excludes the approximately 800 KB of default Xtras, the 1.4 MB IMLLib, and the 500 KB DPLlib, which are all part of the required Shockwave 7 installation and are used by Slim Projectors.

Projector Build Options

You can set the Projector options via the *Options* button in the *Create Projector* dialog box (see Figures 8-1, 8-2, and 8-3) before or after adding Director movies to the file list. In D7, an undocumented config file can override the build options set when the Projector was created. See *http://www.zeusprod.com/nutshell/otto.html*.

Playback

The *Play Every Movie* option applies only to linear presentations with no Lingo. When you control the movie sequence via Lingo, its only effect is to cause Cmd-. (Mac) or Ctrl-. (Windows) to advance to the next movie rather than quit the Projector. Leave it unchecked if incorporating MIAWs in the Projector.

The *Animate in Background* option determines whether Director's playback head continues to advance if the user runs a second application in the foreground.

Options

The *Full Screen* option causes the Projector to cover the entire monitor, even if it is larger than the Stage, preventing the user from clicking on the desktop. In D7.0, MIAWs may disappear behind Full-Screen Projectors. This is fixed in D7.0.1. This option does *not* stretch the movie to fill the screen. Any excess area is filled with the Stage's background color. See "Hiding the Desktop," later in this chapter. In the Macintosh D7.0.1 Projector creation dialog box (not shown), if you uncheck the *Full Screen* option, you can create a moveable Projector window by selecting the *Show Title Bar* option.

The *In a Window* option (Windows only) causes the Projector to play in a Windows-style window with an optional titlebar, close box, and minimize button. If *the exitLock* is TRUE, the close box will not work (even though it still animates), but the minimize button will work.

Refer to Chapter 10, *Keyboard Events*, in *Lingo in a Nutshell* for additional details on *the exitLock* and trapping keyboard events such as Alt-Tab in Windows Projectors.

To create a Macintosh Projector that appears to run in a window, you can use a MIAW as a surrogate Stage or modify the Stage's WIND resource. See Chapter 6.

Stage size, position, and color depth

If your movies don't all use the same Stage size, the *Use Movie Settings* option will change the size of the Stage for each movie. The *Match First Movie* option will prevent the Stage size from changing, and overrides the settings under Modify ▶ Movie ▶ Properties. In practice, your movies should ordinarily all use the same Stage size.

The *Center* option ensures that the movie is centered regardless of the monitor size. Windows Projectors are always centered; for them, the option is dimmed. This is highly recommended in D7 (see the D7.0 and D7.0.1 *ReadMe* files).

The *Reset Monitor to Match Movie's Color Depth* option (Macintosh only) will change the monitor's color depth to match the highest depth of any bitmap cast member in the current movie. This option sets the default value for *the switch-ColorDepth* property. In D7, a bug causes the monitor to flash even if it is already at the correct depth. Leave this option unchecked and set *the colorDepth* manaully instead. See Example 13-1.

During authoring, analogous options are settable under File ➤ Preferences ➤ General.

 If a flash occurs when switching between movies on the Macintosh only, it is probably a result of the monitor depth being switched rather than a palette issue.

Media

The *Compress (Shockwave Format)* option compresses the Director movie assets into Shockwave format. This option is new as of D6. It makes the Projector smaller (if the assets are internal) but increases the load time. Use Xtras ➤ Update Movies ➤ *Convert to Shockwave Movie(s)* to compress external movies and castLibs (DIR and CST files) into DCR and CCT files. In D7, internal GIF and JPEG members are also compressed. See also Table 4-3.

Director 5 supported a *Duplicate Cast Members for Faster Loading* option that is no longer available in D6 or D7. It created additional copies of cast members to reduce seek times for large castLibs.

Xtras (D6 only)

The Xtras-related options determine which Xtras are bundled into D6 Projectors. They use the *XTRAINFO.TXT* file, which must be in the same folder with Director when the Projector is created.

The *Include Network Xtras* option incorporates any Xtras specified in the *XTRAINFO.TXT* file as type *#net* (that is, Net-related Xtras) into the Projector. These are required if you use any of the Net Lingo commands, or any linked media at a remote URL. Xtras of type *#netLib* (the PPC-only NetManage WinSock Lib) are not included by this option.

The *Check Movie for Xtras* option incorporates two unrelated groups of Xtras—those listed under Modify ➤ Movie ➤ Xtras and those specified in the *XTRAINFO.TXT* file as type *#mixin* or *#service*. Xtras of type *#mix* are not necessarily included. In D7, Xtras bundling options are set individually under Modify ➤ Movie ➤ Xtras, and Xtras listed in *XTRAINFO.TXT* as type *#default* are bundled into D7 Projectors by default.

Bundling Xtras is fraught with peril. I recommend manually including any necessary Xtras in an *Xtras* folder external to your Projector. Refer to Chapter 10, *Using Xtras*, for details on determining and including the required Xtras.

Player (D7 only)

Figure 8-3 shows the new D7.0 *Player* options in the *Projector Options* dialog box.

Figure 8-3: Director 7 Projector creation Player options

Use System Player (new as of D7.0)

D7 supports a new standalone Slim Projector (a.k.a. System Player, Shockwave Projector, Shim Projector, or Lite Projector) that relies on the system
components installed with SW7. Slim Projectors are very small (see Table 8-1).
They automatically access SW7's *Xtras* folder (so there is no need to bundle
Xtras with them in most cases), but they'll also access the *Xtras* folder
beneath the Slim Projector itself. Slim Projectors are not subject to the same
security restrictions as the Shockwave plug-in running within a browser, nor
should they be confused with the new ShockMachine. Slim Projectors behave
like standard Projectors, except they are smaller because they use the shared
system components, at the cost of requiring that SW7 be installed on the
machine.

Web Download If Needed (new as of D7.0)

This option attempts to download SW7, if necessary, for use by the Slim
Projector. This is unrelated to the automated downloading of packaged Xtras,
which is controlled by the settings under Modify ➤ Movie ➤ Xtras. Even
absent SW7, the Slim Projector will be able to run if the D7 components
(IMLlib and DPlib on the Macintosh, or *Dirapi.DLL* and *Iml32.DLL* on
Windows) are located in the same folder with it.

D7.0.1 uses somewhat different *Player* options (not shown in Figure 8-3) some of
which parallel the D7.0 Projector creation options:

Standard (D7.0.1)

Creates a standard Projector as would unchecking D7.0's *Use System Player*
option.

Compressed (new feature in D7.0.1)

Creates a Compressed Projector that occupies about half the disk space of the
standard Projectors shown in Table 8-1 (840 KB on Windows and 1,115 KB
on the Macintosh excluding Xtras). They are identical to standard Projectors
but slower to launch, because they must be decompressed at runtime. They
are *larger* than Slim Projectors, but do not require a SW7 installation, and are
appropriate mainly for floppy disk delivery.

Shockwave (D7.0.1)

Creates a Slim Projector that will attempt to download SW7 as needed (same
as checking both D7.0's *Use System Player* and *Web Download If Needed*
options).

Memory

The *Use System Temporary Memory* option (Macintosh only) allows Mac Projectors to access System RAM beyond the fixed memory partitions ordinarily allocated to Macintosh applications. This setting is ignored when the Projector is played back on a Macintosh with Virtual Memory enabled. Leave this option unchecked if supporting 68K Macs, as it can crash 68040 Macs.

Hiding the Desktop

When a Projector is played full-screen, the desktop is covered with a solid background of the same color as the Stage (black is usually best). The color is set using the color chip in the Modify ➤ Movie ➤ Properties dialog box, *the stageColor* property (black is *stageColor* 255), or *the bgColor of Stage* (black is *paletteIndex(255)*).

To use a different color for the Stage's background and the desktop cover, set *the stageColor* to the color you want to use for the *desktop* cover. Then use a colorized shape or bitmap cast member in sprite channel 1 to create the desired Stage background.

Full-screen Projectors cover only the primary monitor with a solid color. The Macintosh XObjects *RearWindow* and *FinderHider* allow you to cover the desktop and multiple monitors with a solid color or a bitmap. My company (Zeus Productions, *http://www.zeusprod.com*) sells *zLaunch* and *zOpen*, which cover the desktop and multiple monitors while launching external applications from Director.

Projector Notes

There is no direct way to tell which options a Projector was built with, although some of them are easily inferred at runtime. Keep careful notes about the options used or rebuild your Projector. You must rebuild your Stub Projector to change the *Create Projector* options, the initial *stageColor*, the initial palette, or the initial Stage size.

To determine the version of a Macintosh Projector, use the Finder's File ➤ Get Info command. To determine the version of a Windows Projector, use File Explorer's File ➤ Properties command, then click on the *Version* tab. To determine the version at runtime, use either *the productVersion* property or the global variable *version*.

To create Projectors on the Macintosh, the *Director 7.0 Resources* file must be in the same folder as Director itself. In D7 for Windows, you'll need the *Projctrc.dll* and *Projec32.skl* files. Under D6 for Windows, you'll need the *Projectr.rsr* file and *Projectr.skl* (for 16-bit Projectors) and *Projec32.skl* (for 32-bit Projectors). When updating to any new version, be sure to update from a folder that contains the correct version of all the old files being patched. (A corrupt *Projec32.skl* file included with the upgrade from D5 to D6.0 created corrupt Windows 95/NT Projectors. D6.0.2 solves this.)

Do not build movies from prior versions of Director into a Projector. Update all movies to the current version using Xtras ➤ Update Movies ➤ *Update* whether leaving them external to or including them in the Projector. See the D7 *ReadMe.html* file for important details.

Avoid running two projectors simultaneously. Use the *go movie* or *play movie* command to play another Director movie. If the source DIR file is not available, the protected DXR version can still be run from a Stub Projector. As a last resort, you can use the Lingo *open* command to launch one Projector from another, although they'll often conflict. The *zLaunch* utility (*http://www.zeusprod.com/products/zlaunch.html*) reduces conflicts between Projectors by allowing you to quit the first one while the second one is running.

See *http://www.zeusprod.com/nutshell/appendices/checklists.html* for a list of files to ship with your Projector, such as Xtras and external digital videos and sounds.

shutDown and restart commands

Table 8-2 shows the platform-dependent behavior of the *restart* and *shutDown* commands.

Table 8-2: Platform-Specific Restart Commands

Platform	restart	shutDown
Macintosh	Restarts Macintosh as would the Finder's Special ➤ Restart command.	Shuts down Macintosh as would the Finder's Special ➤ Shut Down command.
Windows 95/98	Restarts Windows 95/98 as if user chose the *Close all programs and log on as a different user?* option under the *Shut Down* command under the Start Menu.	Same as *restart*.
Windows 3.1	Restarts Windows 3.1.	Reboots the computer as if the user hit Ctrl-Alt-Del twice.
Win NT	Logs off Windows NT, as if the user chose the Program Manager's File ➤ Logoff command.	Same as *restart*.
Shockwave (all platforms)	No effect.	No effect.

The *quit* command will quit both Projectors and the Director authoring environment. The *halt* command will quit a Projector, but will merely halt a Director movie during authoring. It is therefore convenient for testing when you don't want to restart Director after every test. The *quit* command is ignored in Shockwave, but the *halt* command will permanently stop a Shockwave movie, which remains inactive unless the user reloads the page containing the Shockwave tag. Unlike the *quit* command, the *halt* command does not cause the *on stopMovie* handler to be called.

Protecting and Compressing External Movies

The files used by a Projector need not be incorporated directly into the Projector. When using the recommended Stub Projector, your Director movies, castLibs, and Xtras should be left external to the Projector. Use *the movieFileFreeSize* property to determine whether your files have accumulated any clutter from deleted cast members, and use File➤Save and Compact to eliminate it.

Protect external movies and castLibs using Xtras ➤ Update Movies ➤ *Protect*. Compress your movies for Shockwave using Xtras ➤ Update Movies ➤ *Convert to Shockwave Movie(s)*. Shockwave compression is intended for speeding downloads. Avoid using compressed (DCR and CCT) files for local assets; they will load more slowly than DXR and CXT files, because they must be decompressed at runtime. See Table 4–3.

 After you protect your files, maintain the relative position of the external assets relative to the movies and castLibs that use them. If you don't, you may get the dreaded *Where is...?* dialog box when Director tries to find an asset.

Protecting your content from prying eyes

When you protect or compress your Director movie, the Lingo code and internal content is theoretically protected, but all digital video files and streaming sound files (AIFF, WAVE, and SWA) remain external to Director. It is difficult to prevent people from taking screenshots or recording audio while the Projector is running. There have even been reports of utilities to extract the media (but not necessarily the Lingo code) from Projectors and protected files.

If releasing your material to the general public, your technological defenses against ardent thievery are limited and tend to annoy legitimate customers. Your best alternative may be to deter infringement through copyright and trademark notices and threat of legal action. D7 supports QT3 encryption keys (see *qtRegister-AccessKey*) and the Beatnik Xtra supports digital watermarking of audio files. See also D7's *movieCopyrightInfo* property, which will be displayed by ShockMachine.

If you hide your external files as a deterrent, test thoroughly, because some commands may not work properly with invisible files. For example, the *go movie* command will not work with hidden movie files on either platform, and *getNthFileNameInFolder()* detects hidden files on the Macintosh, but not under Windows.

Analyzing the Runtime Environment

Lingo lets you examine many system attributes at runtime, such as the user's monitor depth, monitor size, or platform. A single Director movie can run different Lingo code in response to the runtime environment. Table 8-3 summarizes how to evaluate system attributes at runtime. In some cases, you'll need a third-party Xtra.

Under Windows, MCI commands can be used to analyze and affect many aspects of the Windows environment. See the extensive Macromedia TechNote #03521, "Using MCI for device and media control."

Table 8-3: Analyzing Runtime Environment Properties

Environment Properties	Analyze with
Current movie name	the movie the movieName
Current folder of current movie	the pathName (deprecated in D7) the moviePath
Current folder of Projector or Director	the applicationPath
Current name of Projector	Check *the movieName* or *the movie* from within the *first* movie built into the Projector (doesn't work in D7).
Version of Director, Projector, or Shockwave	the productVersion, or global version
Current product name	the productName (always "Director")
Preferred browser (doesn't work in Shockwave)	browserName()
Distinguish Projector from Director, Shockwave, ShockMachine, or Java Player	the runMode[1], the envronment[1]
Set or check whether security hobbles are in effect	the safePlayer (new in D7)
Macintosh vs. Windows platform	the platform,[1] baVersion("os")[2]
Projector Type	the platform,[1] the environment[1]
Macintosh model	the machineType[1]
Mac CPU (680x0, PowerPC)	OSisPowerPC()[3]
Mac OS Version	OSGestalt ("sysv"),[3] baVersion("mac")[2]
MMX-enabled PC	isDirMMXloaded()[4]
PC CPU (486, Pentium)	cpuidGetCPUType(),[4] or baCpuInfo()[2]
PC chip manufacturer	cpuidIsGenuineIntel()[4]
Windows OS version (3.1/95/98/NT)	zWinVer(),[5] baVersion("windows")[2]
Number and resolution of monitors	the deskTopRectList
Change monitor resolution	Buddy API[3] or DisplayRes[6]
Monitor color depth (get or set)	the colorDepth, the environment, baScreenInfo()[2], baSetDisplay(),[2] or DisplayRes[6]
Director registration	the userName, serialNumber, and organizationName
Movie creation information	the movieCopyrightInfo and the movieAboutInfo (new in D7)

Table 8-3: Analyzing Runtime Environment Properties (continued)

Environment Properties	Analyze with
QuickTime version	See Chapter 16
Video for Windows version	See Chapter 16
Sound capability and volume control	See Chapter 15
Installed Xtras and Movie Xtras	the XtraList and the movieXtraList (new in D7, see Chapter 10)
Installed RAM and available RAM	See Chapter 9
Disk space	OSVolumeFree(),[3] baDiskInfo()[2]
Stage attributes	See Tables 6-1 and 6-2
Windows or Macintosh System folder	getOSdirectory (FileIO Xtra)
Start Menu and other system folders	baSysFolder()[2]
Whether instance of Projector is already running	baPrevious()[2]
Current CD-ROM drive letter	See Example 8-6, CDProXtra, or baDiskInfo("type")[2]
Command-line arguments	baCommandArgs()[2] or DirectOS's getCommandLine()
Disable Windows screen saver	baDisableScreenSaver(),[2] baScreenSaverTme(),[2] or baSetScreenSaver()[2]
Show/hide Windows taskbar	baHideTaskBar()[2]
Disable task switching under Windows 95 (not NT)	baDisableSwitching()[2]
Elapsed time	the ticks, the timer, the milliseconds

[1] See "Determining the Playback Platform" later in this chapter.
[2] Requires Buddy API Xtra (*http://www.mods.com.au/budapi/*). See also the DirectOS Xtra (*http://www.directxtras.com*).
[3] Requires OSutil Xtra (*http://www.magna.com.au/~farryp/director/xtras*). See also the Macintosh version of Buddy API.
[4] Requires the DirMMX Xtra. See "The DirMMX Xtra" later in this chapter.
[5] Requires zWinVer Xtra (*http://www.zeusprod.com/products/zwinver.html*).
[6] DisplayRes Xtra (*http://www.updatestage.com/xtras*).

The *deskTopRectList*

The deskTopRectList property returns a list of rects indicating the size and position of each installed monitor. The coordinates of each rect are relative to the upper-left corner of the main monitor (the monitor with the menubar).

The following indicates two monitors. The first monitor is 1024×768 pixels. The second monitor is 640×480 pixels, and located to the right of the first monitor.

```
put the deskTopRectList
-- [rect (0,0,1024,768), rect(1025,0,1665,480)]
```

Count *the deskTopRectList* to determine the total number of monitors:

```
set numberOfMonitors = count (the deskTopRectList)
```

The colorDepth reads and sets only the depth of the main monitor. There is no way to determine or set the color depth of secondary monitors without a third-party Xtra, such as DisplayRes. Using multiple monitors can increase RAM requirements or cause anomalous behavior if the monitors are set to different color depths. In D7, monitors of different depths may cause the Script window to turn black.

Changing monitor depth and resolution

Director can sometimes change the monitor's color depth, but not its resolution without an Xtra. Xtras can change the resolution of most video cards under Windows 95, depending on the third-party driver. Some video drivers also support switching of the color depth under Windows 95.

The standard video drivers in Windows 98 and Windows NT both support changing the monitor resolution and color depth, so Xtras should be able to set them on most of those machines (and Director's *colorDepth* property may set the depth without an Xtra).

The Buddy API Xtra (*http://www.mods.com.au/budapi/*) checks and sets the Windows monitor resolution and color depth. It also detects whether the computer needs to be restarted after such a change. Buddy API can restart the computer, or you can use the commands listed in Table 8-2. The DisplayRes Xtra (*http://www.updatestage.com/xtras*) similarly will switch the monitor resolution and color depth when possible.

On the Macintosh, set the monitor depth using *the colorDepth* (see Example 13-2). Use ChangeRes (*http://www.toxicorange.co.az*) or Multimixer (*http://www.turntable.com*) to switch the monitor resolution.

Error Checking During Runtime

You can use the properties listed in Table 8-3 to alert the user to various conditions. For example, you might check whether QuickTime is installed. You can take corrective action, launch an appropriate installer using the *open* command, or quit if necessary. If all else fails, ask your user to alter his or her setup as necessary and restart your Projector.

```
if not the quickTimePresent then
  alert "QuickTime is not installed. I can't bear it."
  quit
end if
```

Determining the Playback Platform

There are several commands that determine the platform and environment under which you are running. D7 introduces a new property, *the environment,* containing several properties, with room for expansion.

```
put the environment
-- [#shockMachine:0, #platform: "Macintosh, Power PC",
    #runMode:"Author", #colorDepth:8]
put the environment.runMode
-- "Author"
```

The platform

The platform property distinguishes between the Macintosh and Windows platforms, but does not reliably determine the current OS or CPU type.

Table 8-4 shows the return values for *the platform*. Note that there are no spaces following the commas in the returned strings. The same values are returned in Projectors, Shockwave, and during authoring. Use *the runMode* to determine which of the three modes you are running under.

Table 8-4: The Platform's Return Values

Environment	The Platform
Fat Projectors running on Standard Macs, or Standard Mac Projectors running on any Mac	"Macintosh,68k"
Fat or Power Mac-only Projectors running on Power Macs	"Macintosh,PowerPC"
Windows 3.1 (16-bit) Projectors running under any Windows OS	"Windows,16"
Windows 95/NT (32-bit) Projectors running under Windows 95, 98, or NT.	"Windows,32"
Java Player: *JavaVersion*: 1.0 | 1.1 *browser*: IE | Netscape | UnknownBrowser *OS*: Macintosh | Windows | UknownOS	"Java *javaVersion*, *browser, OS*"[1]

[1] Such as "Java 1.1 IE, Windows" or "Java 1.0, Netscape, Macintosh".

To distinguish between Macintosh and Windows at runtime, use *the platform* (see Example 8-1).

Example 8-1: Distinguishing Between Macintosh and Windows

```
if the platform contains "Windows" then
  -- Windows statements go here
else if the platform contains "Macintosh" then
  -- Macintosh statements go here
else
  -- Unknown OS. Presumably Java Player under Unix
end if
```

 The platform property does not return the platform on which the Projector is running; it returns the Projector type. *The platform* returns "Windows,16", not "Windows,32", when running a 16-bit projector under Windows 95/98 or NT.

See "Determining the Playback Platform at Runtime" (*http://www.zeusprod. com/technote/platform.html*) for additional details. See Table 8-3 to determine the Windows OS version independently of the Projector type.

The machineType

The machineType returns an integer code indicating the Macintosh CPU type, or the code 256 for all Windows PCs. Example 8-2 is *incorrect*, and will take the Windows course of action for Macs with a *machineType* greater than 256 (which now exist):

Example 8-2: Incorrect Use of the machineType

```
if the machineType < 256
  -- Macintosh statements go here
else
  -- This branch will be reached for
  -- PCs or Macs with machineType > 256
end if
```

Unless you are trying to determine a particular Macintosh model, use *the platform* property instead of *the machineType*. For a list of *machineType* codes and additional caveats about their reliability, see *MachineType Codes* at *http://www. zeusprod.com/technote/machtype.html*. The Shockwave 6.0 plug-in returned an incorrect value for *the machineType*. It was fixed in SW6.0.1.

The runMode

Use *the runMode* property to do different things during authoring and runtime or in Shockwave. Example 8-3 jumps straight to the frame labeled "MainMenu" when testing during authoring. From a Projector, it would play the standard introduction.

Example 8-3: Using the runMode to Speed Testing

```
on exitFrame
  if the runMode = "Author"
    go frame "MainMenu"
  else
    go frame "LongBoringIntro"
  end if
end exitFrame
```

This debugging message will be displayed only during authoring:

```
global gSomeGlobal
if the runMode = "Author" then
  alert "The value is" && gSomeGlobal
end if
```

The runMode returns "Author" during authoring, "Projector" in a Projector, "Plugin" in Shockwave, or "Java Applet" in the Director for Java Player.

Version and the productVersion

Director 5 and later support *the productVersion* property in addition to the global variable *version* that indicates the version. In Director 6, the valid versions are "6.0", "6.0.1", "6.0.2", and "6.5". "7.0" or "7.0.1" is returned by Director 7. The version is returned as a string, and cannot be treated as a float because it may contain multiple periods.

The productVersion and *version* return different values in Shockwave. The global *version* includes the word "net" in Shockwave, but *the productVersion* does not. See Chapter 16, *Enumerated Values*, in *Lingo in a Nutshell* for a complete list of return values in Director and Shockwave.

```
put the productVersion    -- Shockwave and Projectors
-- "7.0"
global version
put version   -- Authoring
-- "7.0"
put version   -- Shockwave
-- "7.0 net"
```

Note that these produce incorrect results (the second example ignores the build number):

```
put integer (the productVersion)
-- Void
put float (the productVersion)
-- 6.0000
```

Example 8-4 returns a list of the major, minor, and build version numbers. Use the *checkVersion()* utility in a loader movie created with Shockwave 6 before launching a Shockwave 7 movie.

Example 8-4: Version Number

```
on versionNumber
  global version
  set oldDelimiter = the itemDelimiter
  set the itemDelimiter = "."
  set versionList = [:]
  addProp versionList, #major, integer (item 1 of version)
  addProp versionList, #minor, integer (item 2 of version)
  -- This accounts for the word "net" at the end
  -- of the version string in Shockwave
  addProp versionList, #build, integer (word 1 of item 3 of version)
  set the itemDelimiter = oldDelimiter
  return versionList
end versionNumber

on checkVersion
  set thisVers = versionNumber()
  if not(the major of thisVers > 7) then
    alert "This web page requires Shockwave 7 or later"
  end if
end checkVersion
```

You can also check *the productName* to make sure that your Lingo code is running inside Director, should Macromedia revive its defunct plan to make Lingo a common scripting language across multiple products:

```
put the productName
-- "Director"
```

The DirMMX Xtra

The DirMMX Xtra (Director 6 only) returns some information about PC CPUs. It does not apply to Macintoshes, and works only with 32-bit projectors under Windows 95, 98, and NT. If the DirMMX.X32 Xtra is installed, Director 6 uses MMX acceleration on MMX-capable systems. Earlier versions of the Xtra caused problems with some Cyrix chips that claim to be MMX-capable but are not. Use the latest version of the Xtra included with D6.0.2.

MMX support is built into D7 and the Xtra is obsolete. You can also use the third-party Buddy API Xtra to obtain information about the CPU in D7, as shown in Example 8-5.

Example 8-5: Checking for a Pentium Processor

```
on checkCPU
  -- This assumes that the Buddy API Xtra is installed.
  if the platform contains "Windows" then
    set cpu   = baCPUInfo ("type")
    set speed = baCPUInfo ("speed")
    if (cpu < 5 or speed < 100) then
      alert "A 100 MHz Pentium or better is recommended"
    end if
  end if
end checkCPU
```

Table 8-5 lists the DirMMX Xtra's supported methods.

Table 8-5: DirMMX Xtra Methods

Method	Usage
set *xtraInstance* = new (xtra "DirMMX")	Instantiates the Xtra and returns an instance handle
put mMessageList (xtra "DirMMX")	Displays rudimentary documentation
isDirMMXloaded()	Returns TRUE if CPU is MMX-enabled
cpuidGetCPUFeatureFlags (*xtraInstance*)	Returns 447 on my Pentium[1]
cpuidGetCPUModel (*xtraInstance*)	Returns model (returns 2 on my 100 MHz Pentium) (first model = 0x1B)[1]
cpuidGetCPUStepping (*xtraInstance*)	Returns stepping ID (5 on my Pentium)[1]

Projectors &
Runtime

Table 8-5: DirMMX Xtra Methods (continued)

Method	Usage
cpuidGetCPUType (*xtraInstance*)	Returns code indicating CPU family: 3: 386 4: 486 5: Pentium (586) 6: Pentium II (686)
cpuidIsGenuineIntel (*xtraInstance*)	Returns TRUE if CPU is made by Intel

1 The meaning of these codes is unclear to me. They may be documented at *http://www.intel.com.*

Projectors (Runtime) Versus Director (Authoring)

Although your movie will theoretically operate identically from within a runtime Projector as it did during authoring, this is not always true. Especially if you author on the Macintosh and deliver for Windows, test early and often on all target platform(s). Test on the minimum supported machines, not just on your development machine.

The user's playback environment may be substantially different than your development setup. There is no substitute for thorough compatibility testing to reveal both hardware and software incompatibilities. Professional testing labs will compatibility-test your software on a variety of machines.

The three most common errors in Projectors are:

- "Handler not defined." This is often, but not necessarily, caused by a missing Lingo Scripting Xtra.

- Can't find external files. In D6, you must use the @ operator in place of the current folder in the Cast Member properties dialog box for any files imported via Insert ► Media Element, including QT3, SWA, and Flash members.

- Missing a non-Lingo Xtra, such as a Sprite, Transition, MIX, or sound mixing Xtra required by your Projector.

Non-Lingo Differences

The following differences between Projectors and authoring are not specific to Lingo:

- Projectors can be distributed freely, provided you comply with the Made with Macromedia program (see the *Macromedia:Made with Macromedia* folder on the Director CD). You cannot redistribute the Director authoring environment under any circumstance.

- Windows 3.1 and NT 3.5.1 are supported for runtime playback in D6, but not for authoring. You can test your 16-bit Projector under Windows 95/98 to work out the kinks, but you should ultimately test it on all platforms that you support.

- Because it installs temporary items at runtime, Projectors need write access to the Windows system directories.

- When it first starts, Director for Windows looks for the *DIRECTOR.INI* configuration file in the folder where Director is installed. For Projectors, this file must be renamed to match the Projector's name (such as *PROJECTOR.INI* to match *PROJECTOR.EXE*) and must be placed in the same folder as the Projector.

- Director 7 supports an undocumented *Projector.INI* file on the Macintosh too. See *http://www.zeusprod.com/nutshell/otto.html*.

- When it first starts, Director (for both Macintosh and Windows) looks for the *LINGO.INI* startup file in the folder where Director is installed. Projectors look for *LINGO.INI* in the same folder as the Projector.

- There is no Debugger or Message window at runtime in Director 6. You can use the *alert* command to post messages at runtime, or create a pseudo Message window using a field sprite and the *do* command.

- D7.0 for Windows will open a Message window in a Projector if you pass it any command-line arguments (D7.0.1 fixes the bug). In D7, add these lines to your *PROJECTOR.INI* file to intentionally create a Message window to help debug your Projector:

```
[Settings]
MessageWindow=1
```

- The numeric keypad and function keys (F-keys) are used for command shortcuts during authoring, but can be used for other purposes at runtime. For example, you cannot test for the ENTER key during authoring, because that key halts Director.

- By default, the ESCAPE key aborts a Windows Projector, but does nothing during authoring. Cmd-. (Macintosh) or Ctrl-. (Windows) will ordinarily quit the Projector, but if the *Play Every Movie* option is checked when the Projector is built, Director will go to the next movie. These keys can be disabled by setting *the exitLock* to TRUE. In D7 for Windows, Ctrl-Q does not quit Director or Projectors.

- Cast member thumbnails and the human-readable Lingo scripts are removed from projectorized, protected, or compressed files, making them marginally more secure and smaller than during authoring (apart from any compression).

- Your Projector may be running from a read-only device, such as a CD-ROM. If you store data, it must be written to the user's hard drive, not necessarily the same drive as the Projector. For example, *setPref* won't work in this case.

- Macintosh Projectors have less memory allocated to them by default than does Director during authoring, but they also tend to need less except when using many Xtras.

- Some resources available during authoring are not automatically available during runtime. For example, custom WDEF resources added to the resource fork of Director for Macintosh would not be available unless also copied into a Macintosh Projector's resource fork.

- In earlier versions of Director, not all cursor resources available during authoring were available from Windows Projectors. Instead, use a one-bit cast member as a custom cursor.

- The Stage (and MIAWs) gain and lose focus somewhat differently in authoring versus a Projector. For example, under Windows, MIAWs do not receive *deactivateWindow* messages reliably, especially when losing focus to other applications. See the D7 and D7.0.1 *ReadMe* files for additional issues.

- In D6, rich text cast members can not be created, imported, or edited at runtime. Director 7's new *#text* cast members address this deficiency.

- You can interrupt a transition during authoring with either a mouse click or a keystroke. In a Projector, only a keystroke will interrupt a transition.

- See the optimization checklists in the appropriate chapters and *http://www. zeusprod.com/nutshell/appendices/checklists.html* for a list of files to distribute with a Projector.

Xtras-Related Differences

The following differences exist between authoring and Projectors in relation to Xtras:

- In Director 6 and 7, MIX Xtras are needed to access externally linked sounds and bitmaps from a Projector. Other Xtras are required for NetLingo operations, custom cast member types, and so on. Although transparent during authoring, these Xtras must be included explicitly with your Projector or it may fail.

- Tool Xtras are not available from within a Projector.

- During authoring, Director loads Xtras from the *Xtras* folder where Director is installed. Projectors look for the *Xtras* folder in the same folder as the Projector. Make sure to use the same Xtra with your Projector as during authoring. For example, the D6.5 QT3 Asset Xtra won't work with a D7 Projector.

- If Xtras are bundled with a Projector (which I don't recommend), they are unbundled at runtime, possibly onto the user's system disk if the Projector is running from a read-only medium.

- Xtras are cached during authoring, but always reloaded each time a Projector runs. Trash your Xtras cache file when testing from Director to better simulate the Xtra registration process as performed from a Projector.

- Some demo versions of Xtras may work during authoring, but fail when run from a Projector. Even Xtras you have purchased should be tested from a Projector as soon as possible, as they often require a registration method.

- Some author-time-only Xtras, such as the QT3, Flash Asset, and Custom Cursor Options Xtras from Macromedia should not be distributed. Use their runtime counterparts (see Table 10-4).

- If a "Handler not defined" error occurs only in a Projector, most likely one or more necessary Xtras are missing from the Projector's *Xtras* folder.

- D7 for Windows requires either DirectSound.X32, MacroMix.X32 or QT3Asset.X32 to accompany the Projector in order to play sounds.

Lingo Differences

Lingo that creates, imports, or manipulates D6 *#richtext* attributes won't work in a Projector. The following Lingo commands behave somewhat differently from within a Projector (see *Lingo in a Nutshell* for more information).

the alertHook
> Can be used to open the Script or Debugger window during authoring, but not at runtime.

the applicationPath
> Returns the path to the Projector at runtime and the path to Director during authoring.

on deactivateWindow
> Message is not sent to MIAWs running from a Windows Projector.

the environment
> Returns different *#runMode* and *#shockMachine* properties depending on playback environment.

the frontWindow
> Returns (the stage) if the Stage has focus during authoring. In a Projector, it returns (the stage) only if no MIAWs are open or if the Stage is forced to the front using *moveToFront* (or all MIAWs are moved back with *moveToBack*). In D7.0, it returns the most recently opened window (bug fixed in D7.0.1).

getPref
> Uses a preferences folder whose name and location depend on the application's location and name.

halt
> Stops Director during authoring, but will quit a Projector. Use instead of *quit* to avoid killing Director while authoring.

installMenu
> Doesn't work while movie is halted during authoring. Use only after movie is running.

netStatus
> Prints in the Message window during authoring, but does nothing in a Projector.

the movie and the movieName
> Return the filename of the Projector when checked from the first movie in a Projector in D6. In D7, this is not the case. During authoring in D6, and from Projectors and authoring in D7, they always return the movie's filename, or EMPTY if the movie has not been saved.

the organizationName
> Returns EMPTY from within a D6 Projector and 0 from a D7 Projector.

the platform
> Indicates the Projector type, which may differ from authoring platform in D6.

put

Will not print to the Message window from a Projector (there isn't one unless you use the undocumented *MessageWindow = 1* setting described at *http:// www.zeusprod.com/nutshell/otto.html*. Use *alert* or a field sprite to display results instead.

the runMode

Returns "Projector" from a Projector and "Author" during authoring.

save castLib

Does not work with compressed castLibs or castLibs embedded within a Windows Projector. (It performs an incremental save leading to larger files.)

saveMovie

Does not work with compressed movies or movies embedded within a Windows Projector. (It performs an incremental save leading to larger files.) See Macromedia TechNote #08136.

the scoreSelection

Always returns an empty list ([ ]) from a Projector.

the scriptText of member

Property returns EMPTY from within a Projector to provide a modicum of source code security (except if accessing an external DIR or CST file). The human-readable *scriptText* is removed from any Director movies incorporated into the Projector and from external protected movies and castLibs (DXR, CXT, DCR, and CCT files).

the selection of castLib

Always returns an empty list ([ ]) from a Projector.

the serialNumber

Returns EMPTY from within a D6 Projector and 0 from a D7 Projector.

setPref

Uses the same folder as *getPref*. Not supported on read-only media (CD-ROMs).

the size of member

Property is smaller for script cast members in protected movies (reflecting only the compiled version of the script) than it is during authoring.

the soundKeepDevice

Under Windows during authoring, the sound device is released even if *the soundKeepDevice* is TRUE. In Projectors, it must explicitly be set to FALSE to release the sound device. See Chapter 15.

the trace and the traceLoad

Have no effect in a D6 Projector. In authoring and in D7 Projectors, they output to the optional Message window.

the traceLogFile

Does not write an output file from a D6 Projector but does work from a D7 Projector.

the updateMovieEnabled

Does not work with protected files and should be avoided in Projectors.

the userName

Returns EMPTY from within a D6 Projector and 0 from a D7 Projector.

Other runtime issues

- Any command that creates cast members or assigns media at runtime will consume memory. Using *importFileInto, copyToClipboard,* and *new(#member-Type)* or setting *the media of member* or *the picture of member* properties should be avoided at runtime. Instead, link to external files using *the file-Name of member* property.

- Do not attempt to save entire movies or castLibs during runtime. It is slow and wasteful and can lead to enlarged files, because they are never compacted (and it doesn't work from CD-ROMs). Instead, use the techniques covered in Chapter 14 in *Lingo in a Nutshell* to save only the relevant data, such as global variables, to a file.

- I have seen cases where single-line and two-line *if...then* statements were interpreted correctly during authoring, but misinterpreted in a Projector. Always put your Lingo statements on a separate line from *if* and *else,* and always include a separate *end if* statement.

  Avoid this:

  ```
  if (expression) then statement
  else statement
  ```

  Rewrite it as:

  ```
  if (expression) then
    statement
  else
    statement
  end if
  ```

Projector Utilities

This section covers some of the unique concerns of runtime distribution.

Preventing the User from Quitting

By default, the user can abort a Projector using various platform-specific keyboard shortcuts, such as Escape, Ctrl-Q, Alt-F4, and Ctrl-. (period) under Windows, and Cmd-Q and Cmd-. (period) on the Macintosh. (Ctrl-Q no longer works in D7 for Windows.)

To prevent these key combinations from aborting the Projector, use:

```
set the exitLock = TRUE
```

If you disable the quit key combinations, provide an accessible quit button throughout your presentation. Holding a user hostage is not a good sales technique.

Under Windows, the Buddy API Xtra can prevent the user from using Alt-Tab, Alt-Esc, or Ctrl-Esc to switch to other running applications.

Locating the User's CD-ROM

On the Macintosh, a CD-ROM drive's name is fixed when you create it. Under Windows, the CD-ROM drive is assigned a drive letter (usually between D and Z) that depends on how many other drives the user has installed.

If a Projector is running from the CD-ROM, the Windows drive letter or Macintosh drive name is simply the first portion of *the applicationPath*. See Chapters 7 and 14 in *Lingo in a Nutshell* for many details on file paths.

On the Macintosh, even if the Projector is not on the CD-ROM, the CD-ROM's name should still be known to you (software that burns Macintosh CD-ROMs should allow you to set the CD's name). Give your CD-ROM a unique name, not a generic one like "Demo CD," to distinguish it from other drives.

You can name your Macintosh hard drive the same as your eventual CD-ROM to test before burning a CD-ROM, but be sure to change it back before burning the CD-ROM.

 Two Macintosh drives can have identical names. If your hard drive is named the same as your destination CD during the burning process, some CD-ROM burning software might overwrite it!

When testing the final CD-ROM, make sure that your hard drive has a different name than the CD-ROM to prevent the Mac OS from searching the hard drive for any files that may be missing from the CD-ROM.

Under Windows, if the Projector is not on the CD-ROM with the content, determining the CD-ROM's drive letter is more complicated. Example 8-6 searches all the drives for the specified filename. If you use a unique filename, it is more likely to accurately detect the CD-ROM.

Example 8-6: Searching for the CD-ROM Drive

```
on findCD filename
  global gCD
  if the platform contains "Windows" then
    -- filename should be a strange/unique filename
    -- such as "frobozz.txt" that you've included
    -- in the root of your CD
    set gCD = findDrive (filename)
    if voidP(gCD) then
      alert "Please insert the very cool CD-ROM."
    end if
  else
    -- Macintosh CD is assumed to have the name you gave it
    set gCD = "My Very Cool CD:"
  end if
end findCD

on findDrive filename
```

Example 8-6: Searching for the CD-ROM Drive (continued)

```
    if not (the platform contains "Windows") then
      return Void -- no effort is made on Mac
    end if

    set myFile = new(xtra "fileio")
    -- Search drive letters backward from Z to A
    repeat with driveLetter = 90 down to 65
      set drivePath = numToChar(driveLetter) & ":\"
      set n = 1
      repeat while TRUE
        set nextFile = getNthFileNameInFolder (drivePath, n)
        if nextFile = EMPTY then
          exit repeat
        else if nextFile = filename then
          -- Returns drive letter, such as "D:\"
          return drivePath
        end if
        set n = n + 1
      end repeat
    end repeat
    return void
  end findDrive
```

Reader Exercise: Example 8-6 returns a hardcoded Macintosh CD drive name without actually performing any check. Modify *findCD()* to check whether the Macintosh CD is actually inserted in the CD-ROM drive.

Note in the previous example that we search the drive letters in reverse because CD-ROM drives tend to be the last used drive letter, which prevents unnecessary searching of used drive letters (unused drive letters are searched much faster than floppy drives A and B or full drives such as C). If you expect the CD-ROM to be used with networked drives, you may start your search from drive A in order to search local drives first. You might also start your search with drive C to avoid checking the slow floppy drives A and B. On Japanese systems, drive A may be the first hard drive, so you should eventually check A and B if the file is not found elsewhere.

If you attempt to read from a nonexistent floppy drive, it will cause a "Drive not ready. Abort?, Retry?" error under Windows NT, though not under Windows 95. Some Xtras allow you to disable the disk error message, or you can use an Xtra such as CD Pro Xtra (free at *http://www.penworks.com/xtras*) that returns the CD drive letter directly.

The *getNthFileNameInFolder* command does not recognize hidden files under Windows (unless they are retrieved from a Macintosh server, because it *does* recognize hidden files on the Macintosh). So the unique file used in Example 8-6 must not be hidden. Example 8-6 does not guarantee that the drive letter found is in fact a CD-ROM. You can check a drive's true type using an Xtra such as Buddy API or CD Pro.

Likewise, the FileXtra's *drivesToList()*, *fileExists()*, and *driveIsCD()* methods can be used to find the CD-ROM drive (see *http://www.littleplanet.com/kent/kent.html*).

No general solution exists for determining the CD-ROM from Shockwave without an Xtra, because *getNthFileNameInFolder* is disabled in Shockwave.

Note that the *checkDrive* example in the D6 online Help under "CD-ROM Drives, FAQs" has numerous errors, including typos. It uses the FileIO Xtra, which also searches any files in *the searchPath* and the current folder (if *the searchCurrent-Folder* is TRUE) and might return the wrong drive letter.

Ejecting the CD-ROM

If you are creating a multi-CD project, you might need to prompt the user to switch CD-ROMs. Under Windows, you can simply provide a dialog box asking the user to switch the CD, but to eject the CD automatically under Windows, use:

```
mci "set CDAudio door open"
```

On the Macintosh, the user cannot simply open the CD-ROM drive. The disk must be ejected via software. Use the Enhanced Development Kit's ECDCTRL XObject (won't work in D7) to eject the CD on the Macintosh:

http://www.macromedia.com/software/xtras/director/macromedia.html#ecd

Or use the CD Pro Xtra (both Mac and Windows, D6- and D7-compatible):

http://www.penworks.com/xtras/

Customizing the Projector and CD Icons

Methods for customizing the icon vary markedly on the two platforms.

Customizing Macintosh Projector icons

To add a custom icon to a Macintosh Projector:

1. Create a 32×32 icon in your favorite graphics program. (Photoshop's File ➤ Preferences ➤ Saving Files ➤ Icon option creates a custom icon that matches the document's bitmap.)
2. To copy an icon from another file, single-click its icon and use the Finder's File ➤ Get Info command (Cmd-I) to open its *Get Info* window. Highlight the icon in the *Get Info* window and copy it to the clipboard.
3. Use the Finder's File ➤ Get Info command (Cmd-I) to open the *Get Info* window for the Projector.
4. Select the icon by clicking on it in the *Get Info* window.
5. Paste the replacement icon from the clipboard. If the clipboard bitmap is larger than 32×32 pixels, it will be scaled automatically.

To modify the icon used for all future Macintosh Projectors, replace the icl4, icl8, ICN#, ics#, ics4, and ics8 resources in the *Director 7.0 Resources* file using a resource editor such as ResEdit.

Customizing Macintosh CD-ROM and folder icons

Custom icons can be set for drives or folders using the Finder's *Get Info* command as well. The custom icon for a Macintosh CD must be set by the CD-ROM burning software at the time the CD is created, usually by manually changing the icon of the mounted image. On the Macintosh, custom folder icons are stored in a hidden file named *Icon* within the folder. They can be viewed with ResEdit. When burning a CD-ROM, ensure that these hidden Icon files are copied to (and hidden on) the CD. The freeware *Folder Icon Maker* utility creates a custom folder icon from any file's icon. Mac OS 7.x and Mac OS 8 folder icons work under Mac OS 8, but not vice versa, so create your folder icons in an earlier version of the Mac OS.

Customizing Windows icons

You'll need a third-party Windows resource editor or similar utility to customize the Windows Projector icon. There are shareware icon editors, including Icon-Master and IconEdit. The resource editor that comes with Borland C will not work. See also the following.

Microangelo Librarian (Impact Software) customizes Windows icons. Their site includes all information and tools for managing Windows icons imaginable:

> *http://www.impactsoft.com/muangelo/muangelo.html*

Iconizer (Penworks) customizes Windows Projector icons:

> *http://www.penworks.com/xtras/iconizer/*

MHT-Icon Xtra (Meetinghouse Technologies) sets a Projector's icon and title:

> *http://www.meetinghousetech.com/tools/tls_index.html*

To customize the icon with an appropriate Windows resource editor, edit the ICON resource named APPICON in *PROJECTR.SKL* (for 16-bit Projectors) or *PROJEC32.SKL* (for 32-bit Projectors) before creating the Projector. (Make a backup of these files first.) Editing the Projector's EXE file after it is built will cause an "Invalid Projector File" error (it conflicts with Macromedia's scheme of appending the movie data to the end of the Projector's executable code). See "Icons for Projector files (Windows)" in the D6 online Help and Macromedia TechNotes #00611 and #01107 for additional details.

If you develop with Microsoft Visual C/C++ (MSVC), you can use its resource editor to modify the SKL resource files. AppStudio (part of MSVC++ 1.52) will edit only 16-bit resources.

Under Windows NT 4.0, use MSVC++ 4.0 (Microsoft Developer Studio) to edit both the 16-bit and 32-bit SKL resource files. MSVC++ 5.0 will edit 16-bit resources but not 32-bit resources under Windows NT 4.0.

Under Windows 95, use MSVC++ 5.0 (Microsoft Developer Studio) to edit both the 16-bit and 32-bit SKL resource files. MSVC++ 4.0 will edit 16-bit resources, but not 32-bit resources under Windows 95.

In all cases, edit the large, small, and/or monochrome versions of the icon. When pasting an icon into MSVC, click on the cactus/sun icon to shut off the transparency effect.

Most installers can create a Windows shortcut to a Projector and can specify a separate icon resource (ICO) file, as described in the following section, for the shortcut. If no ICO file is specified, the Projectors APPICON resource is used.

To modify a Windows shortcut icon:

1. Right-click the shortcut on the Windows desktop and choose *Properties*.

2. Choose the *Shortcut* tab in the Property dialog box.

3. Select the *Change Icon* button and select a new icon.

Any competent Windows installer can create shortcuts that use custom ICO files. See *http://www.zeusprod.com/nutshell/appendices/installers.html* for a list of installers for both Macintosh and Windows.

Customizing Windows CD-ROM icons

Icons for Windows CD-ROMs are always stored in external ICO files. The resource editors described earlier will create and edit ICO files, and DeBabelizer Pro for Windows (*http://www.equilibrium.com/ProductInfo/DBPro/ProReadersWriters.html*) will convert from or to ICO format.

The easiest way to associate an icon with a CD is to create an *AUTORUN.INF* file that specifies a file containing an ICON resource, as described later.

Auto-Starting Your Projector

You might want your Projector to start up automatically when the CD-ROM is inserted into the drive.

AutoPlay on the Macintosh

A Macintosh drive can be configured to run a particular file automatically when it is mounted. On the Macintosh, this is controlled by the *QuickTime Settings* Control Panel's *AutoPlay* option for QuickTime 2.5 or later (the default is off for CD-ROMs, but on for audio CDs). The feature is always on for QuickTime versions prior to 2.5.

DropStart is a simple utility included with AutoStart (*http://www.update-stage.com/xtras*); it can add an autostart file to a disk. The *ReadMe* file included with DropStart explains how it modifies the disk's boot blocks.

Some CD-ROM burning software including Adaptec Toast (formerly from Astarte) can also prepare a CD to autostart. See *http://www.adaptec.com/products/over-view/cdrec.html*. The steps for preparing a CD-ROM for automatic startup with Toast are:

1. Select Format ➤ Mac Volume from the Toast menubar.

2. Select the *Data...* button in the main Toast dialog box.

3. Locate and click the small triangle at the left edge of the *Select Volume* dialog box.

4. Select the *AutoStart* checkbox and select a file whose name contains 11 or fewer characters. The file can be either an application or a document.

AutoRun under Windows

Windows 95/98 automatically looks for a file named *AUTORUN.INF* (not *.INI*) in the root of a CD-ROM drive and uses it to start the executable of your choice.

An *AUTORUN.INF* file takes the form:

```
[AUTORUN]
OPEN=PROJECTOR.EXE
ICON=ICONFile,nIconNumber
```

The OPEN entry specifies an application to run when the CD is inserted. The optional ICON entry specifies the file used as the icon of the CD-ROM itself on the desktop. It can be an ICO file with an optional icon number within it (usually 0). To use the icon embedded in your Projector as the CD-ROM's icon, specify the EXE's name as the *ICON File*. If your Projector is named *COOLDEMO.EXE* in a subfolder named *DEMO* on the CD, you might use:

```
[AUTORUN]
OPEN=DEMO/COOLDEMO.EXE
ICON=DEMO/COOLDEMO.EXE
```

The file paths for OPEN and ICON in *AUTORUN.INF* must obey the 8.3 DOS short filename convention.

The AutoRun feature can be disabled under Windows 95/98 by holding down the Shift key while inserting the CD-ROM. It can be disabled permanently as described in *Windows Annoyances* (by David A. Karp, published by O'Reilly & Associates).

GS Technologies (*http://www.connect.net/gstrope/autotest.htm*) offers a free AutoPlay Test Configurator that allows you to test your *AUTORUN.INF* from a floppy or network drive, plus additional tools for creating AutoRun CDs.

Using AutoRun may alter the working directory so that it defaults to the root of the CD-ROM drive. Specify complete paths within Lingo even for items in the same folder. For example, to open a movie in the same folder as the current folder use:

```
go movie the moviePath & "MYMOVIE"
```

It is polite to provide a splash screen asking the user whether they really want to autorun the CD, rather than simply launching into a lengthy presentation.

The AutoRun utility (*http://www.updatestage.com/xtras*) can facilitate starting a CD-ROM, checking whether it has already been installed, and giving the user the option to run it again. It can also prevent multiple copies of a Projector from being launched. Buddy API's *baPrevious()* method can check whether a copy of a Projector is already running, but only after it launches the second Projector. See "How Director Executes your Projector" earlier in this chapter.

Screen Savers

Macromedia TechNote #03112 describes how to create a Windows screen saver by modifying the user's *SYSTEM.INI* file under Windows 3.1. It will not work in Windows 95/98/NT. The TechNote also lists third-party screen saver solutions for other platforms.

Daniel Plaenitz summarizes screen saver utilities for Director and ways to disable the system screen saver at:

http:/www.lingo.de/screensaver.htm

The following all create screen savers in one form or another:

- AnySaver (Windows 3.1 and 95/98/NT):
  - *http://www.dgolds.com/AnySaver.html*
- AutoLaunch and AutoLaunch Pro, by St. Clair Software (Macintosh):
  - *http://www.stclairsoft.com/AutoLaunch/pro_index.html*
  - *http://www.stclairsoft.com/AutoLaunch/index.html*
- Cinemac, by MacSourcery (Macintosh and Windows). Demo versions on Director CD under *Goodies*.
  - *http://www.macsourcery.com/*
- Digital Cafe will convert your Projector to a Windows screen saver:
  - *http://www.digitalcafe.com*
- DirSaver (Windows 95/98/NT only):
  - *http://members.xoom.com/dirsaver/*
- EXE Screen Saver (Windows 95/NT):
  - *http://www.ames.net/bsmith/exe_ss/features.html*
- Way Cool Screen Saver Engine (free; Windows 3.1 and 95/98/NT):
  - *http://www.fullvolume.com/savers.htm*

If playing a long non-interactive animation, you'll want to disable the user's screen saver. Buddy API (*http://www.mods.com.au/budapi/*) and the DirectOS Xtra (*http://www.directxtras.com/do_home.htm*) both have methods that enable or disable the Windows OS screen saver. DirectOS can also change the Windows desktop wallpaper.

Starting a Projector with a Document File

It would be nice to start a Projector by double-clicking a "saved game" file or dragging and dropping one onto the Projector. You can start a Projector by first properly associating a document with it or dropping a file onto it, but you'll need an Xtra to determine the name of the file used to start the Projector. If you always save the game state to a known filename, you need not explicitly determine it (you can just assume its name and location).

Associating a document with a Macintosh Projector

On the Macintosh, you must invent a custom Creator Code for your document and give the same Creator Code to your Projector. A Projector's Creator Code can be modified, as can any file's Creator Code, with ResEdit. Your Creator Code should be unique (that is, not registered by another developer for separate software).

Apple's site explains how to register your own Creator Code:

http://developer.apple.com/dev/cftype/

A database of many but not all existing codes is maintained at:

http://www.angelfire.com/il/szekely/tcdb.html

A text file's Creator Code can be set using the FileIO Xtra's *setFinderInfo()* method. Refer to Chapter 14 in *Lingo in a Nutshell.*

Use the CommandLine Xtra (*http://www.updatestage.com/xtras*) or the Buddy API Xtra's *baCommandArgs()* method to determine the name of the Macintosh document that was double-clicked.

Associating a document with a Windows Projector

Under Windows, file types are associated with applications via the *WIN.INI* file or the Windows Registry. Use an installer or a Windows OS Xtra (Buddy API or DirectOS) to create an association between your chosen three-letter file type and your Projector. The Buddy API documentation includes details on which Registry Keys must be set. Choose a unique three-letter type, not one used by other applications.

Once the association has been made, if the file is double-clicked, the Projector will launch. Under Windows, the Buddy API Xtra can read the command-line parameters (that is, the filename used to start the application). Under Windows, the DirectOS Xtra's *getCommandLine()* method will also retrieve the command-line string passed to your Projector. For example, if you double-click a document, *getCommandLine()* will return the name of the Projector followed by the name of the file that was double-clicked. Example 8-7 extracts the document name using the DirectOS Xtra.

Example 8-7: Parsing Command-Line Arguments

```
set commandLine = GetCommandLine()
put commandLine
-- "D:\Projector.EXE C:\MyFiles\MyDoc.SAVE"
set startDoc = offset (".EXE ", commandLine)
set docName = char (startDoc + 5) to ¬
   char length (commandLine) of commandLine
```

A bug in D7.0 for Windows opens the Message Window whenever starting a Projector with a document or command-line argument. This is fixed in D7.0.1.

CHAPTER 9

Memory and Performance

You must balance the sometimes conflicting requirements of disk usage, download times, memory usage, and runtime performance. Compressed media shortens the download time of a Shockwave movie, but takes longer to decompress. Bitmaps require more memory, but draw more quickly than QuickDraw shapes. There is usually a trade-off between compression and quality for digital video, audio, and bitmaps. Although efficient use of memory often improves performance, the best balance depends on the minimum playback platform and the nature of your project.

See "Determining the Appropriate Minimum Hardware Playback Platform" at *http:// www.macromedia.com/support/director/how/expert/playback/playback.html* for details on specifying the appropriate hardware (and convincing the marketing people to go along with you).

Disk Storage and Memory Management

When you save a movie file, Director saves only the changes made since the last save. The *movieFileFreeSize* indicates the size of old edited or deleted cast members remaining in the movie file. File ➤ Save and Compact rewrites the current data to a temporary file, excluding any old data. Director then deletes the original file and renames the temporary file to match the original file's name. File ➤ Save As also compacts the file. Both operations require enough disk space (at least temporarily) for the compacted file in addition to the original.

Director stores cast members in internal castLibs in the order in which they are used in the Score. Director stores cast members in external castLibs in the order in which they appear in the Cast window.

Each cast member is stored only once, although it may be used multiple times (or not at all) in the Score. For internal Casts, include cast members used solely as *puppetSprites* in a dummy Score frame near the frame(s) to which they relate. They will be stored to disk—along with the other nearby sprite's cast members—

although not loaded when the "live" frame loads. For external castLibs, use Modify ➤ Sort ➤ *Usage in Score* before performing File ➤ Save and Compact.

A cast member's storage order is unrelated to whether it is *loaded* at runtime. By default, Director does not load cast members for frames it never reaches. To load *puppetSprites* along with a "live" frame, place them off-Stage in a sprite channel of the live frame. Director loads cast members for off-Stage sprites, but not for invisible or muted sprite channels (see *the visible of sprite* property and the mute buttons in the Score window).

Memory Management

Director does not usually load all assets into memory at once. The Director movie, external castLibs, and streaming digital video and audio files may be many times larger than the available memory. Director automatically loads cast members as needed and unloads old ones to make room for new cast members.

Test your presentation on your target platform before attempting to tweak the memory loading manually. You can control loading indirectly via *the preLoadMode of castLib* and *the purgePriority of member* properties or explicitly using the preloading, idle loading, and unloading commands described later in this chapter.

Memory Allocations

Windows and the Mac OS allocate memory very differently. This affects the memory available to Projectors and is reflected in several system properties and the Memory Inspector (check *the memorySize* to determine how much memory is allocated to Director or a Projector). Real RAM is much faster than *virtual memory* (VM, in which a *swap file* on the hard drive is used to simulate additional RAM). Director implements its own "virtual memory" scheme, swapping data from the disk to RAM as needed. It is counterproductive for Director to load a cast member from disk only to have it swapped back out to disk by the OS (although it will be accessed faster from a hard disk cache than from a CD-ROM). Tell your users to disable RAM Doubler and similar utilities that degrade performance and confuse Director's memory management.

Multimedia is memory- and processor-intensive. Real RAM is very cheap and strongly preferred. Virtual Memory should be *off* if possible on the Macintosh, but *on* under Windows, although Windows users should also have adequate available RAM.

Macintosh memory allocation

Macintosh applications, including Director and Projectors, request a fixed block of memory when they are launched and will fail to launch unless at least the minimum requested memory is available. Check the minimum and preferred memory allocations by highlighting an application's icon and choosing the Finder's File ➤ Get Info option. These can be edited only when the application is not running.

Increase the preferred memory allocation for Director to allow you to import more cast members during authoring, and to generally improve performance. The Macintosh-only File ➤ Preferences ➤ General ➤ *Use System Temporary Memory* option allows Director to access additional system memory during authoring. You can use this option unless it appears to cause conflicts on your particular development machine.

A D7 Macintosh Projector requests a minimum of 4,096 KB and a maximum of 6,144 KB, by default (see Table 9-1), but some Projectors will fail to launch if the full 6,144 KB is not available. Until it is fixed in D7.0.1, set the minimum allocation to 6,144 KB manually. Adjust these defaults according to your project needs and the limits of your target playback platform.

There is rarely reason to allocate more than about 12 MB to your Macintosh Projector. Allocating 50 MB, for example, will merely consume all available RAM, leaving no headroom for the Mac OS, which will cause problems.

Macintosh Projectors built using the File ➤ Create Projector ➤ Options ➤ *Use System Temporary Memory* option can access additional system RAM beyond their fixed allocation. This setting is ignored when the Projector is played back on a Macintosh with Virtual Memory enabled. Avoid this option if supporting 68040 Macs. If the user has enough RAM, it is strongly recommended that VM be turned off using the *Memory* Control Panel on the Macintosh.

Macintosh Projector memory usage

The amount of memory your Projector will require depends on many factors, such as the monitor color depth and whether you are using digital video. By default, Fat Macintosh Projectors are allocated from 2 MB to 7.3 MB depending on the Director version, processor type, virtual memory setting, and the amount of memory available when the Projector starts. You can adjust the memory allocation manually using the Finder's *Get Info* command after the Projector is built. Mac OS X will adopt a similar approach to Windows, where applications do not use fixed partitions.

Table 9-1 shows how the default memory allocations for each type of Macintosh Projector vary by version and processor type. The minimum and preferred memory allocations adjust automatically when virtual memory is turned on or off. For Director 4.0.4, the minimum and preferred allocations were always 2 MB and 4 MB, respectively.

Table 9-1: Macintosh Projector Default Memory Allocation

Processor[1]	D7 Minimum/Preferred	D6.0.2 Minimum/Preferred	D5.0.1 Minimum/ Preferred
68K Mac	N/A	2,048/6,144 KB	2,048/4,096 KB
PowerMac with VM on	4,096/6,144 KB	2,048/6,1444 KB	2,048/4,096 KB
PowerMac with VM off	4,263/6,311 KB[2]	3,388/7,484 KB	2,986/5,034 KB

[1] A PowerMac running a Standard (68K) Macintosh Projector uses the default memory specifications for a 68K Mac regardless of its VM setting.
[2] The minimum and preferred memory allocations with VM turned off vary slightly depending on the Projector type and Xtras bundled within it.

Use *the memorySize* and *the freeBlock* to check how much RAM the Projector successfully allocated and how much remains available.

Windows memory allocation

Windows applications (including Director and Projectors) request memory as needed from a common system pool. Windows applications do not receive fixed allocations as do Macintosh applications. The Windows-only File ➤ Preferences ➤ General ➤ *Limit Memory Size* option is used during authoring in D5 and D6 to simulate playback on a machine with less memory. It is not available in D7.

Unlike the Macintosh, under Windows, VM (a permanent swap file) should be enabled both during authoring and for Projectors. Some versions of Director can run without VM if more than 64 MB RAM is installed, but VM is required in most cases. D7 will fail to launch if insufficient disk swap space is available.

To configure virtual memory under Windows 95/98, double-click the *System* Control Panel (accessed via Settings ➤ Control Panel from the Start Menu). Choose the *Performance* tab, click the *Virtual Memory* button, and then choose *Let Windows manage my virtual memory settings*. See Macromedia TechNote #03516, "Windows 95 Multimedia Configuration."

Under Windows NT 3.5.1, virtual memory is configured using the *Virtual Memory* tab in the *System* Control Panel. Under Windows 3.1, virtual memory is configured using the *386 Memory* Control Panel and via the *CONFIG.SYS* file. Under Windows 3.1, set the swap file to *None* (if you have enough RAM) or a *Permanent* swap file of about 2 MB, but don't use a *Temporary* swap file.

The *DIRECTOR.INI* file includes two options affecting disk swap space used under Windows for Projectors and during authoring:

```
[Memory]
ExtraMemory = kilobytes
SwapFileMeg = megabytes
```

The *ExtraMemory* option determines the amount of swap space (in KB) a Projector should use at runtime and defaults to 400 KB. Increase this to allocate more swap space to the Projector. The *SwapFileMeg* option determines the amount of swap file space (in MB) to be used during authoring only. It defaults to zero (a special setting that requests disk space equal to half of available physical RAM). Increase *SwapFileMeg* to perhaps 20 MB to import more cast members before running out of memory. See Appendix D, *The DIRECTOR.INI and LINGO.INI Files*, in *Lingo in a Nutshell* for additional details.

Audio buffers

The Macintosh uses a fixed audio buffer of about 400 KB. This means that it buffers less than 3 seconds of CD-quality sound (176 K/sec), but about 18 seconds of 22 kHz, 8-bit, mono sound (22 K/sec). The length of Windows audio buffers can be set via the *DIRECTOR.INI* file. See Macromedia TechNote #03107, which includes some sound buffer size calculations.

Media Sizes

Media elements require a lot of *bandwidth* (capacity) to be stored, loaded, and displayed. The *throughput* (ability to transfer data) of the processor, hard drive,

CD-ROM, network connection, video card, sound card, memory, and Director itself determine whether playback will be instant or delayed, smooth or jerky. You must account for the *latency* (delay) intrinsic to some devices, especially Internet connections, and their limited bandwidth.

The following sections describe each type of asset and how to calculate its size. See *http://www.zeusprod.com/nutshell/glossary.html* for definitions of the words *loaded, preloaded, purged* or *unloaded, streamed* and *streaming, internal castLib, internal asset, external castLib, external asset, linked,* and *unlinked.*

 Internal (unlinked/embedded) and external (linked) cast members are treated similarly whether they reside in internal or external cast-Libs. External assets are generally streamed and internal assets are generally loaded in their entirety into memory when they are needed.

There are four different aspects of an asset's size to consider:

The size of each cast member's header information
For each cast member, Director loads a small header that describes its contents when the movie is first loaded. This header is completely separate from the media for the cast member, which may not be loaded until later. An excessive number of cast members (more than several thousand) can require significant RAM. Although media elements also require a lot of RAM, a cast member's media can be purged, but its header cannot. Likewise, the Score notation, shape cast members, and script cast members are all loaded when a movie or castLib is opened and are not purged until the movie ends. In D7, font cast members are also always loaded.

The size of a loaded asset's media in memory
The size shown in the Cast Member Info window (and by *the size of member* property) loosely indicates the amount of memory a cast member occupies *if* it is loaded (see *the loaded of member*). For cast members that point to other assets, such as film loops, *#digitalVideo*, and linked sounds, it represents the size of the cast member overhead or the *#digitalVideo*'s header data. In such cases, the true size of the asset is usually much bigger than shown. The *size of member* reflects the disk file size for *#QuickTimeMedia* members.

Select multiple cast members and use Modify ➤ Cast Member ➤ Properties to view their cumulative size.

The size of an asset on disk
Whether in an internal or external castLib, or an external file, the time to load or download an asset is determined by its compressed size on disk which is smaller than its size once loaded into memory. There is no easy way to determine the size of internal cast members compressed on disk (see Example 9-1).

The data rate of streaming media
It is possible to play very large external video and sound files that exceed the available memory because they are streamed from disk in "chunks" that are discarded once played. When streaming data, the main concern is not the

entire file's size, but its *data rate* (the amount of data per second that must be loaded). For example, a video compressed to 1 MB/sec requires more throughput than one compressed to 400 KB/sec. Likewise, a CD-quality audio file requires 176 K/sec of data, versus a 22 kHz, 8-bit, mono sound requiring only 22 K/sec. The data rate of *uncompressed* streaming media (standard audio files) depends on the characteristics of the original content (sample rate, number of channels, and so on). The data rate of *compressed* streaming media (digital video and Shockwave audio) is primarily determined by the compression settings and the desired fidelity.

Streaming data

The `Modify` ➤ `Movie` ➤ `Playback` option lets you specify how Director should handle streaming Internet media from within the Shockwave plug-ins within a browser. This also affects the playback of cast members at a remote URL linked into a Projector (streaming options vary slightly in D6 and D7).

Bitmaps and PICTs

Embedded (unlinked) bitmaps are converted to Director's internal bitmap format (unless imported as a PICT). Director's internal format is optimized for a balance between disk size and access speed. It uses *RLE* (Run-Length Encoding) compression. Large areas of the same color compress extremely well, and the number of unique colors in a graphic determines its size on disk. (A 16-bit graphic using 256 colors will compress to the same size as an 8-bit graphic using 256 colors.)

Once a bitmap is loaded, its uncompressed size in RAM can be much larger than the disk storage size. This is calculated (in bytes) as:

(the width of member)× (the height of member)× (the depth of member)/8

Thus, an 8-bit graphic uses one-quarter the RAM of a comparable 32-bit graphic. Bitmaps at a different depth than the monitor must be converted on the fly, which slows performance.

The RAM used by a bitmap depends on its bounding rectangle, so an L-shaped graphic that is 300 pixels on each side takes up the same RAM as a solid 300 × 300 graphic. Cut L-shaped graphics into two cast members to reduce the memory required by upwards of 75%. Likewise, a four-sided framing graphic with a large blank center would occupy much more RAM than four individual sides of the frame.

Linked bitmaps in formats such as JPEG and GIF tend to be smaller on disk but much slower to load, and occupy the same memory once loaded as another bitmap. Linked bitmaps are often so slow as to be unusable. I import bitmaps as unlinked even if I expect the artwork to change. PICT cast members retain their original PICT format and typically require less disk space and less memory, but are slower to load than standard bitmaps. D7 also supports internal JPEG- and GIF-compressed cast members. Import them using the *Include Original Data for Editing* option.

When creating animations, consider the number and size of bitmaps you will need over time and how fast they can be loaded from disk or the Internet.

Shapes, Vector Shapes, and Flash

QuickDraw shape cast members are incredibly efficient and occupy only 64 bytes, as indicated by *the size of member* property. Shapes using a fill pattern or custom tile are much more compact than an equivalent bitmap, although they take slightly longer to draw. A single shape can be stretched and colorized to create multiple sprites. Shapes are always loaded in memory, but this overhead is usually minimal.

Flash and D7's new vector shape cast members are vector-based graphics that require extremely low storage and RAM, but more processor power. Flash and vector shape members are supported on Win32 and Mac PPC systems only.

For information about the Flash Asset Xtra see the HTML help files included with D6.5, the D7 Help, Table 4-10, and *http://www.zeusprod.com/nutshell/appendices/ flash.html.*

Buttons

There are two entirely distinct button types:

Standard buttons
> Built-in Director push button, check box, and radio button cast members created with the Tool Palette occupy only about 250 bytes each.

Custom buttons
> Custom Buttons are inserted via `Insert` ➤ `Media Element` ➤ `Custom Button` in D6. A Custom Button can contain up to eight states, each using a different graphic. The *size of member* property for Custom Button cast members depends on the size of the underlying bitmaps incorporated into it. Unlike film loops, those assets can be deleted once they are incorporated into the Custom Button. Leave unused button states empty to conserve memory. The Custom Button Xtra is obsolete in D7.

Fields

Field cast members are limited to 32,000 (not 32,768) characters in D6, and occupy between about 250 bytes and 35 KB (the character and size limit is eliminated in D7). This includes the cast member header, plus one byte per character, plus overhead for formatting (about 25 characters per style run).

To calculate the length of a field's contents, use:

```
put length (field whichFieldMember)
put the length of the text of member whichFieldMember
```

Field string manipulation can become egregiously slow if a string contains more than a few thousand characters. Copy the contents of a field to a string variable to perform string manipulations, then copy the result back to the field. String variables can contain strings up to about 2 MB, but they too can become slow at those sizes.

Formatted and colorized fields can be slow and may occupy much more memory than unformatted text. Keep the formatting simple.

Rich Text and Text

Rich text cast members in D5 and D6 are stored as *bitmaps*, and their *size of member* property depends mainly on the number of characters and point size. A typical rich text cast member may be from 2 KB to more than 200 KB (25 times larger than a comparable field cast member). Rich text cast members are not compressed when converted to Shockwave format. Prior to D7, convert rich text cast members to bitmaps for better compression, use field cast members (which are always smaller), or use the Flash Asset Xtra, which provides high-quality animated text at extremely low bandwidths. In D7, use the new text and font cast members (as described in Chapter 12), which are space-efficient.

Film Loops and Movie Cast Members

The size of member property for film loops is usually about 1 KB and does not include the cast members that make up the actual film loop. To determine their size, copy the film loop into the Score, and use the *ramNeeded()* function to determine the memory required for the range of frames comprising the film loop. See "Film Loops" in Chapter 3.

The *size of member* property for linked movie cast members is zero and does not reflect the size of the external movie file.

Palettes and Transitions

By using 8-bit custom palettes, you can reduce the RAM required for bitmaps substantially (see Chapter 13). Cast members using built-in transitions require 0 extra bytes. Third-party transition Xtras usually occupy very little memory, although some that use precalculated data may be larger.

Scripts

Script cast members are limited to 32,000 (not 32,768) characters in D6 (this limit is removed in D7), but their *size of member* property may be twice that (about 60 KB), because it includes the size of the compiled script. The original *scriptText* is stripped out of protected movies, which reduces the scripts' size by about half.

During authoring, you can calculate the length of a script's contents using:

```
put length (the scriptText of member whichScriptMember)
```

All the script cast members in a movie and its external castLibs are always loaded and never swapped out until the movie closes. Hundreds of scripts may occupy substantial memory.

Generalize your handlers or use Behaviors to reduce the number of scripts in a project. Refer to Chapter 1, *How Lingo Thinks*, and Chapter 12, *Behaviors and Parent Scripts*, in *Lingo in a Nutshell* for details.

Digital Videos

Digital videos are always externally linked and streamed from disk as they play, enabling a large digital video file to be played without requiring excessive memory. *The size of member* reflects only the size of a *#digitalVideo* member's header, but reflects the true external file size for *#QuickTimeMedia* members. Digital videos should be compressed using MediaCleaner (formerly MovieCleaner), Adobe Premiere, or a similar utility.

A video's average and peak data rates affect performance much more than the total overall size on disk. A video's average data rate can be calculated as:

$$\frac{(size\ of\ the\ external\ digital\ video\ file) \times float(the\ duration\ of\ member)}{(the\ digitalVideoTimeScale)}$$

A video's peak data rate is also of concern, although it is often not significantly higher than the average data rate. Use an external tool such as Adobe Premiere to check a movie's peak data rate. When budgeting for bandwidth, don't forget the size of the audio track(s) within the digital video file.

Sounds

A sound's memory requirements depend on its fidelity, whether it is compressed, and whether it is linked (external) or unlinked (internal). The size of a sound depends partially on the number of channels within the sound (1 for mono, 2 for stereo). See Chapter 15 for additional details and caveats about each type of sound.

Linked external sounds

Externally linked sounds are streamed from disk as they play, enabling a large sound file to play without waiting for it to load and without requiring excessive memory. Only enough memory to buffer the sound is required (usually less than 400 KB). *The size of member* as reported for linked sounds does not accurately reflect the size of the external sound file.

Unlinked internal sounds

Internal embedded sounds are always loaded into memory before being played, and are best limited to small (less than 500 KB) sounds. Large sounds should be externally linked, instead. Use looping sounds to reduce memory requirements. *The size of member* accurately reflects an internal sound's size and can be calculated (in bytes) as:

$$(samples\ per\ second) \times (bits\ per\ sample/8) \times (length\ in\ seconds)$$
$$\times (number\ of\ channels)$$

For example, an 11 kHz, 8-bit, mono sound requires 11 K/sec, and a 44 kHz, 16-bit, stereo sound requires 176 K/sec.

Compressed sounds

Director supports IMA-compressed AIFF audio (4:1 compression). IMA-compressed sound cast members are not further compressed by Shockwave, even when Shockwave audio compression is activated. If Shockwave audio compression is disabled, LZW compression is used for other internal sounds in DCR and CCT files (about 30% savings).

Shockwave audio (SWA)

Naturally, Shockwave audio (SWA) compression is used for external SWA files, but it can be used for internal sound cast members with both Projectors and Shockwave (see the Xtras ▶ Shockwave for Audio Settings option). With SWA, you choose an output bit rate (target bandwidth), not a compression ratio. An SWA sound's download size can be calculated (in KB) as:

$$\frac{(the\ bitRate\ of\ member)}{(8.192) \times (the\ duration\ of\ member)}$$

The MPEG-3 compression algorithm used by SWA yields higher quality sound without additional bandwidth when using a higher fidelity source. Always use either 22 kHz or 44 kHz 16-bit source audio for SWA compression.

Note that SWA sounds requires measurable processing power and may hinder performance on lower-level machines.

Xtras

The amount of memory required for Sprite Asset Xtras is highly dependent on the asset type. The Flash Asset Xtra provides excellent vector-based graphics at extremely low bandwidths and allows fine control over its memory use. Other Xtras, such as the QT3 Xtra, may use substantially more memory and/or use memory-intensive data types.

Determining Asset Sizes via Lingo

The *size of member* property reliably returns the RAM required for most internal cast members, including bitmaps, internal sounds, shapes, buttons, scripts, fields, and text cast members. It does not accurately reflect the RAM used by external sounds (SWA included), digital video, film loops, and movie cast members. Table 9-2 shows cast member properties useful in determining an asset's size.

You can check the size of an external file in the Finder or File Explorer during authoring. Refer to Example 4-6, which calculates an external file's size.

Table 9-2: Size-Related Member Properties

Media Type	Member Size
#bitmap	the *depth*, *height*, *width*, and *size of member*
#button	*length(the text of member)* and *the size of member*
#digitalVideo	the *duration*, *frameRate*, and *preLoad of member*, and *the preLoadRAM*; see Example 4-6
#field	*length(the text of member)* and *the size of member*
#filmLoop	the *media of member* (must be unwrapped)
#movie	see *getSize( )* utility in Example 4-6

Memory & Performance

Table 9-2: Size-Related Member Properties (continued)

Media Type	Member Size
#picture (imported as PICT)	see *getSize( )* utility in Example 4-6
#QuickTimeMedia	*the size of member*; see the *getSize( )* utility in Example 4-6
#richText	*the size of member*
#script	*length(the scriptText of member)* and *the size of member*
#sound (linked)	*the channelCount, sampleRate,* and *sampleSize of member*
#sound (internal)	*the size of member*
#swa	*the bitsPerSample, sampleRate, numChannels,* and *duration of member*
#text	*length(the text of member)* and *the size of member*

Data Throughput

When calculating the acceptable size of an asset, keep in mind the speed of the device (such as a CD) from which it will be loaded. The practical data rate is somewhat lower than the theoretical data rate for a CD-ROM. Table 9-3 shows the approximate time to load 5 MB of data from various CD-ROM drives. Remember that data is often compressed on disk, so that a 300 KB bitmap may require less than half that on disk. Thus, even a quad-speed CD-ROM may be able to load two full-screen (640×480×256-color) images per second. In practice, there may be some latency when first accessing data, due to Director having to find it on the CD-ROM.

CD-ROM performance can also depend on the driver and cache settings. The third-party CD-ROM Toolkit (by FWB) can alter Macintosh CD-ROM drive settings. Under Windows 95, see the *System* control panel (*Performance* tab ➤ *File System* button ➤ *CD-ROM* tab).

Table 9-3: CD-ROM Speeds

CD-ROM Drive	Theoretical Data Rate	Practical Data Rate	Load Time (5 MB)
Single-speed (1X)	150 KB/sec	100 KB/sec	50 sec
Double-speed (2X)	300 KB/sec	200 KB/sec	25 sec
Quad-speed (4X)	600 KB/sec	450 KB/sec	11 sec
Eight-speed (8X)	1200 KB/sec	900 KB/sec	4.3 sec
High-speed (>16X)	> 2400 KB/sec	> 2000 KB/sec	< 2.5 sec

Disk Capacity Budget

A typical CD-ROM holds about 650 MB of data. Table 9-4 shows how much data of a given type will fit on a single CD, but in practice, you will have a mix of various data types, plus some overhead for the installer, Projectors, Xtras, and so on. When using DVD-ROMs, which hold 4 GB or more, you can scale these figures accordingly. For many details on a variety of disc formats (and capacities), see the technical notes from Cinram at:

> http://www.cinram.com/Techlibrary/technical_library.html
> http://www.cinram.com/PDF/capacity.pdf

Table 9-4: CD-ROM Capacities

Asset Type	Storage Requirement	Fits on CD
Digital video (Cinepak—quarter screen)	400 KB/sec	27 minutes
Digital video (Cinepak—full screen)	1600 KB/sec	6.9 minutes
Digital video (Sorenson)	80 K/sec	135 minutes
MPEG-1 full-motion video	150 K/sec	74 minutes
MPEG-2 full-motion video	575 KB/sec	20 minutes
Audio (16-bit, 44.1 kHz, Stereo)	176 K/sec	64.5 minutes
Audio (16-bit, 22.050 kHz, Mono)	44 K/sec	4.3 hours
SWA (MP3) CD-quality	20 K/sec	9 hours
Bitmaps (640 × 480 × 256-color Director internal format)	200 KB/image[1]	3,300 images
Bitmaps (640 × 480 × millions of colors; JPEG compressed)	75 KB/image[1]	8,875 images

[1] A subjective approximation based on typical images with typical compression.

Director Memory Budget

Projectors require less memory than Director because they don't support many authoring-time features. Macromedia's Tech Note #03107, "Projector Memory Requirements," is woefully outdated and has several errors. The default *preferred* Macintosh Projector memory allocation may be adequate (see Table 9-1), but the default *minimum* memory allocation rarely is. Windows Projectors like to allocate at least 10 MB if it is available. Table 9-5 shows a possible memory budget for the Projector, exclusive of media elements. D7 recommends a minimum of 12 MB of RAM available for both Macintosh and Windows Projectors. I recommend a minimum 32 MB of real RAM installed, plus the virtual memory settings described earlier in this chapter.

Table 9-5: Program Memory Budget

Item	Mac	Win
Operating system[1]	5 to 10 MB	2 MB for Windows 3.1 8–24 MB for Windows 95/98/NT
Projector code	1 to 3 MB	1 to 3 MB
Projector misc. memory	1 to 3 MB	1 to 3 MB
Offscreen buffer[2]	300 KB or higher	300 KB or higher
Digital video drivers[3]	500 KB to 1.5 MB	500 KB to 1 MB
Xtras[4]	100 KB/Xtra	100 KB/Xtra

[1] The size of the operating system depends heavily on the extensions loaded.
[2] A $640 \times 480 \times 256$-color (8-bit) Stage requires a 300 KB offscreen buffer.
[3] The size of QuickTime on the Macintosh varies with the version and the QuickTime plug-in components installed and used. For example, the first addition of a QuickTime cast member increases the System memory usage by about 650 KB. Under Windows, it is possible, though unusual, to have a project that uses both Video for Windows and QuickTime for Windows.
[4] This is a very rough estimate, but each Xtra regardless of its type (Scripting, Sprite Asset, Transition, MIX, etc.) consumes a small amount of RAM. Ship only the Xtras you need with your Projector.

Browsers often require 15 MB of memory or more. See Table 11-2.

Table 9-6 outlines the memory requirements that depend directly on media usage. These are arbitrary numbers based on a typical project. You can estimate the RAM needed for your product by performing calculations as shown under "Media Sizes" earlier in this chapter. Internal bitmaps and sounds are usually the biggest consumers of memory. The QuickTime 3 Asset Xtra requires substantial additional RAM. Macintosh Projectors using QT3 may need 15 MB. Your actual requirements may vary widely depending on the nature of your project. Remember that Director will load and unload cast members as needed, so you can survive with less memory at the expense of performance. In extremely low memory, Director may drop out sound or graphics.

Table 9-6: Media Memory Budget

Item	Mac	Win
Score notation and cast member headers	100 KB to 1 MB	100 KB to 1 MB
Script cast members	100 KB to 1 MB	100 KB to 1 MB
Bitmaps and other cast members	2 MB to 3 MB	2 MB to 3 MB
Internal sound cast members	500 KB to 1 MB	500 KB to 1 MB
Digital video[1]	500 KB to 1 MB	500 KB to 1 MB

Table 9-6: Media Memory Budget (continued)

Item	Mac	Win
Streaming buffer for external sounds[2]	400 KB	2.5 × the size of one second of audio (27 KB to 440 KB)
MIAW[3]	500 KB to 1 MB	500 KB to 1 MB

[1] Per typical 400 KB/sec video played concurrently. If *the preLoad of member* is enabled, see *the preLoadRAM*.
[2] Per concurrent sound streamed.
[3] Arbitrary estimate per MIAW. Exact RAM depends on size and complexity of MIAW.

Offscreen Buffer

Director composites sprites in an offscreen buffer whose size depends on the dimensions of the Stage. The size of the offscreen buffer can be calculated (in KB) as:

$$\frac{(\textit{the width of the rect of the stage} \times \textit{the height of the rect of the stage})}{1024 \times (\textit{the colorDepth}/8.0)}$$

For example, a 640×480×8-bit offscreen buffer requires a 300 KB. In D6, if *the fullColorPermit* is FALSE, the size of the offscreen buffer is treated as if *the colorDepth* is 8-bit. Millions of colors is considered 32-bit, though *the colorDepth* reports it as 24-bit under Windows. Larger Stage dimensions and higher color depths usually imply that bitmaps will require more RAM as well.

MIAWs also increase the size of the offscreen buffer. In D6, it appears that MIAWs share an offscreen buffer with the Stage under Windows but have their own offscreen buffer on the Macintosh. In D7, the Stage and MIAWs have separate offscreen buffers on both platforms.

Cast and Score data

Although the Score's notation is fairly compact, the entire Score is loaded into memory when a movie is loaded. The size of the Score data also depends on the number of sprite channels used and the frequency of changes in the Score. Join sprites and eliminate unnecessary keyframes to reduce the Score notation's size markedly (you can save 1 MB over a large, inefficient Score).

There is also overhead associated with each cast member and their thumbnails (although the latter are stripped out when protecting a movie). Split movies containing thousands of frame changes or cast members into multiple movies to reduce the RAM used for the Score and Cast during the life of a given movie.

Data Structure Memory Requirements

Lingo variables and the data they point to require varying amounts of memory, as shown in Table 9-7. Simple types (integers, VOID values, symbols, and floats) always occupy 8 or 16 bytes. Complex types (strings, lists, child objects, and Xtra instances) occupy 8 bytes *plus* additional memory that varies with the size of the structure (such as the number of characters in a string, or the number of elements in a list). You can free the memory used by a complex data type by setting it to simple value, such as VOID, but even a VOID item will occupy 8 bytes.

Table 9-7: Lingo Data Structure Memory Requirements

Item	Minimum Size	Max Size
Integer	8 bytes	8 bytes
VOID	8 bytes	8 bytes
Symbol[1]	8 bytes	8 bytes
Float	16 bytes	16 bytes
String	8 bytes + 1 byte per character	About 2 MB
List	8 bytes + size of elements	About 2 MB
Xtra instance	8 bytes + 180 bytes	No specific limit
Child object (script instance)	8 bytes + 180 bytes	No specific limit

[1] Symbols always persist for the life of Director or the Projector. See *Lingo Symbol Table Archaeology* at *http://www.zeusprod. com/nutshell/chapters/symtable.html*.

Disposing of Objects (Freeing Memory)

All your variables combined may occupy less memory than a single bitmap. However, complex structures such as objects, strings, and lists can consume considerable memory and should be disposed of when no longer needed. Different types of objects are disposed of (freed) in different ways:

Variables

Local variables (those used within a single handler) are allocated when the handler is called and freed automatically when the handler terminates.

Property variables are allocated when the object, such as a Behavior script, parent script, or Xtra instance, is instantiated. They are freed when no variables refer to the object.

Global variables persist indefinitely, but by assigning a global variable to VOID, it occupies minimal memory. Avoid *clearGlobals*, which indiscriminately clears all globals as well as *the actorList* in D6 and D7. Use D7's new *the globals* property as described at *http://www.zeusprod.com/nutshell/d7/ globals.html* to see a list of all globals currently allocated.

XObjects

Use *mDispose* to dispose of XObject instances and *closeXlib* to close XObject libraries. These are not for use with Xtras and are not supported in D7.

Xtra instances, child objects, lists, and strings

Set the variable pointing to the object to zero or VOID, such as:

```
set myInstance = 0
```

MIAWs

Use *forget window* to eliminate a MIAW from memory. *Close window* merely hides the window and does not release its memory. Clear any global variables, properties, and objects in use by the MIAW before disposing of it.

Movies accessed via play movie

Use *play done* to return from a movie that was accessed using *play movie*. The second movie's memory is not released until you return to the first movie using *play done*. Use *go movie* instead to reduce memory usage, as it immediately releases the old movie from memory.

Purgeable Items

Director loads and unloads many entities without your knowledge or instruction. The following items are purgeable if Director needs the memory:

- Cast members with the highest *purgePriority* that are not needed in the current frame are generally purgeable (exceptions follow).

- Objects no longer referred to by any variable can be purged. Thus, a list can be disposed of if no variables refer to it any more.

- Streaming video and sounds (including SWA) are immediately purged after each segment is played. Internal assets are not.

- Forgotten MIAWs will be purged (and disappear from *the windowList*).

The following items are never purged:

- Objects (such as Xtra instances, child objects, lists, and strings) that are still referenced by some variable

- The 8 bytes minimum required for each global, even if set to VOID

- Symbols (see Chapter 19, *The Lingo Symbol Table*, in *Lingo in a Nutshell*)

- MIAWs remaining on *the windowList*, whether visible (open) or not

The following items are not purged until leaving the current movie:

- The Score notation for the movie and cast member header information for each open castLib

- Script, Shape, and Transition, and new D7 Font cast members

- Active puppetSprites

- Cast members used in the current frame (unless RAM is unavailable even after unloading all purgeable assets)

- Cast members with *the purgePriority of member* = 0 (*Never*)

- Cast members that have been imported, created, or modified since the Director movie was last saved (see *the modified of member*)

Cast Member Loading and Unloading

Cast members must be loaded from the disk or the Internet before they can be used. There is always a performance "hit" (delay) when cast members are loaded. You can either manually preload the cast members (and tolerate the delay) before the animation starts or let Director load the cast members as they are needed (and tolerate multiple small pauses as the animation plays).

Optimization of loading will not help if you are demanding too much throughput—reduce your media requirements instead!

Implicit Loading and Unloading

You can control cast member loading in many ways, but regardless, Director will attempt to load cast members when it needs them to draw the current frame. Use Modify ➤ Cast Properties or Modify ➤ Movie ➤ Casts ➤ *Properties* to control cast member loading on a castLib basis. (These equate to *the preLoadMode of castLib* property.) The default setting (*When Needed*) loads cast members on demand, whereas the *Before Frame One* and *After Frame One* modes attempt to preload as many cast members as possible (use these mainly for linear presentations on dedicated hardware).

Automatic cast member unloading and the purgePriority

Director unloads the least recently used cast members as required to make room for new ones. Other unused cast members may remain loaded in case they are needed at a later time. The *Unload* option in the Cast Member Info dialog box (corresponding to *the purgePriority of member*) controls cast member unloading. *Normal* items with the highest *purgePriority* (3) are purged *first*, followed by items flagged as *Next* (*purgePriority* = 2), and finally *Last* (*purgePriority* = 1).

 Don't use the *Never Unload* option (*purgePriority* = 0). It prevents Director from unloading assets even in desperate situations and can cause a crash.

Despite what Macromedia's older manuals and most third-party books erroneously imply, there is no "purge first" setting that purges cast members before *Normal* items. You must use *unLoadMember* explicitly to purge a cast member before other items.

The *Unload* setting is largely irrelevant for streamed assets, such as digital video and externally linked sounds, which are always discarded from memory as they are played. It is ignored for script, shape, transition, and font cast members, which are never unloaded.

Explicit Unloading

You can explicitly unload cast members using the commands in Table 9-8. The *unload* commands attempt to unload the cast members used in one or more frames of the Score, and the *unLoadMember* commands attempt to unload the specified cast members, but they may not be able to unload some of them for the reasons listed earlier. *UnloadMember* is buggy in D7.0, but fixed in D7.0.1.

Table 9-8: Unload Commands

Command	Usage
unload	Unloads only those cast members used in the Score.
unload *fromFrame* {, *toFrame*}	Unloads cast members in a range of frames, or in a single frame, if *toFrame* is omitted.
unload member *fromMember, toMember*	Unloads a range of cast members, as would the *unLoad-Member* command.
unloadCast	Obsolete. See *unLoadMember*.
unLoadMember	Unloads all cast members in D6. In D7.0, but not D7.0.1, you must manually specify a range.
unLoadMember member *fromMember* {of castLib *fromCast*}, {member *toMember* of castLib *toCast*}	Unloads a range of cast members or a single cast member if *toMember* is omitted[1] (*fromCast* and *toCast* can be different castLibs).
unLoadMovie *whichMovie*	Unloads the specified movie (which can be a URL reference). *The result* returns 0 if successful or –1 if movie was not loaded.

[1] *UnLoadMember* requires that *fromMember* and *toMember* be valid member names or numbers. Use *the number of members of castLib* property to find the last valid member.

Reader Exercise: Write your own utility to unload a list of cast members or create an "exclusive unload" utility to unload all cast members *except* those specified.

Analyzing Memory Usage and Cast Member Loading

Director can analyze memory usage and cast member loading to help you track and debug memory problems.

The Memory Inspector

Window ➤ Inspectors ➤ Memory opens the Memory Inspector windoid (shown in Figures 9-1 and 9-2), which shows the memory allocated to various uses and includes a *Purge* button that frees as much RAM as possible. Refer also to the *Memory Inspector* entry in the online Help. The appearance of the Memory Inspector varies across platforms and depends on the *Use System Temporary Memory* (Mac) and *Limit Memory Size* (Windows) options under File ➤ Preferences ➤ General. The values reported in the Memory Inspector are not always reliable, and the area of the bars in the graph are not necessarily to scale.

To determine the installed RAM, virtual memory, and available RAM accurately, use a third-party Xtra, such as Buddy API's *baMemoryInfo()* method or OSutil's *OSGestalt()* method.

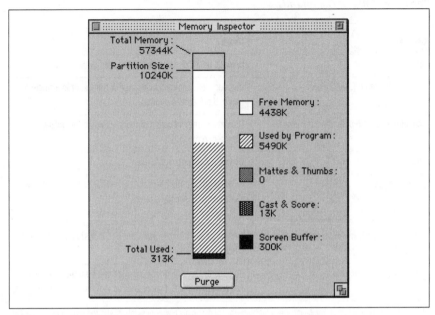

Figure 9-1: Memory Inspector (Macintosh)

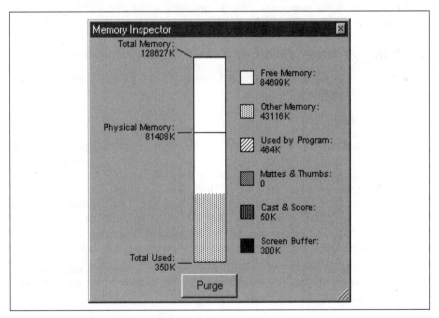

Figure 9-2: Memory Inspector (Windows)

The Memory Inspector displays the following values:

Total Memory
> Installed physical RAM, plus virtual memory (if any).

Partition Size (Macintosh only)
> Memory allocation set in the Finder's File ➤ Get Info window. Memory usage can exceed this if *Use System Temporary Memory* is checked under General preferences (or under File ➤ Create Projector options).

Physical Memory (Windows only)
> Installed physical RAM only. Director can use virtual memory beyond the physical RAM.

Memory Limit (Windows only; not shown in Figure 9-2)
> Reflects *Limit Memory Size* setting, if any, under General preferences.

Total Used
> RAM currently in use for the offscreen buffer, Cast and Score notation, and mattes and thumbnails. This is *not* the total memory used by Director.

Free Memory (see the freeBytes in Table 9-9)
> Unused memory available to Director. On the Macintosh, without *Use System Temporary Memory* enabled, it shows the unused portion of Director's fixed memory partition. On Windows, and on the Macintosh only when *Use System Temporary Memory* is enabled, it shows available system memory (including virtual memory).

Other Memory (shown on Windows, and on Mac if Use System Temporary Memory preference is checked)
> RAM used by OS and other programs.

Used by Program
> RAM currently used by Director. The value shown under Windows is completely wrong in D6.

Mattes & Thumbs
> RAM used to create mattes and display thumbnails.

Cast and Score
> RAM used to hold cast member and Score notation and edited cast members until they are saved to disk.

Screen Buffer
> RAM used for offscreen compositing buffer. Size depends on *the colorDepth* and the Stage's dimensions.

Purge Button
> Use this button to unload any items that are purgeable.

Determining Whether the Necessary Memory Is Available

Table 9-9 lists the commands that analyze RAM and disk space.

Table 9-9: Memory and Disk Space Analysis Commands

Command	Usage
cacheSize *newSize* put cacheSize( )	Gets or sets the cache size for downloadable media in a Projector or during authoring. Does not apply to Shockwave.
the fileName of member *which-Member*	Use this to locate the external file, whose size can then be determined using the FileIO Xtra. See Example 4-6.
frameReady ( )	Returns TRUE if the cast members required for the entire movie have been downloaded, or are local.
frameReady (*startFrame* {, *endFrame*])	Returns TRUE if the cast members required for the specified frame or range of frames have been downloaded, or are local.
the freeBlock	Returns size (in bytes) of the largest contiguous block of RAM.
the freeBytes	Returns total size (in bytes) of RAM available to Director, including Temporary System memory and virtual memory, if applicable.
getStreamStatus (netID or URL)	Get status of specified netID or URL (new in D7).
the loaded of member *whichMember*	Returns TRUE if cast member is currently loaded.
the mediaReady of member	Returns TRUE if cast member has been downloaded, or is local.
the memorySize	Returns size (in bytes) of the RAM allocated to Director or the Projector. Additional memory may be available (see *the freeBytes*).
the modified of member *which-Member*	Returns TRUE if cast member was created or modified since movie was last saved.
the movieFileFreeSize	Returns disk space (in bytes) that can be recovered using File ➤ Save and Compact.
the movieFileSize	Returns the size on disk in bytes of the current movie. Does not include external castLibs.
netDone(*netID*)	Determines whether a network operation, including *preloadNetThing*, has completed.
the purgePriority of member *which-Member*	Affects Director's automatic unloading of cast members. Those members with a higher *purgePriority* are unloaded earliest.
ramNeeded (*fromFrame, toFrame*)	Returns amount of RAM needed for cast members in the given range of frames. Use the same starting and ending frame number to check ramNeeded for a single frame.

Table 9-9: Memory and Disk Space Analysis Commands (continued)

Command	Usage
the size of member *whichMember*	Returns size of a cast member in RAM once it is decompressed from disk. Does not accurately reflect size of externally linked cast members.
the state of member *swaMember*	Returns "ready" if an SWA cast member has downloaded successfully.
tellStreamStatus (*flag*) put tellStreamStatus()	If *flag* is TRUE, Director will call the *on streamStatus* handler periodically, but if *flag* is FALSE (the default), it will not. If *flag* is omitted, *tellStreamStatus( )* returns the current setting. See *getStreamStatus( )*.
set the traceLoad = 0 | 1 | 2	Determines whether cast member loading is shown in the Message window. Highly improved in D7.
set the traceLogFile = *fileName* | EMPTY	Setting *the traceLogFile* directs the output from the Message window to an external text file. Setting it to EMPTY closes the external file.

The FreeBytes, the FreeBlock, and RamNeeded()

If *the freeBlock* is less than *the freeBytes*, RAM has become fragmented, which can happen when cast members of varying sizes are loaded and unloaded repeatedly. In this case, Director may *thrash* (repeatedly load and unload the needed cast members). Clear (and defragment) memory using *unLoadMember* as follows:

```
if the freeBlock < 200 * 1024 then
   unLoadMember
end if
```

The entry under *ramNeeded* in Macromedia's *Lingo Dictionary* includes an example that checks the *ramNeeded()* against *the freeBytes* to determine whether enough memory is available, but this is misleading. The *ramNeeded()* overstates the required memory if some cast members are already loaded (but understates the RAM needed if preloading digital video). Furthermore, *the freeBytes* understates the available memory, unless all purgeable cast members have been unloaded. To get accurate information, you must unload all cast members at the risk of having to reload some of them.

Reader Exercise: Write a *frameLoaded()* utility that checks whether the cast members needed for a frame are loaded. Model its syntax after the *ramNeeded()* and *frameReady()* functions. (Hint: use *the loaded of member* property to check each sprite's cast member. Use *go frame* to move the playback head so that you can check frames other than the current frame.) *FrameReady()* is not helpful because it indicates only whether items are available locally, not whether they are actually loaded.

The traceLoad

The traceLoad can diagnose loading problems by displaying in the Message window those cast members that are being loaded. It has three possible settings:

0:   No output (the default). Loading is not shown.

1:   Shows the cast member name or number of cast members being loaded.

In D6:

```
preLoadMember 200, 201
Loaded cast 200
Loaded cast Roulette Wheel
```

In D7:

```
member 200 of castLib 1("Roulette Wheel") was loaded into memory
```

2:   In D6, shows the cast member name or number, current frame, current movie, and file seek offset of cast members being loaded, such as:

```
Loaded cast 200 frame=1  movie=Test seekOffset=-598
```

In D7, in addition to the information shown when *the traceLoad=1, the traceLoad=2* shows:

```
Time = 1470997 msec (237 msec later)
Movie "test" is on frame X (freeBytes = 26616908, 49200 bytes
consumed)
Member is in movie (or external castLib) "filename"
File Seek Info: No file access occurred
File Seek Info: Seeked between files! Seeked 9014 to final
member at filepos 19262. Read in 4404 bytes.
```

 Using *the traceLoad=2* will crash D7.0 unless you first save the movie and any castLibs. This bug is fixed in D7.0.1.

In D6's *traceLoad* output, the *Loaded cast* indicates only the cast member's *memberNum*, not its *castLibNum*. The *frame* is the current frame, not the frame of the Score for which the cast member was loaded (so it is useless when performing explicit loading via Lingo). The *movie* is the internal or external castLib's name. The *seekOffset* indicates the distance that Director had to seek (forward or backward) in the file to find the requested cast member. Large seek offsets imply that the cast members are stored inefficiently. Perform a File ➤ Save and Compact before using *the traceLoad* to diagnose file seek problems.

In D6, *the traceLoad*'s output does not show cast members being unloaded, nor does it show cast members that are already loaded. Set *the traceLogFile* to capture the output to an external text file for later analysis.

In D7, unloading is shown as:

```
member X of castLib Y ("Name") was purged from memory
```

Determining the compressed size on disk

In D7, use *the traceLoad=2* to analyze disk usage for cast members. In D6, you can't easily tell the size or relative positions of cast members in the Director movie file on disk. Example 9-1 uses the *seekOffset* from *the traceLoad* output in D6 to estimate the disk size of a cast member.

Example 9-1: Guessing an Asset's Size on Disk

```
on checkSeekOffset whichMember
  unLoadMember whichMember
  preLoadMember whichMember
  set the traceLoad = 2
  unload member whichMember
  preLoadMember whichMember
end
```

The result in the Message window will be something like:

```
Loaded cast x  frame=1  movie=test  seekOffset=-76718
```

The first preload positions the disk head at the end of the cast member. The second preload forces Director to seek back to the beginning of the cast member. The absolute value of the *seekOffset* is the approximate size of the asset on disk.

Determining what is loaded

The utility in Example 9-2 reports which cast members are loaded and how much memory they occupy. You may want to save the Director movie and unload all cast members before running *showLoaded*.

Example 9-2: Determining Currently Loaded Cast Members

```
on showLoaded startCastLib, endCastLib
  if startCastLib = void then
    set startCastLib = 1
  end if
  if endCastLib = void then
    set endCastLib = the number of castLibs
  end if
  -- Track count and memory used for various member types
  set memberCount   = 0
  set memSize       = 0
  set scriptCount   = 0
  set scriptMemSize = 0
  set modCount      = 0
  set modMemSize    = 0
  set neverCount    = 0
  set neverMemSize  = 0
  -- Look in all castLibs for loaded cast members
  repeat with x = startCastLib to endCastLib
    repeat with y = 1 to the number of members of castLib x
      -- If a cast member is loaded, try to determine why
      if the loaded of member y of castLib x then
        set thisSize = the size of member y of castLib x
```

Example 9-2: Determining Currently Loaded Cast Members (continued)

```
    set memSize = memSize + thisSize
    set memberCount = memberCount + 1
    set thisType = the type of member y of castLib x
    case (thisType) of
      #script:
        -- Scripts are always loaded
        -- Don't bother printing them out
        set scriptCount = scriptCount + 1
        set scriptMemSize = scriptMemSize + thisSize
      otherwise:
        if the modified of member y of castLib x then
          -- Not unloadable because it has been
          -- modified since movie was last saved
          set append = "(MODIFIED)"
          set modMemSize = modMemSize + thisSize
          set modCount = modCount + 1
        else if the purgePriority of member y ¬
          of castLib x = 0 then
          -- Not unloadable because it is
          -- set to Never Unload
          set append = "(NEVER UNLOAD)"
          set neverMemSize = neverMemSize + thisSize
          set neverCount = neverCount + 1
        else
          -- Not unloaded because it is one of the other
          -- unloadable types (shapes, transitions, fonts)
          set append = EMPTY
        end if
        put member y of castLib x && "Type:" && ¬
            thisType && append
    end case
  end if
  end repeat
end repeat
-- Display some statistics about what is still loaded
put "Total size of" && memberCount && ¬
    "loaded member(s):" && memSize / 1024 && "KB"
put "Including" && scriptCount && "script(s) totaling:" ¬
    && scriptMemSize / 1024 && "KB"
put "Including" && modCount && "modified member(s)" && ¬
    "totaling:" && modMemSize / 1024 && "KB"
put "Including" && neverCount && "unpurgeable" && ¬
    "member(s) totaling:" && neverMemSize / 1024 && "KB"
end showLoaded
```

Manual Preloading

Director allows you to attempt to preload cast members manually from disk into memory. Preloading stops when memory is full, so not all preload attempts succeed completely. Preloading cast members that are not ultimately needed is counterproductive, as is preloading additional cast members after memory is full

---

(items preloaded in the first batch would be unloaded to make room for the second batch). Manual loading of cast members works best when sufficient memory is available and the preloaded members will be used imminently.

 Manual preloading does not appear to be working correctly in D7.0. Upgrade to D7.0.1, which remedies several preloading bugs.

Preloading large amounts of data can be time-consuming. Set the *preLoad-EventAbort* to TRUE to allow the user to interrupt preloading, or set *the idleLoadMode* to use idle loading as described Table 9-11. The preload commands do not generally preload externally linked files. Digital video files are preloaded only if *the preLoad of member* is set. SWA files are preloaded according to *the preLoadTime of member* property using the *preLoadBuffer* command.

The preloading commands shown in Table 9-10 return a status in *the result* that is of dubious value in determining whether they succeeded. Entries preceded by "the" are properties, not commands.

Table 9-10: Preloading Commands

Command	Usage
downloadNetThing URL, localFile	Downloads data from *URL*, so that it is local when needed.
preLoad toFrame	In D6 and D7.0.1, preloads all cast members used in the Score from the current frame to frame *toFrame*. In D7.0, use *preload the frame, toFrame* instead.
preLoad fromFrame, toFrame	Preloads all cast members used in the Score from frame *fromFrame* to frame *toFrame*.
preLoad member fromMember, toMember	Preloads a range of cast members, as would the *preLoadMember* command.
the preLoad of member videoMember	Determines whether a *#digitalVideo* or *#QuickTimeMedia* cast member's external video file can be preloaded. See *the preLoadRAM* entry.
preLoadBuffer member swaMember	Preloads a portion of an SWA as set by *the preLoadTime of member*.
preLoadCast	Obsolete. See *preLoadMember*.
the preLoadEventAbort	If TRUE, allows a mouse click or key press to abort preloading. Defaults to FALSE.
preLoadMember	Preloads[1] all cast members in the current movie in D6. In D7, it preloads only the first castLib.

Table 9-10: Preloading Commands (continued)

Command	Usage
preLoadMember member *from-Member* {of castLib *fromCast*}, {member *toMember* of castLib *toCast*}	Preloads[1] a range of cast members, or a single cast member if *toMember* is omitted (*fromCast* and *toCast* can be different castLibs in D6, but preloading across multiple castLibs fails in D7).
the preLoadMode of castLib *which-Cast*	Determines whether cast members are loaded when needed, or preloaded when the movie starts.
preLoadMovie *whichMovie*	Preloads a movie (URLs allowed) in anticipation of using *go movie* or *play movie*. *The result* returns 0 if successful or a negative error code.
preloadNetThing (*URL*)	Asynchronously preloads an HTML, GIF, or other web-based asset. Check the status with *netDone( )*.
the preLoadRAM	Specifies RAM (in bytes) used for preloading digital videos whose *preLoad of member* property is TRUE. When set to 0, *all* available RAM is used.
the preLoadTime of member *swaMember*	Determines the amount of sound preloaded (in seconds) when using *preLoadBuffer* or otherwise loading an SWA cast member.
the result	Used to access the result of a preload operation.

[1] *PreLoadMember* requires that *fromMember* and *toMember* be valid member names or non-empty member slots. *The number of members of castLib* property returns the last valid member slot, but that slot may be empty if cast members have been moved or deleted. The *number of castLibs* returns the number of the last castLib.

preLoadMember and preLoad

There may be insufficient memory to preload the cast members as requested via the *preLoad* and *preLoadMember* commands. Both return a status via *the result* that ostensibly can be used to check whether the operation succeeded. The following discussion applies mainly to D6. At press time, D7.0's preloading was too buggy to test effectively and D7.0.1 was not yet finalized.

preLoad and *preLoadMember* attempt to preload cast members in the order in which they are saved in the movie file or external castLib on disk, and not in *memberNum* order or the order in which they appear in the Score. Cast members are loaded from the lowest numbered castLib first.

The sequential cast member loading order is efficient when reading from disk, but leads to this oft-repeated potentially incorrect Lingo code:

```
preLoadMember 1, 5
put the result
-- 4
if the result < 5 then alert "Not enough memory to preload"
```

If cast members are used in the Score in the order 1, 2, 3, 5, 4, they will be stored to disk in the same order. *The result* will return 4 (the *last* cast member loaded), and not 5 (the *highest* numbered cast member loaded), implying an error, when in fact the *preLoadMember* command succeeded! (*The result* would return cast member 4, even if member 4 was already loaded, because *the result* indicates the last cast member that would be loaded if needed. It does not necessarily return the highest number member loaded, nor the member that was actually loaded last.) To make *the result* return a meaningful answer, use Modify ➤ Sort ➤ *Usage in Score* and then use File ➤ Save and Compact for internal casts. The sort order doesn't matter for members in external castLibs, because they are stored on disk in the order in which they appear in the Cast window.

Furthermore, if you preload frames 1 to 10, and the Score contains references to both internal and external cast members, members in the lowest number castLib are always loaded first. That is, if you need member 5 of castLib 2 in frame 1 of a movie, it may not be preloaded until after member 1 of castLib 1, even if the latter is not used until frame 2 of the movie! These issues may be more pronounced in Shockwave, where preloading can be slower.

If you attempt to preload items in smaller chunks, it is possible that those items preloaded with the first *preload* command will be unloaded by a subsequent *preload* command. In other words, preloading works best when you perform only one preload before using the newly loaded cast members. You can also unload all cast members before a series of preloads to increase the chance that your new cast members won't be unloaded.

The result of a *preLoadMember* command returns only the cast member's *memberNum*, leaving its *castLibNum* ambiguous:

```
preLoadMember member 2 of castLib 1
put the result
-- 2
preLoadMember member 2 of castLib 4
put the result
-- 2
```

Check *the loaded of member* property to confirm which cast members were loaded.

The *preLoad* command sets *the result* to the number of the last frame for which cast members were successfully preloaded, such as:

```
preLoad 1, 10
if the result <> 10 then alert "Couldn't finish preload"
```

Preloading digital video

A digital video's external data is not preloaded unless the *Enable Preload* option is set in its Cast Member Properties dialog box (or via *the preLoad of member* property). *The preLoadRAM* property determines the amount of memory used for preloading digital videos. The default setting (0) uses *all* available memory. Refer to Chapter 16, *Digital Video*, for more details on proper digital video preparation and optimizing digital video performance in Director.

If a digital video's data rate is sufficiently low, there should be no need to preload data, which should be provided on the fly. One exception might be a very small digital video that must play smoothly without dropping frames. To avoid accessing a CD-ROM in two places at once, preload animations or sounds instead, as they tend to be smaller than digital video.

The example for *the preLoadRAM* in Macromedia's *Lingo Dictionary* prior to D7 was meaningless. You should either specify a fixed value for preloading digital video, such as:

```
set the preLoadRAM = 2 * 1024 * 1024 -- 2 MB
```

or specify a percentage of *the freeBlock* for preloading, such as:

```
set the preLoadRAM = 0.5 * the freeBlock
```

The optimal setting would depend on the length of the video, the video's data rate, the free RAM, and the speed of the drive providing the data, but I prefer not to preload videos at all.

Asynchronous and Idle Loading

Typically, you might preload cast members for a segment in the Score and then wait a considerable time for the user to move onto the next screen. Director will generate one or more *idle* events during each frame as time allows. For example, if the Score's tempo is 10 fps, each frame is allotted six ticks. If Director takes only two ticks to draw the frame, 4 ticks would be left to process *idle* events. Director's idle loading commands (shown in Table 9-11) load cast members without monopolizing Director's attention.

Idle loading works in conjunction with the *preLoad* commands listed in Table 9-10. The frequency and duration of the attention paid to idle loading is controlled by the *idleLoadMode*, *idleHandlerPeriod*, *idleLoadPeriod*, and *idleReadChunkSize* properties.

The frequency of *mouseEnter*, *mouseLeave*, and *mouseWithin* events also depends on *the idleHandlerPeriod*. If *the idleHandlerPeriod* is not zero, rollover event handling becomes unusably sluggish.

Table 9-11: Idle Loading

Command	Usage
cancelIdleLoad *loadTag*	Aborts preloading of cast members with the specified *loadTag*.
finishIdleLoad *loadTag*	Finishes preload command previously tagged by *loadTag*.
on idle	The *on idle* handler is called during each idle event, but need not be used for idle loading.
the idleHandlerPeriod = *numTicks*	Increasing *the idleHandlerPeriod* reduces the frequency with which the *idle*, *mouseLeave*, *mouseEnter*, and *mouseWithin* events are generated. (Default is 0 in D6, which sends these events as frequently as possible and 1 in D7, which reduces Director's monopolization of the processor.)
idleLoadDone(*loadTag*)	Returns TRUE if cast members with specified *loadTag* are all loaded.
the idleLoadMode	Optionally allows idle loading (default is *Never*). See the next section.
the idleLoadPeriod = *numTicks*	Increasing *the idleLoadPeriod* increases the time between idle loads, allowing more time for idle activities other than cast member loading.

Table 9-11: Idle Loading (continued)

Command	Usage
the idleLoadTag = *loadTag*	Creates an arbitrary *loadTag* that identifies the batch of cast members loaded by the next preload command.
the idleReadChunkSize = *chunkSize*	Size (in bytes) of data read each time idle load queue is serviced. Defaults to 32,767 bytes (32 KB).

The idleLoadMode

The idleLoadMode has four possible values:

0:   Cast members are immediately preloaded when a *preLoad* command is issued. (No idle loading. This is the default.)

1:   Performs idle loading when there is free time between the *enterFrame* and *exitFrame* messages in a frame.

2:   Performs idle loading each time Director calls the *on idle* handler. The *idleHandlerPeriod* limits how often *idle* events will be sent (the default is as frequently as possible) and *the idleLoadPeriod* determines whether Director will attempt multiple idle reads during an idle event (the default is to load as frequently as possible during an idle event).

3:   Performs idle loading as frequently as possible (both while idling in a frame, and again after exiting a frame before reaching the next frame).

Each time the idle load queue is serviced, Director reads data equal in size to *the idleReadChunkSize* (defaults to 32 KB).

If you expect the user to follow a particular path, you might preload the cast members used in a range of frames. Example 9-3 shows how to initiate and then wait for idle loading.

Example 9-3: Idle Loading

```
on exitFrame
    -- Idle load as frequently as possible
    set the idleLoadMode = 3
    -- Identify this idle load batch with an arbitrary number
    set the idleLoadTag = 1
    -- Idle load the next scene in the Score
    preLoad marker(1), marker(2)
end
```

Then, in a subsequent frame, you might wait for idle loading to complete before jumping to the new marker:

```
on exitFrame
    if idleLoadDone(the idleLoadTag) then
        -- Turn off idle loading.
        set the idleLoadMode = 0
        -- Go to next marker if all cast members are loaded.
        go marker (1)
```

```
    else if the mouseDown then
      -- Finish idle loading if the user clicked the mouse.
      finishIdleLoad (the idleLoadTag)
      set the idleLoadMode = 0
      go marker(1)
    else
      go the frame
    end if
end
```

Note that we left *the idleHandlerPeriod, the idleLoadPeriod,* and *the idleRead-ChunkSize* at their default values, causing idle reading to occur in 32 KB chunks as frequently as possible.

Memory Optimization

The following sections help you avoid and diagnose memory problems.

Before you can fix a memory problem, you must confirm that the problem is memory-related. The following conditions may indicate a lack of available memory but may also have other causes:

- Warning errors from Director that it has used all available memory.
- Audio not being played or dropping out.
- Background graphics and large graphics not appearing on the Stage.
- Excessive disk access (thrashing). In very low RAM, Director may purge and reload the same graphic repeatedly.
- Sprites leaving trails even when *the trails of member* is FALSE.
- Flickering cursors.
- Printing is extremely slow or delayed until Director quits.
- Poor performance seen only on machines with less installed RAM.

Causes of Memory Errors

There are two types of so-called *memory errors*: either Director is running low on memory due to a known limitation, or there is an unintentional *memory leak* in one or more system components. Director may issue the error, "Warning! The current movie has used all of Director's main memory and some of its reserve memory," or even crash. Save your file immediately if you receive this error.

Not enough memory

You can allocate more memory to Director as described under "Memory Allocations" earlier in this chapter. The following will often lead to low memory situations:

Importing or creating too many cast members during authoring or at runtime
    Allocate more memory to Director, import fewer items, and resave the Director file to free memory. Avoid importing during runtime, or link to external files using *the fileName of member* property instead.

Cast members can not be unloaded

Save the file to allow cast members to be purged. Don't set *the purgePriority of member* to 0 (*Never*). Use *Normal, Next,* or *Last* settings instead.

Director is trying to load a nonexistent cast member

If Director gives the error, "Not Enough memory to load some cast members," it may be trying to load a nonexistent cast member, caused by an erroneous reference in the Score to a cast member that has been deleted. See *the traceLoad* later in this chapter and Example 3-9 to diagnose the problem.

External applications are not leaving enough RAM available to Director

Quit other applications before starting Director or a Projector, and check *the memorySize* and *the freeBlock*.

Director does not leave external applications enough memory to be launched using the Lingo open command

Use zLaunch (*http://www.zeusprod.com/products/zlaunch.html*) to quit the Projector while an external application runs and relaunch your Projector when the external application terminates.

Recursion

Recursion occurs when a handler calls itself or two routines call each other, either directly or indirectly. It often leads to a crash and should be avoided, unless it is intentional. In Example 9-4, the two functions call each other until Director runs out of memory due to an overflowed *handler call stack.* Set breakpoints in each handler to watch the call stack grow in the upper-left pane of the Debugger window (save your work first, as this may crash your computer).

Example 9-4: Bad Mojo Recursion

```
on handlerA
  handlerB()
end

on handlerB
  handlerA()
end
```

Memory leaks

The following are possible causes of memory leaks. Small leaks may never accumulate to the point where they cause trouble. You many need to test for a long time on a machine with little RAM to duplicate the problem. Not all of these things will always cause leaks. but if you suspect a memory leak, you should check these items first:

Using Lingo improperly or not freeing objects

An apparent memory leak may be caused by instantiating an Xtra or child object, creating a large list, or opening a MIAW but never disposing of it. You must eliminate references to objects to allow Director to perform "garbage collection."

A bug in or improper use of an Xtra or XObject

Try to isolate the cause of the problem and contact the Xtra manufacturer for instructions on proper use of the Xtra or to identify known bugs. Leaks from Xtras or XObjects are not uncommon, because C programmers must allocate and deallocate memory explicitly. Multiple layers, such as the ActiveX Xtra interfacing with an ActiveX control, increase the potential sources of error.

Cursor and menu leaks

Switching cursors in D6.0 caused a memory leak (although fixed in D6.0.1, it reappeared in D7.0, but should be lessened in D7.0.1). Switching menus repeatedly under Windows caused a severe memory leak in D5, and it is still recommended that you not switch menus or cursors excessively.

External castLib leaks

There have been reports of Sprite Xtras used in external Casts causing memory leaks. When in doubt, internal Casts are least likely to cause problems.

Sounds not being unloaded

Playing a puppet sound from an external castLib as you go to a new Director movie may cause the sound to stay in memory and never be unloaded (see *http://www.updatestage.com/buglist.html*). Unpuppet any sounds (using *puppetSound 0*) before going to a new movie.

Using play movie without play done

When using the *play movie* command, the first movie is kept in memory until you return from the second movie using *play done*. Avoid the *play movie* command if you can't guarantee that a matching *play done* command will eventually be issued. Use *go movie* and a global variable to store the name of movie to return to instead.

Creating or importing assets dynamically at runtime

Any items created dynamically must reside in RAM. During authoring, these can be purged only when the Director file is saved. From a Projector, they can cause memory to run low. Avoid dynamic linking of content or set *the fileName of member* property instead.

External applications

Anything that uses an external application relies on that application to behave properly. If that external application leaks memory, you won't find the error within your Director project.

External files

When using external files, such as with the FileIO Xtra, close any files when done to allow the OS to deallocate the file handle assigned to the file.

Isolating and Diagnosing Memory Problems

Director performs memory cleanup ("garbage collection") periodically. There is a lag between when Director *could* reclaim memory and when it actually does reclaim it. Decreased available memory does not necessarily indicate a memory leak. Director won't unload cast members unless it needs the memory for something else or until you use *unload* or *unLoadMember*. *The freeBytes* and *the freeBlock* typically drop very low, and then fluctuate at low levels as Director unloads just enough cast members to make room for those it is about to load. In D7, *the freeBytes* shouldn't drop below 300 KB or so.

If memory decreases slowly over time, it may be the cumulative effect of a small memory leak. If memory drops suddenly and can't be reclaimed, it may be due to a large cast member not being freed from memory.

When you suspect a memory leak, try disabling any Lingo that performs any unusual and/or very repetitive operation. For example, if a project using an untested Xtra or unsupported Lingo command is leaking memory, disable those items first. Other suspicious items include dynamically editing properties at runtime that are ordinarily only changed during authoring. This would include changing member properties (as opposed to sprite properties), creating new cast members, Score recording, dynamically linking to external castLibs, and the like.

Use Alex Zavatone's MemMon utility to help diagnose memory problems. For the shareware version, search for "MemMon" at: *http://www.director-online.com/help_ central/DOUGsearch/searches/DWdemo.html*. For technical and ordering information for the professional version, see *http://www.blacktop.com/zav/toolkit*. For Zav's article on memory management, see *http://www.director-online.com/howTo/UD_ articles/UD26.html*.

Checking cast member loading and unloading

To display cast member loading, set *the traceLoad* in the Message window and play the movie:

```
set the traceLoad = 1
```

If a cast member reference is incorrect, you will see Director repeatedly try to load the problematic cast member that it can't find.

Check for *purgePriority of member* settings other than 3 (*Normal*) or 2 (*Next*) using a loop similar to that shown in Example 4-8. Use *the loaded of member* property to determine which cast members are currently loaded (see Example 9-2).

Checking memory usage

Director has several commands to check memory usage. You should save your file, then select an empty Score frame, and use *unLoadMember* or the *Purge* button in the Memory Inspector to clear memory. Use *put the freeBytes* and *put the memorySize* to establish a baseline for the available memory.

Create an *on idle* handler that displays the available memory in the Message window or in field cast members you've placed on the Stage (see Example 9-5).

Example 9-5: Idle Handler Displaying Memory Status

```
on idle
  put the freeBlock into field "FreeBlock Display"
  put the freeBytes into field "FreeBytes Display"
  put the memorySize into field "MemorySize Display"
end
```

At any time you should be able to recover some or all of the memory used by selecting an empty Score frame and using *unLoadMember*. If memory continues to decline, there may be a leak.

 If writing to the Message window to diagnose a memory leak, be aware that each character displayed in the Message window consumes one byte of memory itself!

The diagnostic text printed in the Message window is purged when it exceeds 32 KB, but can appear to indicate a small memory leak when none exists.

Reducing Memory Requirements

Before allocating more memory, try to reduce the memory and bandwidth requirements for your project. Note that many of the following techniques improve performance as the memory use is reduced, which isn't surprising. On the other hand, using bitmaps instead of Flash vector sprites improves performance at the expense of memory usage. Options to reduce memory and bandwidth include:

- Use 8-bit (256-color) graphics with a custom palette instead of higher color depths.
- Use a smaller Stage size.
- Reduce the size of animations and the bitmaps used in them.
- Use fields or D7 text cast members instead of D6 rich text cast members.
- Stream large sounds from disk by linking to them externally, so that they don't remain in RAM.
- Reduce the sampling rate, bit rate, or number of channels for your audio.
- Pre-mix sounds rather than using multiple sound channels.
- Reduce the number of scripts by generalizing handlers or using Behaviors.
- Use shapes, especially shapes filled with tile patterns, rather than bitmaps.
- Never set *the purgePriority of member* to 0 (*Never*) and avoid setting it to 1 (*Last*).
- Don't import external files (using *importFileInto*) or create cast members using *new(member)* at runtime.
- Use *go movie* instead of *play movie* (the latter leaves the first movie partially in RAM).
- Avoid preloading large digital video cast members using *the preLoadRAM* and *the preLoad of member*.
- Set *the preLoadMode* of castLib to 0 (*Load When Needed*) for each castLib to improve startup times.
- Preload only cast members that you know will be needed.
- Reduce the number of MIAWs in use.

Performance

Many developers discover that their titles that ran fine from the hard drive perform poorly when they run from a CD-ROM or on a slower machine. You should have a minimum-capability test box available to you in all circumstances. Refer to Chapter 7, *Cross-Platform and OS Dependencies*, for additional details on how the machine configuration can affect performance and intonations of the "Test Early, Test Often" mantra.

See "Determining the Appropriate Minimum Hardware Playback Platform" at *http:// www.macromedia.com/support/director/how/expert/playback/playback.html*, and also *http://www.zeusprod.com/technote/machspec.html*. These articles discuss how to target the appropriate segment of the installed base to meet both your technical and marketing requirements.

Most developers create a project ad hoc and then see if it runs. You should instead design your project with the optimization principles discussed throughout this book in mind. This will reduce the likelihood and severity of any problems.

Often, a customer will report that your beta version does not run satisfactorily on his machine. Ideally, you can test it yourself on the customer's machine(s) in his presence. If this is impossible (and not just impractical) you must get the customer to tell you precisely which portions are unsatisfactory and the characteristics of the test machine. It is nearly impossible to diagnose and debug a problem that you can't replicate, and you won't know whether you've solved it until the client performs another round of testing. This is egregiously inefficient. Your goal should be to minimize the retesting cycle by installing Director on the machine(s) demonstrating the problem. If you don't see the problem on your test machines, obtain a machine with a comparable—preferably identical—configuration.

If necessary, you can simulate a crippled machine by removing RAM, running a CD-ROM over a network, running other applications at the same time, or using much larger versions of the media (such as 44 kHz, 16-bit, stereo sound) and playing back at higher color depths. You can also limit the amount of RAM in use by a Macintosh Projector or by Director during authoring as described earlier in this chapter. This may place enough of a load on Director that you can see the problems the client describes.

Refer to Chapters 12 through 16 to ensure that you've prepared your content optimally, as improper content preparation often contributes to poor performance.

Macromedia TechNote #08151, "Why does the NT CPU monitor go to 100% when I run Director?", provides excellent details on Director's requests for CPU time under Windows. Director soaks up all available *idle* events. This avoids potentially jerky animation caused by infrequent attention. Director only appears to consume 100% of the processor, because the Windows NT CPU meter measures idle event usage only by applications, not the system. Director does not prevent other applications from receiving time slices when needed. See the D7 *ReadMe* for more information.

Gauging Performance

You can measure the speed of a given operation by starting a timer with *startTimer*, and then checking *the timer* after the operation completes. Example 9-6 checks the speed of 1,000 executions of the *offset()* function. It could be used to compare processor performance or determine whether a particular Lingo command is relatively slow.

Example 9-6: Gauging Performance

```
on testSpeed
  startTimer
  repeat with i = 1 to 1000
    -- Test the offset() function
    set dummy = offset ("st", "test")
  end repeat
  put "Test took" && the timer && "ticks"
end testSpeed
```

Don't include a *put* statement within your timing loop because printing to the Message window is very slow. Store the result in a variable and print it after the timing test completes.

You can also start a timer in one frame, check it in a later frame, and then divide by the number of frames to calculate the approximate frame rate achieved when the movie runs.

Things That Hurt Performance

The following sections list optimization techniques. In some cases, you may need to specify a faster minimum playback platform with more memory and a faster CD-ROM or Internet connection.

Poor performance is often due to a confluence of factors or the cumulative weight of techniques that may not compromise performance in isolation. For example, if you are using SWA sounds, streaming high bandwidth video, and loading large graphics all at once, the cumulative load will overpower low-end machines. Using a high color depth and sprites with alpha channels adds insult to injury. Likewise, eliminating a single culprit may not improve performance measurably, but the cumulative benefit of small changes can be great.

Do not expect optimal performance from versions of Director that predated a given operating system. For example, you should consider upgrading to D7 if you are supporting Windows 98. If you encounter performance problems, perform tests with the latest version of Director.

Lingo scripting techniques or inherent Lingo sluggishness

Following are some Lingo performance tips. Some improve your Lingo code's readability; others compromise it for maximum performance (include comments in your Lingo as necessary):

- Alex Zavatone benchmarked some Lingo variable allocations and simple operations. His Lingo profiler is for sale too. See *http://www.blacktop.com/zav/perf.txt*.

- Avoid tight repeat loops, which lock out other processing, especially in Shockwave.

- Avoid lengthy *on idle* handlers. They can slow performance, because they may be called several times during each frame.

- Printing to the Message windows is slow. Turn off *the traceLoad* and *the trace* commands in the Message window and eliminate extraneous *put* statements.

- Updating fields on Stage is slow, especially if done very frequently.

- Text parsing and searching is slow for long strings. Use the Text Cruncher Xtra (*http://www.itp.tsoa.nyu.edu/~student/yair/texcruncher/HTML/YairText-Cruncher.html*) to parse large amounts of text or use sorted lists for searching.

- String comparisons, especially with long strings and fields, are slow. Use symbols (or integers) instead of strings when possible.

- Leave *the romanLingo* = TRUE (the default for most languages) for faster performance, unless using Japanese or another double-byte language.

- Accessing cast members by number is faster than by name, but referring to them by name is easier, should their cast member number change. Director caches cast member names, so that accessing by name should be fast the second time, but it does not cache script names.

- Accessing a frame by number is faster than accessing it by its marker label name, but referring to it by name is easier, should its frame number change. If you're accessing a frame frequently, assign the number returned by *label("frameName")* to a global variable for future use.

- Change *the cpuHogTicks* and *the idleHandlerPeriod* with caution. Despite accelerating some operations, they can affect others adversely.

- Minimize use of *the actorList* and indiscriminate broadcasting of messages using *sendAllSprites()*.

- The *value()* function and *do* command invoke the Lingo parser to evaluate a string expression, which can be quite slow. For example, use *duplicate()* instead of *value(string())* to duplicate a list.

- List operations tend to be fast. Sorted lists are faster than unsorted lists when accessing elements by value or property name, but not when accessing elements by their index (position).

- Unnecessarily converting between data types, such as converting strings to numbers, can be slow.

- Reduce the number of properties being set. Setting *the rect of sprite* is faster than setting the *width* and *height of sprite* separately. Setting *the loc of sprite* is faster than setting the *locH* and *locV of sprite* separately.

- Reduce the number of calculations by moving static calculations outside repeat loops. Use a global variable rather than calculating a number in a handler that is called repeatedly. Precalculate static numbers. For example:

```
set a = b * 180/pi
```

is not as fast as:

```
set a = b * 57.296
```

- Floating-point calculations take from 1.5 to 3 times longer than integer calculations, with multiplication and division being the slowest. Use fixed-point math whenever possible, but remember that *the maxInteger* is smaller than the maximum floating-point number.

- Eliminate redundant *updateStage* commands that unnecessarily refresh the screen. It refreshes automatically once per frame as the playback head moves or loops.

- Comments have no effect on performance, but the *nothing* command takes a small (but measurable) time to execute. There is no speed difference between D7's new dot notation and the older Lingo syntax.

Media and disk access

There are dozens of reasons why media or disk access might go awry. Here are some common problems:

- Avoid using *the searchPath* (or *the searchPaths*), especially with a long list of paths to search. Linking to external files using an explicit path is much faster.

- Avoid streaming media from two or more external files on the same CD-ROM simultaneously. Preload some data into memory or stream it from the user's hard drive.

- Avoid more than four concurrent Internet streaming operations.

- Stream large sounds from disk by linking to them externally so that they don't need to be fully loaded into RAM before they start playing.

- Avoid playing two or more sounds simultaneously under Windows (mixing sounds causes an initial delay).

- Avoid linked external bitmaps, which are slow to decompress. Import them into the cast instead.

- Don't save in Shockwave (compressed) format for local content, because Shocked data takes longer to decompress.

- Optimize placement of files on a CD-ROM or defragment your hard drive.

- If the CD or hard disk's access light is constantly flickering, it indicates so-called *thrashing*, in which data is constantly being loaded and unloaded. The disk swap file space is much slower than real RAM.

- File access using the FileIO Xtra can be slow for large databases. Use a third-party database Xtra.

- Turn off networking and disable extraneous extensions.

- Too many Xtras or non-Xtra files in the *Xtras* folder will slow down Director or a Projector's startup. It also makes file saves slow during authoring.

- A corrupted Score can cause Director to thrash in an attempt to load a non-existent cast member. See Example 3-9 to detect a corrupted Score.

Digital video

Digital video performance depends primarily on the proper creation of the digital video file in your digital video editing software and proper compression. Some tips to eliminate performance-robbing culprits:

- Incorrect interleaving can be devastating to performance.

- Reduce the data rate to a bandwidth appropriate for the minimum CD-ROM drive speed.

- Play video direct-to-Stage using *Sync to Soundtrack* mode.

- Place digital video sprites on four-pixel boundaries on the Stage.

- Stretch digital video sprites in increments of 100% only.

- Use digital video instead of animation when timing is critical (digital video will drop video frames if necessary).

- Waiting for digital video via Lingo can be more efficient than waiting via the Tempo channel.

Sound

Tips on sound optimization and reducing latency (see also Chapter 15):

- Use a lower sampling rate, bits per sample, or fewer channels.

- SWA uses less disk space and download time, but requires more processing power.

- Use only one sound channel under Windows.

- Use the same sampling rate and bit depth for all sounds played simultaneously. Use the standard sampling rates (11.025, 22.050, and 44.100 kHz).

- Use *updateStage* to trigger *puppetSound* commands.

- Stream large sounds from disk.

Score, Cast, and window usage

There are a number of non-intuitive quirks to Director that can degrade performance:

- Don't loop in a frame with a transition or use a transition while a digital video is playing (especially under Windows).

- Don't loop in the first frame or last frame of the Score. These frames incur an overhead penalty.

- Reduce the number of sprite channels and film loops in use. Set *the lastChannel* in D7 under Modify ➤ Movie ➤ Properties to some number less than the default (150).

- Break up movies with extremely large Casts or Scores into multiple movies.

- Eliminate unneeded cast libraries. An excessive number of linked external castLibs (more than 6 or so) consumes excessive RAM and degrades performance.

- Use a realistic frame rate (10 to 20 fps) for your minimum target platform.

- Reduce the number of animations, sounds, and digital videos playing simultaneously.

- Delete unneeded cast members and perform a File ➤ Save and Compact to optimize the Cast on disk.

- Close any window that refers to data that is being changed at runtime, including the Cast, Score, Control Panel, Message, and Watcher windows (and remove items from the list of watched expressions).

- Cast members in external castLibs are not stored in the most efficient order unless you use Modify ➤ Sort to sort them in the order used in the Score.

 To check whether a sprite or Effects channel is degrading performance, use the *Mute* button in the Score to disable that channel (including sound channels) temporarily.

Graphics and animation

Graphics and animation are at the heart of Director, and a common performance bottleneck:

- The DirMMX Xtra will improve certain graphics performance in D6 on MMX-capable Windows machines.

- Set all monitors to the same color depth, preferably 8-bit (256 colors), and use graphics with the same bit depth as the monitor.

- Reduce and optimize animations.

- Avoid stretched bitmaps. Leave sprites at their cast member's *native* size or use Modify ➤ Transform Bitmap if necessary.

- Avoid slower inks, especially Blend. Use Copy and Background Transparent inks. Mask and Matte inks use twice the memory of any other ink, because Director must create a duplicate of the artwork internally. The allocation required for Matte ink makes it slightly slower the first time it is used for a sprite.

- Setting trails for static images can reduce the number of sprites needed.

- Turn off *the antiAlias of member* or adjust *the antiAliasThreshold* of text members to speed rendering. See also D7.0.1's *preRender* and *saveBitmap* properties in Table 12-8.

- Turn off *the dither* and *the useAlpha of member* for bitmaps when possible.

- When you have a choice, play assets such as Flash and QuickTime direct-to-Stage.

- Improve perceived performance by providing user feedback such as a wait cursor or button feedback.

- QuickDraw shapes use less memory but draw more slowly than bitmaps. Vector shapes and Flash cast members are the slowest to draw, and the speed of drawing depends on their scale to an extent.

- Animations performed via Lingo can be much faster than animations in the Score. Use Lingo to cycle through a series of cast members in a list or in adjacent slots in the Score, using *updateStage* each time you change *the member of sprite* property to display the new cast member.

- Avoid 32-bit graphics.

- Avoid cast members larger than the Stage.

- Set *the useFastQuads* to TRUE to improve performance when using *the quad of sprite*.

Lingo Affecting Performance

There are several commands that affect how Director allocates CPU time. Refer to Chapter 11 for details on asynchronous operations (such as waiting for media to be downloaded from the Internet).

The cpuHogTicks

The cpuHogTicks affects how often Director for Macintosh allows other processes to obtain the processor's attention. It has no effect under Windows, and has been available (although undocumented) since Director 4. The default value (20) allows other processes to interrupt Director every 20 ticks (three times per second). It can be increased (judiciously) to avoid releasing CPU control in the middle of an operation. It will not increase performance as much as it will prevent an operation from being interrupted, and therefore provides smooth animation without an intermittent hitch.

The marginal performance benefit from increasing *the cpuHogTicks* is no substitute for proper optimization. It can also interfere with mouse, clock, keyboard, network, and other system events.

Set *the cpuHogTicks* to 0 to speed auto-repeating *keyDown* events while holding down a key.

The idleHandlerPeriod

The idleHandlerPeriod determines how often Director allows idle events to be processed. If *the idleHandlerPeriod* is increased from the default (0 in D6, and 1 in

D7) idle events are processed *less* frequently. Set *the idleHandlerPeriod* to 0 to allow Director to monopolize the processor. Anything that depends on idle events, including the *on idle* handler, idle loading, and *mouseEnter*, *mouseLeave*, and *mouseWithin* events can become unusably sluggish at higher values.

The netThrottleTicks

The netThrottleTicks affects how often Director for Macintosh allows network operations to be interrupted. It is officially supported in D7, but was undocumented in D6. It has no effect under Windows or in Shockwave. The default value is 15 ticks (which allows net operations to be interrupted four times per second). Lowering *the netThrottleTicks* causes Internet-based media to download somewhat faster. Increasing *the netThrottleTicks* gives priority to local operations such as animation.

The fullColorPermit

The fullColorPermit determines the color depth of the offscreen buffer. To improve performance, set it to FALSE when using 8-bit graphics on monitors with a higher color depth. It is obsolete in D7.

The lastChannel

D7 allows up to 1000 sprite channels, but this degrades performance. Set *the lastChannel* to the smallest number of sprite channels you need under Modify ➤ Movie ➤ Properties. It is not settable via Lingo.

The useFastQuads

This undocumented D7 property renders sprites distorted with the new *quad of sprite* property more quickly but with lower quality. The default is FALSE. Setting it to TRUE also remedies some display bugs in D7.0.

The Big Squeeze (Fitting Your Project on a Floppy)

You'll often want to distribute a portfolio or demonstration piece on a floppy. That is becoming increasingly unrealistic as well as unnecessary. The compromises and time required to fit things on a floppy are rarely warranted these days. To wit:

- CD-R blank disks are very inexpensive (about $1) and CD-ROM burners are under $300. All your clients will have CD-ROM drives.

- Many clients have Zip drives; Zip disks are about $10 apiece (and hold 100 MB or more).

If space is at a premium:

- Use D7's new Slim Projectors (about 200 KB). These require that the user has Shockwave 7 installed or be willing to download it when first launching the Slim Projector.

- Use an older version of Director that creates smaller Projectors (see Table 8-1). Use Windows 3.1 and Mac 68K Projectors, which are smaller than Windows 95/98/NT, PowerMac, or FAT Projectors.

- Compress your files using StuffIt!, WinZip, or a similar utility. Most compression utilities can create self-extracting executable archives. They can also split an archive over multiple floppies.

- Submit a Shockwave version of the file that the user can play in a browser or using ShockMachine, or post it to a URL and let the user play it over the Internet.

- Use external graphics in JPEG or GIF format (the Xtras required for these may undermine any space savings in D6). D7 DCR and CCT files support internal JPEG and GIF compression.

- Use SWA compression for both internal and external sounds.

- Use lower quality graphics, video, or audio, which should require less storage. Crop images, use lower color depths, and compress video more aggressively.

- Use an empty *FONTMAP.TXT* file to save a few kilobytes.

- Omit unnecessary Xtras.

- Use DCR and CCT files, which are the smallest, or DXR and CXT files, which are slightly smaller than DIR and CST files.

- Always perform a File ➤ Save and Compact to purge deleted cast members.

CHAPTER 10

Using Xtras

Xtras allow Macromedia and third-party developers to extend Director's core capabilities and are analogous to the plug-ins available for many software products. This chapter covers the selection, installation, and use of Xtras in D5 through D7, with a focus on non-Lingo Xtras. Lingo Scripting Xtras, which replace the older XObjects supported in D3.1.3 through D6, are covered in Chapter 13, *Lingo Xtras and XObjects*, in *Lingo in a Nutshell*.

Xtras allow Macromedia to update individual components of Director or Shockwave without a major release. Director 7 relies more heavily on Xtras than any previous version. Xtras are well integrated into Director. You may not be able to distinguish a built-in feature from one that uses an Xtra. Even if you don't use Lingo, you can use many non-Lingo Xtras. Some developers want to use an Xtra for everything; some want to avoid Xtras at all costs. Neither extreme is justified. See "Do You Need an Xtra?" later in this chapter.

See *http://www.zeusprod.com/nutshell/xtras.html* for the latest information on D7 Xtras, including Xtras packaging and automatic downloading in Shockwave.

Types of Xtras

There are several distinct types of Xtras supported by Director. Some "Xtras" are actually a combination of more than one Xtra type; a Sprite Xtra may include a companion Lingo Xtra that allows you to manipulate the new Sprite type via Lingo. Xtras that create new custom cast member types (Sprite Xtras or Transition Xtras) are called Asset Xtras. Some Xtras are used during authoring only, but many must be included with your Projector to support specific features. Types of Xtras include:

Lingo Xtras or Scripting Xtras
> Lingo Xtras add new commands to Lingo, such as the ability to read and write external files (provided by the FileIO Xtra). Lingo Xtras are a replacement for older XObjects supported in prior versions of Director (but not in D7). You can also "extend" Director by writing Lingo handlers, but Lingo Xtras are typically written in C/C++.

Sprite Xtras or Asset Xtras

Sprite Xtras add new cast member types, such as QuickTime 3, Flash, ActiveX, or Custom Cursor cast members to the built-in types (bitmaps, fields, and so on). Sprite Xtra cast members can be placed on the Stage like any other sprite. The developer of the Sprite Xtra (Macromedia or a third party) determines its attributes, such as whether it has custom properties, supports a media editor, is imaged direct-to-Stage, and supports ink effects. Macromedia ships two versions of its Sprite Xtras—one for authoring and one for distribution with the Projector.

Transition Xtras

Transition Xtras appear alongside the built-in transitions (which don't require Xtras) in the Transition dialog box. Transition Xtras create custom transition cast members, and are a type of Asset Xtra. The developer of a Transition Xtra determines whether it supports the change area, chunk size, and duration options common to most transitions, and whether it can be interleaved with palette changes.

Tool Xtras

Tool Xtras are made available during authoring, usually via a windoid, and often analyze or modify the Cast or Score. The Animation Wizard (obsolete in D7) is written in Lingo, but most Tool Xtras are written in C/C++.

MIX Xtras (introduced in D6)

Media Information eXchange (MIX) Xtras import and export various graphic and sound formats, such as PICTs. They are required during authoring to import external media via drag-and-drop or File ➤ Import (and must be included with your Projector when using linked graphics and sounds). All MIX Xtras require the MIX Services Xtra.

Photoshop filters

Director can use some Photoshop 3 filters to modify bitmaps in the Paint window during authoring only. Photoshop 4.0 and 5.0 filters will not work. Refer to the *Filter Bitmap, Auto Filter,* and *Auto Distort* options under the Xtras menu. See also Chapter 13, *Graphics, Color, and Palettes.*

Non-Director Xtras

Other Macromedia applications support Xtras, although not necessarily the same ones as Director (some Xtras may support *multiple* Macromedia products). You'll need the SWA Export Xtra for SoundEdit or Peak LE to create Shockwave audio on the Macintosh. (SoundEdit Xtras go in the *System Folder:Macromedia:Xtras* folder and Peak LE Xtras go in the *Peak Plug-ins* folder.)

Sound Mixer Xtras (introduced in D7)

D7 implements Windows sound mixers as Xtras. MacroMix is contained within MacroMix.X32 and QT3Mix is contained within QT3Asset.X32. A DirectSound mixer, DirectSound.X32, was added in D7.0.1. See Chapter 15.

Miscellaneous and third-party Xtras

Some Xtras, including Shockwave Audio, PowerPoint Import, and Java Export, may not fit neatly in another category and show up in the File or Xtras menus. Others are used by Director transparently without showing up in any menu.

Xtras in the Interface

Macromedia places Xtras in subfolders somewhat arbitrarily. Regardless of the subfolder in which an Xtra is installed, the Xtra's internal type (and subtype) determines where it shows up (if at all) in Director's interface. Table 10-1 shows where you can expect an Xtra to appear once it is installed.

Table 10-1: Accessing Installed Xtras

Xtra Type	Accessed Via
Lingo Xtras[1]	Lingo only. See *showXlib, the xtraList, interface( ),* and *mMessageList( )* and Chapter 13 in *Lingo in a Nutshell.*
Sprite Xtras[1]	Insert ➤ Media Element, Insert ➤ Control, or File ➤ Import.
Transition Xtras[1]	Transition dialog box along with built-in transition types. See Modify ➤ Frame ➤ Transition.
MIX Xtras[1]	File ➤ Import and *importFileInto.* See also File ➤ Preferences ➤ Editors.
Export and Import Xtras	The Save as Java command appears under the File menu and requires the Java Export Xtras. The *Import PowerPoint File* option appears under the Xtras menu and requires the Import Xtra for PowerPoint. Other Export Xtras are used under File ➤ Export and are for authoring only.
Tool Xtras	Xtras menu (authoring mode only).
Shockwave Audio[1]	Insert ➤ Media Element, File ➤ Import (in D7), and Xtras menus.
Photoshop Filters	Xtras ➤ Filter Bitmap and Xtras ➤ Auto Filter.
Sound Mixer Xtras[1]	the soundDevice, the soundDeviceList

[1] Can be added to *the movieXtraList* under Modify ➤ Movie ➤ Xtras.

The Xtras menu

The Xtras menu includes items that are only marginally related (in that they use Xtras) and are available only during authoring, not from runtime Projectors. You can reorganize some items in the Xtras menu by changing the file structure within the *Xtras* folder (see following description). The first four options are built into Director and don't require Xtras:

Update Movies
D6 updates movies from D4 or D5. D7 updates movies from D5 and D6 only. After updating from D4 or D5, convert ranges of cells into sprite spans by selecting the cells, choosing Modify ➤ Join Sprite, then choosing Insert ➤ Remove Keyframe.

Update Movies also protects movies and castLibs (creates DXR and CXR files) and compresses movies and castLibs for Shockwave or local use (creates DCR and CCR files). In D5, use the AfterBurner Xtra. In D4, use the AfterBurner standalone executable (see Chapter 11, *Shockwave and the Internet*). See also the File ➤ Save As Shockwave menu option.

In each case, it allows you to make a backup copy of the original files. See Tables 4-1 and 4-3 for additional details.

 Always keep your original source files. Never use the *Delete Original Files* option under `Xtras` ➤ *Update Movies.*

Filter Bitmap, Auto Filter, and Auto Distort

These options allow you to apply Photoshop 3.0 filters or one of Director's built-in transformations to cast members in the Paint window.

Widgets, buttons, Behaviors, wizards, and palette libraries (D6 only)

The Widget Wizard and Button Libraries allow you to add premade Lingo components to your project, such as fancy buttons with existing Behaviors. The Behavior Library lets you add Behaviors to sprites and frames, and the Animation Wizard automates rich text animation for speaker support. The Palette Library includes palettes with reserved colors in the first and last ten palette positions for use under Windows. In D7, the `Window` ➤ `Library Palette` replaces the Behavior library.

Shockwave audio options

`Xtras` ➤ `Shockwave for Audio Settings` determines the compression setting for Shockwave audio. `Xtras` ➤ `Convert WAV to SWA` (Windows only) creates SWA files from WAVE files. On PowerMacs, SWA files are created using SoundEdit 2.0.7 or Peak LE.

Third-party Xtras

Some third-party Xtras such as Beatnik Lite (in D7), PrintOMatic Lite, and ScriptOMatic Lite (in D6) appear under the `Xtras` menu, providing access to custom help files, *About* boxes, and registration information. The Lingo Scripting Xtras that constitute these products don't appear in the `Xtras` menu, but are accessible via Lingo.

Tool Xtras and libraries

You can add your own Director movie Tool Xtras and Cast Libraries to the `Xtras` menu by placing them in the *Xtras* folder. Director for both Macintosh and Windows recognizes any file in the *Xtras* folder with the extensions .DIR, .DXR, .DCR, or .CST (but not .CCT or .CXT). Director 7 for Macintosh also recognizes files with the proper File Types (`MV07`, `M!07`, `FGDM`, or `MC07`), regardless of their extensions or names. Director 5 and 6 for Macintosh used the older File Types `MV97`, `M!97`, `M*97`, `MV95`, `M!95`, and `M*95`. In D5 and D6, Behavior Libraries placed anywhere in the *Xtras* folder will show up in the `Xtras` menu. In D7, they should be placed in the *Xtras/Libs* folder and will appear under the `Window` ➤ `Library Palette`.

Do You Need an Xtra?

Ask around before assuming that you need an Xtra. There is often a built-in Lingo command or Xtra that comes with Director that solves the problem. Macromedia technical support or a competent Lingo consultant can tell you whether Director can accomplish the desired task.

Xtras are not a replacement for proper use of Director or Lingo, nor are they an evil to be avoided.

Identify the Xtras you'll need early in a project. If too many requirements cannot be handled by Director, you may be better off with another tool. Whatever the circumstance, your options become limited if you wait until the last minute (as many do). Allow extra time to research, obtain, implement, and test Xtras.

Don't underestimate the value of managing your client's (or your own) expectations. Many clients would be better served if problematic features were simply dropped or handled via an installer, *Read Me* file, documentation, or training.

Reasons to use Lingo instead of Xtras:

- Lingo is free with Director. Many Xtras cost money, although many are also free or very inexpensive. Some have licensing distribution fees.

- Lingo-only solutions are much more likely to work across all platforms and in future versions of Director and Shockwave. Xtras may need to be rewritten for future operating systems or platforms.

- Shockwave requires Xtras to be downloaded and installed separately (the SW6 download inclues the Flash Asset and SWA Xtras, and the NetLingo, Sound Import Export, PICT, BMP, GIF and JPEG Xtras' capabilities are built into the Shockwave plug-in).

- Shockwave 7 allows automatic downloading of Xtras, but Lingo-only solutions will support Windows 3.1 and 68K Mac users whom SW7 does not support. The Shockwave 7 download includes the Flash, Font, Text, NetLingo, Multiuser, and SWA Xtras, plus built-in support for sounds, GIF, PICT, BMP, and JPEG assets.

- Lingo and Director tend to be more thoroughly tested, more compatible, and more stable than most Xtras. It is sometimes hard to find or obtain an Xtra on short notice, and unwise to introduce one unless sufficient time is available for testing.

Legitimate reasons to use Xtras:

- You're sure that Lingo alone can't do what you want. Sometimes an Xtra drastically simplifies a task that is truly painful via Lingo alone.

- Director is too slow to perform a mission-critical task. Lingo can create databases and manipulate text, but it is not optimized for either.

- You need a new transition type or sprite asset type not supported by Director.

Poor reasons to use Xtras:

- You are having performance or memory problems. An Xtra isn't going to speed up asset loading or reduce memory usage in most cases.

- You don't know how to accomplish something in Director or Lingo. C programmers and inexperienced Linguists often want to use Xtras where Director and Lingo handle the task adequately, even admirably.

- You are stretching Director beyond any logical boundaries. Director is not well-suited for some tasks, no matter how many Xtras you pile on top of it.

Obtaining Xtras

Xtras are available from various sources:

Macromedia
> Macromedia includes numerous Xtras with Director, including the ActiveX, PowerPoint, Custom Cursor, Flash, and Java Xtras sold separately prior to D6.5.

Third-party Xtras
> There are a wide variety of third-party Xtras available from dozens of companies. Many are sold commercially or as shareware, but some are freeware or donationware.

Custom Xtra development
> You may contract with someone to develop an Xtra or develop one in-house. Some Xtra developers will customize their existing commercial Xtras for a separate fee.

 If using an Xtra for a make-or-break portion of your product, allow plenty of extra time and money. Custom Xtra development can be expensive and fraught with delays.

Resources for finding Xtras

There is no single resource that lists all available Xtras, and the list is constantly growing. Try the usual search engines using keywords such as *Macromedia*, *Director*, and *Xtras*, in addition to using the following resources:

The Director 7 CD
> The Director CD includes samples and demonstrations of many third-party Xtras in the *Goodies* and *Xtra Partners* folders. These include Xtras to play MPEG video, manage large databases, and so on. See also previous Director CDs and the Xtras CD distributed at the 1997 Macromedia User Conference. The Director 6 CD includes unsupported Xtras and sample files for Xtra developers. See the *Xtras\Win* and *Goodies\Director\SoundXtr\Xtras* subfolders under *Macromedia\XDK_d6a4* on the D6 CD.

Books
> Many third-party Director books include CDs with demos of various Xtras.

The Director Xtras Book by Rich Shupe (Ventana/Coriolis)
> Rich does a nice job of covering a wide variety of Xtras, and this book is a great place to start your research without trawling the Web. Rich's site (*http://www.fmaonline.com*) has many links to Xtra developer's sites and the book includes a CD-ROM with many demo Xtras.

Xtravaganza! by Chuck Henderson (Macromedia Press/PeachPit)
> Covers Xtras for Director and other Macromedia products. Includes descriptions of 460 Xtras and a CD-ROM with over 100 demos.

Macromedia's web site is a good (but not comprehensive) place to look for third-party Xtras:

> *http://www.macromedia.com/software/xtras/director*

Zeus Productions offers Xtras that open external documents and launch external applications, and custom Xtra development:

> *http://www.zeusprod.com*

UpdateStage sells Xtras from Red Eye Software (Scott Kildall) and Dirigo Multimedia (Glenn Picher), formerly sold via g/matter, plus many other Xtras:

> *http://www.updatestage.com/xtras*

Media Lab sells some of the consistently most useful and coolest Xtras, including Photocaster, Alphamania, and Effector Set:

> *http://www.medialab.com*

Penworks sells a number of utility Xtras, including CastEffects and Iconizer:

> *http://www.penworks.com*

DonationWare (inexpensive utility Xtras for a small donation) can be found at:

> *http://www.trevimedia.com/donationware.html*

Kent Kersten's Little Planet freeware utilities including FileXtra and ScrnXtra are located at:

> *http://www.littleplanet.com/kent/kent.html*

TreviMedia runs an Xtra-related email list (Xtras-L) where you are free to discuss Xtras from any vendor. Send the following in the body of an email to *listserv@trevimedia.com*:

```
SUB XTRAS-L yourFirstName yourLastName
```

Database Xtras

The following Xtras purport to provide database or text access in some form. I have no firsthand knowledge of these Xtras, but have heard frequent praise for V12 and DataGrip. As with all Xtras, your mileage may vary, so ask around.

V12 Database Engine from Integration New Media (cross-platform):

> *http://www.integration.qc.ca/*

DataGrip (MS Access databases, Windows only):

> *http://www.datagrip.com/*

FileFlex (cross-platform):

> *http://www.fileflex.com*

Active XtraBase from Prime Arithmetics (Windows NT servers):

> *http://www.primearithmetics.com*

OpenDBC from Brummell Associates (Windows only):

> *http://www.btinternet.com/~brummell/*

MHTsearch (indexing documents and searching for words):

> *http://www.meetinghousetech.com*

TextCruncher by Yair Sageev (cross-platform text parsing and manipulation):

> *http://www.itp.tsoa.nyu.edu/~student/yair/texcruncher/HTML/*
> *YairTextCruncher.html*

Printing Xtras

PrintOMatic (cross-platform, requires scripting):

> *http://www.printomatic.com*

mPrint (Windows only, visual page layout, no scripting):

> *http://www.mediashoppe.com*

zPrint (Windows only, prints external files with external applications):

> *http://www.zeusprod.com/products/zopen.html*

Utility Xtras

The following Xtras have many OS-level functions for each platform.

Buddy API (cross-platform):

> *http://www.mods.com.au/budapi*

DirectOS Xtra (Windows only):

> *http://www.directxtras.com/do_doc.htm*

OSutil Xtra (Macintosh version is shipping, Windows version is imminent):

> *http://www.magna.com.au/~farryp/director/xtras/*

Shopping for Xtras

The purchase price of an Xtra can be dwarfed by the cost of the time spent trying to implement it or the time lost if it doesn't work. When you purchase an Xtra, ask the vendor to recommend someone to help you implement it if necessary. Assuming you *need* an Xtra, consider the following criteria:

Do you need an Xtra and does it do what you need?
> You must identify the problem before you can decide whether an Xtra will solve it. Obtain a demo version of the Xtra and test whether it solves your problem. Director 7 supports many new features previously requiring a third-party Xtra.

Does the Xtra support the desired platforms?
> It is not unusual for an Xtra *not* to support all the platforms you intend to support. Even so, you may not need an Xtra on all platforms or may use Xtras from different vendors on different platforms. Beware of Xtras that run so poorly

as to be unusable on older platforms. It is increasingly common that Windows Xtras don't support Windows 3.1. Many do not yet fully support Windows NT. Some Xtras don't support older 68K Macintoshes.

 A so-called *cross-platform* Xtra requires separate versions for each platform. Only Xtras written in pure Lingo can use the same file on multiple platforms. Verify that Xtras are compatible with D7.

Is it an Xtra or XObject?

Although D6 supports some older XObjects, XObjects will not work under Windows NT when using a 32-bit Windows Projector, nor are XObjects supported in D7.

Does the Xtra work the same on all platforms?

Many Xtras, such as Macromedia's FileIO Xtra, use identical *commands* on both platforms, but may not *operate* identically in all respects. Anticipate variations across platforms, especially when dealing with external files, applications, or hardware.

Does the Xtra support the desired version(s) of Director?

Many Xtras work in multiple versions of Director, but some do not. Many Xtras that worked in D6 will not work in D7 due to major architectural changes. You may need an updated version of existing Xtras.

Is the Xtra "Shockwave-safe"?

Shockwave 7 recognizes only Xtras marked by the developer as "Shockwave-safe." Any Xtra that provides file access or system API access would be a security risk. Even innocent Xtras that worked with SW6 must be recompiled to work with SW7.

Is the price justified by the added capability?

Xtra prices range from the free to the exorbitant and there is not necessarily a correlation between price and quality. Free Xtras are rarely supported and are less likely to be updated in the future, and even expensive Xtras may be justified by the time they'll save you. Most Director users feel that Xtras are expensive, but a working Xtra is almost always cheaper than custom development. If the Xtra developer provides good support, you are buying a solution, not just an Xtra.

What expertise is required?

Most Lingo scripting Xtras require an average Linguist. Sprite Xtras may also require Lingo to control the sprite asset, but many Xtras require little or no scripting.

Are there good examples and documentation?

Even the simplest Xtra may be hard to use without an example, and even a complicated Xtra can be easy to implement with a proper example. Most companies provide electronic documentation ranging from the inadequate to the excellent. Check their web site and inquire about documentation before you buy. Third-party documentation is sometimes available (see the Xtras books cited earlier).

Always try to obtain a demo version for testing, but do *not* wait until the last minute to purchase and test the live version. Sometimes an Xtra drastically simplifies a task that is truly painful via Lingo alone.

Who is the developer or publisher and who provides support?

Third-party Xtras are sold both directly by developers and via separate publishers and distributors. Some vendors and their products have earned excellent reputations while others have earned poor ones. Ask around.

Support also ranges from non-existent to excellent, and may be provided via phone or exclusively via email. Ask about refund policies, and ask who provides the technical support (engineers, salespeople, the developer, the distributor, or the publisher). Reputable vendors will offer a money-back guarantee.

Can you obtain the Xtra easily and in a timely fashion?

You can't use an Xtra if you need to ship tomorrow and it takes a week to obtain a password. Most Xtras are available electronically but are *not* available in packaged versions or through typical retail or catalog channels. Ask vendors if they provide free downloads of demo versions, accept payment forms convenient to you, and process orders promptly.

What are the licensing requirements?

Most Xtras are designed to be shipped with your Projector (although there may be different versions for authoring and runtime use). Some Xtras require a royalty for each copy distributed, but most charge either a flat rate for an unlimited number of copies, or on a per-product basis.

How long has the Xtra been available?

If an Xtra has been around for some time, it may be more robust or better documented, or it may be painfully obsolete. Whenever a new version of Director or an OS comes out, find out whether the Xtra has been tested or upgraded. You can reasonably expect Macromedia Xtras to work with the current version of Director and latest OS version, although, for example, the Custom Button Xtra is obsolete in D7.

XTRAINFO.TXT

The *XTRAINFO.TXT* file has several purposes. In D6, it determines which Xtras are included when using the *Check Movie for Xtras* and *Include Network Xtras* checkboxes under File ➤ Create Projector ➤ *Options*. In D7, it determines the Xtras added by the *Add Defaults* and *Add Network* buttons under Modify ➤ Movie ➤ Xtras and whether Xtras are downloadable. It also translates the names of Xtras listed under Modify ➤ Movie ➤ Xtras across various platforms.

XTRAINFO.TXT should be placed in the same folder as the Director application (not in the *Xtras* folder). It is used when opening files cross-platform and when a Projector is created. It need not be shipped with the Projector.

Format of XTRAINFO.TXT

Each entry in *XTRAINFO.TXT* specifies a property list defining the name of the Xtra file to be used for each platform, such as:

```
[#name:"XtraName" {, #name:"XtraName",...}, #type:#xtraType]
```

where #*name*:"*XtraName*" is one of the following symbols followed by the name of the Xtra used for the particular platform (only *#namePPC* and *#nameW32* are supported in D7):

```
#name68K: "Mac 68K Xtra"
#namePPC: "PowerMac Xtra"
#nameFAT: "FAT Mac Xtra"
#nameW16: "Win16.X16"
#nameW32: "Win32.X32"
```

The entry for the Windows 16-bit version of the FileIO Xtra in D6.0 was misspelled as *#namwW16* and should be *#nameW16*. See the comments in *XTRAINFO.TXT* (which differs markedly in D6 and D7) for additional information.

Using XTRAINFO.TXT in D6

In D6, *#type:#xtraType* in *XTRAINFO.TXT* specifies the type of the Xtra:

#type:#asset
> Sprite or Transition Xtra

#type:#lingo
> Lingo Scripting Xtra

#type:#mixin
> MIX Xtra, included if *Check Movies for Xtras* is checked

#type:#mix
> Other MIX Xtra, included only if used by linked asset

#type:#net
> Network Xtra, included if *Include Network Xtras* is checked

#type:#netlib
> WinSock Library for PPC only

#type:#service
> MIX Services, included if *Check Movies for Xtras* is checked

See the comments in *XTRAINFO.TXT* (which differs markedly between D6 and D7) for additional information

In the File ➤ Create Projector ➤ *Options* dialog box are two checkboxes:

Include Network Xtras
> Includes all Xtras marked as *#type:#net* in *XTRAINFO.TXT*, but does not include those marked as *#type:#netlib*. See Table 10-2.

Check Movie for Xtras
> Includes all Xtras marked *#type:#mixin* or *#type:#service* in *XTRAINFO.TXT*, but does not include those marked as *#type:#mix*. (See Table 10-3.) This option also includes any Xtras listed under Modify ➤ Movie ➤ Xtras from any of the movies being bundled into the Projector.

Deselecting both checkboxes creates a Projector that contains only the Director movies, castLibs, and Xtras added manually via the file picker in the *Create Projector* dialog box. Xtras can still be distributed separately in an *Xtras* folder to be included with the Projector.

The types specified in *XTRAINFO.TXT* can be edited to your liking. Notice that the GIF Import and JPEG Import Xtras are listed as both *#net* and *#mix* Xtras.

To include an arbitrary Xtra in your Projector when the appropriate checkbox is checked, simply add it to the *XTRAINFO.TXT* file with a *#type* of *#net*, *#mixin*, or *#service*.

Using XTRAINFO.TXT in D7

The entries in the D7 *XTRAINFO.TXT* file include the following optional properties, which supersede the *#type* property specified in D6:

#type: #default
    Included by default with every new movie

#net: #xtra
    Included by *Add Network* button

#net: #netLib
    Not included automatically

#info: "url"
    URL for more information about downloadable Xtras

#package: "url"
    URL from which Xtra package can be downloaded

These attributes affect the following options under **Modify ▶ Movie ▶ Xtras** (see Figure 10-1):

Add Defaults
    Adds Xtras flagged as *#type: #default* to *the movieXtraList*.

Add Network
    Adds Xtras flagged as *#net: #xtra* to *the movieXtraList*.

Info
    Displays information about the Xtras from the URL specified by the *#info* property.

Include in Projector
    Allows Xtras to be included or excluded individually (unlike in D6) when this movie is added to a Projector. (I recommend against this.)

Download if Needed
    Allows an Xtra to be downloaded from the URL specified by the *#package* property. Macromedia packages downloadable Shockwave-safe Xtras beyond those included in the standard Shockwave installation (most notably the QT3 and Animated GIF Asset Xtras, and XML parser). Many third-party developers also make Xtra packages available for download.

Standard Macromedia Xtras

The following sections list the Xtras that come standard with Director. Note that some are not available for all platforms.

Network Xtras

Table 10-2 lists the Xtras that provide network services, such as http and ftp access, and many net-related Lingo commands. The Xtras of type *#net* (but not *#netlib*) are included in the Projector automatically if the *Include Network Xtras* option is checked when creating a D6 Projector. D7 includes all the Xtras in Table 10-2, except WinSockLib, with Projectors by default. You must include the *NetManage WinSock Lib* manually* when shipping a PowerPC or Fat Mac Projector that accesses the Internet.

Table 10-2: Network Xtras Filenames

Type[1]	PowerPC	Mac 68K	Win 32	Win 16
#net	GIF Import	GIF Import 68K	GIF Import.X32	MixGIFf.X16
#net	JPEG Import	JPEG Import 68K	JPEG Import.X32	MixJPEG.X16
#net	INetUrl PPC Xtra	None[2]	INetURL.X32	INetURL.X16
#net	NetFile PPC Xtra	NetFile 68K Xtra	NetFile.X32	NetFile.X16
#net	NetLingo PPC Xtra	NetLingo 68K Xtra	NetLingo.X32	NetLingo.X16
#netlib	NetManage WinSock Lib (D6); WinSockLib (D7)	None[2]	None[3]	None[3]

[1] The GIF and JPEG Import Xtras are listed twice (as both *#net* and *#mix* Xtras) in D6's *XTRAINFO.TXT* file.
[2] The code for the *INetUrl* Xtra and *NetManage WinSock Lib* for 68K Macs is built into Standard and FAT Macintosh Projectors, and does not require an Xtra on 68K Macs or when using Standard (non-native) Projectors on PowerPCs.
[3] WinSock support under Windows is provided by DLLs installed with the OS or by the user's browser in the Windows *System* directory.

Use the Lingo property *the netPresent*, not the *netPresent()* function, to check for the presence of the NetLingo and NetFile Xtras. Shockwave movies do not require these Xtras.

MIX import Xtras

Table 10-3 lists the MIX Xtras that allow Director to import and export various graphic file formats (GIFs, PICTs, and so on). Xtras shown for both PowerPC and Mac 68K are Fat Binary Xtras. The Xtras of type *#mixin* and *#service* (but not *#mix*) are automatically included in the Projector if the *Check Movies for Xtras*

---

* John Taylor reports that when using D6, the Power Macintosh NetManage WinSock Lib can conflict with a file of the same name installed by Quicken 98 in the Macintosh *System* folder. He installs the PowerMac NetManage WinSock Lib in both his *Xtras* folder and the Macintosh *System* folder (over Quicken 98's version) to alleviate the conflict. An alternative is to ship a D6 68K Macintosh Projector, which has its own internal WinSock management.

option is checked when creating a D6 Projector. Those of type *#default* are included with D7 Projectors, unless manually removed from the list of Xtras under Modify ➤ Movie ➤ Xtras.

Table 10-3: Graphic MIX Xtras by Platform

D6 Type[1]	D7 Type	PowerPC	Mac 68K	Win 32	Win 16
#service	#default	Mix Services	Mix Services	MixServices.X32 (D7) mix32.X32 (D6)	Mix16.X16
#mix[2]	N/A	BMP Import Export	BMP Import Export	BMP Import Export.X32	MixBMP.X16
#mix[2]	N/A	GIF Export	None	GIF Export.X32	None
#mix	#default	GIF Import	GIF Import 68k	GIF Import.X32	MixGIF.X16
#mix[3]	N/A	None	None	ImageMark Import.X32	None
#mix[2]	N/A	JPEG Export	None	JPEG Export.X32	None
#mix[2]	#default	JPEG Import	JPEG Import 68k	JPEG Import.X32	MixJPEG.X16
#mix	N/A	LRG Import Export	LRG Import Export	LRG Import Export.X32	MixLRG.X16
#mix	N/A	MacPaint Import	MacPaint Import	MacPaint Import.X32	MixMcPnt.X16
#mix	N/A	Palette Import	Palette Import	Palette Import.X32	MixPal.X16
#mix	N/A	Photoshop 3.0 Import	Photoshop 3.0 Import	Photoshop 3.0 Import.X32	MixPS30.X16
N/A	N/A	Photoshop™ Filters	None	Pshopflt.X32	None
#mix[4]	N/A	None	None	Photoshop Clut Import.X32[4]	None
#mix[2,5]	N/A	PICT Import Export	PICT Import Export	None	None
#mix	N/A	PNG Import Export	PNG Import Export	PNG Import Export.X32	MixPng.X16
#mix	N/A	Targa Import Export	Targa Import Export	Targa Import Export.X32	MixTARGA.X16
#mix	N/A	TIFF Import Export	TIFF Import Export	TIFF Import Export.X32	MixTIFF.X16

[1] The Xtra's type is specified in *XTRAINFO.TXT* and can be modified as desired. The GIF Import and JPEG Import Xtras are listed twice (as both #net and #mix Xtras) in D6.
[2] The GIF Export, JPEG Export, PICT Import Export, and Sun AU Import Export Xtras are new in D6.5 and are used only with the Save as Java Xtra. The JPEG Agent and BMP Agent replace the JPEG Import and the BMP Import Export Xtras in D7.0.1.
[3] The ImageMark Xtra imports PCD, PCX, and WMF files, and the TIFF preview from EPS files (see Chapter 4). It is for authoring only and is not licensed for redistribution. Obsolete in D7.
[4] The Photoshop Clut Import.X32 Xtra was added in D6.0.2, excluded in D6.5, and added back in D7.
[5] Remove the PICT Import Export Xtra except when using Save as Java.

MIX Xtras are required to drag-and-drop certain graphic and sound files from the desktop into the Cast, use linked graphics or sounds, or use *importFileInto* (which isn't recommended within Projectors). Refer to Chapter 4 for details on importing various file types. The *MIX Services* Xtra is required when using any of the other MIX Xtras, or any linked file types.

The Shockwave 6.0 plug-in supported only linked media types for which MIX Xtras were installed in the Shockwave support folder. Shockwave 6.0.1 and 7 recognize GIF, JPEG, PICT, BMP, AIFF (compressed and uncompressed), and WAVE (uncompressed only) files automatically without any Xtras. Other linked media types, such as SWA, QT3, and Flash, require Sprite Asset Xtras, but not MIX Xtras or the MIX Services Xtra. See *http://www.zeusprod.com/nutshell/mix.html* for the complete story on MIX versus non-MIX Xtras. Note also the many Sprite Xtras are included with the Shockwave 7 download.

 The D6.5 PICT Import Export Xtra conflicts with the PICT Agent Xtra when importing bitmaps. Remove it from the D6.5 for Macintosh *Xtras:MIX* folder except when using File ➤ Save as Java.

Secret agent Xtras

The *agent* Xtras in the *MIX Xtras* folder are used when communicating with external editors during authoring. Agents are implemented as separate Xtras when support for importing a file type is already built into Director. (Agents for other file formats are included in the *Import/Export MIX Xtras*.) Agents are for authoring-time only. They are not needed by Projectors or Shockwave and are not included in *XTRAINFO.TXT.*

Agent Xtras include:

- AVI Agent (Windows only)
- PICT Agent
- QuickTime Agent (D6 only)
- xRes Agent
- JPEG Agent and BMP Agent (new in D7.0.1)

Sound and SWA Xtras

The Sound Import Export Xtra is another MIX Xtra needed whenever using external sounds. By convention, the SWA Xtras are kept in the *Media Support* Xtras folder, not the *MIX* Xtras folder. SWA compression is handled by the SWA Export Xtra for SoundEdit or Peak LE on PowerMacs and the Swacmpr.X32 or SWAcnvrt.X32 Xtra under Director for Windows (32-bit only).

You must include all the Network Xtras if using Internet-based SWA files and include the NetFile Xtra even if using local SWA files only. Include the Mix Services Xtra and Sound Import Export Xtra for any external sounds, including SWA. See Macromedia TechNote #12598 if your Sound Import Export Xtra is not being recognized.

Only the SWA decompression and streaming Xtras shown in Table 15-13 are needed at runtime. The following SWA Xtras are used during authoring only.

Windows 95/98/NT development-time-only SWA Xtras:

- Swasttng.X32
- Swaopt.X32
- Swacnvrt.X32
- Swacmpr.X32

PowerMac Director development-time-only SWA Xtras:

- SWA Compression Xtra
- SWA Options Xtra
- SWA Settings (Dir) Xtra

The SunAU Import Export Xtra is another MIX Xtra used to import .au audio files. See Table 15-13 for the sound-related Xtras needed at runtime.

These SWA Xtras are used by SoundEdit and are kept in the *System Folder:Macromedia:Xtras* folder.

PowerMac SoundEdit Development-Time-only SWA Xtras:

- SWA Export Xtra
- SWA Settings (SE16) Xtra

Macromedia Sprite Asset and Lingo Xtras

Table 10-4 lists additional Sprite Asset and Lingo Xtras from Macromedia that ship with Director 6 and 7 and can be distributed with your Projector. Note that the Cursor, Flash, QuickTime 3, and ActiveX Xtras are new to D6.5. Only the distributable version of each of these Xtras is shown in Table 10-4. The authoring-only versions cited in the footnotes to Tables 10-4 and 10-5 must not be distributed.

Table 10-5 lists the new Xtras in D7 that add new asset types and other capabilities.

Table 10-4: Sprite Asset and Lingo Xtras

D6 Type	D7 Type	PowerPC	Mac 68K	Win 32	Win 16
#asset	Obsolete	Button Editor	Button Editor	Buttoned.X32	Buttoned.X16
#asset	Obsolete	QuickDraw 3D Xtra	None	QD3DXtra.X32	None
#asset[1]	N/A	CursorsPPC (D6) Cursor Asset (D7)	None	Cursor.X32	None
#asset[2]	#default	Flash Asset PPC	None	Flash Asset.X32	None
#asset[3]	#default	QuickTime Asset PPC (D6) QuickTime Asset (D7)	None	QuickTime Asset.X32 (D6); QT3Asset.X32 (D7)	None
#asset[4]	N/A	N/A	N/A	ActiveX.X32	None
#lingo[5]	N/A	FileIOXtraFat (D6) FileIOXtraPPC (D7)	FileIOXtraFat	FILEIO.X32	FILEIO16.X16
#lingo	Obsolete	QTVRXtra	QTVRXtra	QTVRW32.X32	QTVRW.X16
#lingo	Obsolete	N/A	N/A	DirMMX.X32	None

[1] The CrOptPPC and CurOpt.X32 Xtras and *Cursor Behavior Library.cst* are for authoring use only and should not be distributed.
[2] The Flash Asset Options PPC and Flash Asset Option.X32 Xtras and *Flash Behavior Library.cst* are for authoring use only and should not be distributed.
[3] The QuickTime Asset Options PPC and QuickTime Asset Option.X32 Xtras and *QT3 Behavior Library.cst* are for authoring use only and should not be distributed.
[4] The ActxPriv.X32 Xtra is for authoring use only and should not be distributed. The *Wintdist.exe*, *Aprxdist.exe*, and *Axdist.exe* installers can be distributed.
[5] Refer to Chapter 14, *External Files*, in Lingo in a Nutshell for details on the FileIO Xtra.

Table 10-5: New Xtras in Director 7

Usage	Type	PowerPC	Win32
Animated GIF sprite	N/A	Animated GIF Asset	Animated GIF Asset.X32
Animated GIF options[1]	N/A	Animated GIF Options	Animated GIF Options.X32
Vector shapes[1,2]	N/A	Shape Xtra	ShapeXtra.X32
Text creation[1]	N/A	Text Asset Options	TextAuth.X32
Text sprites	#default	Text Asset PPC	TextAsset.X32
Text rendering	#default	TextXtra PPC	TextXtra.X32
XML parsing	N/A	XMLParser PPC Xtra	XMLParser.X32
DXR compression[1]	N/A	LZ77 Compression PPC Xtra	LZCompr.X32
DCR compression[1]	N/A	Squish Rules PPC Xtra	Squish.X32
Multiuser server	N/A	Mulitusr	Multiusr.X32

Table 10-5: New Xtras in Director 7

Usage	Type	PowerPC	Win32
Sound mixer	#default	N/A	MacroMix.X32
Font rendering	#default	Font Xtra PPC	Font Xtra.X32
Font management	#default	Font Asset PPC	Font Asset.X32
Font options[1]	N/A	Font Asset Dialog	Font Asset Dialog.X32
MP3 audio	N/A	MPEG 3 Import Export	MPEG3 ImportExport.X32
QT3 export[1]	N/A	QTExportXtra	QTExport.X32
QT3 sprites	#default	QuickTime Asset	QT3Asset.X32[3]
QT3 editing[1]	N/A	QuickTime Asset Options	QTAuth.X32
DirectSoundMixer[4]	#default	N/A	DirectSound.X32

[1] Authoring only.
[2] Vector shapes require the Flash Asset Xtra for playback.
[3] QT3Asset.X32 includes the QT3Mix Sound Mixer.
[4] New in D7.0.1 and included with SW7.0.1.

Miscellaneous Macromedia Xtras

- PowerPoint Import (new in D6.5). The Import Xtra for PowerPoint converts PowerPoint presentation files into Director movie files.

- Java Export Xtra (new in D6.5). The File ➤ Save as Java feature exports Shockwave movies as Java code so they can be played back in browsers without Shockwave. It uses the CompileJavaPPC, JavaConvert, UIHelper PPC Xtra, FileXtra, Sun AU Import Export, PICT Import Export, JPEG Export, and GIF Export Xtras on the Macintosh, and the Javacvnt.X32, UiHelper.X32, Filextra.X32, Sun AU Import Export.X32, JPEG Export.X32, and GIF Export.X32 Xtras under Windows. It uses the *Behavior Library for Java.cst* in D6.5 and the Window ➤ Library Palette in D7, and *Save as Java.dxr* files on both platforms.

- The MUI Dialog Xtra creates custom alert and non-modal dialog boxes. See Chapter 15, *The MUI Dialog Xtra*, in *Lingo in a Nutshell*, and *http://www.zeus-prod.com/nutshell/chapters/mui.html*.

- The Actor Control and Cast Control Xtras are using during authoring to manage sprite, cast members, and castLibs and are not used in Projectors.

- The Cue Card Xtra prompts the developer to run a tutorial the first time Director 6 is launched.

- D7 for Windows includes new Intel Dynamic filters *WDEadd.X32*, *WDEd2Opt.X32*, *WDEdis.X32*, and *WPEopt.X32*. They appear under the Insert menu.

- The D6.5 update CD's *Goodies:Import Goodies* folder includes the unsupported SWA and MPEG3 Xtras, which became official in D7.

- There are numerous unsupported Xtras on the Director 6 CD. Most are simply demonstrations for Xtra developers. See the *Xtras\Win* and *Goodies\Director\SoundXtr\Xtras* subfolders under *X:\Macromedia\XDK_d6a4* on the D6 CD. The CommPort XObject (the Windows analog of the Macintosh Serial Port XObject) is included in the discontinued folder.

- *Xobglu32.DLL* and *Xobglu16.DLL* are a pair of "thunking" DLLs that allow D5 and D6 32-bit Projectors to use older 16-bit XObjects under Windows 95/98. (16-bit XObjects are not supported under Windows NT.) These DLLs are automatically built into 32-bit Windows Projectors and are extracted and used automatically, if necessary. The temporarily extracted files are deleted when the Projector terminates. Search the Macromedia TechNotes for the word "thunk" for details.

- *DLLGLUE.DLL* is an obsolete Windows 3.1 XObject (written by Paul Hamilton) that allowed Lingo to access Windows API functions or DLLs not specifically designed as XObjects. It has been superseded by Xtras such as DirectOS and Buddy API, which access the Windows API, and by RavWare's (*http://www.ravware.com*) GLU32 Xtra for Windows 95/98/NT, which allows Lingo to call the Win32 API.

- The SerialPort and XCMDglue XObjects embedded in Director for Macintosh's resource fork provide serial port access and allow Director to use Hypercard XCMDs in D6, but are obsolete D7.

- The rumored spell-checker and encryption Xtras from Macromedia have yet to materialize.

Third-party Xtras

The third-party Photocaster Lite (*http://www.medialab.com*) and Beatnik Lite Xtra (*http://www.headspace.com*) are included with D7. The third-party PrintOMatic Lite, ScriptOMatic Lite, and PopMenu Lite Xtras are installed by default with D6. The full version of PrintOMatic is now published exclusively by Electronic Ink (*http://www.printomatic.com*) and the PopMenu Xtra has been renamed the Popup Xtra and is available from UpdateStage (*http://www.updatestage.com/xtras*). The full version of ScriptOMatic may be available from *http://www.trevimedia.com*.

There are samples and demonstrations of many other third-party Xtras on the Director 6.0 and 7.0 CDs as described earlier under "Obtaining Xtras."

Loading and Registering Xtras

The preferred way to load Xtras is to include them in the appropriate *Xtras* folder where they will be opened and closed automatically by Director.

You should not access Xtras manually using *openXlib* and *closeXlib*. Use *openXlib* and *closeXlib* with XObjects only.

You can include Xtras in the resource fork of Director for Macintosh or a Macintosh Projector. This is not recommended for Xtras, but was commonly done with the FileIO XObject prior to Director 5.

Director 6 and 7 support bundling Xtras into Projectors on both Macintosh and Windows. I recommend against bundled Xtras, though.

When an Xtra is loaded, Director registers the Xtra in an internal dictionary and identifies it by its unique Xtra ID (and optional Xtra version number) assigned by the Xtra developer.

 Director decides whether to load Xtras based on their external file names (under Windows) and File Types (on the Macintosh), but identifies Xtras by their internal Xtra IDs that are independent of the external filename or type.

Director will issue an error message if it encounters two Xtras with the same Xtra ID, unless one has a later version number. In practice, many Xtra developers omit version numbers. It is best to delete old versions of Xtras and include only the current version in your *Xtras* folder. In some cases, a developer may inadvertently forget to generate a unique Xtra ID when copying a template from one of Macromedia's Xtras. Remove suspicious Xtra(s) from all *Xtras* subfolders (and restart Director) until you locate the culprit. (For Director 5, be sure to check in the multiple Xtras folders described under "The Xtras Folders" later in this chapter.)

When Director requires a particular Xtra, it consults the dictionary to determine whether the Xtra has been registered. When Director loads a movie, it determines whether any cast members require a custom Sprite Xtra. If so, and the Xtra is not present, Director displays an error message.

If a required Sprite Xtra is missing, Director will display a red X on the Stage in place of the sprite. If a Transition Xtra is missing, Director will perform a jump-cut instead of the transition. If a MIX Xtra is missing, Director will not be able to import or use linked assets of the particular type (linked sounds won't play and linked images won't appear).

If a Lingo Xtra is omitted, Director will post a "Handler not Found" error because the required command won't be recognized. For example, if you omit the NetLingo Xtra, net-related Lingo commands such as *downloadNetThing()* will fail.

Once an Xtra is loaded, it is available for the duration of the Projector, not just the current movie. The methods within a Lingo Scripting Xtra can be accessed from any other script.

There are several reasons that an Xtra might not load or register:

Xtras are read only at startup
    You need to restart Director or the Projector to load new Xtras.

Corrupted Xtras cache file
    When in doubt, delete the Xtras cache file and try again.

Corrupted Xtra file
    A corrupted Xtra may be caused by a download problem, a disk error, or an incomplete update of Director. Replace any suspicious Xtras with a fresh copy.

Xtras weren't automatically bundled

I recommend against bundling Xtras, but if you choose to do this, it occurs automatically only if the movie is included in the Projector or if the appropriate options are checked under File ➤ Create Projector ➤ Options in D6. In D7, the *Include in Projector* option must be checked for the relevant Xtra under Modify ➤ Movie ➤ Xtras.

Wrong version of Xtra

Obtain and use the correct Xtras for D7. For example, the D6.5 QT3 Asset Xtra won't work in D7.

Xtra is not Shockwave-safe

Shockwave 7 will only recognize Xtras compiled as "Shockwave-safe" by the Xtra developer.

Not enough memory

For example, the QuickTime Asset Xtra for Macintosh requires that about 15 MB RAM be allocated to Director. The default memory allocations may suffice, but you should probably increase the default allocation when using Quick-Time 3 with Macintosh Projectors.

Xtra requires another Xtra that is missing

The Sound Import Export Xtra and other MIX-related Xtras require the MIX Services Xtra. The error may say that the Sound Import Export Xtra is not loaded, but you actually need to add the MIX Services Xtra to your *Xtras* folder.

Sound Import Export Xtra won't load

This is a known issue addressed by Macromedia TechNote #12598. Also, under Windows NT, rename your Xtras to obey the 8.3 naming convention to ensure that they load properly. The internal name of the Xtra is unaffected.

Xtra requires a missing system component

For example, the Macintosh QuickTime Asset Xtra won't load unless version 3.x of the Macintosh QuickTime extension is installed. And the QTVR Xtra requires a full QT installation, including the QTVR components.

Xtra requires a missing DLL

For example, the Buddy API Xtra requires the accompanying *BUDAPI32.DLL* or *BUDAPI16.DLL* in the same folder. Other Xtras depend on Windows system DLLs, which may in turn depend on other DLLs. If the Xtra registers on some machines but not others, it is a likely culprit. See the next section, "Determining which DLLs are needed."

Conflicting class ID (known as a GUID)

If two Xtras have the same internal class ID, the first one encountered will load, but the second will generate a "Duplicate Xtra" error message and will not load. If you are an Xtras developer, generate a unique ID for your Xtra as described in the MOA documentation. There is no foolproof way to tell which Xtra is the problem, but you can sort all Xtras by name, then make an educated guess. Remove Xtras one by one until you find the two culprits, which may have different names or reside in different subfolders. You won't get the "Duplicate Xtra" error when at least one of them has been removed from the *Xtras* folder.

Wrong filename or File Type

Macintosh Xtras must have the correct File Type (**Xtra**) and Windows Xtras must have an .X16 or .X32 extension. XObjects are not opened automatically (unless embedded in the Macintosh resource fork). XObjects must be opened with *openXlib* instead.

Wrong Xtra for Projector type

Windows 3.1 Projectors require 16-bit Xtras and Windows 95/98/NT Projectors require 32-bit Xtras require 32-bit Projectors. 16-bit Windows Xtras cannot be tested from the D6 authoring environment. You need to test with a D6 Projector or the D5 authoring environment.

Wrong processor or insufficient FPU

Many Xtras won't work on 68K Macintoshes and won't load unless running on a PowerPC. The SWA Xtras require a PowerPC during authoring and at least a 68040 with an FPU (floating-point unit) for playback.

Wrong folder location or folder nested too deep

Projectors don't load Xtras from the same folder as the authoring environment and Shockwave can only access Xtras in the Shockwave plug-ins folder. See "The Xtras Folders" later in this chapter for details on where Xtras must be located. Xtras nested more than five folders deep within the *Xtras* folder will not be found.

Xtras for authoring only

Many Xtras, as a security measure, will refuse to register when used with a Projector. Some require that a registration method be called from Lingo before they can be used in a Projector. Tool Xtras do not register in a Projector. Macromedia's Sprite Xtras come in two different flavors, one for authoring and one for Projector (runtime). See Tables 10-4 and 10-5.

Bundled Xtras interfere with Xtras folder

There have been rumors that bundled Xtras prevent Director from loading Xtras from the *Xtras* folder. I recommend against bundling Xtras.

The proper DEF entries are omitted

If you are an Xtras developer, the Xtra will not be recognized unless you export the proper DEF entries (and remember to compile your DEF). Use **dumpbin /exports** (requires MSVC Developer's Studio) to show what your Xtra exports. If the exports are wrong, the Xtra won't register on any machine.

Determining which DLLs are needed

An Xtra's developer should tell you which DLLs, if any, are required for the Xtra. If not, use **dumpbin** (included with MSVC Developer's Studio) with the **/imports** option to identify the needed DLLs.

Here is the output for Buddy API, filtered to highlight the needed DLLs:

```
G:\MSDEV\bin\dumpbin /imports G:\BudApi\budapi.X32 | find "dll"
        KERNEL32.dll
        USER32.dll
        ADVAPI32.dll
        budapi32.dll
```

You can repeat the process to determine the DLLs that *budapi32.dll* requires "downstream":

```
G:\MSDEV\bin\dumpbin /imports G:\BudApi\budapi32.dll | find "dll"
      kernel32.dll
      user32.dll
      oleaut32.dll
```

Note that future versions of Buddy API reportedly will not require a separate DLL.

The Xtras Cache and Director Preferences

In authoring mode, Xtras are cached, so that Director doesn't need to reregister them every time it starts up (although an Xtra can be designed to allow itself not to be cached). However, all installed Xtras are registered every time a Projector starts (that is, Projectors never cache Xtras). Most Xtras register silently, although demo versions may post a warning dialog box when registering. To perform a clean test of an Xtra, run it from a Projector. If you are having troubles with Xtras, try deleting the Xtras cache file and restarting Director.

On the Macintosh, the cache file is named *dirapi.mch* in D7. In prior versions it is named *Director 6.0 Xtra Cache* (or *Director 5.0 Xtra Cache*) and is located in the Macintosh *System Folder:Preferences* folder. The Preferences file is named *Director 7.0 Preferences*, *Director 6.0 Preferences*, or *Director 5.0 Preferences* in the same folder.

Under Windows, the cache file is named *D70Xtra.MCH*, or *D60Xtra.MCH* and is located in the Director application's folder. (A separate *D50Xtra.MCH* cache file is located in the folders where the 16-bit and 32-bit versions of Director 5 for Windows are installed.) There is no separate D7 preferences file under Windows. Preferences are stored in the Windows Registry file. The D6 and D5 preferences file is named *Director 6.0 Preferences.prf* or *Directr5.prf*, and is in the same folder as Director.

Windows Xtras

There are usually different versions of an Xtra for Windows 3.1 and Windows 95/98/NT, but some Xtras do not support all versions of Windows. The type of Windows Xtra needed depends on the Projector's type, not the version of Windows.

16-bit Projectors require 16-bit Xtras (with an .X16 extension) and 32-bit Projectors require 32-bit Xtras (with an .X32 extension).

Only 32-bit Xtras are used during authoring in Director 6 and 7. In Director 6, you can test 16-bit Xtras only from a Windows 3.1–style Projector (which can be tested under Windows 95).

Windows 3.1

Windows 3.1 requires a 16-bit Projector and 16-bit Xtras. It cannot run 32-bit Projectors. Director 6 and 7 authoring is not supported under Windows 3.1. There is no 16-bit version of authoring-time only Xtras, some of which are shown in Table 10-3. Most of the newer Xtras shown in Table 10-4 are not supported under Windows 3.1. None of the D7-specific Xtras in Table 10-5 is supported under Windows 3.1, as D7 does not support Windows 3.1 at all.

Windows 95/98

A 16-bit projector running under Windows 95/98 requires 16-bit Xtras. A 32-bit projector (the preferred choice) running under Windows 95/98 requires 32-bit Xtras.

Windows NT

32-bit Projectors and 32-bit Xtras are strongly recommended under Windows NT 4.0. Under NT, 16-bit Projectors run under a Windows 3.1 *virtual machine* known as *Windows on Windows*, and use 16-bit Xtras. Windows NT 3.5.1 is not supported as an authoring platform, but will play back 16-bit and 32-bit Projectors with the proper extensions installed. Older 16-bit XObjects are not supported under Windows NT 4.0 when using a 32-bit Projector.

Windows Xtras written in C are only recognized if they have the file extension .X16 or .X32. Both 16-bit and 32-bit Xtras can share the same folder without conflicts. The correct version of the Xtra will automatically be opened to match the Projector (16-bit or 32-bit) regardless of the Windows version in use. Tool Xtras built in Lingo with a .DIR, .DXR, .DCR, or .CST extension are recognized during authoring. Older Windows XObjects used a .DLL extension, but included a message table not found in typical DLLs. Use the GLU32 Xtra to access an arbitrary Windows DLL or API call from Director.

Macintosh Xtras

The type of Xtra needed on the Macintosh depends on the Projector type and not the processor type (68K versus PowerPC). Xtras for both PowerPCs and 68K Macs can reside in the same folder without conflict.

If using a Standard (68K) Macintosh Projector on a PowerPC, both the Projector code and Xtra code run under emulation. Providing both PowerPC and 68K Xtras or a single Fat Binary Xtra is the simplest solution. Some authoring Xtras, such as SWA Compression, are not supported on 68K Macs. See also Table 7-1.

Macintosh Xtras are recognized only if they have the proper case-sensitive four-character File Type (Xtra) and Creator Code (Xown). If you've downloaded an Xtra and it is not being recognized, set its File Type and Creator Code using ResEdit or similar tool. Tool Xtras built in Lingo with a .DIR, .DXR, .DCR, or .CST extension are recognized during authoring as are files with the corresponding Mac File Types shown in Table 4-4. Older Macintosh XObjects used the File Type XOBJ and Creator Code MMDR or MD93 and must be opened manually with *openxlib*. XObjects are not supported in D7. Jason Winshell (*jwins@slip.net*) can convert some older XObjects to Xtras without requiring the source code.

The Xtras Folders

Xtras usually reside in an *Xtras* folder where Director or your Projector will find and open them automatically. The location of the *Xtras* folder depends on the platform, the version of Director, and whether you are running the authoring environment, a Projector, or in Shockwave.

Director for both Macintosh and Windows automatically load Xtras within the *Xtras* folder located below the folder where Director is installed. Projectors automatically load Xtras within the *Xtras* folder located in the folder containing the

Projector. Newly installed Xtras are not recognized until you restart Director or the Projector. (The exception is Xtras downloaded automatically at runtime in D7, which are loaded when the next *goToNetMovie* command is issued.)

You can include both Macintosh and Windows Xtras in the same folder, and Director will load only the appropriate Xtras according to the rules described earlier. Any Xtras inappropriate for the platform or Projector (or any non-Xtras) in the folder are ignored but slow down Director as it checks each file.

Some Xtras install their HTML help files in the *Xtras* folder. Too many files of any type in the *Xtras* folder slows down Director's startup and file saving. Move unused Xtras and any non-Xtra files to other folders to improve performance.

Director and Projectors will scan for Xtras five folders deep below the main folder (don't nest them too deeply, and beware of extremely long folder paths that may exceed the OS limits). Director recognizes *aliases* (Macintosh) and *shortcuts* (Windows) within the *Xtras* folder that point to Xtras elsewhere. See also the TechNote "Installing and Using Xtras" at *http://www.zeusprod.com/technote/ xtrainst.html.*

Table 10-6 lists folders that the Director 5 authoring environment checks for Xtras *in addition to* the *Xtras* folder where Director is installed. Director 5 Projectors check only within the *Xtras* folder in the same folder as the Projector, as do Director 6 and 7 Projectors.

Table 10-6: Supplemental (D5) or Temporary Xtras (D6) Folders

Platform	Xtras Folder
Windows 3.1	C:\Windows\Macromed\Xtras
Windows 95/98/NT	C:\Program Files\Common Files\Macromedia\Xtras
Macintosh	MacHD:System Folder:Macromedia:Xtras

Macromedia's *Using Director* manual incorrectly claims that Director 6.0 recognizes the secondary *Xtras* folders that are recognized only by Director 5.

In a strange twist, Director 6 and 7 Projectors running from read-only (locked) media will unbundle (i.e., unpack) their Xtras temporarily into the same folders shown in Table 10-6. (I've read reports that they are unbundled into invisible temporary folders, but this does not appear to be true.) Other Macromedia applications, notably SoundEdit, may also use these folders.

D7's new Slim Projectors read Xtras from any *Xtras* folder where the Projector is installed, and also from the Shockwave 7 *System Xtras* folder.

When using Director 5, you can test 16-bit Xtras using the 16-bit authoring environment (even under Windows 95), and 32-bit Xtras in the 32-bit authoring environment. Install the 16-bit Xtras in the *Xtras* folder in which the 16-bit version of Director 5 is installed, and the 32-bit Xtras in the *Xtras* folder in which the 32-bit version of Director 5 is installed.

The Xtras menu

Tool Xtras or Libraries within subfolders within the *Xtras* folder appear in submenus (named for the subfolders) under the `Xtras` menu. Use a minus sign to begin a filename to prevent it from appearing in the `Xtras` menu. In D7, Behavior Libraries should be placed in the *Xtras/Libs* folder, where they can be accessed via `Window ➤ Library Palette`.

MIX, Sprite, Lingo, and Transition Xtras are unaffected by the *Xtras* subfolder in which they are placed, as long as they are in a recognized folder. Table 10-1 shows where each type of Xtra appears in the interface.

The SWA Export Xtra used by SoundEdit and Peak LE doesn't appear in Director's `Xtras` menu.

Xtras for Shockwave

Digitally signed packages can be downloadable dynamically in D7 and SW7. Upon acceptance by the user, the Xtras within the package are installed automatically in the Shockwave 7 *System* folder where they are accessible by Shockwave, Shock-Machine, and Slim (system) Projectors. Prior to SW7, the user must download any required Xtras and place them in the browser support folder manually. See the following two sections and Chapter 11 for details.

The Shockwave 6.0 plug-in supports only linked media types for which MIX Xtras are installed in the Shockwave Xtras folder. The Shockwave 6.0.1 plug-in recognizes BMP, PICT, GIF, JPEG, AIFF, AIFC, and WAVE files without requiring any MIX Xtras, but *ignores* any installed MIX Xtras.

The Flash Asset and SWA playback Xtras are not considered MIX Xtras. They are included with the Director for Shockwave download and allow the SW plug-in to play Flash and SWA assets on capable machines.

Only Xtras marked by the Xtra developer as Shockwave-safe are recognized by SW7. Downloaded Xtras are available to all SW movies, not just the one that downloaded them. See *http://www.zeus-prod.com/nutshell/xtras.html* for details on Xtra packaging and downloading.

The Shockwave 7 download installs numerous Xtras. Shockwave includes all the functions built into the NetLingo and other net-related Xtras. They need not be included with Shockwave and are necessary only when using a local Projector that accesses Internet-based content. Shockwave 7 supports the same default graphics and sound types as SW6.0.1, but also recognizes MIX Xtras (although most are inappropriate for SW).

Shockwave for Macintosh Xtras folder

In SW7 for Macintosh, all Xtras are installed under *System Folder:Extensions:Macro-media:Shockwave:Xtras*. For Netscape on the Macintosh, in Shockwave 6, the support folder has the same name as the plug-in with a space and the word "folder" appended. For example, the SW6 Xtras folder would be called:

Netscape Navigator™ Folder:Plug-ins:NP-PPC-Dir-Shockwave folder:Xtras

or:

Netscape Navigator™ Folder:Plug-ins:NP-68K-Dir-Shockwave folder:Xtras

Shockwave for Windows Xtras folder

In SW7, all Xtras are installed under *C:\Windows\System\Macromed\Shockwave\ Xtras.* In SW6, for Netscape on Windows, the support folder has the same name as the plug-in (without the .DLL extension). The 32-bit plug-in name is *NPDSW32.DLL,* so Xtras go under *Netscape\Plugins\NPDSW32\Xtras.*

In SW6, for Microsoft Internet Explorer on Windows 95, the support folder is the entire *Windows\System* directory, but you can place Xtras in *Windows\System\ Xtras* to keep them separated from other files.

Including Xtras with a Projector

When using Xtras with Projectors, you can place them in a Projector-specific *Xtras* folder, bundle them into the Projector, or use some combination of the two. I strongly suggest leaving the Projector's Xtras exclusively in an *Xtras* folder.

Which Xtras to Distribute

Director 6 and 7 use an ungodly number of Xtras. Tables 10-2 through 10-5 and 15-13 list Xtras needed for various operations, but it is still easy to be confused about which Xtras your Projector requires.

The Xtras to distribute are sometimes the same ones as used during authoring, but not always (as with the QT3, Flash, and Custom Cursor Asset Xtras). There are also many Xtras that are needed only at authoring, such as Tool Xtras. Never distribute Xtras meant only for authoring-time such as the agent Xtras or the PowerPoint Import or Java Export Xtras.

See *http://www. zeusprod.com/nutshell/appendices/checklists.html* for a list of Xtras and other files to be included with the Projector.

To include the list of Xtras under Modify ➤ Movie ➤ Xtras automatically in your Projector, check the *Check Movie for Xtras* checkbox when creating your D6 Projector. In D7, each Xtra in the list can be included individually. I prefer to peruse the list and manually include those Xtras in my Projector's *Xtras* folder. In D7, check *the movieXtraList* property.

Network Xtras

If you use any linked cast members, sounds, movies, or castLibs at a URL, you'll need the INetURL and NetFile (and probably NetLingo) Xtras. If using linked GIF and JPEG images, you'll also need the GIF Import and JPEG Import Xtras. When using a PowerPC-native or Fat Projector on a PowerMac, you'll also need the NetManage WinSock Lib file. The D6 *Include Network Xtras* checkbox under File

➤ Create Projector ➤ Options will include the Network Xtras whether needed or not. In D7, Network Xtras are added under Modify ➤ Movie ➤ Xtras. See Table 10-2 for important details.

You'll need the NetLingo Xtra if using any of the Lingo commands shown in Table 11-5. The NetLingo commands are built into the Shockwave plug-in and do not require an Xtra when running under Shockwave. Thus, not every command that requires an Xtra during authoring requires one in Shockwave.

MIX and MIX Services Xtras

The Xtras needed when linking to external graphics are shown in Table 10-3. These assets are typically added via File ➤ Import using the *Link to External File* option.

You do not need any MIX Xtras at runtime if using only internal (embedded) assets. The Modify ➤ Movie ➤ Xtras option should show all the MIX Xtras you need (plus the MIX Services Xtra) automatically. Director updates this list of Xtras whenever you use an externally linked asset. If you have deleted some linked cast members, the list may show Xtras that are no longer needed. If you remove Xtras from the list, Director will re-add them automatically if they are still needed.

For example, if you link to any external sounds (AIF or WAVE files) or use *sound playFile*, you should include the Sound Import Export Xtras and the MIX Services Xtra.

Sprite Asset Xtras and Transition Xtras

If you insert assets that requires Sprite Xtras, include the Xtras with your Projector, as shown in Tables 10-4 or 10-5. Sprite assets are added via File ➤ Import in D7 or the Insert ➤ Media Element or Insert ➤ Control menu in D6 and D7. These include Custom Cursors, Active X controls, QuickTime 3 media, Shockwave audio, and Flash files, plus the new types in Table 10-5. As with MIX Xtras, Director adds the necessary Xtras to the list under Modify ➤ Movie ➤ Xtras automatically whenever you insert a new cast member type that requires an Xtra.

The Flash Asset Xtra is included in the Shockwave for Director download, so you don't ordinarily need to include it in Shockwave projects (it is also needed for D7 vector shapes).

If you use any third-party Sprite Xtras, include them with the Projector, too. Director's built-in Transitions do not require Xtras, but third-party Transitions do.

You do not need Xtras for QuickTime 2 or AVI *#digitalVideo* cast members, or for embedded bitmaps or sounds. You will need a Sprite Xtra for QuickTime 3 cast members.

Lingo Xtras

Lingo Xtras don't show up in the list under Modify ➤ Movie ➤ Xtras unless you add them manually. You need to be aware of which Lingo Xtras you are using and be sure to include them with your Projector. Some are shown in Table 10-4, but you will likely use third-party Xtras as well.

If you omit an Xtra, such as the NetLingo or FileIO Xtra, and try to use a command that requires that Xtra, Director will display a "Handler not defined" error.

You can check the list of commands contained within an Xtra using the Message window, such as:

```
put mMessageList (xtra "NetLingo")
```

or:

```
put interface (xtra "NetLingo")
```

See Chapter 13 in *Lingo in a Nutshell* for additional details on Lingo Xtras.

The Xtras Folder for Projectors

Projectors will load Xtras from the folder called *Xtras* under the folder from which the Projector is running. This allows each Projector to use different Xtras.

Copy the distributable runtime versions of the Xtras, which often differ from the authoring versions used during development, to the Projector's *Xtras* folder.

Xtras Bundled into the Projector

Director 6 and 7 allow you to bundle Xtras into a Projector; Director 5 does not. I see no compelling reason to bundle Xtras, especially because Projectors unbundle their Xtras into a temporary folder at runtime. On writable media, a temporary *Xtras* folder for unbundled Xtras is created within the folder where the Projector resides. For read-only media, a temporary folder on the system disk, as shown in Table 10-6, is used instead.

Reasons not to bundle Xtras:

- Xtras are unbundled at runtime, which slows Projector startup by 15 seconds or more.

- If run from a locked volume (CD-ROM), Xtras are copied onto the user's hard drive, requiring hard disk space and slowing performance. This will fail on systems that prohibit write access to the Windows system folder.

- Xtras could be left behind in the temporary folder if the Projector crashes (the related bug was fixed in D6.0.2).

- Automatic bundling, via File ➤ Create Projector ➤ *Options* checkboxes in D6 or via Modify ➤ Movie ➤ Xtras in D7, includes unnecessary Xtras in some cases. It is better to select exactly the Xtras you need.

- Automatic bundling doesn't necessarily include all needed Xtras, such as Lingo Xtras and the NetFile Xtra needed for local SWA playback.

- Bundling Xtras forces you to rebuild your Projector to add, test, or remove different Xtras.

- Bundling Xtras has been reported to prevent Director from reading Xtras from the *Xtras* folder, but this is unconfirmed.

- Projectors with bundled Xtras cause the error: "Problem opening C:\WINNT," or a similar error under Windows NT if the drive is larger than 4 GB.

- Bundled Xtras are not supported in Shockwave or prior to D6.

- Slim Projectors in D7 use the Xtras in the SW7 *Xtras* folder. Bundling the default Xtras is largely redundant.

If you insist on bundling Xtras, there are several methods:

- Add Xtras to the Projector's build list manually via the file picker when creating the Projector using File ➤ Create Projector.

- In D6, use the *Check Movie for Xtras* checkbox under File ➤ Create Projector ➤ *Options*. It interacts with the Modify ➤ Movie ➤ Xtras option and the *XTRAINFO.TXT* file. Use the *Include Network Xtras* checkbox under File ➤ Create Projector ➤ *Options* in tandem with the *XTRAINFO.TXT* file.

- In D7, use the *Include in Projector* checkbox for individual Xtras under Modify ➤ Movie ➤ Xtras.

Automatic bundling includes only those Xtras used by movies embedded in the Projector (although other Xtras can be added to the Projector build list). I recommend using a Stub Projector containing only one minimal movie.

The Modify ➤ Movie ➤ Xtras options

When you add a cast member that requires a Sprite, Transition, or MIX Xtra, the appropriate Xtras are added automatically to the *Movie Xtras* dialog box accessed via Modify ➤ Movie ➤ Xtras (see Figure 10-1). The Xtras list doesn't include Lingo Xtras unless you add them manually. If you remove an Xtra that is needed, Director will reinstate it the next time you use the menu option to view the list. If you delete all cast members that use a Sprite Xtra, perform a File ➤ Save and Compact to purge the movie of the old assets, then delete the Sprite Xtra from the list manually, as Director won't do this automatically.

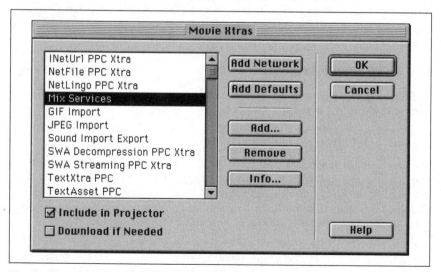

Figure 10-1: Movie Xtras dialog box

In D6, items in the Modify ➤ Movie ➤ Xtras list are bundled with the Projector if the *Check Movie for Xtras* checkbox is checked under File ➤ Create Projector ➤ Options. (Only those Xtras specified for movies included in the Projector are bundled. Xtras for external movies are not.) This checkbox also adds Xtras of type *#mixin* from the *XTRAINFO.TXT* file in the Projector.

Rather than bundle Xtras into the Projector, I use the Xtras list to help determine which Sprite and MIX Xtras to include in the *Xtras* folder.

You can use the *Add* button under Modify ➤ Movie ➤ Xtras to see a list of many (but not all) of the Xtras installed, including Lingo, Sprite, and MIX Xtras. The D7 property *the xtraList* contains all installed Xtras.

In D7, the *Add Defaults* button adds Xtras flagged as #type:#default and the *Add Network* button adds Xtras flagged as #net:#xtra in the *XTRAINFO.TXT* file. I prefer to delete the *#default* flag from the *XTRAINFO.TXT* entries so that unnecessary Xtras are not listed for each movie.

The list of Xtras is stored in each DIR file (Director movie). If (and only if) there is a corresponding entry in the *XTRAINFO.TXT* file, the Xtra names under Modify ➤ Movie ➤ Xtras will be translated to the appropriate platform as needed. In D7, the property *the movieXtraList* contains the Xtras listed there.

When the movie is opened from a Projector or during authoring, this list of Xtras is checked, and an alert dialog box is shown for any missing Xtras. (This dialog box cannot be suppressed via *the alertbook*.) If you delete needed Xtras from the Xtras list, but never reopen the Xtras list via Modify ➤ Movie ➤ Xtras, they will not be added back to the list. This prevents an error dialog box from appearing when the movie is run in a Projector, even if the needed Sprite Xtras are missing. During authoring, you are likely to get an error message.

In D7, the *Download if Needed* checkbox and *Info* button are available only if the *XTRAINFO.TXT* file includes the #package and #info flags for the Xtra. You may experience a long delay or crash if a network connection is not active when using these options.

Detecting Installed Xtras

In D7, the new property *the xtraList* contains a list of property lists showing the name and version of installed Xtras, such as:

```
[[#name:"FileXtra", #version:""], [#name:"UIHelperPPC Xtra",
#version: "7.0"]...]
```

The *showXlib* command lists only Lingo Xtras in the Message window. At runtime, you can use *the netPresent* to determine whether the *NetLingo* and *NetFile* Xtras are installed (it doesn't check for the *INetURL* Xtra). See Examples 13-6 and 13-7 in Chapter 13 in *Lingo in a Nutshell* for a utility that determines which Lingo Scripting Xtras are installed using the *number of Xtra* and *name of Xtra* properties.

See also the list of Xtras displayed via Modify ➤ Movie ➤ Xtras ➤ Add, although it is incomplete in D6. In D6, to determine whether an Asset Xtra is installed, you can attempt to create a new cast member and check the result, as shown in Example 10-1. In D7, you could check *the xtraList* instead.

Example 10-1: Checking Whether an Asset Xtra Is Installed

```
on assetXtraInstalled assetType
  -- Try to create a new cast member
  set asset = new (assetType)
  if ilk(asset, #member) then
    -- Erase it when done
    erase asset
    return TRUE
  else
    return FALSE
  end if
end assetXtraInstalled
```

The following code checks whether the Flash Sprite Asset Xtra is installed:

```
put assetXtraInstalled(#flash)
-- 1
```

CHAPTER 11

Shockwave and the Internet

This chapter explores both Shockwave and Internet-enabled Projectors. Shockwave is an effective way to disseminate net-based content, but the bandwidth bottleneck can not be ignored. Even with Internet-enabled Projectors, you must decide which content to keep local and which to put on the Internet.

For large projects that require updates, you can deliver a CD-ROM containing most of the content and access small updates via Director's NetLingo Xtras. A net-enabled Projector is a controlled environment that avoids the plethora of Shockwave plug-in and browser combinations.

·Conversely, you can distribute HTML-based content to be viewed locally in a Shockwave-capable browser. If your production is too large for Shockwave but has significant HTML components, you can launch a browser alongside the Projector.

Shockwave 7 was released as this book went to press, but Macromedia had not finalized downloadable Shockwave Xtras, and the new ShockMachine. See *http://www.zeusprod.com/nutshell/chapters/shockwave.html* for current information, known bugs, and the inevitable corrections and updates as browsers and plug-ins evolve. There are also many topics including testing and debugging tips, emailing from Director, and embedding a browser within Director that space did not allow me to cover here.* See the URL cited earlier for a treasure trove of additional information.

---

* This chapter touches on a lot of topics, including JavaScript and HTML, that I can't possibly cover in a Director book. Luckily, O'Reilly & Associates publishes terrific books on these topics, and more, including CGI and Perl programming. See *http://www.zeusprod.com/nutshell/biblio.html* for a list of recommended reading or visit *http://www.oreilly.com* for a comprehensive list.

Getting Started with Shockwave

If you are new to Shockwave, this chapter will help you put your first Shockwave movie on the Net. If you are an experienced Shockwave developer, this chapter will expand your understanding of various browser-related issues and the NetLingo commands.

For an overview of Shockwave, refer to the *Shockwave, Shockwave basics, Shockwave movies*, and *Shockwave Audio* topics in the online Help, and to Chapter 17, *Playing Movies Over the Internet*, in Director 7's *Using Director* manual. See also Chapter 14, *Shockwave, the Internet, and Lingo*, in Director 6's *Learning Lingo* manual. Shockwave issues change with each new version of the plug-ins or browsers. The following URLs are good places to keep abreast of the latest information.

Assistance getting Shockwave plug-ins installed:

> *news://forums.macromedia.com/plug-ins*

Shockwave Developer's Center:

> *http://www.macromedia.com/support/shockwave/*

Director—working with Shockwave:

> *http://www.macromedia.com/support/director/how/shock/*

ShockeR-L mailing list:

> MailList: *http://www.shocker.com/shocker/digests/index.html*
> Archive: *http://ww2.narrative.com/shocker.nsf*

Streaming Shockwave Tutorial by O'Reilly author Bob Schmitt:

> *http://www.macromedia.com/support/director/how/expert/stream/
> streaming.html*

Shockwave Tips from DXM by Lee Swearingen and Cathy Clark:

> *http://www.macromedia.com/support/director/how/expert/dxm/dxm.html*

Suggestions for streaming media and working over a network by Jake Sapirstein:

> *http://www.macromedia.com/support/director/how/expert/dxm/dxm.html*

List of files installed by Shockwave (delete these to uninstall):

> *http://www.macromedia.com/support/shockwave/ts/documents/
> uninstall_director_plugin.htm*

Projectors, the Internet, and Shocked Content

Prior to D6, Shockwave-compressed content was exclusively for web browsers. In D6 and D7, files can be compressed using Shockwave's technology but played back via a *local* Projector without the Shockwave plug-in or a browser. Compressed Director files are slower than uncompressed files, so you should compress them only if you are short on disk space. Compressed Shockwave audio (SWA) can be played from a local CD-ROM to allow for both longer sounds and higher fidelity, but SWA requires more processing power than AIFF or WAVE files.

In D6 and D7, Projectors can access remote net-based text, audio, castLibs, Director movie files, GIFs, and JPEG images using the appropriate MIX Xtras and NetLingo Xtras. D6 does not render HTML files, but D7 text cast members can render simple text-only HTML pages. CD-ROM-based Projectors that access net-based content are sometimes called *hybrid CDs*, but should not be confused with the term as it is used for cross-platform CD-ROMs.

D6, D7, SW6, and SW7 support *streaming* Shockwave, meaning that content can be used as it is downloaded, as opposed to earlier versions, which required that the entire SW movie download before playback began. However, QuickTime 3 video does not stream in Shockwave (QuickTime 4 might).

Shockwave Plug-ins and ActiveX Controls

Shockwave (SW) for Director is a plug-in for Netscape Navigator (Netscape) or an ActiveX control for Microsoft Internet Explorer (MIE) that lets users play your Director content via their web browser. The SW6 plug-ins also play SW4 and SW5 Shockwave movies. The SW7 plug-ins also play SW5 and SW6 content.

Macromedia also uses the term "Shockwave" for browser plug-ins that play Flash, Authorware, and FreeHand content, but the term is usually synonymous with "Shockwave for Director." *Shockwave movies* are Director DIR files that have been *burned* (compressed) into DCR format. *Shockwave castLibs* are Director CST files that have been compressed into CCT format. The term "burned" is coined from the original Shockwave compressor (AfterBurner) and should not be confused with burning a CD-ROM. I use the verb "Shocked" synonymously with "burned," and a web site that uses Shockwave is known as a Shocked site. Shocked movies are ordinarily embedded in an HTML page and played via a web browser, but Projectors can also play local and remote Shocked movies (DCR files). Likewise, so-called Shockwave audio (SWA) is compressed audio that can be played through a Shockwave-capable browser or a Projector. D7 also includes a File ➤ Preview in Browser option to preview DIR files in a Shockwave-capable browser.

The Shockwave plug-in may work in other applications that recognize Netscape plug-ins (including MIE and AOL); AOL's installation now includes Shockwave and the ActiveX version of Shockwave is strongly preferred for MIE. The Shockwave ActiveX control can be hosted by any ActiveX-aware Windows application in addition to MIE. Don't confuse the Shockwave ActiveX control or other third-party controls with the ActiveX Asset Xtra, which allows Director to *use* third-party ActiveX controls. I use the terms "Shockwave" and "SW" throughout this chapter to apply to both the Netscape-compatible plug-in and MIE-compatible ActiveX control (for Windows only) unless stated otherwise.

 Director 7, SW7, and SW6.0.1 use the Portable Player's Idealized Machine Layer (IML)—a completely different codebase than SW6.0, Director 6.0.x, or Director 6.5. See *http://www.director-online. com/Features/MI/MI106.html*.

Shockwave 7 introduces a completely new method of downloading and updating the SW plug-in. The major portion of SW7 is downloaded once, after which minor updates can be optionally downloaded automatically. The initial Shockwave 7 installation is in two stages. First, a small browser-specific "shim" is downloaded, along with a "Shockwave Download" program (both are placed in the browser plug-ins folder). If necessary, the shim will download the Shockwave System Libraries (IMLlib and DPlib) and the default Xtras in to the Shockwave System folder. (As SW7 does not support Windows 3.1 and Mac 68K platforms, Macromedia's site will direct such users to the Shockwave 6 download.) Shockwave 7 introduces a massive structural change. Shockwave is now a shared system component that can be accessed from multiple browsers, Slim Projectors, and the new ShockMachine (a local Shockwave-based player).

Supported Plug-ins

Table 11-1 lists the supported browsers for each platform. See Macromedia Tech-Note #03909, "Guide to Shockwave browser and platform compatibility."

Note that MIE 4 is not officially supported on the Macintosh with SW6, but MIE 4.0.1 is supported with SW7. Note that SW7 does not support Windows 3.1 and 68K Macintoshes. Beta versions of Windows 98 are not supported. Macromedia strongly recommends using the final release version of a given browser, not a beta version, which may exhibit inconsistent behavior.

Table 11-1: Supported Platforms

Platform	Supported Browsers	SW Plug-In
Macintosh 68K[1]	Netscape 2.02 through 4.0 MIE 3.0	Netscape 68K plug-In for SW6
PowerMac	Netscape 2.02 through 4.0 MIE 3.0 or MIE 4.0.1 (SW7)	Netscape PPC plug-In
Windows 3.1	Netscape 2.02 through 4.0	Netscape plug-In for SW6
Windows 95/98/NT	MIE 3.0 or MIE 4.0	ActiveX Control[2]
Windows 95/98/NT	Netscape 2.02 through 4.0	Netscape plug-In

[1] 68K Macintoshes must have a 68040 processor and an FPU (math coprocessor) to support streaming Shockwave.
[2] MIE supports Netscape-compatible plug-ins, including Shockwave, but the SW ActiveX control is strongly recommended when using MIE on Win 32 systems.

AOL support

As of January 1999, AOL's browser is based on MIE's engine. It is unclear how AOL's acquisition of Netscape may affect the AOL browser in the near future. AOL recently announced support for Shockwave. AOL users need not use the default browser; they might use Netscape or MIE as with any other ISP.

See Macromedia TechNote #01303, "Can I use AOL's browser to view Director Shockwave movies?" and see "Shockwave for AOL Users" at *http://multimedia. aol.com/internal/dshck.htm.*

Browser Memory Requirements

Shockwave-enabled browsers can be real memory hogs. Under Windows, memory is allocated dynamically. On the Macintosh, the memory to be allocated to an application is specified using the Finder's File ➤ Get Info command (and can be augmented with temporary memory if so configured).

Table 11-2 shows the default memory allocations for Macintosh browsers with and without Shockwave (Windows memory requirements are presumably comparable, although not fixed). The Shockwave installers will update the browser's preferred memory requirements, but if sufficient memory is not available, the Shockwave plug-in may not load. The browser's disk cache should be increased to 15 MB for Shockwave use.

Table 11-2: Macintosh Browser Memory Requirements

Browser	Default Without Shockwave	RAM Required by SW
Netscape 2.0.1	4,296 KB	8,192 KB
Netscape 3.0	6,144 KB	14,000 KB
Netscape 4.0.5	9,630 KB	17,500 KB
MIE 3.0	5,214 KB	8,192 KB
MIE 4.0.1	6,185 KB	8,192 KB
AOL 3.0.1	7,747 KB	8,192 KB

Your First Shockwave Movie

If using Netscape and some versions of MIE with SW installed, you can simply drop your DIR, DXR, or DCR file into an open browser window to test it. In D7, use the File ➤ Preview in Browser option. The steps to create a legitimate Shocked movie for testing and distribution are:

1. Create a standard Director DIR movie, keeping in mind the caveats under "Shockwave Differences" later in this chapter.

2. Set the *Streaming* options under Modify ➤ Movies ➤ Playback.

3. Shock the DIR movie and any external castLibs to create DCR and CCT files (see Tables 11-3 and 4-3).

4. Ensure that the Shockwave plug-in for your browser is properly installed.

5. Create an HTML page for the movie as described under "Running a Shocked Movie on a Web Page" later in this chapter.

6. With most browsers, you can test the Shocked HTML page locally from your hard drive. Linked media must be in the browser support folder or under a folder named *DSWMEDIA* to allow local testing. You can also use a local web server application to test locally.

7. Upload the HTML page, Shocked files (DCR and CCT files), and any external files (SWA, GIF, JPEG) to your server and ensure that the server is properly configured (see "Uploading Shocked Files to a Web Server" later in this chapter).

8. Test the Shocked page in various browsers, platforms, and with various versions of the Shockwave plug-ins.

Table 11-3 lists the common Shockwave-related operations. Shocked movies can also be played as the main movie or as a MIAW from within a Projector.

Table 11-3: Shocking Movie, castLibs, and Audio

Command	Action
Set streaming mode for the movie[1]	Modify ➤ Movies ➤ Playback ➤ Streaming
Shock a single movie[1]	File ➤ Save As Shockwave Movie
Shock a batch of movies[1]	Xtras ➤ Update Movies ➤ Convert to Shockwave Movies
Enable Shockwave compression of internal audio[1,2]	Xtras ➤ Shockwave for Audio Settings ➤ Enable
Shock external audio files on Windows[1]	Xtras ➤ Convert WAV to SWA
Shock external audio files on Macintosh (requires SoundEdit 16 or Peak LE and PowerMac)[3]	In SoundEdit 16 v2.0.7: Xtras ➤ Shockwave for Audio Settings File ➤ Export ➤ Export Type ➤ SWA File In Peak LE: File ➤ Save As ➤ File Type ➤ SWA
Link to SWA cast member at arbitrary URL[1]	Insert ➤ Media ➤ Shockwave Audio
Shock a movie in Director 5	Download and install *AfterBurner* Xtra,[4] then choose Xtra ➤ AfterBurner
Shock a movie in Director 4	Download and use standalone, drag-and-drop AfterBurner executable[4]

[1] New in Director 6 and supported in D7.
[2] By default, internal sounds in DCR and CCT files are not SWA-compressed. See Chapter 15, *Sound and Cue Points*.
[3] Requires SWA Export Xtra and SWA Settings (SE16) Xtra in the Macintosh *System Folder:Macromedia:Xtras* folder or Peak Plugins folder. Shockwave for D5 supports streaming audio creation using D5 for Windows or SoundEdit 16 on Macintosh. Streaming audio Xtras come bundled with the AfterBurner downloads for Director 5.
[4] AfterBurner for Director 4 or 5 is available at no charge at: *http://www.macromedia.com/support/director/how/shock/director_devtools.html*.

Obtaining Test Plug-ins and Browsers

You should obtain both current and older versions of Netscape and MIE for platforms you intend to support, and test your content with the appropriate Shockwave plug-ins. AOL sends out free trial versions of their software, which you can use to test with their custom browsers.

You can download current and older versions of Netscape and MIE at:

http://home.netscape.com/download/index.html
http://www.microsoft.com/windows/ie/download/

Beware when installing MIE4 unless you intend to do so permanently. Users have reported difficulty uninstalling it. Netscape's site provides instructions on setting the default browser and uninstalling various versions of MIE for both Mac and Windows, including MIE4 for Win 95, at:

http://home.netscape.com/download/remove_ie40_win95.html

You can download Netscape-compatible plug-ins for all platforms from:

http://www.macromedia.com/shockwave/download/alternates/index.html

As long as you don't run two browsers at the same time, you can install the SW6 Netscape plug-in once, and create aliases or shortcuts to it as necessary. SW7 plug-ins all use common components stored in a shared system folder. Only a small "shim" plug-in need be downloaded for additional browsers.

ActiveX controls (CAB files), including Shockwave for MIE on Windows 95/98/NT, are designed to be downloaded and installed automatically when needed. Macromedia doesn't provide a manual download, so you can't obtain the ActiveX control from their site, unless you're using MIE on a Win32 system. You can however, download the SW6 ActiveX control installer from:

http://www.microsoft.com/msdownload/ieplatform/shockwave/shockwave.htm

Shockwave is available from many other places, including:

- CD-ROM and OEM versions of Windows, Mac OS, MIE, Netscape, and AOL, plus Internet startup kits distributed by ISPs. (Microsoft's CDs and OEM bundles include the ActiveX control, and Netscape's CDs and OEM bundles include the Netscape plug-in.) See the list of OEM distributions at *http://www.macromedia.com/support/shockwave/info/distribution/*.

- Although not included in the downloadable versions of MIE and Netscape, Shockwave is offered for download on both browsers under *Optional components* on their respective web pages.

- Windows 98 includes the SW ActiveX control, but not the Netscape plug-in.

- CD-ROMs accompanying third-party books on Director may include Shockwave.

- New Macintoshes include Shockwave.

- The current version of AOL includes Shockwave.

Many of these sources include SW6 or even SW5. They should be updated to include SW7 sometime during 1999.

Shockwave installation in Windows 98

The SW6 ActiveX control is included on preinstalled copies of Windows 98 or if the user chooses a Typical installation (SW7 should be included sometime in 1999). It is not included in a Minimal installation and is listed under *Multimedia* during a Custom installation. After installing Windows 98, the ActiveX control can be installed at any time (may require the Windows 98 CD):

1. Select Start ➤ Settings ➤ Control Panel and double-click the *Add/ Remove Programs* icon.
2. Click the *Windows Setup* tab and select *Multimedia* from the list of Components.
3. Click *Details* and select *Macromedia Shockwave.*

Users Obtaining the Shockwave Plug-In

To view your Shocked content, the user must download the appropriate Shockwave plug-in for his particular browser. Some users will inevitably fail and not be able to view your Shocked site. Don't worry, because Shocked sites are usually free and the users won't be able to view other Shocked sites, either. The AfterShock utility included with Director facilitates creating alternative versions of HTML pages for non-Shocked browsers.

The Shockwave 6 download included Shockwave for Director, Shockwave for Flash, the Flash Asset Xtra (for playing Flash content in Director), and two Xtras for streaming SWA. The Shockwave 7 download also includes the Flash, Font, Text, Network, Multiuser, and SWA Xtras (with others optionally downloadable) plus the WinSockLib on PowerMacs. SW7.0.1 also includes the DirectSound Mixer under Windows.

You can leave it entirely up to the user to obtain Shockwave from one of the sources listed earlier or make it easier for them, as described next. If the plug-in is not available, the user will see a broken puzzle piece (in Netscape) or red X (in MIE) and possibly receive an error message.

There are several possibilities when a user enters your site without SW installed or if you want to provide Shockwave for local content to users without Internet connections:

- If you haven't specified appropriate attributes in your HTML OBJECT or EMBED tags (see "HTML Tags" later in this chapter), the user will be prompted to access the default Netscape or MIE plug-ins page where Shockwave is listed.

- If you've included the appropriate attributes in your HTML OBJECT or EMBED tags, Windows 95/98/NT browsers will automatically attempt to download the SW ActiveX control. Other browsers will be sent to the Macromedia's Shockwave Download Center.

- You can rely on the user to click on a *Get Shockwave* button linked to the Shockwave Download Center, or linked to Macromedia's Smart Shockwave JavaScript utility that automates Shockwave installation somewhat.

- You can write your own JavaScript, CGI script, and/or HTML to detect whether the user has Shockwave or to initiate downloading the correct plug-in. This is a complex task considering the number of browsers, some of which don't support JavaScript (most notably MIE on the Mac). Unless you are an expert, you are better off letting the user initiate Shockwave installation via a *Get Shockwave* button.

- You can license Shockwave for distribution from your site or on a CD-ROM, but as of February 1999, it was quite expensive. See *http://www.macromedia.com/support/shockwave/info/licensing/dir_flash/contents.html*. Instead, you can license Navigator or MIE for distribution. Their installers include the Shockwave installer.

- Use the `File` ➤ `Save as Java` feature to create interactive sites that don't require Shockwave.

- Once the user has installed SW7, future updates will be automated.

Netscape Now Button

Provide a *Netscape Now* button to encourage users to view your site with Netscape Navigator. Details on the Netscape Now program can be found at:

> *http://search.netscape.com/comprod/mirror/netscape_now_program.html*

The Netscape Now graphic itself can be obtained from:

> *http://home.netscape.com/download/netscape_now.html*

Your *Netscape Now* button should not link to Netscape's home page, but to:

> *http://search.netscape.com/comprod/mirror/index.html*

Search Netscape's site for the phrase "Netscape Now" for more details on the program and buttons in different languages.

Get Internet Explorer Button

Provide a *Get Internet Explorer* button to encourage users to view your site with Microsoft Internet Explorer (note that MIE is not recommend for Macintosh Shockwave 6 users). Details on the Get Internet Explorer program can be found at:

> *http://www.microsoft.com/sbnmember/ielogo/default.asp*

The Get Internet Explorer graphic itself can be obtained from:

> *http://www.microsoft.com/ie/logo.asp*

Your *Get Internet Explorer* button should link to:

> *http://www.microsoft.com/ie/download/*

Get Shockwave Button

You should alert users that your site requires Shockwave and provide a *Get Shock-wave* button on the HTML page where you expect them to enter your site and before they enter any section requiring Shockwave. The requirements for displaying the *Get Shockwave* button are at:

http://www.macromedia.com/support/programs/mwm/swb.html

The Get Shockwave graphic itself can be obtained from:

http://www.macromedia.com/support/programs/mwm/images/ get_shockwave.gif

Upload the *get_shockwave.gif* file to your server and use it in your HTML pages in one of the following ways:

- You can link your *Get Shockwave* button to Smart Shockwave.

- Link to the Shockwave Download Center (for any Shockwave Player including Flash):

  http://www.macromedia.com/shockwave/download/

- Link to the Shockwave for Director download directly:

  http://www.macromedia.com/shockwave/download/index.cgi?P1_Prod_ Version=Shockwave

To open the Shockwave Download Center in a separate window so that visitors will not leave your site, add a target attribute to your link:

```
<a href="http://www.macromedia.com/
shockwave/download/index.cgi?P1_Prod_Version=Shockwave"
target="_blank"><IMG SRC = "http://www.zeusprod.com/images/get_
shockwave.gif"</a>
```

Smart Shockwave

Smart Shockwave is a JavaScript utility from Macromedia that attempts to intelligently determine which version of the Shockwave plug-ins (for Director and/or Flash) the user has installed. It works best with JavaScript-capable browsers (non-JavaScript browsers simply lead to the Shockwave download page). It opens a small status window to download the appropriate Netscape plug-in or ActiveX control and attempts to install the plug-in without requiring the user to leave your site or restart their browser.

Smart Shockwave attempts to automatically update the user's Shockwave plug-in to the version that you specify in your HTML code (see Example 11-1). If the user has the correct version or a later version, Smart Shockwave does nothing.

Linking to the Smart Shockwave JavaScript library on Macromedia's server increases the likelihood that your page will work with existing and future browsers and plug-ins. Complete details about Smart Shockwave can be found at *http://www.macromedia.com/shockwave/smart.html* as well as *http://www.zeusprod.com/nutshell/chapters/smartshockwave.html*. Also see my quick guide to JavaScript at *http://www.zeusprod.com/nutshell/chapters/javascript.html*.

Shockwave 7's auto-update capability will obviate Smart Shockwave once the SW7 plug-in permeates the user base (probably late in 1999 or early in 2000).

Using Smart Shockwave is easier for the user than manually installing SW and restarting her browser, but it is not ideal. There is little feedback during the long download and installation process, and long pauses give the impression that something has gone awry. Due to the security features surrounding installation of Java or ActiveX components, the user may encounter dialog boxes asking her to grant "high risk privileges" to the installer without explanation or confirmation.

Shockwave 7 provides much better feedback during installation, but you should visit your site with various browsers *without* Shockwave installed to see what the user's experience will be like.

Checking whether the existing Shockwave version is adequate

See Macromedia's documentation on using Smart Shockwave to specify the required version of the Shockwave plug-in. Some browsers support JavaScript to test the version number of installed plug-ins. If the user's browser is not JavaScript-enabled, it cannot run Smart Shockwave. If the user has an old version of Shockwave, you can run a Shocked test movie that checks the plug-in version from Lingo using the global variable *version* or the undocumented *the productVersion* property (see Table 11-4). If the user doesn't have the current version, you can send him to the Shockwave Download Center.

Such a test movie would have to be created in the *oldest* version of Director/Shockwave that you intend to support.

The CODEBASE parameter in the OBJECT tag specifies the desired version of the ActiveX control. To obtain the latest version of the ActiveX control automatically, specify the latest #version in the CODEBASE parameter as shown in Example 11-1.

In SW7, the distinction among revisions will be blurred. Macromedia may post a new update of SW7 without changing the version number. Shockwave installations so configured will check Macromedia's site for updates approximately once per month, but only when visiting Shocked pages.

Java Export (Save as Java)

Alternatives to Shockwave-based delivery range from animated GIFs to other Netscape plug-ins and ActiveX controls. If you require compatibility with non-Shockwave browsers on Macintosh and Windows and even Unix, the `File` ➤ `Save as Java` feature (which requires the Java Export Xtra included with D6.5 and D7) creates a Java applet that can be played by any Java-capable browser. (From the Java Player, *the runMode* returns `"Java Applet"` and *the platform* property returns `"Java javaVersion, browser, OS"` as described in Table 8-4.)

Unlike Lingo and JavaScript, there is no communication between Lingo and Java— just translation. When exporting to Java, all supported Lingo is translated into Java code. See Macromedia's web site for details on embedding your own Java code to be merged into the final output, inside a Lingo script.

There are numerous output and size optimization options in the dialog box that appears under File ➤ Save as Java, including an option to export Java source (creates a .java file in addition to the DJR file). To use Save as Java under Windows, the source Director (DIR) file should be located in a path that obeys MS-DOS eight-dot-three short filename conventions (no long file or folder names). You can edit the Java source files and compile them in a separate Java compiler.

Java Export has a number of deficiencies compared to Shockwave playback, especially in regard to performance and the supported feature set. Complete details can be found in HTML format in the *Help 6_5/Save as Java Help* subfolder where Director 6.5 is installed or *http://www.macromedia.com/support/director/how/ d7/custom.html* and *http://www.macromedia.com/support/director/how/subjects/ appletauth.html.*

For example, the Java Player is pickier than Lingo about the number and type of arguments passed to a handler. Use a single property list argument instead of a variable number of arguments as tolerated by Lingo. Parent script support is limited. Java variable names are case-sensitive! There is no support for symbols, property lists, MIAWs, primary event handlers, multiple casts, Score recording, the *do* command, or the following cast member types: *#digitalVideo, #richText, #movie, #filmLoop, #palette,* or any type requiring an Xtra.

The Java Export Xtra uses a number of new Xtras in D6.5 and D7, including Java-Convert (*JavaCvnt.x32*), CompileJava, FileXtra, and UI Helper Xtras in the *Xtras/Save As Java Files* folder, and the GIF Export, JPEG Export, Sun AU Import Export, and PICT Import Export Xtras in the *Xtras/MIX* folder.

 Initial reports are that the D7.0 *Save as Java* feature is buggy, especially in its text support. The consensus is to stick with D6.5 until the wrinkles are ironed out.

There are several competing versions of Java. Macromedia uses the Metrowerks Java compiler (*http://www.metrowerks.com*). For general Java information, see *http://java.sun.com/.*

Hermes offers a utility that expands the drawing capability of exported Java files:

http://www.hermes.de/heise/peetsdraw/

Running a Shocked Movie on a Web Page

Shockwave movies are usually embedded in web page just as a GIF or JPEG image would be, and uploaded to a server for web playback. Minimal HTML knowledge is required, and many visual HTML editors (such as DreamWeaver) allow you to drag-and-drop Shockwave movies into a web page. The AfterShock utility (see the *Director 7/AfterShock 2.5/AfterShock Help/ContextHelp.htm* included with D7) generates HTML code[*] for a variety of browser configurations.

A Shockwave movie is added to a page using either an EMBED or OBJECT tag. Note the different syntax used for parameters within each tag.

OBJECT tag parameters require the PARAM attribute (see Table 11-7):

```
<PARAM NAME="paramName" VALUE="ParamValue">
```

EMBED tag parameters are treated like any other attribute:

```
paramName = ParamValue
```

Use both tags to ensure optimal viewing regardless of the browser and plug-in. The OBJECT tag is recognized only by MIE on Win32 systems for use with the SW ActiveX control. All other configurations recognize the EMBED tag, as does MIE if the OBJECT tag is absent (but MIE ignores the PALETTE and PLUGINSPAGE parameters of the EMBED tag.)

Without even creating an HTML page you can drag a DIR, DXR, or DCR file to an empty browser window or use D7's **File ▶ Preview in Browser** option.

HTML Tags

Example 11-1 shows a sample OBJECT tag with an equivalent EMBED tag included inside it. All possible options are not shown in the example.

Example 11-1: A Sample OBJECT and EMBED Tag

```
<BODY>
<OBJECT
ID="ShockwaveMovie"
CLASSID="clsid:166B1BCA-3F9C-11CF-8075-444553540000"
CODEBASE=
"http://active.macromedia.com/director/cabs/sw.cab#version=7,0,1"
WIDTH="512"
HEIGHT="480"
NAME="MovieHandle"
TYPE="application/x-director">
<PARAM NAME="SRC" VALUE="http://www.zeusprod.com/shockwave/nutshell.dcr">
<PARAM NAME="swText" VALUE="some text">
<EMBED SRC="http://www.zeusprod.com/shockwave/nutshell.dcr"
HEIGHT="480" WIDTH="512" NAME="MovieHandle"
swText="some text" TYPE="application/x-director"
BGCOLOR ="#FFFFFF" PALETTE="background"
PLUGINSPAGE="http://www.macromedia.com/shockwave/download/
    index.cgi?P1_Prod_Version=Shockwave">
</OBJECT>
</BODY>
```

Use the AfterShock Utility or the *Generate HTML* option under **File ▶ Save as Shockwave Movie** to automatically create HTML tags.

---

[*] For a full discussion of HTML, see O'Reilly's koala-emblazoned *HTML: The Definitive Guide* by Chuck Musciano and Bill Kennedy.

The possible parameters are:

ID

> Used by the browser or other objects to identify this object for hypertext linking.

CLASSID

> The universal class ID identifies the Shockwave 7 ActiveX control and must be typed exactly as shown. Used by MIE on Win 32 only.

CODEBASE

> If the latest version (7.0.1) is not installed, the CODEBASE tells MIE where to download the ActiveX control from. Enter the CODEBASE exactly as shown in Example 11-1, but change the version number for `sw.cab#version` if an updated ActiveX control is made public.

WIDTH and HEIGHT

> Dimensions of the Shocked movie's Stage. These are optional, but adding WIDTH and HEIGHT tags speeds the load time (dimensions need not be multiples of 16 as for D6's Stage). Image is cropped, not scaled, to specified size.

SRC

> Case-sensitive URL of your Shocked movie. Include the .DCR extension, such as *http://www.zeusprod.com/shockwave/nutshell.dcr.*

NAME

> Specifies a name, such as `MovieHandle`, that is required if you are using Java-Script to send events via the *EvalScript()* function to the Shockwave movie, but not otherwise. The browser includes the NAME string and data obtained from the object when submitting a FORM. (See D7's *postNetText* command.)

PALETTE

> Can be either "*background*" (the default and correct setting in most cases), in which case the browser controls the palette; or "*foreground*", in which case the Shockwave movie's palette is obeyed. (MIE does not support PALETTE="foreground".) Use D7's Netscape-safe "Web216" palette. (In D6, see `Xtras ➤ Libraries ➤ Palette Library`.) Refer to the pretty color pictures and stellar coverage of palettes in *Shockwave Studio: Designing Multimedia for the Web* by Bob Schmitt (Songline Studios).

PLUGINSPAGE

> If Shockwave is not installed, Netscape opens the specified URL. If the PLUGINSPAGE parameter is absent, Netscape send users to its own generic plug-ins list page. MIE ignores the PLUGINSPAGE attribute.

BGCOLOR="#RRGGBB"

> Color of the movie rectangle before movie appears. Use standard six-character RGB color codes. *RR*, *GG*, and *BB* are hexadecimal values each ranging from 00 to FF. #000000 is black. #FFFFFF is white.

ALT

> Alternative text label for browsers without the Shockwave plug-in or those set to not load graphics. You could set it to read "This item requires Shockwave."

TEXTFOCUS

Determines whether Shockwave movie has keyboard focus. Has three possible values: *never, onStart*, or *mouseUp*. Most Shockwave movies requiring keyboard input ask the user to click to start, thus guaranteeing keyboard focus.

AUTOSTART

Determines whether movie plays automatically when it is first loaded or when *Rewind()* is called from JavaScript. Can be true or false.

TYPE

Including the TYPE="application/x-director" attribute guarantees that the document type will be identified for the browser regardless of the server configuration. The browser must still be configured to recognize this document type.

swLiveConnect

Add swLiveConnect="TRUE" if using ExternalEvent with Netscape in SW. It enables LiveScript.

There are two dozen special parameters names, such as *swURL*, defined by the Shockwave ActiveX control used to pass information from an HTML page to an embedded SW movie. The reserved parameter names are shown under the *externalEvent* command in Table 11-7. Their conventional uses are detailed at *http://www.macromedia.com/support/director/how/shock/lingoparam.html.*

For example, the *swFrame* parameter is often used to specify a frame to which the Shockwave movie should jump, such as:

```
go to frame getExternalParam("swFrame") of movie "mymovie.dcr"
```

You can also use *gotoNetMovie* with a marker such as:

```
gotoNetMovie "http://www.yourserver.com/sw/mymovie.dcr#marker"
```

Uploading Shocked Files to a Web Server

Netscape can open a local DIR file that is embedded in an HTML page or that has been drag- and-dropped into an open browser window. MIE 4 can open a local DIR file directly, but may require the HEIGHT and WIDTH tags to recognize a Shockwave movie in an HTML page.

Once you've tested from a local drive, you are ready to test your Shocked content from a web server. You can also test using a local personal web server to save upload time. See Alex Zavatone's article on setting up the Mac OS 8 Personal Web Server at *http://www.director-online.com/howTo/archive/Director_Files/Director02.html.*

You must configure your server's MIME types so that the server identifies the files properly when sending them back to a browser. Your webmaster or ISP should be able to configure your server for Shockwave if it is not already so configured. (Including the TYPE="application/x-director" attribute in your EMBED or OBJECT tag will define the Shocked movie's type even if the server is not so configured.)

For example, to configure the Mac OS 8 Personal Web Server to support DCR and SWF files add the following lines to the file *System:Preferences:Web Sharing Folder:Web Sharing MIME Types*, then restart Web Sharing via its Control Panel:

```
*  'MD00'  *  application x-director
*  'MD97'  *  application x-director
*  'MD95'  *  application x-director
*  'MD93'  *  application x-director
*  'SWFL'  *  application x-shockwave-flash
*  'SWF2'  *  application x-shockwave-flash
```

Choose *Binary* mode when uploading the DCR file to your server with your FTP client. If the server doesn't recognize a file, it will send it as text regardless of the file's format. When viewing Shocked pages, the error, "Could not display plug-in for MIME type Text/HTML," could indicate that the file was uploaded as *Text* instead of *Binary*. Upload it again to be sure.

To check an embedded Shockwave movie's MIME type in Netscape:

1. Open the HTML page containing the Shocked movie in Netscape.

2. Use Netscape View ➤ Page Info to display details about items within the page.

3. Click on the link in the upper pane that is the URL to your DCR file. Information about the link appears in the lower frame.

4. The File MIME Type listing in the lower frame should be "application/x-director". If not, the server is not properly configured with the Shockwave MIME type.

5. If the MIME Type is correct, make sure that your browser recognizes it. In Netscape, choose Edit ➤ Preferences, then expand the Navigator ➤ Applications category (in Netscape 3, MIME types are listed under the *Helper Applications* tab).

6. Scroll down the (randomly ordered) list to find *Director*. Highlight *Director* and choose *Edit*. The MIME Type should be "application/x-director," and the Suffixes should be "dcr, dir, dxr." It should be configured to be Handled by *Plug-in–Shockwave for Director*, not *Application*.

In MIE 4, the MIME types recognized by plug-ins aren't shown under Preferences ➤ Receiving ➤ File Helpers. Use MIE's *About...* box to view plug-ins and the MIME types they recognize.

If you are having problems, make sure that you are using the correct case-sensitive URL, especially with Unix or Linux servers (beware of FTP programs that change case). Errors 201 and 208 generally indicate a damaged file. Upload the file again to your server. See also Macromedia TechNotes #03902, "Shockwave for Windows Troubleshooting and Error Messages," and #03907, "Troubleshooting Shockwave for Macintosh."

When testing in a browser, always begin by testing with a known working Shocked site, such as Macromedia's Test Shockwave page (*http://www.macro media.com/shockwave/welcome.html*). When testing changes, be sure to clear the browser cache and reload/refresh the page.

Netscape doesn't show anything (not even a broken puzzle-piece) if the user disables automatic loading of images. Provide an ALT attribute for the EMBED tag, such as "Load Images to see Shockwave."

Using Linked Media and Xtras

You can use several types of external files, including linked media, external castLibs, and Xtras, when playing a movie in a browser.

Suppose you are linking to external JPEG files from your Director movie (and have the necessary Xtras installed). This works fine in authoring mode and from a Projector, because there are no restrictions on linked media in those environments.

But when you Shock the movie and test it locally from a browser, the JPEG images do not appear, because testing linked media locally from a browser has some limitations. Browsers and the Shockwave plug-in are granted only restricted access to local drives (any URLs beginning with *file://* are subject to these limits).

To use local media linked to a local Director movie in a local browser, create a folder named *DSWMEDIA* to create a "safe" area on a local drive. All your local Shockwave content, including your DIR or DCR file, should be within (below) this *DSWMEDIA* umbrella. (URLs using the *http://* protocol and URLs using the *file://* protocol from within a Projector are not limited in this way.)

The *DSWMEDIA* folder is necessary only for local testing of linked media and linked external castLibs. The *DSWMEDIA* umbrella is not required on a web server. Files will work when uploaded to a web folder of any name. Linked assets placed in the browser's "support" folder (explained in next section) need not be under a *DSWMEDIA* folder.

SW6.0 and later plug-ins require that local linked assets reside in the Shockwave support folder or under a *DSWMEDIA* folder. There only two operations that can access data outside of the support folder or *DSWMEDIA* folders: *gotoNetPage* and (perhaps) *gotoNetMovie*.

SW5 could load linked files located in the browser's support folder. Shockwave 5 movies played within a browser could use local linked media in any folder. (Local media could be played without the *DSWMEDIA* folder in SW5, but the convention was to place local linked files into the support folder, which still works in SW6 and SW7.)

Name and path resolution in Shockwave

Certain commands will work from a Projector, but not from SW. For example:

```
go movie "mymovie"
```

will work in Director when running locally, because Director can search for files such as *myMovie.DIR*. But Shockwave can't search a remote directory on a web server. If the filename is not complete, a "404 url not found" error is returned. Use this instead:

```
go movie "mymovie.dcr"
```

Note also that filenames are case-insensitive when tested locally, but case-sensitive on most web servers. The file *ReadMe for Authoring with Shockwave 6.0.1* contains full details on path verification within Shockwave and Director. See *http://www.macromedia.com/support/shockwave/ts/documents/shockwave_601 _readme.htm.*

Support, Preferences, and Xtras Folders

This section lists the names of the plug-ins and the path to the *Prefs* and *Xtras* folders (which vary with the browser and the Shockwave plug-in). The following example folders are for Netscape on a PowerMac.

The browser's *Plug-ins* folder should contain the Shockwave for Director 6 or Director 7 plug-in (although SW7 also places components in the system folder):

> *Netscape Navigator™ Folder:Plug-ins:NP-PPC-Dir-Shockwave*

The *Plug-ins* folder may contain the Shockwave for Flash player (*Shockwave Flash NP-68K, Shockwave Flash NP-PPC*, etc.) and the *ShockwavePlugin.class* and *Shock- waveFlash.class* Java class files.

The support folder contains the *Prefs* and *Xtras* subfolders, plus the Xtras cache file (*dirapi.mch*). For SW7, the preferences folder is called *Prefs* and below the Shockwave 7 System folder cited earlier.

The SW7 for Macintosh support folder is:

> *SystemFolder:Extensions:Macromedia:Shockwave:*

and the *Xtras* and *Prefs* subfolders are within that folder regardless of the browser.

For Windows, the SW7 support folder is:

> *C:\Windows\System\Macromed\Shockwave*

The support folder for Shockwave 6 is named for the plug-in itself:

> *Netscape Navigator™ Folder:Plug-ins:NP-PPC-Dir-ShockwaveFolder*

The *Xtras* folder for SW6 would be called:

> *Netscape Navigator™ Folder:Plug-ins: NP-PPC-Dir-Shockwave folder:Xtras:*

Here are the paths to the support, *Prefs*, and *Xtras* folders for some other plat- forms and browsers when using SW6. (Keep in mind that the path may vary if the user has installed the browser in a different folder.)

SW6 for Netscape on Macintosh 68K:

> *Netscape Navigator™ Folder:Plug-ins:NP-68K-Dir-Shockwave folder:*

SW6 for MIE on PowerMac:

> *Internet Explorer 4.0 Folder:Plug-ins:NP-PPC-Dir-Shockwave folder:*

SW6 for AOL on Mac:

> *America Online v3.0:Plug-ins:NP-PPC-Dir-Shockwave folder:*

SW6 for Netscape for Windows:

> *C:\Program Files\Netscape\Program\Plugins\NP32DSW*

SW6 for Internet Explorer for Windows:

C:\Program Files\Internet Explorer\Program\NP32DSW

Preferences Files

The *getPref* and *setPref* commands are supported in D6 and D7, but were designed primarily for Shockwave, which has supported them since SW4. (*GetPref* and *setPref* can be used from Director or Projectors, but *setPref* won't work from a read-only drive, such as a CD-ROM.)

SetPref writes text to a preferences file, and *getPref* retrieves it (*setPref* will create or overwrite the file as necessary):

```
setPref (prefFile, prefText)
set prefText = getPref(prefFile)
```

The file must have a .TXT or .HTM extension; the default is .TXT. You can have multiple preference files, each up to 32 KB in length. Don't specify a folder as part of the file path, because preferences files always go in a fixed folder.

On the Macintosh, in SW6, the *prefFile* would be:

Navigator Folder:Plug-ins:NP-PPC-Dir-Shockwave folder:Prefs:prefFile.txt

Under Windows, in SW6, it would be:

C:\Program Files\Netscape\Program\plugins\NP32DSW\Prefs\prefFile.txt
C:\Program Files\Internet Explorer\Program\NP32DSW\Prefs\prefFile.txt

From Director or a Projector on the Macintosh, the preferences folder resides beneath Director or the Projector, and is named after the application writing the prefs file such as:

ApplicationName folder:Prefs:

For example the preferences written during authoring might be:

MacHD:Applications:Director 7.0:Director 7.0 folder:Prefs:prefFile.txt

or the preferences written from a Projector in the root of a drive might be:

MyDrive:Projector folder:Prefs:prefFile.txt

From Director or a Projector under Windows, the preferences folder is named *Prefs* and resides beneath Director or the Projector, such as:

C:\Program Files\Macromedia\Director 7\Prefs\prefFile.txt
D:\Prefs\prefFile.txt

For additional details, see Chapter 14, *External Files*, in *Lingo in a Nutshell*.

browserName()

The *browserName()* function can get or set the browser used for *gotoNetPage()*. On the Macintosh, *browserName()* looks in the desktop database, first for Netscape (by both its folder name and its creator code, "MOSS") and then for MIE if it can't find Netscape. It ignores the Internet Config helper application for "http" files.

Under Windows, *browserName()* returns the application registered to handle "open" events for HTML documents in the Windows Registry file.

Use *browserName(newName)* to specify a different browser for use with *gotonetPage*, etc. During authoring, it can be set under File ➤ Preferences ➤ Network and is also used for HTML-based help files. See also the *proxyServer* command in Table 11-5.

Xtras in Shockwave

Shockwave & the Internet

Shockwave 7 adds the ability to automatically download and install digitally signed Shockwave-safe Xtras. Only Xtras compiled as Shockwave-safe by the Xtra developer will be recognized by SW7. The *XtraInfo.TXT* file controls downloading of Xtras. Edit the *#package* property for an Xtra in the *XtraInfo.TXT* file (in the folder in which Director is installed) before creating your DCR files. See *http://www.zeus-prod.com/nutshell/packaging.html* for details on Xtra packaging.

For details on the general use of Xtras, including details specific to Shockwave, see Chapter 10, *Using Xtras*.

Many Xtras are automatically installed with Shockwave 7 and the equivalent of some Xtras needed in Projectors are built into the Shockwave plug-in itself. SW6 does not support automatic Xtra downloading. To use additional Xtras in SW6, the user must manually download each Xtra and place them in the *Xtras* folder inside the browser's support folder described earlier (an *Xtras* subfolder is used by convention, but anywhere within the support folder is adequate).

Once an Xtra is in the appropriate support folder (which differs for SW6 and SW7), *all* Shockwave movies have access to it. For SW6, Macromedia relies on users to avoid dangerous Xtras from unknown sources. In SW7, they rely on Veri-Sign to identify the packager of an Xtra, and they rely on Xtra developers to mark only truly safe Xtras as Shockwave-safe. This is the same security model adopted by Microsoft for ActiveX controls.

Shockwave 6.0 required the MIX Services Xtra (see Table 10-3) to be downloaded into the support folder to allow runtime access to any external graphics and sound files. The GIF Import and JPEG Import Xtras were needed to link to JPEG and GIF images. Other MIX Xtras could be downloaded to access other file types, such as TIFFs.

Support for linked GIF and JPEG images, AIFF files (compressed and uncompressed), Shockwave Audio, and WAVE files (uncompressed only) is built into SW6.0.1. These graphic and sound file formats (and only these formats) can be used in SW6.0.1 without first downloading any Xtras; other MIX Xtras are completely ignored by SW6.0.1 even if present in the browser's support folder. Shockwave 6.0.1 can still use other non-MIX Xtras, such as Sprite Asset Xtras, including the QuickTime Asset Xtra, Alphamania, Lingo Xtras, and Transition Xtras.

SW7 includes built-in support for the same formats as SW6.0.1 (GIF, JPEG, AIFF, SWA, and WAVE), but will also recognize MIX Xtras for enhanced support of additional graphic and sound formats. Macromedia makes the following Xtras available for download in Shockwave 7: Animated GIF, Custom Cursor, MIX Services, MPEG 3, QuickTime 3, Sound, SunAU, SWA Import, and XML Parser. The Text, Font, SWA decompression, Multiuser, and Flash Xtras are installed by default with SW7, and automatic updates are also available. D7.0.1 for Windows also includes the DirectSound Xtra.

Streaming Playback

Shockwave 6 added optional streaming of Shockwave content from the Internet and SW7 content always streams. Unlike earlier versions, in SW6 and SW7 the entire Shockwave movie need not finish downloading before playback begins. This requires special care to ensure that cast members are downloaded before they are needed. Even when streamed, Shockwave first downloads the Score data, script, font, and QuickDraw shape cast members, and the size of each cast member's bounding rectangle. Keep the Score short and the number and size of cast members (especially scripts) small. Shockwave downloads the remaining cast members in the order in which they appear in the Score. When the number of frames specified under Modify ➤ Movie ➤ Playback have been downloaded, the movie begins playing, and Shockwave continues to download cast members in the background.

Use small cast members, preferably shapes, for an introductory animation while the movie continues to download in the background. SW7's support for vector shape cast members and for colorizing, rotating, skewing, quadding, and flipping sprites helps create very compact movies.

See the example of Shockwave streaming at:

> *http://www.macromedia.com/support/director/how/show/geofactsdemo.html*

The D7 Studio's Internet Streaming Behaviors under Window ➤ Library Palette include a number of net-related Behaviors that wait for media to download. (In D6, see the Xtras ➤ Behavior Library menu.)

Use Modify ➤ Movie ➤ Playback to set a movie's streaming options before saving it as a Shockwave movie. These options vary slightly in D6 and D7:

Wait For All Media (D6) or Play While Downloading Movie (D7)
Disables streaming. Movie downloads in its entirety before playing. In D7, streaming is enabled by default.

Use Media as Available (D6 only)
The standard option for streaming playback. Cast members appear on the Stage as they are downloaded, and are blank before that. (Equivalent to leaving "Show Placeholders" unchecked in D7.)

Show Placeholders (D6 and D7)
Movie displays placeholders for media that has not yet downloaded (useful for testing and slow connections).

Pre-Fetch (D6) or Download n Frames Before (D7)
Enter the number of frames to download (perhaps 5) before the movie starts playing. All frames are pre-fetched in SW6's *Wait for All Media* mode.

The new Shockwave pop-up menu in SW7 also allows you to set options for playback in the ShockMachine, including Volume Control, Transport Control, Custom Caching, Zooming, Save Local, and Graphic menu. This menu is accessed via the right mouse button (under Windows) or Ctrl-click (on Macintosh). See *http://www.zeusprod.com/nutshell/shockmachine.html* for the latest ShockMachine details.

StreamStatus Events

StreamStatus events provide rudimentary feedback about a download's progress, but there is no way to force a *streamStatus* event in D6 or SW6. If you enable *streamStatus* events using *tellStreamStatus(TRUE)*, your *on streamStatus* handler (which must be in a movie script) will be called periodically. In D7 or SW7, use *getStreamStatus()* to check a stream at any time.

There is no automatic way to determine the number of active streams or the URLs that are currently streaming. You must check for streams' completion manually using *netDone()* and *netStatus()* with the netID returned by the initial network operation call. You can track streams over time by checking the parameters received by *on streamStatus*.

Do not initiate more than four simultaneous streams. This is the default limit for most browsers and more streams severely degrade performance. Even with fewer streams, foreground animation performance may suffer markedly.

NetThrottleTicks (Macintosh Projectors Only)

The *netThrottleTicks* property (unsupported in D6, and officially supported in D7) determines how frequently Director is interrupted to attend to network operations. The default is 15 ticks (4 times per second). Higher values interrupt Director less often to perform network operations, so it will have more time to perform animation. It affects Projectors under the Mac OS only, not in Windows (whose process management is very different) and not in SW (where the browser allocates time slices).

With the *netThrottleTicks* set to 15, animation may degrade to 2 or 3 fps. Setting it to 30 achieves 15 fps; setting it to 60 may achieve 30 fps; setting it to *the maxInteger* prevents all net activity. However, if you *decrease* the *netThrottleTicks*, Macintosh Projectors will download media faster at the expense of animation performance.

Shockwave Differences

For the most part, Shockwave works the same as Director and for the first time in D7, the authoring tool, Projectors, and Shockwave are based on the same engine (see the interview with David Jennings about the Portable Player's Idealized Machine Layer at *http://www.director-online.com/Features/MI/MI106.html*). (The SW6.0.1 plug-in was the first environment to use the new engine, but D6.5 and previous versions used the old M5 engine.)

Because Shockwave content is downloaded from the Internet, pay particular attention to the size of the compressed file. You should perform a File ➤ Save and Compact before Shocking your file as detailed in Table 4-3. Sacrifice appearance or performance in favor of shorter download time by simplifying animations, stretching sprites to minimize the need for additional cast members, and using transitions, inks, blend, patterns, and shapes. Also use D7's new colorization, rotation, and skewing commands instead of multiple cast members.

Features Disabled in Shockwave

There are many commands that don't work in Shockwave; a complete list is available at *http://www.zeusprod.com/chapters/shockwave/notforsw.html*. See also Chapter 17 in Director 7's *Using Director* manual. Any security limitations regarding external file paths, Xtras, external applications, and system commands also apply whenever *the safePlayer* property is TRUE.

The following do not work in Shockwave:

- Movies-in-a-Window

- Custom menus

- Tempo Channel *Wait* settings (use Lingo instead)

- The Loop setting in the Control Panel (use *go frame 1* instead)

- Accessing external files that are outside the Shockwave support or *DSWMEDIA* folders

- Setting *the colorDepth* of the user's monitor

- Commands that open or run external files, such as *open* or *open...with*

- Commands that affect the machine or browser, such as *restart*, *quit*, or *shut-down*

- Any Xtra that is not marked Shockwave-safe (D7 only)

- FileIO, SerialIO, and XObjects and Xtras that open and access files

- Printing using the *printFrom* command (browser's print option may work)

- Using *saveMovie* or *save castLib*

- Anything that represents a security risk, such as *pasteClipBoardInto*

- Using *getNthFileNameInFolder*, *searchCurrentFolder*, *searchPath* with URLs

- *LINGO.INI* file (*on startUp* not supported)

- Unsupported Lingo as shown in Table 11-4

The following items must be in the browser's support folder (beneath the browser's *Plugins* folder in D6 or in the *System* folder in D7):

- Local linked media such as external casts, QuickTime, and AVI files

- Xtras

- XObjects opened with *openXlib* and closed with *closeXlib* (D6 only)

Custom palettes, palette cycling, and palette fades may operate differently in Shockwave where the browser may control the palette.

SW4 and SW5 recognized net-specific Lingo not recognized by D4 or D5, which made testing in D4 and D5 inconvenient. Table 11-5 lists the commands that require the NetLingo Xtra from within a Projector, but are built into Shockwave. Note that *netLastModDate* and *netMIME* are new as of D6 and *netStatus* doesn't work in MIE.

Lingo That Differs in Shockwave and Projectors

Table 11-4 summarizes Lingo commands that differ measurably when used in Shockwave instead of a Projector. Some of these commands are disabled because they are not applicable to the browser environment. Those that are disabled for security reasons won't work in any environment where *the safePlayer* is TRUE. For a list of commands disabled in SW and when *the safePlayer* is TRUE, see *http://www.zeusprod.com/chapters/shockwave/safeplayer.html*.

Table 11-4: Lingo Differences Between Shockwave and Projectors

Command	Shockwave	Projector
the applicationPath	Error[1]	Returns Projector's path or Director's path
browserName( )	Returns EMPTY	Returns default browser name, including path
cacheDocVerify( )	Returns VOID	Returns #once or #always
cacheSize( )	Used only for SW media, not browser	Used for downloaded assets
the centerStage	No effect	Takes effect on next movie
clearCache( )	Clears SW *getNetText( )* cache only, not browser cache	Clears cached downloaded files
the colorDepth	Can be read but not set	Can be set on most computers
copyToClipboard	*pasteClipBoardInto* doesn't work; Cmd/Ctrl-C shortcut doesn't work	Copies any cast member to clipboard; Cmd/Ctrl-C copies text
do	Can only execute supported commands	Can execute any command
downloadNetThing( )	Can't download to arbitrary location. Use preloadNetThing instead	Downloads Internet-based item to any local folder
ExternalEvent	Sent to browser	Prints in Message window during authoring; no effect in Projector
the filename of castLib	Requires .CCT extension on castLib name	Extension optional; finds CST, CXT, and CCT files automatically
the filename of member	Can only access media in Shockwave support or *DSWMEDIA* folders	Can access media anywhere
the fixStageSize	Size of SW object is always fixed	Takes effect on next movie
getNthFileNameInFolder( )	Doesn't work with URLs	Works with local files
getPref( )	Uses Shockwave support folder	Uses folder beneath Projector

Table 11-4: Lingo Differences Between Shockwave and Projectors (continued)

Command	Shockwave	Projector
go movie	Fails if movie not found; requires .DCR extension for movie name.	Brings up "Where is?" dialog box if file not found
gotoNetMovie()	Goes to new HTML page from within browser; requires .DCR extension for movie name	Launches browser and goes to URL
gotoNetPage()	Replaces the Shocked page	Launches browser and displays the page
importFileInto	Imports from support folder only; requires *preloadNetThing*, and wait for *netDone*	Imports instantly from any local folder
the machineType	Erroneous values returned by SW6.0	Returns same values as SW6.0.1 and SW7
the mediaReady of member	FALSE until media is downloaded	Always true for local media
netDone()	Never returns TRUE if checked in a tight *repeat* loop	May complete even if checked in tight *repeat* loop (not recommended).
netPresent()	Always returns TRUE; no Xtras required	Use *the netPresent* instead
the netPresent	Returns meaningless integer; do not use	Returns TRUE if NetLingo and NetFile Xtras are installed
netStatus	Sends to browser status line	Prints in Message window during authoring
pasteClipBoardInto	Error[1]	Allowed
the picture of member *fieldMember*	SW6.0.1 returns VOID, but SW6.0 returns correct picture handle	Authoring and Projectors return correct picture handle
the platform	Returns plug-in type, such as "Macintosh,PowerPC"	Returns Projector type, even if not native
printFrom	Disabled	Prints the Stage
the productVersion	"6.0", "6.0.1", "7.0", or "7.0.1"	"6.0", "6.0.1", "6.0.2", "6.5", "7.0", or "7.0.1"
the runMode	"Plugin" or "Java Applet"	"Author" or "Projector"
the safePlayer	Always 1 (TRUE)	Defaults to 0 (FALSE)
searchCurrentFolder	Doesn't work with URLs	Works with local files
searchPath or the searchPaths	Doesn't work with URLs	Works with local files

Command	Shockwave	Projector
setPref	Uses Shockwave support folder	Uses folder beneath Projector
version (must declare as global)	"6.0 net", "6.0r59 (pp) net", "6.0.1 net", "7.0 net", or "7.0.1 net"	"6.0", "6.0.1", "6.0.2", "6.5", "7.0", or "7.0.1"

1 Causes "Use of unsupported Lingo command" error.

Projectors That Access the Internet

Projectors can also access remote content on the Internet. Network data often takes a long time to download, and Director allows *background loading* to minimize its effect on animation and user interaction. Note that "loading" from the Internet means that the file has been downloaded to the local disk cache. This is not the same as preloading cast members into memory (although the latter happens much faster once the data is on the local drive).

Network operations tend to be slow, so there is a lag between the time that data is requested and when it is actually available. So-called *NetLingo* commands made possible via the NetLingo Xtra are *asynchronous*. The result of a NetLingo command is generally not available immediately. Additional commands (generally placed in a different handler such as an *idle* handler) are used to check the status of the previous request and to obtain the requested data when it becomes available. All NetLingo commands that eventually obtain data from a network will return a netID that is used to check the status and obtain the final data.

The steps to perform a network operation are:

1. Start the operation, such as *set netID=getNetText(url)*.

2. Use *netDone(netID)* to check at appropriate intervals whether the operation is complete.

3. Use *netError()* to check the status once the operation is done.

4. Read the downloaded data using the appropriate commands.

Using a repeat loop to check whether an asynchronous operation is complete won't work, because the repeat loop monopolizes the processor. Wait for completion in an *on idle* or *on exitFrame* handler instead, as shown in Example 11-2.

Example 11-2: Reading Data from the Internet

```
on mouseDown
   global gNetID
   set gNetID = getNetText("http://www.zeusprod.com/news/new.html")
end mouseDown

on exitFrame
   global gNetID
   if netDone(gNetID) then
```

Example 11-2: Reading Data from the Internet (continued)

```
    if netError(netID)="ok" then
      set the text of member "SomeField" = netTextResult(gNetID)
    endif
  else
   go the frame
  end if
end exitFrame
```

To pass variables to a CGI script and retrieve the result from the CGI script, use:

```
    set netID = getNetText ("http://www.zeusprod.com/cgi_bin/
      some_cgi?var1=val1&var2=val2")
```

followed by *netDone()* and *getNetText()* as in Example 11-2. You can sometimes send email with the browser's email program using, for example, *gotoNetPage "mailto: lingonut@zeusprod.com"*.

Table 11-5 shows all the NetLingo commands built into Shockwave, but which require the NetLingo Xtra during authoring or in a Projector.

Table 11-5: NetLingo Commands

Command	Usage

browserName[1]	Gets or sets the browser used by gotoNetPage, and File ➤ Preview in Browser:
	`set browserPath = browserName()`
	`browserName newBrowserPath`

cacheDocVerify[1]	Determines whether items are cached or re-read every time each time they're requested:
	`cacheDocVerify(#once | #always)`
	`if cacheDocVerify() = #always then...`

cacheSize[1]	Defines Director's cache size in KB. Defaults to 2000 KB (2 MB):
	`put cacheSize()`
	`cacheSize (newSizeInKiloBytes)`

clearCache[1]	Clears Projector cache. Fixes memory leak caused by repeated cells to *getNetText()* in D6.
downloadNetThing (url, localfile)[2]	Downloads a file from the server to a specified file on a local disk for later use. The current movie continues playing while the file downloads. Can also copy local files if the source URL is local.
ExternalEvent	In Shockwave, sends a command to the browser to be interpreted by JavaScript or VBScript.
getLatestNetID()[2]	Returns a unique *netID* for the last asynchronous operation started. It was needed in SW5, because network operations didn't return a *netID*. In SW6 and SW7, obtain the *netID* from the original call to *getNetText*, etc.
getNetText (url{, charSet})[2]	Initiates retrieval of file from *url*. Can also send data to CGI scripts. Use *netTextResult()* to retrieve the text once downloading completes. See *postNetText* in SW7. Optional character set parameter is "AUTO", "ASCII", "JIS", or "EUC".

Table 11-5: NetLingo Commands (continued)

Command	Usage
getStreamStatus (*netID*) getStreamStatus (*url*)	Tracks the status of asynchronous net operations (new in D7). Returns a property list containing the #url, #state, #bytesSoFar, #bytesTotal, and #error values typically received by *on streamStatus* without waiting for a *streamStatus* event.
gotoNetMovie (*url*)[2]	Retrieves and plays a new SW movie from *url*. The current movie runs until the new movie is ready, which then replaces old movie (without warning) in the same display on web page. Subsequent *gotoNetMovie* commands override pending ones. Use *gotoNetMovie( )* after downloading an Xtra in SW7 to load the new Xtra.
gotoNetPage (*url* {, target*})[2]	Loads any URL (SW movie, HTML file, or other MIME type) into current page or *target*. In SW, replaces the current page. From Projector, launches a browser to displays the page. Does not return a value. *target* can be any custom-named frame or reserved names: "_blank", "_self", "_parent", and "_top".
netAbort(*netID*) netAbort(*url*)	Immediately aborts an asynchronous operation identified by *netID* or a URL and clears the value of the operation from the cache. Use *netAbort(url)* before repeating a net operation already in progress with the same URL.
netDone(*netID*)	Returns TRUE if the asynchronous operation tagged by *netID* is complete or FALSE if it is still in progress. Works with *netID* returned by *getNetText( )*, *downloadNetThing( )*, *preloadNetThing( )*, *gotoNetMovie( )*, *gotoNetPage( )*, *postNetText( )*, or *getLatestNetID( )*.
netError(*netID*)	Returns an "OK" (or sometimes 0) for success or an error string. An EMPTY string is returned until the operation is complete as indicated by *netDone( )*.
netLastModDate (*netID*)[3]	Returns the "date last modified" string from the HTTP header for the item denoted by *netID*.
netMIME(*netID*)[3]	Returns the MIME type of the HTTP item denoted by *netID*.
netPresent()	Don't use *netPresent( )* in Director. Use *the netPresent* instead.
netStatus *message*	Displays message on the browser's status line. Include your copyright notice to dissuade infringement.
netTextResult (*netID*)[3]	Returns the text result after *getNetText( )* command completes.

on streamStatus	The on streamStatus handler is called periodically if *tellStreamStatus( )* is TRUE.
	
	`on streamStatus url, state bytesSoFar, bytesTotal, error`
	`    statement(s)`
	`end`
	
	State is "Connecting", "Started", "In Progress", "Complete", or "Error".

*Shockwave &
the Internet*

Table 11-5: NetLingo Commands (continued)

Command	Usage
postNetText[2]	New in D7. Similar to *getNetText( )*. Works with MIE on Mac, contrary to D7 *ReadMe* file. `postNetText(url, propertyList	postText {, serverOS} {,` ` serverCharSet}}` where *serverOS* is "Unix", "Mac", or "Win" and *serverCharSet* is "AUTO", "ASC II", "JIS", or "EUC".
preloadNetThing (*url*)[2]	Preloads a file from server into browser's cache for later use, in the background. Current movie continues to play. Preloading an HTML page does not preload images and movies embedded in the page.
proxyServer	Defines or returns the current proxy http or ftp server. See File ➤ Preferences ➤ Network: `proxyServer #ftp	#http, "ipAddress", portNum` `set portNum = proxyServer (#ftp | #http, #port)` `set IPaddressString = proxyServer (#ftp | #http)` `proxyServer #ftp	#http, #stop`

tellStreamStatus()	Determines whether the *on streamStatus* handler is called during download operations:
	`tellStreamStatus(TRUE | FALSE)`
	`set currentStatus = tellStreamStatus()`

[1] See File ➤ Preferences ➤ Network. Used in Projectors, but not for Shockwave.
[2] The command returns a *netID*. Check the status of the command using *netDone (netID)*.
[3] The *netLastModDate, netMIME*, and *netTextResult* functions can be called only from the time that *netDone* or *netError* reports that the operation is complete until the next operation is started. After the next operation starts, the Director plug-in discards the results of the previous operation to conserve memory.

Communicating with the Browser

Browser scripting, new as of SW6, allows a Shockwave movie to communicate with the browser via LiveConnect (which enables JavaScript in Netscape) or ActiveX (which enables VBScript and JScript in MIE).

 Browser scripting is unreliable in some configurations. *External-Event* calls don't work with MIE on the Macintosh, which does not support browser scripting.

Table 11-6 lists the configurations supporting browser scripting—namely, Java-enabled Netscape 3.0 or 4.0 and 5.0 on PowerMac and Win95/98/NT, and ActiveX-enabled MIE 3.0, 4.0, or 5.0 browsers on Win95/98/NT. Browser scripting fails for Windows 3.1, 68K Macs, MIE on the Mac, Java-disabled or JavaScript-disabled Netscape browsers, MIE on Win95/98/NT using the Netscape plug-in instead of the ActiveX control, browsers low on RAM, and other browser brands. Some commands may not work with older browsers, such as Netscape 2 and MIE3.

Table 11-6: Supported Browser Scripting Configurations

Platform	Browser/Plug-in Combo	Scripting Language
68K Macintosh	Not supported.	N/A
PowerPC	Navigator 3.0 or later with Netscape plug-in. Not supported with IE.	JavaScript (requires Java)
Windows 3.1	Not supported.	N/A
Windows NT 3.5	Not supported.	N/A
Windows 95, 98, and NT 4	Navigator 3.0 or later with Netscape plug-in.	JavaScript (requires Java)
Windows 95, 98, and NT 4	IE 3.0 or later with ActiveX control. (Netscape plug-in not supported).	VBScript

Table 11-7 lists the Lingo commands used to control or react to the browser from within a Shockwave movie. The *externalParamCount()*, *externalParamName()*, and *externalParamValue()* functions use the parameters specified as part of the EMBED or OBJECT tag used to embed the Shockwave movie in the HTML page.

See Table 11-8 for commands issued from a browser to control Shockwave movies.

Table 11-7: Browser Scripting Lingo

Command	Notes
externalEvent "*string*"	Sends event to Netscape or MIE browser (either a built-in method or one defined within the HTML with JavaScript or VBScript).
externalParamCount( )	Returns the number of parameters included in the OBJECT or EMBED tag. Varies by browser. Includes SRC, HEIGHT, and WIDTH.

externalParamName (*n*)	Returns the name of the *n*th parameter passed. There is no limitation on parameter names when using Netscape with an EMBED tag. When used with MIE, *paramName* must be one of the following: "swAudio", "swBackColor", "swBanner", "swColor", "swForeColor", "swFrame", "swList", "swName", "swPassword", "swPreLoadTime", "swSound", "swText", "swURL", "swVolume", "sw1", "sw2", "sw3", "sw4", "sw5", "sw6", "sw7", "sw8", "sw9" Within the OBJECT tag used by MIE, these names must be in quotes: OBJECT Tag:
	`<PARAM NAME="swText" VALUE="some text">`
	 EMBED Tag:
	`swText= "some text"`

Table 11-7: Browser Scripting Lingo

Command	Notes
externalParamValue(*n*) externalParamValue(*name*)	Returns the parameter value by position (*n*) or *name* (*name* is case-sensitive). See *externalParamName( )*. Order of parameters varies with browser. SRC parameter includes full path on MIE 3, but includes DCR movie name only on Netscape and MIE 4.
on EvalScript	The *on EvalScript* handler is called if JavaScript or VBScript issues an *EvalScript* command.

Browser Control of Shockwave

The browser can interact with the Shockwave movie using the commands shown in Table 11-8, which are issued from JavaScript or VBScript and are case-sensitive in JavaScript.

Table 11-8: Browser Control of Shockwave Movie

Command	Usage
AutoStart = true | false	Determines whether movie plays automatically when it is first loaded or when *Rewind( )* is called. Passed in OBJECT or EMBED tag, or set after the movie has loaded. Use lowercase for Boolean constants: *AutoStart = true* or *AutoStart = false*
EvalScript( )	Calls the *on EvalScript* handler in DCR's movie script and returns result. If not present, returns "handler not defined" as return string.
GetCurrentFrame( )	Returns the current frame number whether movie is playing or stopped.
GoToFrame (*frame*)	Moves playback head to specified frame whether movie is playing or stopped.
GoToMovie (*url*)	Goes to an absolute or relative URL. Movie must be playing.
Play( )	Plays the movie from current frame. Runs *on prepareMovie* and *on startMovie* if movie is not already playing.
Rewind( )	Rewinds the movie to frame 1. Movie plays if *AutoStart* is true.
Stop( )	Stops the movie. Window still redraws if necessary. Runs the *on stopMovie* handler. Globals are cleared!

ExternalEvent

The *externalEvent* command enables Lingo to call a function in the browser scripting environment. Keep in mind that *externalEvent* is not supported for all browser and plug-in configurations (see Table 11-6).

To use *ExternalEvent*, a Shockwave movie's OBJECT or EMBED must include the NAME attribute as shown in Example 11-1. JavaScript or VBScript uses this name to communicate with the Shockwave movie. You can also use the *swLiveConnect="true"* attribute to enable LiveScript in Netscape.

In Netscape's LiveConnect environment, *externalEvent* calls the specified JavaScript function, which is case-sensitive.

From Lingo, you might use:

```
externalEvent("someJSFunction()")
```

which would execute a JavaScript function, such as:

```
function someJSFunction() {
  //code goes here
}
```

Pass parameters within single quotes, such as:

```
externalEvent("someJSFunction('parameter1', 'parameter2')")
```

The corresponding JavaScript function would be:

```
function someJSFunction(parameter1, parameter2) {
  //code goes here
}
```

MIE interprets *externalEvent* commands as an event, as it would the *onClick* event. See "Using ExternalEvent and EvalScript with JavaScript and VBScript" at *http://www.zeusprod.com/nutshell/browserscripting.html* for more information.

EvalScript

You can send a string from the browser to Shockwave using *EvalScript* from JavaScript. The movie's *on EvalScript* handler (note the case, including a capital E) will be called and will receive the string as a parameter. Use the *do* command to execute the string, although you should check for specific strings to prevent someone from executing an arbitrary command within your Shockwave movie. See *http://www.zeusprod.com/nutshell/browserscripting.html* for more information.

Network Errors—netError()

The error codes returned by *netError()* depend on the environment. In authoring and Projectors, the errors are generated by the INetURL Xtra (Macromedia's http implementation). In Shockwave, the error codes come from the browser (Netscape or MIE).

Error Handling

Use *netError()* to check the result of network operations. You can use *getNetText()* to check whether an Internet connection is established. If not, *netError()* will return error 4146. In Shockwave, using *preloadNetThing(url)* with an invalid URL—where the server name is valid but the file is simply missing—may still return HTML text stating, "The requested object could not be found on the server." Example 11-3 handles the situation by checking *netError()* before importing the content. You should call *startDownLoad* with the desired URL, and then call *checkProgress* periodically, perhaps from an *exitFrame* or *idle* handler.

Example 11-3: Error Handling

```
global gUrl
global gNetID

-- startDownLoad is called to begin the download
on startDownLoad  url
  set gUrl = url
  set gNetID = preloadNetThing(gUrl)
end startDownLoad

-- checkProgress is called periodically to
-- see if transfer is complete
on checkProgress
  -- Call this periodically
  if netDone(gNetID) then
    case (netError(gNetID)) of
      "OK", 0: importFileInto member "dynamic content", gUrl
      otherwise: alert "Error:" && netError(gNetID)
    end case
  end if
end checkProgress
```

See Macromedia TechNote #12568 for many details on path resolution and URLs in Shockwave. See *http://www.zeusprod.com/nutshell/urls.html* for examples of URLs that may work in browsers, but will fail from Director or Shockwave.

Table 11-9 shows the most common network-related error codes reported by *netError()* in both Shockwave and Director. Codes over 4000 appear to be TCP error codes. Be sure that your URLs include "http://" if applicable and remember that many servers require case-sensitive URLs.

Table 11-9: Macromedia netError() Codes

Code	Meaning
0	"OK"
1	Usually a memory error, but possibly a bus error, or invalid local file path used with *downloadNetThing*.
4	"Bad MOA Class"—network Xtras (NetLingo, INetURL, etc.) or other non-network Xtras may not be properly installed. Check with *the netPresent* property (not the *netPresent()* function).
5	"Bad MOA Interface" (see "Bad MOA Class") in previous entry.
6	Usually a bad URL or unsupported URL redirection (see error 905).
20	"Internal error"—Returned by *netError()* in Shockwave if browser detected a network or internal error.
25	Bad URL when using File ➤ Import. See error 85.
85	Bad URL when using File ➤ Import ➤ Internet. Include "http://" and default document, such as "index.html," within the URL.
905	"Bad URL" or bad file specification.
4144	"Failed network operation"[1]

Table 11-9: Macromedia netError() Codes (continued)

Code	Meaning
4146	"Connection could not be established with the remote host". Establish Internet connection first and ensure proxy server setup is correct.
4149	"Data supplied by the server was in an unexpected format"
4150	"Unexpected early closing of connection"
4154	"Operation could not be completed due to timeout"
4155	"Not enough memory available to complete the transaction"
4156	"Protocol reply to request indicates an error in the reply"
4157	"Transaction failed to be authenticated"
4159	"Invalid URL"
4164	"Could not create a socket"
4165	"Requested Object could not be found"—URL may be incorrect (check for case-sensitivity). Issuing many (100 or more) *getNetText( )* or similar calls would cause this error in D6.0.2. Allegedly fixed in D6.5.
4166	"Generic proxy failure"
4167	"Transfer was intentionally interrupted by client"
4242	"Download stopped by netAbort(url)"
4836	"Download stopped for an unknown reason"—May have been a network error, or the download may have been abandoned.

[1] Other error codes in the range 4145 to 4168, not shown, are the same as code 4144, "Failed network operation."

New Shockwave Features in D7

Shockwave 7 uses a new system player architecture as discussed earlier in this chapter and Chapter 8. It also allows automated downloading of Xtras as discussed in Chapter 10. A local, configurable Shockwave player (ShockMachine) is expected shortly.

See the web page *http://www.macromedia.com/software/director/productinfo/newfeatures/internet.html* or an overview of the new features in Shockwave 7, including HTTPS support. See also the new *postNetText* command in Table 11-5 and the online Help.

Multiuser Server

The Multiuser Xtra allows up to 50 clients to connect to a multiuser server (1000 user licenses are available). Up to 16 users can be connected peer-to-peer without a standalone server. For Macromedia's documentation, see *http://www.macromedia.com/support/director/how/subjects/multiuser.html*. See the Internet ➤ Multiuser Behaviors under Window ➤ Library Palette, or see the source code in the D7 folder under *Libs/Internet/Multiuser.CST* for examples that use the Multiuser Xtra. See *http://www.zeusprod.com/nutshell/chapters/multiuser.html* for many more details and examples. Either the PowerPC or Win32 version of the multiuser server (codename "Mars") ship with the D7 Shockwave Internet Studio, but not the standalone Director 7 upgrade. Unix and Linux versions of the server are anticipated.

Messages transmitted by the multiuser server are sent to the handler defined by *SetNetMessageHandler()* and take the form:

```
[#errorCode: errorCode, #recipients: "users", ¬
    #senderID: "senderName", #subject: "subject", ¬
    #content: content, #timestamp: time]
```

where *errorCode* can be interpreted using *getNetErrorString()* and 0 indicates success. The *senderName* is either "System" or the username of the sender. The *subject* is the message type, such as "ConnectToNetServer". The *content* is specific to the message type and can be any of these types: Void, Integer, Symbol, String, Picture, Float, List, PropList, Point, Rect, Color, Date, or Media. Multiple pieces of data are transmitted as elements within a property list.

Table 11-10 lists the new Lingo elements of the Multiuser Server that can be used to implement a chat room, multiplayer game, or multiuser database.

The Multiuser Xtra's methods can also be viewed in the Message window using:

```
put mMessageList (xtra "Multiuser")
```

Table 11-10: Multiuser Xtra Commands

Command	Usage
muObj = new (xtra "*Multiuser*")	Creates a Multiuser object instance.
breakConnection(*muObj*, "*userID*")	Breaks a peer connection.
checkNetMessages(*muObj*, *maxMessages*)	Processes waiting messages and calls the handlers specified by *SetNetMessageHandler( )*.
connectToNetServer (*muObj*, "*userID*", "*password*", "*server.domain.com*", *portNumber*, "*movieID*" {, *mode*} {, *encryptKey*})	Connects to a server or peer. *PortNumber* is usually 1626. Sends property list to handler specified by *SetNetMessageHandler( )*.
getNetAddressCookie(*muObj* {, *encryptFlag*})	Obtains an optionally encrypted cookie to allow peer-to-peer connections without exposing a machine's IP address.
getNetErrorString (*muObj*, *errorCode*)	Returns the string for an integer error code. 0 indicates success. See D7's *Lingo Dictionary* or online Help for list of error codes.
getNetMessage(*muObj*)	Returns the oldest net message in the queue.
getNetOutgoingBytes (*muObj* {, "*peerID*"})	Returns the size of the outgoing overflow buffer, or a peer connection's outgoing overflow buffer.

Table 11-10: Multiuser Xtra Commands (continued)

Command	Usage
getNumberWaitingNetMessages (*muObj*)	Obtains the number of unread messages.
getPeerConnectionList(*muObj*)	Obtains a list of peer connections.
sendNetMessage (*muObj, toWhom, command {, params}*) sendNetMessage (*muobj, propList*)	Sends a command to *toWhom*, such as "System", "@AllUsers", "@AllServerUsers", or a specific user name. Table 11-11 shows commands recognized by the "System".
setNetBufferLimits (*muObj, bufferSize, maxMessageSize, maxQueuedMsgs*)	Sets memory and message maxima. Increase size if transmitting larger blocks of data.
setNetMessageHandler (*muObj, #handlerSymbol, scriptInstance {, subject} {, sender}*)	Sets the event handler within a script instance that is called when a server message is received. Assign this before using any other commands.
waitForNetConnection (*muObj*, "*userID*", *localPortNumber* {, *maxConnections*})	Waits for peer-to-peer connection from another computer using *ConnectToNetServer( )*. LocalPort-Number is usually 1626. #userId, #password, and #movieID are returned in #content list.

Table 11-11 shows commands and their parameters that can be sent to the multiuser server using *sendNetMessage()*. For example:

```
groupList = sendNetMessage (muObj, "System", ¬
                      "getGroupMembers", "someGroup")
```

Table 11-11: SendNetMessage "System" Commands

Command and Parameters	#Content in Message Sent to Handler Defined by SetNetMessageHandler()
"disableMovie", "*movie* "	Error code, or 0 for success.
"disconnectUser", ["*user*", "*movie*"]	Error code, or 0 for success.
"enableMovie", "*movie*"	Error code, or 0 for success.
"getGroupList"	List of group names (strings).
"getGroupMembers", "*group*"	List containing group name followed by group members.
"getListOfAllMovies"	List of connected movies.
"getNewGroupName"	Unique group name.
"getNumberOfMembers", "*group*"	Number of members in group.
"getServerTime"	Server time in YYYY:MM:DD:HH:MM:SS format.

Table 11-11: SendNetMessage "System" Commands (continued)

Command and Parameters	#Content in Message Sent to Handler Defined by SetNetMessageHandler()
"getServerVersion"	Server version string.
"getUserGroups"	List of groups including predefined groups.
"getUserIPAddress", "*user*"	Property list, [#userID: "*user*", #ipAddress: "123.45.67.890"]
"joinGroup", "*group*"	Message of the form [#errorCode: *errorCode*, #senderID: "*userID*", #subject: "joinGroup", #content: *groupName*]
"leaveGroup", "*group*"	Message of the form: [#errorCode: *errorCode*, #senderID: "*userID*", #subject: " leaveGroup ", #content: *groupName*]

The multiuser database commands shown in Table 11-12 are sent using *sendNetMessage()* and assume that you have an optionally indexed database residing on the server. You must use a separate database program, such as FoxPro or MS-Access to create and index such a database, which should be in DBF format. Sample databases are in included on the Director 7 Studio CD along with the Multiuser Server itself.

The database commands are specified such as:

```
set errCode = sendNetMessage (muObj, "System", "skip", 2)
```

See *getNetErrorString()* in the online Help for a list of the returned error codes, including those pertaining to database operations, or 0 for success.

Table 11-12: SendNetMessage Database Commands

Command and Parameters	Usage
"appendRecord"	Appends an empty record to the database.
"deleteRecord"	Marks current record for deletion. Record must be locked first using *lockRecord* and removed afterward using pack.
"getFields", "#field" | ["#field1", "#field2"]	Property list of field symbols and their values.
"getReadableFieldList"	List of fields that can be read from a database.
"getRecordCount"	Number of records in database.
"getRecords", *numRecords*	List of the next numRecords records.
"getWriteableFieldList"	List of fields that can be written to database.

Table 11-12: SendNetMessage Database Commands (continued)

goToRecord, *recordNum*	Sets current record to specified record number and moves database pointer.
"isRecordDeleted"	Returns TRUE if record is marked for deletion.
"lockRecord"	Locks a record to prevent access by other users. You should lock a record prior to deletion and unlock the record when done.
"pack"	Purges records marked for deletion.
"recallRecord"	Undeletes a deleted record. Record must be locked first.
"reindex", "file"	Reindexes an existing indexed database.
"selectDatabase", "*dbName*"	Specifies a database to open from those listed in *Multiuser.cfg* or movie's configuration file.
"selectDatabase", 0	Closes current database.
"selectTag", "*sortByTag*"	Sorts the database by the specified tag (tags must be created in an external database program.)
"setFields", *propertyList*	Writes data in *propertyList* to current record. Record must be locked first.
"skip", *numRecords*	Repositions the database pointer, where *numRecords* can be positive or negative.
"unlockRecord"	Allows current record to be modified by other users.

Shockwave & the Internet

XML Parser

XML (Extensible Markup Language) gives web developers a way to define their own document formats. It is less restrictive than HTML and is a simplified subset of SGML. See the FAQ at *http://www.ucc.ie/xml/#FAQ-ACRO*. The XML Parser in Director 7 is based on James Clark's "expat" parser (*http://www.xml.com/xml/pub/r/expat*).

Refer to the *XMLTree.DIR* file under *Xtras Partners/Tree View* on the Director 7 CD-ROM for example code using the XML Parser. For a tutorial on using the Xtra, see *http://www.macromedia.com/support/director/how/subjects/xml.html*. See *http://www.zeusprod.com/nutshell/chapters/xmlparser.html* for more details on the XML parser.

You can use *getNetText()* to obtain the contents of an XML-tagged file from the Internet before using *parseString()* to parse it.

Table 11-13 lists the new Lingo elements that pertain to the XML Parser Xtra.

Table 11-13: XML Parser Xtra Commands

Command	Usage
doneParsing (*xmlObj*)	Returns true if parseURL() has completed.
getError (*xmlObj*)	Returns the error string generated by the previous parse command.
ignoreWhiteSpace (*xmlObj*, TRUE | FALSE	Specifies whether the parser should ignore whitespace in the XML document.
makeList (*xmlObj*)	Creates a lingo list from the parsed XML document.
makeSubList (*xmlObj*)	XMLnode.child[n].child[m].makeSubList( ).
set *xmlObj* = new (xtra "XMLParser")	Creates a new parser object.
parseString (*xmlObj*, "*stringToParse*")	Parses the XML-tagged text in "stringToParse".
parseURL (*xmlObj*, "*urlToParse*")) {, *handlerToCall-WhenDone*} {, *paramToPass*})	Parses the XML-tagged document at "urlToParse".

The XML Xtra's methods can also be viewed in the Message window using:

```
put mMessageList (xtra "XMLParser")
```

PART III

Multimedia Elements

CHAPTER 12

Text and Fields

This chapter covers the different types of cast members that can display text in Director. It also covers fonts and character mapping, scrolling text, and text-related Lingo including hypertext functions.*

Rich Text, Fields, and Bitmapped Text

Director 6 had many types of cast members that can contain text in some form: rich text, fields, D7 text, Flash, and bitmaps. Fields were known as "text" cast members prior to Director 5. In D6, "text" usually refers to *rich text* cast members. Lingo error messages in D6 stating that a property can only be set for a *text* cast member usually indicate that Lingo expected a *field* cast member, *not* a rich text cast member.

In D6, rich text can not be created or modified at runtime, because it is stored as a bitmap. It takes up much more memory than fields, and should be used sparingly. In D7, a new type of text cast member replaces rich text. In D7, text cast members and compressed font cast members give the compact size and editability of fields with the anti-aliased appearance and font accuracy of D6 rich text members.

Table 12-1 compares the different types of text supported by Director. The text tool in the Paint window can be used to create bitmapped text. Digital video cast members can also contain one or more text tracks. Refer to the *trackType()* and *trackText()* functions Chapter 16, *Digital Video*. Field cast members are also used to define custom menus.

---

* In *Lingo In a Nutshell*, see Chapter 10, *Keyboard Events*; Chapter 7, *Strings*; and Appendix C, *Case-Sensitivity, Sort Order, Diacritical Marks, and Space-Sensitivity* for important text-related commands.

Table 12-1: Choosing the Right Type of Text

Feature	Text (D7)	Rich Text (D6)	Fields	Flash
Best used for	All types of text in D7	Small amounts of large text	Large amounts of small text	Scaled and rotated text
Not good for	Not supported in D6	Large amounts of small text; not supported in D7	Large text, consistent fonts	Windows 3.1 and 68K Macs
Animation speed	Medium	Fastest, with dynamic anti-aliasing	Slow	Selectable, but processor-intensive
Editable during authoring	Yes	Yes	Yes	No[1]
Editable at runtime	Optional	No	Optional	No[1]
Lingo control over formatting	Yes; HTML and RTF support	Minimal control during authoring only	Yes	No[1]
Hypertext-capable	Yes; see *on hyperlink-Clicked*	No	Manually via Lingo	Yes
Created with	D7 Text window or HTML editor	D6 Text window or MS-Word (RTF format)	Field window or external editor	Flash 2 or Flash 3
Import as	File ➤ Import ➤ Text	File ➤ Import ➤ Text	Copy from clipboard	Insert ➤ Media Element ➤ Shockwave Flash
Character limit per cast member	Unlimited	32,000 characters	32,000 characters (unlimited in D7)	N/A
Storage effciency	Good	Poor	Good	Varies
Usable as custom cursor	No	Yes (D6)	No	No
Requires Xtra	Yes	No	No	Yes

[1] Text can be edited in Flash.

Text Appearance and Attributes

Table 12-2 lists the attributes that you can control for each type of text.

Table 12-2: Supported Attributes for Each Type of Text

Feature	Text (D7)	Rich Text (D6)	Fields	Flash
Anti-aliasing[1]	Yes	Yes	None	Yes
Formatting, margins, and tabs	Yes	Margins, indents, and tabs (per paragraph)	Margins (entire field only)	Margins, columns
Character formatting	Yes	Yes	Yes	Yes
Justification	Per line	Per paragraph	Per entire field only	Yes
Fonts	Compressed fonts	Any font	Required at runtime (D6); Compressed fonts (D7)	Any font
Font styles	Any supported by RTF or HTML, superscript, subscript	Plain, bold, italic, and underline	Plain, bold, italic, underline, shadow, outline, extend, and condense	Plain, bold, and italic
Line spacing (leading)	Per-line basis	Per-line basis	Set for entire field only	Yes
Kerning	Yes	Yes	No	Yes
Box surrounding text	No, use separate sprite	No, must use bitmap or shape cast member	Yes, can set line size and drop shadow	No, must use separate Flash element
Text shadow	No	No	Yes, can set drop shadow offset	No
Ink support	Any	Copy, Background Transparent, and Blend only	All; reverts to Copy ink if scrolled	All, unless direct-to-Stage
Scrollable on Stage	Yes; any ink	Yes; any ink	Yes; Copy ink only	No
Scaling	Bounding box scales, but contents do not	Bounding box scales, but contents do not	Bounding box scales, but contents do not	Yes, with some performance loss
Rotation	Yes	No	No	Yes

[1] Director can anti-alias TrueType and PostScript (outline) fonts, but not bitmapped fonts.

The Paint window has limited text tools. Create fancy text in other programs, such as Photoshop, then import it as a bitmap. You can also create your text as either a field or rich text cast member, then use Modify ➤ Convert to Bitmap to turn it into a bitmap. Once converted to a bitmap, the text cannot be edited. Before converting them to bitmaps, save a copy of the original editable text cast members (perhaps in an external castLib), as the conversion cannot be undone.

Bitmap cast members are created at the current monitor color depth. In D6, transform them to 1-bit cast members (using Modify ➤ Transform Bitmap) to save memory compared to rich text members, and colorize them using the color chips in the Tool Palette.

Fonts and Formatting

Director lets you select the font, font style, and point size for text, fields, and the Paint window text tool. Rich text members are converted to text cast members automatically when upgrading a D6 movie to D7. Conversion is imperfect, so double-check the text appearance carefully.

 Formatting applies to individual characters, not to the cast member itself. Field and text cast members lose their formatting if they are empty. Use at least a SPACE to maintain a field or text cast member's formatting. For fields and new D7 text members, you can set the formatting via Lingo after adding text.

A bug in D6.0 caused font settings to be lost when opening a movie on a different platform. D6.0.2 fixes the bug.

During authoring, you can select from any of the installed fonts, but the Projector will eventually be running on another computer that may not have the same fonts installed. In D7, you can create embedded font cast members using Insert ➤ Media Element ➤ Font to guarantee the fonts needed by your field and text cast members are available. See "Embedding fonts in movies" in the D7 online Help.

In D6, there are several ways to ensure that your text will appear in a specific font and look fairly consistent across multiple platforms from within a Projector:

- Use rich text or bitmapped cast members that retain their font without requiring the font to be present at runtime.

- Use field cast members and rely on fonts that are installed by default on the user's system. Use *FONTMAP.TXT* to substitute fonts if the font is not available at runtime.

- License and install any custom fonts that are required for field cast members at runtime.

- On the Macintosh only, you can add FONT resources to your Projector's resource fork using ResEdit.

Installed fonts

The following Xtras list installed fonts or perform other font-related operations.

Installed Fonts from Red Eye Software:

http://www.updatestage.com/xtras/

FontList Xtra from Andrade Arts (Macintosh-only):

> *http://www.andradearts.com/software*

DirectOS from Direct Xtras (installs and uninstalls fonts as FON, FNT, TTF, and FOT files; Windows-only):

> *http://www.directxtras.com/do_doc.htm*

OSutil by Paul Farry:

> *http://www.magna.com.au/~farryp/director/xtras*

Buddy API by Gary Smith (see the *baFontsInstalled* and *baInstallFont* methods):

> *http://www.mods.com.au/budapi*

TextCruncher Xtra (cross-platform text parsing and manipulation):

> *http://www.itp.tsoa.nyu.edu/~student/yair/texcruncher/HTML/*
> *YairTextCruncher.html*

LoadFont by Pablo Media:

> *http://www.pablomedia.com/*

Mapping fonts with FONTMAP.TXT

Let's assume that you have a large amount of text that you have decided to display in field cast members in D6 (in D7 you'd use embedded fonts with either field or text members). Director's *FONTMAP.TXT* file controls how fonts are *mapped* (translated) from Macintosh to Windows and vice versa. (Open the *FONTMAP.TXT* file in a text editor for reference before proceeding. It is located in the same folder in which Director is installed.)

Table 12-3 shows the default font mapping already included in *FONTMAP.TXT*. Note that both Courier and Courier New under Windows map to Courier on the Macintosh, and that both Palatino and Times on the Macintosh map to Times New Roman under Windows. There is some variation in the size of characters in different fonts and across platforms. *FONTMAP.TXT* also lets you specify a different point size when mapping fonts, as with Times ↔ Times New Roman in Table 12-3.

Table 12-3: Cross-Platform Font-Mapping

Windows to Mac	Mac to Windows	Java[1]
Arial→Helvetica	Helvetica→Arial	Helvetica
Courier→Courier	Courier→Courier New	Courier
Courier New→Courier	Courier→Courier New	Courier
MS Serif[2]→New York	New York→MS Serif	Default
MS Sans Serif[2]→Geneva	Geneva→MS Sans Serif	Dialog input

Text & Fields

Table 12-3: Cross-Platform Font-Mapping (continued)

Windows to Mac	Mac to Windows	Java[1]
Symbol→Symbol[3]	Symbol→Symbol[3]	Zapf Dingbats
System→Chicago	Chicago→System	Dialog
Terminal[2]→Monaco	Monaco→Terminal	Default
Times New Roman→Times	Palatino→Times New Roman	Times Roman

Times New Roman→Times[4]
  12-point→14-point
  14-point→18-point
  18-point→24-point
  24-point→30-point
	Times→Times New Roman[4]
	  14-point→12-point
	  18-point→14-point
	  24-point→18-point
	  30-point→24-point
		Times Roman

[1] Java does not support custom font mapping. See *the font of member* property in the D7 Help index for details on the supported Java fonts. Arial and Helvetica are used for all unsupported fonts.
[2] The Courier, MS Serif, MS Sans Serif, and Terminal fonts are bitmapped (not TrueType). They may not be available if the user has turned off bitmap font display under Windows.
[3] Character-mapping is disabled when using the Symbol font. See the MAP NONE option in the next section.
[4] A larger point size is used for Times on the Mac because it is smaller than Times New Roman under Windows.

Customizing FONTMAP.TXT

Font mapping can be set on a per-movie basis. When you create a new movie, Director incorporates the default *FONTMAP.TXT* file from the folder in which Director is installed. To modify the font mapping:

1. Use **Modify ➤ Movie ➤ Properties ➤** *Save Font Map* to export the font map.

2. Edit the *FONTMAP.TXT* file (or whatever you called it when exporting).

3. Use **Modify ➤ Movie ➤ Properties ➤** *Load Font Map* to import the new font map settings.

This is the general format for specifying a font mapping definition:

```
FromPlatform:OldFontName => ToPlatform:NewFontName {MAP NONE}
{oldPointSize1=>newPointSize1} {oldPointSize2=>newPointSize2}
```

Use **Mac** and **Win** as the platform names. The arrow is made from the = and > characters. The items in curly braces ({}) are optional. Here is a simple example:

```
Mac:Chicago => Win:System
```

Don't forget to provide the reciprocal mapping to map in the opposite direction:

```
Win:System => Mac:Chicago
```

If a font name contains spaces, or is followed by point-size mappings, enclose it in quotes:

```
Win:"MS Serif" => Mac:"New York"
```

The following causes 12-point Times New Roman on Windows to be replaced with 14-point Times on the Macintosh (point-size mappings only apply to the font for which they are specified):

```
Win:"Times New Roman" => Mac:"Times" 12=>14 14=>18 18=>24 24=>30
```

The **MAP NONE** option disables character mapping for that particular font (see the next section, "Character mapping"):

```
Win:Symbol => Mac:Symbol Map None
```

If a font is not available, or a font mapping is not specified, Helvetica is used on the Macintosh and Arial is used under Windows. In D7, fields and text members can use fonts embedded in *#font* cast members. The default *FONTMAP.TXT* file also maps the Japanese Macintosh Osaka font to a Japanese Windows font. All Japanese Windows fonts are mapped to Macintosh Osaka.

Character mapping

FONTMAP.TXT also lets you specify character mapping between platforms, which ensures that nonstandard characters such as bullets, curly quote marks, and accented characters appear correctly. Character mapping affects all fonts for which **MAP NONE** is *not* specified. *FONTMAP.TXT* already includes character mapping for ASCII values between 128 and 255. Refer to the *charToNum()* and *numToChar()* functions, and to the ASCII table in Appendix A, *ASCII Codes and Key Codes,* in *Lingo in a Nutshell*.

This is the general format for specifying a character mapping definition:

```
FromPlatform: => ToPlatform: oldChar1=>newChar1
```

Use **Mac** and **Win** as the platform names, and don't forget the colon after the name. The arrow is made from the = and > characters. You can specify as many character mappings as you like, but you must repeat the platform names on each new line. For example:

```
Mac: => Win: 128=>196 129=>197 130=>199 131=>201 132=>209
Mac: => Win: 133=>214 134=>220 135=>225 136=>224 137=>226
```

Don't forget to provide the reciprocal mapping to map in the opposite direction:

```
Win: => Mac: 128=>222 129=>223 130=>226 131=>196 132=>227
Win: => Mac: 133=>201 134=>160 135=>224 136=>246 137=>228
```

Refer to the comments in the *FONTMAP.TXT* file for additional details.

Table 12-4 shows how to create some common symbols that will work for most, but not all, fonts. Under Windows, the character may appear incorrectly in the Message window, but it will appear correctly when copied into a text or field cast member.

Table 12-4: Creating Common Symbols

Symbol	Macintosh[1]	Windows[2]	HTML[3]
Copyright (©)	Option-g or *numToChar(169)*	Alt+169 or *numToChar(169)*	© or ©
Registered (®)	Option-r or *numToChar(168)*	Alt+174 or *numToChar(174)*	® or ®
Trademark (™)	Option-2 or *numToChar(170)*	Alt+153 or *numToChar(153)*	™

[1] On the Macintosh, create extended characters using the Option key.
[2] Under Windows, create ASCII characters by holding down the Alt key while typing in the ASCII code on the numeric keypad with Num Lock on (i.e., Alt+65 will create a capital "A").
[3] The HTML codes are unrelated to Director or Shockwave, and may not be supported by some browsers. The numeric codes are more likely to be supported than the equivalent names.

Use the Macintosh *Key Caps* desk accessory or the Windows *Character Map* utility (under the Windows 95 Start Menu under **Programs ➤ Accessories**) to view various characters in different fonts.

Manipulating Text in the Interface

You can set the font, style, size, and alignment of text using the Text Inspector, Text Toolbars, and Font dialog box. The Text Inspector modifies text in the Text, Field, Paint, Script, and Message windows, although not all options are supported in all windows. The width of a field or text sprite is determined by the width of the cast member as set by dragging the vertical black line at the right margin of the field or text editing window (or set by resizing the sprite on the Stage).

Director's text-related tools that set font styles, tabs, margins, and so on, are self-explanatory. When in doubt, see *formatting paragraphs, formatting text*, and *formatting characters* in the online Help. You can apply most Text Inspector attributes to multiple text or field cast members simultaneously in the Cast window. The attributes are applied to all the text in the selected cast members. Set the text line spacing to 0 to resume automatic adjustment based on the point size. You can set a custom font size by entering the point size manually instead of using the predefined sizes in the pop-up menu.

Table 12-5 shows how to access and manipulate text in Director. Search and replace operations work only within the currently active cast member type. For example, if the Field window is active, it will search through fields, but not text cast members or scripts. The most inclusive settings perform a wraparound search through all cast members of the same type throughout all castLibs, and ignore word breaks.

 Use the undocumented Cmd-G (Macintosh) or Ctrl-G (Windows) to find an item again.

Table 12-5: Text Manipulation Commands

Action	Command	Macintosh	Windows
Import Text[1]	File ➤ Import ➤ Text	Cmd-R	Ctrl-R
Open Text window[1]	Window ➤ Text, or Text button on main Toolbar	Cmd-6	Ctrl-6
Open Field window	Window ➤ Field	Cmd-8	Ctrl-8
Add Text cast member[1]	Insert ➤ Media Element ➤ Text or open Tool Palette then click Text Tool	Cmd-6, then + button	Ctrl-6, then + button
Set Text attributes[1]	Select Text cast member, then Modify ➤ Cast Member ➤ Properties (must then click Options button in D7)	Cmd-I	Ctrl-I
Add Field cast member	Insert ➤ Control ➤ Field, or open Tool Palette, then click Field tool	Cmd-8, then + button, or Cmd-7	Ctrl-8, then + button, or Ctrl-7
Set Field attributes	Select Field cast member, then Modify ➤ Cast Member ➤ Properties	Cmd-I	Ctrl-I
Show/Hide Text Toolbar	View ➤ Text Toolbar	Cmd-Shift-H	Ctrl-Shift-H
Open Text Inspector (used to set hypertext in D7)	Window ➤ Inspectors ➤ Text	Cmd-T	Ctrl-T
Add Compressed Font (D7)	Insert ➤ Media Element ➤ Font	None	None
Set fonts	Modify ➤ Font	Cmd-Shift-T	Ctrl-Shift-T
Set margins, indents, and paragraph spacing[1]	Modify ➤ Paragraph	Cmd-Shift-Opt-T	Ctrl-Shift-Alt-T
Set tabs and margins with Ruler[1]	View ➤ Rulers	Cmd-Shift-Opt-R	Ctrl-Shift-Alt-R
Set margin, line size, box shadow, and text shadow[2]	Modify ➤ Borders	None	Alt-M,B, then L, M, B, or T
Set Ruler text units[1]	File ➤ Preferences ➤ General ➤ Text Units	Cmd-U	Ctrl-U
Find (and replace) text	Edit ➤ Find ➤ Text	Cmd-F	Ctrl-F
Find again	Edit ➤ Find ➤ Find Again	Cmd-G, or Cmd-Opt-F	Ctrl-G, or Ctrl-Alt-F
Replace again	Edit ➤ Find ➤ Replace Again	Cmd-Opt-E	Ctrl-Alt-E
Find current selection	Edit ➤ Find ➤ Selection	Cmd-H	Ctrl-H
Find Text cast members[1]	Edit ➤ Find ➤ Cast Member ➤ Type ➤ Text	Cmd-;	Ctrl-;

Table 12-5: Text Manipulation Commands (continued)

Action	Command	Macintosh	Windows
Find field cast members	Edit ➤ Find ➤ Cast Member ➤ Type ➤ Field	Cmd-;	Ctrl-;
Colorize text	Select text and use color chips in Tool Palette	Cmd-7	Ctrl-7
Convert text to a bitmap	Select text or field cast member(s), then choose Modify ➤ Convert to Bitmap	None	Alt-M, V
Save font mappings	Modify ➤ Movie ➤ Properties ➤ Save Font Map	Cmd-Shift-D	Ctrl-Shift-D
Load font mappings	Modify ➤ Movie ➤ Properties ➤ Load Font Map	Cmd-Shift-D	Ctrl-Shift-D
Add text in Paint window[3]	Window ➤ Paint, then click Text tool	Cmd-5, T	Ctrl-5, T
Rulers in Paint window	View ➤ Rulers	Cmd-Shift-Opt-R	Ctrl-Shift-Alt-R
Insert Flash element	Insert ➤ Media Element ➤ Shockwave Flash Movie, or File ➤ Import (D7)	None	None

[1] Applies only to rich text members (D6) and text members (D7).
[2] Applies to field members, and possibly button members, but not (D6) rich text members.
[3] Director 6.0.1 added the ability to select the Text tool by typing the letter "T" while the Paint window is active.

Editing Text Sprites on Stage

I find the gestures for editing field, text, and button sprites on the Stage confusing and bet you do too. Table 12-6 clears it all up.

Table 12-6: Manipulating Text and Button Sprites on Stage

Action	Command
Resize a sprite	Single-click the sprite on the Stage. Resize handles should appear (if the sprite has already been double-clicked, click the Stage, then reselect the sprite with a single click). You can only directly control the sprite's width. Its height is usually determined by automatic wrapping.[1]
Edit the text of a sprite	Double-click the sprite on the Stage. A feathered border should appear. Click within the text to edit as usual.
Edit a field or button in the Field window or text in the Text window	Highlight the sprite, and then choose Edit ➤ Edit Cast Member. There is no mouse gesture to open the Field or Text window from the Stage, but you can double-click a thumbnail in the Cast window or Sprite Toolbar, or a sprite in the Score to open it.

[1] The vertical size of a text, field, or button cast member is affected by the number of lines of text. If you can't resize it in the vertical direction, either add or remove text (such as blank lines) and/or change the member's *Framing* option under Modify ➤ Cast Member ➤ Properties. You can't set the bounding rectangle of a field whose *boxType of member* is #adjust. Change the field's *boxType* to #fixed or #scrolling, then use the Sprite Toolbar or Sprite Inspector to set the desired height manually.

Cast Member Properties and Scrolling Text

The Cast Member Properties dialog boxes allow you to specify additional attributes, most notably whether to create a scrolling field.

Both fields and text cast members can be used for scrolling text, although fields are ordinarily used for large amounts of text in D6 (in D7, you can use text members). Refer to *the scrollTop of member* property and *scrollByLine* and *scrollByPage* commands in the online Help. A scrolling field reverts to the Copy ink if it is scrolled by the user (because scrolling is handled by the OS, which ignores ink effects). Use *the rect of sprite* property to change the size of a scrolling text box. Scrollbars' dimensions are included in the *width of member* and *width of sprite* properties.

Rich Text Properties dialog box (D6)

The *Rich Text Cast Member Properties* dialog box allows you to set the following:

Framing
> Adjust to Fit, Scrolling, or *Cropped*.

Anti-Alias
> *All Text, Larger than N points,* or *None.* You'll generally want this set to anti-alias any text larger than 12 points.

Rich text wraps even when *Framing* is set to *Cropped*, and rich text is never editable at runtime. Rich text properties are generally not accessible via Lingo. Other attributes, such as fonts and margins, are set using the Text window (including the Text Toolbar and Text Ruler), Text Inspector, `Modify` ➤ `Font`, and `Modify` ➤ `Paragraph` (see Table 12-5).

Field Properties dialog box (D6 and D7)

The *Field Cast Member Properties* dialog box allows you to set the following:

Framing
> *Adjust to Fit, Scrolling, Fixed,* or *Limit to Field Size.* See *the boxType of member* property.

Editable
> Allows text to be edited at runtime. You can also use the *Editable* checkbox in the Sprite Toolbar or Sprite Inspector to control this on a per-sprite basis. Editable field sprites accept keyboard input without any Lingo programming. See *the editable of member* and *editable of sprite* properties.

Word Wrap
> Determines whether long lines wrap. If this is unchecked, long lines will be cut off. See *the wordWrap of member* property.

Tab To Next Field
> Determines whether the text field accepts the `Tab` character as input, or whether the `Tab` character causes Director to pass focus to the next editable text field. It controls whether a field passes focus, not accepts focus. The latter is determined by whether the field is editable. See *the autoTab of member* property and *the keyboardFocusSprite* property (in D7).

Field text can not be anti-aliased. Other attributes, such as fonts and margins, are set using the *Field* window (including the Field Toolbar), Text Inspector, and Modify ➤ Border options (*Line, Margin, Box Shadow,* and *Text Shadow*) These properties are also generally accessible via Lingo (see Table 12-7).

Text Properties dialog box (D7)

The new D7 text type is implemented as an Xtra; you must click *Options* within its property dialog box to set the *Framing, Editable, Tab to Next Item,* and *Anti-Alias* options (analogous to the field and rich text options of the same names). New options exclusive to D7 text include kerning and the following:

Direct to Stage
  Renders text more quickly, but always in the foreground and with no ink effects. D7.0.1 adds options to Pre-Render and save the bitmap with varied inks.

Use Hypertext Styles
  Causes hypertext links (defined using the Text Inspector) to appear underlined and in blue. See the new *the useHyperTextStyles of member* property.

Keyboard input

The user can switch keyboard focus to a field sprite using the Tab key (if *the autoTab of member* is set) or the mouse. In D6, set keyboard focus for a field sprite by setting its *editable of sprite* property to TRUE or ensuring that it is the only editable field on the Stage. See Chapter 10 in *Lingo in a Nutshell*. In D7, use *the keyboardFocusSprite* property to force focus onto a sprite.

You can also trap keys in an *on keyDown* handler and modify text and field members with Lingo's string functions.

Text and Field Lingo

Most Lingo text commands pertain only to field and new D7 text cast members. D6 rich text cast member properties are generally not accessible via Lingo. Only the *pageHeight of member, scrollTop of member,* and *text of member* properties are accessible at runtime for D6 rich text cast members.

Field and Rich Text Properties

Table 12-7 shows field cast member properties, plus a few sprite properties. Some properties also pertain to rich text cast members; many also pertain to button cast members. In many cases, you can set the contents or style for fields in more than one way, such as:

```
set the text of member "TextField" = "someText"
put "someText" into field "TextField"
```

See Chapter 7 in *Lingo in a Nutshell* for additional details and Table 4-10 for a complete list of properties supported by various cast members and sprite types.

Table 12-7: Field and Rich Text Properties

Member Property	Usage
alignment of member[1,2,3]	Alignment of text within field: "left", "right", or "center". Alignment of D7 text: #left, #right, #center, #full.
autoTab of member[3]	Determines whether Director jumps to the next editable field when the TAB key is pressed. See *the keyboardFocusSprite* property.
backColor of member[3]	Determines the background color of the field.
border of member	Determines width of border of box surrounding text, in pixels.
boxDropShadow of member	Determines field box's drop shadow offset in pixels.
boxType of member[3]	Determines type of field: #adjust, #fixed, #limit, #scroll.
dropShadow of member[1]	Determines text's drop shadow offset in pixels (default 0).
editable of member,[3] or editable of sprite[3]	If either is TRUE, the field can be edited by the user at runtime.
font of member[3,4]	Determines text's font, such as "helvetica".
fontSize of member[3,4]	Determines text's point size.
fontStyle of member[2,3,4]	Determines text style, such as "plain", "bold", "italic", "underline", "shadow", "outline", "extend", or "condense" (Mac only). Multiple attributes are separated by commas within the quotes, such as "bold,italic" or added by separate commands. In D7, use [#plain],[#bold, #italic], etc.
foreColor of member[3,4]	Determines the color of the text.
ink of sprite[3,5]	Determines the sprite's ink effect. Reverts to Copy ink when scrolling fields, but not rich text cast members.
length of *string*[3]	Indicates length of field or other string, such as: `put the length of field "myField"` `put member("myField").text.length`
lineCount of member[3]	Read-only property that indicates the number of lines in the field (wrapped lines count as *multiple* lines). Contrast with *the number of lines in field*.
lineHeight of member[3,6]	Determines the vertical spacing of the text.
margin of member[1]	Determines the margin on all four sides of the text, in pixels.
pageHeight of member[3,5]	Determines the height of the portion of the field cast member visible on the Stage, in pixels.
picture of member[3,5,7]	Returns a PICT handle to the field or rich text cast member's contents.
rect of member[3,5]	Determines the size of the member. Can be set for fields, but only read for rich text cast members.

Table 12-7: Field and Rich Text Properties (continued)

Member Property	Usage
rect of sprite[3,5]	Determines the size of the member on the Stage. Useful for resizing the text box for both field and rich text sprites.
scrollTop of member[3,5]	Determines the distance, in pixels, from the top of the text sprite to the visible portion. Setting it to zero scrolls the text to the top of the field. See the *ScrollByLine( )* and *ScrollByPage( )* commands.
text of member[3,5]	Determines the contents of the field. Limited to 32,000 characters in D6, but not D7. Can be set during authoring for rich text members, and at run time for fields.
textAlign of member	Obsolete. See *alignment of member*.
textFont of member	Obsolete. See *font of member*.
textHeight of member	Obsolete. See *lineHeight of member*.
textSize of member	Obsolete. See *fontSize of member*.
textStyle of member	Obsolete. See *fontStyle of member*.
wordWrap of member[3]	Determines whether long lines are wrapped or truncated.

[1] Pertains to the entire field.
[2] D7 text cast members use symbols instead of strings for this property.
[3] Also pertains to new D7 text cast members.
[4] Can be set for individual chunks.
[5] Also pertains to rich text cast members.
[6] The *lineHeight of member* property can be set, but is not saved when the movie is saved. There are also display problems when the *lineHeight* is set too small, especially with scrolling fields under Windows.
[7] D6.x and the SW6.0 plug-in support *the picture of member* property for field cast members, but the SW6.0.1 plug-in returns VOID for this property for field members. Director and Shockwave prior to D7 support it for rich text cast members.

When setting field contents and styles, use the *field* syntax instead of the *member* syntax. See "Text Anomalies" later in this chapter.

New Text and Font Properties in Director 7

Director 7's new *#text* members replace D6's *#richText* members, but offer some of the features of *#field* members, plus new functions including HTML formatting and hyperlinking. For complete details on *#text* and *#font* members, including known bugs and D7's new chunk expressions, see *http://www.zeusprod.com/ nutshell/chapters/textfonts.html*. Table 12-8 lists properties exclusive to *#text* members beyond those cited in Table 12-7. See also the D7 hyperlink commands in Table 12-11.

Table 12-8: Text Member Properties in Director

Command	Usage
the alignment of member[1]	#left, #right, #center, or #full.
the alpha of member	Undocumented. Same as picture of member.
the antiAlias of member	Boolean indicating whether to anti-alias large sized text at runtime.
the antiAliasThreshold of member	Point size at or below which text is not anti-aliased.
the autoTab of member	Boolean indicating whether TAB key sends cursor to next editable text sprite.
the bgColor of member	Specifies the background color of the member. Cannot be set for chunks.
the bottomSpacing of member	Default spacing between paragraphs is 0. May be positive or negative.
the charSpacing of member[1]	Represents extra spacing in pixels between characters. Defaults to zero (default spacing for the font).
the color of member[1]	*rgb( )* color of text. Can be set for individual chunks.
chunkExpression.chunk.count	Counts the number of *chunks* in *chunkExpression*.
the firstIndent of member	Defaults to 0. Negative number indicates hanging indent. Positive number indicates normal indent.
the fixedLineSpace of member	Default is 0 (natural line spacing dependent on point size).
the font of member	Font name in quotes, such as "Times".
the fontSize of member	Font point size.
the fontSpacing of member	No such property. Documentation is wrong. See *charSpacing of member*.
the fontStyle of member[1]	List of font attributes, such as [#plain] or [#bold, #italic]. Possible values are #plain, #bold, #italic, #underline, #shadow, #extend, #condense, #outline, #superscript, #subscript, #strikeout, #allLower, #allCaps, #smallCaps, #boxed, #overLine, #doubleUnderline, #dottedUnderline, #wordUnderline, #hiddenText.
the html of member	HTML-tagged version of member. Cannot be set or read for individual chunks.
the hyperLinks of member	See Table 12-11.
the kerning of member[1]	Boolean indicating whether to kern large text.
the kerningThreshold of member	Point size at or below which text is not kerned.
the leftIndent of member	Number of pixels that member's left margin is indented from the left edge of the member.
the lineSpace of member	Defaults to 0. Set it to 2 for double-spaced text (undocumented).

Table 12-8: Text Member Properties in Director (continued)

Command	Usage
the missingFonts of member	A list of fonts such as ["esoterica", "grapplemond"] needed for the text member that are not installed or stored in a compressed font member.
paragraph *n* of member	A new chunk expression in D7 separated by a RETURN. See the older *char*, *word*, *item*, and *line* chunks in Chapter 7 of *Lingo in a Nutshell*.
the picture of member	A graphic representation of the text member.
pointToChar (sprite *n*, *point*)	Returns character number under *point*, or -1 if *point* is not within sprite.
pointToItem (sprite *n*, *point*)	Returns item number under *point*, or -1 if none.
pointToLine (sprite *n*, *point*)	Returns line number under *point*, or -1 if none.
pointToParagraph (sprite *n*, *point*)	Returns paragraph number under *point*, or -1 if none.
pointToWord (sprite *n*, *point*)	Returns word number under *point*, or -1 if none.
the preRender of member	New in D7.0.1. Can be set to #none, #copyInk, or #otherInk.
ref	Creates a reference, useful for repeated operations with a text chunk.
the rightIndent of member	Number of pixels that member's right margin is indented from the right edge of the member.
the rtf of member	Rich text representation of contents of member. Cannot be set or read for chunks.
the saveBitmap of member	New in D7.0.1. Boolean indicates whether to store rendered bitmap for better performance.
the selectedText of member	Returns selected chunk of text as an object reference to be used in a further expression.
the tabCount of member	Number of tabs in *the tabs of member*. Read-only.
the tabs of member	A list of tabs including the #type (#left, #center, #right, or #decimal) and the #position. such as: put member("text member").tabs [[#type: #left, #position: 167], [#type: #right, #position: 204]]
the topSpacing of member	Default spacing between paragraphs is 0. May be positive or negative.
the useHypertextStyles of member	See Table 12-11.
the wordWrap of member	Determines whether long lines should be wrapped.

[1] Can be read and set for individual chunks as well as for the entire member.

Despite the new text capabilities, you may use field members in D7 for backwards compatibility (fields don't update automatically when updating movies from D6). D7 fields are the same as D6 fields, except that there is no 32 KB character limit and D7 fields will use embedded font members (but won't be anti-aliased like text members).

Don't convert your old fields to text members unless you're willing to update some of your Lingo. For example, text members don't support borders or box shadows. Support for fields is built into Director, whereas the text engine requires an Xtra, and fields are faster because they are not anti-aliased. In new D7 projects, you'll probably want to use text members for their new features, but to minimize Projector size and maximize performance, use fields.

You can flip, rotate, and distort text using the new D7 *flipH, flipV, skew, rotation*, and *quad of sprite* properties shown in Table 3-2. In both D6 and D7, Pablo Media's Composite Xtra (*http://www.pablomedia.com*) will render rotated text, text around a curve, and multibyte international text. Pablo Media's LoadFont Xtra allows you to use your own TrueType fonts.

ASCII, HTML, and RTF versions of text

A text member has three simultaneous representations: ASCII, HTML, and RTF.

The *text of member* is an ASCII version of the contents, and does not include any formatting codes. Because HTML and RTF include formatting tags and apply to the entire member, not to individual chunks, you must alter the tags manually if attempting to concatenate the formatted text.

The *html of member* property can be used to create basic HTML-formatted text, including simple tables or newspaper style multi-column text using the TABLE tag. HTML files (including those at remote URLs) can be imported via File ➤ Import.

Director 7 does not render embedded <IMAGE> tags for GIFs or JPEGs, nor does it recognize frames, nested tables, applets, or forms. Director ignores any tags it does not recognize (<FRAME>, <APPLET>, <FORM>, <FRAME>, <INPUT>, <IMAGE>, etc.). Formatting, including spacing and layout, is very approximate.

You can't use D7 as a web browser unless you limit yourself to very basic text-based HTML pages and tags. If you need a real browser in Director, you still need an Xtra (MIE4 ActiveX Control and the ActiveX Asset Xtra, WebXtra, LiveCD, etc.).

In D6 you can use Media Connect's HTML Xtra (*http://www.mcmm.com/download/xhtml.htm*) to create HTML-based members.

The *rtf of member* property contains the rich text formatting codes that define the appearance of the field. Changing the *html* or *rtf of member* properties or formatting the text in the Text window or Text Inspector all affect each other.

The format for RTF documents, including conversion to HTML, is described at:

> *http://www.sunpack.com/RTF/*

In D6, to modify RTF text in Projectors or Shockwave, see Zav's RTF engine:

> *http://www.director-online.com/howTo/UD_articles/UD37/UD37.html*

Text chunk expressions in Director 7

For a full discussion of chunk expressions see Chapter 7 of *Lingo in a Nutshell*. Here I cover only the new issues in D7.

D7 text members don't support *the mouseChar, the mouseWord, the mouseItem,* or *the mouseLine* system properties as do fields. Use the new *pointToChar()*, *pointToWord()*, *pointToItem()*, *pointToLine()*, and *pointToParagraph()* sprite functions using *the mouseLoc, clickLoc,* or any point, such as:

```
put pointToChar(sprite n, the clickLoc)
put pointToWord(sprite n, the mouseLoc)
```

The new D7 dot notation can be confusing when working with text members and strings. The *count* property cannot count a string—it can only count chars, items, words, lines, or paragraphs in a string. Therefore, the following fails:

```
set testString = "Thanks I'll Eat Here"
put testString.count
```

The following is a supported use of *count* (note that "char" and "word" are singular:

```
put testString.char.count
-- 20
put member("text member").word.count
-- 4
```

Bugs have been reported in D7.0 when counting lines and paragraphs using this method, especially with longer text contents. Upgrade to D7.0.1 or include the word "text" when using *count,* such as:

```
put member("text member").text.line.count
-- 69
put member("text member").text.paragraph.count
-- 13
```

Note the following chunk expressions use integers in brackets to specify a sub-element:

```
put testString.word[3]
-- "Eat"
put testString.word[1].char[3]
-- "a"
```

Use two dots within brackets to specify a range of chars, words, etc., such as:

```
put member("text member").word[1..2]
-- "Thanks I'll"
```

The *number* and *last* properties don't work with dot notation. Use the old style:

```
put the numbers of chars of testString
put the last char of testString
```

Use the *text* property to extract the contents of a *#text* member. The following is wrong:

```
put member("text member").length
-- 0
```

The following is correct:

```
put member("text member").text.length
-- 21
```

Use the *ref* keyword to create a temporary object that holds a specified chunk, and can be used easily in subsequent repeated chunk operations:

```
set temp = member("text member").word[1..2].ref
put temp
-- <Prop Ref 2 157b9ec>
put temp.text
-- "Thanks I'll"
put temp.char[5]
-- "k"
```

Use *the selectedText of member* as an object that represents the current selection:

```
put member("text member").selectedText.word[1]
-- "Eat"
```

Use *the selection of member* to return a list of the starting and ending characters within the current selection:

```
put member("text member").selection
-- [13, 15]
```

Properties that can be cascaded with chunk expressions (*fontSize, alignment,* etc.) cannot be mixed with the D7's *member(x,y)* notation. The following will not work:

```
set the font of member(2, 3) = "Geneva"
```

You must either use the old-style member syntax for the entire command:

```
set the font of member 2 of castLib 3 = "Geneva"
```

or use the new-style syntax for the entire command:

```
member(2,3).font = "Geneva"
```

Properties that apply to the entire member *can* use the mixed notation, such as:

```
set the editable of member(2, 3) = TRUE
```

A bug in D7.0 prevents a *fontStyle* setting from taking effect if the first character in the chunk already contains the style. Upgrade to D7.0.1 or set the range to [#plain] before setting the desired style.

The *html* and *rtf* properties apply only to members, not chunks. This will fail:

```
put member("text member").paragraph[1].html
```

The following will print out the first paragraph of rtf codes, not formatted text:

```
put member("text member").rtf.paragraph[1]
```

Fonts in Director 7

D7 text members use font outlines stored in compressed font members (a.k.a. embedded or Shocked fonts) rather than font bitmaps as did D6 *#richText* members. To embed a font in D7, use Insert ➤ Media Element ➤ Font. You can only embed an existing font, but once embedded, it can be used during authoring even on a computer without the font installed. You must use True Type or Type 1 fonts instead of bitmap fonts to allow anti-aliasing.

When a D6 project is upgraded, *#richText* members are converted to *#text* members, and any custom fonts used in the *#richText* member must be available at the time of the conversion. Check the converted text carefully as conversion is somewhat inconsistent. The *missingFonts of member* property indicates needed fonts.

You should embed the needed fonts in your movie to allow Director to display text in the specific font even if it is not installed at runtime. Embedded fonts are cross-platform and add about 15 to 25 KB each to the Director movie depending on the character set. They are used for both text and field members although the latter are not anti-aliased. There are no font licensing restrictions with embedded fonts because the font is available to Director only, and not installed in the system

In most cases, you should use the original font name followed by an asterisk as your *New Font Name* in the font dialog box. You should include a bitmap version of the font (using the *Bitmap* option) if using small text (7 to 12 points), although this makes the font member somewhat larger. Specify only the subset of characters (using the *Characters* option) and point sizes needed (such as 9, 10, 12) to keep file size down. D7.0.1 conveniently lets you add partial character sets (punctuation, numbers, or Roman characters) using new checkboxes in the *Font Cast Member Properties* dialog box.

Select the *Bold* or *Italic* options for better-looking bold and italic text only if you are including a bitmap version of the font (otherwise, leave them off).

Table 12-9 lists D7's new font member properties, all of which are read-only, but can be set via the font member's property dialog box. See also *the missingFonts of member* text property in Table 12-8.

Table 12-9: Font Member Properties

Command	Usage
bitmapSizes of member	List of point sizes for which bitmaps were generated, such as [8, 10] or <Null> if none specified.
characterSet of member	String containing characters explicitly embedded for the font, such as "0123456789" (or "" for all characters).
font of member	User-specified name of font. Usually *originalFont* followed by an asterisk.
fontStyle of member	Face style of bitmapped point sizes, such as [#plain] or [#bold,#italic].
name of member	Same as *font of member*.
originalFont of member	Original font face name.

Use the *recordFont* command to change a font cast member's attributes:

```
recordFont(fontMember, font {, [face]} ¬
    {,[bitmapSizes]} {,"characterSubset"})
```

Use the *substituteFont* command to change the font used for a specific text cast member:

```
substituteFont (textMemberRef, originalFont, newFont)
```

Hypertext Functions and Highlighted Text

Table 12-10 lists D6 commands that identify the position of the cursor within a field, and can therefore be used to create hypertext. You can highlight text or create hyperlinks based on the string under the mouse. Most of the commands and system properties pertain only to field cast members, not D6 rich text or D7 text cast members.

Table 12-10: Hypertext Commands

Command	Usage
charPosToLoc(member *which-Member, nthChar*)	Returns a point relative to the upper left of the field, at which the specified character resides. The first character might be at *point (1, 10)*.
hilite *chunkExpression* of *chunkExpression*	Highlights any chunk of a field, such as *hilite word 5 of field "myField"*. See *selStart* and *selEnd*.

locToCharPos(member *which-Member*, point(*x, y*))	This is the opposite of *charPosToLoc( )* and returns the closest character to a given point, such as:
	`set nearestCharNum = locToCharPos (member ¬`
	`   whichMember, point(x, y))`

locVToLinePos(member *which-Member, V*)	Returns the closest line to a given vertical distance in pixels, such as:
	`set nearestLineNum = locVToLinePos(member ¬`
	`   whichMember, vOffset)`

the mouseCast	Obsolete. Returned –1 if the mouse was not over a sprite. See *the mouse-Member*.
the mouseChar[1]	Returns the number of the character over which the mouse resides, or –1 if it is not over a field sprite.
on mouseEnter	This handler is called when the mouse enters a sprite's bounding box. You can use it to set *the editable of sprite* property when the mouse is over a field.
the mouseH	This indicates the mouse's horizontal offset from the left of the Stage. Other properties in this table are measured relative to the upper left of the field.
the mouseItem[1]	Returns the number of the item over which the mouse resides, or –1 if it is not over a field sprite.
on mouseLeave	This handler is called when the mouse leaves a sprite's bounding box.
the mouseLine[1]	Returns the number of the line over which the mouse resides, or –1 if it is not over a field sprite.
the mouseMember[2]	This indicates the member of the sprite under the cursor. Returns VOID (not –1 as returned by *the mouseCast*) if it is not over a sprite.

Table 12-10: Hypertext Commands (continued)

Command	Usage
the mouseV	This indicates the mouse's vertical offset from the top of the Stage. Other properties in this table are measured relative to the upper left of the field.
on mouseWithin	This handler is called while the mouse is over a sprite's bounding box. You can use it to perform actions while the mouse is over a field.
the mouseWord[1]	Returns the number of the word over which the mouse resides, or –1 if it is not over a field sprite.
the selection	Returns a string containing the highlighted portion of the current editable field. See *the selStart* and *the selEnd*.
the selEnd	Determines the last character selected in the currently editable field. See *hilite*.
the selStart	Determines the first character selected in the currently editable field. See *hilite*.

[1] The *mouseChar, mouseItem, mouseLine,* and *mouseWord* properties return –1 if the mouse is over the scrollbar of a scrolling field sprite. See the definition of *chars, words, items,* and *lines* that have an impact on these properties in Chapter 7 of *Lingo in a Nutshell*.
[2] In D6.0 the *mouseMember* returned a member number even if the cursor was off-Stage. In D6.0.1 and later, it returns VOID in that case.

The *selStart* and the *selEnd* properties determine the currently selected text of the field currently with keyboard focus. They are specified as *the selStart* and *the selEnd* (without the keywords of member or of sprite) and can be both tested and set. Setting them to the same value creates a blinking insertion point. Set the *selEnd* before setting the *selStart* for reliable results. See Examples 10-5 and 10-6 in *Lingo in a Nutshell*. Use the *hilite* command or *the selStart* and *the selEnd* properties to highlight a portion of a field and *the selection, the selStart,* and *the selEnd* properties to determine the currently highlighted characters. The Message window will steal keyboard focus and cancel field selections, so set and test the selection using handlers attached to buttons, not from the Message window.

James Newton points out that there are two distinct types of Director text selection and highlighting; native OS text selection (user-controlled) and Lingo-based highlighting (programmer-controlled). Only editable fields can be highlighted by the user, but Lingo can highlight even uneditable text fields (a field is editable if either *the editable of member* or *editable of sprite* property is TRUE).

Native OS highlighting can conflict with Lingo highlighting, so Lingo-based highlighting is sometimes best accomplished with uneditable fields (you can write Lingo to simulate user-selection gestures). But Lingo-based selections in uneditable fields disappear when the field scrolls (either via scrollbars or by setting *the scrollTop of member*). During scrolling, you can simulate the highlight using shape sprites (you'll need three rectangles for multiline selections) with an appropriate ink effect and colorization applied, or simply reset the highlight once scrolling completes.

Assuming the *editable of sprite* is FALSE, toggling the *editable of member* property to FALSE temporarily unhighlights the selection, but setting *the editable of member* back to TRUE restores the selection. On the other hand, toggling the *editable of sprite* while the *editable of member* is FALSE kills the last selection and highlights the entire field. Furthermore, Lingo selections made while a field is uneditable disappear if the field is made editable. That is, only selections made while the field is editable are preserved if the field's *editable of member* is toggled (and you should avoid changing the *editable of sprite* property if trying to preserve a selection).

Hyperlinks in Director 7

To create a hyperlink in a D7 text member:

1. Enter the text in a text member and select the text for the hyperlink.

2. Choose Window ➤ Inspectors ➤ Text (Cmd-T or Ctrl-T).

3. In the *Hyperlink Data* field (the one with the link icon) in the Text Inspector, enter the data for the link, such as a URL. If creating simple hypertext, you may want to enter the same text as you highlighted in the Text window.

4. Attach an *on hyperlinkClicked* handler in a sprite script as shown in Example 12-1 (cast, frame, and movie scripts also receive *on hyperlinkClicked* events).

5. Hyperlinks can only be tested while the movie is running and the sprite is on the Stage. Clicking them in the Text window has no effect.

The hyperlink data is passed to the *on hyperlinkClicked* handler, but you must manually implement the desired action (this provides maximum flexibility).

In Example 12-1, *data* contains the hyperlink data to be acted upon and *range* is a two-element list specifying the starting and ending characters of the link. We might execute any text preceded by the string "lingo:" and pass any URL preceded by "http://" to *gotoNetPage( )*. We assume other links are relative URLs, and prefix them with the desired domain name.

Example 12-1: Hyperlinks

```
property spriteNum
on hyperlinkClicked me, data, range
  set currentMember = sprite(spriteNum).member
  set anchorString = currentMember.char[range[1]..range[2]]
  put "The hyperlink on" && anchorString && "was just clicked."
  if data starts "lingo:" then
    delete char 1 to 6 of data
    do data
  else if data starts "http://" then
    gotoNetPage(data)
  else
    -- Assume it is a relative url. Add a domain.
    gotoNetPage ("http://www.zeusprod.com/" & data)
  end if
end
```

The *Hypertext–General* Behavior under *Text* in the Library Palette executes any link prefaced by "lingo:", such as, "lingo: go to frame 5". Enclose nested strings in single quotes, such as "puppetSound 1, 'spoken word'", when using that Behavior and they will be replaced as necessary.

If you import an HTML member, HREF attributes within <A> tags automatically generate the correct hyperlink text, but you still need to set up the *on hyperlink-Clicked* handler.

Reader Exercise: Write a utility to add URL hyperlinks to any text starting with the letters "http://" or "ftp://". Write another utility to add hyperlinks to any underlined text. Hint: In both cases, once you've determined the relevant text, set the hyperlink data to be the same as the text itself, such as:

```
setHyperlink(member(x), word[n], member(x).word[n])
```

or:

```
member(x).word[n].hyperlink = member(x).word[n]
```

Table 12-11: Hyperlink Commands in Director 7

Command	Usage
on hyperlinkClicked	Handler called when linked text is clicked.
chunkExpression.hyperLink	The contents of the hyperlink. Can be tested or set. See *setHyperLink( )*.
chunkExpression.hyperLinkRange	The range of characters of the hyperlinked text, such as [150, 175].
chunkExpression.hyperLinkState	#normal, #active, or #visited.
the hyperLinks of member	A list of characters containing hyperlinks in the text, such as [[12, 50], [92, 108]]
pointInHyperlink (sprite *n*, *point*)	Boolean indicating whether *point* is within a hyperlink area. Useful for rollovers.
setHyperLink (member *n*, *textRange*, *dataString*)	Turns *textRange* into a hyperlink using link specified by *dataString*.
the useHyperlinkStyles of member	No such property. Documentation is wrong. See *the useHypertextStyles of member.*
the useHypertextStyles of member	Boolean indicating whether to display text underlined and in blue. Has no effect under Windows.

Text Anomalies

See the quirk list at *http://www.updatestage.com/buglist.html* for a list of some text quirks, many of which were fixed in D6.0.1 and D6.0.2 and new ones in D7.

Field anomalies when using *member* syntax

Although using either *field* or *member* when referring to a field cast member is supported, many problems have been reported when using the *member* syntax. Symptoms include crashing Director or the entire computer, and incorrect text display (extra line breaks, incorrect styles, or disappearing text). Use the *field* syntax instead of the *member* syntax, especially when using chunk expressions to refer to a subset of a field's contents.

These syntax examples are good:

```
put "someText" into field "TextField"
set the foreColor of line 1 of field "TextField" = 255
set the fontStyle of line 3 of field "TextField" = "bold"
```

These syntax examples can cause problems and should be avoided:

```
set the text of member "TextField" = "someText"
set the foreColor of line 1 of member "TextField" = 255
set the fontStyle of line 3 of member "TextField" = "bold"
```

Note that in some cases where you are setting a property for the entire member, it may work fine. This is okay:

```
set the font of member "TextField" = "helvetica"
```

But if setting a separate chunk's style, always use the *field* syntax:

```
set the font of word 1 of line 4 of field ¬
    "TextField" = "helvetica"
```

Losing text styles

The text style formatting for a field or text member is lost whenever the member's text is EMPTY. Leave at least a space in the member to retain formatting or set the formatting via Lingo after the member has some contents. Setting the *text of member* to EMPTY is an effective way to intentionally clear any style formatting within the field or text member.

Undesired field updates

Changes to fields are not like changes to bitmap sprite properties. When a field changes, it updates immediately on the Stage, even if *the updateLock* is TRUE. (This can be an annoyance during Score Recording.) There is no need to issue an *updateStage* command after modifying a field's contents. D7 text members address this annoyance.

Can't create or import rich text at runtime

In D6, rich text can not be created using *new(#richText)* or imported using *import-FileInto* at runtime. D6 Projectors do not include the rendering engine necessary to render text as a bitmap, which is how Director handles rich text. Use field cast members instead. D7 can create new text members at runtime. Alex Zavatone has posted a workaround for runtime rich text creation in D6 at *http://www.director-online.com/howTo/UD-articles/UD37/UD37.html*.

Rich text appearance problems

Director automatically re-renders D6 rich text into a bitmap whenever the rich text cast member changes, but incorrect text display has been reported. Problems may be exacerbated by rich text members residing in external casts or if the original font used for the cast member is not available (such as when re-editing the text on a different platform). Rich text members with multiple lines, different line heights, wrapped lines, and tabs appear most prone to error. Try simplifying your text, recreating the rich text cast member, adding a RETURN character at the end of each line, using a field cast member, or creating the text in the Paint window or Photoshop. Consider upgrading to D7 text members.

Picture of member

D6.x and the SW6.0 plug-in support *the picture of member* property for field cast members, but the SW6.0.1 plug-in returns VOID for this property for field cast members. D7 and SW7 return a valid picture object for both field and text members.

Copy and paste in Shockwave

Editable fields automatically implement the basic keyboard editing commands. But the copy and paste keyboard shortcuts do not work in Shockwave, because the clipboard is disabled for security reasons. You can manually trap the desired key combinations to copy the text to and from a global variable to the field. See Chapter 10 in *Lingo in a Nutshell* for more information and see *http://www.behaviors.com* for a copy and paste Behavior.

Internationalization and non-English language issues

Director is available in localized versions in Japanese, Spanish, German, and French. For double-byte languages, set *the romanLingo* to FALSE.

Plan ahead for localization by leaving extra room for text strings in various languages, and by placing text strings (and bitmapped text) in an external castLib for easy substitution. Director handles diacritical marks, as described in Appendix C in *Lingo in a Nutshell*. Refer to the downloadable examples (*http://www.zeus-prod.com/nutshell/examples.html*) for a utility that strips diacritical marks from a string. It is very cool. See "Internationalization" in Chapter 7, *Cross-Platform and OS Dependencies*, for more localization issues.

European systems may prevent a @ character from being entered in Shockwave. If you must ask the user for his email address, provide separate fields for the username and domain name, separated by a @ character. SW7 may address this annoyance.

D7 text member anomalies

The anomalies in D7 cast members will probably be addressed in the D7.0.1 maintenance release by the time you read this. Anomalies include incorrect paragraph and line counts, incorrect application of font styles, and differences between text and field nomenclature. This works for fields, but not text:

```
put the fontStyle of char 1 of member 7
```

Fields use the following D7 dot notation:

```
put member(7).fontStyle.char[1]
```

But text members use:

```
put member(7).char[1].fontStyle
```

Bugs have also been reported in *the selection of member* and the appearance of the insertion point in editable sprites.

CHAPTER 13

Graphics, Color, and Palettes

This chapter covers Director's commands and interface options pertaining to graphic elements, color management, the Paint window, and color palettes. This chapter assumes that you are familiar with Director's Paint window, ink effects, and using color palettes. (If you are not, see Macromedia's *Using Director* manual.)

For Director-related tips using Photoshop and DeBabelizer, see the web pages *http://www.zeusprod.com/technote/photoshop.html* and *http://www.zeusprod.com/technote/debabel.html.* See *http://www.zeusprod.com/xtras/medialab.html.* for tips on using MediaLab's Alphamania and Photocaster Xtras.

Color-Related Lingo Commands

Table 13-1 lists all the Lingo commands that pertain to palettes and colors.

Table 13-1: Color-Related Lingo

Command	Notes
the backColor of member	Specifies background color in D6's old color model.
the bgColor of member	Specific background color in D7's new RGB model.
the color of member	Specifies forecolor in D7's new RGB model.
the colorDepth	Returns and sets monitor color depth. See "Colors Schemes and Color Depths" later in this chapter.
the colorQD	Determines whether computer supports color. Always TRUE for supported computers.
the depth of member	Cast member bit depth. May differ from *colorDepth*. Bit depth is shown under Modify ➤ Cast Member ➤ Properties and in the Paint window.

Table 13-1: Color-Related Lingo (continued)

Command	Notes
the framePalette	Indicates the current palette (either the most recent palette set in the Score or the *puppetPalette* in effect). Sets the palette during Score Recording.
the filled of member	If TRUE, the shape cast member is filled with pattern specified by the *pattern of member*.
the foreColor of member	Specifies foreground color in D6's old color model.
the fullColorPermit	If TRUE, uses offscreen buffer at same depth as monitor. If FALSE, uses an 8-bit offscreen buffer for better performance. Obsolete in D7.
the palette of member	Indicate member's palette as set by Modify ➤ Cast Member ➤ Properties palette pop-up. Returns an integer. See Table 13-8.
#palette[1]	The *type of member* for a palette cast member.
the paletteMapping	If TRUE, Director tries to remap graphics in the wrong palette to the current palette by nearest color. See D7's new *dither of member* in Table 13-17.
the paletteRef of member	Indicates member's palette as set by Modify ➤ Cast Member ➤ Properties palette pop-up. Returns symbolic value. See Table 13-8.
the pattern of member *shapeMember*	Specifies fill pattern (1–64) from Tool Palette's pattern chip. Custom tiles are patterns 57–64.
puppetPalette	Changes current palette via Lingo. See Table 13-8.
the scoreColor of sprite	Specifies color of sprites in Score (0–5: purple, yellow, green, blue, pink, orange). Uses nearest colors in current palette. Lingo changes to *the scoreColor* are canceled if playback head moves backwards or loops in a frame.
the scoreSelection	Indicates those channels selected in the Score. –4 represents the Palette channel. See Table 3-22.
the stageColor	Set the Stage's background color. Sets the border's color for full-screen projectors. In D7, you can use *the bgColor of the stage*. See Table 6-2.
the switchColorDepth	Allows the Macintosh monitor depth to switch to the highest *depth of member* property for any cast member.

[1] Using *new(#palette)* creates a new palette matching the default movie palette, but it is not editable. The *#palette* symbol can also be used as the *#format* property within *on getPropertyDescriptionList*. In that case, the Parameters dialog box displays a pop-up menu of the built-in palettes, plus custom palette cast members.

Graphics Types

Graphics can be created in an external program, such as Photoshop, FreeHand, Flash, or Fireworks (designed for web graphics), or with Director's internal Paint window. The categories of graphics in Director are shown in Table 13-2.

Table 13-2: Graphics Formats

Format	Characteristics	Added Via
Bitmaps and imported files	Imported (unlinked) graphic cast members and those created in the Paint window are stored as bitmaps. See Tables 4-4 and 10-3 for a list of supported file formats and required Xtras.	File ➤ Import ➤ Bitmap Image; File ➤ Import ➤ PICT; Window ➤ Paint
Animated GIFs	New in D7	File ➤ Import; Insert ➤ Media Element ➤ Animated GIF
Flash and Vector graphics	Flash files can include bitmaps, text, and animations that can be scaled and rotated while remaining anti-aliased. Vector shapes can be polygons and Bézier curves.	Insert ➤ Media Element ➤ Shockwave Flash Movie (D6); Insert ➤ Media Element ➤ Flash Movie (D7); Insert ➤ Media Element ➤ Vector Shape (D7); Window ➤ Vector Shape (D7)
QuickDraw shapes	QuickDraw shapes are very efficient for areas filled with a sold color, pattern, or custom tile.	Window ➤ Tool Palette
Digital video	QuickTime 2 and 3 import various still image formats including JPEG.	File ➤ Import ➤ QuickTime; File ➤ Import ➤ Video Clip; Insert ➤ Media Element ➤ QuickTime 3 (D6.5 and D7)
Third-party Xtras	Major third-party Xtra graphic formats include Alphamania (*http://www.medialab.com*), which imports bitmap cast members with an alpha channel.	Insert ➤ Media Element ➤ Alphamania; Insert ➤ Media Element ➤ Media Lab Media ➤ Photocaster (D7)

Bitmap Formats

Director imports many different bitmap file formats. To import most formats or use linked cast members at runtime, Director requires the MIX Xtras (as shown in Table 10-3).

Director does not recognize a Photoshop document's multiple paint layers as separate elements. It flattens the image when importing. Either export the layers as separate images in Photoshop or use the Photocaster Xtra (*http://www. medialab.com*) to import the layers as separate cast members automatically. (Photocaster Lite is included with D7.)

There are four possible import modes under File ➤ Import as described later in this chapter. When a graphic containing a custom palette is imported, you are given the option of importing the palette as well (see Figure 13-3).

The size of a bitmap on disk depends on the content of the bitmap and its bit-depth (*the depth of member* property). Thus, an 8-bit graphic uses one-quarter the disk space of a comparable 32-bit graphic. Director's internal bitmap format uses *RLE* (Run-Length Encoding) compression; large areas of the same color, such as a black rectangle, compress extremely well. A 16-bit graphic using only 256 colors will compress on disk to the same size as an 8-bit graphic using 256 colors, but it will use twice the RAM once loaded.

Once loaded from disk, the uncompressed size in bytes of a bitmap in RAM is:

```
width×height×depth/8
```

When creating web graphics, consider throughput requirements. A single JPEG 20 KB image might take 10 seconds to download via a 28.8 Kbps modem. Reduce the dimensions (resolution), bit depth, or quality as necessary to reduce the file size. Use JPEG compression for most complex images, but consider GIF compression for line drawings or graphics with large areas of solid color.

When budgeting for performance, consider the series of bitmaps required by an animation or film loop. For example, a 10-frame film loop lasting one second may require 10 or more bitmaps per second. If each graphic occupies 100 KB on disk, approximately 1 MB of data per second is needed, requiring a hard drive or a fast CD-ROM; such a data stream won't download fast enough via modem. You can reduce the frame rate, number of graphics, or size of each graphic to reduce an animation's bandwidth.

 The size of a member in RAM depends on the bitmap's *depth of member*, not the monitor's *colorDepth*. Bitmaps at a different depth than the monitor must be converted on the fly to the monitor depth, which slows performance. Bitmaps are always imported at 72 dpi.

Note that the size of a cast member in RAM depends on the bitmap's bounding rectangle. Therefore, a 300×300 pixel L-shaped graphic requires the same RAM as a 300×300 pixel rectangle. Cut L-shaped graphics into two cast members to reduce the total memory required by up to 75%. Likewise, a four-sided framing graphic with a large blank center would occupy much more RAM than four individual sides of the frame. Use prudence when splitting a graphic into multiple pieces, as there is minor overhead associated with additional cast members and sprites.

Standard Import mode

Regardless of their original format, all graphics are converted to Director's internal device-independent bitmap (DIB) format when imported as *unlinked* cast members (*Standard Import* mode). This format balances disk size and access speed; it is less compressed than some formats such as JPEG, but it loads more quickly. D7 supports internal JPEG and GIF compression as well. You might use JPEG or GIF images for Shockwave where download time is at a premium, and the internal bitmap format for local Director movies for better performance.

Import PICT File as PICT mode

PICT files imported in *Import PICT File as PICT* mode become internal to the Cast but retain their PICT format (their *type of member* is #picture, not #bitmap). PICTs draw more slowly but take up less RAM than if imported in *Standard Import* mode (their *size of member* is the size of the external PICT on disk).

Link to External File mode

Graphics imported in *Link to External File* mode are linked (remain external) to the Cast and retain their original file format. Their external size depends on their format, but *the size of member* property is the same as for an internal bitmap (because it is converted to a bitmap once loaded). External files must be included with, and remain in the same relative position to, the movie or Projector as during authoring. You must also include the appropriate MIX Xtras with your Projector (see Table 10-3). Linked bitmap cast members can be extremely slow and should usually be avoided.

Include Original Data for Editing option

Files imported with the *Include Original Data for Editing* option can be edited with an external application (as set under `File` ➤ `Preferences` ➤ `Editors`) instead of the Paint window. *The size of member* property for these cast members is identical to that of an internal bitmap, although I suspect that the original data requires some extra storage during authoring. Use this option to maintain JPEG or GIF compression when Shocking movies in D7.

Animated GIFs

D7 can import Animated GIFs with a global color table (i.e., custom palette), in either GIF89a or GIF87 format, via `File` ➤ `Import` or `Insert` ➤ `Media Element` ➤ `Animated GIF`. Animated GIFs require the Animated GIF Xtras shown in Table 10-5, which are not included with Shockwave 7, but can be automatically downloaded as necessary.

The first frame (but not subsequent frames) of an animated GIF can be imported as a bitmap by choosing "Bitmap Image" when prompted during import. Aftershock for D7 no longer exports animated GIFs due to licensing constraints. The GIFtrader Xtra from Integration New Media (*http://www.integration.qc.ca*) will export animated GIFs and import multiple bitmaps from an animated GIF.

Table 13-3 lists the new properties for animated GIFs, plus the commands to rewind, pause, and resume playback of the GIF.

Table 13-3: Animated GIF Lingo

Command	Usage
directToStage of member	Boolean indicating whether member is played direct-to-Stage. Set to TRUE to allow the animated GIF's frame rate to be greater than the Score's tempo.
fileName of member	Indicates file path or URL to external animated GIF if *the linked of member* is TRUE.
fixedRate of member	Integer frames per second; used only if *playBackMode of member* is #fixed.
linked of member	Boolean indicating whether animated GIF content is external or internal to castLib.

Table 13-3: Animated GIF Lingo (continued)

Command	Usage
playBackMode of member	#normal, #fixed, or #lockStep
type of member	The *type of member* is #animGif for an Animated GIF cast member
pause (sprite n)	Pauses an Animated GIF
resume (sprite n)	Resumes playback of an Animated GIF
rewind (sprite n)	Rewinds an Animated GIF to its first frame

An animated GIF has three possible playback modes as set by *the playBackMode of member* property:

#normal

GIF animates at the rate set when then GIF was created, independent of the Score's tempo.

#fixed

GIF animates at the rate specified by the *fps* field in the Animated GIF properties dialog box, or *the fixedRate of member* property.

#lockStep

GIF animates at the same rate as other Director content based on the Score's tempo.

In *#normal* and *#fixedRate* modes, the Animated GIF's update rate is limited by the Score's tempo unless *the directToStage of member* is TRUE.

Flash Members

Flash members must be created using either Flash 2, Flash 3, or Flash Generator, sold separately by Macromedia. Director 6.5 supports Flash 2 files (imported using Insert ➤ Media Element ➤ Shockwave Flash Movie). Director 7 supports Flash 3 files (imported using File ➤ Import or Insert ➤ Media Element ➤ Flash Movie).

The Flash Asset Xtra must be shipped with your Projector if using Flash cast members (or vector shape members). But the Xtra is included in the Shockwave for Director download and automatically placed in the Shockwave *Xtras* folder, so you need not ship it with your Shockwave project.

The *Shockwave for Flash* plug-in (which is included with some browsers) can play both Flash 2 and Flash 3 files in a web browser, but is unrelated to Shockwave for Director or the Flash Asset Xtra.

For information about the Flash Asset Xtra's usage, see the HTML help files included with D6.5 and *http://www.zeusprod.com/nutshell/appendices/flash.html*. See Table 4-10 for a summary of Flash member and sprite properties. See also Appendix B, *Changes in D6 through D6.5*, in *Lingo in a Nutshell* for details on the Lingo related to Flash cast members. Table 13-4 lists numerous properties that pertain to Flash members in addition to vector shapes.

Vector Shapes

D7 supports new vector shapes, created via `Window ➤ Vector Shape` or `Insert ➤ Media Element ➤ Vector Shape`. They can be used to create Bézier curves, polygons, and line graphs. For an introduction to vector shapes, see *Vector Shapes and Bitmaps* in the online Help (or in Chapter 13 of Director 7's *Using Director* manual).

Vector shapes share many properties with Flash cast members (see Table 4-10). Display the properties for a vector shape or Flash member or sprite during authoring using:

```
showProps(member flashOrVectorShapeMember)
showProps(sprite flashOrVectorShapeSprite)
```

Vector shapes require the Shape Xtra (see Table 10-5) during authoring, but require only the Flash Asset Xtra at runtime or in Shockwave.

Table 13-4 shows vector shape member and sprite properties, most of which take their default values from the Vector Shape window and properties dialog box. Unless otherwise noted, the properties are member properties only. Sprite properties override member properties of the same name.

Table 13-4: Vector Shape Properties

Property	Usage
antiAlias[1]	Boolean indicating whether to anti-alias the vector shape's border for better appearance, but poorer performance. Default is TRUE.
backgroundColor	*rgb (red, green, blue)* color used for area of bounding rectangle surrounding the vector shape sprite.
broadcastProps[2]	Boolean indicating whether to change all vector shape sprites when a member changes. Default is TRUE.
centerRegPoint[2]	Boolean indicating whether to recenter *regPoint* if vector shape is resized. Default is TRUE.
closed	Boolean indicating whether vector shape is open (a curve) or closed (a shape). See the *Closed* checkbox in the Vector Shape window.
defaultRect[2]	Default rect *(l, t, r, b)* for new sprites if *defaultRectMode* is #fixed.
defaultRectMode[2]	Determines default size of new sprites created from member: #flash (default; uses rect specified by *flashRect*) or #fixed (uses rect specified by *defaultRect*).
directToStage[1,2]	Boolean indicating whether member is played back direct-to-Stage, in which case it is rendered in the foreground.
endColor[3]	*rgb (red, green, blue)* destination color used for gradient fill.
fillColor	*rgb (red, green, blue)* color for solid fill, or starting color of gradient fill.
fillCycles[3]	Number of repetitions in fill pattern; default is 1.
fillDirection[3]	Direction of fill, from 0.0 (default) to 360.0.

Table 13-4: Vector Shape Properties (continued)

Property	Usage
fillMode	#none, #solid, or #gradient; relevant only if *closed of member* is TRUE.
fillOffset[3]	point (*x*, *y*) for offset of gradient fill; default is point(0, 0).
fillScale[3]	Size of fill pattern, 0.0 to *n* percent. Default is 100.0.
flashRect[2]	Default rect (*l*, *t*, *r*, *b*) for new sprites if *defaultRectMode* is #flash.
gradientType[3]	Specifies #linear or #radial fill pattern.
imageEnabled[1,2]	Boolean indicating whether sprite is visible. Default is TRUE.
originH[1,2]	Horizontal component of *originPoint*. Default is 0.0.
originMode[1,2]	Determines origin for rotation and scaling: #center (default), #topLeft, or #point (see *originPoint*).
originPoint[1,2]	point (x, y) of origin around which rotation and scaling occur if *originMode* is #point. Default is point(0, 0).
originV[1,2]	Vertical component of *originPoint*. Default is 0.0.
regPoint[2]	Registration point (*x*, *y*) for positioning sprite on Stage.
rotation of sprite[2]	Rotation angle in degrees (sprite property only for vector shapes; member and sprite property for Flash assets).
scale[1,2]	Magnification for both horizontal and vertical scaling. Default is 100.0 (normal size).
scaleMode[1,2]	Indicates mode in which scaling is performed: #showAll, #noBorder, #exactFit, #noScale, or #autoSize (default).
static[1,2]	Boolean indicating whether sprite is fixed over time and does not need to be redrawn. Default is FALSE (non-static).
strokeColor	*rgb (red, green, blue)* color of border of shape.
strokeWidth	Width of border of shape.
type	The *type of member* is #vectorShape for vector shape members and #flash for Flash members.
vertexList	List of vertices and optional control handles.
viewH[1,2]	Horizontal component of *viewPoint*. Default is 0.0.
viewPoint[1,2]	point (*x*, *y*) that determines which portion of the shape or Flash member is displayed in the bounding rect. Default is point(0, 0).
viewScale[1,2]	Scale from 0.0 to n for magnification within its bounding rect. Default is 100.0.
viewV[1,2]	Vertical component of *viewPoint*. Default is 0.0.

[1] Both a member and a sprite property.
[2] Supported by Flash cast members too.
[3] Relevant only if *fillMode* is #gradient.

Graphics & Color

Vector shapes and Flash members share the same scaling modes, as described in the ondline Help under *the scaleMode* property. For a visual depiction of *the scaleMode's* effect, see "Using Flash Movies" under *Using Interactive Media Types* under *Contents* in the online Help. Note that in D7, the default *scaleMode* is the new *#autoSize* option, not *#showAll* as it was for Flash members in D6.5. The *#noScale* scale mode is also new in D7.

Setting *the scale of sprite* does not change the size of the sprite's rect on Stage, it only scales the member within the existing sprite rect as defined by the Score or the *rect of sprite*. That is, the *scale* is a percentage relative to *the rect of sprite*, not *the rect of member*. Even stretched sprites have a default *scale* of 100.0.

The *#autoSize* mode allows a sprite to be rotated, skewed, and flipped, using the properties in Table 3-2. It works properly only if the *scale* is 100.0, the *originMode* is *#center*, and *the originPoint* is point(0,0) (*the originH* and *originV* are both 0.0). Otherwise, the sprite will be clipped instead of scaled.

Vector shape vertices

Unlike a Flash member, a vector shape can contain only one continuous curve. The *vertexList of member* property contains a list of the vertices in a vector shape of the form:

```
[[#vertex: point(x1, y1)], [#vertex: point(x2, y2), ¬
    #handle1: point(x3, y3), #handle2: point(x4, y4)]]
```

where each *#vertex* is a fixed point, and the optional *#handle1* and *#handle2* properties are control points that determine the shape of the curve between vertices. Vertices without handles are "corners" and are connected by straight lines to other vertices without handles. Vertices with handles are connected to adjacent vertices by Bézier curves whose slope is controlled by the handles' position relative to the vertex. Corners are indicated by square dots, and vertices with handles are indicated by round dots in the Vector Shape window. See the "Creating a vector shape" Show Me movie for a demonstration.

You can also use the rectangle, round rectangle, and oval tools in the Vector Shape window to draw shapes, but these tools are available only prior to other vertices being added.

Table 13-5 shows the keyboard and mouse commands used to manipulate vertices.

Table 13-5: Vector Shape Keyboard Commands

Action	Tool	Command
Open Vector Shape window	N/A	Cmd-Shift-V (Macintosh) or Ctrl-Shift-V (Windows)
Create corner vertex	Pen	Click.
Create a vertex with handles	Pen	Click and drag.
Delete a vertex	Arrow	Select with arrow, then delete (Mac), backspace (Windows).

Table 13-5: Vector Shape Keyboard Commands (continued)

Add a vertex in the middle of a line	Pen	Wait until the cursor changes to indicate that pen is exactly over line, then click on line.
Move a vertex	Arrow	Click and drag or use arrow keys.
Close a shape	Pen	Click on first vertex or use *Closed* checkbox.
Unclose a shape	Close button	Uncheck the *Closed* checkbox.
Extend a line	Arrow, then Pen	Click on one of the end vertices with the arrow, then add new vertices with pen.
Extend a line at both ending vertices (adds two vertices; works with open shapes only)	Pen	Option-click (Mac), Alt-click (Windows).
Add handles to an existing vertex	Arrow	Option-click (Mac), Alt-click (Windows).
Move both handles in unison	Arrow	Click and drag either handle.
Move one handle independently of the other	Arrow	Cmd-click (Mac), Ctrl-click (Windows). (Use Shift to constrain; useful to align two handles.)
Delete handles	Arrow	Drag handle onto vertex to make it act like a corner.
Scale entire shape	Arrow	Cmd-Option-drag (Mac), Ctrl-Alt-drag (Windows)
Constrain drag to circle, square, etc.	Shape Tools	Shift-drag.
Select Tools	Various	Arrow (0), Pen (6), RegPoint (G), Hand (H), Rect (r or R), RoundRect (p or P), Oval (o or O). See Table 3-12.

Elements of *the vertexList of member* can be read, but not set, using the standard Lingo list functions. To modify *the vertexList*, use the following commands or assign an entire vertex list at once. A vertex location is relative to the origin of the vector shape (see the *originMode* property).

To add a vertex via Lingo, use:

```
addVertex(member memberRef, indexToAddAt, pointToAddVertex )
```

The *indexToAddAt* should be between 1 and the number of vertices plus 1. The new vertex can be a *point* structure or a two-element list, such as:

```
addVertex(member 5, 1, point(57, 72))
addVertex(member 5, 1, [57, 72])
```

This adds a vertex at the *originMode* position, such as the center or top left:

```
addVertex(member 5, 1, point(0, 0))
```

To specify control handles, include two additional points, which are relative to the vertex (not to the vector shape's origin):

```
addVertex(member memberRef, indexToAddAt, pointToAddVertex, ¬
    handle2Point, handle1Point)
```

Setting control handles via *addVertex()* is buggy in D7.0. The fourth parameter seems to be ignored and the fifth parameter is erroneously used for *#handle1* instead of *#handle2*. The *#handle2* property of the newly created vertex is erroneously created as point(0, 0).

```
addVertex(member 5, 1, [57, 72], [0,0], [10, -40])
put member(5).vertexList
-- [[#vertex: point(57.0, 72.0), #handle1: point(10.0, -40.0),
    #handle2: point(0.0, 0.0)]...
```

Use *moveVertexHandle()* to move the handles instead or upgrade to D7.0.1.

To delete a vertex, use:

```
deleteVertex(member memberRef, indexToRemove)
```

This deletes the last vertex:

```
deleteVertex(member 5, member(5).vertexList.count)
```

You cannot delete the only remaining vertex. Attempting to delete a non-existing vertex results in a –2147221503 error ("Invalid parameter passed").

To move a vertex, use:

```
moveVertex(member memberRef, vertexIndex, xChange, yChange)
```

such as:

```
moveVertex(member 5, 1, 25, -75)
```

To move a vertex's handles, use:

```
moveVertexHandle(member memberRef, vertexIndex, ¬
    handleIndex, xChange, yChange)
```

To move *#handle1* of vertex 4 of member 5 left 10 pixels and up 20 pixels, use:

```
moveVertexHandle (member 5, 4, 1, -10, -20)
```

To move *#handle2* of the same vertex right 15 pixels and down 18 pixels use:

```
moveVertexHandle (member 5, 4, 2, 15, 18)
```

The *moveVertexHandle()* function is ignored if the existing vertex does not have control handles.

To edit multiple vertices or add handles to existing vertices, reassign a new list to *the vertexList of member*, such as:

```
temp = member(5).vertexList
temp [1] = [#vertex:point(27,52)]
temp[2] = [#vertex:point(75,92), #handle1:point(-10,0), ¬
    #handle2:point(10,0)]
member(5).vertexList = temp
```

QuickDraw Shapes

Use the Tool Palette (Cmd-7 on Macintosh or Ctrl-7 under Windows) to create QuickDraw shape cast members. Shape cast members are very efficient, occupying only a few bytes, but they are drawn marginally slower than an equivalent bitmap. A shape sprite can be stretched without degrading performance (whereas stretching bitmaps is very slow). Shapes drawn in the Paint window are immediately converted to bitmaps, and should not be confused with "live" QuickDraw shapes.

Use an unstroked (zero-width border), unfilled shape sprite with a *mouseUp* or *mouseDown* handler attached to create invisible hotspots. See Table 4-10 for shape cast member properties. Refer particularly to *the shapeType of member* (*#rect*, *#roundRect*, *#oval*, or *#line*).

The registration point of a shape is always its upper-left corner, in contrast to a bitmap whose registration point defaults to its center. To swap a shape cast member with a bitmap cast member, it is easiest to first set the bitmap's registration point to its upper-left corner using the registration tool in the Paint window.

Shapes are drawn using the foreground color and fill pattern set in the Tool Palette. You can use custom tiles created with other cast members to create very efficient backgrounds, such as a basketball court or tile floor.

Hold down the Shift key to constrain proportions while drawing or resizing a shape (to create circles, squares, and lines at incrementss of 45 degrees).

Shape sprites highlight only if their *ink of sprite* is set to 8 (Matte).

The foreground color chip in the Tool palette (see Figure 13-1) can colorize shape cast members. See "Color Chips" later in this chapter.

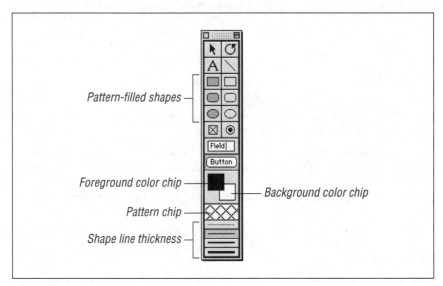

Figure 13-1: Tool palette

Drawing at Runtime

You cannot use the authoring mode's drawing tools at runtime. To draw at runtime, one typically uses a colorized shape cast member (such as an oval) as a paintbrush by turning on *the trails of sprite*. You can switch *the member of sprite* property to switch brushes and set *the ink of sprite* for different effects.

You can set *the rect of sprite* of shape sprites dynamically to create ovals and rectangles and *the rect of sprite* of a line sprite to connect two points. There are two types of line shapes: those that slant from the upper left to the lower right and those that slant from the lower left to the upper right. Because Director allows you to specify a sprite's rectangle but not the endpoints of a line, you must use a line cast member of the appropriate slant to draw lines in Director 6. In D7, you can set *the lineDirection of member* dynamically (0 indicates a line sloping from top left to bottom right; 1 indicates opposite slope).

DrawXtra (formerly XtraDraw), published by Tabuleiro da Baiana (*http://www.tbaiana.com*) embeds a complete drawing tool inside Director. Basic drawing can be achieved at runtime using the Cast FX Xtra (*http://www.penworks.com*). RavWare (*http://www.ravware.com*) has a drawing Xtra under development as of January 1999.

Colors Schemes and Color Depths

The monitor's color depth determines how many colors can be displayed simultaneously. Computers represent colors with numeric codes. The terms *8-bit*, *16-bit*, and *32-bit* color refer to the size of the number used to represent the color of each pixel. (These are unrelated to 16-bit and 32-bit Projectors under Windows.) Note that there are 8 bits to a single byte (see calculations later in this chapter).

Because the monitor's color depth determines how many bits are used to display each pixel, the term *bit depth* is often used interchangeably with color depth or monitor depth; however, graphics might have a different bit depth than the monitor color depth.

Color Models

There are different notations for specifying color, including RGB (Red, Green, Blue), HSB (Hue, Saturation, Brightness), HLS (Hue, Lightness, Saturation), and CMYK (Cyan, Magenta, Yellow, and Black).

See Chapter 10, *The Image Menu*, of *Photoshop in a Nutshell* (Donnie O'Quinn and Matt LeClair, O'Reilly & Associates) for a discussion of different color models; see "Poynton's Color FAQ" at *http://www.inforamp.net/~poynton/notes/colour_and_gamma/ColorFAQ.html* for more than you ever wanted to know about different color schemes.

Director uses RGB color notation, but the other color schemes are indirectly equivalent. For example, you can specify either RGB or HSB values in the Macintosh and Windows color pickers.

Keep in mind that the units in any scheme are somewhat arbitrary. RGB values range from 0 to 100, 0 to 255, or 0 to 65535 depending on the color depth and the program. Photoshop 3.0 uses Hue (0–360), Lightness (0–255), Saturation (0–255). The Mac OS 7.6 Color Picker uses HSB and RGB values from 0 to 65535. The Windows Color Picker uses HSL values from 0 to 240, and RGB from 0 to 255. Other color pickers and applications may use different ranges.

I'll first examine *direct color* (non-palettized 16-bit and 32-bit modes), and then discuss monitor color depth. Later I'll discuss the use of palettes in *palettized* color mode (8-bit).

Director 7's new RGB color model and color picker

Prior to D7 there was no easy, consistent, cross-platform method to specify colors independently of the monitor depth. D7 introduces a different color model in which colors can be specified either as absolute RGB values or as palette indices whose color depends on the current palette. (See "Direct Color" in the next section and "Palettes" later in this chapter.)

The D7 color palette pop-up, explained in Chapter 8 of Macromedia's *Using Director* manual, is accessed via the color chips specified in Table 13-20. The user can select from a palette index, specify RGB colors by their hexadecimal equivalent, add favorite colors to the palette, or access the OS color picker.

The color mode (*RGB* or *Palette Index)* selected using Modify ➤ Movie ➤ Properties ➤ *Color Selection* determines whether the palette pop-up displays hexadecimal (hex) RGB values or palette indices. Hold down Option (Macintosh) or Alt (Windows) for the opposite setting (although the Paint window always shows hex RGB values).

Director 7 introduces the concept of a color object, which takes the form:

```
color (#rgb, red, green, blue)
```

or the equivalent notation:

```
rgb (red, green, blue)
```

where *red*, *green*, and *blue* indicate the amount of each primary color used to achieve the final color, and range from 0 to 255. Or, in hex notation:

```
rgb ("#RRGGBB")
```

where *RR*, *GG*, and *BB* are hexadecimal numbers from 00 through FF (equivalent to 0–255 in decimal).

Macromedia may support additional color models, such as *#cmyk* and *#hsv*, in the future. Alternatively, to specify a color by palette position instead of RGB value, use:

```
color (#paletteIndex, index)
```

or the equivalent notation:

```
paletteIndex (index)
```

where *index* is from 0 to 255 and represents a position in an 8-bit palette.

Note that RGB colors are independent of the monitor depth or current palette, whereas palette indices point to a position in the current palette.

D7's new *color* and *bgColor of sprite* properties replace the deprecated *foreColor* and *backColor of sprite* properties, which supported only palette indices, and are maintained for backward compatibility only.

All color objects support the *red, green, blue, colorType,* and *paletteIndex* properties as shown in the following examples:

```
set the color of sprite 1 = color(#rgb, 255, 122, 0)
put the color of sprite 1
-- rgb( 255, 122, 0 )
put sprite(1).color.colorType
-- #rgb
put sprite(1).color.green
-- 122
sprite(1).color = rgb("#FF0000")
put sprite(1).color
-- rgb( 255, 0, 0 )
```

Note that you *cannot* use the decimal equivalent of a hex RGB value, such as:

```
sprite(1).color = 16711680
```

To find the closest palette index for an RGB color, use:

```
put sprite(1).color.paletteIndex
-- 69
```

To change the color mode from RGB to using a palette index, use:

```
sprite(1).color.colorType = #paletteIndex
put sprite(1).color
-- paletteIndex (69)
```

There is no easy way to obtain the RGB components of an index within an arbi-
tary palette. The *paletteIndex()* function works only with the current palette, as
indicated by *the framePalette.* To determine the red, green, or blue component of
the RGB triplet associated with a palette index in *the framePalette,* use:

```
put paletteIndex(69).red
-- 255
```

Don't confuse the red, green, and blue components of an RGB triplet, which each
range from 0 to 255, with a palette index, which coincidentally also ranges from 0
to 255. Each palette index points to a different RGB triplet that indicates a 24-bit
color.

There are also two undocumented (and very slow) commands in D7 to get and set
the color of individual pixels in a bitmap. Unfortunately, these use the decimal
equivalent of the hex notation.

This retrieves the color of the pixel at point(27, 67) in bitmap member 5, which is
equivalent to the hex color #FFFF99, or rgb (255, 255, 153):

```
put getPixel (member 5, 27, 67)
-- 16777113
```

This sets the color of the pixel at point(60, 50) in bitmap member 5 to the hex
color #CC3300, or rgb (204, 51, 00):

```
setPixel (member 5, 60, 50, 13382400)
```

Direct Color

Graphics take up a lot of space because the color of each pixel must be stored separately. In *direct color* modes (16-bit and 32-bit), a pixel's value specifies the RGB components to create the desired color.

So-called 16-bit color uses only 15 bits (5 bits for each RGB component) and doesn't use the 16th bit. This leads to 2^{15} (32,768) possible colors constructed by mixing 2^5 (32) shades of each primary color.

So-called 32-bit color uses only 24 bits (8 bits for each RGB component) and leaves the last 8 bits for an alpha channel. This leads to 2^{24} (16.77) million possible colors constructed by mixing 2^8 (256) shades of each primary color. D7 can specify colors as an RGB triplet as described in the previous section.

In 16-bit color (2 bytes per pixel), a 640×480 bitmap in RAM requires:

$640 \times 480 \times 2 = 614,400$ bytes = 600 KB

In 32-bit color (4 bytes per pixel), a 640×480 bitmap in RAM requires:

$640 \times 480 \times 4 = 1,228,800$ bytes = 1.2 MB

So 32-bit graphics allow you 16.77 million colors to choose from, but 16-bit graphics still afford 32,768 possible colors while requiring only half the memory space (and somewhat less disk space, depending on the nature of the graphic and file format).

Choosing a Color Depth

Even though most computers support higher color depths, I recommend using 256 colors (8-bit) when practical, for increased performance and compatibility. If using 8-bit images, you are advised to learn DeBabelizer or a similar tool that creates custom palettes and super-palettes for batches of images. Using 8-bit color requires planning, because you are limited to 256 colors onscreen at any one time. Digital video quality usually suffers noticeably at 256 colors, but a proper custom palette can limit the damage. See "Palettes" and "Palette Problems Under Windows" for details on palette management and conflict resolution.

A 16-bit color depth offers an acceptable compromise between the competing needs of visual quality, storage space, and performance; most current systems support 16-bit color, although older systems may not or the user may have his monitor set to 256 colors. Digital video will look better in 16-bit than in 8-bit color, and there is no need to fuss with palettes. Although suitable in most cases, there may not be enough colors available in 16-bit for very subtle gradients. (Introduce noise into a gradient to make it appear smoother.)

Use 32-bit color only for presentations where performance is secondary to color fidelity (such as for art portfolios or color-matching applications), or in cases where you need alpha channel support (D7 supports alpha channels, but you'll need the Alphamania Xtra in D6). But 32-bit color is not universally supported and causes severe performance degradation on slower systems. See *http://www.zeus-prod.com/nutshell/alpha.html* for details on using alpha channels.

Monitor Color Depth

Ordinarily, you will create assets that match the desired monitor's color depth, but the user's monitor may be at the wrong depth.

 Director converts cast members of the wrong depth to the monitor's color depth each time they are drawn to the Stage, which slows performance.

The colorDepth system property indicates the color depth of the monitor and is optionally used as the depth for imported graphics. In a multi-monitor setup, *the colorDepth* reflects the monitor containing the Stage; the depth of other monitors may be different.

Animations are generally slower at higher color depths, but graphics perform best at their "natural" depth. For example, 16-bit cast members will perform best (even better than 8-bit graphics) when the monitor is set to thousands of colors (16-bit).

Use the code in Example 13-1 to check for cast members that have the wrong color depth.

Example 13-1: Finding Cast Members of the Wrong Depth

```
on checkDepth desiredDepth
  -- Search for cast members of the wrong color depth
  if voidP(desiredDepth) then
    set desiredDepth = the colorDepth
  end if
  -- Loop through all the cast members in all the castLibs
  repeat with i = 1 to the number of castLibs
    repeat with j = 1 to the number of members of castLib i
      if (the type of member j of castLib i) = #bitmap then
        set thisDepth = the depth of member j of castLib i
        -- Print members with aberrant color depths
        if (thisDepth <> desiredDepth) then
          put "Depth of" && member j of castLib i && ":" ¬
            && thisDepth
        end if
      end if
    end repeat
  end repeat
end checkDepth
```

The colorDepth and depth of member properties

Table 13-6 lists the values for *the colorDepth* property. The number of possible colors at a given depth is 2^n where n is the bits per pixel. For example, in 8-bit color, there are 256 possible colors (ranging from 0 to 255), because 2^8 equals 256 (but recall that in 16-bit and 32-bit modes, only 15 bits and 24 bits are actually used). Not all monitors and video cards support all color depths.

The values in Table 13-6 also pertain to *the depth of member* property, which is usually 1, 8, 16, or 32. 1-bit bitmaps can be colorized and are also used for custom cursors. 2-bit and 4-bit cast members are rarely used, because 8-bit cast members using the same number of colors will compress just as well on disk and display more quickly on an 8-bit monitor.

Table 13-6: The colorDepth Property Values

Bits/pixel	Simultaneous Colors	Notes	Mode
0	N/A	Restores user's Control Panel setting under Windows 98/NT (rarely works in Win95).	N/A
1	2	Black and white. Rarely used.	N/A
2	4	Rarely used.	N/A
4	16	Windows VGA palette is the only 4-bit palette available under Windows. Rarely used.	Palettized
8	256	Palette of 256 colors can be customized.	Palettized
15	32,768	16-bit color is reported as 15-bit on some Windows systems.	Direct color[1]
16	32,768	"Thousands" or "high color."	Direct color[1]
24	16,777,216	32-bit color is reported as 24-bit on some Windows systems.[2]	Direct color[1]
32	16,777,216	"Millions" or "true color."[2]	Direct color[1]

[1] Palette fades don't work in modes above 8-bit. Within Windows 3.1 Projectors (even when played under Windows 95/98/NT), 16-bit and 32-bit graphics are dithered to the current 8-bit palette even if the monitor is set to a higher color depth, although digital video will display at the higher depth.
[2] Recommended only for projects requiring perfect color matching (Pantone, etc.) or alpha channels.

Checking and setting the monitor color depth

There are three ways to set the monitor color depth. When a monitor depth change is successful, there is a very noticeable flash:

Tell the user to change the monitor manually if you detect it is incorrect
   The monitor's bit depth can be set via the *Monitors* or *Monitors and Sound* Control Panel by Macintosh users, but it is also settable via Lingo on the Macintosh. It can be set using the *Settings* tab in the *Display* Control Panel under Windows 95/98/NT, or the *System Configuration* option under Windows 3.1. The MS QuickRes utility (part of MS Power Toys) may allow the Windows 95 color depth to be set without rebooting, but rebooting is often necessary. Windows 98/NT support switching the *colorDepth* via Lingo for most video cards.

Build a Projector that automatically changes the color depth (Macintosh only)
   If you create your Macintosh Projector using the *Reset Monitor to Match Movie's Color Depth* option, the Projector will change the monitor's color

depth to match the highest depth of any bitmap cast member in the current movie (see Example 13-1). If using this option, the monitor's color depth may not automatically return to its original value when the Projector quits. The Projector's setting for this option determines the default value of *the switch-ColorDepth* property, which controls whether Director attempts to change the monitor's color depth when a new movie starts. This option is the easiest to implement, but also offers the least control. I recommend avoiding it.

 If a flash occurs (on the Macintosh only) when switching between movies, it may be that Director is switching the monitor depth, and it's not a so-called "palette flash." In D7.0, it will flash even if the monitor is already at the correct depth.

Attempt to change the colorDepth via Lingo or an Xtra

Setting *the colorDepth* usually works on Macintosh computers, Windows 98 and Windows NT, but it usually has no effect under Windows 95, and it never works under Windows 3.1. Instead, use an Xtra such as *DisplayRes* (*http://www.updatestage.com/xtras*) or BuddyAPI to change the color depth (this may not work with all Windows video cards).

Example 13-2 includes routines to save and restore the monitor's color depth. Call *setMonitorDepth* once, perhaps from your *startUp* handler, and call *restoreMonitorDepth* before quitting, perhaps from your quit button.

Example 13-2: Checking and Setting the Monitor's Color Depth

```
on setMonitorDepth newDepth
  global gOrigColorDepth
  -- Check for multiple monitors, and ask user to set them.
  if count (the deskTopRectList) > 1 then
    alert "Please ensure that all monitors are set to" ¬
      && newDepth && "-bit color."
  end if
  -- Save the old color depth, so that we can restore it later
  set gOrigColorDepth = the colorDepth
  if not isDepthOK(newDepth) then
    -- Try to set the colorDepth. May fail under Win 95.
    set the colorDepth = newDepth
    -- Check if we succeeded
    if not isDepthOK(newDepth) then
      alert "The attempt to set your monitor to" && newDepth ¬
        & "-bit color failed. Please set your monitor accordingly."
    end if
  end if
end setMonitorDepth

on isDepthOK newDepth
  set depthOK = FALSE
  set depth = the colorDepth
  case (newDepth) of
```

Example 13-2: Checking and Setting the Monitor's Color Depth (continued)

```
    8:   -- Is it already set to 8-bit?
      if depth = 8 then set depthOK = TRUE
    16: -- Both 15 or 16 are acceptable color depths
      if depth = 15 or depth = 16 then set depthOK = TRUE
    32: -- Both 24 and 32 are acceptable color depths
      if depth > 16 then set depthOK = TRUE
    end case
    return depthOK
end isDepthOK


on restoreMonitorDepth
  global gOrigColorDepth
  set the colorDepth = gOrigColorDepth
end restoreMonitorDepth
```

Reader Exercise: Modify Example 13-2 to tolerate any *colorDepth* greater than or equal to *newDepth*. You must gracefully handle PCs that report *the colorDepth* as 15 or 24 instead of 16 or 32.

In Example 13-2, if *setMonitorDepth* fails to set *the colorDepth*, it gives up and posts an error (you can modify it to return an error code instead or try using an Xtra to set it under Windows). Some Macintosh video cards can be set to 32-bit color, but not 16-bit color. Example 13-3 attempts to set the monitor to 32-bit mode if 16-bit mode failed. 32-bit mode will giver poorer performance, but is preferable to the palettized (8-bit) mode if using non-palettized graphics.

Example 13-3: Setting Monitor to Greater Than 256 Colors

```
if the colorDepth <= 8 then
  set the colorDepth = 16
  -- Check whether the action succeeded
  if the colorDepth <= 8 then
    set the colorDepth = 32
    -- Check again whether the action succeeded
    if the colorDepth <= 8 then
      alert "Couldn't set depth to 16-bit or higher"
    end if
  end if
end if
```

Reader Exercise: Modify Example 13-3 for the case of 32-bit graphics. Try to set the monitor to 32-bit mode; if that fails, try to set it to 16-bit mode, in which case 32-bit graphics are displayed using the closest 16-bit colors available. D7.0 did not provide runtime dithering from 32-bit to 16-bit, but D7.0.1 does.

In D4.0.4 there was a known bug in which PowerPCs operated very slowly in bit depths greater than 8-bit. Example 13-4 solves the problem by resetting *the colorDepth*. Note that it uses *the machineType* to determine the platform because *the platform* property was not supported in D4.

Example 13-4: Resetting Monitor for PowerPCs in D4.0.4

```
if the colorDepth <> 8 and the machineType <> 256 then
  -- Switch and restore the color depth on PowerPCs
  set oldDepth = the colorDepth
  set the colorDepth = 8
  set the colorDepth = oldDepth
end if
```

Caveats with the colorDepth

There are a number of caveats with the monitor set at different color depths and with *the colorDepth* command itself:

- *The colorDepth* can be read but not set from Shockwave. It can be set from MIAWs.

- Setting *the colorDepth* will do nothing on the Macintosh if the new depth is not supported, and may have no effect under Windows 95 even if the new depth *is* supported. Test *the colorDepth* again after you've tried to set it, as shown in Examples 13-2 and 13-3.

- Using multiple monitors at different depths may cause unpredictable results. In D7.0, it will cause scripts to appear black during authoring. Use *count (the deskTopRectList)* to determine the number of monitors. There is no way to determine or set the color depth of multiple monitors via Lingo alone; it requires an Xtra, such as DisplayRes.

- *The colorDepth* doesn't distinguish between 256 colors and 256 shades of gray on the Macintosh. Set *the colorDepth* to another value and then back to 8 to ensure that the monitor is set to 256 colors rather than shades of gray.

- Some Windows PCs report a *colorDepth* of 15 instead of 16, and 24 instead of 32. Check *the colorDepth* in a way that will work for any valid variation, as shown in Examples 13-2 and 13-3.

- Not all monitor resolutions are supported at all color depths. Because there is generally a limited amount of video RAM (VRAM), the higher color depths support lesser monitor resolutions. Use *the deskTopRectList* to check the monitor resolution.

- Color depths higher than 8-bit (256 colors) may not be supported on all user systems, require more memory, can severely degrade performance, and are not fully supported under Windows 3.1. To support higher color depths, use Windows 95/98/NT, or use QuickTime, which bypasses Director's offscreen buffer and can display 16-bit or 24-bit video and JPEG images even under Windows 3.1.

- New cast members created in the Paint window use *the colorDepth* as their default depth. Cast members created with Edit ➤ Duplicate or via copy and paste use the same depth as the original cast member. (In D4, copying and pasting always created a new cast member with *the colorDepth* as its depth.)

- Test your presentation at 8-bit, 16-bit, and 32-bit color depths on all platforms. The same graphic may look fine in 8-bit, but be problematic in higher color depths, or vice versa. Watch for colorized sprites (see Table 13-21) and anomalies during palette fades, which vary at different color depths.

- Earlier versions of PrintOMatic may not print under Windows using the *draw-StagePicture* method if *the colorDepth* is greater than 8. Obtain the latest version from *http://www.printomatic.com*.

- Some Xtras may not work at all color depths or with all cast member bit depths. For example, Alphamania requires 32-bit graphics and works best at 16-bit and 32-bit monitor depths, but also supports 8-bit dithering.

- QuickTime and QTVR perform best at a 16-bit monitor depth, although they also support 8-bit and 32-bit monitor depths.

- If *the colorDepth* is greater than 8, the *Switch Colors* command and *Switch* ink in Paint window do not work in D6. In D7, they work in all color depths.

- If *the colorDepth* is greater than 8, palette fades perform jump cuts instead and erase all graphics on Stage until they are redrawn due to a change in the Score. Check *the colorDepth* before executing a palette fade.

- Theoretically, palettes apply only when the color depth is 8 bits or less, but Director uses palettes in some respects even when the monitor is set to a higher color depth. (See Table 3-21.)

- Under Windows 3.1, 16-bit and 32-bit graphics are dithered through the current 8-bit palette even if *the colorDepth* is greater than 8. The Microsoft DIB driver for Windows 3.1, which Director uses prior to D7, performs real-time compositing only in 8-bit mode, so 16-bit and 32-bit graphics cannot be composited in Windows 3.1 Projectors.

- Even if *the colorDepth* and *the depth of member* are greater than 8, the foreground and background color chips in the D6 Paint window allow you to paint only with colors in the cast member's 8-bit palette. D7 allows painting in any color.

- Likewise, the Tool Palette color chips can use color only from the active palette in D6. The *backColor* and *foreColor* member and sprite properties vary by platform and with the monitor's color depth (see Table 13-21). D7's new *color* and *bgColor* properties remedy this deficiency.

- *The stageColor* uses an index of 0–255 into an 8-bit palette at all color depths.

- In D6, setting *the stageColor* doesn't affect the background surrounding a full-screen Projector until the next movie starts. In D7, it changes the background color immediately.

- On some video cards, with monitors set to thousands of colors (16-bit color), some rounding will occur in RGB conversion when using D6's DirMMX Xtra, and colors in the Paint window may be somewhat darker than expected. Remove the Xtra from the *Xtras* folder and restart Director.

- D7 may not print, and *the picture of the stage* may not function, in 24-bit color.

Palettes

You might know that 8-bit color mode allows you to use 256 colors. But why only 256 colors and which 256 colors? Suppose you are an amateur artist who paints by numbers. You buy a picture in which each area is marked with a number from 0 to 255 (the name of each color is not indicated). The kit includes a set of color paints also marked 0 to 255. You assume that someone has numbered the picture and the paints such that if you follow the numbers the picture will be colored correctly. The paint set includes all the colors you need or are allowed to use (you cannot mix the paints together). To make it easy to find the right color paint, arrange them numerically from 0 to 255. You "look up" the correct paint color (based on its number) and fill in the appropriate areas of the picture.

 Using a *palette* is analogous to painting by numbers. An indexed pixel's "color" (0 to 255) does not represent a color directly. It represents the position (*index*) in a palette of 256 colors that contains the full RGB color information.

The full color information is not stored for each pixel. Director "looks up" each pixel's 8-bit index (0 to 255) in a palette containing the full RGB colors, as shown in Figure 13-2. A palette is sometimes called a *CLUT* (color look-up table). An *adaptive or custom palette* is one whose colors are chosen to best represent the variety of colors used in one or more graphics.

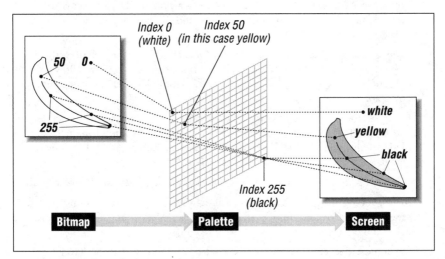

Figure 13-2: Color palette example

A palette is stored only once, but is used to look up the correct color for each pixel. If you can survive with only 256 simultaneous colors, an 8-bit bitmap (which uses 1 byte per pixel) requires only 1/4 the space of a comparable 32-bit image:

$640 \times 480 \times 1 = 307,200$ bytes = 300 KB

See the MacroMedia TechNotes "Creating and Using Custom Palettes," "Creating Super Palettes," "Getting Predictable Color in Cross-Platform Director Movies On-Screen and on the Web," and "Switching Palettes," all by Leslie Alperin at *http://www.macromedia.com/support/director/how/expert.*

Importing Custom Palettes

Although Director can import Windows PAL files, palettes are typically imported *indirectly* by importing a bitmap with a custom palette via File ► Import. Such a palette can be created in Photoshop using *Indexed Color* mode with an adaptive 8-bit (256 color) palette. (See *Photoshop in a Nutshell* for details.) To import a palette for a digital video, create a dummy bitmap and piggyback the custom palette onto it.

To import a custom palette, import the bitmap to which it is attached, and then choose *Color Depth: Image* and *Palette: Import* from the Image Options import dialog box, shown in Figure 13-3. If the image has a custom palette that hasn't already been imported, the palette will be imported as a separate cast member. If the exact palette already exists in the Cast, the new cast member will use the existing palette. The custom palette for an animated GIF imported as a D7 *#animGIF* member remains hidden. Importing an animated GIF as a *#bitmap* imports its palette as a separate cast member.

Import custom palette

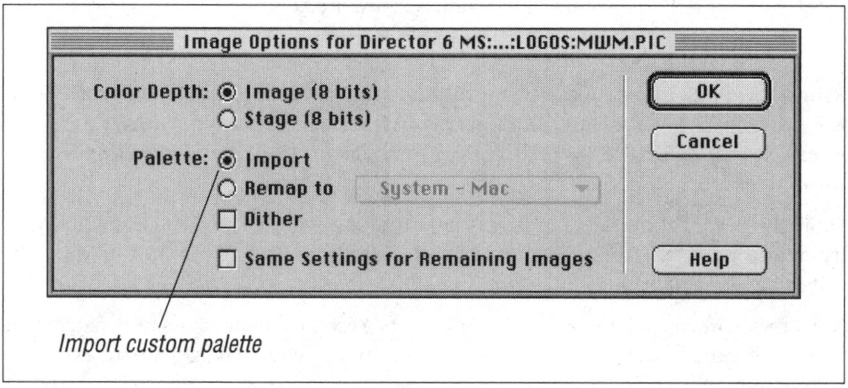

Figure 13-3: Bitmap import image options dialog box

If new custom palettes appear in the Cast, your newly imported bitmaps have different palettes than existing bitmaps. If they're not supposed to, adjust their palette in Photoshop or DeBabelizer and re-import them.

Director 4 would post a palette mismatch alert whenever importing a bitmap with a custom palette, but would import the palette only if it did not already exist in the Cast. (In D4, graphics were imported at the monitor color depth and custom palettes could be imported only in 8-bit.)

All Director palettes must have white in the first position (index 0) and black in the last position (index 255). If you attempt to import a palette with other colors in those positions, Director may refuse to import the palette or will move the colors to other positions in the palette. If you import a palette with black in the first position and white in the last position, Director may reverse the entire palette when it's imported. Adobe has released a "Force Black and White Extension" plug-in (*http://www.adobe.com/supportservice/custsupport/LIBRARY/536a.htm*) that ensures that white and black are present in the first and last positions of any adaptive palette created in Photoshop 5.

Don't use the first palette position for your transparency color in Photoshop. Instead, assign a transparency color after it is imported in Director using the background color chip in the Tools Palette.

Avoid palettes with pure white or pure black in multiple palette positions. Director will remap such pixels to positions 0 and 255, respectively. (Likewise, any duplicate colors in multiple palette positions may cause pixels to be remapped to a different index.) Use off-white and off-black colors, RGB (0,0,1) and RGB (255, 255, 254), in other palette positions, if necessary.

If the *Import* option in the dialog box is dimmed or intones "Image Has an Invalid Palette," the image may not have a custom palette, white and black may not be in the first and last palette positions in the palette, or there may be an Xtras conflict.

 Director 6.5 for Macintosh's PICT Import Export Xtra causes the "Invalid Palette" error. Remove it from the *Xtras:MIX* folder (leave the PICT Agent Xtra alone) and restart Director.

Return the PICT Import Export Xtra to the *Xtras* folder and restart Director before using the File ➤ Save as Java option. (Other alternatives are to use the PICT Agent Xtra from D6.0.x instead of D6.5, or remove the entire *Java Xtras/Save As Java* folder.)

Similarly, if a custom palette will not import along with a bitmap under Windows, try removing the Bitmap Import Export Xtra from the *Xtras\MIX* folder and restarting Director.

Note that Director's version of the Windows System palette may not match that shown in other programs, such as Photoshop, so you may get an unexpected palette mismatch.

Mark Sandau reports that Director 6.5, unlike Director 5, deletes colors in an incoming custom palette if they are not used in the bitmap being imported. Allegedly only the used colors are retained in the custom palette cast member. I have not confirmed or disproved this, nor tested it in other versions.

Palette Types

Let's return to the same paint-by-numbers picture discussed earlier, labeled with the numbers 0 to 255. You assume that the provided paint set matches the picture, but suppose you received the wrong paint set (palette). If "color 50" should be yellow in the correct paint set but it is red in your erroneous paint set, you would end up painting anything labeled "color 50" with the wrong color. Your bananas might end up red instead of yellow!

See the D6 *Color Palettes Show Me* demonstration movie for an interactive overview of palettes, and the "Experts Speak" section at *http://www.macromedia.com/support/director/how/show/colorpaletts.html*.

There are numerous different palettes that affect Director. The *active* or *current* palette is the one set in the Score Palette channel to the left of the current frame (but it can be overridden temporarily by the *puppetPalette* command). If no palette is set in the Palette channel, the movie's default palette (see Modify ➤ Movie ➤ Properties) is used. Even so, the active palette is ignored in some cases (see caveats later in this chapter).

When colors are looked up through the wrong palette, it is called a *palette mismatch* or *palette conflict.* You must take steps to ensure that the appropriate palette is asserted at all times. Note that there are over a dozen possible palettes to consider:

Built-in palettes
Director provides a number of predefined 8-bit palettes and one 4-bit palette (VGA), as shown in Table 13-8. These are accessible via pop-up menus throughout Director's interface. Attempting to modify a built-in palette automatically creates a new custom palette. Built-in palette types do not appear as separate cast members, but custom palettes do.

Custom palettes
Director can import or create an unlimited number of custom palettes, each of which appears as a separate cast member in the Cast window. Custom palettes are automatically added to the palette pop-up menus beneath the built-in palette types. They can be edited in the Color Palettes window.

Palette used in Score Palette channel (the "Active" Palette)
The Score Palette channel can be used to assert a built-in or custom palette. This becomes the "active" palette through which all graphics on Stage are displayed (remember our paint-by-numbers analogy). It is also used to colorize sprites with the Tool Palette color chips. This is reflected in *the framePalette* property and can be set during Score recording. The Palette channel can also be used to create palette fades and color cycling effects.

puppetPalette
The *puppetPalette* command can temporarily override the Score Palette channel (i.e., *the framePalette*). See Table 13-8 for details.

Cast member palette
The *#bitmap* and *#picture* cast member types (but no others) have a palette associated with them, as reflected by the *palette of member* and *paletteRef of member* properties (see Table 13-8). The palette can be set during import or changed via the Palette pop-up under Modify ➤ Cast Member ➤ Properties or *the palette of member* and *paletteRef of member* properties. Bitmaps can be transformed to a new palette using Modify ➤ Transform Bitmap.

If a cast member is dragged to the Score or the Stage, its palette is placed in the Palette channel (is used as the active palette) if no palette exists in the frame. Ideally, all graphics in a frame will use the same *palette of member*, which you can assert as the active palette. If not, set *the paletteMapping* to

TRUE or use the Modify ➤ Movie ➤ Properties ➤ *Remap Palettes when Needed* option to remap bitmaps to the active palette on the fly. D7 can dither graphics to the current palette if *the dither of member* is TRUE (but this is slow).

A cast member's palette is also used by the Paint window color chips.

Default palette of Projector

A Projector's default palette is set in the Modify ➤ Movie ➤ Properties dialog box of the first movie built into the Projector. It is used to determine *the stageColor* and thus the desktop color of full-screen Projectors.

Default movie palette of current movie

Each movie can have a default palette set in its Modify ➤ Movie ➤ Properties dialog box. (This is not accessible via Lingo, but in the MOA XDK it is referred to as the *defaultPalette*.) At higher color depths, the default palette tends to revert to "System – Mac" or "System – Win" without warning. In D3 and D4, the movie palette was set under File ➤ Movie Info.

Digital video palette

Digital video cast members don't have their own palettes, but will usually be dithered to the active palette if running in 8-bit color. Custom palettes within digital video files are ignored; import a custom palette attached to a dummy bitmap if necessary.

The same palette was not always used by both QuickTime 2 and Director in earlier versions. On the Macintosh, the QuickTime palette was set to the palette in effect when a digital video was first played. Subsequent palette changes were ignored by QuickTime on the Macintosh. See the FixPalette XObject under "Video palette problems" in Chapter 16, *Digital Video*. This is no longer a problem using QT3 and D7.

QuickTime never uses a palette at 16-bit and 32-bit monitor depths, even though Windows 3.1 Projectors dither graphics through an 8-bit palette at 16-bit and 32-bit monitor depths.

Palette of direct-to-Stage assets and sprite Xtras

Cast member types that can be played direct-to-Stage (such as digital video) and third-party Sprite Xtras may interact in unexpected ways with the active palette, and may not obey it at all. They will usually use Director's palette if played non-direct-to-Stage.

Palette of externally linked files imported at runtime

Any custom palette within an external file cannot be accessed at runtime. The palette must be imported ahead of time into Director. When Director accesses an externally linked file, the graphic adopts the currently active palette. If the active palette changes, the bitmap will be mismapped, because it continues to obey the palette that was active when it was imported. Either import the graphics as unlinked assets during development or assert the custom palette before setting *the fileName of member* or using *importFileInto* to access an external image. Avoid changing the active palette after an external image has been loaded.

System palette used by the operating system

Windows itself uses the "System – Win" palette and the Mac OS uses the "System – Mac" palette. You can use any palette on either platform, but it may conflict with the interface colors and system dialog boxes, particularly under Windows.

Browser palette

When used with Netscape Navigator, a Shockwave movie can control the palette rather than allowing the browser to do so. If the HTML EMBED tag's PALETTE attribute is foreground, the Shockwave movie controls the palette; the default setting (background) allows the browser to control the palette. The PALETTE attribute is not supported when using the HTML OBJECT tag with Microsoft Internet Explorer.

In Shockwave, consider using a browser-safe palette, such as the "Web216" palette in D7, or the Netscape Palette under Xtras ➤ Libraries ➤ Palette Library in D6.

Palettes used by other applications

Other applications (such as Acrobat) running simultaneously with Director may be affected by Director's custom palette and vice versa. Most, but not all, applications use the operating system's palette. Director for Macintosh continually attempts to assert its palette. If you have two copies of Director running on a 256-color monitor, the palette may flicker continuously.

Palette Operations

There are various palette transformations that one can perform in Director, but there are only two basic processes at work: palette remapping and palette transformation (although Director uses the terminology very loosely).

Palette mapping

A bitmap's pixels can be "looked up" through any palette. The colors may change (depending on the old and new palettes), but the each pixel's index remains unchanged. Asserting a palette via the Score's Palette channel (see *the framePalette*) or via *puppetPalette* changes the palette through which a cast member's data is looked up. It can produce hideous results if using the wrong palette. Setting *the palette of member* or *the paletteRef of member* affects palette mapping for the given cast member in the Paint window only.

The Modify ➤ Movie ➤ Properties ➤ *Remap Palettes When Needed* option attempts to remap bitmaps with the wrong palette to the currently active palette on the fly.

Palette transforms

Director can find the closest available color in a new palette and alter each pixel's index in an attempt to preserve its previous color. Modify ➤ Transform Bitmap and File ➤ Import both give the option to transform a bitmap to a different color depth or to a different palette with optional dithering.

`Modify`►`Transform Bitmap` has two options:

Remap
> Converts image to use a new palette. Indices (0–255) are changed to use the index of the closest available color in the new palette.

Dither
> Converts image to use a new palette. Colors for which an exact match doesn't exist in the new palette are simulated with a combination of dots using the colors available in the new palette.

`File`►`Import` can achieve similar results with these options:

Remap
> Converts the image to the specified existing palette instead of importing a new palette.

Dither
> If this option is checked, colors are dithered instead of being remapped to the closest color.

Although Director can transform bitmaps, you might get better results using another tool. The standard tool for palette and image transformation on either platform is DeBabelizer (*http://www.equilibrium.com*) although alternatives, including Photoshop, exist. See Macromedia TechNote #03174, "Color Palettes in Director."

D7.0 won't dither 32-bit images to 16-bit when importing as did D6 on the Macintosh. Either import the images using D6 for Macintosh (D6 for Windows won't work) or upgrade to D7.0.1.

D7 also supports a new *dither of member* property in 8-bit color mode. It is slower than the default mode (remapping) but may give better visual results.

Palette Conflicts

When the monitor is set to 8-bit, there is always one and only one active palette. By default, the OS uses its system palette, but you can create a custom palette of any 256 colors out of the possible 16.77 million colors. Unless a bitmap uses more than 256 different colors, there is no visible difference between a 32-bit image and an 8-bit image displayed with an optimal palette.

Because only one palette can be active at any time, all graphics that appear simultaneously should use the same palette. Always retain your 32-bit original art so that you can re-dither it to an appropriate 8-bit palette or to 16-bit color if needed.

To display more than 256 colors simultaneously, you *must* use a higher color depth. You can instead create a *super palette* containing the best 256 colors from the batch of images you wish to display (use DeBabelizer, Photoshop, or the Planet Color Xtra to create a super palette). An insufficient range of colors tones in the palette may cause a graphic or video to appear blocky. For example, a palette must have sufficient fleshtones to show the subtle gradations of skin color or a range of blue tones for sky and water.

See "Palette Transitions" later in this chapter for details on managing palette changes.

Reserving colors in a palette

You may want to use common interface elements (such as navigation arrows) with a variety of custom palettes. To do so, you must reserve (set aside) some indices in each palette and use only those palette positions when creating your common interface elements. It is typical to reserve the first and last 10 colors in each palette for the standard Windows system colors. See the Xtras ➤ Libraries ➤ Palette Library in D6 or the Windows System palette for examples.

When designing multiple palettes with common colors, you should ensure that the reserved colors appear at the *same index* in each palette. (Photoshop tends to sort all palettes by HSB, which is undesirable.)

Palette Problems Under Windows

The same palette typically appears somewhat darker under Windows than on the Macintosh. (Windows uses a lower gamma. The Macintosh monitor's gamma can be set in the *Monitors and Sound* Control Panel.) You can simply tweak the palette's brightness in the Color Palettes window (make a backup first, as the palette changes are not reversible) or remap the bitmaps to a brighter palette using Modify ➤ Cast Member ➤ Properties (in which case the new palette should have similar but brighter colors in each palette position).

Colors corrupted in Windows dialog boxes

Windows expects the first and last ten colors in a palette to be occupied by specific "reserved" colors shown in the "System – Win" palette and under D6's Xtras ➤ Libraries ➤ Palette Library option.

Under Windows, system dialog boxes are drawn using these reserved Windows interface colors in the first and last ten positions in the palette. Windows system dialog boxes include but are not limited to those generated using:

*   *alert*
*   *displayOpen* or *displaySave* (FileIO Xtra)
*   *Alert, FileOpen, FileSave*, or *GetURL* (MUI Xtra)
*   Any commands from third-party Xtras that create alert or file dialog boxes
*   *Where is* . . . dialog boxes generated by missing assets

When using a custom Director palette, the system dialog boxes will often be unreadably dark. (Most custom palette have their darkest colors towards the end of the palette; Windows uses these indices for its dialog boxes.) Reserve the 20 Windows system colors when you create a palette in DeBabelizer, Photoshop, or in Director's Color Palette's window, or see Chapter 14 for alternatives to system dialog boxes.

Colors corrupted in Director following a Windows dialog box

Reserving colors guarantees that the Windows dialog boxes are readable. Unreadable dialog boxes (due to unreserved system colors) are often confused with the prior problem, in which a Windows system dialog box will override Director's active palette (if not using the "System – Win" palette) and prevent future palette changes. The prior problem relates to the appearance of the Windows dialog box itself, but the second relates to the appearance of Director *after* returning from a Windows dialog box.

There are four ways to solve the second problem:

- Avoid using any Windows system dialog boxes (again see Chapter 14).

- Use the "System – Win" palette throughout your Director movie.

- Use *go movie* or *play movie* to start a new movie or restart the current movie to fool Director into re-instantiating the palette as follows:

  ```
  go frame (the frame) of movie (the movie)
  ```

  This will execute any *stopMovie*, *prepareMovie*, and *startMovie* handlers.

- Modify the *Animation* option in the *DIRECTOR.INI* file, which has two possible values:

  0 (more compatible)
  > Prevents Director from seizing control of the palette. Director palette fades will be much slower, but the Windows system palette will not lock out Director's custom palette, and vice versa.

  1 (default)
  > Director seizes control of the palette for faster palette fades and color cycling, causing palette conflicts with the OS or other applications.

To configure *DIRECTOR.INI* to reduce palette conflicts, follow these steps:

1. Locate and edit the *DIRECTOR.INI* file (included in the folder in which Director for Windows is installed). Use a plain text editor such as Notepad. Find the [Palette] section within the INI file.

2. Change the line Animation = 1 to Animation = 0. Be sure to remove the semicolon (;) at the beginning of the line. Save the file.

3. Copy the *DIRECTOR.INI* file to your Projector's folder and rename it to match the Projector's name (i.e., if your Projector is *PROJECTOR.EXE*, rename the *DIRECTOR.INI* file to *PROJECTOR.INI*).

If Colors or Palettes Still Look Wrong

There are many easily solvable problems that can cause the wrong colors to appear:

- You may have asserted the wrong palette or no palette in the Score Palette channel. The *puppetPalette* command is not permanent; it must be reiterated whenever the playback head moves backward or loops in a frame.

- You may be using multiple bitmap cast members that require multiple different palettes. See the next section, "Quick and Dirty Fixes."

- If the palette is overrideen by a Windows dialog box, see the fix in the previous section.

- The custom palette used for digital video (see Chapter 16) may need to be refreshed on the Macintosh.

- The monitor depth or cast member depth may be incorrect. See Example 13-1.

- It may not be a palette issue. Set the sprite's ink to Copy, and set its *foreColor* to black and its *backColor* to white (using the Tool Palette color chips) to rule out these factors. For example, on the Macintosh, if the *foreColor* is not black, 16-bit bitmaps appear as if there is a palette mismatch.

- Your Lingo may be wrong. It may be setting the desired properties in unexpected ways or may not be setting them at all. Changes to a sprite's properties do not take effect until the Stage is updated and are lost when the movie is halted.

- When working with palettes, the interface colors may be affected. Work with the monitor set to a higher (non-palettized) color depth or use the File ➤ Preferences ➤ General ➤ *Classic Look (Monochrome)* option.

- In D5, 16-bit and 32-bit sprites sometimes look wrong even though they are supposed to be independent of the current palette (and even though their *foreColor* and *backColor* are correctly set to black and white). Set the monitor to 8-bit mode and try changing the member's palette using Modify ➤ Cast Member ➤ Properties (not Modify ➤ Transform Bitmap). In D6 and D7, 16-bit and 32-bit cast members always use the system palettes.

- Palettes of externally linked files imported at runtime will not be read. Import all custom palettes for bitmaps and digital videos beforehand during authoring and place them in the Palette channel where applicable.

- PCs tend to have a lower gamma, so graphics may look darker than they do on the Macintosh when using the same palette on a PC. The D6 DirMMX Xtra can cause some darkening of 16-bit graphics in the Paint window on MMX-capable Windows PCs and should be removed to remedy the problem.

Quick and Dirty Fixes

Ideally, you have planned ahead, but sometimes you'll discover a big problem late in the game. If you've used the wrong palettes or bit depth, try one of the techniques in the following sections.

 Make a backup before performing the following irreversible transformations.

Adjusting from thousands or millions of colors to 256 colors

One common problem is that performance in 16-bit or 32-bit is unacceptably poor, and you've decided to switch to 8-bit color at the last minute. Ideally, you'll return to DeBabelizer or Photoshop and redither your art to an appropriate super palette.

This task is not particularly onerous and can be accomplished with DeBabelizer's batch processing mode. If you don't own or know DeBabelizer or are pressed for time, convert all graphics to 8-bit inside Director using Modify ➤ Transform Bitmap. Transform them to the most appropriate available palette, such as the Macintosh or Windows system palette. It won't be pretty, but it may be adequate. D7.0 for Macintosh does not perform 32-bit to 16-bit dithering as did D6 for Macintosh, but D7.0.1 performs dithering under both Macintosh and Windows.

Adjustments using 256 colors

Another common problem is when graphics that need to be on the Stage simultaneously use two or more different palettes. Again, the ideal solution is to redither the source material to a common palette in DeBabelizer or Photoshop and re-import it all.

First, try checking the *Remap Palettes When Needed* option in the Modify ➤ Movie ➤ Properties dialog box. This may be enough to make your graphics look acceptable, even though they are in the wrong palette.

If that option doesn't provide adequate quality, select all the cast members that you need to remap to a particular palette and choose Modify ➤ Transform Bitmap. This can transform all your graphics to any available palette. Use this option to transform your bitmaps to new palettes that might be similar to an existing palette, but might have all the Windows system colors reserved or might contain identical colors in different index positions.

In D7, you can also try setting the *dither of member* to TRUE for bitmaps in the wrong palette. This is slow, but reversible.

Adjusting from lower to higher color depths

Remember that bitmaps always display fastest if the monitor is set to the same color depth (see Examples 13-1 and 13-2). You can use Modify ➤ Transform Bitmap to convert graphics from 8-bit to 16-bit or 32-bit, but remember that graphics at higher depths require more RAM.

If all your graphics are 8-bit, instead of converting them to higher depths, try setting *the fullColorPermit* to FALSE to improve animation speed without consuming RAM. (The *fullColorPermit* is obsolete in D7.)

Palette Issues

Certain palettes are dimmed in the palette pop-up menu depending on the color depth. Most palettes are available in 8-bit color. The VGA palette is available only when using 4-bit color. In 16-bit and 32-bit color, only the "System – Mac" and "System – Win" palettes are selectable.

You cannot delete palette cast members that are being referenced by bitmap cast members. If necessary, use Edit ➤ Find ➤ Cast Member to find all cast members that use a given palette. Select those cast members and use Modify ➤ Cast Member ➤ Properties to map them to a different palette. If no cast members refer to a palette, you can delete it from the cast (ensure that it is not used in the Score before deleting it).

At 16-bit and 32-bit color depths, Director for Macintosh tends to switch the default palette to the "System – Mac" palette and Director for Windows tends to switch the default palette to "System – Win," even when working with 8-bit images. Work with an 8-bit monitor or reset the palette under Modify ➤ Movie ➤ Properties as needed.

Palette-Related Interface Options

Table 13-7 shows the interface options pertaining to palettes and colors.

Table 13-7: Palette-Related Interface Options

Option	Macintosh	Windows
File ➤ Import ➤ Bitmap Image; File ➤ Import ➤ PICT; File ➤ Import ➤ Palette	Import bitmap with custom palette or .PAL ('8BCT') files	Import bitmap with custom palette or separate palette (PAL) files
File ➤ Create Projector ➤ Options ➤ Reset Monitor to Match Movie's Color Depth[1]	None	N/A (Mac only)
File ➤ Preferences ➤ General ➤ Reset Monitor to Match Movie's Color Depth[1]	Cmd-U	N/A (Mac only)
File ➤ Preferences ➤ General ➤ Classic Look (Monochrome)	Cmd-U	Ctrl-U
File ➤ Preferences ➤ Score ➤ Director 5 Style Score Display ➤ Allow Colored Cells	Ctrl-click in Sprite Toolbar	Right-click in Sprite Toolbar
Open Palette window and use Edit ➤ Duplicate; Insert ➤ Media Element ➤ Color Palette	Cmd-D	Ctrl-D
Edit ➤ Invert Selection (in Palette window)	None	None
Edit ➤ Find ➤ Cast Member ➤ Palette[2]	Cmd-;	Ctrl-;
Modify ➤ Cast Member ➤ Properties ➤ Palette[2,3]	Cmd-I	Ctrl-I
Modify ➤ Frame ➤ Palette[2,4]	None	None
Modify ➤ Movie ➤ Properties ➤ Default Palette[2]; Modify ➤ Movie ➤ Properties ➤ Stage Color; Modify ➤ Movie ➤ Properties ➤ Remap Palettes When Needed[5]	Cmd-Shift-D	Ctrl-Shift-D
Modify ➤ Font ➤ Color (color chip)	Cmd-Shift-T	Ctrl-Shift-T
Modify ➤ Transform Bitmap[2]	None	Alt-M-T
Xtras ➤ Library ➤ Palette Library (D6 only)[2]	None	None
Window ➤ Color Palettes[2,6]	Cmd-Opt-7	Ctrl-Alt-7
Window ➤ Tool Palette	Cmd-7	Ctrl-7

Table 13-7: Palette-Related Interface Options (continued)

Option	Macintosh	Windows
Help ➤ Show Me ➤ Color Palettes (D6 only)	Help button	F1
File ➤ Preferences ➤ Editors ➤ Microsoft Pal	None	None

[1] See the switchColorDepth property.
[2] Command opens a window containing a palette pop-up menu that lists both built-in and custom palettes.
[3] You can change the palette only if all selected members share the same initial palette.
[4] Inserts an existing palette, as does double-clicking in the Palette channel or dragging a bitmap with a custom palette to the Score.
[5] See the paletteMapping property.
[6] Double-click the foreground or background color chips in the Paint window or Tool Palette to open Color Palettes window.

Palette Channel Properties

To add an effect to the Palette channel using an existing palette, use Modify ➤ Frame ➤ Palette, double-click in the Palette channel, or drag a bitmap with a custom palette to the Score or the Stage. (The Palette channel and *puppetPalette* commands are ignored within MIAWs.)

The Frame Palette options are covered in Chapter 8 in Macromedia's *Using Director* manual and in the online Help. The Palette channel can perform color cycling over one or more frames to create pseudo-animation appropriate for water effects or flashing banners.

The Frame Properties Palette dialog box allows you to select from a list of both built-in palettes and custom palette cast members. You must first select a range of frames and then choose Modify ➤ Frame ➤ Palette to use the *Span Selected Frames* option.

If you jump to a frame without a palette in the Palette channel, the most recent palette to the left of the current frame is used. Add a palette to the Palette channel at the beginning of each scene to ensure that the proper palette is asserted. Palette effects in the first frame of the Score are executed whenever the movie is first reached.

Palette Transitions

To switch palettes, specify the new palette to assert, and the speed or number of frames over which to assert it. Simultaneous effects in the Palette and Transition channels in the same frame of the Score may be very slow.

It is easiest if your entire project uses a single palette (whether it is a built-in or custom palette doesn't matter). You can use different palettes (each with up to 256 colors) in different frames of the Score, but when you switch to the new palette, all the colors on the screen are going to be mapped through it. To avoid a *palette flash* or psychedelic effect, any graphics on screen during the palette switch must use only those indices that map to the same colors in both the old and new palettes. One solution is to switch palettes while the screen is black or white (or contains only black and white art). These colors are in the same positions in all palettes, and thus the palette switch will not be evident. In this case, use the *Don't*

Fade option and set the rate to the maximum (30 fps). See also *the puppetPalette* command.

Another solution is to use the Palette channel to fade to white or fade to black while performing the palette switch. (See the caveats on palette fades later in this chapter.)

Yet another solution is to use a subset of color indices that are identical in two or more palettes. Suppose that the first 50 colors in your two palettes are the same. As long as any artwork on screen uses only the first 50 color indices, they will appear identical in either palette. Thus, the palette switch will be invisible. (Use the Color Palettes window's *Select Used Colors* option to determine which color indices a bitmap uses.)

Transitioning slowly between two palettes can produce an interesting color blending effect. In that case, you can specify the a slower *Rate* for your palette transition. Select multiple frames and use the *Span Multiple Frames* option to allow animation to continue while the palette transition occurs.

Palette Fades

Palette fades are designed to hide palette switches and are performed in the Score's Palette channel, not the Transition channel. Palette fades temporarily fade to either white or black, after which they assert the new palette. Don't loop in a frame with a palette fade. In the next frame, assert the new palette again, this time using the *Don't Fade* option to "stop" the fade and improve performance.

 Palette fades don't work in color depths higher than 8-bit; they will perform a jump cut and erase everything on the screen. Check *the colorDepth* before using a palette fade, and skip the Score frame in which the fade occurs if necessary.

In higher depths, there are no palette switches (the Palette channel is ignored). If you still want to perform a pseudo-fade, you can use a true transition, such as *Dissolve Pixels*, in the Transition channel to dissolve to a solid white or black screen.

Under Windows, when using *Fade to Black* in the Palette channel, pure white pixels will not fade (they will remain white). Likewise, when using *Fade to White*, pure black pixels will not fade to white (they will remain black). Use off-white or off-black pixels at a different position in the palette instead. (See the *Switch Colors* command in the Paint window to alter such pixels.)

Palette fades under Windows will be egregiously slow if the *Animation* option in the *DIRECTOR.INI* file is set to 0. See "Colors corrupted in Director following a Windows dialog box" earlier in this chapter.

Lingo Palette Properties

Table 13-8 lists the codes for the *palette of member, paletteRef of member,* and *framePalette* properties and the *puppetPalette* command. Note that setting these properties affects only the display in the Paint window or on the Stage. None of these permanently transforms the data as does Modify ► Transform Bitmap.

Table 13-8: Palette Property Codes

Palette	Palette of Member and FramePalette	PaletteRef of Member	puppetPalette
Custom palette	member number > 0	member *palMem* {of castLib *whichCast*}	member number > 0 or "*paletteName*"
Macintosh system	-1	#systemMac	-1 or "system"
Rainbow	-2	#rainbow	-2 or "rainbow"
Grayscale	-3	#grayscale	-3 or "grayscale"
Pastels	-4	#pastels	-4 or "pastels"
Vivid	-5	#vivid	-5 or "vivid"
NTSC	-6	#NTSC	-6 or "NTSC"
Metallic	-7	#metallic	-7 or "metallic"
VGA (4-bit *colorDepth* only)	-8	#VGA	-8 or "VGA"
Windows System (D4)	-101	#systemWinDir4	-101
Windows System (D5 and later)	-102	#systemWin	-102
Web 216 (Director 7)	-8	#web216	-8 or "web216"

puppetPalette

The *puppetPalette* command temporarily overrides the Score's Palette channel and takes the form:

```
puppetPalette "paletteName" {, speed}{, numFrames}
```

where *speed* corresponds to the Rate in the *Frame Palette Properties* dialog box and ranges from 1 (5 seconds) to 30 (instant); higher numbers are faster and the default is approximately 28. The *numFrames* parameter apparently doesn't work; the palette switch is executed within one frame regardless of *numFrames*.

You can also use the form:

```
puppetPalette memberNumber {, speed}{, numFrames}
```

where *memberNumber* is a positive integer representing a palette cast member or a negative integer representing a built-in palette. If *memberNumber* is 0, the *puppet-Palette* command is canceled and palette control is returned to the Score.

The *puppetPalette* command is not permanent. Any *puppetPalette* is canceled when the playback head pauses, goes backwards in the Score, or loops in a single frame. Specify your *puppetPalette* immediately following a *go frame* command to prevent the palette from reverting, such as:

```
on exit Frame
  go loop
  puppetPalette the number of member "myPalette"
end
```

When the *puppetPalette* is canceled, the palette will revert to the previous palette set in the Palette channel to the left of the current frame. Place the equivalent palette in the Score to prevent a visible palette switch at that time. Check *the framePalette* at any time to determine if your *puppetPalette* is still in effect.

The *puppetPalette* command does not accept a member reference, such as:

```
puppetPalette member whichMember
```

You cannot perform color cycling or palette fades using the *puppetPalette* command as you can with the Score's Palette channel.

Color Palettes Window

The Color Palettes window (opened via Window ➤ Color Palettes and shown in Figure 13-4) is used to view and edit custom palettes. It is covered in great detail in Chapter 8 in Macromedia's *Using Director* manual.

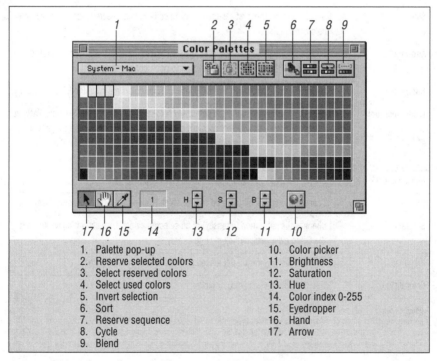

1. Palette pop-up
2. Reserve selected colors
3. Select reserved colors
4. Select used colors
5. Invert selection
6. Sort
7. Reserve sequence
8. Cycle
9. Blend
10. Color picker
11. Brightness
12. Saturation
13. Hue
14. Color index 0-255
15. Eyedropper
16. Hand
17. Arrow

Figure 13-4: Color Palettes window

Table 13-9 explains the Color Palettes window's tools.

Table 13-9: Color Palette Window Options

Tool	Notes
Editing	Use the standard Cut, Copy, Paste, and Select All commands from the Edit menu (or the keyboard equivalents) to modify color cells in a palette.
Palette pop-up	Selects an existing built-in or custom palette to edit.
Reserve selected colors[1]	Reserves (or unreserves) the selected palette indices. Reserved indices won't be used when importing or pasting bitmaps or using Modify ➤ Transform Bitmap.
Select reserved colors	Highlights indices already reserved.
Select used colors	Highlights palette indices used by the selected cast members. (Select bitmaps in Cast or open Paint window first.)
Invert selection[1]	Reverses currently selected palette indices. Use after *Select Used Colors* to select all unused colors, which can then be reserved with *Select Reserved Colors*.
Sort[2]	Sorts selected range of indices by hue, brightness, or saturation. You can also manually rearrange the colors.
Reverse sequence[2]	Reverses selected range of indices.
Cycle[2]	Cycles selected range of indices one position to the left.
Blend[2]	Blends from color of first selected index to color of last selected index. Intermediate colors are replaced.
Arrow tool	Selects one or more color cells. Cmd-click (Macintosh) or Ctrl-click (Windows) to select discontiguous cells. Double-click to open color picker.
Hand tool	Moves selected color cells to new location. Other colors are reshuffled. See *Sort* entry.
Eyedropper tool	Click the eyedropper tool, then select any color cell in Color Palettes window. Without releasing mouse, drag cursor over any pixel in the Paint window or the Stage. Color palette selection and foreground color chips in Paint Window and Tool Palette reflect color (index) of pixel under the cursor. In D7, affects Tool palette only.
Index readout[1]	Shows index (0 to 255) of first selected color cell in range.
Hue[1,3]	Changes the hue of all selected colors, which is akin to rotating the color wheel.
Saturation[1,3]	Changes the saturation (intensity) of all selected colors. Less saturation washes out the color, eventually turning it white or gray.
Brightness[1,3]	Changes the brightness. Decreased brightness tends towards black.
Color Picker[1]	Opens platform-specific color picker.

[1] Requires selection of one or more color cells in palette.
[2] Requires selection of two or more contiguous indices in palette. *Blend* requires three or more selected cells to be useful.
[3] You can also adjust the hue, saturation, and brightness in the Color Picker or specify colors by RGB values instead. Changes to HSB may not be easily reversible. If the saturation is reduced to 0, all colors turn gray; increasing it again turns the grays to red.

Custom palettes are stored as *#palette* cast members. To create a new palette, edit one of the built-in palettes, or use Edit ➤ Duplicate or Insert ➤ Media Element ➤ Color Palette. See also "Importing Custom Palettes" and Figure 13-3.

Paint Window

Some people hate the Paint window, whereas others love it. The main complaint about the D6 Paint window is that it does not truly support 16-bit and 32-bit paint operations but D7 remedies this deficiency. In D6, if you select a color with the eyedropper tool from a 16-bit or 32-bit image, Director uses the nearest color in the current 256-color palette. (Director 6 paints only with the 256 colors in the current palette, which often don't match the colors in 16-bit and 32-bit images.)

Table 13-10 shows the interface options pertaining to bitmaps and the Paint window. Photoshop filters can be used to modify cast members in the Paint window during authoring, but not at runtime. D7 for Windows supports runtime effects using Insert ➤ Intel Web Design Effects.

Table 13-10: Paint-Related Interface Options

Option	Macintosh	Windows
File ➤ Export	PICT, PICS, Scrapbook	BMP
File ➤ Preferences ➤ Editors	BMP, GIF, JPEG, MacPaint, Microsoft Palette, Photoshop 3.0, PICT, PNG, Targa, TIFF, xRes LRG	All Mac formats, plus EPS, PCD, WMF (D6 only)
Modify ➤ Convert To Bitmap[1]	None	Alt-M,V
Xtras ➤ Filter Bitmap[2] Xtras ➤ Auto-Filter[2] Xtras ➤ Auto-Distort[2]	None	Alt-X,B Alt-X,F Alt-X,D

[1] The Modify ➤ Convert to Bitmap command converts text and field cast members to bitmaps without warning and cannot be undone. Make a copy of the cast members first to allow you to edit the live text at a later date.
[2] See Chapter 13 in Macromedia's *Using Director* manual.

Paint Tool–Related Preferences

There are many paint tool–related preference dialog boxes, as shown in Table 13-11.

Table 13-11: Paint Tool–Related Preferences

Preference Dialog Box	Shortcut	Notes
File ➤ Preferences ➤ Paint	Double-click *Other Line Width* in Paint window.	See Figure 13-5.
Paint brush settings	Double-click paintbrush tool in Paint window.	Customize size and shape for five brushes.

Table 13-11: Paint Tool–Related Preferences (continued)

Preference Dialog Box	Shortcut	Notes
Airbrush settings	Double-click airbrush tool in Paint window.	Customize spray pattern for five airbrushes.
Gradient settings	Double-click paint bucket, filled shape tools, or gradient color chips in Paint window.	Customize direction and nature of gradient.
Pattern settings	Double-click pattern chip in Paint window (triple-click in D7).	Customize foreground and background contribution to pattern.
Custom tile settings	Double-click pattern chip in Tool Palette (triple-click in D7).	Use cast members as custom patterns.

Figure 13-5 shows the main Paint window preference dialog box.

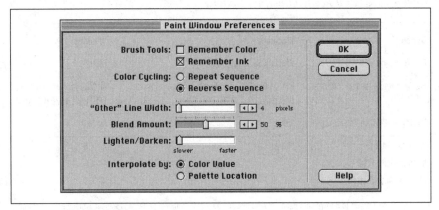

Figure 13-5: Paint Window Preferences window

Paint Window Tools

Figure 13-6 shows the Paint window drawing tools; Table 13-12 shows the shortcuts for the Paint tools. It includes the single-key accelerators for choosing each tool, which are new as of D6.0.1—no modifier keys (Cmd, Ctrl, etc.) are required. These were chosen for compatibility with Photoshop, Studio/8, and other graphics programs. Some of these shortcuts also work in the Vector Shape window.

To check the colors used in the current bitmap, open the Paint window or select one or more bitmaps in the Cast, then use the *Select Used Colors* command in the Color Palettes window.

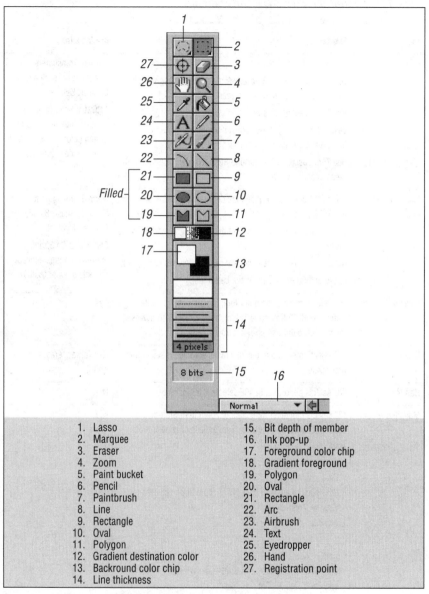

1. Lasso
2. Marquee
3. Eraser
4. Zoom
5. Paint bucket
6. Pencil
7. Paintbrush
8. Line
9. Rectangle
10. Oval
11. Polygon
12. Gradient destination color
13. Backround color chip
14. Line thickness
15. Bit depth of member
16. Ink pop-up
17. Foreground color chip
18. Gradient foreground
19. Polygon
20. Oval
21. Rectangle
22. Arc
23. Airbrush
24. Text
25. Eyedropper
26. Hand
27. Registration point

Figure 13-6: Paint window drawing tools

Table 13-12: Paint Window Tools and Shortcuts

Tool	Shortcuts	Available Inks
Lasso[1]	"L" selects lasso tool. Option-drag (Mac) or Alt-drag (Win) to select using straight lines; double-click to close polygon. *No shrink:* selects area bounded by lasso. *Lasso:* selects only those pixels of a different color from the first pixel you clicked. *See Thru Lasso:* shrinks around area bounded by lasso; white areas become transparent	Normal, Transparent, Reverse, Ghost, Blend, Darkest, Lightest. Activates Smooth, Invert, Lighten, Darken, Fill, and Switch Colors tools in Paint toolbar (see Figure 13-7).
Marquee (selection)[1]	"M" or "S" selects marquee tool; double-click to Edit ➤ Select All. *Shrink:* selection shrinks to bounding rectangle, ignoring white pixels. *No shrink:* selection does not shrink and includes white pixels. *Lasso* and *See Thru Lasso:* see Lasso tool.	Normal, Transparent, Reverse, Ghost, Blend, Darkest, Lightest. *Shrink* and *No Shrink* marquee options activate all tools in Paint toolbar.
Registration point	"G" selects registration point tool; double-click to center registration point. Option-arrow (Mac) or Alt-arrow (Win) moves registration point one pixel in arrow direction.	N/A
Eraser[2]	"E" select eraser; double-click erases graphic, or select and press Delete.	N/A (always erases to white)
Hand[2]	"H" selects hand tool; SPACE selects it temporarily.	N/A
Magnifier (Zoom)	"Z" selects magnifier tool; click to zoom in or Shift-click to zoom out. Other shortcuts work regardless of current tool. Zoom In: · + · Cmd-+ (Mac), Ctrl-+ (Win) · Cmd-click (Mac), Ctrl-click (Win) zoom in on selected area · View ➤ Zoom ➤ In Zoom out: · – · Cmd-- (Mac), Ctrl-- (Win) · Cmd-Shift-click (Mac); Ctrl-Shift-click (Windows) · View ➤ Zoom ➤ Out · Click in Paint window inset Other shortcuts: · 1 or View ➤ Zoom ➤ 100% · 2 or View ➤ Zoom ➤ 200% · 4 or View ➤ Zoom ➤ 400% · 8 or View ➤ Zoom ➤ 800% · Double-click pencil to toggle zoom	N/A

Table 13-12: Paint Window Tools and Shortcuts (continued)

Tool	Shortcuts	Available Inks
Eyedropper	Set foreground color: · "i" (permanent) · "d" (temporary) · Option (Mac), Alt (Win) Set background color: · Shift-D Set gradient destination color: · Option-D (Mac), Alt-D (Win)	N/A
Paint bucket (fill)	"F" or "K" selects paint bucket; double-click for gradient settings. Paints with foreground color or gradient color.	Normal, Gradient, Reveal.
Text	"T" selects text tool; double-click for Modify ➤ Font or use Cmd-Shift-T (Mac), Ctrl-Shift-T (Win). Use Text Inspector, Cmd-T (Mac), Ctrl-T (Win), to modify text styles.	Normal, Transparent, Reverse, Ghost, Gradient, Blend, Darkest, Lightest.
Pencil[2]	"Y" or "." (period) selects pencil; double-click to zoom in/out. Draws with foreground color usually. Draws with background color if first pixel clicked matches foreground color.	Normal.
Airbrush[2]	"A" selects airbrush; double-click for airbrush settings. Hold mouse down for airbrush options.	Normal, Transparent, Reverse, Ghost, Reveal, Cycle, Blend, Darkest, Lightest.
Paintbrush[2]	"B" selects paint brush; double-click for brush settings. Hold mouse down for paintbrush options.	Normal, Transparent, Reverse, Ghost, Gradient, Reveal, Cycle, Switch, Blend, Darkest, Lightest, Darken, Lighten, Smooth, Smear, Smudge, Spread, Clipboard.
Arc[3]	"C" selects arc tool.	Normal, Transparent, Reverse, Ghost, Blend, Darkest, Lightest.
Line[4]	"N", "/", "\", or "|" selects line tool.	Normal, Transparent, Reverse, Ghost, Blend, Darkest, Lightest.
Filled rectangle[3]	"Shift-R" selects filled rectangle tool; double-click for gradient settings.	Normal, Transparent, Reverse, Ghost, Gradient, Reveal, Blend, Darkest, Lightest.
Rectangle[3]	Lowercase "r" selects rectangle tool.	Same as filled rectangle.

Graphics & Color

Table 13-12: Paint Window Tools and Shortcuts (continued)

Tool	Shortcuts	Available Inks
Filled oval[3]	"Shift-O" selects filled oval tool; double-click for gradient settings.	Same as filled rectangle.
Oval[3]	Lowercase "o" selects oval tool.	Same as filled rectangle.
Filled polygon[4]	"Shift-P" selects filled polygon tool; double-click button for gradient settings. Double-click point to close polygon.	Same as filled rectangle.
Polygon[4]	Lowercase "p" selects polygon tool; double-click point to close polygon.	Same as filled rectangle.

[1] See Table 13-13 for other shortcuts that can be performed with a selection once selected with the lasso or marquee tool, including the Shift key to constrain movement.
[2] Shift key constrains to horizontal or vertical movement, whichever is performed first.
[3] Shift key constrains to proportional shapes (square, circle, circular arc).
[4] Shift key constrains lines to drawing at 45-degree intervals.

Table 13-13 lists the modifier keys that affect the current selection in the Paint window. Some of these gestures work on the Stage or in the Score as well.

Table 13-13: Paint Window Selection Modifier Keys

Result	Macintosh	Windows
Move selection from original location	Drag	Drag
Copy selection, leaving original in place	Opt-drag	Alt-drag
Stretch selection[1]	Cmd-drag	Ctrl-drag
Proportional stretch (scale) selection[1]	Cmd-Shift-drag	Ctrl-Shift-drag
Constrain movement or proportions while dragging selection (horizontal, vertical, or 45-degree lines)	Shift	Shift
Move selected portion of bitmap 1 (or 10) pixels	Arrow keys (or Shift-arrow)	Arrow keys (or Shift-arrow)

[1] Works with marquee tool's Shrink or No Shrink options only, not the lasso tool (cursor must be inside selection, not at corner of selection to stretch). Can be combined with Shift key and Option key (Macintosh) or Alt key (Windows) to copy the selection and then stretch or scale it.

Paint Window Tips

Refer to Chapter 13 of Macromedia's *Using Director* manual for basic Paint window operations.

Registration point and selections

When copying and pasting bitmaps *between* cast members, the *regPoint* of the source image is ignored. But, if you duplicate an entire cast member and then edit the new cast member in the Paint window, the *regPoint* of the original image will be intact.

To cut out pieces of a graphic while maintaining registration, first duplicate the entire cast member as many times as there are pieces to be cut out. Then, create each separate cast member by cutting away the unwanted portions. You will be left with multiple cast members all registered perfectly.

If you erase a bitmap by double-clicking the eraser tool in the Paint window, the registration point is lost, unless the onion skinning feature is currently active.

Double-click the marquee tool to select the entire graphic in the Paint window and show its extent. This helps to locate stray non-white pixels that may increase the bounding rectangle unnecessarily.

If the hand tool or the rectangular marquee is used to select the entire bitmap, the registration point moves with the object. If the lasso tool is used to move the bitmap (or a partial selection is made with the marquee tool), the registration point doesn't move.

Click the *regPoint* point tool once to display crosshairs to help locate graphics in the Paint window.

The *regPoint* is always recentered in the Paint window to facilitate onion skinning (but it can remain off-center relative to the graphic). Use the arrow buttons to page through bitmap cast members to recenter the *regPoint* in the Paint window.

Erasing and cropping

Use white as the foreground color with the paint bucket, paintbrush, airbrush, filled rectangle, filled oval, or filled polygon tool to erase large or irregular areas. Use the pencil tool to erase individual pixels.

Use the *Switch Colors* command, or the Switch ink with the paintbrush (with white as the destination color) to erase a single color while leaving other pixels untouched. Use ink effects (see Table 13-18) to remove white and black regions.

To crop a graphic in the Paint window while maintaining its registration point, follow these steps:

1. Open the Onion Skinning windoid using View ➤ Onion Skin.

2. Turn on onion skinning by depressing the leftmost push-button in the Onion Skinning windoid.

3. Select the portion of the image that you want to keep in the Paint window and copy it to the clipboard using Edit ➤ Copy, Cmd-C (Mac), or Ctrl-C (Windows).

4. Double-click the eraser tool to erase the image in the Paint window.

5. Paste the saved portion from the clipboard using Edit ➤ Paste, Cmd-V (Mac), or Ctrl-V (Windows).

6. If you don't need to preserve the registration point, you can turn off onion skinning or double-click the registration point tool to recenter the registration point.

Resizing bitmap cast members

Director can scale sprites dynamically, but scaling the member ahead of time yields better runtime performance. You can use Modify ➤ Transform Bitmap to resize bitmap cast members. But if the new dimensions differ less than 1% from the old dimensions, Director won't resize the graphic. To enlarge a bitmap by 1 pixel, duplicate one row or column in the Paint window. To shrink a bitmap by 1 pixel, use the eraser tool while holding down the Shift key to constrain its motion along one axis. Double-click the registration tool to recenter the registration point after changing the size of a bitmap. Director does a poor job of scaling bitmaps, especially those containing text. Use an external graphics program such as Photoshop instead.

Other Paint Window Shortcuts

Table 13-14 shows Paint window shortcuts affecting the color chips. See also the eyedropper tool in Table 13-12.

Table 13-14: Paint Window Color Chips Shortcuts

Result	Mac and Windows
Set black foreground color chip and white background color chip	W
Swap foreground and background color chips	X
Set foreground color and starting gradient color chips to next/previous index in palette	↑ and ↓ keys
Set background color chip to next/previous index in palette	Shift-↑ and Shift-↓

Table 13-15 shows additional Paint window shortcuts not related to a specific tool.

Table 13-15: Other Paint Window Shortcuts

Result	Macintosh	Windows
Window ➤ Paint[1]	Cmd-5	Ctrl-5
Edit ➤ Undo (doesn't undo all operations)	` or ~, or Cmd-Z	` or ~, or Ctrl-Z
Edit ➤ Repeat (repeats last Paint operation)	Cmd-Y	Ctrl-Y
View ➤ Onion Skin[2]	None	Alt-M,O
View ➤ Rulers (click in corner of rulers to change units to pixels, cm. or inches)	Cmd-Shift-Opt-R	Ctrl-Shift-Alt-R
View ➤ Paint Tools	Cmd-Shift-H	Ctrl-Shift-H
Next/previous bitmap cast member (if no portion of bitmap is selected)	→ and ← keys or arrow buttons	→ and ← keys or arrow buttons

Table 13-15: Other Paint Window Shortcuts (continued)

Result	Macintosh	Windows
Modify ➤ Transform Bitmap	Double-click *Bit Depth* readout in Paint Window	Double-click *Bit Depth* readout in Paint Window
Modify ➤ Convert To Bitmap	None	None

[1] The Director Toolbar includes a button to open the Paint window. D5, D6, and D7 allow only one Paint window to be open at a time. Use onion skinning to view multiple cast members in the Paint window semi-concurrently. D4 allowed up to 50 Paint windows to be open at once.

[2] See the D6 *Onion Skinning Show Me* in the online Help or Chapter 13 in Macromedia's *Using Director* manual.

Paint Window Effects Tools

Table 13-16 lists the Paint window effects tools shown in Figure 13-7. In D4, these options appeared under the Effects menu. In D5, D6, and D7 use the effects toolbar in the Paint window (use View➤ Paint Tools to toggle the toolbar). You can also use the context-sensitive pop-up menu by selecting the graphic and then Ctrl-clicking (Macintosh) or right-clicking (Windows) on the selection. The Paint window tools are only available during authoring. See "Drawing at Runtime" earlier in this chapter, and see the third-party Xtras at the end of the chapter to perform similar operations at runtime. Director 7 introduces new sprite properties to flip, rotate, and skew sprites at runtime as shown in Table 3-2. See also the filter options described in Table 13-10.

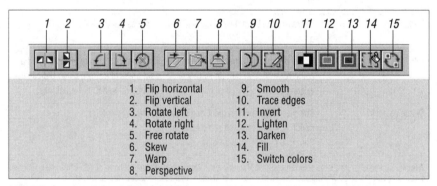

1. Flip horizontal
2. Flip vertical
3. Rotate left
4. Rotate right
5. Free rotate
6. Skew
7. Warp
8. Perspective
9. Smooth
10. Trace edges
11. Invert
12. Lighten
13. Darken
14. Fill
15. Switch colors

Figure 13-7: Paint window toolbar

Table 13-16: Paint Window Transformation Options

Tool	Action	Notes
Flip horizontal[1]	Mirror from left to right (across vertical axis)	Can't be used with Auto Distort
Flip vertical[1]	Mirror from bottom to top (across horizontal axis)	Can't be used with Auto Distort

Graphics & Color

Table 13-16: Paint Window Transformation Options (continued)

Tool	Action	Notes
Rotate Left[1,2]	Rotate counter-clockwise 90 degrees	See Xtras ➤ Auto Distort[3]
Rotate Right[1,2]	Rotate clockwise 90 degrees	See Xtras ➤ Auto Distort[3]
Free Rotate[1,2]	Arbitrary rotation (grab handles and drag)	See Xtras ➤ Auto Distort[3]
Skew[1,2]	Parallelogram skew	See Xtras ➤ Auto Distort[3]
Warp[1,2]	Arbitrary distortion in X-Y plane	See Xtras ➤ Auto Distort[3]
Perspective[1,2]	Perspective distortion in Z-plane	See Xtras ➤ Auto Distort[3]
Smooth[4]	Blends adjacent colors to smooth jagged edges	Same as *Smooth* ink
Trace Edges[4]	Creates a one-pixel thick outline of the graphic using the color(s) along its edge. Existing graphic is deleted.	Use the no-shrink marquee tool to select an area larger than the graphic to create a complete outline.
Invert[4]	Colors are reversed based on their palette position (in 8-bit)	Same as *Reverse* ink
Lighten[4]	Increases the brightness of the selected area.	Same as *Lighten* ink
Darken[4]	Decreases the brightness of the selected area.	Same as *Darken* ink
Fill[4]	Fills entire selected area with foreground color, regardless of pattern setting or existing pixels in Paint window.	The Paint Bucket tool fills in only adjacent areas of a single color, but can use Normal, Gradient, or Reveal inks.
Switch colors[4]	Switches foreground gradient and destination gradient colors in selected area. Prior to D7, works in 8-bit only.	Same as Switch ink.

[1] Requires portion of graphic to be selected using the Marquee tool's *Shrink* or *No Shrink* option by double-clicking the Marquee tool or using Edit ➤ Select All. Will not work with Lasso tool or Marquee tool's *Lasso* or *See Thru Lasso* option.
[2] Click one of the rotation or distortion tools to undo the effect of the previous tool and start the distortion afresh. Can't use Edit ➤ Undo (or ~ or ` keys).
[3] Perform rotation or distortion, then use Auto Distort to create intermediate steps as new cast members. When using Auto Distort to rotate a selection, select an area larger than the graphic of interest to prevent clipping pixels at the edges when it is rotated.
[4] Requires at least partial selection using Lasso or Marquee tool.

New bitmap properties in D7

Director 7 introduces new functions and properties pertaining to bitmaps as shown in Table 13-17. See also the undocumented *setPixel()* and *getPixel()* functions described earlier in this chapter, the new sprite transformation properties in Table 3-2, and the complete list of bitmap properties in Table 4-10.

Table 13-17: Director 7 Bitmap Functions and Properties

Property	Usage
alphaThreshold of member	Property for 32-bit bitmaps with an alpha channel. A number from 0 to 255, below which the sprites ignores mouse clicks. Set it to 0 to trap all mouse clicks. See *the useAlpha* and *the antiAlias of member*.
blendLevel of sprite	Blend transparency from 0 to 255. Similar to *the blend of sprite* whose range differs (0 to 100).
crop (member *whichBitmap*, *cropRect*)	Crops a member to the specified *cropRect*.
dither of member	If TRUE, bitmaps in the wrong palette are dithered to the current 8-bit palette (slower than remapping). Defaults to FALSE. No effect at bit depths above 8.
picture of member	Capture the Stage or a MIAW using one of these: (new(#bitmap)).picture = the stage.picture (new(#bitmap)).picture = window(*n*).picture
thumbnail of member	Get or set the thumbnail image of a cast member. Seems reliable in D7.0 for setting only, such as: member(*dest*).thumbnail = member(*source*).picture
useAlpha of member	If TRUE, D7 uses the alpha channel information in 32-bit bitmap members when compositing them on Stage.

Inks

There are two distinct types of inks in Director: Paint window inks are applied during authoring, and sprite inks can be set in the Score or controlled via Lingo at runtime.

Paint window inks

Table 13-18 explains the ink effects available in the Paint window. The Paint window has a number of inks not supported for sprites on the Stage, most notably *Gradient, Reveal, Cycle, Switch*, and *Clipboard*. See the online Help for details. If the Paint window's *Remember Ink* Preference is checked, the last ink used for each tool or brush is reinstated when the tool is reselected.

Table 13-18: Paint Window Inks

Ink	Effect	Works Best With
Normal[1]	Draws using foreground color, usually analogous to a sprite's *Matte* ink effect. *Normal* text is surrounded by a rectangular area colored by background color chip, analogous to a *Copy* ink.	Brushes, filled shapes
Transparent[1]	Draws patterns with opaque foreground color and transparent background color. Allows background items to show through patterns and text.	Text, filled shapes

Table 13-18: Paint Window Inks (continued)

Ink	Effect	Works Best With
Reverse[1]	Reverses each pixel's color index (sets it to 255 – index). Black becomes white; white becomes black.	Brushes, filled shapes
Ghost[1]	Draws using background color (if solid) or switching background and foreground colors (if using a pattern). When used with selection tools, black becomes white. Selection becomes invisible over white areas.	Brushes, filled shapes
Gradient[1]	Paints according to gradient settings using the pattern.	Paintbrush, paint bucket, filled shapes
Reveal[1]	Non-white pixels reveal artwork used in previous cast position. See online Help.	Paintbrush, filled shapes
Cycle	Cycles through colors in palette set by the gradient foreground and destination color chips (see Paint window preferences *Color Cycling* option).	Solids and patterns
Switch	Switches pixels of foreground color to gradient destination color. Prior to D7, works only in 256 colors (8-bit).	Paintbrush
Blend	Translucent percentage blend, as set by Paint window preferences *Blend Amount* setting.	Solids and patterns
Darkest	Uses the darkest color from the paintbrush and background graphic for each pixel. Useful for colorizing black and white artwork.	Patterns
Lightest	Uses the lightest color from the paintbrush and background graphic for each pixel.	Patterns
Darken	Reduces pixel brightness.	Paintbrush
Lighten	Increases pixel brightness.	Paintbrush
Smooth	Non-directional blur used to smooth jagged edges. Affects only boundary between two colors.	Paintbrush
Smear[2]	Spreads color in the direction of the brushstroke, fading slowly with distance.	Paintbrush
Smudge[2]	Smears color in the direction of the brushstroke, fading rapidly with distance (carries less color than Smear).	Paintbrush
Spread[1]	A copy of area under the paintbrush when you start to drag is used as the brush. Similar to Clipboard ink. Does not mix colors or fade with distance.	Paintbrush
Clipboard[1]	Uses the Clipboard's contents as the brush. Similar to dragging a sprite with trails on stage.	Paintbrush

[1] Also works in black and white.
[2] The Smear and Smudge inks reflect the Paint Window Preferences *Interpolate by* setting.

Sprite inks

Table 13-19 shows possible values for *the ink of sprite* property. Any sprite, such as digital video or Flash assets, played direct-to-Stage are rendered using the Copy ink effect in the foremost paint layer. QuickTime 3 also supports a new mask option that allows for uniquely shaped digital video sprites (see Chapter 16).

Only the Copy, Background Transparent, and Blend inks are supported for D6 rich text sprites. Convert rich text to a bitmap using Modify ► Convert to Bitmap to apply other inks. You can set a scrolling field sprite to Background Transparent ink, but it reverts to Copy ink when the user scrolls. See Chapter 3, *The Score and Animation*, for details on how sprites are drawn in the offscreen buffer. The ink effect can also affect whether a sprite highlights. For example, shape sprites with a Matte ink highlight when clicked, but those with other inks applied do not.

Only Copy, Background Transparent, Transparent, and Blend inks are supported for Flash and vector shape sprites. (Unlike bitmaps, the latter three inks use the outline for mouse-click detection when used with Flash and vector shape members.) The transparency color is defined in Flash when the object is created.

See the *Demonstrating Ink Effects Show Me* movie for a demonstration of sprite inks. Unlike Paint window inks, sprite inks can affect runtime performance markedly. Try to stick with the fastest inks (Copy, Background Transparent, and Matte). Avoid slow inks such as Blend if performance is an issue. The Reverse ink reverses the colors beneath a sprite, not the colors of the sprite itself. Blend is especially slow under Windows and with stretched sprites. Use inks such as Not Copy to create highlights and similar visual effects. Refer also to the *trails of sprite* property.

Use the ink pop-up menu in the Sprite Toolbar or Sprite Inspector to set the sprite ink. Use Cmd-click (Mac) or Ctrl-click (Windows) to set the sprite ink on Stage.

An alpha channel is an 8-bit value (0 to 255) used to give varying transparency to a 32-bit sprite. D7 supports alpha channels only for sprites using Matte ink for which *the useAlpha of member* is TRUE. The new *alphaThreshold of member* property erty determines how mouse-clicks are registered over sprites using an alpha channel. See *http://www.zeusprod.com/nutshell/alpha.html* for more details.

Table 13-19: Sprite Ink Effects

Code	Ink Name	Effect	Black	White	Others
0	Copy	Sprite's bounding rectangle is filled with the background color. Use for rectangular sprites and backgrounds. Fastest ink.	Opaque	Opaque	Opaque
1	Transparent	Black pixels can be colorized using the foreground color chip in the Tool palette.	Opaque	Transparent	Semi-transparent
2	Reverse	Any color except white reverses pixels behind sprite. Good for making custom masks.	Reverses pixels	Transparent	Reverses pixels

Table 13-19: Sprite Ink Effects (continued)

Code	Ink Name	Effect	Black	White	Others
3	Ghost	Hides a sprite while over a white background. Colors are transparent over white and dimmed and reversed over other colors.	Opaque white	Transparent	Varies
4	Not Copy	The foreground image is reversed, then the Copy ink is applied.	Opaque white	Opaque black	Opaque inverted
5	Not Transparent	The foreground image is reversed, then the Transparent ink is applied.	Opaque white	Opaque black	Inverted and Semitransparent
6	Not Reverse	Colors reverse over any non-white colored background.	Transparent	Reverses any color	Reverses
7	Not Ghost	Colored areas create tints over non-white background.	Transparent	Opaque	Tinted
8	Matte[1]	Traces the outline of the object instead of using the bounding box. The interior of the image remains opaque.	Opaque	Opaque, except around edges	Opaque
9	Mask[1]	Uses the next cast member (must be 1-bit in D6, or 2-, 4-, or 8-bit in D7) in the Cast window to define transparent and opaque areas.	Black pixels in mask are opaque	White pixels in mask are transparent	Unchanged
32	Blend[2]	Opacity depends on blend percentage in the Sprite Properties dialog box, Sprite Inspector, Sprite Toolbar, or set via *the blend of sprite*. 0 is transparent; 100 is opaque.	Varies	Varies	Varies
33	Add Pin	Adds pixel indices. If sum exceeds 255, the color is set to white.	Transparent	Opaque	Varies
34	Add	Adds pixel indices. If sum exceeds 255, it wraps around to 0.	Transparent	Varies	Varies
35	Subtract Pin	Subtracts foreground index from background index. If less than 0, the color is set to black.	Transparent	Opaque black	Varies
36	Background Transparent	Pixels of background color (set with background color chip in Tools Palette) are transparent. Slower than Copy, but faster than Matte. Good for holes in doughnuts and coffee mug handles.	Opaque	Transparent if background color is white	Opaque, except background color is transparent

Table 13-19: Sprite Ink Effects (continued)

Code	Ink Name	Effect	Black	White	Others
37	Lightest	Uses lightest color from the foreground or the background (or the Stage).	Transparent	Opaque	Lightest prevails
38	Subtract	Subtracts foreground index from background index. If less than zero, it wraps around to 255.	Transparent	Varies	Varies
39	Darkest	Uses darkest color from the foreground or the background (or the Stage).	Opaque	Transparent	Darkest prevails
40	Lighten[3]	Colors in a sprite are lightened as the background color gets darker the foreground color tints the sprite.	Foreground color tinted with background color	White	Varies with foreground and background colors
41	Darken[3]	Background color used as filter. Foreground color tints the sprite.	Foreground color	White	Varies with foreground and background colors

[1] Mask and Matte inks require twice the memory of other inks because Director creates a duplicate of the artwork. There is a small delay when a sprite with Matte ink is first drawn as the matte is calculated.
[2] *The blend of sprite* property controls the display of sprites whose *ink of sprite* is set to 32 (*Blend*). See Example 13-5. It is most reliable at color depths above 8-bit.
[3] New in D7. Neither darken nor lighten has any effect unless the foreground and background colors are changed from the default black and white. See "inks, using sprite inks" in the D7 online Help.

Prior to D7, *the blend of sprite* property does not increment smoothly from 0 to 100. Example 13-5 creates a smooth blend from the starting *blend of sprite* property to the specified `endBlend` (0 to 100) using only the 55 valid values. D7 also supports *the blendlevel of sprite*, which ranges from 0 to 255, but is otherwise equivalent to *the blend of sprite*.

Example 13-5: A Smooth Blend

```
on blendSprite spriteToBlend, endBlend
    set the ink of sprite spriteToBlend = 32    -- Blend ink
    set startBlend = (the blend of sprite spriteToBlend*55)/100
    set endBlend   = (endBlend*55)/100
    if startBlend <= endBlend then
        repeat with i = startBlend to endBlend
          set the blend of sprite spriteToBlend = (i*100)/55
          updateStage
        end repeat
    else
        repeat with i = startBlend down to endBlend
          set the blend of sprite spriteToBlend = (i*100)/55
          updateStage
```

Example 13-5: A Smooth Blend (continued)

```
    end repeat
  end if
end blendSprite
```

```
blendSprite 5, 0      -- Fade sprite 5 to transparent
blendSprite 6, 100    -- Transition sprite 6 to opacity
```

Paint Window Issues

Here are some common problems with graphics:

Halo effect or jagged edges

The halo effect is caused by near-white pixels around the edges or the graphic, created when it was anti-aliased (or feathered) against a white background (perhaps in Photoshop). Only true white pixels (or whatever color is chosen for the background color) will be transparent when using the background transparent ink.

To remove the halo, change off-white pixels to pure white pixels (palette index 0) in the Paint window using the tools described in Table 13-12. Place the graphic against a black Stage to make the offending edges more apparent. Alternately, you can defringe the graphic in Photoshop and re-import it.

Either don't anti-alias the graphic, or anti-alias it in Photoshop against a color similar to the background on which it will eventually be placed. Use text, Flash, or Alphamania cast members for real-time anti-aliasing. D7 anti-aliases 32-bit bitmaps with an alpha channel if *the useAlpha of member* is TRUE.

Switch Colors command or other tools won't work in Paint window

You must select all or part of the graphic to activate many of the Paint tools. Prior to D7, *Switch Colors* only works reliably on 8-bit graphics (256 colors). At other color depths, it would switch only colors that match a color in the 8-bit palette exactly.

Importing

Director treats pure white as a background color and ignores white pixels when determining the size of a bitmap. Double-click the marquee tool in the Paint window to view the extent of a graphic's bounding box. Add off-white pixels in the surrounding area and apply a Copy ink to simulate a white border.

Bitmaps wrong size

Make sure that your images are saved in 72 dpi. If you save them at 300 dpi, they will appear about four times larger once imported into Director.

Performance and scaling

Sprites draw fastest when the sprite is the same size as the original cast member. Create assets in appropriate sizes or scale them using Modify ➤ Transform Bitmap (leave the palette and bit depths at their defaults). Other programs such as Photoshop or DeBabelizer may provide better scaling.

Rotation

Director 6 does not provide real-time rotation. Use **Xtras ➤ Auto Distort** to create a series of rotated cast members during authoring, use a third-party Xtra for realtime rotation, or upgrade to D7 and use *the rotation of sprite* property.

Unwanted holes in background transparent sprites

Use a color different from the background color to create opaque areas in a background transparent sprite (i.e., use off-white instead of white).

Wrong colors or colors too dark

The D6 Paint window supports only 8-bit color brushes. When painting 16-bit and 32-bit cast members, the exact brush color may not be available. If colors appear too dark in D6 for Windows, remove the DirMMX.X32 Xtra from your *Xtras* folder and restart Director to solve the problem. D7 addresses both of these problems, because it can paint using any 16-bit or 32-bit color and does not use the MMX Xtra.

Color Chips

Director uses a number of so-called *color chips* to select the colors for various operations, as described in Table 13-20. Click and hold on a color chip to display its associated palette.

See the eyedropper tool in Tables 13-9 and 13-12, plus Table 13-14 for additional commands that affect the color chips.

Table 13-20: Color Chips

Chip	Effect
Foreground chip in Tool palette[1,2]	Colorizes 1-bit bitmap, QuickDraw shape, and Flash cast members.[3] Used for border of QuickDraw shape cast members and foreground of fill pattern (see *the foreColor of sprite*). Determines color of text, fields, and buttons (see *foreColor of member*). In D7, colorizes sprites of any bit depth (see *the color of sprite*).
Background chip in Tool palette[1,2]	Determines transparent color used for background transparent ink (see *the ink of sprite* code 36) and background of fill pattern for shapes (see *the backColor of sprite*). Determines color of background for fields and buttons (see *backColor of member*). Affects the background color of text cast members. In D7, sets *the bgColor of sprite*.
Pattern chip in Tool palette[1]	Determines pattern (1 to 64) used to fill QuickDraw shape cast members. See *the pattern of member* and *the filled of sprite*. Pattern color relies on foreground and background color chips.
Foreground chip in Paint window[4,5]	Determines drawing color for Normal ink (see Text, Pencil, and Brush tools) and foreground color used by fill pattern (paint bucket and shapes). Used for border of shapes; starting color for Cycle and Gradient inks; swapped with Destination color by Switch ink or *Switch Colors* command.
Destination chip in Paint window[5]	Determines ending color for Cycle and Gradient inks; swapped with Foreground color by Switch ink or *Switch Colors* command.

Table 13-20: Color Chips (continued)

Chip	Effect
Background chip in Paint window[5]	Determines background color used for fill pattern. Used to draw in Ghost ink. Pencil draws in background color if first pixel clicked is colored with foreground color.
Pattern chip in Paint window[5]	Determines pattern used for filled shapes; combines with gradient settings for Gradient ink.
Stage color chip	Select Stage's background color (see *the stageColor* and the D7 *bgColor of the stage* property) from the movie's default palette (see Modify ➤ Movie ➤ Properties). The color is an index into the movie's 8-bit palette even if *the colorDepth* is greater than 8. On the Win32 platform at 16-bit color depth, it appears to use an index into the default palette of the first movie contained within the Projector. In D7, an *rgb( )* color can be specified. Also used for desktop cover when creating a full-screen Projector. In D4, the stage color chip is in the Control Panel.
Font color chip[1]	Set in Modify ➤ Font. Same as foreground color chip in Tool Palette. Sets *the foreColor of member* color for field and buttons members and sets text color for text, field, script, and button members. Double-click to access Tile Setting dialog box (see Table 13-11).
Score channel colorization[6]	Color chips in bottom left of Score window colorize selected sprite(s) in Score window. See File ➤ Preferences ➤ Score ➤ *Allow Color Cells*, and *the scoreColor of sprite*.
Sprite Toolbar and Sprite Inspector color chips[2]	In D7, the Sprite Toolbar and Sprite Inspector color chips match those present in the Tool Palette when a sprite is selected in the Score or on the Stage. Double-click or triple-click them to open the Color Palettes window.
Text Inspector color chips[2]	In D7, the Text Inspector color chips match those present in the Tool Palette when editing a text, field, button, or script member. Also colorizes text in Message window.
Script colorization	In D7, scripts can be auto-colored using the color chips under File ➤ Preferences ➤ Script. If enabled, the Tool Palette color chips and Text Inspector won't affect script text.
Sprite Overlay	You can choose the color of the Sprite overlay text using View ➤ Sprite Overlay ➤ Settings.

[1] Chips in the Tool Palette and the Font color chip always use the active palette, ordinarily set in the Score's Palette channel, or the movie's default palette if none is set.
[2] In D7, the Tool Palette color chips also appear in the Text Inspector, Sprite Toolbar, and Sprite Inspector.
[3] If you colorize Flash sprites, white areas take on the color specified by *the foreColor*, non-white pixels are tinted, and black pixels remain black. Flash's color model is the opposite of QuickDraw's (also used by 1-bit bitmaps) in which colorizing black yields the specified color, and colorizing white always yields white.
[4] The two Foreground color chips in the Paint window (for gradients and patterns) are always the same. See Figure 13-6.
[5] Chips in the Paint window always use the cast member's palette set in the Cast Properties dialog box. 16-bit and 32-bit cast members use the "System - Mac" or "System - Win" palette depending on the platform. See Table 13-14.
[6] Score channel colors are cosmetic only and have no effect on the Sprite's appearance on Stage.

D7 adds the ability to specify RGB values from #000000 to #FFFFFF in the movie properties dialog box, Sprite Inspector, and Sprite Toolbar. Hold down the mouse on any color chip and choose *Edit Favorite Colors* to specify RGB values that appear atop the current palette or choose *Color Picker* to select a specific color.

ForeColor and BackColor Properties

Use the Tool Palette's foreground and background color chips to colorize shapes and bitmap sprites and set the background transparent color for sprites using the background transparent ink. In D7, you can use the color chips in the Sprite Toolbar or Sprite Inspector instead. First select the sprite in the Score or on the Stage, then choose a color from the color chip. The Tool Palette color chips also apply color to the selected text in the Field, Text, and Message windows and to the Script window if auto-coloring is disabled in the Script Preferences.

Foreground colors other than black and background colors other than white will affect the appearance of various ink effects and may produce unpredictable results when applied to bitmaps with depths above 1-bit in D6. However, using a background color other than white with the *Background Transparent* ink effect is reliable in 8-bit color, even in D6. In D7, sprites of any bit depth can be colorized and colors can be tweened (see Modify ➤ Sprite ➤ Tweening).

Table 13-21 shows the quirky values for the *backColor* and *foreColor* member and sprite properties. Note that the value for Windows 3.1 Projectors apply even if such Projectors are run under Windows 95/98/NT. See also Macromedia Tech-Notes #00760 and #12118 covering the *backColor* and *foreColor* sprite and member properties.

In D7, the *bgColor* and *color* member and sprite properties, which are specified as RGB triplets, produce accurate colorization regardless of the monitor or bitmap color depth.

Table 13-21: BackColor and ForeColor Properties

Platform (Color Depth)	backColor and foreColor of member[1] Index (0 to 255) Into	backColor and foreColor of sprite[2] Index (0 to 255) Into
Mac (8-bit)	Active palette[3]	Active palette[3]
Mac (16-bit)	No palette (0 to 32767)	Movie palette[4]
Mac (32-bit)	No palette (0 to 16777215)	Movie palette[4]
Win3.1 (8-bit)	Active palette[3]	Active palette[3]
Win3.1 (> 8-bit)	Active palette[3]	Movie palette[4]
Win95/98/NT (8-bit)	Active palette[3]	Active palette[3]
Win95/98/NT (> 8-bit)	Windows system palette	Movie palette[4]

[1] The member properties are used for field and button cast members (also for rich text cast members, although not accessible via Lingo in D6).
[2] The spite properties are used for shapes and 1-bit bitmaps. Default *foreColor* is 255 (black) and default *backColor* is 0 (white). Values higher than 255 are set to *value mod 256*. Negative values are "wrapped around" to (*256 - value*).
[3] The "active" palette is set in the Score's Palette channel (*the framePalette*), although it can be affected temporarily by the *puppetPalette* command. If no palette is set, the movie palette is used.
[4] The movie's "default" palette is set under Modify ➤ Movie ➤ Properties.

BackColor and ForeColor of Member Settings

The default *backColor of member* is white. The default *foreColor of member* is black. Director automatically changes the values for these properties on the Macintosh at different monitor color depths to maintain a given color. Under Windows, the values are always indices (0–255) into the active palette or Windows System palette. You should check *the platform and colorDepth* before setting any value for the *backColor* or *foreColor of member* properties. In D6, you can create a list in which to look up each color at different color depths or create reference cast members with the desired colors and use their member properties as a reference. In D7, you can avoid the issue altogether by specifying RGB colors for the *color of member* and *bgColor of member* properties. The *backColor* and *foreColor of member* are as follows.

In 8-bit color on the Macintosh:

- 0 = white
- 255 = black
- Invalid values are set to 255

In 16-bit color on the Macintosh:

- 0 = black
- 32767 = white
- Other colors are 15-bit RGB values
- Overflow values are set to *value mod 32768*
- Negative values are wrapped around to *32768 – value*

In 32-bit color on the Macintosh:

- 0 = black
- 16777215 = white
- Other colors are 24-bit RGB values
- Overflow values are set to *value mod 16777216*
- Negative values are wrapped around to *16777216 – value*

Xtras

There are numerous third-party Xtras and applications to address some deficiencies in Director. The sprite rotation Xtras in the following list may provide superior appearance to D7's native rotation feature.

Cast Effects: Penworks (http://www.penworks.com)
Lingo manipulation of 8-bit bitmap images: extract subportions of images to create new cast members, flip images, rotate images in 90-degree increments, determine color of any pixel in a bitmap and split the RGB channels of a cast member as in Photoshop.

Precision Xtra (http://www.penworks.com)
Create irregular or multiple clickable areas within a sprite. Return RGB value of any point on screen.

Color Picker

Use the Microsoft Common Dialog ActiveX Control's *ShowColor* command to create a Color Picker under Win32.

MediaLab Xtras (http://www.medialab.com)

Photocaster: multi-layer import from Photoshop. Splits RGB channels. Lite version included with D7.

Alphamania: alpha channel support and blend effects.

Effector Set: scale, rotate, resize fully anti-aliased cast members.

Color Genie (XObject): Dynamically modify palettes. Incompatible with D7.

Planet Color—Lizard Tech (http://www.lizardtech.com)

Creates optimized palettes from within Director.

Gamma Fade—Scott Kelley (http://www2.connectnet.com/~sakelley)

Macintosh-only transition Xtra.

ScrnUtil Xtra—Little Planet (http://www.littleplanet.com/kent/kent.html)

Screen grab utility; copies Stage to cast member, clipboard, or file. D7 captures the Stage using *the picture of the stage*.

Picture Xtra—Geoff Smith (http://fargo.itp.tsoa.nyu.edu/~gsmith/Xtras)

Extracts subsections of bitmap cast members; Macintosh only. D7 crops images using the new *crop()* command.

DeBabelizer—Equilibrium Technologies (http://www.equilibrium.com)

Standalone application to batch process images in myriad ways.

Fast Eddy (shareware) also by Lizard Tech (http://www.lizardtech.com)

Uses a human perception–based conversion algorithm to create optimal palettes for fine gradients, rather than the statistical approach used by Photoshop and DeBabelizer.

CHAPTER 14

Graphical User Interface Components

This chapter covers the standard Director user interface (UI) elements, including buttons, cursors, menus, and dialog boxes. Audio can also be an important UI element. Many UI Behaviors are included with the full Director 7 Shockwave Internet Studio, but not with the standalone D7 upgrade. The Lingo Behavior Database has many example button and UI Behaviors. See *http://www.behaviors.com/ lbd/*.

Most user interfaces are terrible. Test your UI on someone unfamiliar with the product and make adjustments based on their feedback.

Make the interface consistent:

*   All buttons should behave the same way. Make consistent use of rollover, highlighted, and depressed button states. Use *mouseDown* or *mouseUp* handlers consistently so that all buttons behave similarly.

*   The size and position of buttons should be consistent. For example, the *exit* or *back* button should be in the same place on each screen.

*   Clickable buttons should be intuitively obvious (round, oval, or rectangular, with a raised appearance). Adjacent text labels should also be clickable. Non-clickable elements, such as titles, should not look button-like.

*   Provide consistent, immediate, and useful feedback, such as sounds, wait cursors, progress bars, confirmation prompts, or text screens.

*   Create a logical hierarchy of screens or submenus. The user should be able to navigate anywhere in three or four clicks and easily find his way back.

Respect the user:

*   Allow the user to interrupt, pause, or replay lengthy animations and videos.

*   Avoid timed screens. Allow the user to dismiss help screens immediately or read them at his leisure. Allow users to repeat any audio instructions.

- Provide a friendly installer, if appropriate. Minimize the disk space required and don't install any system software without the user's approval.

- Allow the user to save his work or place in the presentation, if applicable. Children should always be allowed to save and restore their creations.

- Allow the user to print his work, if applicable.

- Certain symbols, graphics, animals, hand gestures, colors, music, and depiction of gender roles are considered offensive, inappropriate, or simply may not translate to different cultures. Consult a localization expert.

- Include a *ReadMe* file with relevant quirks or installation issues.

Special considerations for children or inexperienced kiosk users might include:

- Young users have trouble manipulating the mouse and keyboard. Avoid gestures such as double-clicking, click-and-drag, Shift-click, or keyboard commands (especially ones requiring modifier keys).

- Avoid hierarchical menus, which require more dexterity.

- Make buttons and hotspots large. Provide clues such as rollovers, sounds, or cursor changes to indicate clickable items.

- Use a large and colorful cursor with a hotspot in the middle of the cursor itself. Children don't understand that they need to point with the tip of the arrow or paint bucket. Consider a touch-screen if appropriate. (Note that touch screens do not generate mouse rollover events.)

- Expect children to click repeatedly. If a double-click halts an animation started by the first click, the child may never see it. Some designers opt to ignore multiple mouse clicks and always play an animation to completion. Avoid this, especially for lengthy animations, by ignoring double-clicks but allowing a delayed click to abort the animation.

- Children like to interact. Avoid "click and wait" syndrome. Kids love to repeat things; allow them to repeat animations indefinitely.

- Provide kooky sounds. Kids love sounds.

- Young children can't read. Use graphics instead of text boxes. In confirmation dialog boxes, provide an audio cue and an animation of characters shaking their heads "Yes" or "No."

- Provide automatic help or hints after a reasonable timeout period. See Chapter 11, *Timers and Dates*, in *Lingo in a Nutshell*.

- Eliminate screen clutter, distracting backgrounds, text-heavy interfaces, and unnecessary animations.

Some good references include:

- *The Non-Designers Design Book: Design and Typographic Principles for the Visual Novice*, by Robin Williams. Peachpit Press, 1994. (A very approachable overview of design concepts.)

- *The Macintosh Human Interface Guidelines.* Apple Computer, 1992.

- *The Windows Interface: An Application Design Guide,* Microsoft Press.

- *Demystifying Multimedia: A Guide for Multimedia Developers*, Apple Computer. Random House, 1994.

- *Envisioning Information & The Visual Display of Quantitative Information*, by Edward Tufte. Graphics Press, 1990.

- *Guide to Macintosh Software Localization*. Apple Computer, 1992.

- *Internationalization Handbook for Software Design*. Microsoft Corp., 1993.

Buttons

There are numerous types of buttons in Director, none of which do anything until you attach a script to them. Refer to Chapter 9 in *Lingo in a Nutshell* for details on adding *mouseUp* and *mouseDown* handlers to buttons. Any graphic element including digital video, text, and field cast members can be used as buttons, but the cast member types described in the following sections are more commonly used. A sprite's ink setting determines whether it responds to mouse clicks within its bounding box (Copy ink) or only within its outline (Matte ink). Refer also to the new *alphaThreshold of member* property in D7, which determines how mouse-clicks are detected for sprites using an alpha channel.

Don't confuse Director's built-in button cast members (whose *type of member* is *#button*) with the D6 custom buttons made possible via the Button Editor (whose *type of member* is *#btned*). Only *#button* cast members are found when searching for Button cast members via Edit ➤ Find ➤ Cast Member. Search for cast members of type *Xtras* to find custom *#btned* buttons (along with other Xtra cast members). Macromedia's *D6 Lingo Dictionary* does a poor job of differentiating between properties of the two types of buttons. Unless listed in Table 14-1, a so-called "button" property relates only to Custom Buttons, which are obsolete in D7. Implement fancy buttons using bitmaps with attached Behaviors instead.

In D6, the *Widget Wizard* and *Button Library* (both under the Xtras ➤ Widget Wizard menu) provide numerous premade buttons, some of which use Custom Button cast members. In D7, refer to the Window ➤ Library Palette.

Bitmaps

Any bitmap cast member can be used as a button. The *Bitmap Cast Member Properties* dialog box's *Highlight When Clicked* option causes the bitmap to invert when clicked if there is any script attached to the sprite. You'll typically want to provide fancy rollover and depressed button states using Behaviors to change the *ink* or *member of sprite*. See Director 6's Behavior Library, the D7 Library Palette, the Lingo Behavior Database, Example 4-3, or Chapter 12, *Behaviors and Parent Scripts*, in *Lingo in a Nutshell* to create your own multi-state buttons.

Shapes and Invisible Hotspots

The Tool Palette, opened via Windows ➤ Tool Palette and shown in Figure 14-1, is use to create QuckDraw shapes and various styles of button cast members (or use Insert ➤ Control to create buttons). It also colorizes shapes and text and sets the background color used by the background transparent ink

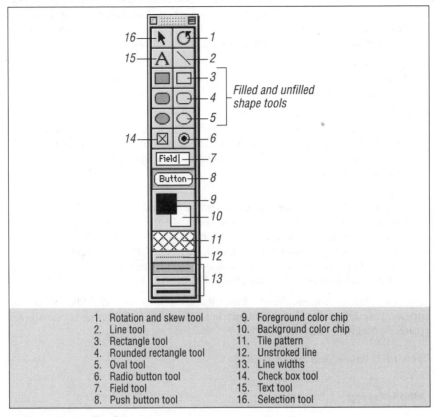

1. Rotation and skew tool	9. Foreground color chip
2. Line tool	10. Background color chip
3. Rectangle tool	11. Tile pattern
4. Rounded rectangle tool	12. Unstroked line
5. Oval tool	13. Line widths
6. Radio button tool	14. Check box tool
7. Field tool	15. Text tool
8. Push button tool	16. Selection tool

Figure 14-1: Tool Palette

effect. In D7, the new rotation and skew tool can distort bitmap, text, animated GIF, Flash, and vector shape sprites.

Shape cast members can be used as buttons. An unstroked (zero-width border), unfilled shape sprite will still respond to mouse events and can be used to add invisible hotspots. Use the Precision Xtra (*http://www.penworks.com*) to create irregular hotspots or multiple hotspots on an image.

Push Buttons, Check Boxes, and Radio Buttons

Push buttons, check boxes, and radio buttons are three variations of the same type of cast member. (You can alter a button's type in the *Button Cast Member Properties* dialog box.) All three button types include a text label that can be edited on the Stage or using the Field window (Window ➤ Field). Use the Text Inspector (Cmd-T or Ctrl-T) to alter the button text's style and size and the Tool Palette's color chips (while the button's contents and not the entire sprite are selected) to colorize the text or the button's background. The D7 Text Inspector includes these color chips as well.

Unlike most asset types, changes to push button, check box, and radio button sprites always affect the underlying cast member, and hence affect all sprite instances created from it. You must use separate button cast members to create independent push button, check box, and radio button sprites:

Push buttons

Simple push buttons are created using the Button tool. Push buttons always invert when clicked.

Check boxes

Simple check boxes are created using the Check Box tool. Check boxes have two states (checked and unchecked). The checked state can be shown as an X in a square, a semi-filled black square, or a solid black square (see *the checkBoxType* property).

Radio buttons

Simple radio buttons are created using the Radio Button tool. Radio buttons can have two states (checked and unchecked); the checked state is shown as a small black dot inside a larger black circle. In D6, refer to the Radio Button Group widget that uses the UI Radio Button Behavior to create groups of radio buttons that are mutually exclusive. In D7, see the Radio Button Group Behavior under *Controls* in the Library Palette.

Table 14-1 covers button-related Lingo. Radio buttons and checkboxes always appear to the left of the button text and are always black. Use custom bitmaps for greater flexibility.

Table 14-1: Button-Related Lingo Usage

Button-Related Lingo	Usage
#button	Standard buttons return *#button* as their *type of member*. See the *buttonType of member* entry.
the buttonStyle[1]	Determines whether *mouseUp* and *rightMouseUp* messages are sent following a *mouseUpOutside* message: 0: list style (default) 1: dialog box style
the buttonType of member	Determines the button type (*#checkBox*, *#pushButton*, or *#radioButton*).
the checkBoxAccess[1]	Determines the behavior of check boxes: 0: User can toggle buttons on and off (default). 1: User can toggle state on, but not off. 2: User cannot change toggle state. Control is via Lingo only.
the checkBoxType[1]	Determines checked appearance of check boxes: 0: Marked with an "X" (default) 1: Marked with a small solid black square 2: Filled with solid black

Table 14-1: Button-Related Lingo Usage (continued)

Button-Related Lingo	Usage
the highlight of member	Determines whether a radio button or checkbox is checked (TRUE) or unchecked (FALSE), not whether a button or bitmap highlights when clicked. Can be both tested and set via Lingo or changed by the user depending on *the checkBoxAccess*. (Not meaningful for push buttons.)
the text of member	Determines text label for button. Button text can be manipulated from Lingo as can field text.

1 The *buttonStyle, checkBoxAccess,* and *checkBoxType* properties are systemwide. They cannot be set for individual members or sprites.

Custom Buttons

Director 6's Button Editor Xtra created custom buttons that automatically handled their rollover, depressed, toggled, and inactive states. In D6, Custom Buttons are inserted using Insert ➤ Control ➤ Custom Button. Custom Buttons are obsolete in D7. Due to a number of unresolved bugs, you should use Behaviors instead. See the web page *http://www.zeusprod.com/nutshell/custombuttons.html* if you are a die-hard fan of Custom Buttons.

Widgets

There are a number of third-party vendors that offer higher-level premade widgets (UI components).

Math Xtras by Maxwell Technologies (sliders, tables, counters, graphs, speedometers, and an onscreen calculator):

> *http://www.maxwell.com/MathXtras/*

StageHand Xtra by T-Tools (creates buttons, scrollbars, dials, and other widgets):

> *http://www.t-tools.com*

Instant Buttons and Controls by stat media:

> *http://www.statmedia.com*

Multimedia Tackle Box by Vicious Fishes Software:

> *http://www.viciousfishes.com*

Director 7 Shockwave Internet Studio includes Behaviors to implement common UI components. Open the Windows ➤ Library Palette menu and then select the *Controls* or *Text* castLib.

Director 6 included numerous premade widgets via the Widget Wizard. Refer to the *Widget Wizard ReadMe* file in the *Xtras:Wizards:Widget Wizard* subfolder where Director 6 is installed.

The D6 Widget Wizard is more a starting point and a teaching tool than a robust production tool. Open the Widget Wizard movie from the File ➤ Open menu to examine its scripts. See *http://www.zeusprod.com/nutshell/widgetwizard.html* for details on using the Widget Wizard.

Cursors

Director can change the cursor's appearance while the mouse is over the Stage, a MIAW, or Shockwave movie, or over a specific sprite (in which case it obeys the Matte ink outline). The new cursor can be set to one of the cursor resource IDs built into Director using:

```
cursor cursorResourceID
```

The most important cursor resource IDs are shown in Table 14-2. Using *cursor 0* or *cursor –1* sets the global system cursor to the arrow pointer. Setting *the cursor of sprite = 0* reverts the sprite to use the global cursor, but setting *the cursor of sprite = –1* uses an arrow for the sprite's cursor regardless of the global cursor.

Table 14-2: Cursor Resource IDs

ID	Cursor	Macintosh	Windows
–1	Arrow pointer	▲	▲
0	Default[1]	▲	▲
1	I-beam	I	I
2	Crosshair	+	+
3	Crossbar	✥	✥
4	Wait	⌚	⌛
5	Black Arrow	▲	▲
200	Blank (hidden)	<None>	<None>

Only cursor resource IDs numbered –1 through 4 are available on all platforms in earlier versions of Director. Figure 14-2 shows additional cursor (CURS) resources that are supported in Director 6 and 7 during both authoring and playback. On the Macintosh, the basic cursor resources shown in Table 14-2 are embedded in the Macintosh System file. The extended CURS resources shown in Figure 14-2 are stored in the resource fork of the Director 7 application or the Director 7.0 Resources file. Use ResEdit to examine the CURS resources of any Macintosh application and copy them to Director's Paint window.

The hotspot and mask of an existing cursor resource (see Figure 14-3) are intrinsic to the resource definition, and cannot be altered inside Director.

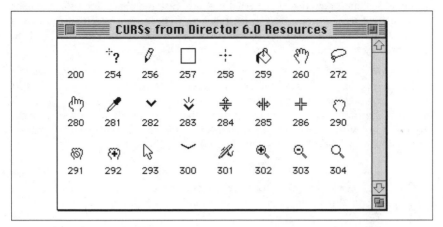

Figure 14-2: Additional cursor resources

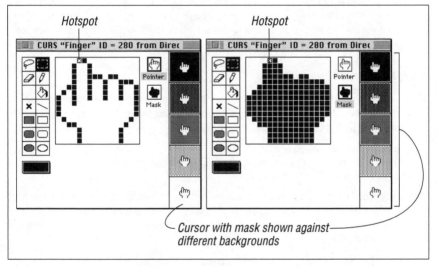

Figure 14-3: A cursor and its mask

Windows cursors can be edited with a Windows resource editor (see "Customizing Windows Icons" in Chapter 8, *Projectors and the Runtime Environment*.) Windows system cursors are stored in CUR files in the *C:\Windows\Cursors* folder. The default cursors shown in Table 14-2 can be modified under the *Pointers* tab of the Windows *Mouse* control panel.

Cast Members as Cursors

You can also use black and white bitmaps as custom cursors, such as:

```
cursor [member cursorMember, member maskMember]
```

(Director assumes that the specified items are cast members and not a cursor resource ID if they are enclosed in list brackets.) The *cursorMember* must be a 1-bit cast member no larger than 16×16 pixels. (Bitmaps can be converted to 1-bit using Modify ➤ Transform Bitmap.)

The *maskMember* is optional on the Macintosh, Windows 3.1, and Windows 95/98, but is apparently mandatory under Windows NT. A mask should be used in all cases to improve the cursor's visibility over various backgrounds. Black pixels in the mask become opaque, whereas white pixels in the mask allow the background to show through. A mask is often the same size as the *cursorMember*, but filled in with solid black as shown in Figure 14-3.

 The registration point of *cursorMember* determines the cursor's hotspot (arrow tip, crosshair center, and so on).

Both the cursor resource ID and the 1-bit cast member approach work with both the *cursor* command and *the cursor of sprite* property. Use bitmap cast members instead of cursor resources to guarantee cross-platform compatibility in all versions of Director and Shockwave.

System Cursor

The *cursor* command determines which cursor is displayed whenever the mouse is over the Stage or the area covered by a full-screen Projector. The cursor can be set separately within MIAWs. The *cursor* command takes one of the following forms:

```
cursor cursorResourceID
cursor [member cursorMember, member maskMember]
cursor member "CustomCursor"
```

The last form can be used with a 1-bit member, but is intended for the Custom Cursor Xtra included with D6.5 and D7. The default system cursor is 0 (an arrow). You can use the undocumented *the cursor of sprite 0* to set or read the current system cursor, such as:

```
set currentCursor = the cursor of sprite 0
```

Sprite Cursors

The cursor of sprite property overrides the system cursor whenever the mouse is over the sprite in the specified channel. The default setting is 0, meaning that it assumes the value of the system cursor set with the *cursor* command. Don't set *the cursor of sprite* to –1 unless you want to use an arrow cursor for the sprite even when the system cursor is something different.

To set the cursor for a sprite, use one of the following:

```
set the cursor of sprite whichSprite = cursorResourceID
set the cursor of sprite whichSprite = ¬
        [member cursorMember, member maskMember]
set the cursor of sprite whichSprite = member "CustomCursor"
```

The last form is best used with the Custom Cursor Xtra included with D6.5 and D7.

The cursor of sprite property is not automatically reset when the sprite span ends; it pertains to the entire channel. Reset the cursor in an *on endSprite* handler to prevent a phantom sprite cursor from appearing over the bounding rectangle of the last sprite used in the channel.

Example 14-1 is more efficient than setting the cursor repeatedly using *on mouseEnter* and *on mouseLeave* handlers, which may cause memory leaks in Shockwave 6.0.1 and 7.0 and Director 7. Reducing the number of cursor switches is prudent.

Example 14-1: Setting a Temporary Cursor

```
on beginSprite me
  -- Set some custom cursor, in this case, a crosshair
  set the cursor of sprite (the spriteNum of me) = 2
end

on endSprite me
  -- Reset the sprite to follow the system cursor setting
  set the cursor of sprite (the spriteNum of me) = 0
end
```

Creating Special Cursors

Standard Director cursors are limited to 16×16–pixel, black-and-white static images. Attach the script in Example 14-2 to a sprite to simulate a color cursor larger than 16×16. Use a sprite in the highest number channel and set its ink effect to *matte* or *background transparent.*

Example 14-2: Simulating a Cursor with a Sprite

```
on beginSprite
  -- Hide the real cursor
  cursor 200
end

on exitFrame me
  -- Track the mouse's movement to position "cursor"
  set the loc of sprite (the spriteNum of me) = ¬
          point (the mouseH, the mouseV)
end

on endSprite
  -- Reset arrow cursor
  cursor 0
end
```

You can animate the cursor by changing the sprite's *member of sprite* property periodically, but the Custom Cursor Xtra included with D6.5 and D7 can handle this for you automatically.

Cursor operations

Table 14-3 shows some commonly performed cursor operations.

Table 14-3: Common Cursor Operations

Action	Command
Hide the cursor	Use *cursor 200*. Appropriate when using a touch-screen.
Create a color cursor	Use the Custom Cursor Xtra, or simulate a cursor using a sprite.
Create an animated cursor	Use the Custom Cursor Xtra, change the 1-bit cursor, or change the sprite used to simulate a cursor.
Create a large cursor	Simulate a cursor using a sprite. See Example 14-2.

Watch cursor

Example 14-3 sets a watch or hourglass cursor during some time-consuming operation.

Example 14-3: Setting a Wait Cursor

```
-- Save state of old cursor
set oldCursor = the cursor of sprite 0

cursor 4 -- Watch/Hourglass cursor
-- Perform some time-consuming operation here
statement(s)

-- Revert to previous cursor, or use cursor 0 to revert to arrow
if oldCursor <> 4 then
  cursor oldCursor
else
  cursor 0
end if
```

Cursor Caveats

There are numerous cursor quirks (most surmountable or ignorable), including:

- The cursor will flicker during transitions or while over a playing digital video sprite. Hide the cursor at these times.

- The cursor will flicker even after an AVI file completes, because AVI files do not automatically set *the movieRate* to zero when done. See *http://www.mmii.com/directorhelp* for Greg Griffith's solution. George Langley recommends setting *the movieRate* of the offending sprite to 0, then to 1, then back to 0 to clear the flickering cursor.

- Avoid using cursor resource IDs because all are not supported in all versions of Director. Create 1-bit cast members from the cursor resources you need instead.

- Director may not recognize the cursor change made by another program or the QTVR or QuickTime 3 Xtras. Director will ignore any request to switch the cursor to what it thinks is already the current setting. Force an update by switching the cursor to a different value and then back.

- To cancel a custom cursor for a sprite, reset it to 0 (zero), not –1. The latter will always use an arrow, rather than matching the system-wide cursor setting.

- Reset *the cursor of sprite* to 0 (zero) when a sprite is no longer on Stage, or risk the custom cursor appearing over the old sprite's bounding rectangle.

- The Tempo channel's *Wait for Mouse Click* option changes the cursor to a blinking icon. Use Lingo to wait if you prefer a different cursor.

- Cursors are reset between movies. Set them in the *on startMovie* handler.

- Setting the cursor to a bitmap cast member leaked memory in D6.0, but was fixed in D6.0.1. Unfortunately, cursor leaks resurfaced in D7.0, but are again remedied in D7.0.1. Minimize cursor switches to reduce leaks.

- Sprite cursors are ignored for invisible sprites as of D6.0.1. Prior to that, the cursor might change over an invisible sprite's bounding rectangle.

- See the Quirk List at *http://www.updatestage.com* for additional cursor caveats.

- Myron Mandell reports that when using a cast member as a cursor, a mask cast member must also be specified under Windows NT.

- Cursors flicker over any sprites played direct-to-Stage. D7.0.1 fixes problems in D7.0 with flickering cursors in editable text sprites.

Cursor doesn't appear

If the cursor is not visible, check the following possible causes.

The cursor is hidden automatically if there are no sprites that include scripts on-Stage. If necessary, attach a dummy script to at least one sprite, such as:

```
on mouseDown
-- do nothing
end
```

The cursor may have been disabled by setting it to resource 200 (hidden cursor). Reset the cursor using the code in Example 14-4.

Example 14-4: Resetting All Cursors

```
on resetAllCursors start, end
  cursor -1
  repeat with whichSprite = start to end
    set the cursor of sprite whichSprite = 0
  end repeat
resetAllCursors
```

The cursor may not appear if it is assigned to an invalid value:

- The cursor may be set to an incorrect or nonexistent *cursorResourceID*.

- The cursor may be set to incorrect or nonexistent cast member(s) or to cast members that are not 1-bit bitmaps or Custom Cursor assets.

Cursor Lingo Commands

Table 14-4 explains Lingo related to standard cursors.

Table 14-4: Cursor-Related Lingo Commands

Command	Usage
closeResFile {resFile}	Close a resource file potentially containing cursor resources (Mac-only, obsolete).
#cursor	Used with *on getPropertyDescriptionList*'s *#format* option to bring up a list of cursor types. See Chapter 12 in *Lingo in a Nutshell*.
cursor *cursorResourceID*	Uses the specified resource as the new system cursor.
cursor [member *cursorMember*, {member *maskMember*}]	Uses the specified 1-bit cast member and optional mask cast member as the new system cursor.
the cursor of sprite 0	Returns the current system cursor as set by the *cursor* command.
the cursor of sprite *whichSprite* = *cursorResourceID*	Uses the specified resource as the new cursor while the mouse is over a specific sprite.
the cursor of sprite *whichSprite* = [member *cursorMember*, {member *maskMember*}]	Uses the specified 1-bit cast member and optional mask cast member as the new cursor while the mouse is over a specific sprite.
the depth of member *cursorMember*	The depth of member must be 1 for black-and-white cursor cast members and masks.
the mouseH	Returns the horizontal position of cursor's hotspot relative to left edge of Stage.
the mouseLoc	Returns the point of the cursor's hotspot relative to the upper left of the Stage (new in D7).
the mouseV	Returns the vertical position of cursor's hotspot relative to top edge of Stage.
openResFile {resFile}	Opens a resource file containing cursor resources (Mac-only, obsolete).
the regPoint of member *cursorMember*	*The regPoint of member* of a 1-bit cast members acts as the cursor's hotspot.
showResFile {resFile}	Shows resources in a resource file (Mac-only, obsolete). Use mouse click to abort output listing in Message window.

The Custom Cursor Xtra

The Custom Cursor Xtra included with D6.5 and D7 uses one or more bitmaps (similar to a film loop) to create a color animated cursor. In D6.5, its HTML-based help files are installed along with the Xtra in the *Xtras:CustomCursor:Help* folder. In D7, refer to the online Help and to *http://www.macromedia.com/support/xtras_essentials/cursor/how/tutorial/*.

To create a custom cursor, follow these steps:

1. Ensure that the Custom Cursor Xtra is installed.

2. Choose `Insert`➤`Media Element`➤`Cursor`.

3. In the *Cursor Properties Editor* add one or more 8-bit cast members to be used as frames in the animated cursor.

4. Set the interval (in milliseconds) for animating the cursor.

5. Set the cursor's hotspot relative to its upper left corner.

6. Use the Custom Cursor cast member with *cursor* or *the cursor of sprite*, as:

```
cursor [member customCursorMember]
set the cursor of sprite whichSprite = ¬
     [member customCursorMember]
```

7. Distribute the Cursor Asset Xtra with your Projector. It is not included by default with SW7, but can be auto-downloaded.

Custom cursor caveats

- The Custom Cursor Xtra requires D6.0.1 or later and a PowerMac or Windows 95/98/NT (32-bit projectors only). It won't work with 16-bit (Windows 3.1) Projectors, on non-PPC Macs, or in SW6.

- All cast members used within an animated cursor should be the same size, although oversized cast members will be scaled down. Do not delete the original bitmaps from the Cast after incorporating them into the custom cursor, as they are still referenced by it.

- All cast members used within an animated cursor must be 8-bit (256-color) bitmaps. 1-bit, 4-bit, 16-bit, 24-bit, or 32-bit cast members won't appear in the *Cursor Properties* dialog box for inclusion.

- D6.5 allowed rich text members to be used in custom cursors, but D7 does not. Rich text cast members are scaled if they are wider than the cursor; thus the text may become almost invisible. Narrow the rich text cast member's width in the Text window to eliminate any whitespace.

- The bitmap cast members used should contain only colors present in the native platform's system palette (Macintosh or Windows).

- Macintosh cursors must be 16×16 pixels or smaller. Windows cursors can be up to 32×32 pixels on most machines, depending on the video card.

- Animated cursors are limited to 50 frames (elements) in the animation.

- Don't place a custom cursor cast member on the Stage; it appears as a red X. Use the *cursor* or *cursor of sprite* commands instead.

- When using custom cursor in a Windows MIAW, you must reset the cursor to a system cursor before closing the MIAW or it will become invisible and unchangeable.

- Custom cursors will not animate while in authoring mode when over a MIAW (works fine in Projector mode).

- You must include the Cursor Asset Xtra with your Projector, but not the Cursor Options Xtra.

Custom cursor Lingo

Table 14-5 shows the Lingo to control custom cursor cast members.

Table 14-5: Custom Cursor Xtra Commands

Command	Usage
the automask of member *cursorMember*	Specifies whether white pixels in the custom cursor cast member are transparent (default is TRUE).
the castMemberList of member *cursorMember*	Specifies a Lingo list of cast members used as frames of the animated cursor. (Only 8-bit bitmaps allowed.)
#cursor	Custom cursor cast members return *#cursor* as their *type of member*.
cursor [member *cursorMember*]	Uses a custom cursor cast member as the new system cursor.
the cursor of sprite *whichSprite* = [member *cursorMember*]	Uses a custom cursor cast member as the new cursor while the mouse is over a specific sprite.
the cursorSize of member *cursorMember*	Determines size of cursor in pixels. Can be 16 for Macintosh, and 16 or 32 for Windows.
the hotSpot of member *cursorMember*	Indicates the cursor's hotspot relative to its upper-left corner. Returned as a point such as point (0,0).[1]
the interval of member *cursorMember*	Interval (in milliseconds) between animated cursor frames.[2] Default is 100.
new(#cursor)	Creates a new cursor cast member.

[1] The hotspot can range from *point(0,0)* to *point(15,15)* for 16 × 16 pixel cursors, or *point(32, 32)* for 32 × 32 pixel cursors. For 16-pixel cursors, you can set the hotspot to *point(16,16)* via the cursor properties dialog box; it will be reported via *the hotspot of member*, but you can't set it to *point(16,16)* via Lingo.

[2] Use the same cast member more than once within an animated cursor to create the appearance of uneven intervals in its animation.

Controlling Cursor Position

Lingo does not provide a way to move the cursor. You can simulate cursor movement by using a sprite as a surrogate cursor as shown in Example 14-2.

To move the real system cursor, use one of these Xtras:

- The DirectOS Xtra (*http://www.directxtras.com/do_doc.htm*) sets the cursor position and can generate a mouse click for any one of three buttons under Windows.

- The Buddy API Xtra (*http://www.mods.com.au/budapi*) sets the cursor position under Windows and can also restrict the cursor to certain subsections of the screen.

- The free SetMouse Xtra (*http://www.scirius.com*) sets the position of the cursor (cross-platform).

Other cursor-related Xtras can be found at:

- *http://members.aol.com/XtraTools/index.html* (cross-platform)
- *ftp://ftp.tbaiana.com/pub/Goodies* (Windows only)
- *http://netnow.micron.net/~enzo* (Windows only)

Menus

Director can define custom menus in the menubar. The Macintosh menubar always appears at the top of the primary monitor, regardless of the Stage's location or size or whether it is played full-screen. If a Windows Projector is played in a window, the menubar appears below the window's titlebar (this requires that the *Show Title Bar* option be used when the Projector is built). The window's titlebar has its own menu with the Move, Minimize, and Close options active, and the Restore, Size, and Maximize options disabled. If the Windows Projector is played full-screen, the menubar appears at the top of the monitor. Shockwave does not support custom menus but the right mouse button (Windows) or Ctrl-click (Macintosh) is reserved for a user menu in Shockwave 7 and ShockMachine.

Lingo directly supports pull-down menus only. Use custom Lingo or the Popup Xtra to create hierarchical or pop-up menus. See the DropDownList control in the D7 Library Palette. Use the MUI Xtra to create pop-ups within a dialog box.

A custom menubar is created in four steps:

1. Create the commands or handlers to be called from each menu item.
2. Define the menu by entering the menu's text in a field cast member.
3. Install the menu using installMenu *whichMenuMember*.
4. Remove the menu using installMenu 0.

Defining and installing a menu determines only its initial state. You can optionally modify the menu via Lingo after it is installed. *InstallMenu* is buggy in D7.0 for Macintosh. Only every other *installMenu* command works, so you must issue it twice, or preferably upgrade to D7.0.1.

Menu Definition

To define a custom menu, enter appropriate text in a *field* cast member. A menu definition takes the general form:

```
menu: menuName
<F menuItem /K | script
<F menuItem /K | script
menu: menuName
<F menuItem /K | script
<F menuItem /K | script
```

where:

- *F* is one of the formatting codes (see Table 14-6).
- *K* is a keyboard shortcut (see "Keyboard shortcuts" later in this chapter).
- *script* is a command or script to be executed when the menu item is chosen.

I have left space in the previous example for readability. Don't include spaces or blank lines in the menu definition, as it is whitespace-sensitive.

Table 14-6 lists the menu definition codes. Experiment with them until the menu appears as desired. If necessary, widen the field cast member holding the menu definition to avoid wrapped lines, which are treated as separate menu items even if no carriage return is used.

Table 14-6: Menu Definition Codes

Symbol	Usage
menu:@	Specifies menu:@ as the first menu to add the standard Apple menu to the menubar.[1]
menu: *menuName*	Defines a menu name. Subsequent lines define the menu items under the menu.
menuItem	Each line of text below the menu heading creates another entry in the menu.
| *script*	Specifies a script to be executed when a menu item is selected (see *the script of menu-Item*).
/K	Specifies a shortcut key for the menu option (using Cmd on the Mac, Ctrl on Windows).
(*menuItem*	Disables a menu item (see *the enabled of menuItem*).
(-	Creates a disabled horizontal line separator in the menu.
(empty line)	Creates a blank line as a menu item.
!✓	Adds a checkmark next to the menu item.[1,2]
<B	Displays the menu item in boldface.[1,3]
<I	Displays the menu item in italic.[1,3]
<O	Displays the menu item in outlined text.[1,3]
<S	Displays the menu item in shadowed text.[1,3]
<U	Displays the menu item in underlined text.[1,3]

[1] Macintosh-only.
[2] Create the checkmark using an exclamation point followed by the ✓ character created with Option-v on the Macintosh (ASCII code 195). See *the checkMark of menuItem* property and "Checkmarked menu items" later in this chapter.
[3] You can use multiple formatting codes in a single menu item.

Table 14-7 lists the cross-platform custom menu differences.

Table 14-7: Cross-Platform Custom Menu Differences

Operation	Macintosh	Windows
Menu location	Always displayed at top of main monitor, even if Stage is smaller than screen or played *In a Window*.	Displayed at top of window if played *In a Window*, otherwise at top of screen.
@ character in menu definition	Creates Apple menu at the left of the menubar.	Unsupported.

Table 14-7: Cross-Platform Custom Menu Differences (continued)

Operation	Macintosh	Windows
checkMark of menuItem	Supported.	Unsupported.
Bold, italic, outlined, shadowed, and underlined menu items	Supported.	Unsupported.
Maximum number of items in a menu	At least 255; menu scrolls automatically.	Limited to number that fit on screen. *More* button not supported.
Maximum total length of strings in menus	No practical limit.	May be limited under Windows 3.1.
Switching menus dynamically	Supported. Buggy in D7.0; fixed in D7.0.1.	Supported, but not recommended (may leak memory, especially in D5).
Menu shortcuts use	Cmd key.	Ctrl key.
Activate menu via	Mouse only.	Alt key or mouse.

Menu names and the Apple menu

Menu names may be exceedingly long (at least 100 characters). Any wrapped lines in the menu definition field are treated as menu items and not as part of the menu name. A blank menu name appears as whitespace in the menubar and may contain menu items. The number of menus is limited only by the width of the monitor. Menu names do not accept formatting codes as do menu items.

Example 14-5 defines a field cast member that includes the Apple menu, along with a custom *About...* entry, in your Macintosh menubar.

Example 14-5: Creating an Apple Menu

```
menu:@
About... | aboutBox()
menu: Second Menu
menuItem
menuItem
```

Specify the Apple menu (menu:@) before other menus in the definition. The *About...* entry appears at the top of the Apple menu, before the default entries. In Example 14-5, selecting the *About...* item runs a custom *aboutBox()* handler that you should create in a movie script.

The Apple menu option (@) is buggy in D7.0 but fixed in D7.0.1.

When menu:@ is used under Windows, the Apple logo is replaced with an unprintable block character and the menu contains only user-defined entries.

Menu item names cannot contain the (, <, |, !, and / characters, which are used for formatting. If the menu item name is empty, a blank line appears in the menu.

Very long Macintosh menus scroll automatically, and the number of entries is at least 255. Windows menus are limited to the number of entries that can fit on screen, which depends on the monitor resolution (although *the number of menu-Items* may report more items than can actually fit on the screen).

Menu commands

Use a vertical bar (|) to separate the menu item's name from the command to be executed when it is chosen. In the following example, the custom `File ➤ Quit` option executes the Lingo *quit* command:

```
menu: File
Quit | quit
```

To execute a multiline command, call a handler instead, such as:

```
menu: File
Quit | quitHandler()
```

The script associated with each menu item is run when that item is selected from a menu. You cannot determine the last menu item selected via Lingo. If you need to track the last menu item selected, do so in the handlers called from each menu item.

Any formatting codes should precede the vertical bar in the menu definition, and the Lingo command or handler to execute should follow it. The vertical bar is ASCII code 124 on both platforms. Director 5 and earlier used ASCII code 197 instead, which appeared as ~ on the Macintosh (and was created using `Option-x`), and appeared as Å under Windows (and was created using `Alt-0-1-9-7`).

Keyboard shortcuts

Use a forward slash (/) to separate the menu item name from a single character to use as a keyboard shortcut in combination with the Macintosh `Cmd` key or Windows `Ctrl` key. In Example 14-6, choosing `Cmd-L` or `Ctrl-L` executes the Sound ➤ Low option.

Example 14-6: Using Keyboard Shortcuts for Menus

```
menu: Sound
Off/0| set the soundLevel = 0
Low/L| set the soundLevel = 1
Medium/M| set the soundLevel = 4
High/H| set the soundLevel = 7
```

Keyboard shortcuts are always one character plus either the `Cmd` or `Ctrl` key. If you use more than one forward slash in a line, the character following the *last* forward slash becomes the keyboard shortcut.

Although characters are shown in the menu as entered, both upper- and lower-case keys are recognized (that is, the state of the `Shift` key is ignored). Any keyboard shortcuts override the default keyboard combinations, such as:

```
menu: File
Quit/Q | quitHandler()
```

Refer to Chapter 10 in *Lingo in a Nutshell* for ways to trap more sophisticated key combinations and for details on *the exitLock* property.

Windows menus can be accessed using the `Alt` key followed by the first letter of the menu name, and then the first letter of any menu item. The arrow keys also navigate among the menus and menu items after the `Alt` key is pressed.

Checkmarked menu items

Use an exclamation point (!) to add a checkmark (or other character) to the left of any item in the menu. Create the checkmark using an exclamation point followed by the ✓ character created with `Option-v` on the Macintosh (ASCII code 195). The same character appears as Ã under Windows, and can be created using `Alt-0-1-9-5` (but the function is primarily designed for the Macintosh). If you specify a different character after the exclamation point, it is shown to the left of the menu item instead of a checkmark.

```
menu: menuName
!✓someItem |handleCheckedItem("someItem", "someMenu")
```

Adding a checkmark to a menu item does *not* automatically toggle the checkmark each time the item is selected. You must do so manually (see Example 14-7).

Example 14-7: Setting a Menu Item Checkmark

```
on handleCheckedItem whichItem, whichMenu
  -- whichItem can be an item name or number
  -- whichMenu can be a menu name or number
  set newValue = not (the checkMark of ¬
      menuItem whichItem of menu whichMenu)
  -- This toggles the checkmark on and off
  set the checkMark of menuItem whichItem ¬
    of menu whichMenu = newValue
  if newValue then
    -- Do something here because the item is checked
  else
    -- Do something here because the item is unchecked
  end if
end
```

Line separators

Use the characters (- on a line by themselves to create a simple horizontal rule to separate menu items. Such lines are counted in the *number of menuItems*:

```
menu: menuName
menuItem | script
(-
menuItem | script
```

Disabled Items

If the (character appears anywhere in an item name, it disables the menu item (prevents it from being selected). Use *the enabled of menuItem* to enable or disable a menu item dynamically:

```
menu: menuName
(disabledMenuItem | menuCommand
```

Menu item formatting

You can specify one or more case-sensitive formatting codes (<B, <I, <O, <S, <U) to create bold, italic, outlined, shadowed, or underlined menu item entries on the Macintosh (they are ignored under Windows). The code(s) can occur before or after the menu item name, such as:

```
menu: Style
Bold Item<B /B | boldIt()
<IItalic Item /I | italicizeIt()
<U<BUnderlined Bold Item /U | emphasizeIt()
```

Any characters following a < but preceding the next valid formatting character (B, I, O, S, or U), will be ignored, such as:

```
menu: menuName
<ithis won't appear in menu because i is lower case| script
menu: menuName
<Ithis is correct for italic| script
```

InstallMenu

The *installMenu* command activates a custom menu using:

```
installMenu whichMember
```

where *whichMember* is the name or number of the field cast member containing the menu definition. Director 5 and earlier may require a field number when calling *installMenu*, and not allow a field name. In that case, use:

```
installMenu the number of member "fieldName"
```

You can change the custom menu by specifying a different field cast member.

Remove the custom menu by using:

```
installMenu 0
```

InstallMenu doesn't work while the movie is halted. Set it once the movie is playing. (*InstallMenu* can also interfere with the Macintosh Director Help menu.)

 Installing menus repeatedly under Windows can slow performance and lead to a system crash. *InstallMenu* is buggy in D7.0 for Macintosh. It must be called twice to switch menus. Upgrade to D7.0.1.

Minor changes to a menu should be made via Lingo instead of using *installMenu* repeatedly. At a minimum, use *installMenu 0* to uninstall one menu before installing another.

Example 14-8 installs different menus under Macintosh and Windows.

Example 14-8: Installing Platform-Specific Menus

```
if the platform starts "Windows" then
  installMenu member "WindowsMenus"
else
  installMenu member "MacMenus"
end if
```

Lingo Menu Commands

Table 14-8 shows the Lingo commands that modify menus that have already been installed using *installMenu*. They will not work when Director is halted. They can determine whether a menu item is active, whether a checkmark is displayed, and even change a menu item name or the command it executes. To modify the name of a menu, number of menus, number of items in a menu, menu item formatting (bold, italic, outline, shadow, or underline), or to change keyboard shortcuts, you must install a new menu with *installMenu*.

Menus are numbered from 1 to *the number of menus*, starting with the leftmost menu; menu items are numbered within each menu from 1 to *the number of menuItems* of that particular menu. In Table 14-8, menu items are generally specified as:

> the *property* of menuItem *whichItem* of menu *whichMenu*

The undocumented use of *in* instead of *of* also works:

> the *property* in menuItem *whichItem* in menu *whichMenu*

where `whichItem` is a menu item's name or number, and `whichMenu` is a menu's name or number. The menu and menuItem properties do not support the D7 dot notation.

Table 14-8: Menu-Related Lingo Commands

Command	Usage
the checkMark of menuItem *whichItem* of menu *whichMenu*	If TRUE, the menu item will have a checkmark next to it (see the "!" operator). Can be tested and set. (Default is FALSE.)
the enabled of menuItem *whichItem* of menu *whichMenu*	If TRUE (the default), the menu item is selectable. Otherwise, it is dimmed and inactive; see the (operator. Can be tested and set.
installMenu *fieldMember*	Specifies the name or number[1] of a field cast member from which to construct a custom menu.
installMenu 0	Removes any custom menu in effect.

Table 14-8: Menu-Related Lingo Commands (continued)

Command	Usage
menu:*menuName*	*menu* is not a Lingo command. It is used within a field cast member to define a menu (see Table 14-6).
the name of menu *whichMenu*	Returns the name of a particular menu based on its number.[2]
the name of menuItem *whichItem* of menu *whichMenu*	Determines the name of a menu item. Can be tested or set.
the number of menuItems of menu *which-Menu*	Returns the number of menu items within a menu, including line separators created with (– and blank lines.[2,3]
the number of menus	Returns the number of menus in the menubar,[2,4] including the Apple menu, if applicable.
the script of menuItem *whichItem* of menu *whichMenu*	Determines the command executed when the menu item is chosen. Can be tested or set.

[1] Director 5 and earlier may require a field number when calling *installMenu* and not allow a field name.
[2] This property cannot be set directly. It can be affected indirectly by installing a different menu with *installMenu*, and returns 0 if no custom menu is installed.
[3] *The number of menuItems* reported may not match the number of visible items in the menu. Under Windows, a menu will display only as many items as fit on the screen, even though more items are installed within the menu.
[4] *The number of menus* reported may exceed the number that are visible in the menubar if the installed menus are too wide to fit on the screen.

Hierarchical and Pop-up Menus

Director does not directly support hierarchical or pop-up menus. You can create simple pop-up menus using the D7 DropDownList Behavior:

The MHT Pop Up Xtra (*http://www.meetinghousetech.com*) allegedly creates pop-up menus under Windows, but I haven't tested it.

Complex hierarchical pop-up menus can be created with the Popup Xtra (the Xtra formerly known as PopMenu), which is sold via UpdateStage (*http://www.update-stage.com/xtras*). I refer to it here as PopMenu for convenience and because the cast member type is still *#popMenu*. PopMenu Lite ships with Director 6, but is merely a demo version; you cannot save any PopMenu cast members until you purchase the full version of the Xtra. PopMenu Lite is installed in the *Xtras:ScriptOMatic Lite* subfolder on the Macintosh and the *Xtras\GrayMatter\ScriptOMatic Lite* subfolder under Windows in D6.

The Popup Xtra supports all platforms and offers the following features not available with standard Director menus:

- Create pop-up menus on the Stage to be used like any other sprite assets
- Create hierarchical menus nested up to five levels deep
- Colorize menu background and text

- Specify custom fonts and point sizes for the text in the menu
- Modify the number and content of menu items dynamically at runtime
- Modify menu item styles (bold, italic, etc.) dynamically (Mac-only)
- Include customized icons beyond the standard checkmark (Mac-only)

There are many commands and properties that control PopMenu cast members, and I've outlined the most important ones in the following sections. See Xtras ➤ PopMenu ➤ Help for details. *The Director Xtras Book* by Rich Shupe also covers the PopMenu Xtra in some detail.

Using the PopMenu (Popup) Xtra

Unlike standard Director menus, PopMenus are cast members that are placed on Stage like any other sprite. Therefore, you don't specify the commands to be executed as part of the menu definition, but instead attach a script to the PopMenu sprite.

The steps to create a hierarchical menu with PopMenu are:

1. Enter the menu definition text (explained later) in a field cast member.
2. Choose Insert ➤ Red Eye Xtras ➤ PopMenu (or Popup in later versions).
3. Double-click the new PopMenu cast member to bring up its options dialog box:
    a. Choose a castLib from the pop-up (even if there is only one).
    b. Choose your menu text cast member from the *Member* pop-up.
    c. Set the other attributes to control the menu's appearance.
4. Drag the PopMenu cast member to the Stage or Score.
5. If using PopMenu 3.0 or earlier, attach an *on mouseDown* handler to detect mouse events. If using PopMenu 3.10 or later, use an *on menuItemSelected* handler.

Defining pop-up menus

As with standard Director menus, PopMenu cast members read their initial menu definitions from field cast members, but there is only one top-level menu per PopMenu sprite. Menu items are separated by semicolons (;) or carriage returns. Submenus are indicated by brackets, such as:

```
topItem1[subItem1A;subItem1B]
```

or:

```
topItem2[subItem2A [tertiaryItem]]
```

The same format styles (<B, <I, <O, <S, <U) used in standard Director menus are supported by PopMenu on the Macintosh, such as:

```
topItem1<I[subItem1A<B;subItem1B<U]
```

Keyboard shortcuts are supported on the Macintosh only and are specified with a slash (/) as with standard Director menus. They should be used only for the last item in a menu hierarchy, not the interim submenus:

```
topItem2[subItem2A [tertiaryItem/T]]
```

The – character creates a separator line, the ! indicates a checkmark, and the (disables an item, as with standard Director menus.

Configuring a PopMenu cast member

The PopMenu cast member options are a bit confusing, and are best understood via some examples. To create a pop-up menu that behaves like Director's ink pop-up menu in the Sprite Inspector, set each option in the PopMenu cast member's option dialog box as shown in the second column of Table 14-9. To create a fixed menu, set each option as shown in the table's third column. The font, font size, foreground color, and background color may also be specified.

Table 14-9: Configuring a PopMenu Cast Member

PopMenu Option	Ink Example	Fixed Menu
Display Text	Initial value, such as "Copy"[1]	Menu title, such as "Click Me"[1]
Auto-Align Menu	TRUE	FALSE
Menu Location[2]	Upper-Left	Upper-Right[1]
Auto-Select Text[3]	TRUE	FALSE
Menu Indicator[4]	Diagonal Arrow	No Indicator[1]
Look[5]	Macintosh Standard	Macintosh Standard
Auto-Mark Selections[6]	TRUE	TRUE
Mark Type[6]	Bullet (·)	No Mark[1]

[1] These are merely suggestions. You may want different settings.
[2] Determines where upper-left corner of menu appears relative to sprite. Possible values are *Mouse location, Center, Upper-Left, Upper-Right, Lower-Left, Lower-Right*.
[3] Unchecking *Auto-Select Text* prevents the selection from replacing the *Display Text*.
[4] Adds small graphic to sprite to visually emphasize that it contains a pop-up menu. Possible values are *No Indicator, Down Arrow, Diagonal Arrow*.
[5] Possible values are *Macintosh Standard* and *Invisible*. The latter hides the menu, which can still be activated when the user clicks within the sprite's area.
[6] Checkmarks are available only on the Macintosh. Possible values are *No Mark, Check, Filled Diamond, Command, Bullet, Serif Check, Prompt, Open Diamond*.

PopMenu Lingo

The PopMenu Xtra provides extensive Lingo control over all aspects of the PopMenu cast members. After inserting a PopMenu cast member, the following commands print out brief documentation of PopMenu's properties and functions:

```
put the help of member popUpMember
put the propertyNames of member popUpMember
put the functionNames of member popUpMember
```

The most interesting properties are:

the selectedSpec of member
> This returns a string identifying the last menu item selected. For example, "1;2;3" indicates that the third item from the second submenu of the first menu item was chosen. Use the following to determine the text of the selected menu item or an arbitrary menu item:

```
put getItem (member popUpMember, ¬
    the selectedSpec of member popUpMember
put getItem (member popUpMember, "1;2;3")
```

the selectedText of member
> This returns the text of the last menu item selected. It contains the terminal item name, and doesn't include intervening submenu names from a hierarchical menu. Even numeric menu items are returned as strings, and must be converted using *value()*.

the menuDisplayText of member
> This returns the text currently displayed in the menu. It contains the last selected text item if the *Auto-Select Text* option is checked. Otherwise, it returns the initial *Display Text* (or that last specified with *setDisplayText*).

The *selectedSpec* and *selectedText* properties represent the most recent choice, not the current menu setting. They are EMPTY if the user rolled off the menu without selecting an item.

Example 14-9 contains a sample handler that can be attached to a pop-up menu to respond to user events. In this case, let's assume that the pop-up is a list of external sounds files that the user can play.

Example 14-9: Choosing an Item from a PopMenu

```
on menuItemSelected me
  -- Retrieve the text of the selected item
  set thisPopup = the member of sprite (the spriteNum of me)
  set textChoice = the selectedText of thisPopup
  -- If EMPTY, the user rolled off without making a choice
  if textChoice = EMPTY then
    beep
  else
    alert "User choose" && textChoice
  end if
end menuItemSelected
```

For PopMenu 3.0 or earlier, use an *on mouseDown* handler instead of the *on menuItemSelected* handler in Example 14-9, as shown at *http://www.zeusprod.com/nutshell/popup.html*. In PopMenu 3.0, the *mouseDown* handler is not executed until after the menu selection is made. In PopMenu 3.10 and later, *on mouseDown* is called before the menu selection is made (and therefore should not be used), but *on menuItemSelected* is called afterward.

The *selectedText* includes only the menu item, not the menu name. Example 14-10 concatenates a string built from the menu and submenu names leading to a menu choice. For example, if the user selected Desks ➤ Marquise ➤ Model6972, it would return "Desk Marquise Model 6972". You might use this code to select a cast member with a matching name.

Example 14-10: Constructing a String from a Hierarchical PopMenu

```
on menuItemSelected me
  global gMenuChoice
  set thisPopup = the member of sprite (the spriteNum of me)
  -- menuChoice is a string such as "2;3;1;2"
  set menuChoice = selectedSpec (member thisPopup)
  -- Exit if the user did not make a choice
  if menuChoice = EMPTY then
    exit
  end if
  -- We'll extract the name from each level of the menu
  -- to build a complete name.
  set oldDelimiter = the itemDelimiter
  set the itemDelimiter = ";"
  set gMenuChoice = EMPTY
  set itemCount = the number of items in menuChoice
  -- Construct the name based on the menu choice
  repeat with x = 1 to itemCount
    set subText = getItem (member thisPopup, ¬
      item 1 to x of menuChoice)
    put subText after gMenuChoice
    if x < itemCount then
      put SPACE after gMenuChoice
    end if
  end repeat
  set the itemDelimiter = oldDelimiter
  alert "Choice was" && gMenuChoice
end menuItemSelected
```

Dialog Boxes

You'll often need to present a user with a dialog box to:

- Alert him of an error condition
- Allow him to make a choice from a small number of alternatives
- Allow him to select a file or folder to read from or write to

---

 System dialog boxes under Windows may appear in the wrong colors, and may prevent Director from using the desired custom palette. See Chapter 13, *Graphics, Color, and Palettes*, for solutions.

Simple Alert Dialog Boxes

The Lingo *alert* command causes a system beep and posts a modal dialog box with the specified message and a single *OK* button. It is convenient for providing warning messages or for debugging from a Projector. It does not allow any user choices and is limited to displaying 255 characters.

The *alert* command takes the form:

```
alert message
```

For example:

```
if not (the platform contains "Mac") then
  alert "I don't do Windows. I'll quit now."
  quit
end if
```

To include a variable's or property's value in the alert message, concatenate it into the alert string, such as:

```
set x = 5
alert "The value of X is" && x
```

or:

```
alert "The current folder is" && QUOTE & the pathName & QUOTE
```

Alert requires a string. Convert nonstring data using the *string()* function:

```
alert string (the number of members of castLib 1)
```

The *alertHook* property can be used to intercept alert messages generated by the *alert* command or by other system errors. Refer to Chapter 3, *Lingo Coding and Debugging Tips*, in *Lingo in a Nutshell* for more information.

Custom Dialog Boxes via Lingo

If you use a series of sprites to simulate a custom dialog box, it can be any size, contain graphics elements, and allow the user to choose between multiple alternatives. A sprite-based dialog box can be implemented using:

- Multiple sprites, including puppetSprites or film loops

- A MIAW with the appropriate *windowType*

- A linked Director movie cast member (see *the scriptsEnabled of member*)

You can also use the MUI Dialog Xtra's *Alert* method to create a simple multibutton dialog box or use its other methods to create a fully customized dialog box. See Example 15-1 in *Lingo in a Nutshell* or *http://www.zeusprod.com/nutshell/chapters/mui.html*.

The Buddy API Xtra's *baMsgBox()* method creates multibutton platform-compliant dialog boxes.

The DialogBoxer (*http://www.coderiders.com*) is a customizable MIAW solution that creates cross-platform dialog boxes, with widgets including pop-up menus and various button types.

See also Media Connect's Border Xtra cited in Chapter 6.

File selection dialog boxes

The FileIO and MUI Xtras can display file browser dialog boxes for saving or opening files. (The MUI Xtra can also display a dialog box for entering a URL.) Refer to Chapter 14, *External Files*, in *Lingo in a Nutshell* for details.

Various third-party Xtras can set the default folder from which the file browser begins or allow you to choose a folder instead of a specific file. See the Dialogs Xtra (*http://www.updatestage.com/xtras/*).

The donationware FileXtra (*http://www.littleplanet.com/kent/kent.html*) shipped with D6.5 and D7 includes both *FileOpenDialog* and *FileSaveAsDialog* methods that can display file dialog boxes.

CHAPTER 15

Sound and Cue Points

Director is not a sound editing tool. You will usually create your sound files in an external application, and then import them into Director. For testing, you can use the sample sound files on the Director 7 CD in the *Macromedia/Support* folder.

D7 includes the Beatnik Lite Xtra (see `Xtras` ➤ `Beatnik Lite` or *http:// www.headspace.com/to/?xtra0support*). The D7 Studio for Macintosh includes Bias Peak LE (see *http://www.bias-inc.com*) instead of SoundEdit, which was bundled with previous Studio versions. The D7 Studio for Windows includes Sonic Foundry's Sound Forge XP, as did the D6 Studio.

Digital Audio Primer

A brief primer on digital audio is in order. In the real world, sound is continuous. For computer use, sound is digitized by sampling it at many points throughout each second of audio. A sound's *sample rate* is typically 11.025, 22.050, or 44.100 kHz (kilohertz, or thousands of samples per second), although many variations exist. Higher sampling rates require more storage, but typically sound better (have higher fidelity). The *bits per sample* or *sound bit depth* is usually 8 or 16, meaning that each sample requires 1 or 2 bytes of storage (there are 8 bits per byte).

Downsampling refers to lowering a sound's sample rate or bit depth, which can be done in a sound editor, but not in Director. Downsampled audio uses less storage at the expense of quality. *Resampling* is the process of changing the sampling rate, either up or down. The fidelity of resampled audio can vary measurably between different sound editors.

Sounds typically contain one or two channels: mono (or monaural) or stereo. To *fold* or *flatten* a sound is to convert it from stereo to mono, sometimes at the expense of quality.

The size of an uncompressed sound can be determined as:

```
size in K = (bits per sample)/8 × (sample rate in kHz) ×
    (number of channels) × (duration in seconds)
```

For example, 22.050 kHz, 16-bit mono sound occupies:

$$16/8 \times 22.050 \times 1 = 44.1 \text{ K/sec}$$

And 44.100 kHz, 16-bit stereo sound occupies:

$$16/8 \times 44.100 \times 2 = 176.4 \text{ K/sec}$$

For compressed Shockwave audio (SWA), the important factor is the streaming data rate, which is chosen when you compress your SWA, measured in Kbps (thousands of bits per second):

$$(\text{bit rate in Kbps})/8 = \text{data rate in K/sec}$$

Audio data is typically measured in K/sec. Memory is typically measured in increments of 1024 bytes (KB). Throughout this chapter, I use *K* to indicate 1000, and *KB* to indicate 1024. For example, CD-quality audio (16-bit, 44.1 kHz, stereo) requires 176.4 K/sec, which is technically 172.27 KB/sec. Divide by 1.024 to convert from K to KB, and divide by 8.192 rather than by 8 to convert from Kbps to KB, to account for the 2% discrepancy.

To calculate the disk space required for any type of sound, multiply the rate in KB/sec by the duration in seconds. These calculations exclude the small header associated with each sound. Unless the sound is very short, has a low data rate, and contains numerous cue points, the header size is insignificant relative to the audio data.

Sound Playback in Director

Director uses two Sound channels in the Score that correspond to the first and second system sound channels. But SWA sprites, which are placed in the sprite channels, can also use system sound channels 1 and 2. I use the uppercase *Sound channel* when referring to the channels in the Score, and the lowercase *sound channel* when referring to the System sound channels accessible via Lingo.

 See "Xtras needed to play external sounds in Director 6 and 7" later in this chapter to ensure that you've included the necessary Xtras with your Projector.

Supported Sound Formats

Sound cast members may be imported (embedded) into Director's cast or may be externally linked. Table 15-1 lists the supported audio formats as well as cross-platform differences. Note that the same AIFF, WAVE, and SWA files can be used on both Macintosh and Windows in D6 and D7. QuickTime and AVI files can also contain audio tracks. The Java player supports Sun AU format only.

Director does not export sound files, and sounds may be lost when exporting to QuickTime or AVI formats. To export a sound, cut and paste from the Cast to your sound editing program, set an external sound editor under File ➤ Preferences ➤

`Editor`, or rely on a third-party Xtra. There should be no need to export sounds in most cases, as you should retain the original source files imported into Director.

Table 15-1: Cross-Platform Audio Comparison

Feature	Macintosh	Windows
Formats supported for import into Cast[1]	SWA, AIFF, AIFC,[2] WAVE, System 7 sounds, Sun AU,[3] MPEG3	Same as Mac, except for System 7 sounds
Formats supported for external linking	Same as above (except System 7 sounds), plus QuickTime (AVI imported as QT3 only)	Same as above, plus QuickTime, AVI
Supported sampling rates[4]	5.564, 7.418, 11.025, 11.127, 22.050, 22.255, 32.000, 44.100, and 48.000 MHz	11.025, 22.050, and 44.100 MHz
Multichannel audio	Built-in (zero latency)	Supported via *MacroMix*, DirectSound, or *QT3Mix*[5] (non-zero latency)
Maximum number of sound channels	8	Up to 8 (set by *MixMaxChannels* in *DIRECTOR.INI*)
Multiple simultaneous audio sources	Yes	Not necessarily[5]
System audio buffer size[6]	System's audio buffer size is fixed	Settable via *DIRECTOR.INI* file.
the soundLevel (0 to 7)	Matches settings in *Sound* or *Monitors & Sound* Control Panel	Matches *SoundLevel* settings in *DIRECTOR.INI*. See also *Volume Control* in Task Bar[7]

[1] Any internal sounds are stored in Director's internal format, and are completely cross-platform. D7 can import SWA files via File ➤ Import, but they are converted to Director's internal format.
[2] AIFC is an AIFF file with IMA compression.
[3] The Sun AU Import Export Xtra included with D6.5 and D7 is required for Sun AU file support.
[4] Unsupported audio sampling rates under Windows are resampled to the nearest supported rate on the fly, distorting the pitch in some cases. The Macintosh supports just about any sampling rate, including variants such as 11,126, 22.253, and 22.254 MHz.
[5] Windows does not necessarily allow Director-based and QuickTime or AVI-based audio to be played simultaneously and multiple sounds introduce latency. See "Sound Mixing Under Windows" later in this chapter for details.
[6] The system audio buffer size is unrelated to the SWA buffer length, which can be set for each SWA member.
[7] The Windows Volume Control accessory can be opened by double-clicking the speaker icon in the Task Bar or running *C:\Windows\SNDVOL32.EXE*, which is accessed via Start ➤ Programs ➤ Accessories ➤ Multimedia ➤ Volume Control.

SoundEdit's native SE16 format was supported by D5, but is not supported in D6 or D7. Likewise, sounds compressed with MACE 3:1 and MACE 6:1 are not supported. D6 and D7 support IMA-compressed WAVE files, but not WAVE files compressed with Microsoft's proprietary compression. Sun AU files must have the .au extension (the equivalent Mac file type, `ULAW`, was not recognized prior to D7.0.1). See Table 4-4.

User Interface Issues

High-quality audio enhances a multimedia experience more than you might realize. When designing your audio, keep the following in mind:

- Director will automatically continue playing sounds at the end of one movie when branching to another movie. This provides an audio "transition."

- Use professional-quality sound effects and voice-overs (sound effects collections and professional voice talent are widely available).

- Avoid loud, annoying sound loops.

- Not all computers have a sound card and speakers, or the volume may be muted (and some users are deaf).

- Include text prompts for vital operations and allow the user to replay important audio messages.

- Sound cards and speaker quality vary. Not all systems support CD-quality stereo sound. The highest quality sounds may be a waste of bandwidth.

- Provide a volume control with a mute option. It is exceedingly rude to increase the system volume level automatically. If necessary, check the volume level via Lingo and suggest that the user change it.

Comparison of Sound Playback Methods

The various sound playback options are shown in Tables 15-2 and 15-3. The optimal method depends on the playback platform, the format of the sound, the size of the sound, the number of sound channels in use, the presence or absence of simultaneous animation and video, and whether a sound is triggered by an event, used as background music, or played in synchronization with a video or animation.

Table 15-2: Audio Playback Method Comparison

Method	Pros	Cons
Score Sound channel	Easy and intuitive. No scripting. Can use Tempo channel to wait for sounds.	Limited control and poor synchronization; only two sound channels.
puppetSound	Control over sound triggering.	Sounds must be explicitly unpuppeted.
sound playFile	Sounds don't require a cast member. Can be played in any sound channel.	Slows loading of video or graphic media.
Sound tracks in digital video cast member	Can start and stop sound at any point, or play sound fast, slow, or backward.	QT and AVI audio may not mix with other audio under Windows
SWA	High quality at low bandwidth (good compression). Accesses up to 8 sound channels.	Processor-intensive. Requires 68K with FPU, or Pentium for playback.
Flash Audio	Compact and integrated with Flash file.	Low quality. Conflicts with Director sounds.

Table 15-2: Audio Playback Method Comparison (continued)

Method	Pros	Cons
MIDI	Small size with excellent fidelity. Instruments can be changed dynamically.	Not well supported. Requires QT with MIDI extension or third-party Xtra.
MCI	Control over external devices, such as video disks and RedBook CDs.	Windows-only. Not universally reliable.
Third-party Xtras	The free CDPro Xtra (*http://www.penworks.com*) plays RedBook audio. Beatnik adds many capabilities.	Beatnik Xtra is expensive.

Table 15-3 compares features of the various playback methods. The Macintosh supports up to eight sound channels. The number of channels on the PC is set by the *MixMaxChannels* option in the *DIRECTOR.INI* file.

Table 15-3: Audio Playback Method Features

Method	Streamed	Loopable[1]	Channels	Cue Points
Score Sound channels	Only if external	Only if internal	2	AIFF, and WAVE (D6.5 or later)
puppetSound	Only if external	Only if internal	Up to 8	Same as above
sound playFile	Always	No	Up to 8	Same as above
Audio track in digital video	Always	No	Uses separate video mixer	Same as above
SWA	Only if external	Only if internal	Up to 8	Yes, for QT and AVI
Flash audio	N/A	No	N/A	No
MIDI	Varies	Yes	N/A	No
Third-party	Usually	Varies	Varies	Xtra-dependent[2]

[1] Internal sounds are generally loopable, whereas external sound files are not. Even sounds that are not automatically loopable can be looped manually via Lingo, although the loop may not be as seamless as with internal sound cast members.
[2] The third-party MPEG Xtra supports cue points, as may other Xtras.

Sound Cast Members

Sound cast members may be imported (embedded) into Director's Cast or externally linked (see "Import Options: To Link or not To Link" in Chapter 4). Import short and frequently used sounds into the Cast. Leave longer sound files on disk and link to them instead. See Example 4-7, which imports small external sounds into the Cast and warns about large internal sounds.

Standard sound and SWA cast members are indicated by a speaker icon (see Figure 4-3). Find sound cast members under Edit ➤ Find ➤ Cast Member by searching for members of *Type: Sound*; find SWA members using *Type: Xtras* in D6 and *Type: Shockwave Audio* in D7. Find QT2 or AVI members (which often contain audio) using *Type:Digital Video*. Find QT3 members using *Type:Xtra* in D6.5 and *Type:QuickTime 3* in D7.

External sound files can be changed without altering your Director movie and allow you to easily ship audio in different languages or audio of varying quality. Similar flexibility can be achieved by using an externally linked castLib to hold your internal sound cast members.

During development, either of these techniques prevents your main movie from growing large due to the inclusion of sounds. As sounds don't often change, this allows you to transfer, back up, or distribute only those portions of the project that have been altered.

Internal (embedded) sounds

Embed small sounds (those under approximately 500 KB) in the Cast using the *Standard Import* mode under File ➤ Import. An internal sound is preloaded in its entirety before it plays (or can be preloaded manually ahead of time), so any disk access occurs before, not during, playback. Internal sounds remain in memory after being played (until being unloaded when Director needs the RAM), and need not be reloaded each time they are played. Thus, internal sounds are convenient for button-click noises and small looping sounds. These same attributes make embedded sounds inappropriate for large sounds; large internal sounds cause long load delays and consume excessive memory.

Externally linked (streaming) sounds

Link to large AIFF and WAVE sounds using the *Link to File* mode under File ➤ Import. Externally linked sounds are streamed from disk and begin to play as soon as the first data is available. A streamed sound can be of arbitrary length without requiring significant RAM. Linked sounds are most appropriate for long sounds used only once, such as narration.

However, streamed sounds are not kept in RAM, cannot be looped automatically, and must be reloaded to be repeated. Because a CD-ROM can't access data from two places simultaneously, streaming audio will hinder the loading of other data such as digital video or bitmaps. The key factor for external streaming sounds, including SWA, is the *bandwidth*, not the total file size; as Buzz Kettles puts it, "It's not the size, it's the motion."

When using linked sounds, include the external sound files and sound-related Xtras with your Projector (see "Sound-Related Xtras" later in this chapter).

Sounds played via *sound playFile* behave similarly to linked sounds, although they need not be imported at all.

The path to external sounds as indicated by *the fileName* or *streamName of member* updates automatically for the current platform if the sound was imported via File ➤ Import or inserted via Insert ➤ Media Element ➤ Shockwave Audio in D7. Assuming that the external sound file remains in the same position relative to the movie or castLib and that *the fileName* or *streamName* is valid for the current platform, Director 7 will find the external audio file. However, the path to SWA files inserted via Insert ➤ Media Element ➤ Shockwave Audio in D6 (as indicated by *the streamName of member*) will not update automatically when files are moved, even if the same relative positions are maintained. See "Common importing and linked file problems" in Chapter 4 for the solution.

Place external sound files close to the appropriate Director movie when burning a CD to reduce the seek time (and latency) for accessing external sounds.

Differentiating between a sound's type and the playback method

In most cases, a sound's format or cast member type dictates whether it will be internal or external, but a standard sound cast member can be either. However, a cast member's or sprite's type (*#sound*, *#SWA*, *#digitalVideo*, or *#quickTime-Media*) will determine which commands support it. For example, *puppetSound* and the Score Sound channels support only *#sound* cast members (linked or unlinked). See Table 15-4 for a comparison of Lingo commands used with the different sound formats.

So-called "streaming" sounds are not necessarily located on a remote server. All external sound files are streamed, whether from the Internet, CD-ROM, or hard drive. Likewise, although SWA compression is usually associated with streamed Internet audio, SWA sounds can be streamed from a local drive, and internal Director sounds can be SWA-compressed, in which case they are not streamed.

Sound Playback Methods

Your presentation will probably use more than one method to play sounds. They can be combined, subject to these limitations:

Sound channel conflicts
Each sound channel can play only one sound at any time. You can't use Sound channel 1 in the Score while simultaneously using *sound playFile* or *puppetSound* to also play a sound in channel 1.

Sound device or sound driver conflicts
Only one device or driver can access the sound card at any given time. Under Windows, because QuickTime and Director audio often play through different mechanisms, the two types of audio cannot always be combined. See "Sound Mixing Under Windows" later in this chapter. The Macintosh handles multiple sound sources transparently, but even there, Director can not access the data track of a CD while a RedBook audio Xtra is accessing RedBook audio tracks on the same CD.

Sound in the Score

Sound cast members are placed in one of the two Sound channels of the Score. SWA and digital video (DV) cast members, including audio-only QuickTime movies, are placed in sprite channels, not the Sound channels.

Score-based sounds do not play unless the Score's playback head is moving or looping in a frame (avoid the *pause* command). Because Director's frame rate is not exact, you should use cue points to synchronize sounds with Score animations.

Sound playback is not affected by the Tempo channel's frame rate setting or the *puppetTempo* command. Standard and SWA sounds always play back in real time, although the speed of a DV sprite, including the audio tracks, can be changed via *the movieRate of sprite*. (Slower playback lowers the pitch of the audio track; faster playback raises the pitch.)

Sounds in the Score Sound channels

Score Sound channels are best used for fixed sounds that accompany animations, but the triggering and synchronization of Score sounds is insufficient for lip-synching or other time-critical uses.

Sounds in the Score are triggered when a sound is first encountered in a Sound channel or an SWA or DV sprite span is encountered in a sprite channel. Sounds ordinarily terminate after playing once through, even if they are tweened out over additional frames. To re-trigger a sound, you must either use Lingo or create a break of at least one empty frame in the Sound channel. Internal sounds that are looped will play as long as they occupy a sound channel or until the Tempo channel's *Wait for Cue Point:End* option causes them to "play out."

puppetSound

Use *puppetSound* to trigger a sound cast member (whether linked or unlinked) at an arbitrary time, such as in response to button-clicks or timeouts. *PuppetSounds* played in channels 1 and 2 override the corresponding Score Sound channel. Use:

```
puppetSound channel, "soundMemberName"
puppetSound channel, member "whichMember" {of castLib whichCast}
```

where *channel* is a number from 1 to 8. If *channel* is specified, the sound will trigger immediately. Otherwise, the default channel is 1, and the *puppetSound* is not triggered until the playback head advances (or loops) or an *updateStage* command is issued. Here, the default channel 1 is assumed:

```
puppetSound "soundMemberName"
puppetSound member "whichMember" {of castLib whichCast}
```

Specifying 0 as the "sound" unpuppets a *puppetSound*. Unpuppetting halts the current *puppetSound*; unpuppetting channel 1 or 2 also returns control to the corresponding Score Sound channel. These commands unpuppet a sound channel:

```
puppetSound channel, 0
puppetSound 0 -- Unpuppets sounds channel 1 by default
```

Sound playFile

The *sound playFile* command streams an external AIFF, AIFC, or WAVE file from disk, similar to a linked sound cast member. The sound need not be imported into the Cast nor appear in the Score, but it must reside on disk. *Sound playFile* can play a file at a remote URL, but it does not support SWA files, so you should use linked SWA cast members for net-based sounds. If you choose to play a remote AIFF or WAVE, the file should be downloaded first with *downloadNetThing*.

Using *sound playFile* with channel 1 or 2 overrides the corresponding Score Sound channel, but control automatically returns to the Score when the sound terminates. *Sound playFile* even overrides puppeted sound channels. *Sound playFile* assumes that the external sound file has an .AIF extension, if none is specified. It takes the form:

```
sound playFile channel, soundFilePath | url
```

where *channel* is from 1 to 8. If the *channel* is omitted, channel 1 is assumed:

```
sound playFile 1, the moviePath & "mysound.aif"
sound playFile 3, "http://www.zeusprod.com/examples/sound.wav"
```

The path to the external file specified by *sound playFile* does not update automatically. You must manually specify the path on each platform, as shown in Example 15-1, or use the @ operator to create a generalized path. Note that we constructed a path relative to the current movie's location.

Example 15-1: Specifying a Path to a Sound

```
if the platform contains "Windows" then
  sound playFile 1, the moviePath & "audio/mysound.aif"
else
  sound playFile 1, the moviePath & "audio:mysound.aif"
end if
```

Example 15-2 shows how to construct a central convenience function to play voice-overs from a subfolder named *VO*, and ambient sounds from a subfolder named *AMBIENT*, each below the folder containing the current movie.

Example 15-2: Centralized Sound PlayFile Commands

```
on playVoiceOver someSound
  -- Play voice-overs in channel 1
  set pathSeparator = the last char of the moviePath
  sound playFile 1, the moviePath & "VO" & ¬
    pathSeparator & someSound & ".AIF"
end playVoiceOver

on playAmbient someSound
  -- Play ambient sounds in channel 2
  set pathSeparator = the last char of the moviePath
  sound playFile 2, the moviePath & "AMBIENT" & ¬
    pathSeparator & someSound  & ".AIF"
end playAmbient
```

In Example 15-2, the sound files are assumed to have an .AIF extension and reside in the *VO* or *AMBIENT* subfolder. When using these routines, we can specify sound filenames without the .AIF extension or the folder name, such as:

```
playVoiceOver ("intro")
playAmbient ("mood")
```

As with all external sound playback, *sound playFile* is appropriate for long sounds. Such sounds won't automatically loop; you must use *sound playFile* again to retrigger them.

Digital video sounds

Digital video (DV) cast members are played in sprite channels, not the Sound Score channels, and may contain audio tracks (*#sound* or *#midi*) even if no *#video* track is present. DV (QT or AVI) provides better synchronization than other audio playback methods, provided that the audio and video being synchronized are properly interleaved in a single DV file. See Chapter 16, *Digital Video*, for complete details.

DV sprites, including their audio tracks, are played automatically when a DV sprite is encountered, provided that *the pausedAtStart of member* is FALSE. Lingo commands can start, stop, rewind, or fast forward to any point in the DV file. DV files, which are always external, can be played at different speeds or even backward. But DV audio may not be playable simultaneously with other standard Director sounds under Windows. See "Sound Mixing Under Windows" later in this chapter.

Shockwave Audio (SWA)

SWA cast members are played in sprite channels, not the Sound Score channels. Shockwave audio offers high quality at low bandwidths, but requires more processing power at runtime and isn't supported on some low-end machines. (SWA compression requires a Pentium or PowerMac.) SWA requires several Xtras (see Table 15-13) that must be distributed with your Projector. If using SWA from Shockwave 6 or 7, the Xtras are included with Shockwave browser plug-in.

Flash audio

Audio can be added to a Flash cast member prior to import into Director, but Flash-based audio is low-fidelity and may conflict with Director. (Flash-based audio and Director-based audio can't play at the same time under Windows.) Instead, trigger Director-based sounds from your Flash sprite, offering Lingo control over volume, better integration with other Director sounds, and optional SWA compression.

Sound Operation Comparison

Table 15-4 compares the inconsistent sound control commands across the different sound-related cast member types. Digital Video includes AVI and QuickTime prior to version 3 (QuickTime 2.5 on Macintosh or QuickTime 2.1.2 under Windows). QuickTime 3 requires the new QT3 Asset Xtra in D6.5 or D7. See also Chapter 16, *the digitalVideoType of member*, and Table 4-10.

External files played via *sound playFile* do not support any sprite or member properties. They obey only the *SoundBusy(), sound level, sound stop,* and *sound close* commands.

Table 15-4: Common Sound Operations

Operation	Sound	SWA or MP3	QuickTime 3 or Digital Video
Type of member	#sound	#SWA	#digitalVideo or #quickTimeMedia
Number of channels in asset	channelCount of member	numChannels of member	trackCount(), trackType = #sound
Specify sound channel	Place in Score or puppetSound or sound playFile	soundChannel of member (0 assigns highest)	Allocated by OS
Volume[1]	volume of sound	volume of member, volume of sprite	volume of sprite, sound of member, volumeLevel of sprite
Play in Score	Sound channel	sprite channel	sprite channel
Play via Lingo	sound playFile, puppetSound	play ()	movieRate of sprite, mRate of sprite[3]
Stop a sound	sound stop, puppetSound 0, sound close	stop(), pause()	set movieRate of sprite = 0, or set mRate of sprite = 0
Sound playing	soundBusy()	state of member = 3	movieRate of sprite, mRate of sprite, pausedAtStart of member
Wait for sound[2]	soundBusy()	state of member	movieRate, movieTime, mRate, or mTime of sprite[3]
Samples per second	sampleRate of member	sampleRate of member, bitRate of member	Not available
Bits per sample	sampleSize of member	bitsPerSample of member	Not available
Current position	currentTime of sound	percentPlayed, percentStreamed, and currentTime of sprite	movieTime, mTime, or currentTime of sprite
Length in seconds	See Example 15-3	duration of member × 1000	duration of member × the digitalVideoTimeScale

[1] See "Volume Levels and Sound Fades" later in this chapter.
[2] You can use the Tempo channel or cue points to wait for any type of media that supports them. See "Cue Points and Timing" later in this chapter.
[3] In D6.5, use *the volumeLevel, mRate,* and *mTime of sprite* properties for QT3 sprites. In D7, these properties are deprecated; use *the volume, movieRate,* and *movieTime of sprite* instead.

There is no *duration of member* property for standard sound cast members. Example 15-3 calculates the duration of a sound based on its other attributes. The *size of member* property is accurate only for internal (embedded) sounds, but can be calculated for external sounds (see Examples 4-6 and 4-7).

Example 15-3: Calculating the Duration of an Internal Sound

```
on soundDuration whichSound
  -- Returns the duration in seconds
  set duration = the size of member whichSound / ¬
        (the sampleRate   of member whichSound * ¬
         the channelCount of member whichSound * ¬
         the sampleSize   of member whichSound / 8.0)
  return duration
end soundDuration
```

Sound Channels and Sound Mixing

Director supports up to eight sound channels, although only two are shown in the Score. The remainder are accessible via *puppetSound* or *sound playFile* or are used implicitly by SWA sprites, film loops, and MIAWs (which all share the same sound channels). Digital video and Flash sprites do not use the same sound channel numbers as standard Director sounds.

Director's Score Sound channels do not correspond to the left and right channels of a typical stereo. Monaural sounds are split equally between the left and right speakers regardless of the Director sound channel used. A so-called *stereo* sound uses only one of Director's sound channels because the left and right audio tracks are interleaved into a single data stream (think of Director's sound channels as *data* channels, rather than *audio* channels). The sound card knows how to split a stereo data stream between the right and left speakers, but a sound's left/right balance can not be set in Director without an Xtra (or you change the balance using an external sound editor before importing into Director).

Avoid sound channel number conflicts by simply specifying different channel numbers for *puppetSounds* or *sound playFile* commands (both use channel 1 by default, which will override the Score's Sound channel 1). If *the soundChannel of member* of an SWA member is 0 (the default) it automatically sidesteps conflicts by using the highest available channel number.

Most Macintoshes support eight sound channels, although older Performas may support only four. On the Macintosh, all sound playback is handled seamlessly by the Sound Manager, which is a QuickTime component. You can play almost any type or number of sounds without regard to conflicts at the Mac OS level.

The number of audio channels supported under Windows is generally at least four, but even assuming that you have not used conflicting channel numbers, other audio sources (digital video and Flash) can cause conflicts at the so-called Windows device level.

Sound Mixing Under Windows

Windows PCs have only one *hardware* sound channel. Multichannel sound is simulated by premixing multiple audio sources before sending the resultant audio stream to the sound card. There are a number of competing and complementary sound drivers, mixers, and devices that ameliorate the latency and conflicts arising from playing multiple sounds under Windows. The best method and achievable results vary with the software configuration, Windows version, and Director version. For an overview of sound mixing under Windows, see Macromedia Tech-Note #03191, "Windows and Multichannel Sound."

Sound mixing latency

Playing two or more sounds simultaneously under Windows may cause a delay as the sounds are mixed together for output. Sound latency varies with the sound card, but can be up to 500 milliseconds. To reduce latency:

- Play only one sound at a time (zero latency).

- Preload short sounds, if possible.

- Use uncompressed sounds (not SWA or IMA-compressed).

- Use one of the preferred PC sampling rates (11.025, 22.050, or 44.1 kHz) and not the variations that are Macintosh-specific (see Table 15-1).

- Use sounds of the same bit depth and sampling rate. The suggested sound format is 16-bit, 22.050 kHz, mono in most cases.

- Avoid changing the volume or performing sound fades when using multiple sounds.

- Combine the sounds in an external sound editor before importing into Director.

- Use a sound mixer with less latency, such as QT3Mix in D7, the DirectSound mixer (new in D7.0.1), the Beatnik Xtra, or MacroMix with RSX/DirectSound (in D6.x)

Sound output devices

Before we talk about audio sources, understand that there are two *mutually exclusive* sound output "devices" under Windows 95/98/NT: WaveOut and DirectSound ("device" refers to a virtual device driver, not the physical sound card). Only WaveOut is supported under Windows 3.1. DirectSound (part of the DirectX suite of Microsoft drivers) comes standard with later versions of Windows 98, and has been installed by many users on other Windows 95/98 systems. The latest version can be downloaded from *http://www.microsoft.com*. Windows NT supports the older DirectSound 3, which behaves as if the sound device is WaveOut.

All Windows audio must pass through one of these two devices, which sends the data onto the sound card driver and eventually the sound card itself. The sound output device can change dynamically at runtime, although only one device can be active at a given time. (Some IBM PCs support two simultaneous sound devices, but you can not rely on this unless all users have identical equipment.)

WaveOut supports only one input at a time. DirectSound 5 or later under Windows 95/98 can handle multiple simultaneous inputs. Windows NT with Service Pack 3 uses DirectSound 3, which, like WaveOut, supports a single input only.

Macromedia TechNote #13249, "Director sound playback mixing under Windows" contains detailed information (mainly regarding D6.5) on the differences between sound mixing under Windows 95/98 and Windows NT. It includes a helpful overview and informative diagrams of WaveOut and DirectSound mixing schemes:

> *http://www.macromedia.com/support/director/ts/documents/d6_sound_
> mixing01.htm*

Prior to Director 6, all Director sounds used WaveOut; although there *was* competition among multiple sources for the WaveOut device, there was not contention between the WaveOut and DirectSound devices (unless another application was using DirectSound).

Director 6 introduced support for RSX/DirectSound in addition to WaveOut. To reduce latency, D6.x Projectors keep the current device loaded even after a sound completes, unless specifically configured to release the device. If your sounds play during authoring but not in a Projector (and it is not caused by a missing Xtra) use the following to "offer-up" the device to WaveOut following playback via Direct-Sound, or vice versa:

```
set the soundKeepDevice = FALSE
```

Even if *the soundKeepDevice* is **FALSE**, the device is not released until all previously playing sounds complete. Set it to **TRUE** to decrease latency if only one output device is being used (see the following sections to determine whether WaveOut, DirectSound, or both are used by your Projector).

Potential conflicts from multiple sound input sources

Consider the following sources (classes) of audio used in Director for Windows and the sound mixing mechanism they use:

Director sounds
> Standard *#sound* and *#SWA* sprites in the Score, *puppetSounds*, and WAVE and AIFF sounds played via *sound playFile* commands are considered "Director sounds." These are always passed through Director's sound mixer (either MacroMix or QT3Mix) and may be played either via WaveOut or DirectSound as described under "Windows Sound Mixers." D7.0.1 can also use DirectSound via the new DirectSound mixer.

Flash sounds
> Sounds embedded in *#flash* members are always played via WaveOut and do not pass through Director's sound mixer.

VFW and QTW2 audio tracks
> Audio tracks contained in #digitalVideo members imported via File ➤ Import in D6.5 or earlier are known as "Traditional DV sounds." These are always played via WaveOut and do not pass through Director's sound mixer or the QuickTime for Windows Sound Manager.

QTW3 or later sound tracks
> Sound tracks contained in QTW3 #quickTimeMedia members imported via File ➤ Import (in D7) or inserted via File ➤ Insert Media Element ➤

`QuickTime` 3 (in D6.5 or D7) are known as "QT3 sounds." These are always played via the QuickTime for Windows Sound Manager, which sends the audio to either DirectSound or WaveOut based on the *Sound Out* setting in the QuickTime Control Panel.

Third-party Xtras

Third-party Xtras may use their own sound mixer, Director's sound mixer, the QuickTime Sound Manager, or some combination of the three. (Beatnik uses MacroMix or its own sound mixer, but not the QTW Sound Manager.)

Playing multiple sounds of a single class is always supported, but may cause latency as they are mixed. Sound conflicts (where the second sound never plays) arise primarily from playing sounds of different classes under the following conditions:

- Playing sound from multiple sources to WaveOut under any Windows version. Director-based sounds in Windows 3.1, Flash-based sounds, and traditional DV audio (*#digitalVideo* sprites) can never be mixed with each other or with QTW3 (*#quickTimeMedia*) sprites.

- Playing sound from multiple sources to DirectSound 3 (which is the highest version supported under Windows NT).

- Playing sound to one device (WaveOut or DirectSound) when the other is actively playing a sound or "locked in" because *the soundKeepDevice* is TRUE (the default).

- Conflicts with the sound output of other applications. (See Macromedia Tech-Note #12180, "How does Director's use of sound on Windows affect other applications?")

There are several ways to avoid conflicts:

- Avoid playing sounds from a second source before sounds from the first source have completed. This allows Director to switch the sound device as needed, provided that *the soundKeepDevice* is FALSE.

- Use DirectSound 5 or later, which handles multiple input streams, as the output device for all sounds. In D6.x this requires that RSX and DirectSound 5 or later be installed and, if using QT3 sounds, that the QuickTime Control Panel specify DirectSound for *Sound Out*. This scheme will not work in D7.0, because RSX/DirectSound output is not supported for D7.0 sounds, nor will it work in D6.5 if the QuickTime Control Panel uses WaveOut, nor will it work under Windows NT with DirectSound 3 or under Windows 3.1. D7.0.1 with DirectSound 5 or later installed can use Macromedia's new DirectSound mixer without the need for RSX.

- Manually specify that Director should use QT3Mix, which sends sounds to the QuickTime Sound Manager where they can be mixed with QTW3 audio into a single stream before being sent to either the WaveOut or DirectSound device. (This requires a Windows 32 system with QTW3 installed and D6.5 or D7.)

Windows Sound Mixers

Sound mixers are a middle layer that mix multiple sound channels or input sources into a single data stream to be sent to the output device. The mixer for Director sounds is the only one that can be changed—QuickTime 3 sprites always play via the QuickTime Sound Manager, and other non-Director sounds always play directly to the WaveOut device (bypassing Director mixing).

Sound mixing with MacroMix

MacroMix transparently mixes multiple #sound, #SWA cast members, AIF and WAV files under Windows, but doesn't mix audio tracks from #flash, #digitalVideo, or #quickTimeMedia cast members.

MacroMix automatically configures itself based on the current sound card, although the settings in the *DIRECTOR.INI* file (see Table 15-11) can customize it. In most cases, the default *MixMaxFidelity* (99) is appropriate. The maximum number of mixable channels is determined by *MixMaxChannels* (the default is 4 in prior versions, and 8 in D7). See *Appendix D* in *Lingo in a Nutshell* for details on working with the *DIRECTOR.INI* file.

Windows 3.1 Projectors always uses the 16-bit *MacroMix.DLL* to play sound. This DLL is bundled into Windows 3.1 Projectors (assuming that it is present when the Projector is built). It is unbundled temporarily into the Windows System folder at runtime and deleted when the Projector terminates.

MacroMix and other mixers for Windows 95/98/NT Projectors are implemented as Xtras in D7 and can be configured via Lingo at runtime. D6.5 and prior versions of Windows 95/NT Projectors used an internal version of MacroMix, which could be overridden using the *DLLname* option in the *DIRECTOR.INI* file in D6.5. (Except for the *DLLname*, all [Sound] settings in *DIRECTOR.INI* pertain only to MacroMix, and not to QT3Mix.)

In Director 4 through Director 6.0.2, MacroMix was the only sound mixer available under Windows. MacroMix is not a single mixer, it is a Sound API (application programmer's interface). The actual mixer used by MacroMix depends on the Director version and software configuration. D4, D5, 16-bit Projectors in D6, and D7 support only the WaveMix implementation of MacroMix. In D6.0 through D6.5, when using 32-bit Projectors, MacroMix uses its RSXMix implementation if RSX is installed.

WaveMix

An implementation of MacroMix that uses WaveOut. It is a lowest common denominator mixer to ensure that multiple sounds can be mixed without requiring RSX, DirectSound, or QTW3, but it is characterized by latency and potential conflicts with other sound sources. To combat latency, refer to the tips under "Sound Mixing Latency." You may choose to initiate the sound early to make it play on time under Windows (in which case it would play early on the Macintosh). The 16-bit version of WaveMix is located in the *MacroMix.DLL* file. In D7, the 32-bit version is stored in *MacroMix.X32*.

RSXMix

> An implementation of MacroMix that uses RSX, available only in Director 6.x. The system–level RSX service will use DirectSound if installed. It will use WaveOut if DirectSound is not installed or if *rsxDontUseDirectSound* is set to 1 in the *DIRECTOR.INI* file. RSX with DirectSound offered low latency but was tempermental, especially prior to D6.0.2, and not all users have RSX and DirectSound properly installed. RSXMix is not supported in D7.0 or later, but D7.0.1 includes a separate DirectSound mixer that does not require RSX.

QMix

> A QT3-based mixer (typically referred to separately as QT3Mix) and described in the next section.

For more details on MacroMix, see Macromedia TechNote #13010, "How does Director play sound on Windows?" (pertains primarily to D6.5).

Sound mixing with QT3Mix

QT3Mix uses the QuickTime Sound Manager to mix Director sounds and requires that QTW3 (or the upcoming QTW4) be installed. QT3Mix is available only in D7 and D6.5 with the Service Pack installed, and is referred to as "QMix" in some Macromedia TechNotes.

The QuickTime Sound Manager will use DirectSound (if it is installed) under Windows 95/98; it uses WaveOut if DirectSound is missing or if running under Windows NT. The user can also set the preferred *Sound Out* device in the Quick-Time Control Panel (and some developers report better results using WaveOut). There is no documented way to detect or switch the QuickTime Control Panel setting, but it is contained in the QuickTime Preferences file (*C:\Windows\System\QuickTime.qtp*) if you want to hack it.

QT3Mix allows Director and *#quickTimeMedia* sounds to play simultaneously under Windows 95/98/NT. QT3Mix is contained in the QT3Asset.X32 Xtra in D7, and the *QT3Mix.DLL* in D6.5 with the Service Pack. QT3Mix is the recommended (but not the default) mixer in D7.0. The D7 version of QT3Mix is much-improved over the D6.5 version, offering near-zero latency on faster computers (and reduced latency on slower Pentiums). See the following sections for complete details on activating QT3Mix under D6.5 and D7. In D7.0.1, if DirectSound 5 or higher is installed under Windows 95/98, the new DirectSound mixer should yield better performance than QT3Mix.

There is no need to change your Lingo when using QT3Mix instead of MacroMix. All sounds are played with the same familiar commands and methods.

QT3Mix is not supported under Windows 3.1 or with 16-bit Projectors under Windows 95/98/NT because they do not support QTW3. QT3Mix ignores the [Sound] settings in the *DIRECTOR.INI* file (except for the *DLLname* option).

RSX and DirectSound

RSX is a system-level service for Windows 32 systems from Intel. Obtain the latest version of RSX (*http://www.intel.com/ial/rsx/*) for best results when using D6.x. To determine whether RSX is installed, look for the *C:\Windows\System\RSX.DLL* file.

If RSX is enabled, a pair of red headphones appears in the Windows Start Menu tray.

DirectSound is a Microsoft sound driver that is part of the DirectX driver suite (which includes Direct3D, DirectDraw, etc.) and is not related to Director, per se. DirectSound version 5 or later is installed under Windows 98 by default, and most Windows 95 users have it too. DirectSound is compatible with Windows NT, but only up to DirectSound 3, which is implemented in software and has the same problems as WaveOut (latency and only one input source allowed). DirectSound is never supported under Windows 3.1.

D6.x required RSX to use DirectSound, and D7.0 never uses it. D7.0.1's new DirectSound mixer will use DirectSound without RSX.

Sound mixing with the Beatnik Xtra

The Beatnik Xtra (*http://www.beadspace.com*) provides near-zero latency mixing with extremely low CPU overhead under both Macintosh and Windows, plus it includes sound effects, sound panning, support for additional sound formats (RMF, MIDI, and MOD in addition to AIF, WAVE, and AU) and much more.

The Beatnik Xtra is "Shockwave-safe" and is appealing for Shockwave delivery because it supports extremely compact sound formats for fast downloading and does not require RSX, QTW3, or DirectSound to be installed.

The major drawback is the licensing fee (which ranges from $495 to $1295 at press time, but may change) as you are not allowed to distribute the Lite version included with D7. Unlike QT3Mix, the Beatnik Xtra requires custom calls to play sounds, although the pro version includes premade Behaviors to play sounds.

Beatnik optionally uses the custom Headspace Audio Engine mixer (up to 32 channels without latency) or MacroMix (up to eight channels), but doesn't currently support QT3Mix or the QuickTime Sound Manager. Its MacroMix compatibility mode enables Beatnik audio to be intermixed with normal Director audio including SWA, *sound playFile* commands, and *puppetSounds*.

Sound Mixing Under Director for Windows

Table 15-5 summarizes the preferred sound mixer configurations under Windows for both Director and Shockwave if you are playing multiple sounds. It is a matter of considerable dispute whether the RSX/DirectSound combination available in D6.X is the preferred method of mixing sound. If RSX and DirectSound are installed properly, it works well, but some well-respected developers prefer using QT3Mix in D6.5, and using WaveOut by disabling RSX in D6.0.X.

Table 15-5: Preferred Sound Mixer Configurations

Environment	MacroMix and DirectSound	QT3Mix
D4, D5, SW4, SW5	WaveOut only[1,2,3]	N/A
D6.0.x, SW6.0	DirectSound[1] (requires RSX) or WaveOut[2,3]	N/A

Table 15-5: Preferred Sound Mixer Configurations (continued)

Environment	MacroMix and DirectSound	QT3Mix
SW6.0.1	WaveOut only (RSX ignores DirectSound)	N/A
D6.5 without Service Pack	Buggy, don't use.	Buggy, don't use.
D6.5 with Service Pack	DirectSound[1] (requires RSX) or WaveOut[2]	DLLname = QT3Mix.DLL[3]
D7.0, SW7.0	WaveOut only[4]	the soundDevice = "QT3Mix"[1,3]
D7.0.1, SW7.0.1	WaveOut (the soundDevice = "MacroMix") DirectSound[1] (the soundDevice = "DirectSound")	the soundDevice = "QT3Mix"[3]

[1] Preferred method in most Windows 95/98 configurations.
[2] Only supported method under Windows 3.1.
[3] Preferred method under Windows NT with SP3 and DirectSound 3.
[4] WaveOut is the only supported configuration in SW7.0 unless QTW3 is installed and the QT3Asset.X32 Xtra is downloaded.

MacroMix is the default mixer for Director-based sounds (*#sound*, SWA, AIFF, and WAVE files) in all versions of Director for Windows prior to D7.0.1. But its capabilities, whether it is the best method of mixing sounds, and how to override it varies with each version. Even if using a later version of Director, you'll find the following descriptions of sound mixing in earlier versions relevant.

Sound mixing in Director 4 and Director 5 for Windows

Director 4 and 5 always use MacroMix for Director-based audio. MacroMix will mix up to 8 Director sounds (the default is 4 in D4, D5, and D6.x), but exhibits marked latency in D4, D5, and D7. Traditional #digitalVideo sound tracks (QTW2 and AVI files) can not play simultaneously with Director sounds (AIFF, WAVE or sound cast members) in any version of Director for Windows, and are limited to one sound track per video.

In Director 4 and 5, *#digitalVideo* and Director sounds conflicted because both types use WaveOut. Whichever type took control of the WaveOut device first prevented sounds of the other type from playing. When one component finished playing its sounds, the other component could gain access to the WaveOut device.

Therefore, to allow a new type of audio to play, ensure that all sounds of the other type are stopped (see Table 15-4). Use the *puppetSound 0, sound close,* or *sound stop* commands to stop all Director sounds before attempting to play *#digitalVideo* sound tracks. Stop a video by setting *the movieRate of sprite* to 0, or disable its sound track using the *sound of member* property or *setTrackEnabled* command before attempting to play other Director sounds.

These limitations don't necessarily apply in D6, which can use DirectSound, or in D7 which doesn't typically use *#digitalVideo* members (*#quickTimeMedia* members are preferred).

Sound mixing in Director 6.0.x for Windows

Even in D6, Windows 3.1 Projectors always use the WaveMix implementation of MacroMix to play sounds to WaveOut, and therefore exhibit marked latency and conflicts with *#digitalVideo* audio (which uses WaveOut, as in D4 and D5).

For D6.x Windows 95/NT Projectors, the RSXMix implementation of MacroMix will be used if RSX is installed. RSXMix reduces latency substantially in the typical case where a button triggers a sound while a background track is playing. Absent RSX, the older WaveMix implementation (with the familiar latency and device conflicts) will be used.

Even RSXMix will resort to using WaveOut if DirectSound is not installed, but the RSX/DirectSound combination has the lowest latency (best performance). The performance is maximized by never releasing the DirectSound device (locking out *#digitalVideo* sounds, which always use WaveOut). To force RSX/DirectSound to release the sound device, you must set *the soundKeepDevice* to FALSE.

Some conflicts were reported between Director and RSX, especially prior to D6.0.2. If using D6.0 or D6.0.1, obtain the free update to D6.0.2 from Macromedia's site. RSX will use DirectSound by default, but because RSX and DirectSound have been plagued by installation and version issues, you can force RSX to use WaveOut (with reduced performance) by including the following line in the [Sound] section of your *DIRECTOR.INI* file:

```
[Sound]
rsxDontUseDirectSound = 1
```

Sound mixing in Director 6.5 for Windows

D6.5 was the first version to allow the developer to manually choose the mixer used for Director-based sounds. It allows you to specify QT3Mix using the *DIRECTOR.INI* file during Projector initialization.

If using D6.5, obtain the D6.5 Service Pack Update from: *http://www.macromedia.com/support/director/upndown/updates.html.*

The initial release of D6.5 (prior to the Service Pack) included an erroneous version of QT3Mix (a.k.a. "QMix"), mistakenly named "MacroMix.DLL." For Windows 3.1 Projectors, the bogus file overrode the default 16-bit *MacroMix.DLL* and prevented all sound from playing. Windows 95/NT Projectors ignored the external DLL and continued to use their internal version of MacroMix, but mistakenly set *the soundLevel* to 0.

The Director 6.5 Service Pack (unrelated to Windows 95/98/NT OS Service Packs) addresses the sound errors caused by the initial release of D6.5. It includes the same 16-bit *MacroMix.DLL* used in D6.0.2, and a copy of the correct 32-bit *QT3Mix.DLL* that is recognizable by Windows 95/NT Projectors.

QT3Mix allows Director and QT3 (*#quickTimeMedia*) sounds to be mixed together via the QuickTime Sound Manager regardless of the Windows 32 version or *Sound Out* setting in the QuickTime Control Panel. Unfortunately, it requires QTW3, still exhibits some latency, and can not mix *#digitalVideo* and *#flash* sounds. (See also Macromedia TechNote #13416, "Director 6.5 sound playback options, by cast member type.")

To use QT3Mix in D6.5+SP, include the following line in the [Sound] section of your *DIRECTOR.INI* file (or just remove the semicolon that acts to comment it out):

```
[Sound]
DLLname = QT3Mix.DLL
```

Include the *QT3Mix.DLL* file, and a copy of *DIRECTOR.INI* renamed to match your Projector's name, in the same folder as your Windows 95/98/NT Projector. If QTW3 isn't installed, no DLLname is specified, or *QT3Mix.DLL* does not accompany the Projector, QT3Mix will not load and MacroMix will be used instead.

The RSX/DirectSound combination has lower latency (better performance) than QT3Mix in D6.5. It allows QTW3 and Director sounds to play simultaneously under Windows 95/98 (but not Windows NT) if the QuickTime Control Panel specifies DirectSound as *Sound Out* (the default if it's installed). In this case, the two input sources are mixed by DirectSound instead of by the QuickTime Sound Manager.

Even if RSX and DirectSound are installed, setting the *rsxDontUseDirectSound* flag to 1 in the *DIRECTOR.INI* file, or configuring the QuickTime Control Panel to use WaveOut, would prevent Director sounds from mixing with QTW3 sound tracks if not using QT3Mix.

Sound mixing in Director 7.0 for Windows

Sound mixers are implemented as Xtras in Director 7, but should not be confused with the unrelated MIX Xtras used to import external media. At least one of the sound mixer Xtras must be included in the *Xtras* folder or bundled into the Projector in order to play sound in D7 under Windows. D7 allows sound mixers to be specified on the fly, whereas D6.5 configured the sound mixer during Projector start up only.

D7.0 includes two initial sound mixers for Windows: an implementation of MacroMix that always uses WaveOut, and QT3Mix (which uses DirectSound or WaveOut depending on the *SoundOut* setting in the QT3 Control Panel). D7.0.1 includes a third sound mixer, DirectSound, which offers improved mixing if DirectSound 5 or higher is installed. Unlike D6.x, D7.0.1 does not require RSX to access DirectSound; D7.0 and D7.0.1 ignore RSX in all cases.

MacroMix is contained in the *Xtras\Drivers\MacroMix.X32* Xtra. QT3Mix is contained in the *Xtras\QT3\QT3Asset.X32* Xtra and can be used to mix sounds even if you are not playing any QuickTime videos. The DirectSound mixer is contained in the *Xtras\Drivers\DirectSound.X32* Xtra included with D7.0.1.

There are two new properties related to sound mixing in D7—*the soundDevice* and *the soundDeviceList*—that affect the sound mixer selection, and thus indirectly affect whether the WaveOut or DirectSound device is used.

The *soundDeviceList* is a read-only list of the installed sound mixer Xtras:

```
put the soundDeviceList
-- ["MacroMix", "QT3Mix", "DirectSound"]
```

If no sound mixer Xtras are installed, *the soundDeviceList* returns an empty list. Although they may appear in *the soundDeviceList,* QT3Mix can not be used unless QTW3 is installed, and the DirectSound mixer cannot be used unless an appropriate version of the DirectSound drivers are installed. MacroMix, which doesn't depend on any system components, is always available if the *MacroMix.X32* Xtra is installed.

Use the *soundDevice* property to identify or set the current sound mixer. The default mixer depends on the installed Xtras and system components. In D7.0, before DirectSound mixing was offered, the default sound mixer was MacroMix, followed by QT3Mix if MacroMix was not installed. In D7.0.1, DirectSound is the default mixer if the DirectSound 5 drivers or higher are installed. If not, MacroMix becomes the default mixer, because older versions of the DirectSound drivers (such as DirectSound 3 under Windows NT) offer no benefit over MacroMix. If none of the necessary Xtras and system components are installed, *the soundDevice* will be 0, and sounds will not play.

 When *the soundDevice* defaults to "DirectSound," it will offer the best available sound mixing. If *the soundDevice* defaults to "Macro-Mix" because DirectSound 5 is not installed, switching *the sound-Device* to "DirectSound" may kill sound playback if the DirectSound drivers are old or improperly installed.

If QTW3 is available, but DirectSound 5 or higher is not, setting *the soundDevice* to "QT3Mix" may be preferable to the default MacroMix mixer. QT3Mix provides reduced latency and conflict-free mixing of frame sounds, *puppetSounds, sound playFiles,* SWA, and QT3 sound tracks, regardless of whether RSX or DirectSound is installed. There may be a one-time delay of several seconds when changing *the soundDevice* to "QT3Mix." Use the following in D7.0.1 to take advantage of QT3Mix in the above scenario:

```
if the soundDevice = "MacroMix" and the quickTimePresent ¬
    and string (the soundDeviceList) contains "QT3Mix" then
  set the soundDevice = "QT3Mix"
end if
```

This example will work in both D7 and SW7 on all platforms. It will leave Direct-Sound as the default mixer if DirectSound 5 or later is installed, or attempt to load QT3Mix otherwise. It has no effect on the Macintosh. The checks in the example for *the quickTimePresent* and QT3Mix's presence are extraneous; setting *the soundDevice* to an unavailable mixer leaves its value unchanged (in some cases it may set *the soundDevice* back to its default). You can verify *the soundDevice* after attempting to set it.

The Modify ➤ Movies ➤ Xtras dialog box includes the MacroMix.X32 Xtra by default in D7. Although new movies created in D7.0.1 will also include Direct-

Sound.X32 by default, you may need to add it manually to the list of Xtras when upgrading movies from D7.0 to D7.0.1. Although the sound mixer Xtras are for Windows-only you should not remove them from the Xtras list, even on the Macintosh.

On the Macintosh, the only supported sound mixer is the MacSoundManager, which uses the Sound Manager system extension:

```
put the soundDevice
-- "MacSoundManager"
put the soundDeviceList
-- ["MacSoundManager"]
```

Sound mixing in Shockwave 6 and Shockwave 7

SW6.0 uses RSX with DirectSound to speed sound mixing, if available, and WaveOut otherwise. But very few users have both RSX and DirectSound properly installed, so sound latency and conflicts were common. SW6.0.1 uses RSX (if available) but always uses the WaveOut sound device, even if DirectSound is installed. SW6.x never uses QT3Mix and does not allow the developer to select the sound mixer manually.

SW7.0 and SW7.0.1 never use RSX. SW7.0 includes the MacroMix.X32 sound mixer in the default installation. In SW7.0, you can set *the soundDevice* to "QT3Mix" to reduce latency, provided that both the QT3Asset.X32 Xtra and QTW3 are installed. But the QT3Asset.X32 Xtra must be downloaded separately, and there is no convenient way to provide a QTW3 installer to Shockwave users (as there is when shipping a CD-ROM).

The DirectSound.X32 Xtra offers improved sound mixing in SW7 if DirectSound 5 or higher is installed (as it is on most Windows 95/98 systems, but not Windows NT). Set the *Download if Needed* checkbox under Modify ➤ Movie ➤ Xtras to auto-download the DirectSound.X32 Xtra for SW7.0 users (it is downloaded by default with SW7.0.1).

You can also use the Shockwave-safe Beatnik Xtra to mix sounds, as it doesn't require QTW3 or DirectSound, although it does have a licensing fee.

Controlling Sound Position and Playback

Director does not allow random access to any position within most sounds. SWA sounds can be paused and restarted, but AIFF, WAVE, and internal sounds always start from the beginning whenever played. They can be stopped, but not paused or cued. However, audio-only QuickTime or AVI movies allow full control over sound positioning and playback.

Cue points can be used for synchronization, but they are read-only. You can't jump to an arbitrary point in a AIFF or SWA file (although, see the wildly unsupported *setSoundTime* command in Table 15-14), but you can jump to an arbitrary point in a QuickTime or AVI movie. (MCI calls can be used to set an arbitrary location in a WAVE file under Windows, but it is not universally reliable.)

See Table 15-4 for commands to position sounds.

Sound Tools and Interface Options

Table 15-6 summarizes the interface options related to sounds.

Table 15-6: Sound-Related Interface Options

Action	Command
Edit or play the sound cast member in the external editor	File ➤ Preferences ➤ Editor (AIFF, MPEG3, snd, AU, SWA, WAVE) Edit ➤ Launch External Editor Command-, (Mac) or Ctrl-, (Windows)
View or edit a sound cast member's properties	Modify ➤ Cast Member ➤ Properties Double-click a sound cast member or sprite.
Import sound	File ➤ Import ➤ Sound (see Table 4-4)
Record a new sound (Mac only)	Insert ➤ Media Element ➤ Sound
Import SWA sound	Insert ➤ Media Element ➤ Shockwave Audio (retains SWA format) File ➤ Import ➤ Sound (D7; converts to non-SWA format)
Export Sound	Copy to Clipboard, or use Edit ➤ Launch External Editor, then save from your sound editor.
Export sound channels	Under File ➤ Export, use *Format: QuickTime Movie*, then choose *Options* and export Sound Channels 1 and 2.
Place a sound in the score	Modify ➤ Frame ➤ Sound Drag sound cast member to sound channel, or drag SWA or DV member to sprite channel.
Add cue points to a sound	See "Cue Points and Timing" and "Sound Editing Applications and Utilities" later in this chapter.
Create SWA cast member	See "Shockwave Audio (SWA)" later in this chapter.
Wait for sound or cue point	Modify ➤ Frame ➤ Tempo ➤ Wait for Cue Point. (In D5, use Wait for End of Sound or Wait for End of Digital Video options.)
Play sounds in the cast (internal, linked external, and SWA sounds)	*Play* button under Modify ➤ Cast Member ➤ Properties or Modify ➤ Frame ➤ Sound
Preview external sound files	*Play* button under File ➤ Import
Find sound cast members in Cast	Edit ➤ Find ➤ Cast Member ➤ Sound
Find SWA cast members in Cast	Edit ➤ Find ➤ Cast Member ➤ Xtra (D6) Edit ➤ Find ➤ Cast Member ➤ Shockwave Audio (D7)
Find Sound or SWA members in Score	Highlight member in Cast and use Edit ➤ Find ➤ Selection
Volume levels or mute a sound[1]	Control ➤ Volume, or volume button in Control Panel. Mute buttons to left of Score Sound channels.

[1] Cmd-Opt-M (Mac) or Ctrl-Alt-M (Windows) toggles the *soundEnabled* and does not affect the *soundLevel* property.

Sound Cast Member Properties Dialog Box

Some sound cast member's properties can be viewed and set via the *Sound Cast Member Properties* dialog box (see Figure 15-1) or set via Lingo, but a sound's sampling rate, bit depth, and number of channels are read-only in Director. The original sound must be modified in a separate sound editing program.

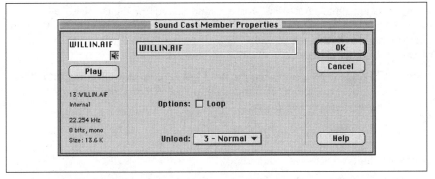

Figure 15-1: Sound Cast Member Properties dialog box

If multiple sound cast members are selected, the cast member properties dialog box will contain summary information, such as the total size of selected cast members.

The *Sound Cast Member Properties* dialog box can be used to play a sound. It also shows the sample rate (see *the sampleRate of member*), the number of channels (see *the channelCount of member*), and the bit depth (see *the sampleSize of member*). See Example 15-3 to determine the duration of an internal sound.

The size listed for internal sounds is accurate, but the size listed for externally linked files is merely the size of the cast member's header. See Example 4-6 to determine an external sound file's size.

The following sound properties are also shown in the dialog box:

Name and filename
> If the sound is linked, an external filename is shown. Click on the name to browse to another filename. *The fileName of member* includes the complete path to the file and updates automatically for the current platform.

Loop
> *Loop* controls whether Director obeys the loopback points set in an external sound editor. Absent any loopback points, the sound loops back to its beginning after it has completed. The Tempo Channel's *Wait for Cue Point:{End}* option causes Director to ignore the *loop* setting and play the sound until it ends. To wait indefinitely, use *Wait for Cue Point:{Next}* or the *soundBusy()* function. When creating a looping sound, ensure that the beginning and end of the loop combine seamlessly. External sounds won't loop automatically. See also the equivalent *loop of member*.

Unload

Set *Unload* to "Next" to keep a small sound in RAM (avoid this for larger sounds). Director often unloads sounds if it is low on memory, regardless of this setting. This setting has no effect on linked (streamed) audio.

Cue Points and Timing

Cue points are timing notations stored within sounds or digital video files. They were introduced in D6 and are used to synchronize audio or video with Score animations. Use sound tracks within QuickTime or Video for Windows when lip-synching or other close synchronization is required.

Director 6.5 and later supports cue points in WAVE files, as well as the AIFF, SWA, and digital video cue points supported in D6.0.x. Third-party Xtras such as the MPEG Xtra also support cue points.

Waiting for Godot's Audio

There are three ways to wait for audio:

- The Score's Tempo channel

- Checking the current playing time or audio state via appropriate Lingo properties, or using a Lingo function such as *soundBusy()*

- Waiting for a *cuePassed* event or checking the *isPastCuePoint()* function or the *mostRecentCuePoint* property

Tempo channel settings

The Tempo channel's *Wait for Cue Point* option can be used to wait for a sound to end or to reach a particular cue point. In the *Frame Properties: Tempo* dialog box (see Figure 15-2), choose the Sound channel or sprite channel to wait for, and choose from the list of available cue points within the sound, or *{Next}* or *{End}*.

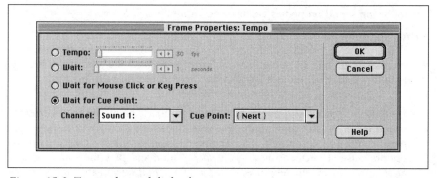

Figure 15-2: Tempo channel dialog box

Waiting for sounds via the Tempo channel in D5 (which used separate *Wait for End of Sound* and *Wait for End of Digital Video* options) locked out other events, such as mouse clicks. In D6, it locks out events for Custom Buttons, but otherwise allows events to be processed. In D7, Custom Buttons are obsolete, and Director continues to process other events while waiting via the Tempo channel.

Waiting for sound via Lingo

Use Lingo for finer control over waiting for sounds. For example, the Tempo channel cannot be used to wait for sounds played via *sound playFile*. Use the *soundBusy( )* function instead, as shown in Example 15-4.

Example 15-4: Waiting for a Sound by Sound Channel Number

```
on exitFrame
  -- This waits for a sound in channel 2 to complete
  if soundBusy(2) then
    go the frame
  end if
end
```

As a general rule, you should *not* wait in a repeat loop, as it locks out all interactivity. Avoid this:

```
repeat while soundBusy(2)
  -- Waiting for the sound in channel 2 to end
end repeat
```

Avoid waiting for a sound to start unless you are sure it will actually start. For example, *sound playFile* will not give an error if you specify a missing or invalid filename; the sound will simply fail to play. The following will cause an infinite loop if the sound in channel 1 never starts.

```
puppetSound "someSound"
repeat while not soundBusy(1)
  -- Waiting for the sound to start
end repeat
```

To avoid an infinite loop in the prior example, trigger the *puppetSound* using an *updateStage* command before the *repeat* loop.

You can wait for a specific time in an SWA sprite by using *the currentTime* property in a script attached to the sprite of interest. Example 15-5 waits for 10 seconds (10,000 milliseconds) of the SWA to play. It will cause an infinite loop if *the currentTime* never reaches that point.

Example 15-5: Waiting for a Specific Point in an SWA Sound

```
on exitFrame me
  if the currentTime of sprite the spriteNum of me < 10000 then
    go the frame
  end if
end
```

Synchronizing with Cue Points

You can use cue points to wait in, leave, or jump to a particular frame in the Score. Create your cue points in a sound editing program with your Score layout and frame labels in mind. Create a cue point *before* the sound segment of interest if you'll be jumping to a new frame when the cue point is reached. Create a cue point *after* the sound segment of interest if you'll be waiting in a frame until a cue point is reached.

 To simplify your Lingo code, name your cue points the same as the frame label to which you wish to jump.

The Tempo channel's *Wait for Cue Point* option waits for a cue point in a Sound channel, digital video sprite, or SWA sprite. If the *Cue Point* option is {*Next*}, Director will wait for the next cue point to be reached. Use the {*End*} setting to wait for the end of a sound, even one without cue points. The {*End*} setting will not cause an infinite loop if a sound's *loop* option is set, but the {*Next*} setting will. The *Channel* parameter in the Tempo dialog box does not update automatically, so you must update it manually if you move a sound or sprite to a different channel.

Example 15-6 is a frame script that waits for a cue point. It then jumps to a frame whose label matches the cue point name.

Example 15-6: Using Cue Points to Synchronize with Score Animation

```
on exitFrame
  go the frame
end

on cuePassed me, channelID, cueNumber, cueName
  go frame cueName
end
```

Creating Cue Points

Cue points must be added to a sound before it is imported into Director. SoundEdit 16 (Macintosh only) can add cue points to AIFF and QuickTime files. You should use the SoundEdit v2.0.7 update at *http://www.macromedia.com/ support/soundedit/updates*. Earlier versions may not create cue points correctly and will fail under Mac OS 8.

In D6.0.x, QuickTime cue point support was through a custom mechanism. Quick-Time cue points appeared in SoundEdit as "markers" as they do for other file formats, but in MoviePlayer the same cue points appeared as a text track. (You must enable the track in MoviePlayer to see the text cue points, but Director reads the cue points even if the text track is disabled.)

Director 6.5 and 7 use the standard QT3 chapter tracks (which can be created and edited in any program that supports them) for cue point support in QuickTime.

AVI and WAVE cast members cannot contain cue points in D6.0.x, but Director 6.5 supports cue points in WAVE files (AVIs support cue points only if played via QT3). For example, cue points created in Sound Designer for Windows are ignored by Director 6.0.x, but recognized by D6.5. WAVE files use markers ("MARK" chunks) to represent cue points. Any sound editor that supports markers can be used to create and edit cue points for D6.5.

To add cue points to a sound using SoundEdit 16 v2.0.7, follow these steps:

1. Open the sound file and click the location in the sound track at which you want to create the cue point.

2. Choose Insert ➤ Cue Point.

3. Enter a cue point name and/or change the cue point time. Director will always read cue points in milliseconds, regardless of the units used in SoundEdit.

4. You can move cue points by dragging them along the sound track, or delete them by dragging them off the sound track. Use Windows ➤ Cue to bring up SoundEdit's Cue Points inspector.

5. Save the file from SoundEdit in Audio IFF or QuickTime movie format or use the SoundEdit SWA Xtra from SoundEdit's Xtras menu to save an SWA file (requires PowerPC). Cue points added to a QuickTime file appear as text elements in a text track in QT2 and as chapter tracks in QT3.

To add cue points using Sound Forge or Cool Edit under Windows, see the *ReadMe Windows Sound Loop-Cue* file that comes with D6 and D7. To add cue points in Peak LE and for more tips on cue points, see *http://www.zeusprod.com/nutshell/cuepoints.html*.

To use cue points:

1. Import the asset into Director's Cast or File ➤ Import using Insert ➤ Media Element as appropriate.

2. Insert a sound into one of the Score's Sound channels or insert an SWA or QuickTime member into a sprite channel. *Sound playFile* and *puppetSound* also work with cue points.

3. Use the Tempo channel's *Wait for Cue Point* option to wait for a cue point or wait in a frame until a *cuePassed* event is sent to your *on cuePassed* handler.

Cue point caveats

Cue points trigger off the actual data buffers sent to and returned from the sound card under Windows. If there is no sound card (such as is common under Windows NT), cue points will not work.

A muted Sound channel in the Score will not load the specified sounds and those sounds won't generate cue point events. Similarly SWA or QuickTime sprites in muted sprite channels will not generate cue point events.

Cue point events *are* sent even if the volume is muted via the Control Panel or via Lingo.

Cue points near the end of a sound may not be recognized. Add silence to the end of the sound if necessary.

Avoid putting cue points beyond the end of an audio track in either a sound file or QuickTime movie. *The duration of member* reflects the position of the last cue point, not merely the end of audio data.

Cue Point Lingo

The cuePointNames of member property returns a Lingo list of cue point names for any cast member type that supports cue points. Unnamed cue points are shown as `""` (EMPTY). If no cue points are present, an empty list (`[]`) is returned. The *cuePointTimes of member* property returns a Lingo list of cue points times (in milliseconds), or an empty list (`[]`) if no cue points are present:

```
put the cuePointNames of member "mySound"
-- ["Intro", "Bridge", "Chorus", "", "Coda"]
put the cuePointTimes of member "mySound"
-- [4466, 7300, 13000, 17000, 21500]"
```

 The *cuePointNames* and *cuePointTimes* of an SWA, sound, or QuickTime cast member are returned as empty lists (`[]`) until the sound is playing. See *the state of member* property.

The lists of cue point names and times is read-only, but can be manipulated with Lingo's list functions, such as:

```
set numCues = count (the cuePointNames of member "mySound")
set lastCue = getLast (the cuePointTimes of member "mySound")
```

The *isPastCuePoint()* function takes the general form:

```
isPastCuePoint (sprite n | sound n, cuePointNumber | cuePointName)
```

The first parameter is either a sprite channel or a sound channel. If the second parameter is a *cuePointNumber*, *isPastCuePoint()* returns a Boolean value indicating whether the current media playback position is beyond the specified cue point (regardless of how many times it may have passed that point). If the second parameter is a *cuePointName*, *isPastCuePoint()* returns an integer count of the number of times that the cue point with the given name has been passed (including multiple cue points with the same name).

The *mostRecentCuePoint* takes the form:

```
the mostRecentCuePoint of {sprite n | sound n}
```

It indicates the number of the last cue point passed for the specified sprite channel or sound channel. It returns 0 if no cue points have been passed.

Table 15-7 summarizes cue point-related operations.

Table 15-7: Cue Point Functions

Action	Command
Wait for cue point	Tempo channel, isPastCuePoint( ), or see Examples 15-6 and 15-7
Determine names of cue points	the cuePointNames of member
Determine times of cue points	the cuePointTimes of member
Determine whether a cue point has been reached	isPastCuePoint( )
Check the last cue point passed for a sprite or sound channel	the mostRecentCuePoint of sprite, the mostRecentCuePoint of sound
Trigger an event when a cue point is reached	*on cuePassed* event handler (see Examples 15-6 and 15-7)
Identify the sprite triggering a cue point	See the *the spriteNum of me* or *channelID* passed to the *on cuePassed* handler
Forces preloading of list of cue points (highly undocumented and unsupported in D6.5, and removed in D7)	forcePreloadCuePoints (member *whichMember*)

Cue Point Events

Director generates *cuePassed* events whenever it passes a media cue point in an appropriate sound or sprite. The beginning and end of the media do not automatically generate *cuePassed* events, although the Tempo channel's *Wait for Cue Point* option will wait for the end of a sound without cue points. As shown in Example 15-6, the declaration of an *on cuePassed* handler takes the form:

```
on cuePassed {me,} channelID, cuePointNumber, cuePointName
```

The *on cuePassed* handler receives three or four parameters as follows:

me

> The script instance of the sprite that triggered the event, *me*, is sent to *on cuePassed* handlers in sprite scripts and frame scripts, but not to *onCuePassed* handlers in cast scripts or movie scripts. Use *the spriteNum of me* to determine the sprite's number.

channelID

> *channelID* is the sprite channel or sound channel of the asset that reached a cue point. If the cue point is triggered by an SWA or QuickTime sprite, *channelID* is an integer from 1 to 120 in D6, or 1 to 1000 in D7. If triggered by a sound in a sound channel, channelID is *#sound1* or *#sound2* representing the Score's Sound channels; *#sound3* through *#sound8* represent *puppetSound* and *sound playFile* commands played in channels 3 through 8.

cuePointNumber

> The number of the cue point within the asset triggering this event, starting at 1.

cuePointName

> The name of the cue point triggering this event, or EMPTY (" ") for unnamed cue points.

Example 15-7 can be used to analyze or diagnose cue point problems from any type of script. It automatically adjusts to whether 3 or 4 parameters are passed in (which depends on the script type). Ordinarily, you wouldn't use most of the information available, except perhaps the cue point name. See Example 15-6 for a typical cue point handler.

Example 15-7: Diagnostic Cue Point Event Handler

```
on cuePassed
  -- Sprite and Frame scripts receive four parameters
  -- Movie and Cast scripts receive three parameters
  if the paramCount = 4 then
    set me = param(1)
    put "on cuePassed handler reached for sprite" && ¬
      the spriteNum of me
  end if
  set channelID = param(the paramCount - 2)
  set cueNumber = param(the paramCount - 1)
  set cueName   = param(the paramCount)
  put "Channel ID:" && channelID
  put "Cue Number:" && cueNumber
  put "Cue Name:"   && cueName
  -- Print the cue point time
  case(channelID) of
    #sound1:
      set thisMember = the frameSound1
    #sound2:
      set thisMember = the frameSound2
    #sound3, #sound4, #sound5, #sound6, #sound7, #sound8:
      put "Cue point times not available for" && channelID
      set thisMember = 0
    otherwise:
      set thisMember = the member of sprite channelID
  end case
  if thisMember <> 0 then
    put "This cue time:" && getAt (the cuePointTimes of ¬
        thisMember, cueNumber)
  end if
end cuePassed
```

Shockwave Audio (SWA)

Shockwave audio (SWA) could be renamed *compressed audio*, because SWA can be used with a standalone Projector as well as with the Shockwave browser plug-in. For both Projectors and Internet delivery, SWA compression can be used to create external streaming SWA files or to compress *internal* sound cast members.

Compressing Sounds for SWA

When using SWA compression, you don't select a compression ratio—you select an output bandwidth. The throughput of users' Internet connections varies tremendously. You should pick a data rate that is sustainable over the slowest expected connection. Table 15-8 lists suggested output bit rates for SWA.

Even the highest quality SWA (160 Kbps) requires less than 20 KB/sec. Divide Kbps (1000 bits per second) by 8.192 (that is, $8 \times 1024/1000$) to convert to kilobytes per second.

Converting very large sound files to SWA may crash Director or SoundEdit. Refer to the Shocker-L archives (see the Preface) circa August 19, 1998 for comments about it.

Table 15-8: Shockwave Audio Delivery Rate Comparison

Delivery	Bit rate	Quality[1]
T1 or CD-ROM	64–160 Kbps (8–20 K/sec)	Equal to source material
ISDN	48–56 Kbps (6–7 K/sec)	FM stereo to CD-quality audio
28.8–56 Kbps modem[2]	16–32 Kbps (2–4 K/sec)	FM mono or good quality AM
14.4 Kbps modem[2]	8 Kbps (1 K/sec)	Telephone

[1] All SWA is decompressed as 16-bit audio. Stereo sounds are automatically folded (flattened) to monaural if an output rate of 32 Kbps or lower is used.
[2] Only external SWA files can be compressed to 8, 16, or 24 Kbps as is necessary for streaming over a modem. Internal Director sounds can be compressed only to 32 Kbps or higher.

If you expect approximately 2 K/sec through a 28.8 Kbps modem, you should use a compression rate of 16 Kbps (equal to 2 K/sec). The goal is gapless delivery, but if the stream cannot keep up, the audio will pause or drop out.

Internal sound cast members can be compressed to rates of 32 to 160 Kbps (4 to 20 K/sec). External SWA sounds can be compressed as low as 8 Kbps (1 K/sec). You might use 8 Kbps or 16 Kbps SWA for uninterrupted streaming of large sounds over a 28.8 Kbps modem and 64 Kbps for high-quality smaller internal sounds.

During streaming or downloading, only the bandwidth (i.e., *the bitRate of member*) is important. Streaming sound is discarded as it is played, so it doesn't use much RAM.

The disk size of an SWA file is only relevant if calculating the CD-ROM space required when using local SWA files. Its size depends only on the duration of the source audio and the bit rate chosen for SWA compression, regardless of the source material's sample rate and sample size. The size of an SWA file on disk can be calculated in KB as:

```
(the duration of member) * (the bitRate of member) / 8192
```

Compressing internal sounds

Standard internal sound cast members can be compressed as follows:

1. Fully import (unlinked) sounds into Director using File ➤ Import ➤ *Standard Import*.

2. Enable compression under Xtras ➤ Shockwave for Audio Settings and choose 32, 48, 56, 64, 80, 112, 128, or 160 Kbps as the final output rate.

3. Compression does not occur until the DCR or CCT file or Projector is created using `File` ➤ `Save As Shockwave Movie`, `Xtras` ➤ `Update Movies`, `File` ➤ `Create Projector` ➤ *Options* ➤ *Compress (Shockwave format)*.

4. If Shockwave compression is not enabled, internal sounds in DCR and CCT files are compressed about 30% using LZW compression. Internal sounds in DIR, DXR, CST, and CXT files are never compressed.

Internal non-streaming sounds that are SWA-compressed using `Xtras` ➤ `Shockwave for Audio Settings` are blown up fully into RAM when needed. They use the standard properties for *#sound* cast members, not those for *#SWA* members, as shown in Tables 15-4 and 4-10. Likewise in D7, SWA cast members imported via `File` ➤ `Import` are converted to Director's internal sound format. Insert SWA via `Insert` ➤ `Media Element` ➤ `Shockwave Audio` to retain the SWA format.

Compressing external sounds

External SWA sounds can be compressed to 8, 16, or 24 Kbps (which are designed for very low bandwidth), in addition to the higher quality rates (32–160 Kbps) available for internal sounds.

Director for Macintosh compresses internal sounds only. Use SoundEdit 16 or Peak LE to compress external sounds on the Macintosh.

The steps for SWA compression of external sounds in SoundEdit 16 (PowerMac-only) are:

1. Import or create sound files within SoundEdit v2.07.

2. Within SoundEdit, choose `Xtras` ➤ `Shockwave for Audio settings`.

3. Compression occurs when using `File` ➤ `Export` (sound format *Shockwave Audio*).

4. Import sounds as linked SWA cast members into Director using `Insert` ➤ `Media Element` ➤ `Shockwave Audio`.

For an SWA Tutorial, examples, and SWA players, click the "Working With Shockwave" option and then the "Download the example movies" option at *http://www.macromedia.com/support/soundedit/*. The following two links include the SWA Xtras for SoundEdit 16 (also included with the D6 Studio).

SWAtomator—batch processes files to SWA:

http://www.macromedia.com/support/soundedit/SE16SWA.hqx

SoundEdit 16 updater to version 2.0.7 (supports Mac OS 8.x):

http://www.macromedia.com/support/soundedit/SE16v207.hqx

To export SWA from Peak LE:

1. Install Peak LE from the *Peak LE 2.0* folder included on the Director 7 Shockwave Internet Studio CD.

2. Copy the SWA Export Xtra from that same folder to the *Peak LE Plugins* folder (where Peak LE is installed).

3. Choose *Shockwave .swa* format under `File` ➤ `Save As`.

SWA compression of external sounds in Director (Windows only) requires a Pentium and operates on WAVE files. Choose `Xtras ➤ Shockwave for Audio settings` and then `Xtras ➤ Convert WAV to SWA`.

SWA compression hints

SWA uses MPEG3 compression (SWA files can be previewed in MacAmp or WinAmp) and is optimized to deliver high quality audio at reasonable bandwidths, but it also delivers fair quality audio at minuscule bandwidths. Whether compressing internal or external sounds, use at least 16-bit, 22.050 kHz source audio. Do *not* downsample the audio to 8-bit first. After SWA compression, 8-bit, 11 kHz monaural audio occupies the same space as 16-bit, 22 kHz monaural audio (or even 16-bit, 44 kHz).

There is no benefit to reducing either the bit depth or the sample rate before compression. Quite the contrary, higher fidelity source audio results in higher quality SWA without any additional bandwidth. All SWA-compressed sounds *reconstruct* (decompress) into 16-bit audio regardless of the source material's bit depth (which is why *the bitsPerSample of member* property always returns 16).

The numChannels of member is 1 (monaural) if *the bitRate of member* is 32000 bps or less. SWA properties can be checked only after the SWA begins playing, as indicated by *the state of member* property (see Table 15-9).

Use the highest output rate that your Internet connection will tolerate (see Table 15-8). Output rates below 32 Kbps are intended only for compatibility with slower modems. As compression increases, the absolute savings are only marginally better.

For example, a CD-quality (16-bit, 44 kHz, stereo) source file requires 176 K/sec (1400 Kbps). Compressing it to 160 Kbps reduces the size by 89% with no detectable loss of quality. Compressing it to 32 Kbps (4 K/sec) saves a whopping 172 K/sec and it can still play over a fast modem. But compressing it to 8 Kbps (1 K/sec) saves only an additional 3 K/sec, and the loss in quality to achieve the marginal savings is *immense* (according to Macromedia).

SWA Decompression

SWA decompression is processor-intensive, so SWA is most appropriate over the Internet, where download time is at a premium. For local content, SWA may simply hinder performance, especially on slower machines.

Decompression time is not significantly different at different data rates (as with most compression schemes, decompression is much faster than compression). The propensity to drop sounds seems independent of the bit rate. On 68K Macs (which require an FPI to play SWA), SWA decompression ignores some of the data when using 8 Kbps and 16 Kbps bit rates. This provides adequate performance at the expense of lesser quality than on PowerMacs.

All SWA is decompressed as 16-bit audio (which is why you shouldn't downsample to 8-bit). Internal sounds that were compressed with SWA are reconstructed in their entirety in RAM before playback; they are blown up to their original size, so a 44 kHz source will occupy twice the memory of a comparable

22 kHz source once decompressed. Regardless, streaming external sounds don't remain in memory—they use only a small temporary buffer—so the size is only relevant for internal sounds.

SWA Lingo

Table 15-9 lists the commands and properties pertaining to SWA cast members. All the properties are read-only and apply to externally linked #SWA cast members, not to internal cast members compressed when the Director movie or castLib is compressed as a whole. All SWA commands are new as of D6; although some were supported in Shockwave for D5, none were supported during authoring in D5.

Table 15-9: Shockwave Audio Lingo

Property	Usage
the bitRate of member[1]	0 (not ready) | 8000 | 16000 | 24000 | 32000 | 48000 | 56000 | 64000 | 80000 | 112000 | 128000 | 160000
the bitsPerSample of member[1,2]	Bit depth of expanded media, *not* the bit depth of the original file that has been SWA encoded. It always returns 0 (not ready) or 16.
the copyrightInfo of member[1,2]	Copyright text for sound file.
the cuePointNames of member[1,2]	List of names of cue points.
the cuePointTimes of member[1,2]	List of cue point times in milliseconds.
the currentTime of sprite[1,2]	Current point in playback in milliseconds.
the duration of member[1]	Duration of SWA file in seconds (different units than property of the same name for #digitalVideo, #quickTimeMedia, and #transition members).
getError (member *swaMember*)	Error status for SWA cast members. The integer value returned by *getError( )* corresponds to the string returned by *getErrorString( )*: 0: returns EMPTY string ""[3] 1: "memory" 2: "network" (or "Network software error") 3: "playback device" 99: "other"
getErrorString (member *swaMember*)[3]	See *getError( )*.
isPastCuePoint(member, cueID)[2]	Returns a positive integer if the cue point has been passed.
the mediaReady of member	Indicates whether media has been completely downloaded. Appropriate only for internal nonstreaming SWA-compressed sounds.
the mostRecentCuePoint of member[2]	Returns number of most recent cue point passed.
the numChannels of member[1,2]	Number of channels (usually 1 or 2). Returns 1 when *the bitRate of member* is <= 32000.

Table 15-9: Shockwave Audio Lingo (continued)

Property	Usage
pause (member)	Pauses SWA stream, but not instantly.
the percentPlayed of member	Percentage of bytes played (0 to 100). Should be less than or equal to *percentStreamed*.
the percentStreamed of member	Percentage of bytes streamed from server (0 to 100).
play (member)	Begins playing SWA (initiates preload, too).
preLoadBuffer (member *swaMember*)	Begins preloading amount of data specified by *the preLoadTime of member*. Use *stop( )* to "rewind" the media after preloading before using *play( )*.
the preLoadTime of member	Duration of SWA audio (not download time) in seconds to be downloaded before playback begins (prevents skipping).
the sampleRate of member[1,2]	Sample rate of original sound source (in Hz) before compression, such as 11025, 22050, or 44100.
the soundChannel of member[1,2]	System sound channel in which to play SWA (0 uses highest available channel). Avoid using 1 and 2, the Score Sound channels.
the state of member	*The state of member* must be 2, 3, 4, or 5 before checking other SWA properties accurately: 0: Stopped 1: Preloading 2: Preloading completed 3: Playing 4: Paused 5: Done 9: Error 10: Insufficient CPU
stop (member)	Stops SWA stream, but not instantly. Also rewinds SWA.
the streamName of member[1,2]	URL of SWA file. Can be local. (Same as *URL of member*.)
the url of member[1]	URL of SWA file. Can be local. (Same as *streamName of member*.)
the volume of member	Volume of SWA, from 0 to 255.

[1] Returns 0, [], EMPTY, or meaningless data unless *the state of member* is 2, 3, 4, or 5.
[2] Appears for the fist time in Director 6. Not supported in Shockwave for Director 5.
[3] *GetErrorString(0)* returns the EMPTY string in my tests, not "OK" as claimed by Macromedia's documentation.

Pausing an SWA and playback gaps

When you use *pause()* or *stop()* to halt an SWA, a certain amount of audio data is still in the SWA buffer and continues to "play out." Therefore, the sound does not pause immediately. To stop the sound from being heard, you must set *the volume of member* to 0. When you use *play()* to start the sound again (don't forget to reset the volume), the sound will have skipped the portion that was played out of the buffer after the last *pause()* command. No ideal solution exists.

If an SWA sprite is streaming, there may be times when the Internet connection does not provide data fast enough and gaps in the audio occur. Even though the audio is momentarily interrupted, *the state of member* still returns 3 (playing).

Likewise, the *soundBusy()* function indicates whether a sound channel has been allocated and is presently "in use," not whether sound is currently audible.

There is no random access to an arbitrary point in an SWA stream, which is incompatible with streaming playback. The data would have to be either stored to disk or preloaded to allow such access, as is done by various MP3 players. However, see the highly unsupported Din Xtra commands in Table 15-14.

Streaming live audio sources via Shockwave

According to John "jd" Dowdell of Macromedia, there are two alternatives to encode and broadcast SWA in realtime:

- Use the Telos AudioActive (*http://www.audioactive.com*) real-time encoding and multicasting equipment. It works under Windows and with the SW6.0 on the Mac. (It doesn't work with SW6.0.1 and Netscape 3 and 4 on the Macintosh; the audio stream downloads but never plays.)

- Use RealAudio's real-time compression and multicasting hardware. The Real-Audio Xtra requires installation in the browser plug-in folder. You can instead use a RealPlayer element in a web page and use LiveConnect and ActiveX scripting from Shockwave to control it. (Some have reported poor results with this solution.)

Details on these solutions using Shockwave 7 were not available at press time. The RealAudio Xtra won't work in SW7 unless a Shockwave-safe version is made available by Real Networks, and no such plans appear likely.

Other Sound-Related Lingo

Table 15-10 lists system-level sound-related Lingo properties and commands.

Table 15-10: System-Level Sound-Related Lingo

Command	Usage
beep {*n*}	Beeps *n* times (*alert* also causes a beep). If *the soundEnabled* is FALSE, beep flashes the Macintosh menubar. *n* defaults to 1, and multiple beeps don't usually work under Windows.
the beepOn	If TRUE, Director beeps when the user clicks on an inactive sprite (one without a mouse script attached). Useful for debugging.
sound close *channel*	Closes the specified sound *channel*. This requires the sound buffer to be reallocated for the next sound.

Table 15-10: System-Level Sound-Related Lingo (continued)

Command	Usage
sound stop	Stops the sound playing in the specified *channel*.
the soundEnabled	If FALSE, all sounds are muted.
the soundLevel	System volume from 0 (mute) to 7 (loudest).
the multiSound	If TRUE, the computer supports stereo sound.

The *DIRECTOR.INI* file has numerous settings that affect the audio buffers and sound-mixing under Windows. Ordinarily, you shouldn't change any except the *DLLname* and *rsxDontUseDirectSound*, which are both obsolete in D7, anyway. Refer to Appendix D in *Lingo in a Nutshell* for additional details on setting the items listed in Table 15-11.

Table 15-11: DIRECTOR.INI File Sound-Related Settings

Command	Usage
DLLname (D6.5 only)	Default is MacroMix.DLL. Change to QT3Mix.DLL to use QT3 Sound Mixing (requires D6.5 with Service Pack).
rsxDontUseDirect-Sound (D6.x only)	If set to 1, RSX will output to WaveOut instead of DirectSound. Default is 0. SW6.0 treats this as 0; SW6.0.1 treats it as 1.
MixMaxChannels	Maximum number of sound channels allowed to be mixed. Default is 8 in D7 and 4 in previous versions; max is 8.
MixMaxFidelity	Maximum sound fidelity that MacroMix will need to mix. The default, 99, determines max on the fly: 0: 22.050 kHz, 8-bit, mono 1: 22.050 kHz, 8-bit, stereo 2: 44.100 kHz, 16-bit, stereo 99: Switch formats on the fly (default)
MixServiceMode	0: Interrupt Mixer based on MixIntPeriodMs and MixIntResolutionMs (default) 1: Use polling to drive mixer (may cause drop out if other tasks hog CPU access) 2: Use waveout buffer-completion callback to drive mixer. Set MixBufferBytes to multiple of 1024
MixWaveDevice	Ranges from 0 (default) to the number of devices – 1.
MixBufferBytes	Defaults to 0. Set MixBufferMs to 0 and then set MixBufferBytes to multiple of 1024 to specify a buffer size in bytes.
MixBufferCount	Number of mixing buffers from 2 to 16 (default is 4).

*Sound &
Cue Points*

Table 15-11: DIRECTOR.INI File Sound-Related Settings (continued)

Command	Usage
DLLname (D6.5 only)	Default is MacroMix.DLL. Change to QT3Mix.DLL to use QT3 Sound Mixing (requires D6.5 with Service Pack).
rsxDontUseDirect-Sound (D6.x only)	If set to 1, RSX will output to WaveOut instead of DirectSound. Default is 0. SW6.0 treats this as 0; SW6.0.1 treats it as 1.
MixBufferMs	Defines sound buffer length in milliseconds. Default is 200 milliseconds (size in bytes varies with sound format). To define buffer size in bytes using MixBufferBytes, set MixBufferMs to 0.
MixIntPeriodMs	Interrupt interval, defaults to 200 milliseconds. Used only when MixServiceMode is 0.
MixIntResolutionMs	Interrupt duration, defaults to 50 milliseconds. Used only when MixServiceMode is 0.
SoundLevel0 through SoundLevel7	Specifies "wave output" volume corresponding to *the soundLevel* property. Default values for the soundLevel = 0 to 7 are shown:[1] SoundLevel0 = 0 SoundLevel1 = 24770 SoundLevel2 = 35030 SoundLevel3 = 42903 SoundLevel4 = 49540 SoundLevel5 = 55388 SoundLevel6 = 60674 SoundLevel7 = 65535
HighSpoolBufferMs	Length of one 16-bit spool buffer; default is 1500 milliseconds.
LowSpoolBufferMs	Length of one 8-bit spool buffer; default is 2500 milliseconds.
SpoolBufferAlloc	0: Allocates/deallocates spool buffers dynamically, when sound starts/stops (default) 1: Allocates spool buffer once at startup and keeps them it entire session
SpoolBufferCount	Number of spool buffers to allocate, from 2 (default) to 10.

[1] *The soundLevel* settings in the *DIRECTOR.INI* file can range from 0 to 65,535, but the output response is nonlinear. The default settings for *soundLevel1* through *soundLevel3* are inaudible on some PCs.

Volume Levels and Sound Fades

Volume levels vary tremendously across platforms and even on different machines running the same OS. Perform tests to determine an appropriate volume level and then record all your sounds for a project at the same level. You can later adjust their relative volumes in Director (this is simplified greatly if all background sounds or voiceovers are played in a specific channel).

There are many commands that control sound volume in Director, including system-level volume controls, plus those at the sprite or cast member level. On the Macintosh, Lingo can set the master volume, but under Windows, Lingo controls only the "wave output" volume.

Provide a volume control with a mute option to the user. Macromedia provides an example volume slider in the D6 Behavior Library. You can use the keyboard characters 0 through 7 to set *the soundLevel*, as shown in Example 15-8.

Example 15-8: Setting the soundLevel via the Keyboard

```
on keyDown
  -- 0 though 7 set the soundLevel.  Keys 8 and 9 set it to 7.
  if charToNum(the key) >= 48 and charToNum(the key) <= 58 then
    set the soundLevel = min(integer(the key), 7)
  end if
end keyDown
```

It is exceedingly rude to increase the system volume level automatically. If necessary, check *the soundLevel* or sprite volume via Lingo and suggest that the user change it. If you do set *the soundLevel*, set it to 5, not 7.

Table 15-12 lists commands that pertain to sound volumes in Director. See also Control ➤ Volume and the volume button in the Control Panel.

Table 15-12: Volume-Related Lingo

Command	Usage
sound fadeIn *channel* {, *ticks*}	Fades volume up from 0 to the current *volume of sound* setting, not up to 255, as in D5. See the D6 *ReadMe*.
sound fadeOut *channel* {, *ticks*}	Fades volume down from the current *volume of sound* setting to 0, not from 255 to 0, as in D5. See the D6 *ReadMe*.
the sound of member *videoMember*	Boolean indicating whether sound is enabled for a digital video or Flash cast member.
the soundEnabled	If FALSE, all sounds are muted.
the soundLevel	System volume from 0 (mute) to 7 (loudest). See Table 15-11.
the visibility of sprite	Muting a Sound channel or sprite channel in the Score prevents the sound, SWA, or digital video sprite from playing.
the volume of member	Volume level for SWA members (0 to 255). Doesn't work for Flash.
the volume of sound	Volume level for Sound channel 1 or 2 (0 to 255).
the volume of sprite	Volume level for digital video, AVI, QT2 in D6, QT3 in D7, and SWA sprites. Nominal range is 0 to 255, but can be set much higher.
the volumeLevel of sprite	Volume level for QT3 digital video sprites in D6.5. Use *volume of sprite* in D7. Nominal range is 0 to 255, but can be set much higher.

Sound & Cue Points

Volume levels

The soundLevel command sets the volume for the overall system on the Macintosh and it matches the settings in *Sound* or *Monitors & Sound* Control Panel. Under Windows, *the soundLevel* controls the "wave output" volume matching the

SoundLevel0 through *SoundLevel7* settings in the *DIRECTOR.INI* file (see Table 15-11). Note that human audio perception is nonlinear. The default settings for *SoundLevel0* through *SoundLevel3* are usually indistinguishable from each other and undesirably soft. Consider respecifying the range of *SoundLevel1* to *SoundLevel7* from 45,000 to 65,535 in the *DIRECTOR.INI* file for more useful control via Lingo's *the soundLevel* property.

For complete control of the master volume under Windows, either open the Windows Sound mixer or use a third-party Xtra.

Burak Kalayci's bkMixer Xtra adjusts the Windows master volume level:

> *http://www.updatestage.com/xtras/bkmixer.html*

Buddy API Xtra—see the *baGetVolume()* and *baSetVolume()* methods:

> *http://www.mods.com.au/budapi/*

Some Windows sound cards' volume mixers can be controlled via *mci* commands. Bear in mind that the volume can also be changed by the user on some speakers with external volume knobs.

The soundLevel affects all sounds; you can adjust the relative volumes of individual members or sprites using the commands shown in Table 15-12.

There is no volume control over Flash sprites beyond shutting sound off using the *sound of member* property. Use native Director sounds instead.

Modal MIAWs reportedly prevent *the soundlevel* from being set under Windows NT in D7.0.

Sound fades

Prior to D6, *sound fadeIn* and *sound fadeOut* always faded between the minimum and maximum volumes (0 to 255). In D6 and later they fade from the current *volume of sound* for the specified channel towards either 0 or 255 as appropriate.

Interrupting sound fades under Windows tends to freeze *the volume of sound* at the level it held when the fade was interrupted. For example, if a sound terminates in the Score before a *sound fadeOut* completes, it might lock the volume for that channel to a near-zero level. Use this to reset the problem:

```
set the volume of sound channel = 255
```

You can manually construct your own *fadeIn* and *fadeOut* commands to fade between two arbitrary volume levels and avoid the buggy sound fade commands altogether. See *http://www.zeusprod.com/nutshell/fade.html*.

Some conflicts have been reported when fading sounds with different sampling rates at the same time. Always use sounds of the same rate at the same time.

Sound-Related Xtras

There are two broad categories of sound Xtras: those required by Director to play external sounds and those that add additional sound-related features of interest, but are not mandatory for most users.

Xtras needed to play external sounds in Director 6 and 7

Director 5 does not require any Xtras for sound playback. In Director 6 and 7, as with most external media, MIX Xtras are required to access external sounds at runtime. Note that in D6 the MIX Services and Sound Import Export Xtras are automatically added under Modify ➤ Movie ➤ Xtras when your cast includes linked sounds, but sometimes additional Xtras are needed. These Xtras, plus the SWA Xtras, are added by default to all D7 Projectors unless deleted from the Modify ➤ Movies ➤ Xtras list. This list also includes the MacroMix and Direct-Sound mixers. Regardless, I recommend against bundling Xtras with your Projector, so you should distribute the Xtras listed in this section with your Projector in a separate *Xtras* folder.

If all your sounds are embedded (unlinked) internal sounds, you don't need any Xtras unless you are using internal SWA compression.

Following is a list of Xtras needed in certain situations. See Table 15-13 for the exact names of the Xtras needed on the various platforms. The Xtras can be found in the *MIX, Media Support, Net Support, Device,* and *QT3* subfolders within the *Xtras* folder where Director is installed.

Playing any sounds in D7 or SW7 under Windows
D7 and SW7 for Windows require the MacroMix.X32, DirectSound.X32, and/or QT3Asset.X32 Xtras, depending on the user's installed software.

Linked sounds played via sound playFile, puppetSound, and the Score
To use *sound playFile* or to play any externally linked sound cast members via the Score Sound channels or via *puppetSound*, include the MIX Services and Sound Import Export Xtras with your Projector.

Local SWA audio played from a Projector
To play SWA from a local drive, include the MIX Services, Sound Import Export, SWA Streaming, SWA Decompression, and NetFile Xtras with your Projector. (NetFile is needed even when not using the Internet.)

SWA streaming over the Internet played from a Projector
To play SWA from a remote server via a Projector, include the MIX Services, Sound Import Export, SWA Streaming, SWA Decompression, NetFile, INetURL, and NetLingo Xtras (and the NetManage Winsock Lib, for PowerPC only) with your Projector.

Table 15-13 lists sound-related Xtras.

Table 15-13: Xtras Needed for Sound Playback.

PowerPC	Mac 68K	Win 32	Win 16
MIX Services	MIX Services	mix32.X32	mix16.X16
Sound Import Export	Sound Import Export 68k	Sound Import Export.X32	mixsound.X16
SWA Streaming PPC Xtra	SWA Streaming 68K Xtra	swastrm.X32	swastrm.X16

Table 15-13: Xtras Needed for Sound Playback. (continued)

PowerPC	Mac 68K	Win 32	Win 16
SWA Decompression PPC Xtra	SWA Decompression 68K Xtra	swadcmpr.X32	swadcmpr.X16
NetFile PPC Xtra	NetFile 68K Xtra	NetFile.X32	NetFile.X16
InetUrl PPC Xtra	None needed	INetUrl.X32	INetUrl.X16
NetLingo PPC Xtra	NetLingo 68K Xtra	NetLingo.X32	NetLingo.X16
NetManage WinSock Lib	None needed	None needed	None needed
MPEG 3 Import Export	MPEG 3 Import Export 68K	MPEG3 Import Export.X32	N/A
N/A	N/A	QT3Asset.X32[1] (contains QT3Mix)	N/A
N/A	N/A	MacroMix.X32[1]	N/A
N/A	N/A	DirectSound.X32[2]	N/A

[1] D7 only. MacroMix.X32 is bundled with SW7.0.
[2] D7.0.1 only. MacroMix.X32 and DirectSound.X32b are bundled with SW7.0.1.

If you choose to bundle Xtras with your Projector instead of shipping them separately, you can check the *Check Movies for Xtras* option in the D6 Projector creation dialog box in all of the previous cases. If playing SWA files either locally or remotely, you can also check the *Include Network Xtras* D6 Projector option. Instead of using these checkboxes, you can manually add the specified Xtras to your Projector file build list. In D7, individual Xtras can be flagged for inclusion under Modify ➤ Movie ➤ Xtras. All the previously listed Xtras are included by default for all D7.0.1 movies, whether needed or not. (Again, I recommend removing them from the list and placing them in an *Xtras* folder.) D7.0 movies will not include the DirectSound.X32 Xtra until upgraded to D7.0.1.

Xtras needed for sound in Shockwave

The equivalent of the MIX Services, Sound Import Export, and network-related Xtras (NetFile, INetURL, NetLingo, and the NetManage Winsock Lib for PowerPC) are built into Shockwave 6 and 7. These Xtras are needed only during authoring or in a Projector.

To play SWA from within Shockwave, the SWA Streaming and SWA Decompression Xtras must be installed in the Shockwave *Xtras* folder. These Xtras are both installed by default with Shockwave 6 and 7. Shockwave 7 for Windows also installs MacroMix.X32. SW7.0.1 installs DirectSound.X32 in addition. These Xtras are needed to mix sounds under Windows.

See Chapters 10 and 11 for more details on Xtras and Shockwave.

Other third-party sound-related Xtras

Besides the Xtras mentioned throughout this chapter, here are some that support more esoteric functions. See *http://www.zeusprod.com/nutshell/links* for a larger list of sound-related Xtras and other URLs of interest.

Audio Xtra (formerly sold as the Sound Xtra)—sound recording at runtime:

http://www.updatestage.com/xtras

DirectSound Xtra from DirectXtras:

http://www.directxtras.com

Speech Recognition—XtrAgent for Windows 95/98/NT support for speech input:

http://www.directxtras.com/xtragent.htm

Multimixer Xtra—extensive control over QuickTime audio tracks:

http://www.turntable.com

Beatnik Xtra (multichannel sound mixing):

http://www.headspace.com

Din Xtra (unsupported)

The completely unsupported Din Xtra, which has some interesting methods for controlling streaming audio and checking sound channels, is found on the Director 6 CD under:

D:\Macromedia\XDK_d6a4\Goodies\Director\SoundXtr\Xtras\Din.X32

or:

Director 6 CD:Macromedia:XDK for Director 6\Authorware 4:
Goodies:Director:SoundXtr:Xtras:Din

To see the Din Xtra's help text, type this in the Message window:

```
put mMessageList (xtra "Din")
```

Table 15-14 explains the Din Xtra commands. Note that many of these commands appear highly unreliable, and none are officially supported. The Xtra is absent in D7.

Table 15-14: The Unsupported Din Xtra

Din Command	Description/Usage
getChannelCount()	Returns maximum number of sound channels. `set numSoundChannels = getChannelCount()`
getFreeChannel()	Returns number of highest free sound channel: `set highestFreeSoundChannel = getFreeChannel()`

Table 15-14: The Unsupported Din Xtra (continued)

Din Command	Description/Usage
getPlayStatus( )	Determines if the sound is playing in specified channel: set *soundPlaying* = getPlayStatus (*soundChan*) Buggy; seems to always return TRUE. Use *soundBusy( )*.
getSndLength( )	Returns sound stream's total length in milliseconds: set *length* = getSndLength (*DinInstance*)
getSndPosition( )	Returns sound stream's current time in milliseconds: set *currentTime* = getSndPosition (*DinInstance*)
pauseRawSound( )	Pauses stream played through *playRawSound*: pauseRawSound (*DinInstance*)
playRaw( )	Plays the list of files through raw sound as one stream. Returns sound channel: set *soundChan* = playRaw (*DinInstance*, ¬ 　　　　[*file1, file2, ...*], "aif" | "wav")
playRegular( )	Plays sound through *playSound* mechanism. Returns sound channel: set *soundChan* = playRegular (*DinInstance*, ¬ 　　*soundFileName*, "aif" | "wav")
setSoundTime( )	Sets stream to specified time (in milliseconds): setSoundTime(*DinInstance, time*)
stopSound( )	Stops stream played through *playSound* or *playRawSound*: stopSound (*DinInstance*)
stopSoundInChan( )	Stops sound in *soundChan*. Returns current time: set *currentTime* = stopSoundInChan(*soundChan*)

Detecting the Sound Card at Runtime

All Macintosh models should include sound capabilities, but not all Windows PCs do. There are several techniques of varying reliability to detect whether a sound card is installed.

You can try playing a sound and then checking its status. For example, you might play a sound via *puppetSound* (remember to trigger it using *updateStage*) and then check whether *soundBusy()* returns TRUE for that channel. You can use a dummy sound containing silence for this test. Make it long enough to give you a chance to check it before it terminates.

Under Windows, you can use *mci* commands as follows:

```
mci "capability waveaudio can play"
set soundCardInstalled = the result
```

But it has been reported that some Windows 3.1 machines return TRUE as the result even though they do not have sound cards installed. Furthermore, if the MCI drivers are not properly installed (as is common under Windows 3.1), the result will be FALSE even though the system may be sound-capable.

For the highest accuracy, use the Buddy API Xtra's *baSoundInstalled()* method to check for a sound card, or perform a combination of these checks.

MIDI and MCI Device Control

There are a number of ways to play MIDI sounds under Director. The Beatnik Xtra will play MIDI files (and MOD as well).

QuickTime 3 Pro will import a MID file and convert it to a *#midi* track in a Quick-Time 3 movie. Any such QT3 movie can be played in D6.5 or D7 via the QT3 Asset Xtra (also requires the QuickTime Musical Instruments extension).

Allegedly, RMI and MID files can be imported as OLE cast members under Windows and played with the MIDI OLE controller.

The Yamaha MIDI Xtra plays back MID files under Windows.

Windows sound cards have a separate MIDI port (configured via the Multimedia Control Panel), which should be independent of the DirectSound/WaveOut device discussed earlier. However, the Yamaha MIDI Xtra will lock out Director sounds. As long as the software synthesizer device is open (even if *soundBusy()* returns FALSE), Director can't play sounds via *puppetSound*, for example. Wait for a second (either via Lingo or via extra frames in the Score) after closing the software synthesizer to allow the sound card to switch sound drivers before playing *puppetSounds*.

MIDI files can be played under Windows via appropriate MCI calls. Playing MIDI via MCI is covered in the otherwise outdated "Windows 3.1 Multimedia" once published by QUE, or search Macromedia's TechNotes for the words "MCI" and "MIDI."

You can also use *mci* commands to control WAVE files under Windows (but Director commands won't affect it; for example, *the soundLevel* and *volume of sound* commands won't affect its volume).

Other sound formats

The MOD sound format was designed to store music for video games, especially background music, but is not supported by Director. The MOD Hypercard XCMDs work in D5. In D6 and D7, use the Beatnik Xtra to play MOD files and also RMF (Rich Music Format) files, which are very compact.

Enhanced CDs and RedBook Audio

Director is the dominant application used to create so-called *Enhanced CDs* that combine music and multimedia. *RedBook* is the standard format used for music CDs that are commonly played in home stereo systems. Enhanced CDs (ECDs) known variously or formerly as "CD Extra" or "CD Plus," combine RedBook audio with a separate computer-only (data) session on the same physical disc.

Most CD-ROM burning software, such as Toast, can create Enhanced CDs. Various hardware and software issues ensued before the preferred Enhanced CD format was ironed out a few years ago. The favored format is currently "Stamped Multi-session" that conforms to the so-called BlueBook specification, and replaces older approaches such as "Track-Zero."

Cinram (*http://www.cinram.com*) has detailed white papers available on the various CD formats and specifications, including RedBook and BlueBook.

> Director can access the RedBook session (via an appropriate Xtra) or the multimedia (data) session, but not both simultaneously.

To access the RedBook audio from within Director requires an Xtra or MCI commands under Windows. To ensure smooth performance, you should not attempt to load multimedia content and play RedBook audio simultaneously or in rapid succession. Here are some possible alternatives:

Load multimedia content into RAM

If you have sufficient RAM to preload your multimedia content, it can play back from RAM while the RedBook audio is accessed off the CD. The upper limit for RAM playback is probably about 5 to 10 MB.

Load multimedia content onto hard drive

If the multimedia content is copied to the hard drive, it will not conflict with the attempt to read the RedBook audio from the CD. That said, users don't want large presentations loaded on their hard drive. Keep the content under 20 MB or (preferably) 10 MB. Copying 50 MB of content to someone's hard drive borders on the offensive.

Play RedBook audio at limited times

Playing RedBook audio throughout your entire presentation might require that the entire presentation to be preloaded or copied to the hard disk. Instead, play RedBook audio only within a small portion of Projector, perhaps via a single jukebox-like interface that can be loaded into RAM. If the remainder of the multimedia content does not require RedBook audio, it can be streamed from the CD as needed.

Use limited non-RedBook Audio

To simulate RedBook audio being played concurrently with your multimedia content, you can duplicate one or more RedBook tracks as typical Director WAVE or AIFF files on the multimedia session. Most computers don't do justice to CD-quality audio, so you can use 16-bit, 22 kHz, mono tracks or even SWA to save space. You may wish to provide alternate bonus tracks or even music videos instead of mere duplicates of the RedBook tracks available on the album.

Use a caching Xtra

LRU Cache Xtra (*http://www.mca.com/newumg/lrucache.html*) is designed for making Enhanced CDs. It caches parts of your program so you don't have to copy it to the hard drive.

To calculate how much room will be available on the CD for multimedia content, subtract the size of the RedBook audio from the CD's capacity.

CD-quality audio occupies 176 K/sec or about 10.3 MB per minute. For example, 55 minutes of RedBook audio would require 567 MB of CD-ROM space, leaving about 100 MB for multimedia. The capacity of CD-ROMs vary from about 650 to 720, depending on the format, manufacturer, and CD-burning software. (See *http://www.cinram.com* for more information.)

ECD resources

Refer to the following ECD resources in addition to the LRU Cache Xtra mentioned earlier.

CD Pro Xtra (free Xtra plays RedBook Audio cross-platform and replaces ECD Control and ECD File):

> *http://www.penworks.com*

Macromedia ECD Control and ECD File XObjects (obsolete toolkit that plays RedBook audio and optionally copies files to hard drive):

> *http://www.macromedia.com/*

ECD mailing list (and links to FAQs):

> *http://www.turntable.com/ecd/*

ECD support web site (includes a database of enhanced CDs):

> *http://www.musicfan.com/ecd/making.html*

Apple Interactive Music Toolkit:

> *http://www.apple.com*

Troubleshooting Sound Problems

If your sound problem is widespread and not exclusive to a particular platform or configuration, then it can usually be addressed by restructuring your Lingo. Unfortunately, many sound problems are configuration-specific, especially under Windows. If the problem occurs under Windows, but not on the Macintosh, refer to the platform-specific caveats under "Sound Mixing Under Windows" earlier in this chapter and in Table 15-1.

Windows sound issues often depend on the sound card or sound driver. Conflicts with RSX and DirectSound are also sometimes reported. When in doubt, obtain the latest device driver for your sound card and the latest versions of RSX and Direct-Sound if you are using them. In all cases, you should perform compatibility testing on a variety of sound cards with various software installed (with and without RSX and DirectSound). Windows laptops tend to have nonstandard sound cards. Obtain the latest drivers and test on any laptops you are specifically targeting (as for a sales presentation).

Your *ReadMe* file should instruct your Windows users to update their sound card drivers (and RSX and DirectSound if applicable) if they encounter problems.

Sounds may skip during transitions or other processor- or disk-intensive activities. Either preload the sounds or avoid too much concurrent activity, such as loading or streaming other media. Refer to the distinctions between internal and external in Chapter 4 for additional insights.

Here are some common problems that are not specific to a given sound card:

Sounds play in authoring mode, but not in a Projector
> You have most likely omitted the necessary Xtras. See "Xtras needed to play external sounds in Director 6 and 7" earlier in this chapter. You may also have failed to include the external sound files (AIFF, WAVE, or SWA) required by *sound playFile* or linked cast members.

Director asks, "Where is xxxx?"
> You must include external sounds files in the same relative position to your Projector or Director movie as they were during authoring.

Sounds can't be heard at all
> Check *the soundLevel* and *soundEnabled* properties and the volume for the particular item(s) of interest. See Table 15-12. Check the speakers by playing a test sound in the Windows Sound Control Panel.

Sounds drop out in somewhat arbitrary fashion
> In low-memory situations, Director drop outs the sound first. Reduce and optimize memory usage as described in Chapter 9, *Memory and Performance*.

Sound plays too late, particularly under Windows
> If using *puppetSounds*, issue an *updateStage* command to trigger the sound. Playing multiple sounds under Windows introduces a delay (see "Sound mixing latency" earlier in this chapter). Trigger sounds earlier in the Score or premix the audio into one sound using a sound editor.

Sound synchronization is not accurate
> Sound synchronization in Director's Score is never guaranteed, especially when mixing multiple sounds under Windows. Use cue points for improved synchronization and ensure that they are located at the proper points within the audio file (build in some lead time if necessary). Use an audio track in a digital video file for optimal synchronization.

Sounds pop and click or make screeching noises
> Use a clean audio source. Corrupt audio will sound like static or glass shattering and must be replaced or recompressed. Include about 100 to 500 milliseconds of silence at the beginning and end of sounds to reduce popping. RSX and/or DirectSound may also cause popping.

Very short sounds don't play under Windows
> Sounds shorter than 250 milliseconds (1/4 second) may not play at all. Add at least 50 milliseconds of silence to the beginning of the sound and pad the end with some silence if the sound is very short.

Problems playing both QT-based and Director-based sounds simultaneously
> Playing both QuickTime audio and Director audio is not reliably supported under Windows. See "Sound Mixing Under Windows" earlier in this chapter.

Problems switching between QT-based and Director-based sounds
> Make sure that all Director sounds are stopped using *sound stop*, *sound close*, and *puppetSound 0* before playing a QT sound. Ensure that QT sound is stopped by setting *the movieRate of sprite* to 0 or setting *the sound of member* to FALSE before playing a non-QT sound. Allow Director to release the sound device by setting *the soundKeepDevice* to FALSE.

A digital video's audio can't be heard even though no other sounds are playing
Ensure that the video contains an audio track and that *the sound of member* is TRUE and *the volume of sprite* is 255. Ensure that *the movieRate of sprite* is 1. Check *the soundLevel* property. Under Windows, you may need to stop all non-QuickTime sounds to free the sound card for QuickTime usage if not using QT3Mix.

Multiple audio tracks in a digital video cannot be heard
QuickTime 2 for Windows can't handle more than one audio track inside a single QuickTime movie. If necessary, separate the excess audio tracks into distinct audio-only QT movies. QuickTime 3 should handle multiple tracks within a single QuickTime movie and multiple QuickTime movies with separate audio tracks.

Sounds play at the wrong pitch (chipmunk-like or very low-pitched)
If using a non-standard rate, such as 15 KHz, Director will resample audio to the closest rate that the sound card supports. Use the standard Windows sampling rates: 11.025, 22.050, or 44.100 kHz.

Last few seconds of SWA or MP3 don't play
An SWA won't play the final few seconds of its sound if there is a cue point at the very end of the file. Use an alternate method for timing near the end of an SWA stream, such as checking *the currentTime of sprite* manually. The last few seconds of an MP3 file won't play in D7.

Can't import AIFF, WAVE, or SWA files
The MIX Services and Sound Import Export Xtras are needed to import sound files both during authoring and at runtime. Director won't import some compressed WAVE files, depending on the type of compression.

Tempo channel Wait setting interferes with interactivity
In Director 5, the Tempo channel locked out interactivity. In Director 6, using the *Wait for Cue Point* option may prevent Custom Buttons from behaving as expected. In either case, use Lingo alternatives to the Tempo channel, such as manually checking *soundBusy()* or waiting for *cuePassed* events as shown in Examples 15-4 and 15-6.

Exported QT or AVI files missing sounds
Sound tracks are often omitted during QuickTime export. Even if exported successfully, Director sometimes creates an excessive number of separate audio tracks in the QuickTime movie. Add the sound track to the exported digital video with a separate QuickTime editing application.

Sound Editing Applications and Utilities

Many applications can be used to create Director-ready sound files in either AIFF or WAVE format. SWA files can be created via SoundEdit, Peak LE, or Director for Windows.

SoundEdit is made by Macromedia and is included with Director 6 Multimedia Studio for the Macintosh (see also the SoundEdit Automator and SWAtomator utilities that come with it):

http://www.macromedia.com/support/soundedit/

Peak LE is included with the Director 7 Multimedia Studio for the Macintosh. The full version is sold by Bias Inc., which also sells Sound Designer:

http://www.bias-inc.com

Sound Forge XP (included with Director Multimedia Studio for Windows) is made by Sonic Foundry:

http://www.sfoundry.com

Cool Edit 96 shareware and professional versions (Windows only):

http://www.syntrillium.com

BarbaBatch by MacSourcery (Mac only) converts batches of sounds between various formats:

http://www.macsourcery.com/web/BarbaBatch/barbabatch.html

CHAPTER 16

Digital Video

Director is not a video editing tool. Although you can make minor edits to DV files within Director, you will ordinarily create your DV files in an external application such as Adobe Premiere and then import them into Director. See "Applications and Tools" later in this chapter and *http://www.zeusprod.com/nutshell/dvtools.html* for additional information on external digital-video related applications.

Digital Video in Director

The term "movie" is used to indicate Director movies (DIR files), QuickTime movies (MOV files), Video for Windows movies (AVI files), and also Movies-in-a-Window. My use of the word "movie" in this chapter should be clear from context, but be explicit when asking for technical assistance.

AVI is a file format that is supported by Video for Windows (VFW), or its successors, ActiveMovie and DirectShow. Director supports only the Video for Windows API. The DirectMedia Xtra (*http://tbaiana.com*) can take advantage of DirectShow. This chapter focuses primarily on QuickTime, although most of it applies to AVI files as well. For information on AVI, VFW, and ActiveMovie, see *http://www.mmii.com/directorhelp/avi01.htm* and also *http://camars.kaist.ac.kr/~jaewon/special/avi/avi.html*.

As of February 1999, QT4 has not yet shipped. There are no major architectural changes between QT3 and QT4 on either platform, so D7 should work with QT4 using the QT3 Asset Xtra, as it does with QT3.

Digital Video Cast Members

Director supports QuickTime on the Macintosh and both QuickTime for Windows (QTW) and Audio Video Interleave (AVI) under Windows, referred to collectively as digital video (DV). The QuickTime 3 Asset Xtra adds QuickTime 3 (QT3) support to Director 6.5 and 7 on both Macintosh and Windows. Director 7 supports QT3 and QT4, but no longer supports QT2.x. Versions prior to Director 6.5 supported QT 2.x or earlier only.

Note that there are two distinct types of DV cast members: old *#digitalVideo* members and newer *#quickTimeMedia* members. DV files imported via `File ➤ Import` create *#digitalVideo* (QT2 or AVI) members in D6. DV files inserted via `Insert ➤ Media Element ➤ QuickTime 3` or via `File ➤ Import` in D7 ordinarily create *#quickTimeMedia* (QT3) members (but AVI files under Windows can be imported as either *#digitalVideo* or *#quickTimeMedia* members in D7). All DV files are always externally linked.

DV cast members use the first frame of the external video file as their thumbnail, and are distinguished by a small video camera or QuickTime 3 icon as shown in Figure 4-3.

Sprites in the Score and Playback on the Stage

DV sprites can be placed in any sprite channel. When Director is not running, the first video frame of the DV cast member is displayed on the Stage, even if the DV sprite spans multiple Score frames. The DV sprite will not update or play until the Score's playback head is moving.

 A DV sprite will play at the frame rate intrinsic to the digital video file (see Example 16-4) unless overridden by the commands in Tables 16-12 and 16-13. A video's playback rate is not affected by the Tempo channel's frame rate setting or the *puppetTempo* command.

When a DV sprite is tweened out over multiple Score frames, one Score frame will *not* correspond to one frame of the digital video. See Chapter 1, *How Director Works*, for a discussion of Director's frame-based animation model, and Chapter 3, *The Score and Animation*, for details on the Tempo channel.

To wait for a DV sprite to reach a particular cue point, use the Tempo channel's *Wait for Cue Point* option. Indicate the channel containing the DV sprite of interest and choose from the list of available cue points within the DV, or {Next} or {End}. Use Lingo instead for more flexible and powerful control of DV sprites (see Tables 16-13 and 16-16).

When a DV sprite is played direct-to-Stage, it appears in the foremost paint layer, using the Copy ink effect, and leaves trails. Director does not automatically refresh the Stage area within the DV sprite's bounding rectangle. You must force a refresh by moving a non-DV sprite over the affected area, by performing a transition, or using *set the stageColor = the stageColor*.

Compression and Decompression (Codecs)

The *uncompressed* size of a single video track, in bytes, can be calculated as:

```
(the width of member) × (the height of member) ×
(bits per pixel/8) × frames per second × duration in seconds
```

This calculation does not include other tracks in a digital video file, such as secondary video tracks, multiple sound tracks, text tracks, and so on. For example, uncompressed CD-quality audio adds 176 K/sec to a digital video's data rate.

Because uncompressed video requires too much bandwidth, video is usually compressed with an appropriate algorithm called a *codec* (COmpressor-DECompressor). The DV file's *compressed* data rate is determined by the nature of the source material and the chosen codec, output file's dimensions, bit-depth, frame rate, keyframe interval, and output quality (lossless or lossy).

Use Media Cleaner Pro (*http://www.terran-int.com*) or a similar utility to compress your video. A typical compression ratio might be 9:1 for Cinepak, 50:1 for Sorenson, and possibly 100:1 for animation compression assuming clean source. QuickTime also supports compressed sound tracks, but the audio bandwidth is usually minor compared to the video bandwidth.

The MPEG and DirectMedia Xtras (*http://ww.tbaiana.com*) play back MPEG-1 and MPEG-2 compressed video.

A full discussion of codecs is beyond the scope of this book. See the information at *http://www.zeusprod.com/quicktime/codecs.html* for a list of codecs supported by QT2 and QT3 and a comparison of different codecs.

If you are using a proprietary Xtra, codec, or engine for video playback, contact the manufacturer for licensing and distribution issues.

Digital Video Performance

The CPU, available RAM, drive performance, video card, VRAM, video driver, OS version, QuickTime or Video for Windows version, monitor depth, and software configuration all affect digital video performance.

DV data is streamed from disk as it is played, enabling a large file to be played without requiring excessive RAM (although SW7 and QT3 don't support Internet streaming, QT4 might). The video and audio tracks are interleaved in a DV file, so that they can be read in quick succession as time passes. (Improper interleaving of audio and video severely degrade DV playback.) If the disk's transfer rate cannot keep up with the video file's data rate, QuickTime or Video for Windows will skip video data to maintain sound synchronization, unless the *Play Every Frame (No Sound)* option is set. This will cause the video to appear jerky and in extreme cases may cause the audio to drop out.

All else being equal, DV performance is affected primarily by its data rate.

A video's *average* data rate (in KB/second) can be determined by:

```
(size of the external data file in KB) ×
float(the duration of member) / (the digitalVideoTimeScale)
```

(See Example 4-6, which determines the size of an external file.) A video's *peak* data rate is sometimes of more concern, although the peak data rate should not be significantly higher than the average data rate if the movie is properly prepared. Table 9-3 lists acceptable video data rates for various speed CD-ROM drives.

Use Adobe Premiere or a similar utility to determine a movie's peak data rate or detect improper interleaving.

Playing DV sprites non-direct-to-Stage or stretching DV sprites in increments other than 100% is *very* slow. Avoid moving a video sprite while it is playing—use a still frame from the video when performing animations or transitions. Place DV sprites at an offset that is evenly divisible by 8 relative to the upper left of the monitor for improved performance. Prior to D7, the upper-left coordinate of the Stage should always be an even multiple of 8, so position your sprite such that its upper-left edge is at an offset of 160 pixels (for example), not 159 pixels. In D7, the Stage is no longer constrained to offsets that are multiples of 8, but you should position the Stage at an even multiple anyway. The width and height of the external DV file (and the DV sprite if stretched) should also be evenly divisible by 8, such as 320×240 pixels.

Even if a DV file performs adequately in MoviePlayer, it may lag within Director due to additional overhead or suboptimal Score or Lingo techniques. Minimize other activities, such as loading or animating large cast members or playing additional sounds or video while playing a DV sprite. If applicable, interleave your audio and video within a single DV file, rather than attempting to play separate audio and video files simultaneously. Test DV performance early in the design process within a realistic Director prototype (not simply in isolation) on all supported platforms.

Preloading digital video

The preLoad of member property (equivalent to the *Enable Preload* option in the DV Properties dialog box) determines whether a digital video's data is preloaded into RAM before it is played. The amount of RAM used for preloading is set by *the preLoadRAM* (which is a system-wide property, not a cast member property).

I'm not convinced that preloading DV (often called *pre-rolling*) has ever worked correctly in Director or that it would be terribly useful if it did. If the DV data rate is sufficiently low, there should be no need to preload the data; it should be provided as needed on the fly. Preloading is only of practical use for very small videos that must play smoothly with no frames dropped, such as a simulated visual transition or animation.

Preloading entire videos can cause a long delay and consume excessive RAM. Preloading a portion of a video may result in a noticeable "hiccup" when the preloaded data runs out. In most cases, you are better off preloading other assets instead. For example, to avoid accessing a CD-ROM in two places at once, preload any animation or audio, and stream the video from disk as usual.

 If *the preLoad of member* is TRUE, the default setting for *the preLoadRAM* (0) uses all available memory for preloading.

If you insist on preloading digital video, you can specify a fixed amount of RAM, such as 2 MB:

```
set the preLoadRAM = 2 * 1024 * 1024 -- 2 MB
```

Or use a percentage of *the freeBlock*, such as:

```
set the preLoadRAM = 0.5 * the freeBlock
```

To avoid the characteristic hiccupping of a QT movie when it first starts, include about a 0.5 second lead-in to your video track (perhaps some extra black frames followed by a dissolve). A second technique is to load the cast member header before the video data is needed. Set *the pausedAtStart of member* to TRUE and use *the preLoad member* command to preload the header information (or place the DV sprite off-Stage before the frame in which it is needed). Set *the movieRate of sprite* to 1 to start the video in the following frame of the Score. If hiccupping remains evident, add a few extra Score frames between the frame in which the video sprite first occurs and the frame in which you start it playing.

The purgePriority of member property (equivalent to the *Unload* option in the *DV Properties* dialog box) is largely irrelevant for DV cast members, because their data is always unloaded immediately after playback. Only the header information (several hundred bytes) is unloaded based on this property.

QuickTime 2, QuickTime 3, and QuickTime 3 Pro

Prior to QuickTime 3, the latest Macintosh release was QT 2.5 and the latest Windows release was QTW 2.1.2 (referred to here collectively as *QT2*). Director 6.5 and earlier for both Macintosh and Windows support QT2 (as long as the system software is installed) without requiring any Xtras.

The QuickTime 3 Asset Xtra (see Table 16-3) is required to use QT3 (*#quickTime-Media*) members in D6.5 and D7. Director 6.0.x does not support QT3.

Apple's QT3 Extension supports all Macintoshes, but Macromedia's QT3 Xtra requires a PowerMac (or G3). On the Macintosh, the QT3 extension replaces QT2.x entirely; the two versions can not cohabitate. In D6.x, existing Macintosh QT2-style (*#digitalVideo*) cast members will work whether QT2 or QT3 is installed. The Macintosh QT3 System Extension and QT3 Xtra add support for QT3-specific features, such as importing QTVR, QD3D, and AVI files.

 Director 7 supports only QT3 members. QT2-style *#digitalVideo* members are converted to *#quickTimeMedia* members when updating DIR files from D6 to D7.

QTW3 requires Windows 95/98/NT and does not support Windows 3.1. Windows 95/98/NT support *simultaneous* installation of up to 3 versions of QTW—16-bit and 32-bit versions of QTW2, plus the 32-bit QTW3. QTW3 has a completely new architecture and is not backward-compatible with QTW2 cast members under Windows. Therefore, older *#digitalVideo* cast members won't play unless QTW2 is installed, regardless of whether QTW3 is installed. Windows 3.1 supports only the older 16-bit version of QuickTime for Windows (QTW 2.1.2). As on the Macintosh, D7 for

Windows supports only QT3 cast members, and the *#digitalVideo* type is supported only for AVI files in D7.

Table 16-1 lists the versions of QT supported on each platform for Director 6.5 and Shockwave 6.0.1. D7 and SW7 support only QT3 and D6.0 supports only QT2.

Table 16-1: Supported QuickTime Versions in D6.5

Platform	Supported QT Versions in D6.5	D6.X #digitalVideo Members Require	D6.5 and D7 #quickTimeMedia Members Require
Macintosh 68K	QT2 or QT3	QT2 or QT3	Never supported
PowerMac/G3	QT2 or QT3	QT2 or QT3	QT3 and QT3 Xtra
Windows 3.1	16-bit QTW2 only	QTW2	Never supported
Windows 95/98/NT	16-bit QTW2, 32-bit QTW2, QTW3 concurrently installed	16-bit or 32-bit QTW2 matching Projector	QTW3 and QT3 Xtra
Shockwave movie	QT2 (SW6); QT3 (SW7)	SW6[1]	QT3 and QT3 Xtra[1]
Browser outside Shockwave	QT2 and QT3	QT2 browser plug-in	QT3 browser plug-in[2]

[1] Shockwave 6 does not require an Xtra or plug-in to play QT2 video. It requires the same QT system software as is needed by a Projector on that platform. Likewise, QT3-style cast members require the same Xtras as Projectors, but placed in the Shockwave *Xtras* folder. QuickTime video doesn't stream in Shockwave. It must be downloaded in its entirety first.
[2] The QuickTime 3 browser plug-in is installed by the QT3 Installer from Apple and also comes with the major browsers.

Differences in QT2 and QT3 capabilities

QT3 cast members support new features in Director, including:

- Many new file formats, including QTVR 2.0, QD3D, AVI, and GIF.

- New codecs, most notably the Sorenson codec (*http://www.s-vision.com*) which yields better compression than Cinepak in most cases.

- Loop points within QuickTime media.

- A 1-bit mask cast member can be used as a non-rectangular mask for direct-to-Stage video.

- Ability to rotate, scale, and offset QuickTime media within a sprite's bounding rectangle.

- Non direct-to-Stage playback under Windows 95/98/NT in addition to the Macintosh (although it's not recommended, for performance reasons).

- Under Windows, Director-based and QT-based sounds can be mixed if the system is properly configured. See "Sound Mixing Under Windows" in Chapter 15.

- QT3 itself offers special effects and transitions within QT movies. These must be added in a third-party video editor such as Adobe Premiere before the video is inserted into Director's cast.

Differences in QT2 and QT3 usage in Director

You must use QT2 cast members to retain support for Windows 3.1 and 68K Macintoshes, as neither are supported by the QT3 Xtra.

To take full advantage of QT3 on both platforms, QT3 cast members must be imported via Insert ► Media Element ► QuickTime 3, instead of imported via File ► Import. Unlike File ► Import, Director 6.5's Insert function hard codes the path to external files. Manually substitute in the @ relative path operator for the current folder in the *QT3 Cast Member Properties* dialog box. See Chapter 4, *CastLibs, Cast Members, and Sprites*.

In D7, File ► Import will import QT3 members on both platforms. QT3 uses the *mRate, mTime,* and *volumeLevel of sprite* properties instead of the *movieRate, movieTime,* and *volume of sprite* properties. Throughout this chapter, when I refer to the *movieTime* and *movieRate* properties, it is implicit that you should use *the mTime of sprite* and *mRate of sprite* properties for QT3 sprites in D6.5.

QT3 can read QT2 movie files, but not vice versa. However, some QT2 movies may display artifacts when played with QT3. Resave files in QT3 format with the QT3 Movie Player for best results.

Under Windows, QTW3 is much more processor-intensive; it may drop audio and video during playback on machines on which QTW 2.1.2 played well, such as Pentiums below 133 MHz. The performance hit occurs both inside Director and in the standalone MoviePlayer. QTW3 performs noticeably better under Windows if DirectX is installed/enabled. DirectX can be obtained online from *http://www.microsoft.com/directx.*

Determining the Installed Digital Video Software

Ideally, you will include an installer that guarantees that the necessary version(s) of QuickTime or Video For Windows are installed. Regardless, you should check for the presence of the required DV software via Lingo and warn the user or run an installer if it is not available.

Detecting Video for Windows

Example 16-1 detects the presence of Video for Windows (VFW) and its version. It returns EMPTY is VFW is not installed and returns a text string containing the version, such as "4.0.95", if VFW is installed.

Example 16-1: Checking the VFW Version

```
on getVFWversion
  if the videoForWindowsPresent then
    MCI "open AVIVIDEO alias filename.avi"
    MCI "info filename.avi version"
    return the result
  else
      return EMPTY
  end if
end getVFWversion
```

As not all Windows system are MCI-enabled, you can also use the Buddy API Xtra's *baVersion()* method:

```
put baVersion("vfw")
-- "4.0.95"
```

Detecting QuickTime 2 and QuickTime 3

To detect the QuickTime's version and presence, use the *quickTimeVersion()* method (requires the QT3 Asset Xtra) and *the quickTimePresent* property. These indicators vary markedly across platforms and in D7, as shown in Example 16-2 and Table 16-2.

The number of digits displayed of the value return from *quickTimeVersion()* depends on *the floatPrecision.*

Example 16-2 sets two separate global variables: *gHasQT3*, indicating whether QT3 is installed; and *gHasQT2*, indicating whether QT2 (or prior) is installed—and is necessary only in D6.5. It checks for the presence of the QT3 Xtra before calling *quickTimeVersion()*. See the following sections for an explanation of its pretzel-like contortions. In D7, the QT2 is never supported and *the quickTimePresent* indicates whether QT3 is installed.

Example 16-2: Checking for QT2 and QT3 Presence in D6.5

```
on checkQTversions
  global gHasQT2, gHasQT3
  if integer (char 1 of the productVersion) >= 7 then
    set gHasQT3 = the quickTimePresent
    set gHasQT2 = FALSE
    exit
  endif
  --Remainder of code pertains to D6.5
  if the platform contains "Windows" then
    -- Windows may have both QT2 and QT3!
    set gHasQT3 = (quickTime3check() >= 3.0)
    set gHasQT2 = the quickTimePresent
  else
    -- Macintosh has only one version of QT installed
    if the quickTimePresent then
      set gHasQT3 = (quickTime3check() >= 3.0)
      set gHasQT2 = not (gHasQT3)
    else
      set gHasQT3 = FALSE
      set gHasQT2 = FALSE
    end if
  end if
end checkQTversions

on quickTime3check
  -- This checks whether the QT3 Xtra is installed
  -- before attempting to call quickTimeVersion()
  repeat with x = 1 to the number of Xtras
    if the name of xtra x = "QuickTimeSupport" then
```

Example 16-2: Checking for QT2 and QT3 Presence in D6.5 (continued)

```
      return quickTimeVersion()
    end if
  end repeat
  if the quickTimePresent then
    -- Assumes QT 2.x is installed if pre-QT3 version is found
    return 2.0
  else
    return 0
  end if
end
```

To determine the installed browser QT plug-in, you must use JavaScript.

Detecting QuickTime 2 or QuickTime 3 on the Macintosh

In D6 and earlier versions on the Macintosh, *the quickTimePresent* indicates whether any version of the QuickTime Extension (plus the QuickTime PowerPlug on PowerPCs) is installed in the *System:Extensions* folder. In D7, it returns TRUE only if QT3 or higher is installed.

The *quickTimeVersion()* function returns the QT version if QT3 or higher is installed. If not, *quickTimeVersion()* returns a –2147483648 error during authoring. Furthermore, if QT3 or higher is not installed, the QT3 Asset Xtra for Projectors won't load, and calling *quickTimeVersion()* causes a "Handler not defined" error.

If the QuickTime Extension but not the QuickTime PowerPlug is installed, MoviePlayer will still function, but Director will not allow you to import, insert, or open QT cast members. When changes are made to the QuickTime Extensions, the Macintosh must be rebooted before they take effect.

Unlike the *quickTimeVersion()* function on the Macintosh, the Buddy API Xtra's *baVersion()* method won't fail if QT3 is not installed:

```
put baVersion("qt")
-- "3.0"
```

Detecting QuickTime 2 and QuickTime 3 under Windows

In D6 and D6.5 under Windows, *the quickTimePresent* indicates whether the version of QTW2 (16-bit or 32-bit) matching the Projector is installed. (It looks for either *QTW.DLL* or *QTW32.DLL* in the *Windows\System* folder.) In D7, *the quickTimePresent* is TRUE only if QTW3 is installed. *QuickTimeVersion()* checks for the necessary QTW components, including *QuickTime.qts* in the *Windows\System* folder.

You must restart Director, but not Windows, to make it recognize any changes to the QuickTime installation. The QTW3 uninstaller provided by Apple unregisters the QTW3 components, but deletes only those items in the *C:\Program Files\QuickTime* folder, not the actual QTW3 software drivers (specifically *Quick-Time.qts*) in the *Windows\System* folder. Therefore, even after an uninstall, *quickTimeVersion()* will report that QTW3 is still installed. To perform a complete "uninstall," use the QTW3 uninstaller, then delete all the files listed at *http://www.zeusprod.com/quicktime/qtfiles.html*. (The QTW3 control panel doesn't include a list of installed component files as did QTW2.x.)

Digital Video

Table 16-2 explains testing *the quickTimePresent* and *quickTimeVersion()* under Windows.

Table 16-2: The QuickTimePresent and QuickTimeVersion()

Projector	16-bit QTW2	32-bit QTW2	QTW3	quickTimePresent		quickTimeVersion()[1]
				D6	D7	
16-bit		N/A	N/A	FALSE	N/A	Error[2]
16-bit	✓	N/A	N/A	TRUE	N/A	Error
32-bit	N/A			FALSE	FALSE	0.0000
32-bit	N/A	✓		TRUE	FALSE	2.0000,[3] 2.1200, etc.
32-bit	N/A		✓	FALSE	TRUE	3.0000, 3.0100, 3.0200
32-bit	N/A	✓	✓	TRUE	TRUE	3.0000, 3.0100, 3.0200

[1] The number of digits of the returned value displayed depends on *the floatPrecision*.
[2] The QuickTime Asset.X32 Xtra doesn't load when running a 16-bit projector under any version of Windows. There is no .X16 (16-bit) version.
[3] The *quickTimeVersion( )* method reports 2.000 for any versions of QTW prior to version 2.0.

Example 16-3 detects QTW2's presence and version. It returns EMPTY if QTW2 is not installed and returns a text string containing the version, such as "2.11", if QTW2 is installed. It does not recognize or check for QTW3.

Example 16-3: Checking the QTW2 Version

```
on getQTW2version
  MCI "open QTWVIDEO alias filename.mov"
  MCI "info filename.mov version"
  return the result
end getQTW2version
```

You can also use the Buddy API Xtra's *baVersion()* method to check the QTW2 and QTW3 versions separately. It returns a different string than the MCI call:

```
put baVersion("qt")
-- "2.1.1.50 Beta 1"
put baVersion("qt3")
-- "3.0.2"
```

The QuickTime 3 Asset Xtra

Table 16-3 lists the QT3 Xtras you'll need for authoring and distribution. The authoring-time QuickTime Asset Options version of the Xtra will prevent a Projector from launching; distribute the QuickTime Asset instead. Windows 3.1 and 68K are not supported by the QT3 Xtra. Director D6.5 or D7 is required when using the QT3 Xtras.

The QuickTime Asset Xtra shipped with Projectors will not load on PowerMacs unless QT3 is installed, causing an error when Director encounters movies using *#quickTimeMedia* cast members.

To avoid an error message, delete the QuickTime 3 Xtra from the list under Modify ➤ Movie ➤ Xtras before saving each movie using *#quickTimeMedia* members. Don't bundle the movie into the Projector. Check whether the Quick-Time 3 Xtra is available as shown in Example 16-2 before using a Director movie or castLib containing *#quickTimeMedia* members.

Table 16-3: QuickTime 3 Xtras

Projectors	Xtra Name
Power Macintosh Authoring	QuickTime Asset Options PPC (D6.5) QuickTime Asset Options (D7)
Power Macintosh Distribution (Projectors or Shockwave)	QuickTime Asset PPC (D6.5) QuickTime Asset (D7)
Windows 32-bit Authoring	QuickTime Asset Options.X32 (D6.5) QTAuth.X32 (D7) QTExport.X32 (D7)
Windows 32-bit Distribution (Projectors or Shockwave)	QuickTime Asset.X32 (D6.5) QT3Asset.X32 (D7)

The QT3 Xtra requires at least 15 MB allocated to Director on the PPC. Although Projectors seem to work with the default allocation (less than 7.5 MB), you should consider increasing it when using QT3.

The QT3 Asset Xtra can import many data types, including QTVR 2.0 and QD3D. QTVR 1.0 files may not work with the QT3 Asset Xtra. Update your QTVR files to QTVR 2.0 or higher. On the Macintosh, Macromedia recommends deleting all old versions of QTVR and QT-related extensions and doing a clean install of QT3.

In D6.5, the QT3 Asset Xtra does share CPU cycles with Director to allow sufficient time to animate other sprites while a QTVR sprite is playing direct-to-Stage. The D7 version of the Xtra is a bit friendlier.

The QT3 Asset Xtra provides new Lingo commands and properties, but all older digital video properties also work with media inserted as QuickTime 3 cast members. See *Show Me 6_5/QT3/qt3_showme.dir*, which comes with D6.5. Also see Macromedia's web site.

Note that QuickTime 3 itself implements many features that are not supported fully by Macromedia's QT3 Xtra.

Cross-Platform Digital Video Issues

QuickTime allows you to use a single QT movie (MOV) file on both Macintosh and Windows. To use QT2 movie files under Windows, simply flatten and de-fork them by saving them with the *Self-Contained* and *Playable on non-Apple Computers* options with MoviePlayer (other DV editing software has similar options). This collects all DV data into a single file and removes the resource fork (such files will still play on the Macintosh). See Macromedia TechNote #12113, "Supported Digital Video Formats." All QT3 movies are cross-platform by design, and for performance reasons they should be self-contained.

There are some substantial platform differences pertaining to DV, as shown in Table 16-4. See Table 16-5 for more details on importing and exporting.

Table 16-4: Cross-Platform Digital Video Differences

Feature	Macintosh	Windows
Video formats for import	QT2 (.MOV, 'MooV'); D6.5 or later imports QT3, VFW (.AVI, 'VfW '),[1] and MPEG, .MPG ('MPEG').[2]	QTW2 (.MOV),[3] VFW (.AVI), QT3 Xtra (D6.5) imports QTW3 formats, but not MPEG.
Video formats for export	QT2 (prior to D7); QT3 (D7 or later).	VFW (.AVI).
Direct-to-Stage video	Optional for QT2 and QT3.	Optional for VFW and QTW3. Mandatory for QTW2.
Standard video controller	Optional for QT2 and QT3.	Optional for QTW, not supported for AVI files.
QuickTime movie format	Allows file dependencies and resource fork.	QT2 movies must be flattened and de-forked. QT3 allows file dependencies.
QuickTime software	Extension is included with Mac OS, but can be disabled.	Must install QTW version to match Projector. (16-bit or 32-bit). D7 requires QTW3 (32-bit).
the timeScale of member property	Defaults to 600 for QuickTime.	Defaults to 30 for QTW and to 60 for VFW.
Multiple audio track support	Yes for QT2 and QT3.	No for AVI and QTW2; yes for QTW3.
Simultaneous Director and DV audio	Yes.	Not always. See "Sound Mixing under Windows" in Chapter 15.
Different custom palettes for multiple digital videos	QT2 requires Fix Palette Xobject to reset palette between movies. QT3 does not.	Does not require any special accommodations.

[1] An AVI (digitalVideoType #videoForWindows) cast member imported via D6 for Windows will be converted to a QT cast member (digitalVideoType #quickTime) on the Macintosh if QT3 is installed. In D7, an AVI member will be converted to a #quickTimeMedia member on the Macintosh if QT3 is installed. If QT2.x only is installed, Director will issue a –2048 error when trying to use the AVI member on the Macintosh.
[2] MPEG import requires the QuickTime MPEG extension.
[3] QT2 files must be "flattened and deforked" for Windows playback.

Once you have settled on your DV format, bear in mind:

- Non-direct-to-Stage video is not always cross-platform-compatible (nor recommended). See Table 16-7.

- The same video with the same palette may appear slightly darker under Windows than on the Macintosh. Test under both platforms to avoid problems.

- Video performance is rarely the same on different machines and different platforms. Test on a variety of machines, including ones with different video cards, to detect any problems.

- Proprietary video playback schemes may involve a runtime royalty fee, may not be cross-platform, and may not work as advertised.

- Video for Windows is not fully supported on the Macintosh (although AVI files can be played via QuickTime 3).

- Sound and transitions are not always exported when using QT export. Add the sound track to the exported digital video in a separate video editing tool. Add transitions in a separate tool such as Adobe Premiere.

Installation and Licensing Issues

QuickTime 3 can be be downloaded for free (*http://www.apple.com/quicktime*) and is also available for $10 on a CD.

The QT3 installer will create a folder named *QuickTime Folder* in the root of the System disk on the Macintosh, and named *C:\Program Files\QuickTime* under Windows. That folder includes the MoviePlayer and PictureViewer utilities and some sample files, but the QuickTime software itself is installed in the Macintosh *Extensions* folder or *C:\Windows\System* directory. See *http://www.zeusprod.com/quicktime/qtfiles.html* for a complete list of files and where they are installed.

The *Get QuickTime Pro* movie is a special advertisement that is copied to your desktop by the QT3 installer. It does not behave properly in Director. Use the *Sample* movie installed in the *QuickTime* folder if you need a test video to debug QT3 problems.

QT3 Pro is not a different version of QuickTime; it is an enhancement to QT3 that adds the ability to import and export multiple formats from MoviePlayer and PictureViewer. Upgrade to QT3 3 Pro ($30 per platform) via the *Get QuickTime Pro* demo movie, via the *Registration* option in the QuickTime 3 Control Panel, or at:

> *http://www.apple.com/quicktime/rights/*

Macintosh users usually have the QuickTime extension installed, but you should provide a QT3 installer if requiring QT3. Many but certainly not all Windows users have QTW installed, so you should license and distribute the Apple QTW installer (currently free). At least until QTW4 is released, Apple licenses both the QTW3 and older QTW2.1.2 installers.

You can install the older 16-bit QTW 2.1.2 under Windows 3.1. You can optionally QTW 2.1.2 in addition to QTW3 on Windows 95/98/NT systems.

If creating a custom installer for other components, have it launch the Apple QT installer. (Most commercial installers will check for specified files on disk or entries in the Windows Registry file to determine whether components need to be installed.)

A Macintosh must be rebooted after installing QT; Windows does not need to be rebooted, but you must restart Director or your Projector for it to recognize the updated QT installation. The QTW installer cannot install QTW while a Projector using QTW is running. Use zLaunch (*http://www.zeusprod.com/products/ zlaunch.html*) to quit and restart a Projector after QTW is installed. You *must* use the Apple QT3 Installer in its entirety if you intend to install any QT components. Apple's QT3 installer will check which versions of QuickTime are already installed, and install only what is needed.

When using AVI files, you may want to provide an installer. VFW is included with Windows 95, but some Windows 3.1 users may not have it. VFW's successors, ActiveMovie or DirectShow, are included with Win95 OSR2, Win98, and WinNT, so all of these can play AVI files. You can distribute the VFW installer from the Director 6 CD if necessary. The DirectMedia Xtra (*http://www.tbaiana.com*) will check if DirectShow is installed (see its *isDirectShowInstalled()* function).

QT2 or QT3 can be played in a browser without Shockwave if the user has the Netscape-compatible QT2 or QT3 plug-in installed (and the appropriate version of QT installed). Shockwave 6, like D6 Projectors, can play QT2 content without an Xtra, but QT3-specific content requires the QT3 Xtra (see Tables 16-1, 16-2, and 16-3).

Licensing

Apple licenses the basic QT installer for Macintosh and Windows for free, assuming the installer displays their *Get QuickTime Pro* advertisement, but you must fill out a licensing agreement. For an additional fee, you can distribute QT3 without the advertisement or even QT3 Pro, but there is rarely a need for this in Director.

The current QuickTime Licensing terms are available at:

> *http://gemma.apple.com/mkt/registering/swl/agreements.html*
> *http://developer.apple.com/mkt/registering/swl/qtannouncement.html*

To license the QT installer(s), download the PDF file:

> *http://developer.apple.com/mkt/registering/swl/agreements.html#QuickTime*

Print out the PDF file using Acrobat Reader, fill it out, and mail signed copies to:

> Apple Computer, Inc.
> Software Licensing M/S 198-SWL
> 2420 Ridgepoint Drive, Austin, TX 78754

Follow up an email to *sw.license@apple.com* or with a phone call to 800-793-9378 or 512-919-2645 and ask for an FTP address from which to download the file once they have received your contract. The licensed installer includes a *QTSETUP.INI* file that can customize the installation prompts somewhat.

User Interface Issues

DV sprites may affect your product design. Bear in mind the following:

- DV sprites are ordinarily played direct-to-Stage, which ignores any ink effects (Copy ink is used) and displays the DV sprite in front of all other sprites regardless of their sprite channel numbers.

- The cursor will flicker when it passes over a DV sprite. Either hide the cursor or tolerate the flicker.

- Transitions are very slow under Windows when a DV sprite is playing. Stop the DV sprite before performing a transition. Do not attempt to use transitions with other sprites while a DV sprite is playing; any transition will include the DV sprite's bounding rectangle, because a DV sprite is always changing. Either bring the other sprites in from off-Stage or imitate a transition with a series of cast members or by using a blend ink (see Example 13-5).

- DV sprites will play back using the custom palette in effect, but certain caveats apply. Refer to Chapter 13, *Graphics, Color, and Palettes,* for details on palette management.

Sound Issues

The Macintosh has multiple sound channels, so you can play audio tracks within QT files simultaneously with Director-based sounds (AIFF, WAVE, SWA, and internal sounds).

Windows has only one true sound channel, and QuickTime for Windows and Video for Windows seize it when playing audio tracks within DV files. This may prevent Director from playing Director-based sounds while a DV file with an audio track is playing. Director's MacroMix technology mixes Director-based sounds together to simulate multichannel audio, and it too seizes the sole Windows sound channel when it plays a sound.

Whichever component takes control of the sound channel first may lock out the other from playing sounds. D6.5 or D7 in conjunction with QT3 can sometimes mix QT-based and Director-based sounds simultaneously. See "Sound Mixing under Windows" in Chapter 15 for details on avoiding sound conflicts.

Digital Video Tools and Options

This section describes the digital video cast member properties and user interface options.

Video Playback and Editing Window

Use Director's Digital Video window, shown in Figure 16-1, to preview or perform simple edits on DV cast members. Don't confuse the Digital Video window with a DV sprite placed on the Stage, which does not have its own window, or with movies-in-a-window (MIAWs) which are Director files, not digital videos.

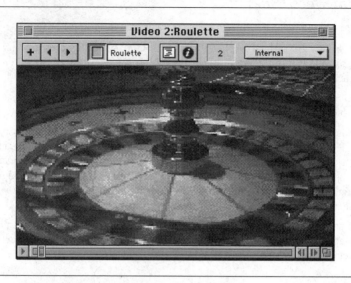

Figure 16-1: Digital Video playback window

The DV window contains the standard buttons common to all media editing windows (see Figure 2-1). It also includes the standard QT controller, which allows you to test videos and perform simple edits on QT cast members. The controller includes a volume slider if the QT movie has an audio track. The DV window does not display a standard controller for AVI cast members, which automatically play once through when they are viewed in the DV window. The D6 video window shows *#digitalVideo* members only. In D7, the Video window was renamed as the QuickTime window and shows *#quickTimeMedia* members only. D7 for Windows has a separate AVI Video window (accessible via Window ➤ AVI Video) for AVI (*#digitalVideo*) members.

Playback in the DV window does not obey the cast member property settings, such as *directToStage, crop, frameRate, center,* or *sound,* so it is not an accurate test of these attributes. Test these by placing a DV sprite on the Stage and running Director.

In D6, only QT2-style cast members imported via File ➤ Import appear in the DV window; QT3 Assets inserted via Insert ➤ Media Element ➤ QuickTime 3 include a preview in the QuickTime Xtra Properties dialog box only. In D7, the DV window supports QT3 members.

Table 16-5 summarizes digital video-related commands in the user interface including importing and exporting.

Table 16-5: Digital Video Interface Options

Action	Command
Edit or play a *#digitalVideo* member (D6) or a *#quickTimeMedia* member (D7) in the Video window	Choose Window ➤ Video.[1] Command-9 (Mac). Ctrl-9 (Windows). Double-click on a DV or QT3 cast member or sprite.
View or edit a *#digitalVideo* member's properties (D6) or a *#quickTimeMedia* member (D7)	Use the "i" button in the DV editing window or the Cast window. See Tables 2-8 and 4-8. Modify ➤ Cast Member ➤ Properties
View or edit a *#quickTimeMedia* member's properties in D6.5	Double-click the QT3 thumbnail in the Cast window. Click the *Options* button in the Xtra Cast Member Properties dialog box. Edit ➤ Edit Cast Member
Find *#digitalVideo* cast members (D6 and D7)	Edit ➤ Find ➤ Cast Member ➤ Type: Digital Video
Find *#quickTimeMedia* (QT3) cast members	Edit ➤ Find ➤ Cast Member ➤ Type: Xtra (includes all Xtra types in D6.5 and D7). Edit ➤ Find ➤ Cast Member ➤ Type: QuickTime 3 (D7).
Import *#digitalVideo* (QT2 or AVI) cast members (D6)	Drag and drop from desktop. File ➤ Import: ➤ Show: QuickTime (Mac) or Files of type: Video Clip (Windows).
Insert *#quickTimeMedia* (QT3) cast members	In D7, drag and drop from desktop. File ➤ Import ➤ QuickTime. Insert ➤ Media Element ➤ QuickTime 3 (D6.5 and D7) In D7, but not in D6.5, click the "i" button, then the Options... button, before clicking the *Browse* or *Internet* button or enter a fileName by hand.
Export QuickTime or AVI movies	File ➤ Export[2,3] Format: QuickTime Movie (Mac: D6, D7; Windows: D7 only) Format: Video for Windows (Windows only) Xtras ➤ QuickTime Sprite Export[4]

[1] This option is dimmed if QuickTime and AVI are not installed, depending on the version of Director and the platform.
[2] QuickTime export *Options* include setting the frame rate, codec, and size. Transitions will be lost. Director may create multiple audio tracks in the QT movie even when exporting only one sound channel. Add a silent audio track that runs the length of the entire QT movie (to fill any gaps between audio tracks) and use SoundEdit 16 to combine all the sound tracks into one.
[3] QT3 Export requires D7 and the QT3 Export Xtra under both Mac and Windows.
[4] Exports QT3 *#sprite* tracks and requires Apple QuickTime Sprite Export Xtra (*http://www.apple.com/quicktime/developers/tools.html*).

NTSC output

NTSC output resolution is ostensibly 640×480, but the usable screen area is smaller. Leave plenty of border space, avoid one-pixel horizontal lines, and avoid over-saturated colors when creating content for NTSC output.

Prepackaged NTSC filters and NTSC palettes may not give an accurate color. Tweak your colors in Photoshop as you interactively watch the output using a video card that supports an NTSC monitor. Although you can transform graphics to an NTSC palette using Modify ➤ Transform Bitmap, Photoshop's Filter menu includes video options to de-interlace images and transform them to NTSC-safe colors.

Editing in the Digital Video window

Director's video window can be used for minor edits. Don't expect to use Director for serious DV editing—use an external application instead (see "Applications and Tools" later in this chapter). In D6, you can edit QT2 members (but not QT3 members) on the Macintosh, but cannot edit QTW or AVI cast members under Windows. In D7, you can edit QT3 members both on the Macintosh and under Windows.

You can select a range of frames by Shift-clicking in the QT's controller bar in the Video window or by Shift-dragging the sliding shuttle. Use the standard Edit menu commands to cut, copy, and paste video frames (and the accompanying audio). The QT cast member's duration will update to reflect the video's new length.

 Editing a QT cast member inside Director will also modify the original external video file to which it is linked. Make a backup and work on a separate copy of the video instead. If you make a mistake and use File ➤ Revert, you'll lose your other changes since your Director file was last saved.

Digital Video Cast Member Properties Dialog Box

The *QuickTime Xtra Properties* dialog box (shown in Figure 16-2) sets QT3 member properties in D6.5 and D7. The *Digital Video Cast Member Properties* dialog box (not shown) is nearly identical, and sets QT2 and AVI member properties.

If multiple DV cast members are selected, you will see only a dialog box with summary information about the multiple cast members (editable properties are settable via Lingo, as indicated in Table 16-8).

Digital video file information

The *Digital Video* and *QuickTime Xtra Properties* dialog boxes include information about the external video file. The first includes a thumbnail, and the latter includes a full video preview. Information includes:

Filename
  The external filename for QT2 members in D6, and QT3 members in D7, is set when importing and will adjust automatically as long as the external video file remains in the same position relative to the Director movie or external castLib. For QT3 members, you may need to click the *Browse* or *Internet* buttons or enter a filename by hand. In D6.5, substitute @ for the current folder in a QT3 cast member's file path to make it a relative, platform-independent path.

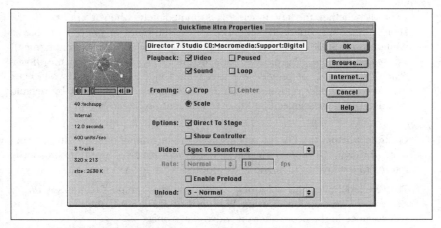

Figure 16-2: QuickTime 3 member properties dialog box

Duration

> The duration of the external DV file is listed in seconds. Note that *the duration of member* is measured in units that depend on *the digitalVideoTimeScale* (usually ticks), not seconds.

Dimensions

> The width and height should each be a multiple of eight for optimal performance. Refer to *the width of member* and *height of member* properties.

Size

> The size listed in the *QT Xtra Properties* dialog box is the true size of the external file. The size listed in the *DV Properties* dialog box is the size of the cast member's data structure and is not related to the size of the external digital video file (see Example 4-6).

The *QT Xtra Properties* dialog box also lists *the timeScale of member* property (usually 600) and the number of tracks.

Playback options

The playback options control whether the audio and video portion of a DV movie play, whether it starts playing automatically, and whether it loops when done:

Video

> Controls whether the video tracks(s) of the DV movie are shown. Uncheck this option to improve performance for audio-only DV files.

Sound

> Controls whether all audio tracks(s) of the DV movie are audible. In D7, audio-only QT3 members must be played direct-to-Stage. Uncheck this option to improve performance and to prevent sound conflicts with non-QT sounds under Windows for DV movies without audio tracks. To disable an individual audio track, use the *setTrackEnabled* command.

Paused

    Controls whether the DV movie plays immediately when it appears in the Score. Check this option to set a DV sprite's attributes or preload the media while it is off-Stage, before bringing it onto the Stage in a subsequent frame. If *Paused* is checked, you must either start the DV sprite by setting the *movie-Rate of sprite* to 1, or provide the user with a video controller. If you check the *Show Controller* option, the QT movie is paused at the start by default, because Director assumes that the user will control the movie.

Loop

    Controls whether the DV file repeats from the beginning or stops after playing once through. If *Loop* is unchecked, *the movieRate of sprite* automatically returns to 0 when a QT movie ends (doesn't work for AVI movies).

    To wait indefinitely for a looping video, use the Tempo Channel's *Wait for Cue Point:{Next}* option. If using *Wait for Cue Point:{End}*, the playback head will advance in the Score after the video plays once.

Framing options (cropping and scaling)

The framing options determine the appearance of the digital video cast member within the sprite's bounding box on the Stage:

Crop

    Crops the video if the sprite box is smaller than the DV cast member's dimensions. If the sprite box is larger than the cast member, the video is not stretched and the excess area is filled with gray.

Scale

    Stretches or shrinks the DV cast member to match the sprite's dimensions. DV sprites will perform better if you stretch/shrink them only in even increments that are multiples of $1/2$ or 2 (i.e., 25%, 50%, 100%, or 200%, but not 67%, 125%, or 150%).

Center

    Determines whether the video is centered or aligned in the upper-left corner of the sprite box when it is cropped.

QT2 and QT3 assets treat scaling somewhat differently, as shown in Table 16-6. QT3 supports *the scale of member* property that ironically is ignored when the Framing is set to *Scale* mode (*the crop of member* is FALSE). The scale of member is set as a list [*xScale, yScale*] where each dimension defaults to 100.0 (normal size), and ranges from 0 (zoom out) to over 50000 (zoom in); 50 is half-size. See also *the translation of member* property.

Table 16-6: QT2 and QT3 Framing Options

Framing	Center	Display	QT2	QT3
Crop[1]	TRUE	Center of video displayed; edges may be cropped.	Cropped, not scaled.	Scaled by *scale of member*, then cropped.
Crop[1]	FALSE	Upper left of video displayed; lower right may be cropped.	Cropped, not scaled.	Scaled by *scale of member*, then cropped.
Scale[2]	N/A	Video stretched or shrunk to match sprite's rect (no cropping).	Scaled based on size of sprite. No cropping.	Same as QT2. *The scale of member* is ignored.

[1] The crop of member is TRUE.
[2] The crop of member is FALSE.

Stage display options

Table 16-7 summarizes the supported modes for direct-to-Stage video and the DV Controller.

Table 16-7: Support for Direct-to-Stage Video

Platform	DV Format	Direct-to-Stage Setting	Controller	Ink Effects
Macintosh	QuickTime 2	True	Optional	Copy only
Macintosh	QuickTime 2	False	No	Limited[1]
Windows	QuickTime 2	Always true	Optional	Copy only
Windows	QuickTime 3	True	Optional	Copy or custom mask only
Windows	QuickTime 3	False	No	Limited[1]
Windows	VFW (AVI)	True	No	Copy only
Windows	VFW (AVI)	False	No	Limited[1]

[1] Blend is not supported, nor are other processor-intensive inks.

The following options determine whether DV playback bypasses Director's compositing buffer and whether the QT controller is visible.

Direct To Stage

Determines whether the video is played directly to the Stage, or whether it is first passed through Director's offscreen compositing buffer. Direct-to-Stage sprites are always displayed using the Copy ink in the foremost paint layer and always leave trails. See "Drawing to the Stage" in Chapter 1.

Use non-direct-to-Stage playback, which may be very slow, only when you absolutely must overlay other sprites atop, or apply non-Copy ink effects to, a DV sprite. You are ordinarily better off re-designing your product instead.

Director will not automatically refresh the DV sprite area, even after the video terminates. Force Director to redraw the Stage by using a different cast member (a *cover* sprite) in a subsequent frame in the same sprite channel, a fast transition, or using *set the stageColor = the stageColor*.

Show Controller

Determines whether the standard QT controller is shown below a QT sprite, enabling the user to control video playback. This option is available only for QT cast members played direct-to-Stage. For non-direct-to-Stage QT or AVI files, which do not support controllers, you must provide a custom controller via Lingo. The standard QT controller includes a sound volume control only if the QT file contains an audio track. D7 provides a custom QuickTime Control Slider Behavior under Window ➤ Library Palette ➤ Media ➤ QuickTime.

The standard controller appears in the foremost paint layer, as does the entire video sprite when played direct-to-Stage. The controller itself is drawn using the colors from positions 1, 7, 248, and 256 of the palette. If you are using a custom palette under Windows, reserve the first and last ten colors to be the same as those in the Windows System palette to avoid conflicts.

When *Show Controller* is checked, the QT sprite is automatically paused at first, and will not play until started by setting *the movieRate of sprite* to *1* or via the controller. See the *Paused* option and *the pausedAtStart of member* property.

Video rate

The following options determine the speed and synchronization mode of DV playback. The frame rate at which a DV sprite plays is completely independent of the Score's Tempo channel, *the frameTempo*, and *the puppetTempo*.

Video

Controls the playback synchronization mode of the DV movie, and has two possible settings:

Sync to Soundtrack

Plays the DV file in the customary time-based manner. The QuickTime and Video for Windows playback engines drop video frames to maintain audio synchronization if necessary. The playback rate is determined by the DV movie's intrinsic frame rate, which is defined when the video is created in your DV editing software.

Play Every Frame (No Sound)

Plays the DV file as if it were a straight animation, and QT or VFW does not drop frames to maintain synchronization. This mode disables the audio track(s), and is most appropriate for visual transitions in which you want to see every frame of the animation. The apparent frame rate is ordinarily slower than in the *Sync to Soundtrack* mode, as frames are never dropped.

Rate

Determines how fast Director attempts to play the video in *Play Every Frame (No Sound)* mode (ignored in *Sync to Soundtrack* mode). Video frames will not be dropped if the target rate cannot be met, so the actual playback rate might be slower.

Normal

Plays every frame of the DV file, but no faster than its intrinsic frame rate.

Maximum

Plays every frame of the DV file as fast as it can.

Fixed

Plays every frame of the DV file at the rate specified in the adjacent *Frames Per Second* field.

Frames Per Second

Specifies the rate for *Fixed* playback of the DV file when using *Play Every Frame (No Sound)* mode. The default value is the DV file's intrinsic frame rate, which is defined when the video is created in your DV editing software.

Memory management options

The *Enable Preload* and *Unload* options control how the DV cast members are loaded and unloaded from memory.

The Lingo equivalent for each of the options in the *Digital Video and QuickTime Xtra Properties* dialog box are shown in Table 16-8.

Table 16-8: Lingo Equivalents to DV and QT Xtra Property Dialog Box

Dialog Option	Lingo Equivalent	See Also
Cast Member Name	the name of member	castLibNum of member
File Name	the fileName of member (includes path)	name of member
Dimensions	the width, height, and rect of member	width, height, and rect of sprite
Duration	the duration of member / float (the digitalVideoTimeScale)	movieTime of sprite
Size	Size of header for QT2 and external file size for QT3. See Example 4-6.	size of member, duration of member
FrameRate/ Frames Per Second	the frameRate of member. See "Determining a DV's intrinsic frameRate."	movieRate of sprite
Video	the video of member[1]	sound of member
Sound	the sound of member[2]	video of member, volume or volumeLevel of sprite, soundLevel, soundEnabled, trackEnabled, setTrackEnabled

Dialog Option	Lingo Equivalent	See Also
Paused	the pausedAtStart of member (unrelated to the *pause* command)	controller of member, movieRate of sprite
Loop	the loop of member	movieTime of sprite, duration of member
Crop	the crop of member = TRUE	center of member, scale of member
Scale	the crop of member = FALSE	center of member, width, height, stretch, and rect of sprite
Center	the center of member	crop of member
Direct to Stage	the directToStage of member	ink, controller, invertMask, and mask of member
Controller	the controller of member	directToStage, pausedAtStart of member
Sync to Soundtrack	the frameRate of member = 0	movieRate of sprite
Play Every Frame (No Sound)		
Normal	the frameRate of member = -1	movieRate of sprite
Maximum	the frameRate of member = -2	movieRate of sprite
Fixed fps	the frameRate of member = *n* (*n* > 1, specified in fps field)	fps field in dialog box
Enable Preload	the preLoad of member	the preLoadRAM, preLoad-Member
Unload Settings (Normal/Next/Last/Never)	the purgePriority of member = *n* $0 <= n <= 3$	unLoad, unLoadMember

[1] Changing *the video of member* also resets *the movieTime of sprite* to 0, which restarts the movie at the beginning.
[2] Setting *the sound of member* to FALSE initializes *the volume of sprite* to 0. Changing *the volume of sprite* via Lingo or the QT controller overrides *the sound of member* setting.

Digital Video Properties and Functions

Table 16-9 lists the properties for both *#digitalVideo* (QT2 and AVI) and *#quick-TimeMedia* (QT3) cast members, including those that are new or behave differently with *#quickTimeMedia* cast members than with *#digitalVideo* cast members. Consult Table 4-10 for a list of other sprite and member properties that are not specific to digital video cast members. See also the HTML documentation that comes with the D6.5 QT3 Asset Xtra and the D7 online Help.

In Table 16-9, with the exception of *the digitalVideoTimeScale*, which is a system property, it is implied that each property takes the form:

    the *property* of member *qtMember*

and/or:

    the *property* of sprite *qtSprite*

For example, *the movieRate* is a sprite property and can be set using:

    set the movieRate of sprite 5 = 1

or in D7 syntax:

    sprite(5).movieRate = 1

Note that sprite properties override any member property of the same name on a per-sprite basis. The default value, if any, is shown in italic in the *Value* column. QT3 imports many media types, but not all commands and properties are applicable for all media types (see Table 16-10).

To create a QT3 cast member in D6.5, choose Insert ➤ Media Element ➤ QuickTime 3. Use File ➤ Import to create QT3 members.

Table 16-9: Digital Video and QuickTime 3 Properties

Command	Value	Read-Only	Member	Sprite	Notes
bottom	Pixels from top of Stage.			✓	Includes height of controller, if any.
center	TRUE | *FALSE*		✓		Used only if *crop* = TRUE.
controller	TRUE | *FALSE*		✓		Used only if *directToStage* = TRUE.
crop	TRUE | *FALSE*		✓		See *center, scale, translation* entries. If *crop* is FALSE, movie is scaled to sprite box.
digitalVideoTime Scale	Default is 60 units/second.				A system property, not a sprite or member property.
digitalVideoType	#quickTime | #videoFor-Windows	✓	✓		Always *#quickTime* for QT3 members.
directToStage[1]	*TRUE* | FALSE		✓		See *controller, mask, mouseLevel* entries.
duration	Measured in ticks.	✓	✓	✓	See *mTime, movieTime* entries.
fileName[2,3]	Path to external video.		✓		Replace folder name in file path with @ in D6.5.
frameRate of member	0 | -1 | -2 | *n*		✓		See *mRate and movieRate* entries.

Table 16-9: Digital Video and QuickTime 3 Properties (continued)

Command	Value	Read-Only	Member	Sprite	Notes
height	Measured in pixels.		✓	✓	Should be multiple of 8.
ink	Default is 0 (Copy).			✓	Copy ink is used for direct-to-Stage sprites.
invertMask[4]	TRUE | FALSE		✓		See *mask* entry.
isVRmovie[4]	TRUE | FALSE	✓	✓	✓	See Table 16-10.
left	Pixels from left of Stage.			✓	Should be multiple of 8.
loaded	TRUE | FALSE		✓		Indicates only whether header is loaded, not data.
loop	TRUE | FALSE		✓		See *loopBounds* entry.
loopBounds[4]	[*startTicks, endTicks*]			✓	[0, 0] indicates no *loopBounds*.
mask[4]	member *oneBitMember*		✓		Set to 1-bit cast member or zero to disable; Only if *directToStage* = TRUE.
media	Not useful in most cases.		✓		Does not access external DV file data.
modified	TRUE | FALSE		✓		Indicates whether video has been edited in Video window.
mouseLevel[4,5]	#none | #controller | #all | #share			✓	See *VRTriggerCallback* in Table 16-10.
movieRate[6]	0 – n, default is 1.0.			✓	Use *mRate* instead for QT3 sprites in SW6.0.1 and D6.5.
movieTime	Measured in ticks by default.			✓	Use *mTime* instead for QT3 sprites in SW6.0.1 and D6.5.
mRate[4,6]	0 – n, default is 1.0.			✓	See *pausedAtStart*; use for SW6.0.1 and D6.5 instead of *movieRate*.
mTime[4]	Measured in ticks.			✓	Use for SW6.0.1 and D6.5 instead of *movieTime*.
name	String.		✓		Defaults to initial external file name, excluding the path.
purgePriority	0 | 1 | 2 | 3 (default is 3: Normal)		✓		Indicates whether header is purged. Streamed media is always purged.

Table 16-9: Digital Video and QuickTime 3 Properties (continued)

Command	Value	Read-Only	Member	Sprite	Notes
rect	Measured in pixels.		✓	✓	Dimensions should be multiple of 8, and sprite rect should be even multiple of member rect.
regPoint	point (*x*, *y*)		✓		Defaults to center.
right	Pixels from left of Stage.			✓	Should be multiple of 8.
rotation[4]	0.0 to 360.0 degrees.		✓	✓	Default is 0.
scale[4]	[*xScale, yScale*]		✓	✓	Used if *crop* = TRUE. Default is [100.0, 100.0].
size[2]	Bytes.				Size of header for QT2. Size of external file for QT3.
sound	*TRUE* | FALSE		✓		Ignored if *frameRate* is not 0 (sync to soundtrack).
startTime	Ticks.			✓	Unreliable.
stopTime	Ticks.			✓	Unreliable.
timeScale	Units/second.	✓	✓	✓	Defaults to 600 for QT on Mac. See the *digitalVideoTimeScale* entry.
top	Pixels from top of Stage.			✓	Should be multiple of 8.
trails	TRUE | FALSE			✓	If *directToStage* = TRUE, DV leaves trails.
translation[4]	[*hPixels, vPixels*]		✓	✓	Used if *crop* = TRUE.
type[2]	#*digitalVideo* (QT2 or AVI) | #*quickTimeMedia* (QT3)	✓	✓		See *digitalVideoType* entry.
video	*TRUE* | FALSE		✓		See *sound* entry.
volume	0 to 255 (or higher)[7]			✓	Always reports 0 for QT3 in D6.5; see *volumeLevel* entry.
volumeLevel[4]	0 to 255 (or higher)[7]			✓	Use in D6.5 instead of *volume*.
width	Measured in pixels.			✓	Should be multiple of 8.

1 If *the directToStage of member* is FALSE, the user cannot interact with QTVR movies automatically. You must manually simulate callbacks with *VRPtToHotSpotID( )*.
2 Different for QT3 cast members and sprites than for QT2 cast members and sprites.
3 The default *fileName* for QT3 cast members in D6.5 is an absolute path. In the *QuickTime Xtra Properties* dialog box, replace the current folder in the path with the "@" operator to create a relative path (not necessary in D7).
4 New as of D6.5. Applies to QT3 cast members and sprites, not QT2 members and sprites.
5 If *the mouseLevel of sprite* is #*none*, callbacks are not sent. You must use *VRPtToHotSpotID( )* to manually handle the callbacks. The docs are ambiguous, the correct syntax is *VRPtToHotSpotID(sprite n, point(the mouseH, the mouseV))*.
6 The *mRate* and *movieRate* return 0 if *the frameRate of member* is not 0 (*Sync to Soundtrack* mode).
7 Setting *the volumeLevel* or *volume of sprite* higher than 255 causes distortion.

Digital Video

Table 16-10 lists the sprite properties that pertain only to QTVR assets imported as *#quickTimeMedia* members. All are settable except *the VRNodeType*. For example:

```
set the VRmotionQuality of sprite 5 = #minQuality
```

The VR prefix for each property is unnecessary in D7. For example:

```
sprite(5).motionQuality = #minQuality
```

Table 16-10: QTVR-Specific Properties of QT3 Assets

Command	Value	Notes
VRFieldOfView	*degrees*	Current field of view.
VRHotSpotEnterCallback	#enterHotspot | 0	on *enterHotspot* me, *hotSpotID* *actions* end
VRHotSpotExitCallback	#exitHotspot | 0	on *exitHotspot* me, *hotSpotID* *actions* end
VRMotionQuality	#minQuality | #maxQuality | #normalQuality	See VRStaticQuality entry.
VRMovedCallback	#movedVR | 0	on *movedVR* me *actions* end
VRNode	nodeID	Current node ID being displayed.
VRNodeEnterCallback	#nodeEnter | 0	on *nodeEnter* me, *nodeID* *actions* end

VRNodeExitCallback	#nodeExit | 0	on nodeExit me, oldNode,
		newNode
		  actions
		  return 0 | 1
		end
		
		0: cancel (not implemented)
		1: allow (go to new node)

VRNodeType	#panorama | #object | #unknown	#unknown means non-QTVR; see isVRMovie entry in Table 16-9.
VRPan	*degrees*	See VRTilt entry.
VRStaticQuality	#minQuality | #maxQuality | #normalQuality	See VRMotionQuality entry.
VRTilt	*degrees*	See VRPan entry.

Table 16-10: QTVR-Specific Properties of QT3 Assets (continued)

Command	Value	Notes

VRTriggerCallback	#triggerVR | 0	MouseLevel must be #all or #share, not #none or #controller.
		
		`on trigger VR me,`
		`hotSpotID`
		  `actions`
		    `return 0 | 1`
		`end`
		
		0: cancel
		1: continue

VRWarpMode	#none | #partial |#full	See VRStaticQuality, VRMotion Quality entries.

Table 16-11 lists the supported QuickTime 3 functions. See the HTML help files included with Director 6.5 under the *Help 6_5/QT3 Help* folder, or the D7 online Help. QT3 also supports the track sampling and time functions in Tables 16-15 and 16-16.

Table 16-11: QuickTime 3 Asset Xtra Commands and Functions

Command	System	Member	Sprite
canUseQuicktimeStreaming()[1]	✓		
isUsingQuicktimeStreaming()[1]	✓		
interface (xtra "QuickTimeSupport")	✓		
mMessageList (xtra "QuickTimeSupport")	✓		
new (#quickTimeMedia)	✓		
qtRegisterAccessKey (*category, key*)	✓		
qtUnRegisterAccessKey (*category, key*)	✓		
quickTimeVersion()[2]	✓		
setTrackEnabled (sprite *qtSprite, track*)			✓
trackCount (member *qtMember*) trackCount (sprite *qtSprite*)		✓	✓
trackEnabled (sprite *qtSprite, track*)			✓
trackText (sprite *qtSprite, track*)			✓
trackType (member *qtMember, track*) trackType (sprite *qtSprite, track*)		✓	✓

Table 16-11: QuickTime 3 Asset Xtra Commands and Functions (continued)

Command	System	Member	Sprite
useQuickTimeStreaming (TRUE | FALSE)[1]	✓		
VREnableHotSpot (sprite *qtvrSprite*, *hotSpotID*, TRUE | FALSE)[3]			✓
VRGetHotSpotRect (sprite *qtvrSprite*, *hotSpotID*)[3]			✓
VRNudge (sprite qtvrSprite*qtvrSprite*, #left | #upLeft | #up | #upRight | #right | #downRight | #down | #downLeft)[3]			✓
VRPtToHotSpotID(sprite *qtvrSprite*, point(the mouseH, the mouseV))[3]			✓
VRswing (sprite *qtvrSprite*, pan, tilt, fieldOfView)[3,4]			✓

[1] Streaming QT is "not implemented and extremely unsupported" in D6.5 and D7, according to Macromedia. For streaming video, see RealVideo from Real Networks (formerly Progressive Networks) at *http://www.real.com.*
[2] See Table 16-2.
[3] The "VR" prefix is deprecated in D7. Use *enableHotSpot( )*, *getHotSpotRect( )*, *nudge( )*, *ptToHotSpotID( )*, and *swing( )* in D7.
[4] The *pan*, *tilt*, and *fieldOfView* are in degrees.

Masks

QT3 adds support for 1-bit cast member masks (see *the mask of member*), which allow non-rectangular QT movies to play direct-to-Stage. If *the invertMask of member* is FALSE, black areas of the mask show the QT cast member, and white areas hide it. If *the invertMask of member* is TRUE, the reverse holds.

Don't use a duplicated member as a mask. (Duplicating a member doesn't always generate a unique internal ID, which the QT3 Xtra uses to track the mask.) Use copy and paste to create a new cast member with a unique internal ID.

The registration point of the mask member is placed at the upper-left corner of the QT3 sprite. This allows you to use a shape cast member as a mask. If using a bitmap, set the mask's registration point to its upper-left corner.

Controlling Digital Video Playback

The *movieRate of sprite* and *frameRate of member* control the playback rate of DV sprites. In D6.5, QT3 cast members use *the mRate of sprite* instead of *the movieRate of sprite*. In all other versions, including D7, use *the movieRate* property instead of *the mRate*.

Synchronous Video Playback

Digital videos are usually played synchronously, using *Sync to Soundtrack* mode, in which audio and video are synchronized to a time code, and QuickTime (QT) or Video for Windows (VFW) will drop frames if necessary to achieve the requested frame rate. The *movieTime of sprite* is used to start and stop the video and even play it backward.

If the natural frame rate of the movie is 10 fps, setting the *movieRate* to 1 will play the movie at 10 fps; setting the *movieRate* to 2 will play the movie at 20 fps, and so on. Table 16-12 summarizes the different playback settings. For the purposes of Table 16-12, *the frameRate of member* should be zero (0), and *the movieRate of sprite* should be set to the value *n* shown in the table.

Table 16-12: Synchronous Playback Speeds

DV Speed	movieRate or mRate	Notes
Stopped	$n = 0$	See *pausedAtStart* and *controller of member* in Table 16-9.
Normal speed	$n = 1$	DV plays at intrinsic frame rate defined when it was created.
Reverse normal speed	$n = -1$	Backward video playback is inefficient and may be jerky. Sounds play in reverse.[1]
Fast forward	$n > 1$	Sound plays quickly and at a higher pitch. Video may be jerky at high multiples.
Fast reverse	$n < -1$	Sounds play quickly, at higher pitch, and in reverse. Video will be jerky.
Slow-motion forward	$0 < n < 1.0$	Sounds play slowly and at a lower pitch.
Slow-motion reverse	$-1.0 < n < 0$	Video may be jerky. Sounds play slowly, and at a lower pitch.[1]

[1] Sounds play in reverse and occasionally sound like the word "Satan."

Asynchronous Video Playback

To play back every frame of a DV file without regard to the time code, use the *Play Every Frame (No Sound)* option. This is commonly used for animations or visual transitions when you don't want QT or VFW to drop frames, and don't care about speed.

Table 16-13 summarizes the possible settings for asynchronous video playback using *the frameRate of member*. Setting *the frameRate of member* at runtime is not reliable; use the *DV Cast Member Property* dialog box to set it instead. Set *the movieRate of sprite* to 1 to play the video forward, to 0 to pause the video, and to −1 to play the video backward.

Table 16-13: Asynchronous Playback Speeds

Playback Speed	frameRate	Video	Audio
Synchronized	$f = 0$	Drops frames, if needed, to achieve intrinsic rate, multiplied by *movieRate of sprite*. See Table 16-12.	Yes[1]
Normal	$f = -1$	Played at the DV file's intrinsic frame rate without dropping frames.	None
Maximum	$f = -2$	Played as fast as possible without dropping frames.	None
Fixed	$1 <= f <= 255$	Played at the specified frame rate without dropping frames.	None

[1] Audio is synched to the video, if audio track is enabled. See *the sound of member* property and *setTrackEnabled( )* function.

Determining a DV's intrinsic frameRate

Example 16-4 determines the frame rate that was assigned to a QT2 (*#digitalVideo*) video file when it was created in Adobe Premiere, for example. It makes use of a trick that doesn't work with QT3 (*#quickTimeMedia*) members. For QT3 members, examine the frame rate in MoviePlayer.

Example 16-4: Reading a DV File's Intrinsic Frame Rate

```
on getFrameRate DVmember
  set oldRate = the frameRate of member DVmember
  -- Set an invalid frame rate and it will revert to the true rate.
  set the frameRate of member DVmember = -3
  set intrinsicRate = the frameRate of member DVmember
  set the frameRate of member DVmember = oldRate
  if intrinsicRate > 0 then
    return intrinsicRate
  else
    return 0
  endif
end getFrameRate
```

Playing Digital Video from/to a Specific Point

The *startTime of sprite* (which defaults to zero) and *stopTime of sprite* (which defaults to the duration of the DV cast member) properties can be used to cue specific segments of a digital video file. I have found them to be unreliable (they work best if set once the video is playing). Instead, use *the movieTime of sprite* property to set or read the position in a DV file.

The movieTime of sprite property can be set when the video is playing or stopped, as indicated by *the movieRate of sprite*. Table 16-14 assumes that *the digitalVideoTimeScale* is set to 60, its default. Note that D6.5 QT3 members use the *mRate* and *mTime of sprite* properties instead of the *movieRate* and *movieTime*. The *movieTime of sprite* is affected by the *digitalVideoTimeScale*, but the *mTime of sprite* is not.

Table 16-14: Digital Video Timing

Position Within DV	movieTime or mTime of sprite Equivalent
Beginning of video	0
t ticks from the beginning	*t*
s seconds from the beginning	*s* * 60
Current time of DV (usually in ticks)	the movieTime of sprite *dvSprite* the mTime of sprite *dvSprite*
Current time of DV in *milliseconds*	the currentTime of sprite *dvSprite*
Current time − *s* seconds	(the movieTime of sprite *dvSprite*) − *s* * 60 (the mTime of sprite *dvSprite*) − *s* * 60

Table 16-14: Digital Video Timing (continued)

Position Within DV	movieTime or mTime of sprite Equivalent
Current time + *s* seconds	(the movieTime of sprite *dvSprite*) + *s* * 60
	(the mTime of sprite *dvSprite*) + *s* * 60
Midpoint of DV	0.5 * (the duration of the member of sprite *dvSprite*)
s seconds from the end of video	(the duration of the member of sprite *dvSprite*) – *s* * 60
t ticks from the end of video	(the duration of the member of sprite *dvSprite*) – *t*
End of video	the duration of the member of sprite *dvSprite*
*n*th Photo – JPEG still frame	*n* *60 / (video frame rate in fps[1])
Previous keyframe	trackPreviousKeyTime(sprite *dvSprite*, *whichTrack*)
Next keyframe	trackNextKeyTime(sprite *dvSprite*, *whichTrack*)

[1] See Example 16-4.

Analyzing and Controlling Individual Digital Video Tracks

A DV file can contain multiple tracks—often one video track and one audio track. There can be 0 to 7 video or audio tracks, plus other media types, including text, MIDI, and sprites (unrelated to Director's sprites).

Lingo provides track-specific commands, summarized in Table 16-15. Although Lingo may report that a track exists and is enabled, this may not reliably reflect whether it will actually be played. QuickTime for Windows Version 2.1.2 and earlier support only one audio track and one video track and do not support text tracks. AVI files are limited to one audio and one video track.

Table 16-15: Track-Specific Digital Video Commands

Action	Command	Notes
Count the number of tracks in a DV sprite or cast member	trackCount (sprite *y*) trackCount (member *x*)	See trackType( )
Determine the type of data in a track	trackType (sprite *y*, *t*) trackType (member *x*, *t*)	Returns #video, #sound, #text, #music, #sprite[1], #unknown, #chapter, or VOID if out of range.
Retrieve the text content of a text track	trackText (sprite *y*, *t*)	Applies only to text tracks.
Determine whether a track is enabled in a DV sprite[2]	trackEnabled (sprite *y*, *t*)	See setTrackEnabled( ), the video, and the sound of member.
Enable/disable a track in a DV sprite	setTrackEnabled (sprite *y*, *t*) = TRUE | FALSE	See trackEnabled( ), the video, and the sound of member.

Digital Video

Table 16-15: Track-Specific Digital Video Commands (continued)

Action	Command	Notes
Determine when a track starts within a DV sprite or cast member[3]	trackStartTime (sprite *y*, *t*) trackStartTime (member *x*, *t*)	See the startTime, movieTime, and mTime of sprite.
Determine when a track ends within a DV sprite or cast member[3]	trackStopTime (sprite *y*, *t*) trackStopTime (member *x*, *t*)	See the stopTime, movieTime, and mTime of sprite, the duration of member.
Enable/disable all video tracks in a cast member, and any sprites that reference it	set the video of member *x* = TRUE | FALSE	See setTrackEnabled( ), trackEnabled( ), sound of member.
Enable/disable all audio tracks in a cast member, and any sprites that reference it	set the sound of member *x* = TRUE | FALSE	See setTrackEnabled( ), track Enabled( ), video of member.

[1] The #sprite tracks create by the QuickTime Sprite Export Xtra return VOID when imported as a QT2-style #digitalVideo member, but return #sprite when inserted as a QT3-style #quickTimeMedia member.
[2] Tracks are enabled/disabled on a per sprite basis, not a per cast member basis.
[3] The *trackStartTime( )* specifies the offset of a track within the digital video file, which is ordinarily 0 (the beginning of the DV file). The *trackStartTime( )* and *trackStopTime( )* are *not* analogous to *the startTime* and *stopTime of sprite*.

Timing Within Digital Video Tracks

Lingo provides the *trackPreviousKeyTime*, *trackNextKeyTime*, *trackPreviousSampleTime*, and *trackNextSampleTime* functions to access specific data points within individual tracks as shown in Table 16-16. These functions do not appear to return reliable data. Lingo also allows you to query the time scale being used to play digital video files. See also Chapter 11, *Timers and Dates*, in *Lingo in a Nutshell*.

Table 16-16: Track Sampling and Time Functions

Action	Command
Determine time of next keyframe	set nextKey = trackNextKeyTime(sprite *y*, *trackNum*)
Determine time of previous keyframe	set prevKey = trackPreviousKeyTime(sprite *y*, *trackNum*)
Determine time of next sample	set nextSample = trackNextSampleTime(sprite *y*, *trackNum*)
Determine time of previous sample	set prevSample = trackPreviousSampleTime(sprite *y*, *trackNum*)
Determine or set the time units used to measure time for digital video cast members	the digitalVideoTimeScale, where scale = 1/t (i.e., 60 = 1/60th of a second)
Determine or set the time units on which the digital video's frames are based	the timeScale of member, where scale = 1/t (i.e., 600 = 1/60th of a second)

Common Digital Video Operations

Although you can wait for a video via the Tempo channel, here are some Lingo variations. Example 16-5 waits for a digital video by comparing the current time to the overall length of the video. Waiting in a *repeat* loop devotes all the time to video playback, but locks out other interactivity.

Example 16-5: Waiting for a Video in a Repeat Loop

```
on waitForVideo channel
  set end = the duration of the member of sprite channel
  repeat while the movieTime of sprite channel < end
    updateStage
  end repeat
end
```

Example 16-6 waits until a digital video stops by itself or until the user clicks the mouse. *The movieRate of sprite* automatically becomes 0 when a QT sprite ends, but when using AVI sprites, the playback head won't advance until the user clicks.

Example 16-6: Allowing a Mouse Click to Interrupt a Video

```
on exitFrame
  global gVideoChan
  if the movieRate of sprite gVideoChan then
    if the mouseDown then
      set the movieRate of sprite gVideoChan = 0
    end if
    go the frame
  end if
end
```

Table 16-17 lists common digital video operations that can be achieved via Lingo. Refer also to Table 16-14. The last two entries in the table can be used to reduce audio conflicts under Windows.

Table 16-17: Common Digital Video Operations

Action	Command
Rewind a video	`set the movieTime of sprite x = 0`
Determine whether a video is currently playing	`if the movieRate of sprite x <> 0 then...`
Determine whether a video file has reached its end	`if the movieTime of sprite x >= the duration of the member of sprite x then...`
Wait until a specific cue point has been reached in the DV file	See the Tempo channel's *Wait for Cue Point* option or *the mostRecentCuePoint of member* and *isPastCuePoint( )*.
Wait until a specific time in seconds is reached in the DV file	`if the movieTime of sprite x ¬` `  <= t * 60 then go the frame`

Wait until a specific time in seconds is reached in the DV file while in a repeat loop	`repeat while the movieTime of sprite x <= t * 60`
	`  updateStage`
	`end repeat`

Digital Video

Table 16-17: Common Digital Video Operations (continued)

Action	Command
Shut off all DV-related audio	`set the movieRate of sprite x = 0`

Shut off all non-DV related audio	`repeat with x = 1 to 8`
	   `puppetSound x, 0`
	   `sound stop x`
	`end repeat`

Digital Video Resources

There are many QT-related URLs of interest. Here are a select few. See *http://www.zeusprod.com/nutshell/links.html* for many more.

Information

Getting started with QuickTime 3:

http://www.apple.com/quicktime/information/index.html

QuickTime Gazette:

http://www.Blackstone.ca/QuickTimeGazette/Latest_News.html

QuickTime FAQ (outdated but worthwhile):

http://www.QuickTimeFAQ.org/

Creating QuickTime content:

http://www.apple.com/quicktime/authors/index.html

QuickTime developer mailing list (free, informal support):

http://lists.apple.com/quicktime-dev.html

QuickTime announce mailing list (news and announcements):

http://lists.apple.com/quicktime-announce.html

Applications and Tools

Here are some of the most common digital video editing, management, compression, and analysis tools. Recall also that Director for the Macintosh exports QT files and Director 7 for Windows exports AVI or QT files. When timing is critical, you can export the Score animation to a digital video file, then reimport the resulting video for playback in Director.

Adobe Premiere creates and edits DV files (Mac/Win):

http://www.adobe.com

SoundEdit 16, included with Director 6 Multimedia Studio for Macintosh manipulates QT audio tracks, and adds cue points (Mac only):

http://www.macromedia.com

QuickTime 3 Pro (upgrades to MoviePlayer and PictureViewer) plays and performs minor edits on DV files, converts between formats, and prepares files for Windows playback (Mac/Win):

> *http://www.apple.com/quicktime/information/qt3pro.html*

deBabelizer by Equilibrium creates custom palettes for video, etc. (Mac/Win):

> *http://www.equilibrium.com*

MediaCleaner Pro (formerly MovieCleaner) from Terran Interactive—the standard CD compression tool. Not an editing tool:

> *http://www.terran-int.com*

QT Gallery 1.0, Lakewood Software is an image editor and browser tool supporting QT3's image import options (PICT, JPEG, TIFF, GIF, and Photoshop, etc.), editing filters, and transition effects:

> *http://www.lakewoodsoftware.com*

Make Effects movie—adds QT3 transition effects:

> *http://www.apple.com/quicktime/developers/tools.html*
> *ftp://ftp.apple.com/Quicktime/developers/makeeffectmovie.sea.hqx*

Video-Related Xtras

Besides the QT3 Xtra from Macromedia included with D6.5 and D7, see the following Xtras.

MPEG and DirectMedia Xtras—Tabuleiro da Baiana:

> *http://www.tbaiana.com*

MultiMixer Xtra by TurnTable controls the pan of a QuickTime movie's sound:

> *http://www.turntable.com/multimixer*

RobinHood Xtra for QT3:

> *http://www.hermes.de/heise/robin.html*

Focus 3 Xtra—captures and displays video from device connected to a Macintosh:

> *http://www.focus3.com*

VSnap—video capture:

> *http://www.penworks.com*

Digital Video Troubleshooting

When troubleshooting DV, you must narrow down the problem. Does the problem occur in MoviePlayer or only in Director? Does the problem occur under Windows 3.1, Windows 95/98, Windows NT, and the Macintosh? Does it occur with all videos, or only some? Does it depend on whether there are other sounds or other videos playing? Does the problem depend on the version of QuickTime or the sound or video card installed? Are RSX and DirectSound installed under Windows? By answering these questions, you'll reveal the most likely culprit.

Test your video in an external application, such as MoviePlayer, before blaming Director. Test with a known working video—one with one video track, one audio track, and a low data rate—that you can substitute for a suspicious video during testing. Have a known working test machine available.

Lingo errors

The Lingo script errors "Not a digital video sprite," "Digital video sprite expected," or "Property not found" indicate that you are attempting to check or set an invalid member or sprite property.

For example, *the movieTime of sprite* is valid for only digital video sprites. Ensure that you are in the correct frame in which the DV sprite appears and that you are using the correct sprite channel. Check *the type of the member of sprite n* to ensure it is a *#digitalVideo* or *#quickTimeMedia* member.

Many QT3 properties (see Tables 16-9 and 16-10) are not supported for older QT2-style cast members.

Video doesn't appear

Ensure that other videos play and that the proper version of QT, QTW, or VFW is installed (see Examples 16-1 and 16-2 and Tables 16-1 and 16-2). During authoring, Director will display an error message if QuickTime or Video for Windows is not loaded and cast members requiring those extensions are present. Projectors may simply fail to display digital video sprites if the required extensions are missing.

Include the externally linked DV file in the correct relative path.

Test the video in an external video application. Ensure that it contains a video track that is enabled (see the *trackCount()*, *trackType()*, *trackEnabled()*, and *setTrackEnabled()* functions in Table 16-15). When using QTW2 under Windows, ensure that the video was prepared specifically for Windows playback (i.e., flattened and deforked).

Test the video in Director's Video window. The beginning of many videos is black, so you may not see an image on Stage until they play. Ensure that the DV sprite is located on the Stage, not off-Stage, and make sure that the Director playback head is moving.

Set *the video of member*, *the visible of member*, and *the directToStage of member* to TRUE. Set *the puppet of sprite* to FALSE. If playing the video non-direct-to-Stage, ensure that the DV sprite is not obscured by another sprite. See "Drawing to the Stage" in Chapter 1 for generic reasons why a sprite may not appear, such as the wrong size, width, or location.

Some versions of QuickTime for Windows and Video for Windows may not support multiple video tracks.

Video doesn't play from a different drive (can't find video)

If Director asks, "Where is movie *xxxx?*" be sure that you've included the external DV files with you Projector. Maintain the same relative path position after protecting your Director files or creating your Projector.

In D6.5, QuickTime 3 cast members will not adjust their paths automatically, as will QT2 cast members, unless you use the @ operator to specify the path relative to the Director movie's current folder. In D7, this is not an issue.

Cast members inserted via Insert ➤ Media Element ➤ QuickTime 3 in D6.5 or D7, or imported via File ➤ Import in D7, require the appropriate runtime version of the QuickTime 3 Asset Xtra.

Video works on Macintosh but not under Windows

Ensure that the movie was flattened and deforked. (Save it as *Self-Contained* and *Playable on non-Apple computers* using MoviePlayer.)

If you imported the video using File ➤ Import in D6.5 or earlier versions, it is treated as a QT2-style *#digitalVideo* member. It will play if either QT2 or QT3 is installed on the Macintosh, but requires QTW2 under Windows. (You must install the 16-bit version of QTW2 when using a 16-bit Projector and the 32-bit version of QTW when using a 32-bit Projector.) QTW2-style *#digitalVideo* members will not work under Windows if only QTW3 is installed.

Similarly, *#quickTimeMedia* members require QT3 and the QT3 Asset Xtra. QT2 or QTW2 will not play *#quickTimeMedia* members.

Any video using any new features of QT3 (see the next section) must be imported using Insert ➤ Media Element ➤ QuickTime 3 to be supported in D6.5 for Windows. In D7, all QuickTime videos are imported as QT3 members by default.

Sorenson video caveats

The Sorenson Video Codec is much more processor-intensive than Cinepak compression. However, Sorenson-compressed video at 70 KB/sec may look better than Cinepak-compressed video at 320 KB/sec. Therefore, use a lower data rate when using the Sorenson codec.

Sorenson Video is a QT3-specific codec requiring the QT3 Xtra under Windows. If you import a Sorenson-compressed QT movie as a QT2-style cast member using File ➤ Import in D6.x, it *will* work on a Macintosh with QT3 installed, but will *never* work under Windows regardless of the QTW version(s) installed. You must use Insert ➤ Media Element ➤ QuickTime 3 in D6.5 to create a *#quickTime-Media* cast member to make a Sorenson video playable under Windows (assuming QTW3 and the QT3 Asset Xtra are installed). Again, in D7, all videos are imported as QT3 by default.

Video palette problems

If, on the Macintosh, the first QT movie played looks fine, but the second QT movie has the wrong palette, you need the FixPalette XObject. It is necessary only when using multiple QT movies with different custom palettes on the Macintosh. It is not necessary in D7, under Windows, or when using a single custom palette. See "Using the FixPalette XObject" online at *http://www.zeusprod.com/technote/patchpal.html*.

If your digital video appears to be using the wrong palette under Windows, it is probably a general palette issue, and not specific to DV. There are several fixes that work for both standard graphics and DV, discussed in Chapter 13.

Poor visual appearance

Remember the phrase "Garbage in, garbage out." You can't get high-quality video from a low-quality source (such as standard VHS tape). The video won't look any better in Director than it does in MoviePlayer. If the video looks acceptable in 16-bit (thousands of colors) but not in 8-bit (256 colors), create a custom palette.

If necessary, recapture the video from a cleaner source to allow for better compression, or use a different codec or custom palette. Don't confuse poor performance with poor visual quality. Increasing the frame rate, decreasing the keyframe interval, or choosing higher quality settings will improve the appearance of individual frames, but may worsen overall playback if they increase the data rate unacceptably. Poor appearance may be preferable to poor performance.

Audio track doesn't play

Test the video in an external video application. Ensure that it contains a soundtrack that is enabled (see the *trackCount()*, *trackType()*, *trackEnabled()*, and *setTrackEnabled()* functions).

Check that *the movieRate of sprite* or *mRate of sprite* is 1 and *the frameRate of member* is 0. Audio plays only if the video is set to *Synch to SoundTrack* mode. In D7, the sound in an audio-only QuickTime File won't be heard if the video is not played direct-to-Stage.

Ensure that other QT sounds play. Set *the soundLevel* to 7, *the sound of member* to TRUE, and *the volume of sprite* or *volumeLevel of sprite* to 255.

QTW2 and VFW may not recognize multiple soundtracks in a single digital video file. Mix the multiple tracks into a single track using SoundEdit 16 or use separate audio-only QT or AVI files.

Under Windows, you may need to stop all other sounds to free the sound device for QTW or VFW. Set *the soundKeepDevice* to FALSE, and see Chapter 15.

Sound is dropped out by Director in very low memory situations. Unload other cast members and do not preload the entire digital video.

Director runs out of memory

The default value for *the preLoadRAM*, 0, uses all available RAM when preloading DVs for which *the preLoad of member* is TRUE. Ensure that no cast members are using the "Never" or "Last" unload settings (*the purgePriority of member* should be 2 or 3, not 0 or 1).

Poor digital video performance

Test the video in MoviePlayer; if the movie is not compressed and interleaved properly, or plays poorly in MoviePlayer, it will only be worse in Director. Ensure that the DV file is not fragmented on disk and that there is adequate working disk space on the system disk.

QuickTime performs best in 16-bit (thousand of colors), although this can compromise performance of Director animations designed for other depths.

If the video plays back well in an external application, it should play adequately in Director. Test video playback in the Score by itself. Minimize other activities while playing videos. Set *the directToStage of member* to TRUE, and ensure that the DV sprite is not stretched, or is stretched only in 100% increments. Ensure that the *width of member, height of member, width of sprite, height of sprite, top of sprite,* and *left of sprite* properties are evenly divisible by 8. Do not use *on idle* handlers or other time-consuming Lingo while playing digital video. Reduce Director's frame rate in the Tempo channel to about 5 fps, so that Director spends less time trying to redraw the Stage.

 The most common culprits of poor performance are an excessive data rate (see Table 9-3) and improper interleaving of the audio and video tracks. Some codecs are more processor-intensive.

If the video plays well from a hard drive, but not from a CD-ROM, specify a faster minimum CD-ROM speed drive or reduce the date rate of the digital video. Return to your DV compression program and increase the keyframe interval, reduce the frame rate to 10 to 15 fps, reduce the height and width (to, say, 320×240), or reduce the quality setting to lower the data rate. If necessary, recapture the video with a cleaner source to allow for better compression or use a different codec.

The QuickTime 3 Xtra uses DirectDraw under Windows in D6.5 when it is enabled. But DirectDraw causes problems with some video cards when using QTW3. The QuickTime Control Panel *Video Settings* defaults to *Options (Enable DCI, Enable DirectDraw, Enable DirectDraw Acceleration)*. This causes the cursor to disappear and severely degrades performance of non-video elements. Change it to *Safe Mode (GDI Only)* to solve the problems (this doesn't adversely affect video playback outside Director).

If using QTW3, install DirectX. It improves performance dramatically. Director plays AVI files via the VFW interface, ActiveMovie, and DirectShow, but does not explicitly use the optimized DirectShow API.

Repeatedly setting *the volume of sprite* under Windows degrades performance, and repeatedly setting the *mRate* or *movieRate of sprite* may cause stuttering. Avoid setting the property if it has not changed, as shown in Example 16-7.

Digital Video

Example 16-7: Setting a Property Only When Needed

```
on exitFrame
  global gNewVolume, gVideoSprite
  -- Set the new value only if it represents a change
  if the volume of sprite gVideoSprite <> gNewVolume
    set the volume of gVideoSprite = gNewVolume
  end if
end
```

Video appears, but does not update or play

Ensure that Director is playing (don't use *pause*, use *go the frame*), and that *the movieTime of sprite* is 1. If looping in a *repeat* loop (not necessarily recommended), include *updateStage* within the repeat loop to redraw the video. Stop the video (set *the movieRate of sprite* to 0) before performing any transitions.

Video sprite conflicts or redraw problems

If a video is being played direct-to-Stage (which it usually should be), it will play in front of all other sprites and ignore ink effects, because it bypasses Director's offscreen compositing buffer. It will also leave trails. Refresh the screen as described under "Stage display options" earlier in this chapter.

To place other sprites over a DV sprite, set the DV to non-direct-to-Stage (not available with QTW2 for Windows). This is not recommended, because it severely degrades performance. Modify your interface instead.

Other Video and Non-Video Formats

The spectrum of QT3-supported formats and related digital video issues is enormous, and well beyond the scope of this book. In the following sections, I touch on the key points. More information can be found by searching the Macromedia TechNotes or visiting *http://www.zeusprod.com/nutshell/chapters/digvid.html*.

MPEG, Video CD, DVD, VideoDiscs

MPEG (Motion Picture Expert Group) is a standard for playing compressed audio and video data. MPEG 1 is designed for digital media that can supply data at rates up to 1.5 Mbits/sec, and MPEG 2 is a compatible extension of MPEG 1 designed for digital media that can supply data at rates of 4 to 10 Mbits/sec.

MPEG playback can be achieved via software alone or augmented with hardware decoders (necessary on less powerful computers). QuickTime supports software-only MPEG 1 playback on the Macintosh, provided the QuickTime MPEG Extension is installed. It is unclear whether QT4 will support software-only MPEG 2.

MPEG playback is not supported directly by QTW2 or QTW3. Under Windows MPEG video can be played using *mci* commands, the MPEG Xtra or DirectMedia Xtra both from Tabuleiro da Baiana Multimedia (*http://www.tbaiana.com*), or the MPEG ActiveX control (requires the ActiveX Xtra included with D6.5 and D7).

See Macromedia TechNote 03531, "MPEG Video FAQ," and the article on MPEG at *http://www.director-online.com*; see *http://www.zeusprod.com/nutshell/mpeg.html* for additional links.

Video CD (the so-called WhiteBook format) is a specification for playing MPEG 1 and MPEG 2 video and audio from a CD-ROM platter. Likewise, DVD-Video is an specification for playing MPEG 1 and MPEG 2 video and audio from a DVD-ROM platter. These are typically used in videodisc players.

Don't confuse DVD-Video with DVD-ROM. DVD-ROM is a storage medium (essentially a large CD-ROM) using the UFS (universal file system) supported by Windows 98 and DVD-ROM drives. The capacity varies with the media type (DVD-5, DVD-10, etc.). DVD-ROMs can be played back in any computer with the appropriate hardware and software (Real Magic's Hollywood board with a DVD-ROM drive is about $400).

DVD-Video is a video playback standard. Although DVD-Video discs allow some interactivity, they typically contain cinematic movies, such as *Titanic*, and are played on separate DVD-players attached to large-screen TVs. DVD-Video decoder cards are available for computers, but the DVD-Video format is not suitable for typical Director-style applications involving a lot of interactivity and a custom GUI. Controlling an external device such as a video disc player from Lingo usually requires an Xtra that is specifically designed to communicate with that device. Under Windows, you can issue *mci* commands if the device is MCI-compliant.

DVD-ROM burners ($15K) and media ($50 each) are currently very expensive, as are "one-off" pre-masters ($1,000), which you can obtain at a service bureaus in lieu of buying a burner. Creating the output files for a DVD-Video requires a separate authoring and compression system ($40–50K), such as the one from Sonic Solutions (*http://www.sonic.com*).

See *http://www.cinram.com* for details on these formats and media and see *http://www.zeusprod.com/nutshell/dvd.html* for additional links.

Director 7 does not add any new support for MPEG or DVD beyond the support in prior versions. The DirectMedia Xtra (*http://www.tbaiana.com*) will play. VOB files designed for DVD-Video discs.

QTVR and VRML

QTVR is just one of the many non-video formats supported by the larger Quick-Time architecture. QTVR files should have "MooV" file type or .MOV extension, but unfortunately the same file type is used by standard QT movies.

There are two distinct types of QTVR files movies: so-called *panoramas* (also called *navigable* or *pano* movies), in which the user can explore a 360-degree view as if spinning in the middle of a room, and *object* movies in which the user can rotate an object and view it from all angles as if it were in his hands. The pano or object movies are created with software from Apple or third parties by warping and stitching one or more photographic images together. (See *http://www.apple.com/qtvr* for details.) Some rendering programs output QTVR files, too.

Digital Video

There are several ways to import QTVR content (but you should *not* import QTVR files as QT2-style cast members using `File ➤ Import` in D6.5 and earlier versions):

- In D6.5, use `Insert ➤ Media Element ➤ QuickTime 3` and then click *Browse* to choose a QTVR file. In D7, use `File ➤ Import`. Either of these imports the QTVR file as a QT3-style cast member and is recommended for QTVR 2.0 and later. See *the isVRMovie of member* property in Table 16-9 and the QTVR-specific properties in Table 16-10.

- Use a third-party Xtra such as the full-featured QTVR 2 Sprite Xtra (*http://www.glink.net.bk/~gemmay*). Obtain the latest version if using D7.

- Use the QTVR 1.0 Xtra included on both the Director 5 and Director 6 CDs. See the "QTVR 1.0 Xtra" later in this chapter.

All QTVR-related Xtras require a full QT installation, including the QTVR system omponents. Using QTVR files as *#quickTimeMedia* members requires the QT3 Asset Xtra and D6.5 or D7. Because the content visible in a QTVR movie changes as the user navigates, you can't use standard Director hotspots with QTVR. Hotspots are painted over the desired clickable areas in the stitched panoramic image just before it is turned into a QTVR movie. Tools including Apple's QTVR Authoring Studio will embed the hotspots in the QTVR movie when it is created (the hotspot colors become invisible). When the user clicks a hotspot, Director will receive the event, including the hotspot ID (equivalent to the hotspot's color index, 0 to 255) and pass it to the specified callback handlers, allowing you to take appropriate action.

A full discussion of QTVR is beyond the scope of this book. See the following resources and *http://www.zeusprod.com/chapters/qtvr.html* for more information.

QTVR, 3D, and VRML Xtras

Help on integrating QTVR into Director:

> *http://www.geocities.com/SiliconValley/Heights/6791/*

QTVR 2 Sprite Xtra—full-featured:

> *http://www.glink.net.bk/~gemmay/*

RealVR Xtras from RealSpace—QTVR and VRML:

> *http://www.rlspace.com*

3D Dreams—Shells Interactive VRML Xtra for Shockwave:

> *http://www.shells-ifa.com/index.html*

QTVR 1.0 Xtra

The obsolete QTVR Xtra is a Lingo *scripting* Xtra, not a Sprite Asset Xtra like the QT3 Asset Xtra. The QTVR Xtra does not "import" QTVR files or create QTVR cast members, but it accesses external QTVR 1.0 files via Lingo.

The QT3 Sprite Xtra can import QTVR 2.0 panorama or object movies, but it won't work with QTVR 1.0 movies nor support the oldest Macs and PCs. The older

---

QTVR Xtra supports QTVR 1.0 files on Director 5 and Director 6 (and supports 68K Macs and Windows 3.1, but does not work with Shockwave).

The QTVR Xtra gives finer control over QTVR 1.0 (i.e. it has more Lingo commands) than offered by the QT3 Sprite Xtra for QTVR 2.0 files. If using QTVR 2.0 files, consider the third-party QTVR 2 Sprite Xtra cited earlier in this chapter.

Table 16-18 shows only a few of the commands supported by the QTVR Xtra. The QTVR Xtra's full documentation and examples can be found under the *Macromedia:QTVR Xtra* folder on the D6 CD or printed in the Message windows using:

```
put mMessageList (xtra "QTVRXtra")
```

Notice that a QTVR 1.0 file is opened via Lingo, not stored as a cast member or used in the Score. Note also that the newer QT3 Asset Xtra has replaced many of the QTVR Xtra's function calls with properties. For example the QT3 Asset Xtra's *VRwarpMode of member* property replaces the QTVR Xtra's *QTVRGetWarpMode()* and *QTVRSetWarpMode()* functions. Furthermore, the QTVR Xtra often used strings, instead of the symbols or integers used by the QT3 Asset Xtra. For example, the QTVR Xtra's *QTVROpen* command requires the window dimensions as a string of four integers.

Table 16-18: QTVR 1.0 Xtra Commands

Command	Notes
QTVREnter (xtra "QTVRXtra")	Call once to initialize the Xtra.
set *instance* = new (xtra "QTVRXtra")	Create an instance.
put mMessageList (xtra "QTVRXtra")	Display documentation.
QTVRExit (xtra "QTVRXtra")	Close the Xtra.
QTVROpen(instance, "vrMovie.mov", "*left,top,right,bottom*", "visible" | "invisible")	Opens QTVR in specified rectangle; returns error string, or EMPTY for success.

QuickDraw 3D

QuickDraw 3D (QD3D) is another cool offshoot of Apple's QuickTime/Quick-Draw technology that never caught fire. QD3D does amazing things such as manipulate 3D objects in real time and use a QT video as a texture for an object.

Because it is processor-intensive, it is supported only on PowerPCs and Windows 32-bit systems. It requires that substantial extra RAM be allocated to Director, and naturally requires the QuickDraw 3D System Extensions (QuickDraw 3D, Quick-Draw 3D Viewer, QD3D Custom Elements, QuickDraw 3D IR, QuickDraw 3D RAVE, Apple QD3D HW Driver, and Apple QD3D HW Plug-in).

As with QTVR files, there are several options for importing QD3D content:

- Install the QuickDraw 3D Xtra included on the D5 and D6 CD and use Insert ➤ Media Element ➤ Media Element ➤ QuickDraw 3D Model to import a 3D model file (file type "3DMF"). This creates a custom cast member of type #QD3D_Xtra, whose supported properties are shown in Table 16-19.

- In D6.5, use Insert ➤ Media Element ➤ QuickTime 3 and then click *Browse* to choose a QD3D (3DMF) file. In D7, use File ➤ Import. Either of these imports the QD3D file as a QT3-style cast member (requires the Quick-Time Asset Xtra). Unfortunately, the QuickTime Asset Xtra doesn't support any meaningful commands or properties specific to QD3D assets.

- Use a third-party Xtra such as the Focus3's QD3D Xtra, which supports multiple simultaneous QD3D models on the Stage.

The QuickDraw 3D Xtra

The QuickDraw 3D Xtra is not installed automatically with Director. It has been orphaned, but is still offers good, clean, scandal-free fun. It prefers the older QD3D drivers (included in *Drivers* folder on the Director 6 CD).

The Apple QD3D drivers installer installs sample QD3D model files in the *Apple Extras* folder. Macromedia's sample DIR movie on the Director 6 CD includes the infamous spinning dinosaur. Macromedia's defunct Extreme 3D software can also create 3DMF models.

Note that a QD3D cast member's model file can be external (linked) or internal to the cast (embedded) as set under the *Modeling* tab in the *QD3D Properties* dialog box. For performance reasons, you should set *the directToStage of member* to TRUE (or use the *Direct To Stage* option under the *Rendering* tab in the *QD3D Properties* dialog box).

Table 16-19 lists the member and sprite properties supported by the QuickDraw 3D Xtra. None of these properties are supported when using QD3D models imported as *#quickTimeMedia* cast members using Insert ➤ Media Element ➤ QuickTime 3 in D6.5 or File ➤ Import in D7.

Note that *the type of member* of QD3D cast members is *#QD3D_Xtra*, and that the external file's name is stored in the *modelFile of member* property, not *the fileName of member* as with most other cast member types. Although not shown, note that all Lingo symbols used by the QD3D Xtra begin with "#q3". See the HTML documentation included with the QuickDraw 3D Xtra for more details.

Table 16-19: QD3D Xtra Member and Sprite Properties

QD3D Member Properties	QD3D Sprite Properties
ambientBrightness, ambientColor, autoRotate, autoRotateAngle, backColor, backFacing, badge, buttonDistance, buttonMove, buttonRotate, buttonZoom, cameraAspectRatio, cameraDirection, cameraFOV, cameraHeight, cameraHither, cameraPosition. cameraInterest, cameraType, cameraUpVector, cameraWidth, cameraYon, controller, diffuseColor, directManipulation, directToStage, dragAndDrop, fillStyle, frame, interpolation, lightBrightness, lightColor, lightDirection, modelCenter, modelFile, modelSize, position, rotation, scale, shading, specularColor, specularCoeff, texture, textureType, type	autoRotate, autoRotateAngle, badge, buttonDistance, buttonMove, buttonRotate, buttonZoom, cameraAspectRatio, camera Direction, cameraFOV, cameraHeight, cameraHither, cameraPosition. cameraInterest, cameraType, cameraUpVector, cameraWidth, cameraYon, controller, directManipulation, dragAndDrop, frame, modelCenter, modelSize, position, rotation, scale

Index

Symbols and Numbers

B

CD-ROM drive
  access, performance of, 290
  customizing icons, 246–248
  data throughput, 262
  digital video performance from, 577
  disk storage capacity, 263
  Enhanced CDs (ECDs), 531–533
  locating for user, 244–246
cells
  Director 6/7 changes, 68
  duplicating, 67
center of member property, 560, 561
Center option, 225
center property, DV sprites, 142
centering (see alignment)
centerRegPoint property, 402
centerStage property, 19, 162, 169, 351
changeArea of member property, 73
Channel parameter (Tempo dialog), 512
channelCount of member property, 509
channels
  Effects (see Effects channels)
  examining all, 99–100
  sound (see sound)
  sprite (see sprite channels)
Character Map utility, 376
character mapping, 375
characterSet of member property, 388
charPosToLoc( ), 389
charSpacing of member property, 383
check boxes, importing, 115
"Check Movie for Xtras" option, 305,
    306, 322, 226
checkBoxAccess proeprty, 460
checkboxes, 459–461
checkBoxType property, 460
checkDepth( ) (example), 412
checkLinks( ) (example), 145
checkMark of menuItem property, 477
checkmarking menu items, 475
CheckNetMessages( ), 362
checkQTversions( ) (example), 544
checkScore( ) (example), 78
checkSeekOffset( ) (example), 275
chunk expressions (text), 385–387
chunkSize of member property, 73
Cinemac utility, 250

Classic Look (Monochrome) option, 427
CLASSID attribute, 341
clearCache( ), 351, 354
clearFrame command, 95
clearGlobals command, 171, 266
clickLoc property, 159
clickM( ), clickV( ) (examples), 160
clickOn property, 143
Clipboard ink effect, 446
close box (windows), 180
close window command, 188, 189, 192
closed property, 402
closeDA command, 212
closeHandler event, 180
closeResFile( ), 212, 468
closeWindow event, 189
closeXlib( ), 212, 266, 314
closing external files, 284
closing Stage window (D7), 42
closing windows, 42–44, 187
CLUT files, importing, 114
Cmd key (see shortcuts)
CMYK color model, 408
CODEBASE attribute, 341
codecs, 539
collaboration, 103, 105
color chips, 451–454
color depth, 19, 206, 225, 265, 408
  animation, 62
  choosing, 411
  converting to higher depths, 428
  determining and changing, 233
  palettes and, 5
  performance and, 292
Color Genie Xtra, 455
color models, 408–410
color of member property, 383, 396,
    453, 454
  color depth and, 417
color of sprite property, 409, 453
  color depth and, 417
Color Palettes window, 39, 433
Color Picker Xtra, 455
colorDepth property, 206, 231, 351,
    396, 412
  fullColorPermit property and, 265
  multiple monitors and, 233
  troubleshooting, 416–417

union( ), 162
units, choosing, 164
Unix support for Director, 200
unlinked cast members, 102
unlinked castLibs, 103
    copying cast members, 128
    external, 105
unlinked media types, 115–121
unload command, 268, 510
Unload option, 559
unloadCast command, 269
unloading (see loading)
unLoadMember command, 268, 269,
    285
unLoadMovie command, 269
unpuppeting (see puppeting)
unused cast members, deleting, 124
Update Movies (Xtras menu), 298
updateFrame command, 95
updateLock property, 3, 13, 95
updateMovieEnabled property, 96
    Director vs. Projectors, 242
updateStage command, 3, 13
    redundant, 290
updateStage event, 9
UpdateStage web site, xxii
updating
    digital video, 578
    fields, 393
    Score references to external castLibs,
        108
    Stage, Lingo execution and, 13–14
    (see also redrawing)
upgrading Director, 32
uploading Shocked files to web server,
    342–345
uppercase characters, platform
    differences, 210, 214
"url not found" error, 344
url of member property, 213, 521
URLs for source movies, 177
"Usage (Not Used in Score)" option,
    124
Use Hypertext Styles option, 380
Use Media as Available option, 348
Use Movie Settings option, 225
Use System Player option, 227
Use System Temporary Memory option,
    228, 253, 271

Use System Temporary Memory
    Projector creation option, 203
useAlpha of member property, 293,
    445, 447
Used by Program (Memory Inspector),
    271
useFastQuads property, 293, 294
useHyperlinkStyles of member
    property, 392
useHypertextStyles of member
    property, 384, 392
useQuickTimeStreaming( ), 566
user events
    delay command and, 92
    Lingo interference with, 14
    sprite properties changes after,
        143–144
    Tempo frame rate and, 5
    waiting for, 71, 93
    (see also runtime; interactivity)
user interface, 456–484
    buttons (see buttons)
    cursors (see cursors)
    dialog boxes, 482–484
    digital video and, 551–566
    menus (see menus)
    Paint window options, 435
    palette-related options, 429
    platform differences, 209–211
    references on, 457
    sounds, 488, 508–510
    text manipulation, 376–380
    widgets, 461
userName property, 231, 242

V

V12 Database Engine, 302
value( ), performance, 289
variables, disposing of, 266
vector graphics, 398, 401
    (see also Flash files)
vector shapes, 402–406
    performance, 293
    storage space, 258
version (global variable), 236
version of Shockwave, checking if
    adequate, 338
version property, 353

About the Author

Bruce A. Epstein first learned Director when it became apparent that no one would fund his desire to wander aimlessly unless he was doing so in front of a keyboard. Since that time he has become a recognized Director and Lingo expert, spouting unsolicited advice in various books, magazines, and multimedia fora. Bruce has programmed and optimized dozens of cross-platform multimedia products, such as children's edutainment titles, enhanced audio CDs, and interactive advertisements, including the Chrysler/Plymouth Virtual Auto Plaza. He writes voraciously about multimedia development, software design, and project management, and refers to himself in the third person. In his copious spare time, Bruce runs Zeus Productions (*http://www.zeusprod.com*), which offers Lingo consulting and Xtras for Director. *Director in a Nutshell* is Bruce's brain in a book, distilling years of Director and Lingo expertise into a concise desktop reference.

Colophon

Our look is the result of reader comments, our own experimentation, and feedback from distribution channels. Distinctive covers complement our distinctive approach to technical topics, breathing personality and life into potentially dry subjects.

The bird on the cover of *Director in a Nutshell* is an ostrich (*Struthio camelus*). The ostrich is the largest living bird, measuring up to 10 feet tall and weighing up to 340 pounds. In addition to its size, the ostrich's long, featherless neck, long, powerful legs, and small head with its large eyes and short, flat bill, ensure that you'll probably never mistake an ostrich for another bird. Males have black and white plumage, while females have gray-brown plumage. These big birds are unable to fly, but they can run up to 30 miles per hour, with bursts of over 40 mph when pursued. They outrun most of their natural predators. In order to hide from predators, ostriches sit with their neck and head outstretched on the ground. It is this defensive position that led to the incorrect belief that ostriches hide their heads in the sand to avoid detection. Should a predator spy and catch up to an ostrich, the ostrich's strong legs and clawed toes provide an excellent defence. An ostrich kick can be powerful enough to kill a lion.

Once widespread throughout Africa, Asia, and Europe, ostriches now live only in Africa. They live in arid, open country and feed on succulent plants, grasses, leaves, and fruit, and occasionally insects, lizards, small birds, or small rodents. They can survive without water for long periods of time, but when there is water available they enjoy not only drinking but bathing in it. They usually live in small, loosely organized flocks, often alongside other grazing animals such as zebras and antelopes. At mating time, a male ostrich will mate with three to five females; the eggs will be laid in a communal nest, and they hatch after about 40 days. Despite the 15–60 eggs in the nest, each female is apparently able to identify her own eggs. A single ostrich egg weighs approximately 3 pounds, and is the equivalent of 24 chicken eggs. They are considered to be quite tasty. Native African tribes create jewelry and containers to carry water out of ostrich eggs.

Ostrich feathers have been in demand by humans for ornamentation purposes for thousands of years. By the late 19th century they were on the verge of extinction because of overhunting. The development of ostrich farms has helped to curb the hunting of wild ostriches and to bring them back from the brink of extinction. Still, the four subspecies of ostrich are carefully watched by preservationists.

Nancy Kotary was the production editor and copy editor for *Director in a Nutshell*; Sheryl Avruch was the production manager; Clairemarie Fisher O'Leary, Jane Ellin, Nicole Gipson Arigo, and Ellie Cutler provided quality control; Betty Hugh, Tricia Manoni, and Sebastian Banker provided production support. Robert Romano created the illustrations using Adobe Photoshop 5 and Macromedia FreeHand 8. Mike Sierra provided FrameMaker technical support. Seth Maislin wrote the index.

Edie Freedman designed the cover of this book, using a 19th-century engraving from the Dover Pictorial Archive. The cover layout was produced with Quark XPress 3.32 using the ITC Garamond font. Whenever possible, our books use RepKover™, a durable and flexible lay-flat binding. If the page count exceeds RepKover's limit, perfect binding is used.

The inside layout was designed by Nancy Priest and implemented in FrameMaker 5.5.6 by Mike Sierra. The text and heading fonts are ITC Garamond Light and Garamond Book. This colophon was written by Clairemarie Fisher O'Leary.

In a Nutshell Quick References

Web Authoring and Design

Designing with JavaScript

By Nick Heinle
1st Edition September 1997
256 pages, Includes CD-ROM
ISBN 1-56592-300-6

Written by the author of the "JavaScript Tip of the Week" web site, this new Web Review Studio book focuses on the most useful and applicable scripts for making truly interactive, engaging web sites. You'll not only have quick access to the scripts you need, you'll finally understand why the scripts work, how to alter the scripts to get the effects you want, and, ultimately, how to write your own groundbreaking scripts from scratch.

Information Architecture for the World Wide Web

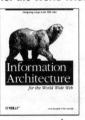

By Louis Rosenfeld & Peter Morville
1st Edition January 1998
226 pages, ISBN 1-56592-282-4

Learn how to merge aesthetics and mechanics to design web sites that "work." This book shows how to apply principles of architecture and library science to design cohesive web sites and intranets that are easy to use, manage, and expand. Covers building complex sites, hierarchy design and organization, and techniques to make your site easier to search. For webmasters, designers, and administrators.

Web Navigation: Designing the User Experience

By Jennifer Fleming
1st Edition September 1998
288 pages, Includes CD-ROM
ISBN 1-56592-351-0

This book takes the first in-depth look at designing Web site navigation through design strategies to help you uncover solutions that work for your site and audience. It focuses on designing by purpose, with chapters on entertainment, shopping, identity, learning, information, and community sites. Comes with a CD-ROM that containing software demos and a "netography" of related Web resources.

HTML: The Definitive Guide, 3rd Edition

By Chuck Musciano & Bill Kennedy
3rd Edition August 1998
576 pages, ISBN 1-56592-492-4

This complete guide is chock full of examples, sample code, and practical, hands-on advice to help you create truly effective web pages and master advanced features. Learn how to insert images and other multimedia elements, create useful links and searchable documents, use Netscape extensions, design great forms, and lots more. The third edition covers HTML 4.0, Netscape 4.5, and Internet Explorer 4.0, plus all the common extensions.

How to stay in touch with O'Reilly

1. Visit Our Award-Winning Site

http://www.oreilly.com/

★ "Top 100 Sites on the Web" —*PC Magazine*
★ "Top 5% Web sites" —*Point Communications*
★ "3-Star site" —*The McKinley Group*

Our web site contains a library of comprehensive product information (including book excerpts and tables of contents), downloadable software, background articles, interviews with technology leaders, links to relevant sites, book cover art, and more. File us in your Bookmarks or Hotlist!

2. Join Our Email Mailing Lists

New Product Releases

To receive automatic email with brief descriptions of all new O'Reilly products as they are released, send email to:
listproc@online.oreilly.com
Put the following information in the first line of your message (*not* in the Subject field):
subscribe oreilly-news

O'Reilly Events

If you'd also like us to send information about trade show events, special promotions, and other O'Reilly events, send email to:
listproc@online.oreilly.com
Put the following information in the first line of your message (*not* in the Subject field):
subscribe oreilly-events

3. Get Examples from Our Books via FTP

There are two ways to access an archive of example files from our books:

Regular FTP

• ftp to:
  ftp.oreilly.com
  (login: anonymous
  password: your email address)
• Point your web browser to:
  ftp://ftp.oreilly.com/

FTPMAIL

• Send an email message to:
  ftpmail@online.oreilly.com
  (Write "help" in the message body)

4. Contact Us via Email

order@oreilly.com
To place a book or software order online. Good for North American and international customers.

subscriptions@oreilly.com
To place an order for any of our newsletters or periodicals.

books@oreilly.com
General questions about any of our books.

software@oreilly.com
For general questions and product information about our software. Check out O'Reilly Software Online at **http://software.oreilly.com/** for software and technical support information. Registered O'Reilly software users send your questions to:
website-support@oreilly.com

cs@oreilly.com
For answers to problems regarding your order or our products.

booktech@oreilly.com
For book content technical questions or corrections.

proposals@oreilly.com
To submit new book or software proposals to our editors and product managers.

international@oreilly.com
For information about our international distributors or translation queries. For a list of our distributors outside of North America check out:
http://www.oreilly.com/www/order/country.html

O'Reilly & Associates, Inc.

101 Morris Street, Sebastopol, CA 95472 USA
TEL   707-829-0515 or 800-998-9938
       (6am to 5pm PST)
FAX   707-829-0104

International Distributors

UK, EUROPE, MIDDLE EAST AND AFRICA (EXCEPT FRANCE, GERMANY, AUSTRIA, SWITZERLAND, LUXEMBOURG, LIECHTENSTEIN, AND EASTERN EUROPE)

INQUIRIES
O'Reilly UK Limited
4 Castle Street
Farnham
Surrey, GU9 7HS
United Kingdom
Telephone: 44-1252-711776
Fax: 44-1252-734211
Email: josette@oreilly.com

ORDERS
Wiley Distribution Services Ltd.
1 Oldlands Way
Bognor Regis
West Sussex PO22 9SA
United Kingdom
Telephone: 44-1243-779777
Fax: 44-1243-820250
Email: cs-books@wiley.co.uk

FRANCE

ORDERS
GEODIF
61, Bd Saint-Germain
75240 Paris Cedex 05, France
Tel: 33-1-44-41-46-16 (French books)
Tel: 33-1-44-41-11-87 (English books)
Fax: 33-1-44-41-11-44
Email: distribution@eyrolles.com

INQUIRIES
Éditions O'Reilly
18 rue Séguier
75006 Paris, France
Tel: 33-1-40-51-52-30
Fax: 33-1-40-51-52-31
Email: france@editions-oreilly.fr

GERMANY, SWITZERLAND, AUSTRIA, EASTERN EUROPE, LUXEMBOURG, AND LIECHTENSTEIN

INQUIRIES & ORDERS
O'Reilly Verlag
Balthasarstr. 81
D-50670 Köln
Germany
Telephone: 49-221-973160-91
Fax: 49-221-973160-8
Email: anfragen@oreilly.de (inquiries)
Email: order@oreilly.de (orders)

CANADA (FRENCH LANGUAGE BOOKS)
Les Éditions Flammarion ltée
375, Avenue Laurier Ouest
Montréal (Québec) H2V 2K3
Tel: 00-1-514-277-8807
Fax: 00-1-514-278-2085
Email: info@flammarion.qc.ca

HONG KONG
City Discount Subscription Service, Ltd.
Unit D, 3rd Floor, Yan's Tower
27 Wong Chuk Hang Road
Aberdeen, Hong Kong
Tel: 852-2580-3539
Fax: 852-2580-6463
Email: citydis@ppn.com.hk

KOREA
Hanbit Media, Inc.
Sonyoung Bldg. 202
Yeksam-dong 736-36
Kangnam-ku
Seoul, Korea
Tel: 822-554-9610
Fax: 822-556-0363
Email: hant93@chollian.dacom.co.kr

PHILIPPINES
Mutual Books, Inc.
429-D Shaw Boulevard
Mandaluyong City, Metro
Manila, Philippines
Tel: 632-725-7538
Fax: 632-721-3056
Email: mbikikog@mnl.sequel.net

TAIWAN
O'Reilly Taiwan
No. 3, Lane 131
Hang-Chow South Road
Section 1, Taipei, Taiwan
Tel: 886-2-23968990
Fax: 886-2-23968916
Email: benh@oreilly.com

CHINA
O'Reilly Beijing
Room 2410
160, FuXingMenNeiDaJie
XiCheng District
Beijing
China PR 100031
Tel: 86-10-86631006
Fax: 86-10-86631007
Email: frederic@oreilly.com

INDIA
Computer Bookshop (India) Pvt. Ltd.
190 Dr. D.N. Road, Fort
Bombay 400 001 India
Tel: 91-22-207-0989
Fax: 91-22-262-3551
Email: cbsbom@giasbm01.vsnl.net.in

JAPAN
O'Reilly Japan, Inc.
Kiyoshige Building 2F
12-Bancho, Sanei-cho
Shinjuku-ku
Tokyo 160-0008 Japan
Tel: 81-3-3356-5227
Fax: 81-3-3356-5261
Email: japan@oreilly.com

ALL OTHER ASIAN COUNTRIES
O'Reilly & Associates, Inc.
101 Morris Street
Sebastopol, CA 95472 USA
Tel: 707-829-0515
Fax: 707-829-0104
Email: order@oreilly.com

AUSTRALIA
WoodsLane Pty., Ltd.
7/5 Vuko Place
Warriewood NSW 2102
Australia
Tel: 61-2-9970-5111
Fax: 61-2-9970-5002
Email: info@woodslane.com.au

NEW ZEALAND
Woodslane New Zealand, Ltd.
21 Cooks Street (P.O. Box 575)
Waganui, New Zealand
Tel: 64-6-347-6543
Fax: 64-6-345-4840
Email: info@woodslane.com.au

LATIN AMERICA
McGraw-Hill Interamericana
Editores, S.A. de C.V.
Cedro No. 512
Col. Atlampa
06450, Mexico, D.F.
Tel: 52-5-547-6777
Fax: 52-5-547-3336
Email: mcgraw-hill@infosel.net.mx

O'REILLY®

TO ORDER: **800-998-9938** • **order@oreilly.com** • **http://www.oreilly.com/**

OUR PRODUCTS ARE AVAILABLE AT A BOOKSTORE OR SOFTWARE STORE NEAR YOU.

FOR INFORMATION: **800-998-9938** • **707-829-0515** • **info@oreilly.com**